Right from the Start

Right from the Start

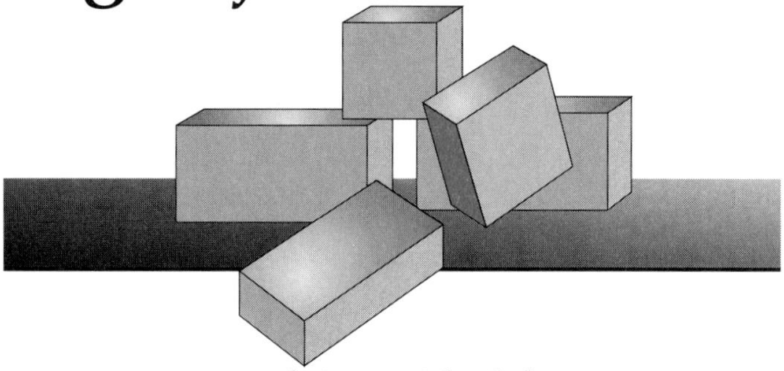

Teaching Children Ages Three to Eight

Bernard Spodek
University of Illinois

Olivia N. Saracho
University of Maryland

Allyn and Bacon
Boston / London / Sydney / Toronto

TO OUR PARENTS,

David Spodek
and
Pablo and Francisca Villareal

Series Editor: Nancy Forsyth
Editorial Assistant: Christine Nelson
Cover Administrator: Linda Dickinson
Manufacturing Buyer: Louise Richardson
Editorial-Production Service: Karen Mason
Cover Designer: Susan Paradise

A Division of Paramount Publishing
160 Gould Street
Needham Heights, Massachusetts 02194

Library of Congress Cataloging-in-Publication Data
Spodek, Bernard.
Right from the start: teaching children ages three to eight / Bernard Spodek, Olivia N. Saracho.
p. cm.
Includes references and index.
ISBN 0-205-15281-3
1. Early childhood education—United States. 2. Early childhood education—United States—Curricula. I. Saracho, Olivia N. II. Title.
372.21—dc 20 93-36708
CIP

Printed in the United States of America

10 9 8 7 6 5 4 3 2 1 98 97 96 95 94 93

Photo credits: p. 17, Jim Pickerell; p. 220, Stephen Marks; p. 230, Jim Pickerell; p. 398, Stephen Marks; p. 436, Stephen Marks

Illustrations: pp. 62, 64, 68, 70, 71, 74, 76, 78, by Lyrl C. Ahern

Brief Contents

Contents

Preface

When we began developing *Right from the Start: Teaching Children Ages Three to Eight,* we wanted to produce a different sort of book. We had written and edited texts before: Bernard Spodek had written the venerable text, *Teaching in the Early Years;* both of us wrote *Foundations of Early Childhood Education* with Michael D. Davis and *Mainstreaming Young Children* with Richard C. Lee. We also wrote and edited a number of scholarly books. But, we wanted this book to be different from all the rest.

We started our project by reviewing *Teaching in the Early Years.* Though there were many excellent parts to the book, we considered it out of date. In addition, we were not happy with its design. It was stuffy, with too much straight narrative. We wanted our new book to be authoritative—based on the best professional knowledge we could garner from research, theory, and practice. We accomplished this, and the text is clearly referenced throughout. We feel we succeeded in our efforts to make the book more accessible without watering down and trivializing the vast amount of knowledge and information in the field.

We wanted to highlight important material in the book, explain professional terms, and give examples and suggestions for teaching in practice. Thus, we designed a textbook that we felt would be a good learning tool. We tried to accomplish this in a number of ways:

- Providing concrete examples of complex ideas,
- Illustrating examples by placing them in boxes throughout the text,
- Including photographs and sketches of classroom practices,
- Highlighting pioneers in early childhood education and theorists of child development through pictures, which gives the reader a background of the people who helped create the field, and
- Explaining terms the reader might encounter for the first time—a marginal glossary is provided where these terms are first used.

But features alone in a book are not enough to make it worthwhile. The content has to be significant. And for a book like this, the content needs to be related to what a person needs to know in order to become a good early childhood teacher. The first few chapters include materials that represent the foundation for early childhood practice:

- A view of early childhood teachers and the preparation required. This is provided so that novice teachers will be more conscious of the process and more self-reflective as practitioners.

- A review of the history and theory of early childhood education. The reader can become aware of the roots of current practice and the relationship of the field of child development to early childhood education.
- A review of ideas about curriculum in early childhood education. The reader should become aware that education at this level requires considerably more than filling time with activities. Learning experiences need to be goal oriented. They also need to be educationally worthwhile.
- A chapter on individual differences in young children is presented. This focus is important because a greater range of children are entering early programs today.
- Throughout the text there is a continuing focus on multicultural education. Children today are being raised in a global society. They need to become increasingly aware of cultures that are different from their own.

Chapters in the middle of the text deal with the activities of teaching young children. Some of these activities require the attention of teachers when children are not in the classroom. These include:

- planning and organizing the classroom,
- evaluating the overall program, and
- working with their parents.

The chapters on content in early childhood education are concerned with providing educationally appropriate experiences for children in preschool, kindergarten, and primary classrooms. Following is a clarification of these terms.

Early childhood programs are called by many names. In the United States, programs for young children ages six and above are typically primary classes in elementary schools. Programs for five-year-olds are called *kindergartens* in our country, though in other countries kindergarten may refer to programs for children from ages three to six.

Extended day programs for young children are provided in *child care centers.* Originally, these programs were called day nurseries. In about the 1920s, "day care center" replaced that term. The term *child care center* is used now to distinguish these programs from day programs for other populations, such as senior citizens or persons with disabilities. Half day programs for children before kindergarten were offered by *nursery schools* in the United States. Recently, the term *preschool* has supplanted that term. But the term preschool has also been used to identify any programs for prekindergarten age children, including child care programs, nursery school programs, and Head Start programs.

The term *prekindergarten* has been used by public school personnel more recently. As programs for children below kindergarten age are added to the public school programs, this term has become more popular.

In the chapters on content, each begins with a foundations section, which identifies the important issues relating to each content area and provides the background and the theoretical basis for the practical activities of teaching. Separate chapters are provided for teaching mathematics, science, social studies, and the expressive arts. Two chapters are provided on language and literacy, since we think this is a very valuable content area for young children. A separate chapter on play is provided, since play is one of the most important ways that young children learn.

In early childhood education, teachers need to take a more holistic approach to education, often through themes using units or projects that integrate content areas. Separating subject areas into individual chapters is important for teachers, not for children. Suggestions for ways to integrate subjects are presented throughout these chapters.

Teaching as a profession requires continued professional development. The final chapter presents resources for ongoing development. Teachers need to continue their quest for knowledge about the field.

While writing a textbook is, in many ways, a very lonely act, a book like this is never written alone. We wish to acknowledge our gratitude to the many individuals who directly and indirectly contributed to this book. We owe much to the many teachers, undergraduate and graduate students, and children with whom we have worked—the ideas expressed here have grown out of our interactions with them over the years. I-Hui Lee, Mary Ellen O'Ferrall, Juanita Garcia, and Elida De La Rosa helped identify some of the resources we used. Michael J. Bell, University of North Texas; Linda C. Edwards, College of Charleston, South Carolina; Sherry L. Kirksey, Shelton State Community College; Joseph T. Lawton, University of Wisconsin at Madison; Patricia K. Lowry, Jacksonville State University; Judith H. Reitsch, Eastern Washington University; Mary Snyder, University of Iowa; and Paul B. Woods, Delaware State College reviewed earlier versions of our manuscript and provided us with valuable suggestions. We would also like to thank Sean Wakely and, especially, Nancy Forsyth, our editors at Allyn and Bacon, for their encouragement, support, help, and an occasional prodding in getting this book published.

We also wish to thank the staff, children, and families of George Washington School and Martin Luther King Elementary School in Urbana, Illinois, and especially those in the classes of Joyce Bezdezek, Linda Campbell, Phyllis Erikson, and Gloria Rainier. The bulk of the photographs of children in school were taken in these classes by Bernard Spodek.

Most important, we wish to acknowledge the support and encouragement we received from our families during the period we wrote this book—from Prudence Spodek, and from Francesca S., Pablo J., Saul Villareal, and Lydia Gonzales.

Bernard Spodek
Olivia N. Saracho

1

Teaching

CHAPTER OVERVIEW

This chapter presents:

- Qualities needed to become a teacher of young children
- Ways to become a teacher of young children
- Ways to assure quality in teachers of young children
- The roles of early childhood teachers
- Qualities of early childhood teachers

INTRODUCTION

Whether standing in front of the classroom commanding the attention of all the children or sitting quietly in a corner working with a small group, teachers are central to all classroom activity. Directly or indirectly, teachers control much of the activity and are responsible for all that happens to children at school. They must respond to the children's many needs as those needs become apparent during the day. They must plan activities that produce educational benefit for the children.

Teachers perform many different tasks. They function as lecturers, storytellers, group discussion leaders, traffic directors, mediators of conflicts, psychological diagnosticians, custodians, assigners of academic work, and file clerks. Teachers also serve as curriculum designers, organizers of instruction, managers of learning, counselors and advisers, and makers of decisions about the education of children. Most importantly, they directly interact with children, either verbally, as in a discussion, or physically, as when they place an arm around a child's shoulders. The interactions may be obvious ones, such as directing a child from one part of the room to another, or subtle ones, such as giving a child a knowing look.

Many things determine what teachers do in classrooms. Teachers must always make decisions that are appropriate for a particular group of

Teachers support activities that produce educational benefits.

children in a particular setting. Even within the limited age range of early childhood education—as defined in this book, between birth and eight years of age—children of different ages demand different responses from teachers. Teaching in a day-care center requires greater concern for the physical well-being of children than does teaching in a half-day preschool. In addition, institutional requirements often involve teachers in activities that have nothing directly to do with children's learning, such as keeping attendance or collecting money for lunch and milk. Thus, teachers' duties vary according to the nature of the educational institution and its program.

READINESS FOR TEACHING

What does it take to become a teacher of young children? Few people are born with a desire to teach young children or with the necessary competencies, yet both desire and competencies are required for successful teaching. There are other important requirements as well.

Qualities of Teachers

Over the years early childhood educators have stressed different requirements for teachers of young children. Millie Almy and Agnes Snyder (1947) suggested that early childhood teachers need physical stamina, world mindedness, an understanding of human development, a respect for personality, and a scientific spirit. More recently, Millie Almy (1974) suggested such qualities as patience, maturity, energy, warmth, and ingenuity. Lilian Katz (1969) included such characteristics as flexibility and an ability to enjoy and encourage children. All of these are laudatory qualities. However, they are not things that can be taught in a teacher education program, though they can be used in selecting teachers or students for teacher education.

Teacher Competencies

More recently, educators have attempted to specify particular competencies as requirements for early childhood personnel. **Teacher competencies** are not personal qualities but skills that individuals can learn. The Child Development Associate (CDA) Credentialing Program has identified six general areas and thirteen functional areas of competence as requirements for teaching young children (see box on p. 4). Determining whether an individual possesses these competencies is a complex process. A team judges teaching performance through direct observation as well as through assessment of a portfolio of professional materials.

Teacher competencies are skills that can be learned.

Other ways to characterize a good teacher of young children include identifying what such teachers should know as well as what they should be able to do. We suggest that the following knowledge is fundamental for early childhood teachers:

1. **Knowledge of Basic Health and Safety Measures.** The teacher's prime responsibility is to keep children safe and healthy. If this responsibility is not met, then all of the teacher's attention to planning and programming is wasted. Child-care centers can easily become sources of contagion. Improper handling of food and inadequate concern for cleanliness on the part of caregivers can be a source of serious illness for children. Children can also infect one another. There are also many potential physical dangers for children in a center. Electrical outlets present a shock hazard. Children can misuse equipment, and broken furniture or equipment can lead to accidents. Teachers must keep children healthy and whole. They must understand the nature of disease and infection, proper handling of food and materials, and proper sanitary procedures, especially in relation to toileting. Teachers must be alert to the potential causes of accidents in classrooms.
2. **Techniques to Present Activities to Children.** A classroom teacher must know the techniques for planning and guiding learning activities. Some of these techniques are simple, such as mixing paints or playdough properly or showing children how to use scissors. Some are more complex, such as setting up learning centers and organizing activities for children to engage in during the day.

CDA COMPETENCIES AND RELATED FUNCTIONAL AREAS

Competency Area I: *Setting Up and Maintaining a Safe and Healthy Learning Environment*

Functional Areas:

1. **Safe:** Candidate provides a safe environment by taking necessary measures to prevent accidents.
2. **Healthy:** Candidate provides an environment that is free of factors which may contribute to or cause illness.
3. **Environment:** Candidate selects materials and equipment and arranges the room to correspond to the developmental level of the children.

Competency Area II: *Advancing Physical and Intellectual Competence of Children*

Functional Areas:

1. **Physical:** Candidate provides a variety of appropriate equipment, activities, and opportunities to promote the physical development of children.
2. **Cognitive:** Candidate provides activities and experiences which encourage questioning, probing, and problem-solving skills appropriate to the developmental level of the children.
3. **Language:** Candidate helps children acquire and use language as a means of communicating their thoughts, feelings, and understanding.
4. **Creative:** Candidate provides a variety of experiences and media that stimulate children to explore and express their creative abilities.

Competency Area III: *Building Positive Self-Concept and Individual Strength in Children*

Functional Areas:

1. **Self-Concept:** Candidate helps each child to know, accept, and appreciate him- or herself as an individual.
2. **Individual Strength:** Candidate helps each child develop a sense of independence and acquire the ability to express, understand, and control his or her feelings.

Competency Area IV: *Organizing and Sustaining the Positive Functioning of Children and Adults in a Group in a Learning Environment*

Functional Areas:

1. **Social:** Candidate helps children learn to get along with others and encourages feelings of mutual respect among the children in the group.
2. **Group Management:** Candidate provides a positive routine and establishes simple rules with the group that are understood and accepted by children and adults.

Competency Area V: *Bringing About Optimal Coordination of Home and Center Childrearing Practices and Expectations*

Functional Area:

1. **Home/Center:** Candidate establishes positive and productive relationships with parents and encourages them to participate in the center's activities.

Competency Area VI: *Carrying Out Supplementary Responsibilities Related to the Children's Programs*

Functional Area:

1. **Staff:** Candidate works cooperatively with other staff members concerning plans, activities, policies, and rules of the center.

Source: Child Development Associate Consortium, *Competency Standards* (Washington, DC: Author, 1977.

3. **Classroom Management Techniques.** Classroom management is always important, but it is difficult for the novice. Proper transitions between activities can reduce discipline problems. Teachers must know how to establish rules for the classroom, how to deal with unruly children, and how to influence children without being punitive. Inappropriate punishment can be both harmful to children and ineffective in helping them learn appropriate behavior.
4. **Knowledge of the Content of the Early Childhood Curriculum.** To teach young children well requires knowing more than how to keep children safe and how to arrange interesting activities. The teacher must know what young children should know both for their current lives and as preparation for later learning. The teacher must also know how to teach this knowledge in ways that are appropriate to the children in a particular class to insure that these children are successful in meeting the goals of the program. The areas of learning include language and literacy, quantitative ability, understanding social processes, understanding scientific processes, and ability to express themselves in a variety of media. Evaluation is integral to instruction: teachers need to know how to judge what children are capable of learning as well as whether the children have successfully achieved the goals of the program.

The knowledge described here represents a foundation upon which increased knowledge and skills can be built.

PROFESSIONALISM AND THE EARLY CHILDHOOD PRACTITIONER

There are many kinds of practitioners in the field of early childhood education. Some of these practitioners are at the preprofessional level and have relatively little training. Other early childhood practitioners have considerable preparation, including advanced degrees, as well as many years of experience. Some even have specialties within the field of early childhood education. The National Association for the Education of Young Children (NAEYC) has identified the roles of early childhood practitioners, characterizing teaching assistants or aides as nonprofessional or preprofessional. The **professional roles** include assistant teachers, teachers, master teachers, and family child-care providers. These roles require different levels of preparation and are characterized by different levels of professionalism. In addition to these roles, NAEYC has identified specialty roles in early childhood education, including special educators, subject-area teachers (in such areas as art, music, physical education, or foreign language), parent education coordinators, social service coordinators, education coordinators, program administrators, and unit administrators. These specialist roles generally require preparation beyond that required of early childhood teachers.

Professional roles in early childhood education include assistant teacher, teacher, master teacher, and family child care provider.

EARLY CHILDHOOD PROFESSIONAL CATEGORIES

Level 1 ***Early Childhood Teacher Assistants*** are entry-level personnel who implement program activities under direct supervision of professional staff. This level would require a high school diploma or the equivalent. Once employed, teacher assistants should participate in professional development programs.

Level 2 ***Early Childhood Associate Teachers*** independently implement program activities and may be responsible for the care and education of a group of children. They must be able to demonstrate competency in six basic areas as defined by the national Child Development Associate (CDA) Credentialing Program.

Level 3 ***Early Childhood Teachers*** provide care and education for groups of children. They must demonstrate all Level 1 and Level 2 competencies and possess greater theoretical knowledge and practical skills. A bachelor's degree in early childhood education or child development would be required.

Level 4 ***Early Childhood Specialists*** supervise and train staff, design curriculum, and/or administer programs. They are expected to have at least a bachelor's degree in early childhood education or child development as well as three years of full-time teaching experience with young children and/or an advanced degree.

NAEYC (1984) has identified different levels of preparation and responsibility for practitioners. It recognized four levels of early childhood education practice, delineated the levels of knowledge and skill corresponding to each level, and disseminated recommendations on ways to attain such knowledge and skill.

The concern for the professionalization of the field of early childhood education continues. Recently NAEYC established a National Institute for Early Childhood Professional Development. The Institute has held several conferences related to professionalizing the early childhood field. One of the major issues relates to inclusion and exclusion. Many persons enter the early childhood field with little or no preparation. A major question is whether such individuals should continue to be included in the field or whether increased preparation should be required of practitioners. On the one hand, the requirement of increased preparation will lead to increased status for the field as well as better experiences for young children. On the other hand, such a move may exclude many individuals who could make a significant contribution to the lives of young children.

PREPARING TO BECOME AN EARLY CHILDHOOD TEACHER

Teachers of young children are prepared in colleges and universities, often in early childhood education or child development programs. Sometimes early childhood teachers are prepared in elementary education programs that require additional courses for an early childhood or kindergarten endorsement. Junior colleges also offer associate degrees or one-year programs in child development or early childhood education.

While early childhood teacher preparation programs vary, the majority meet a general set of requirements for content. The early childhood education major is designed to prepare students to be certified as teachers of young children. Since the period of early childhood spans the years from birth through age eight, programs may prepare teachers to work in that entire age span or just some portion of it. Most programs require that students receive a broad general education background. They may also require students to complete a concentration in one of these areas. In addition, students must complete a core of professional courses that includes educational foundations, curriculum knowledge, teaching methods in the general subject areas appropriate to the education of young children, and opportunities to observe, participate, and student teach under supervision, in a variety of settings and at a variety of age and grade levels.

Early childhood teachers are teachers of general education. They should be well grounded in broad areas of knowledge. Since they teach those areas of knowledge, general education is also professional knowledge. The areas of general education include language and literacy, mathematics, science, social studies, art and music, and health and physical education. General education can constitute two-thirds to three-fourths of the undergraduate program, with professional preparation rounding out the program. Increasingly, the teacher preparation portion of the program is being offered after completion of the bachelor's degree and may lead toward a master's degree.

The portion of the program dedicated to professional preparation begins with educational foundations, which includes study of the history and philosophy of education and of child growth and development. Prospective teachers study the early childhood curriculum and classroom organization in order to learn how to plan, organize, implement, and evaluate a program that is appropriate for young children. Courses in teaching language arts and reading, mathematics, science, social studies, art, and music—either taught separately or integrated in some way—are required. All programs also focus on teaching children with disabilities in the regular classroom.

Field experiences are an important part of the teacher preparation program. These experiences allow students to observe and participate in preschool, kindergarten, and primary-grade programs. Settings might include public elementary schools, child-care centers, Head Start programs, and other preschools. Field experiences include student teaching, in which students take on increasing responsibility for a class of children until they acquire full responsibility. In student teaching, students integrate the technical knowledge gained from the various professional courses with the practical knowledge that comes of working directly with children in an educational setting. The result should be a core of professional knowledge on which good teaching is based. Teacher preparation programs often require several student teaching experiences at different levels (College Board, 1992).

Many programs in two-year and community colleges may parallel early childhood teacher training programs at the university level, although they offer fewer course hours in each area of preparation and a much smaller general education component. Often community college programs for early childhood practitioners are vocational programs that focus more on the practical and less on the theoretical and foundational levels of teaching. Such programs do not lead to teacher certifications but are designed for persons who wish to work in preschools, day-care centers, or child-development centers. Often these programs follow the Child Development Associate guidelines and lead to the CDA credential.

NAEYC has developed a set of guidelines for four-year and five-year programs of early childhood teacher education (NAEYC, 1982) that are being provisionally implemented by the National Council for the Accreditation of Teacher Education. Successful completion of a four- or five-year teacher education program should lead to state certification as an early childhood teacher. While similar guidelines have been developed for programs at two-year and community colleges, they are advisory only, since no form of program accreditation exists at this level.

CERTIFICATION AND CREDENTIALING

One of the greatest concerns in the field of early childhood education is to ensure the quality of programs for young children. One way to assure quality is to set standards for early childhood practitioners. Standards for teachers are established through state teacher certification. Certification standards apply in all states to teachers in public schools and in some states to teachers in private schools as well. However, certification is generally not required for teachers in child-care centers or preschools. These early childhood programs are regulated by social service agencies rather than by educational agencies. Unfortunately, as noted in Table 1–1 on pages 10–11, there is no consistency in how states certify teachers or in the definition of early childhood education. Indeed, while some states offer an endorsement for kindergarten or early childhood teaching on an elementary teacher certificate, other states offer no early childhood certification. Not all states presently certify early childhood teachers. Because certification requirements have been changing so rapidly in recent years, persons interested in the current certification standards for early childhood education might wish to consult their college or university's certification officer or to check the library for the most recent edition of Tryneski's *Requirements for Certification of Teachers, Librarians, and Administrators for Elementary and Secondary Schools* (Chicago: University of Chicago Press).

Requirements for practitioners in preschools are usually embedded in the licensing standards in the various states. These requirements may include a high school diploma and a small number of child-related courses taken beyond high school. Since the 1970s a Child Development Associate credential has been required by Head Start programs and by some child-care licensing agencies to demonstrate practitioners' competence. This credential is currently administered by the Council for Professional Development, an affiliate of the National Association for the Education of Young Children (NAEYC). Presently, 26 states plus the District of Columbia require the CDA credential for at least one category of day-care center staff.

Another way of ensuring the quality of teachers in early childhood programs is to ensure the quality of programs that prepare these teachers. This is accomplished in two ways. State departments of education usually approve programs leading to teacher certification. In addition, accreditation of programs that prepare teachers in four-year colleges and universities is provided by the National Council for the Accreditation of Teacher Education (NCATE), which approves both institutions and the individual programs these institutions offer. Review of early childhood programs is done through NAEYC just as other professional associations review programs in their areas of specialization.

As shortages of teachers have become apparent in certain specialties, some states have adopted alternative certification procedures for those who have not been prepared in traditional teacher education programs. Lutz and Hutton (1989) indicate that alternative certification can assist in addressing the problem of teacher shortage. However, there seems little hope that this process can have a major impact on a general teacher shortage without drastically lowering professional standards.

In addition to alternative certification, some states and local school districts are allowing teachers of three- and four-year-olds to teach without early childhood certification. Although this procedure might alleviate the shortage of teachers of young children, it does not help to ensure quality education. These individuals might have a degree, or even certification in another area, but they may not understand child development and the use of appropriate teaching strategies for young children.

Table 1.1

Early Childhood Teacher Certification: A National Perspective

	State	Range of Applicability	Required Competency Tests P&P	OTJ
1.	Alabama	N–Grade 3	x	
2.	Alaska	no		
3.	Arizona	no	x	
4.	Arkansas	no (K endorsement)	x	
5.	California	no (K endorsement)	x	
6.	Colorado	3–8 years	x	
7.	Connecticut	no	x	
8.	Delaware	N–K and K–Grade 3	x	
9.	Florida	no (K endorsement)	x	x
10.	Georgia	K–Grade 4	x	x
11.	Hawaii	no	x	
12.	Idaho	no	x	
13.	Illinois	birth–Grade 3	x	
14.	Indiana	0–4 years (K–Grade 3)	x	x
15.	Iowa	PreK–K		
16.	Kansas	0–4 years	x	
17.	Kentucky	no (K–Grade 4)	x	x
18.	Louisiana	(N–K)	x	
19.	Maine	no	x	x
20.	Maryland	(N–K)	x	
21.	Massachusetts	K–Grade 3	x	
22.	Michigan	no		
23.	Minnesota	(PreK–K)	x	
24.	Mississippi	no	x	x
25.	Missouri	N–Grade 3	x	
26.	Montana	no	x	
27.	Nebraska	birth–K	x	
28.	Nevada	no	x	x

Table 1.1 (continued)

29.	New Hampshire	birth–Grade 3	x	
30.	New Jersey	(N–K)	x	
31.	New Mexico	no	x	
32.	New York	no	x	x
33.	North Carolina	K–Grade 4	x	x
34.	North Dakota	no (K endorsement)	x	
35.	Ohio	(PreK–K and K–Grade 3)		
36.	Oklahoma	N–Grade 2	x	x
37.	Oregon	no	x	x
38.	Pennsylvania	N–Grade 3	x	x
39.	Rhode Island	N–Grade 2	x	
40.	South Carolina	K–Grade 4	x	x
41.	South Dakota	(N endorsement)	x	x
42.	Tennessee	(K–Grade 3)	x	
43.	Texas	(PreK–Grade 3)	x	x
44.	Utah	N–Grade 3		
45.	Vermont	birth–age 8	x	x
46.	Virginia	N–K–Grade 4	x	x
47.	Washington	N–Grade 3		x
48.	Washington, DC	N–K		
49.	West Virginia	N–K	x	
50.	Wisconsin	(EC and K endorsements)		
51.	Wyoming	K–Grade 3	x	

NOTE: ( ) = Endorsement, not early childhood certification
P&P = Paper and pencil test
OTJ = On-the-job performance test
N = Nursery school
K = Kindergarten

(Cooper, J. M., & Eisenhart, C. E. (1990). The influence of recent educational reforms on early childhood teacher education programs. In B. Spodek & O. N. Saracho (Eds.), *Early childhood teacher preparation: Yearbook in early childhood education,* Vol. 1. New York: Teachers College Press, pp. 186–187).

Certification Testing

Traditionally, persons who successfully completed an approved teacher education program in a given state were recommended for certification in that state. Today, teacher competency tests are increasingly being required for certification in the United States. The testing is usually of the paper-and-pencil type, although teacher performance assessment, which involves observing and assessing teachers' performance on the job, has been gaining momentum.

Certification testing is designed to provide quality control in teacher selection. Most states rely on the services of outside testing contractors. Eighteen states currently have some type of testing program in place. Ten states are developing such programs. Several other states have decided to test competence, but have not yet made commitments regarding which tests they will use. Certification tests may include tests of knowledge of the field of education in which the individual specializes, tests of basic academic skills, or both.

Beginning Teacher Assistance Program

Some educators have questioned whether a graduate of a teacher education program is actually prepared to assume responsibility for a class of children. McNergney, Medley, and Caldwell (1988) briefly describe the Beginning Teacher Assistance Program (BTAP), which aims to (1) assure that beginning teachers possess the necessary competencies to teach and (2) assist beginning teachers in developing these competencies.

Another approach to the problems of beginning teachers is to identify mentors to work with novice teachers. These mentors are experienced, exemplary teachers who are willing to take new teachers under their wings and provide them with the guidance necessary to smooth the transition to competence as a teacher. In some districts, mentors are formally identified and may receive additional salary and released time to work in this role.

THE ACT OF TEACHING

Preactive teaching happens away from the children. It includes planning, evaluating, and making decisions. It is more deliberate than interactive teaching.

Interactive teaching takes place with children. It is more intuitive than preactive teaching.

Early childhood teachers perform many functions, and teacher-child interactions serve many purposes. However, the classroom behavior of teachers is not all there is to teaching. Much of the activity of teaching occurs away from children. Such activity includes determining what to teach; selecting, procuring, and organizing materials and equipment for teaching; evaluating learning; and recording and reporting children's progress. Philip Jackson (1966) differentiated between two modes of teaching behavior—***preactive* teaching** and ***interactive* teaching:**

> Preactive behavior is more or less deliberate. Teachers, when grading exams, planning a lesson, or deciding what to do about a particularly

> difficult student, tend to ponder the matter, to weigh evidence, to hypothesize about the possible outcomes of a certain action. During these moments teachers often resemble, albeit crudely, the stereotype of the problem solver, the decision maker, the hypothesis tester, the inquirer. At such times teaching looks like a highly rational process. . . . In the interactive setting the teacher's behavior is more or less spontaneous. When students are in front of him, and the fat is in the fire, so to speak, the teacher tends to do what he *feels*, or *knows*, rather than what he *thinks*, is right. (p. 13)

The intuitive nature of interactive teaching helps to explain why this form of teaching is so resistant to change through the tactics used in most teacher education programs. The behavior of teachers, however, does have a rational basis. How people behave is a function of how they feel they ought to behave, and what they feel is right cannot be fully separated from what they think is right. Teachers' behaviors go hand in hand with teachers' beliefs.

Teachers' Thought Processes

In his book *Life in Classrooms*, Philip Jackson (1968) reported the mental constructs and processes that underlie teachers' behavior. He illustrated the full complexity of teachers' tasks, distinguished teachers' conceptual frame of reference (such as the distinction between preactive and interactive phases of teaching), and made researchers aware of the importance of describing teachers' thinking and planning as a means to understand classroom processes more fully.

Clark and Peterson (1986) suggest a model for understanding the teaching process. The model represents two fields, teachers' thought processes and teachers' actions with their observable effects, that are critical in the teaching process. Teachers' thought processes take place inside the teachers' heads and cannot be observed. Teachers' behaviors can be observed and measured.

Three major groupings of teachers' thought processes include teachers' planning (preactive and postactive thoughts), teachers' interactive thoughts and decisions, and teachers' theories and beliefs. The difference between the first two groups reflects a difference between whether the thought processes occur outside classroom interaction (preactive and postactive thoughts) or during classroom interaction (interactive thoughts and decisions). These groupings proceed from Jackson's (1968) distinction among the preactive and interactive phases of teaching. This distinction has been used to categorize teachers' thought processes because it represents the types of thinking that teachers do before, during, and after classroom interaction.

Classroom teaching is observable. The model presented by Clark and Peterson (1986) assumes that the relationships among teacher behavior, student behavior, and student achievement are reciprocal. These relationships have been studied by researchers on teaching effectiveness (for example, Brophy & Good, 1986; Wittrock, 1986).

Teacher Characteristics

The characteristics of early childhood personnel that have been found to affect the quality of teaching include age, educational level, training in child development or early childhood education, and years of experience (Vondra, 1984; Feeney & Chun, 1985; Whitebook, Howes, Phillips, & Pemberton, 1989). In child care, the teacher's education is the most important characteristic, affecting the quality of teacher/child interactions and, to a lesser degree, child outcomes (Berk, 1985; Whitebook et al., 1989). Some studies indicate that teachers' age and years of experience affect child outcomes (Feeney & Chun, 1985), but others do not support this finding (Jambor, 1975). In addition to such characteristics as age, experience, and education, other components such as "burnout," dynamics of the work force (Peters, 1993), organizational commitment (Krueger, Lauerman, Graham, & Powell, 1986), job satisfaction (Jorde-Bloom, 1986; McClelland, 1986; Stremmel & Powell, 1990), professional orientation (Jorde-Bloom, 1989), tenure or separation rate (Whitebook & Granger, 1989), and turnover (Whitebook et al., 1989) are also important. Russell, Clifford, and Warlick (1991) suggest a practical model for examining the interrelation of these characteristics with individual behavior as it is encouraged or restricted by the community and work environment.

The National Child Care Staffing Study found that important influences on teacher performance included (1) formal education, specialized early childhood education training, and work experience; (2) the general work environment (wages, benefits, auspices, accreditation); and (3) the classroom environment (teacher/child ratio, group size). These contribute to such outcomes as (a) job satisfaction and turnover, (b) quality of the early childhood program (for instance, the presence of developmentally appropriate activity and appropriate caregiving), and (c) the nature of teacher/child interactions (such as sensitivity, harshness, or detachment); they also influence directly assessed child outcomes (attachment, security, sociability, communication skills, Peabody Picture Vocabulary Test scores, time with peers, and aimless wandering).

NAEYC's *Survey of Child Care Salaries and Working Conditions* (1984) reported the results of its survey in which 3,818 NAEYC members responded to questions about their work environment. The report noted that "Hundreds of thousands of individuals are employed in early childhood programs" (p. 10).

Although many early childhood teachers, especially those outside the public schools, are discouraged with the low pay, lack of benefits, and poor working conditions, they have a high level of organizational commitment (Jorde-Bloom, 1989; Powell & Stremmel, 1989; Stremmel, 1990).

Teachers' Roles

Teachers of young children act out their many roles in response to the expectations of the school, the profession, and the teachers themselves. Teachers may be involved in all the major decisions relating to children and what they learn, or teachers may be told what to do. Some schools place great stress on *caring* for children, others, only on *instructing*. The extent to which a range of teaching styles is encouraged varies among schools.

In all situations, to a greater or lesser extent, teachers seem to serve a nurturing role, an instructional role, and a relational role. Each role contains elements of both action and decision making. An analysis of teachers' roles could provide an alternative basis for assessing teachers' professional knowledge. Saracho (1984) has analyzed the following roles of a teacher:

1. **Diagnostician.** Teachers need to assess children's strengths and needs in order to plan successful learning experiences.
2. **Curriculum Designer.** Teachers develop curricula within the capabilities of young children based on theories and practice of early childhood education as well as on the learning that the community considers important.
3. **Organizer of Instruction.** Teachers use long-range and short-range planning to organize the classroom activities in order to achieve educational goals. Teachers inquire about appropriate available resources and make the best possible use of them.
4. **Manager of Learning.** Teachers facilitate learning by creating a learning environment and offering learning experiences that are relevant and interesting to the children.
5. **Counselor/Advisor.** Teachers continuously interact with children and provide them with caretaking, emotional support, and guidance as well as instruction. Teachers also help children to learn socialization skills.
6. **Decision Maker.** Teachers constantly make a range of decisions about children, materials, activities, and goals. Some are instantaneous decisions, while others reflect planning, as teachers select from among alternatives and implement their choices.

These roles are directly related to both preactive and interactive professional performance. If the role of teachers is extended beyond classroom responsibilities, other roles (for example, child advocate, adult educator, or supervisor), may be added. The successful performance of each role requires that teachers of young children acquire a range of knowledge, skills, and attitudes. As teachers acquire knowledge and understanding, they can apply the principles of early childhood education to practical situations.

Teaching as Nurturing Young children are relatively dependent on adults for their health, care, and safety. Teaching in the early years requires one to be nurturing. Children cannot learn if they are hungry, ill, frightened, or uncomfortable. From its inception, the nursery school provided for the care of children. Day-care centers were specifically designed to provide such care. Kindergartens and elementary schools have accepted responsibility for caring elements as well, feeding breakfast and lunch to children and providing various screening tests to identify developmental problems. The responsibility for this care often falls on the classroom teacher.

Teachers of young children have to go beyond these basic nurturing responsibilities. They need to provide love and comfort. They may, in a limited sense, serve as parent substitutes. They may even be called upon provide toilet training. All these are important and reasonable educational requirements. However, problems arise when nurturing acts become the only interests of the teacher. It is easy to become aware of the children's needs for nurturing; in some circumstances they cry out for response. Though these needs should never be ignored, some of the other educational needs of children are less apparent and thus more easily overlooked. When the teacher's only role is the nurturing one, the program is apt to be more a child-minding operation than an educational endeavor, and the children are shortchanged.

Teaching as Instructing When we think of teaching, we usually think of the instructional role of the teacher. The conventional view of a teacher is of a person who transmits knowledge to others. Telling and demonstrating are direct forms of instruction. Other, more indirect, forms of instruction can also elicit learning. Indirect instruction includes creating learning situations, planning for encounters with instructional resources, and asking questions that cause children to think and test perceptions of reality. These techniques cause the children to act upon their perceived world to create their own knowledge.

Each view of instruction is based upon a set of assumptions about knowledge and schools that often remains unexamined. One assumption is that knowledge consists of a body of facts and information to be assimilated by an individual. The teacher must determine what knowledge is important. Then the teacher tells the children what they must know through lectures, storytelling, demonstrations, or the use of computers, films, sound recordings, or television. During the years that children attend school, they accumulate more facts and information, and thus become more knowledgeable.

Other views of education and the development of knowledge require different forms of instruction. Knowledge is not the result of an accumu-

One role of the teacher is to instruct children.

lation of facts and information but rather the result of integrating information within some structure that gives it meaning. Facts are the raw data from which knowledge is developed, and they may be easily discarded once used. To create knowledge, a person must do something to these facts, become an active seeker and creator of knowledge. Passively receiving information is not enough to create knowledge.

A variety of curriculum models have been developed in the field of early childhood education, based on different assumptions about the nature of schooling, of knowledge, and of young children. Teachers can select from among those models and modify them to fit the particular circumstances. In selecting and modifying existing programs, teachers design a curriculum for a particular group of children after carefully considering issues of scope, sequence, and balance.

Once teachers have designed a program for a group of children, they must turn to assessing the learning capabilities of the children. Teachers must come to know each child in order to create an appropriate match between children's learning abilities and styles and the teaching methods and materials to be used. In this process, teachers draw on their knowledge both of how children learn and develop and of early childhood practices and procedures.

As diagnosticians, teachers collect relevant information about each child for use in program planning. Some of this information comes from others, including parents, psychologists, learning specialists, and former teachers. In addition, teachers continually collect their own information about the children in their class through observing children's behaviors, analyzing children's products, and administering both standardized and teacher-made tests. Teachers should systematically record the information they collect. They can use this information in program planning from the beginning of the school year and, as the school year progresses, use further information to modify the evolving curriculum.

Once these tasks are performed, teachers are responsible for delivering the educational experiences they have designed. They must gather and use appropriate physical and human resources. They must orchestrate the activities of the classroom to meet each child's individual needs within the total class milieu. Teachers must organize physical space, collect and deploy materials, establish a daily schedule, and choose and implement strategies for learning activities. Especially in the beginning of the year, teachers should make children aware of the resources available to them. Teachers can use both direct and indirect methods of teaching. The concept of the teacher as instructor is adequate for understanding only one of the teacher's roles. It represents part of the whole picture.

Teaching as Relating While some educators view the instructional role of the teacher as crucial, others view the relational aspect of teaching as being of primary importance. The teacher continually interacts with children during the school day, and the quality of these interactions may be more important than the specific instructional practices.

Arthur Combs (1965) defines effective teachers as unique human beings who use themselves effectively and efficiently to carry out personal and social purposes in the education of others. Using one's self in carrying out the purposes of education goes beyond professional competence to involve the teacher's total self, personal as well as professional, in the educational process. Developing ways of relating to and interacting with people is an important part of becoming a teacher. In addition to providing instruction, the teacher serves as a guide and a helper to children. Teachers create an atmosphere in the classroom in which children gain a sense of trust. They help children feel secure as learners and as persons, guiding children in making decisions and providing a rich environment for learning.

Each teacher brings a set of values to a classroom. These values help determine what the teacher considers important and how the teacher deals with individual children. They even determine the selection and use of materials and the arrangement of the classroom. Ultimately, these values will influence the children's values. Values are often "caught rather than taught" because they are expressed and transmitted in personal ways. Above all, teachers provide warmth and support for children. They accept children as whole human beings with strengths and weaknesses. Through personal relationships with children, teachers help them grow.

The relational aspects of teaching are not contained in a prescribed set of actions; what is important is that teachers manifest their personalities

The relational aspect of teaching is important.

in authentic ways. Teacher training programs must go beyond conventional courses in educational methods and foundations; they must help students explore what education and teaching mean to them and how they relate to others.

Teaching as Thinking and Acting Much of what teachers do can be observed in the classroom. Because teachers' actions are so accessible, they have been the focus of attention and research for many years. Indeed, until recently, most of the research on teaching has focused on teacher behavior (see, for example, Rosenshine, 1976). More recently, however, researchers have focused on teachers' thinking. Teachers' thought processes are less accessible than are their behaviors and can often be studied only through teachers' reports of what they think. Analyzing such research requires a higher level of inference than does analyzing teachers' behavior. Teachers' thought processes are no less real, however; nor are they less important. In fact, much of what teachers do is driven by what they think. Among the areas of teachers' thought that have been studied are teacher planning, teacher judgment, interactive decision making, and teachers' implicit theories (Clark & Yinger, 1979).

The research summarized by Clark and Yinger suggests that teachers begin their planning by considering the content of what is to be taught and the setting in which teaching will take place. Teachers then focus their attention on the need for student involvement. The activity itself, rather than its goal, is the focal point of planning. In thinking about teaching, teachers make judgments about their students, about the materials available to them, and about themselves. Evidence indicates that teachers' judgment are responsive to training.

Among the studies of teachers' thinking are several studies about teachers' implicit theories. Teachers hold a variety of curriculum constructs (Bussis, Chittendon, & Amarel, 1976), or theories in use (Argyris & Schon, 1975), that drive their actions. Teachers sift the knowledge they gain from university courses, in-service training sessions, or their professional reading through their belief systems, accepting or rejecting the information they gather. The theories they hold help teachers create meaning from the information they receive. Such theories allow teachers to behave in a consistent manner as they work under a variety of circumstances with different children. Within this consistency, however, teachers must respond flexibly to particular conditions.

In becoming a teacher, each individual constructs his or her own set of theories of education. Implicit theories are built out of the information gained in teacher training programs: theories of learning and development along with knowledge of methods and materials. Practical experience in classrooms with children provides a test for the theoretical knowledge gained in teacher preparation as well as another source of information with which to build and modify a personal set of theories of education. Finally, teachers must match their professional knowledge with their personal and social values related to the importance of childhood, the importance of the individual, the importance of the school, and the effectiveness of all that they do with and for children (Spodek, 1989).

The process of becoming a teacher may begin in a college course, but it should not end there. It includes the continued development and modification of theories about education as well as the continued improvement of teaching skills. Teaching reaches its highest professional stage by integrating thinking and acting.

A **Code of ethics** provides guidelines for practice to protect clients and to minimize a professional's temptation to perform in an unprofessional manner.

Teaching as Ethical Behavior A profession usually has a **code of ethics** to protect the best interests of the clients and to minimize any temptations inherent in the practice of the profession. Most professional societies institute a system to discipline members who violate the profession's code of ethics (Katz, 1984, 1988). Thus, a lawyer can be disbarred and a doctor can be banned from practicing because of unethical professional behavior.

While NAEYC has no way to bar an unethical teacher from practicing, it did develop a code of ethical conduct. This is presented in Appendix A at the end of the book. The code sets forth a conception of professional responsibilities related to children, families, colleagues, and community and society. It is hoped that this code will guide practitioners' conduct and help to resolve dilemmas.

While NAEYC cannot enforce this code of ethics, it does print a "Commitment to Children" on the back of each membership card, with the hope that its members will adhere to it.

Commitment to Children

- I know about, abide by, and advocate for laws and regulations that enhance the quality of life for young children.
- I will support the rights of childrpen to live and learn in environments that are responsive to their developmental needs.
- I will improve my competencies in providing for children's needs.
- I will appreciate each child's uniqueness, thus enhancing the child's self-respect.

Summary

Teaching is a complex task that requires ethical behavior. Teachers of young children must develop the appropriate knowledge and skills, which can be gained in teacher education programs. States try to insure the quality of teaching by establishing standards for teacher certification.

Not all early childhood practitioners are certified teachers. Some may be credentialed by the Child Development Associate Consortium. Others may have little or no preparation. However, there is an increasing movement to professionalize the field.

Preparation to teach does not end with completion of a program and certification. It requires continued professional development.

References

Almy, M. (1974). *The early childhood educator at work.* New York: McGraw-Hill.

Almy, M., & Snyder, A. (1947). The staff and its preparation. In *Early childhood education.* 46th Yearbook of the National Society for the Study of Education, Part II. Chicago: University of Chicago Press.

Argyris, C., & Schon, D. A. (1975). *Theory in practice: Increasing professional effectiveness.* San Francisco: Jossey-Bass.

Berk, L. E. (1985). Relationship of caregiver education to child-oriented attitudes, job satisfaction, and behaviors toward children. *Child Care Quarterly, 14*(2), 103–109.

Brophy, J. E., & Good, T. L. (1986). Teacher behavior and student achievement. In M. C. Wittrock (Ed.), *Handbook of research on teaching* (3rd ed.) (pp. 328–375). New York: Macmillan.

Bussis, A. M., Chittendon, E. A., & Amarel, M. (1976). *Beyond surface curriculum.* Boulder, CO: Westview Press.

Child Development Associate Consortium. (1977). *Competency standards.* Washington, DC: The Consortium.

Clark, C. M., & Peterson, P. L. (1986). Teachers' thought processes. In M. C. Wittrock (Ed.), *Handbook of research on teaching* (3rd ed.) (pp. 255–296). New York: Macmillan.

Clark, C. M., & Yinger, R. J. (1979). Teachers' thinking. In P. L. Peterson & H. J. Walberg (Eds.), *Research on teaching: Concepts, findings and implications.* Berkeley, CA: McCutcheon.

College Board (1992). *Guide to 150 popular college majors.* New York: College Entrance Examination Board.

Combs, A. W. (1965). *The professional education of teachers.* Boston: Allyn and Bacon.

Cooper, J. M., & Eisenhart, C. E. (1990). The influence of recent educational reforms on early childhood teacher education programs. In B. Spodek & O. N. Saracho (Eds.), *Early childhood teacher preparation: Yearbook in early childhood education* (Vol. 1). (pp. 176–191). New York: Teachers College Press.

Feeney, S., & Chun, R. (1985). Research in review: Effective teachers of young children. *Young Children, 41*(1), 47–55.

Feeney, S., & Sysko, L. (1986). Professional ethics in early childhood education. *Young Children, 42*(1), 15–20.

Jackson, P. W. (1966). *The way teaching is.* Washington, DC: Association for Supervision and Curriculum Development.

Jackson, P. (1968). *Life in classrooms.* New York: Holt, Rinehart & Winston.

Jambor, T. W. (1975). Teacher role behavior: Day care versus nursery school. *Child Care Quarterly, 4*(2), 93–100.

Jorde-Bloom, P. (1986). Teacher job satisfaction: A framework for analysis. *Early Childhood Research Quarterly, 1*(2), 167–184.

Jorde-Bloom, P. (1989). Professional orientation: Individual and organizational perspectives. *Child and Youth Care Quarterly, 18*(4), 227–242.

Katz, L. G. (1969). *Teaching in preschools: Roles and goals.* Urbana, IL: ERIC Clearinghouse on Early Childhood Education.

Katz, L. G. (1984). The education of preprimary teachers. In L. G. Katz, P. J. Wagemaker, & K. Steiner (Eds.), *Current topics in early childhood education* (Vol. 5). (pp. 1–26). Norwood, NJ: Ablex.

Katz, L. G. (1988). Where is early childhood education as a profession? In B. Spodek, O. N. Saracho, & D. L. Peters (Eds.) *Professionalism and the early childhood practitioner* (pp. 75–83). New York: Teachers College Press.

Krueger, M., Lauerman, R., Graham, M., & Powell, N. (1986). Characteristics and organizational commitment of child and youth care workers. *Child Care Quarterly, 15*(1), 60–72.

Lutz, F. W., & Hutton, J. B. (1989). Alternative teacher certification: Its policy implications for classroom personnel practice. *Educational Evaluation and Policy Analysis, 11*(3), 237–254.

McClelland, J. (1986). Job satisfaction of child care workers: A review. *Child Care Quarterly, 15*(2), 82–89.

McNergney, R. F., Medley, D. M., & Caldwell, M. S. (1988). Making and implementing policy on teacher licensure. *Journal of Teacher Education, 39*(3), 38–44.

National Association for the Education of Young Children (1982). *Early childhood teacher education guidelines for four- and five-year programs.* Washington, DC: NAEYC.

National Association for the Education of Young Children (1984, November). Results of the NAEYC survey of child care salaries and working conditions. *Young Children*, pp. 9–14.

Peters, D. L. (1993). Studying teachers and teaching in early childhood settings. In B. Spodek (Ed.), *Handbook of research in early childhood education* (pp. 493–505). New York: Macmillan.

Powell, D. R., & Stremmel, A. J. (1989). The relation of early childhood training and experience to the professional development of child care workers. *Early Childhood Research Quarterly, 4,* 339–355.

Powell, D. R., & Stremmel, A. J. (1988). Managing relations with parents: Research notes on the teacher's role. In D. L. Peters & S. Kontos (Eds.), *Continuity and discontinuity of experiences in child care* (pp. 129–146). Norwood, NJ: Ablex.

Rosenshine, B. (1976). Recent research on teacher behaviors and student achievement. *Journal of Teacher Education, 27,* 61–64.

Russell, S., Clifford R., & Warlick, M. (1991). *Working in child care in North Carolina.* Carrboro, NC: Daycare Services Association.

Saracho, O. N. (1984). Perception of the teaching process in early childhood education through role analysis. *Journal of the Association for the Study of Perception International, 19*(1), 26–29.

Spodek, B. (1989). Implicit theories of early childhood teachers: Foundations for professionalism. In B. Spodek, O. N. Saracho, & D. L. Peters (Eds.), *Professionalism and the early childhood practitioner* (pp. 161–172). New York: Teachers College Press.

Stremmel, A. J. (1990, April). Predictors of intention to leave child care work. Paper presented at the annual meeting of the American Educational Research Association, Boston, Massachusetts.

Vondra, J. I. (1984). A consideration of caregiver age variables in day care settings. *Child Care Quarterly, 13*(2), 102–113.

Whitebook, M., Howes, C., Phillips, D., & Pemberton, C. (1989, November). Who cares? Child care teachers and the quality of care in America. *Young Children,* pp. 41–45.

Whitebook, M., & Granger, R. C. (1989). Assessing teacher turnover. *Young Children, 44*(4), 11–14.

Wittrock, M. C. (Ed). (1986). *Handbook of research on teaching.* New York: Macmillan.

2

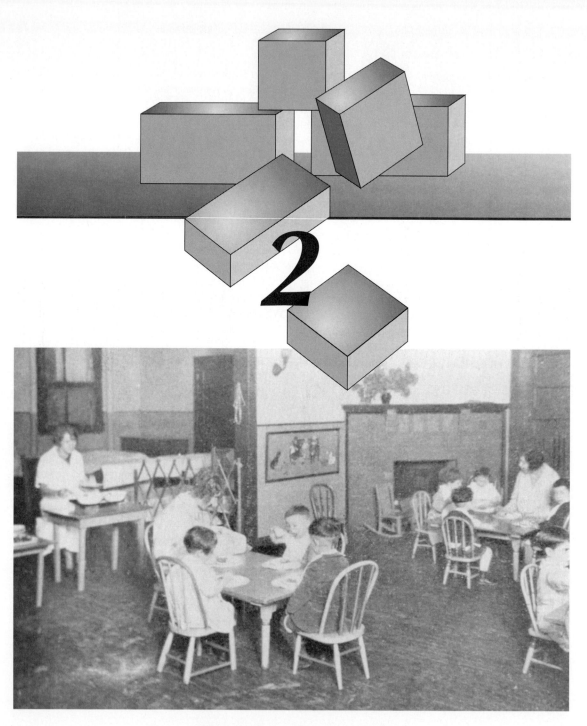

Beginnings of Early Childhood Education

CHAPTER OVERVIEW

This chapter presents:

- The primary school
- The kindergarten
- The infant school
- The nursery school
- The Montessori school
- The child care center
- Project Head Start
- Early childhood special education programs
- Programs for children at risk

INTRODUCTION

Early childhood education programs have been offered in one form or another in the United States since colonial times. While the proportion of children enrolled in primary schools has remained constant since World War II, the proportion of children enrolled in preprimary school (preschool and kindergarten) has increased. In 1991, 28.2 percent of all three-year-olds, 53 percent of all four-year-olds, and 86 percent of all five-year-olds were enrolled in school. About 12.6 percent of kindergarten children, about the same percentage as for all elementary and secondary students, were enrolled in private school. Enrollment in full-day early childhood programs has increased significantly over the last several years, with about 38 percent of three- and four-year-olds enrolled in full-day programs in 1991 compared with 16 percent in 1969. The proportion of three- and four-year-old African-American children enrolled in school was higher than that of white children, while the proportion of children of Hispanic origin was lower than that of white children. A significantly higher proportion of African-American girls than of all other children were enrolled. What makes the increase in preprimary enrollment especially significant is that it occurred at the same time that enrollments in elementary and secondary schools were declining (Snyder & Hoffman, 1992).

The proportion of women with young children who are in the work force has risen sharply since 1970. These women make various arrangements for caring for their children. In 1987, 22 percent of children whose

Figure 2–1 Preprimary Enrollment of 3- to 5-Year Olds, by Attendance Status: October 1970 to October 1991

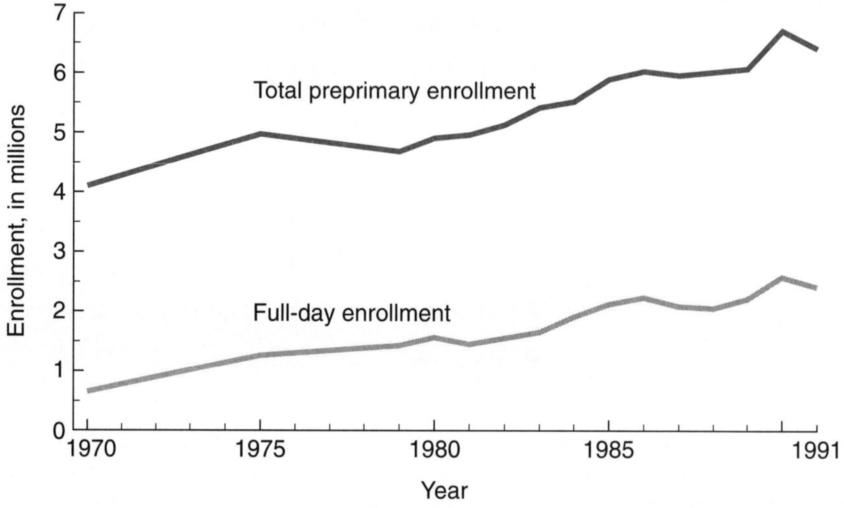

Source: T. D. Snyder and C. M. Hoffman, *Digest of Educational Statistics* (1991). (Washington, D.C.: National Center for Educational Statistics, 1992), p. 45.

mothers worked outside the home were cared for in family day care homes and 25 percent in child care centers or preschools. An even higher proportion of children whose mothers work full time are enrolled in school (Children's Defense Fund, 1991). The exact number of children in nonpublic early childhood programs is not available, since these programs do not have to report enrollment or attendance figures. However, surveys of the Bureau of Census provide reasonably accurate estimates. They show that attendance in early childhood programs has become the rule rather than the exception for children in the United States.

A variety of institutions provide early childhood education in the United States. These include preschools, nursery schools, child care centers, Head Start programs, prekindergartens, kindergartens, and primary classes. These institutions share many common elements but may differ in institutional setting, ages of children served, traditions from which the programs developed, goals set for programs, and psychological theories to which they subscribe, all of which influence the programs. A look at the traditions of early childhood education and contemporary schools should help in understanding the organization of the field.

THE ROOTS OF EARLY CHILDHOOD EDUCATION

When did early childhood education begin? Children have been educated and cared for at least since the beginning of recorded history, but only in modern times were schools established specifically to educate and care for young children. At first there was no difference between the education of young children and the education of older children. Only at the beginning of the nineteenth century was the education of young children separated from that of older children, and methods appropriate for children in their early years were developed.

We could go back in time to identify the education of young children that has taken place since the beginning of the human race. But this education was informal; educating and caring for young children was the responsibility of families. We could easily identify the concerns of educational philosophers about young children at least as far back as the ancient Greeks. Plato, for example, wrote extensively about education. But the education we find in schools today is a product of the work of modern educators and philosophers rather than of ancient ones. Modern early childhood education began when schools were especially designed for young children and when institutions were created to care for groups of young children outside the home.

Early Educational Philosophers

In 1628, John Amos Comenius wrote *School of Infancy*, which included his idea of the "school of the mother's lap," where the child from birth to age six learned the rudiments of all knowledge (Osborn, 1991). Comenius' course of study included "Simple lessons in objects, [as children were] taught to know stones, plants, and animals; the names and uses of the members of the body; to distinguish light and darkness and colors; the Geography of the cradle, the room, the farm, the street, and the field; trained in moderation, purity and obedience, and taught to say the Lord's Prayer" (Monroe, 1908, p. ix). In 1658 Comenius wrote the first children's picture book, *Orbis Pictus* (*Visible World*, 1887), which used illustrations and was translated into every major European language.

Jean Jacques Rousseau's classic book, *Emile* (1762), written a century later, discussed the value of early childhood education. Rousseau believed that education should begin at birth and continue until the individual reached age 25. He emphasized the need to support children's natural development instead of using instruction to socialize children and prepare them for life: ". . . freedom, not power, is the greatest good. That man is truly free who desires what he is able to perform, and does what he desires. This is my fundamental maxim. Apply it to childhood, and all the rules of education spring from it" (Rousseau, 1762, p. 48). Rousseau viewed sense perception as the foundation of human knowledge. This

Figure 2–2 Time Line of the History of Early Childhood Education, 1647–1965

1965	The creation of Head Start
1941	The establishment of Lanham Act child care centers
1933	WPA nursery schools
1914	The creation of the nursery school—Margaret Macmillan
1913	Reform of the kindergarten (International Kindergarten Union Report)
1907	Maria Montessori's *casa dei bambini*
1856	America's first kindergarten
1854	First American day nursery opened in New York
1837	Friedrich Froebel's kindergarten
1816	Robert Owen's infant school
about 1767	Frederick Oberlin's knitting school
1647	Puritan School Law of 1647

idea is also found in Robert Owen's Infant School, in Maria Montessori's *casa dei bambini,* and in contemporary early childhood programs.

Our story of how the different institutions devoted to the education and care of young children developed will begin in colonial America. Other parts go back to European origins.

SCHOOLS FOR YOUNG CHILDREN

The **common school** provided basic education for all children during colonial times.

In the United States, young children were initially enrolled in the primary school or **common school,** as it was called. This school provided basic education for all the children in the community. Most children completed their education in this common school. Common schools did not prepare children for secondary school or college. Of the few young persons who went to college at that time, many never attended the common school but were tutored at home in their early years.

The Primary School

The goals of contemporary primary education descend directly from those of colonial primary education. Especially in the New England colonies, religious belief required that persons be able to read the Scriptures in English. This led to the establishment of primary schools, under the supervision of community churches, to teach reading. Instruction in spelling, grammar, and arithmetic were added later.

The preamble to the Puritan School Law of 1647 gives evidence of the religious roots of colonial primary education:

> It being one chief point of that old deluder, Satan, to keep men from the knowledge of the Scriptures, as in former times, by keeping them in an unknown tongue, so in these latter times, by persuading from the use of tongues, that so at last the true sense and meaning of the original might be clouded by false glosses of saint-seeming deceivers, that learning might not be buried in the grave of our fathers in church and commonwealth, the Lord assisting our endeavors—It is therefore ordered that every township in this jurisdiction, after the Lord has increased them to the number of fifty householders, shall then forthwith appoint one within their own town to teach all such children as shall resort to him to write and read (Nohle, 1924, pp. 24–25).

As the American colonies became a nation after the Revolutionary War, schools lost their religious flavor. The U.S. Constitution, which provided for the separation of church and state, prohibited government support of religion. Because the Constitution does not mention education as a function of the federal government, schools became the responsibility of the states. At the same time, patriotism increased in the country. The content of primers used for reading instruction in the late eighteenth century shifted from excerpts from the Bible and simple prayers to tales of patriotism and morality. In the nineteenth century, the content of the primary school became secular. Also at this time, the concept of universal education began to take hold, and children of varied backgrounds were admitted into publicly supported schools.

The primary school was designed to provide instruction in the basic skills. Reading, writing, and arithmetic were the core of learning and teaching at this level, as they continue to be today. Although other areas of study may be included in the primary grades, they have never been as important as the basic skills.

In this early period very young children were often enrolled in primary schools. Children were believed to be capable of high levels of intellectual development. They often learned to read at age three or four, while Latin instruction might begin at age five or six.

By the beginning of the nineteenth century, most towns in Massachusetts, for example, offered private and public schooling to the young. School attendance by the very young was high. In 1826, 5 percent of all the children enrolled in public schools were below the age of four, including 20 percent of all three-year-olds. By the end of the first third of the nineteenth century, enrollment of young children began to decline. The reasons given for the declining enrollment of the young include

(1) an increased emphasis on the role of the mother at home, including her role in educating her young children; (2) a greater concern for the balanced development of young children, including a fear that excessive intellectual activity in young children would cause insanity; and (3) the growing bureaucracy of the public schools, which, in the 1840s and 1850s, sought to exclude not only children under four, but four- and five-year-olds as well, because of concern for the well-being of both the young children and the school. Reformers were hoping that excluding young children would bring better attendance, more disciplined classes, and financial savings (May & Vinovskis, 1977).

While the primary school of the early nineteenth century was basically concerned with teaching the "Three Rs," new elements of instruction were slowly added to the curriculum: arts and crafts, nature study (later to be supplanted by science), geography (later to be incorporated into the social studies), music, and physical education. Many of these new subjects became part of the primary curriculum, at least in part as a result of the influence of the kindergarten, as it came to be included in the elementary school.

Teachers in the colonial primary schools were hired with little regard for professional qualifications or credentials. Indentured servants and widowed women often served as teachers simply because they were available, without concern for their qualifications. The method of instruction consisted mainly of recitation and rote memorization. Few textbooks were available to provide the core of the instructional program.

New educational methodologies that were developing in Europe during the nineteenth century affected the American primary school. Interpretations of the Pestalozzian system of education, with its emphasis on education through objects, led to new developments in German primary education. Johann Heinrich Pestalozzi (1746–1827) was a Swiss educator and reformer who developed a system of education that was related to the organic development of the child. He based his approach to education on humanistic priniciples and on firsthand experience as the basis for children's learning (Silber, 1965). Reports about the changes in German schools influenced American educators to modify their methods of teaching and to enrich their curricula. An increased concern on the part of American educators about teaching methodology led to the establishment of normal schools for the preparation of teachers.

During the latter half of the nineteenth century, the philosophy of the German educator Johann Friedrich Herbart greatly influenced the American primary school. The Herbartian system organized lessons in five steps: (1) preparation, (2) presentation, (3) association, (4) generalization, and (5) application. All lessons were to start with an introduction to prepare the class. All were to culminate in the children's demonstration of their ability to apply new learning. Remnants of the Herbartian method still inform the way teachers today organize their lesson plans, which may begin with motivating the children and end in a culminating activity.

The progressive education movement had a great impact on primary schools in the United States during the first half of the twentieth century. In many cases the Herbartian lessons gave way to the more organic *project* method, which in turn led to the *unit* approach (see Chapter 6).

The move toward urbanization and the development of large schools and school systems in the nineteenth century also led to a change in the organizational patterns of primary education. The nongraded structure of the one-room common school was supplanted by the multiroom school organized by grade, with instructional objectives being determined for each grade level and with all children of like age being grouped into a single class.

The "Knitting School"

The **knitting school** was an early school for young children created by Jean Frederick Oberlin.

The earliest school especially for young children was developed by Jean Frederick Oberlin about 1767. Oberlin was a Protestant minister who lived in Alsace, a province in eastern France. Although Oberlin founded the school, he did not teach in it. That responsibility rested with his wife, Madeleine Oberlin, until her death in 1784, and with Sarah Banzet and Louise Scheppler, who also managed the Oberlin household. The Oberlin school enrolled children as young as two or three years old. The school program included handicrafts as well as exercise and play. The children gathered in a circle around Louise Scheppler, who would talk to them as she knitted. In time, older children took on some of her teaching responsibilities.

The curriculum consisted of showing pictures of subjects taken from nature and history to children and talking about these pictures. At first the teacher would simply show the pictures. When the children were familiar with the pictures, the teacher told them the names of the objects in their regional dialect. Later, the teacher would speak the names of the objects in French while showing the picture. Thus, the children learned to speak French as well as the dialect spoken in their home while learning about the world (Deasey, 1978).

This "knitting school" was so popular that it expanded to five neighboring villages before Oberlin's death. Oberlin's methods were not adopted more generally in other sections of France, however. With the coming of the French Revolution, religious clerics and their work became suspect. Since Oberlin was a minister, French citizens were concerned that his teaching might be both religious and antirevolutionary. Although Oberlin was respected both during and after the revolution, the knitting school remained an isolated phenomenon in France, and the idea never expanded into the rest of Europe. Perhaps the time was not yet ripe for a major effort in support of education for young children.

The Infant School

The **infant school** provided a humane and innovative approach to the education of young children in the early nineteenth century.

The **infant school**, a form of primary education that developed in Britain, was founded in 1816 in New Lanark, Scotland, by Robert Owen, the social reformer. The original principles of infant education were

> that the children were to be out of doors as much as possible and to learn "when their curiosity induced them to ask questions," to dance and sing and not to be "annoyed with books." They were to be educated and trained without punishment or the fear of it, no unnecessary restraint was to be imposed on them and they were to be taught only "what they could understand." The teachers were told to think about such matters as forming good habits and helping the children to treat each other kindly. (Gardner, n.d., p. 6)

Robert Owen, influenced by Pestalozzi and Rousseau, founded schools and a child care center for children of families associated with his mill in New Lanark. He banned very young children from working in his mill and limited the working hours of older children. Children under 12 years of age were restricted to work only six hours a day while children over 12 years of age worked between 12 and 14 hours a day. The common practice in mills at that time was for six-year-old children to work 12 hours a day without a lunch break. They were also not provided with any education (Osborn, 1991). Owen's school was conceived as a part of a broader program of social reform. Owen's conception of the Infant School foreshadowed the concerns of many contemporary educators.

The use of the infant school to serve the needs of poor and working-class children spread beyond Owen's mill town. By 1825 there were at least 55 infant schools in England, Scotland, and Ireland, along with a number of infant school societies. Owen's books circulated throughout Continental Europe and the United States. By 1827 infant schools were

Robert Owen, developer of the infant school

being established in Hartford, Connecticut; New York City; Philadelphia; Boston; and other American cities. Robert Owen himself came to the United States during this period and lectured extensively about his new views of society and about education. He purchased the settlement of New Harmony, Indiana, from the Rappites, a religious group, and established a communitarian society there. He also established an infant school. Both the school and the community had serious problems and failed after a few short years. Infant schools did flourish in New England and in mid-Atlantic communities for about another decade. By the mid–1830s the infant school movement in America had faded (Strickland, 1982).

The infant schools embodied humane innovations and principles of education that proved valuable to the public primary schools. More importantly, these infant schools were underwritten by social reformers who saw them as ways of combatting the evils of urban life. Infant schools, it was felt, could permanently eliminate poverty by educating and socializing young children from poor families. They provided both moral and literary instruction for the children of the urban poor while at the same time freeing mothers for work (May & Vinovskis, 1977). Less than a quarter of a century after the demise of the infant school movement, the Froebelian kindergarten was introduced in the United States.

While Froebel's kindergarten reflected a very different philosophy of education and served a different purpose than the infant school, there were some close connections. Elizabeth Peabody, one of the earliest advocates of the kindergarten in America, had been a part of Bronson Alcott's infant school in Boston. She wrote a book on the infant schools' approach to education, which continued to be revised as late as 1874, long after the schools ceased to exist (Peabody, 1874). Bronson Alcott, the father of the novelist Louisa May Alcott and an American social reformer, was an infant school educator.

Friedrick Froebel, creator of the kindergarten

The Kindergarten

Froebel's **kindergarten** provided symbolic education based on a philosophy related to the unity of humanity, God, and nature.

The **kindergarten** is a unique educational entity. It was developed in Germany in the first half of the nineteenth century. The kindergarten curriculum was based upon a mystical religious philosophy of the unity of nature, God, and humanity. Friedrick Froebel designed a series of activities for children aged three to six to symbolize these relationships. The Froebelian kindergarten was designed to use the *Gifts*, the *Occupations*, and the *Mother's Songs and Plays*, as well as to help children learn to care for plants and animals.

Froebel's ***Gifts*** are manipulative educational materials.

The ***Gifts*** were sets of small manipulative materials to be used by children in prescribed ways. The first set was a series of six yarn balls, each a different color. The single surface of the ball—a sphere—symbolized the unity and wholeness of the universe. The next set—a wooden sphere, a cylinder, and a cube—represented unity, diversity, and the mediation of these opposites, with the sphere and cube representing the opposites and the cylinder representing a mediating shape. Other *Gifts*,

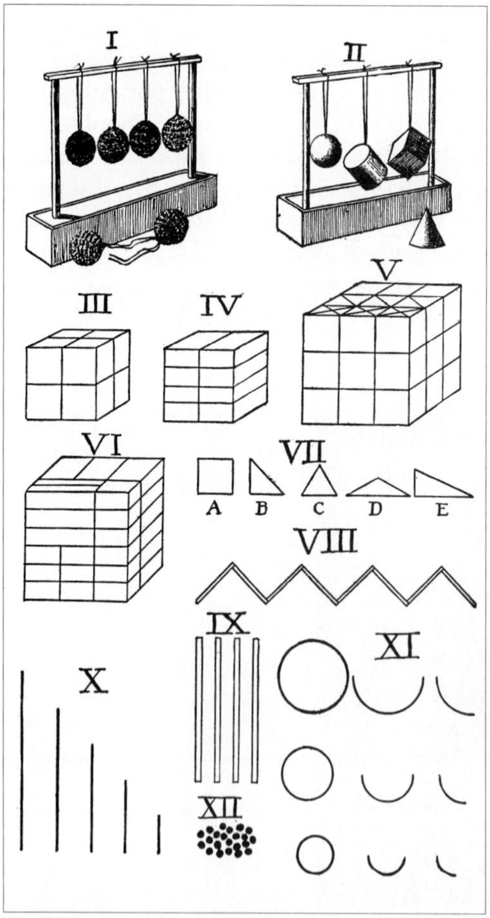

Froebel's kindergarten Gifts

including cubes broken up into smaller parts and then square and triangular tablets, were presented to children in a prescribed sequence. At each stage, children were supposed to build specific forms, each representing some deeper meaning. Throughout the manipulations, little attention was paid to the physical properties of the objects, for sensation and perception of the real world were not considered important.

The ***Occupations,*** consisting of paper weaving, paper folding, paper cutting, sewing, drawing, painting, and clay modeling, reflected the activities of primitive people. They also provided the children with opportunities for artistic expression. The ***Mother's Songs and Plays,*** specially designed songs and games, were derived from the play of peasant women with their young children and from the activities of the social and natural world.

Froebel's ***Occupations*** are craft activities.

Froebel's ***Mother's Songs and Plays*** are songs and games for children.

In time, the Froebelian kindergarten began to expand as an educational movement. With the extension of kindergarten education came a need to train kindergarten teachers. Soon kindergarten training institutions began to attract a number of young German women as students.

In the wave of German migration in the mid-nineteenth century, many women with kindergarten training came to the United States. Their desire to apply the principles of the Froebelian kindergarten to their own children led many to establish kindergartens in their homes. Margarethe Schurz, who was trained in Germany as a kindergartner, as kindergarten teachers were then called, invited the children of relatives into her home to join her children. This became the first kindergarten in the United States, established in Watertown, Wisconsin, in 1856 (Swart, 1967). Other

America's first kindergarten, Watertown, Wisconsin, 1856

German-speaking kindergartens were established in various communities in the United States in the 1860s and 1870s.

Elizabeth Peabody, who became interested in kindergarten education through her reading and through contact with Margarethe Schurz, established the first English-speaking kindergarten in Boston in 1860. Froebel's philosophy was compatible with that of New England Transcendentalism, a philosophic movement that provided intellectual support for the establishment of kindergarten programs in America (Snyder, 1972). American transcendentalism was a philosophy that asserted the superiority of intuitive thought over sensory knowledge. Although kindergartens were first introduced into public schools in St. Louis by 1873, their full inclusion in public education took about a century longer. However, private kindergartens were established in many cities in the interim, sponsored by various associations, mothers' clubs, and philanthropic agencies.

The kindergarten was seen as especially useful to the children of the poor in these early days. In response to the rapid rise of urban centers, the immigration of Europeans to America, and the growth of large city slums, philanthropic kindergartens were established in many areas. Arguments not unlike those heard today in support of Project Head Start were used to support kindergarten education for the poor:

> Centering among, and concerning itself with, the children of the poor, and having for its aim the elevation of the home, it was natural that the kindergarten as a philanthropic movement should win great and early favor. The mere fact that the children of the slums were kept off the streets, and that they were made clean and happy by kind and motherly young women; that the child thus being cared for enabled the mother to go about her work in or outside the home—all this appealed to the heart of America, and America gave freely to make these kindergartens possible. Churches established kindergartens, individuals endowed kindergartens, and associations were organized for the spread and support of kindergartens in nearly every large city. (Fisher, 1908, pp. 19–20)

By the beginning of the twentieth century, a significant rift had developed in American kindergarten education. Traditional kindergarten educators felt that Froebel had discovered the significant elements of education for young children that were relevant to all children for all time. A more liberal group saw greater meaning in Froebel's educational philosophy than in the specific educational activities and methods derived from it. This liberal group felt that, although the original kindergarten program was a step in the right direction, specific activities ought to be discarded when inappropriate. The emergence of the child study movement, which was then establishing an empirical base of knowledge about childhood, and the progressive education movement, with its emphasis on freedom and activity in the classroom, lent support to the liberal kindergartners.

The emerging philosophy of the kindergarten reform movement was probably best stated by Patty Smith Hill in the second report of The Kindergarten: Reports of the Committee of Nineteen on the Theory and Practice of the Kindergarten (1913). According to Hill, the content of the kindergarten program should be related to the present life of the children rather than to the life of children of another culture and another generation. Children should acquire the knowledge of their civilization by using their personal experiences as a means of achieving insight. Hill proposed using concrete child-oriented experiences and classroom play based on the natural activities of childhood. Children were to be free to reconstruct their own reality.

The reform movement tried to retain Froebel's philosophy while doing away with the unnecessary formalism of kindergarten method. Some of the elements of Froebelian philosophy these educators supported included the following:

1. **The Concept of Development in Childhood.** Development was seen as a process of unfolding. Education takes place as the human organizm unfolds. The child's educational activity supports this unfolding process. While Froebel's conception of child development is incompatible with present knowledge, the assumption that education ought to be developmentally oriented remains sound.
2. **Education as Self-Activity.** Froebel suggested that education for young children ought to differ in form and content from that offered to older children. Young children were seen as educating themselves through engaging in activities with the *Gifts* and *Occupations.* While child development has moved away from an acceptance of an "unfolding" process, the concept of education as self-activity is still supported in education.
3. **The Educational Value of Play.** Froebel saw play as an important activity in helping the child mature and learn. In play, Froebel observed the child's symbolic reproductions of adult activity. He attempted to abstract the significant elements of these and provide them in a meaningful order in his educational program. This idea of the use of play in the education of young children is still supported by educators.

The kindergarten reformers felt that many of the Froebelian *Occupations* were too tedious and required hand movements that were too small for young children. They also felt that other arts and crafts activities could profitably be included in the kindergarten program. Since the play of American children was different from that of German children, the reformers wanted to encourage different kinds of play activities. In addition, the reformers felt that children's current lives should provide a source of learning. Because of the reformers' efforts, school play became freer and more reflective of children's lives. Large blocks replaced the *Gifts*, and dolls and miniature housekeeping materials were included in the program.

The reform of kindergarten education continued through the 1920s and 1930s, leading to the creation of kindergartens much like those we find in schools today. A number of factors have influenced the development of kindergarten education since the 1920s. The changing economy of the 1930s and 1940s brought a decrease in the number of public school kindergartens, as shortages in funds and building space led to the exclusion of this level of education from the public schools. The influence of the mental health movement led to an increase in concern for social-emotional learnings and a deemphasizing of the "habit training" of the 1920s. In the late 1950s and 1960s, kindergarten education began to receive more positive attention. A concern for intellectual development in children led to a reexamination of kindergarten curricula. In addition, psychological theories emphasizing the importance of early education gave support to increased public aid for kindergartens and to increasing availability of kindergarten education in many states.

The Nursery School

The nursery school movement developed from a different cultural context from that of the kindergarten. Out of their experience in English health clinics for poor children, Rachel and Margaret Macmillan conceived of the nursery school as a preventive for the children's illnesses, both mental and physical, that were prevalent in the slums. The basic philosophy of nursery education was one of *nurturance.*

Nurturance is a form of education that responds to the social, physical, intellectual, and emotional needs of each child.

Nurturance meant dealing with the whole child—the social, physical, emotional, and intellectual aspects of the human being. The responsibilities of the original nursery school included bathing the children, dressing

Margaret Macmillan, founder of the nursery school

them in clean clothing, resting them, feeding them, and seeing that they got plenty of fresh air—all while educating them. The original nursery schools were single-story buildings, with large doorways or French windows opening into gardens and large outdoor play spaces. Children's play flowed freely between indoors and outdoors.

The educational program developed by the Macmillans was social rather than religious in origin. It was concerned with helping the child learn about observable rather than symbolic phenomena. The Macmillans were influenced more by Edward Seguin than by Friedrich Froebel. Seguin, a French educator, had developed many activities to improve the sensory education of retarded children. His influence can be seen in current programs for children with disabilities as well as in the Montessori method.

For three- and four-year-olds, the program of the nursery school included learning the skills involved in caring for oneself (washing, tying shoelaces, and so forth). Caring for plants, keeping animals, and cleaning the school were also important. In addition, specific activities were included to develop the senses. These included music and rhythmic activities, language activities, and activities to teach form and color. Margaret Macmillan recommended activities leading to reading and writing, as well as to arithmetic and science, while Grace Owen, another nursery school pioneer, opposed the introduction of the "Three Rs" and object lessons in the curriculum. Free play activities were included in the program, along with opportunities for art construction and work with water, sand, and other nonstructured materials.

The work of the Macmillans was so successful that it led to passage of the Fisher Act of 1918, which allowed for the establishment of nursery schools in local school systems throughout England. Unfortunately, the funds needed to establish these programs were not forthcoming, and the expansion of nursery education was a slow process.

About 1920, a number of teachers who had worked with Margaret Macmillan and Grace Owen came to the United States to demonstrate English nursery education. Nursery schools were started at Teachers

Early nursery school

College, Columbia University, the Merrill Palmer School of Motherhood and Home Training, and several other institutions in the United States.

During the next decades nursery schools spread slowly throughout the United States. A survey listed 203 nursery schools in existence in 1931. About half of these schools were related to colleges and universities, a third were private schools, and a fifth were part of child welfare agencies. This diversity of sponsorship, a continuing characteristic of nursery schools, paralleled their diversity of function. All nursery schools were concerned with educating children. Additional purposes varied with the sponsorship of the school:

> A large number of colleges and universities use the nursery school as a laboratory for the preparation of teachers and for research. The schools sponsored by departments of home economics in college and universities act as laboratories and demonstration centers for preparental education and instruction on home management. Relief of parents from daytime care of their children is chiefly supported by nursery schools connected with day nurseries and conducted by family welfare or philanthropic organizations. (Davis, 1933, p. 31)

The Great Depression of the 1930s had its impact on the development of nursery education. With incomes low and tax collections down, many school systems curtailed educational services and released teachers whose salaries they could no longer pay. In 1933, the federal government, first under the Federal Emergency Relief Act (FERA) and then under the Works Projects Administration (WPA), provided money to establish nursery schools to provide work for unemployed teachers. These nursery schools operated through public schools. Emergency teacher training programs were instituted to provide teachers of older children with the necessary skills for working with young children.

WPA nursery schools provided work relief for unemployed teachers and education for children.

Many communities provided **WPA nursery schools**. These schools offered not only relief to unemployed teachers, but also a valuable educational experience to children. Federally sponsored schools were operated in most states in the United States and numbered in the thousands, far outstripping the number of nursery schools that had been in existence up to that time.

The end of the Depression and the beginning of World War II ended the need to provide work for unemployed teachers. This brought an end to the WPA nursery schools. The burgeoning economy and the needs of the armed services and the defense industry required additions to the labor force. As women were hired for war work, agencies were needed to care for their children. Under the Lanham Act, the federal government established child care centers in most centers of war industry. These centers provided care and education for the children of mothers working in war-related industries. Support for these programs was withdrawn shortly after the end of World War II. In many cases, however, since the need for child care remained, the centers continued to operate under the sponsorship of local governments or philanthropic agencies.

The 1950s saw the expansion of parent-cooperative nursery schools. Many of these parent-cooperatives still exist today. The desire for high-quality, nursery education at a reasonable cost and for increased parent education supported this development. Parents own parent-cooperative nursery schools and may participate in the program as well. Adult classes or parent meetings relating to child development, childrearing practices, or other topics are often included in the program (Taylor, 1968).

Nursery school education continued to develop slowly under its varied sponsorship until the mid–1960s, when the federal government became involved in providing preschool education for children from low-income families under the Economic Opportunity Act and the Elementary and Secondary Education Act. This was the beginning of Project Head Start, which signaled a major change in early childhood education in the United States.

While nursery school education went through a series of changes, its development did not elicit the deep theoretical conflict that characterized the development of the kindergarten. For one thing, the nursery school movement was preceded by the establishment of the field of child development. Additionally, the original eclectic approach to nursery education was broad enough to encompass modification and diversity without serious conflict.

Among the important changes that took place in nursery school thought are the following:

1. **The Change From Nursery Education as a Program for the Poor to One for the Affluent.** The originators of nursery schools conceived of their programs as an antidote for problems caused by poverty. In the United States, the nursery school became a source of information about children, a place for young women to practice for motherhood and home management, a place to "keep" children, and a place to educate middle-class children. This change was a consequence of how nursery schools were supported in the United States. Without government support, most nursery schools outside of philanthropic agencies were supported by tuition payments, so that opportunities for nursery education were limited primarily to children of the affluent.
2. **A Deemphasis of the Health Aspects of Nursery Education.** Because the children served by American nursery schools had less need for the total care provided by the English nursery schools, programs were shortened to half days or school hours. The responsibility for nutrition, health, and hygiene was omitted. Only in child care centers and Head Start programs do we see a manifestation of the original concept of nurturance.
3. **A Shift from the Emphasis on "Training the Senses" to a More Broadly Based Education.** The same conditions that led to the reform movement in the kindergarten led to the shift in emphasis in nursery education. As compared to the kindergarten, the

nursery school has been less concerned with cognitive learning and more concerned with emotional and social learning. Because of the current concern for intellectual learning in young children, nursery educators have generally supported the development of broad cognitive skills and strategies rather than using the too-specific learning tasks of the original nursery school.

The **Montessori method** is a form of self-education that focuses on sensory training.

The Montessori Method

Paralleling the development of the nursery school in England was the development of the *casa dei bambini* in Italy. Dr. Maria Montessori, the originator of this new educational institution, attempted to break from traditional Italian education just as Macmillan had broken from the formalism of the British primary schools. While Montessori education has developed separately from nursery and kindergarten education, interesting parallels exist between the systems, and their ideas have intertwined.

Montessori began her work as a physician dealing primarily with children with mental disabilities. Impressed by her study of the work of such educators of children who were retarded as Seguin, she began to use and modify some of their methods and materials. She moved from working with children who were retarded to creating an educational program for normal children in the slums of Rome (Kramer, 1988).

The target population and the root methods of the nursery school and Montessori school were basically the same. They both worked with children of the poor, were influenced by the work of Seguin, and stressed sensory education. The British nursery school was more broadly conceived,

Maria Montessori with a child studying shapes.

Sensory education in the Montessori school.

however, and took responsibility for aspects of child development and work with parents that were essentially ignored in the Montessori system. Freedom from a specific dogma also allowed nursery educators to develop programs flexibly, utilizing new knowledge that became available and responding to new social situations. The Montessori method, however, strongly influenced the content and method of nursery schools.

Montessori philosophy also shows some interesting parallels with Froebelian education. Montessori saw the development of the young child as a process of unfolding and conceived of education as self-activity, as did Froebel. The ideas of self-discipline, independence, and self-direction could also be found in the writings of both educators. Significant differences in philosophy were Montessori's emphasis on sensory education, which was less important to Froebel than was symbolic education, and her identification of **sensitive periods** of instruction in the development of the child. Sensitive periods are periods in children's development when they are most receptive to a particular kind of learning.

Sensitive periods are periods in children's lives when they can most easily learn certain things.

The Montessori movement expanded, first in Italy and then throughout the world, with Montessori schools being established in several communities in the United States in the 1920s. While Montessori schools remained well established in Europe, most such schools disappeared in the United States during the 1930s and 1940s, either closing down or becoming nursery schools like the others around them.

A resurgence of Montessori education occurred in the United States in the 1960s. Montessori schools were reestablished, as were training programs for teachers. Some of these schools adhere exactly to the regimen of activity set down by Montessori in her original writings. Others modify these activities or include additional activities found in non-Montessori nursery schools, such as block building and dramatic play.

The genius of early childhood education in the United States has been its eclectic nature. Rather than rejecting new or foreign methods and theories, American educators and the American public have been willing to accept them, at least in some limited form. Seldom, however, has any form of early childhood education remained pure. As a result of the interaction of ideologies and the pragmatic approach of many educators, an American form of early childhood education emerged, a form that was consistent yet flexible, taking the best from Froebel, Montessori, Macmillan, and other European theorists and incorporating American theories and techniques. Just as the above-mentioned European educators influenced early childhood education, so did Americans such as John Dewey, Patty Smith Hill, Caroline Pratt, and a host of others.

Today many educators view the kindergarten and the nursery school as a downward extension of the primary school. The goals for the nursery school and kindergarten are like the goals set for all schooling. The differences in activities found at these earlier levels stem from developmental differences in the children rather than from philosophic differences or differences of purpose. The form and content of early childhood education must be related to how we define the goals of the school and how we conceive of schooling.

Child Care Centers

Unlike the other institutions, child care center—or day care centers or day nurseries, as they have alternatively been called—were originally designed to serve a custodial rather than an educational need. The American day nursery was fashioned after the French *créche*, which literally translates as "crib." The first créche was established in Paris in 1844 to help working mothers, fight infant mortality, and teach hygiene. The first American day nursery was established in New York City in 1854 by the New York Nursery and Child's Hospital (Forest, 1927).

Child care centers are a product of the Industrial Revolution. Prior to that period, women worked, even for pay, in a home—their own or someone else's—where they could keep children near at hand. When the

A day nursery in the 1920s

Table 2.1

Definitions of Child Care

Center Care: Establishments where children are cared for in a group in a nonresidential setting for all or part of the day. Centers can be categorized by their legal status and auspice [into] nonprofit centers, both sponsored and independent; and for-profit centers, both independent and members of a chain. Nonprofit, sponsored programs are further categorized by auspices, including those sponsored by Head Start, public schools, religious organizations, or other sponsors, such as employers or community agencies.

Family Day Care: Care provided for a small group of children in the caregiver's home. . . Family day care may be regulated or nonregulated. . .

In-Home Care: Care provided by a nonrelative who comes into the home. Sometimes the providers bring their own children along into the home.

Relative Care: Care provided by a relative in the child's home or the relative's home.

No Supplementary Care: Parents provide all care for their children or use nonparental arrangements only on an irregular basis.

Source: B. Willer, S. L. Hofferth, E. E. Kisker, P. Divine-Hawkins, E. Farquhar, and F. B. Glantz. *The Demand and Supply of Child Care in 1990.* (Washington, DC; National Association for the Education of Young Children, 1991), p. 3.)

factory system was established and factories hired large numbers of women and children, young children who were separated from their mothers during the long work day needed care. The day nurseries filled this need for the working class. The middle and upper classes had servants to care for their young.

During the latter half of the nineteenth century, a number of day nurseries were established in the United States, often by settlement houses or philanthropic groups wishing to help the children of immigrant and poor working women. Sometimes the nurseries provided Froebelian activities for the children. Often the caregiver's only responsibility was to keep the children fed, clean, and safe. Matrons cleaned the house and prepared meals, in addition to caring for the children. A broad age range of children was enrolled, including infants, toddlers, and preschool-age children.

Not until the 1920s, with the introduction of nursery schools in the United States, did day nurseries begin to implement educational programs. Child care centers began to structure their age groups much as the nursery schools did, limiting the age range to children already toilet trained. Staff members prepared as nursery school teachers began to work with more informally trained caregivers.

During World War II the number of child care centers in the United States dramatically increased. The Lanham Act of 1941 provided federal funds for child care on a matching basis to communities affected by the war, in order to increase the number of women in war work. Many of the Lanham Act centers were high-quality programs, even though they were created in response to an emergency. They provided staff training and adequate funding for materials and equipment. Some centers operated as many as 24 hours a day to match the three shifts on which mothers worked (Hymes, 1972).

In 1946, shortly after the end of the war, the Lanham Act was terminated and with it federal support for child care services. Where child care continued to be provided, it was much more limited. Often it was considered a child welfare service, a temporary aid to a family in difficulty that could not assume traditional childrearing responsibilities.

In the past three decades, the demand for child care as a normal service to families has increased. Women from all social classes have been seeking greater equality and finding that lack of child care interferes with continual employment and promotion to positions of greater responsibility.

The history of child care centers includes several periods of growth and reconceptualization. Margaret O'Brien Steinfels (1973) has identified three periods in the history of the field. In the first, prior to 1920, child care centers were seen as an essential service to poor working mothers. The availability of such a service often allowed both fathers and mothers to work, thus increasing their upward mobility. From about 1920 to 1940, child care services were curtailed, being provided only in cases of special need. A stigma was attached to child care services through the 1960s. Since the mid-1960s, child care services have again been seen as essential to working women, poor or not. The feeling that this service should be available to mothers who want to work as well as to those who need to work has increased.

The change in attitudes toward child care centers is the result of many diverse factors. Certainly the changing status of women in our society has contributed, as have the increase in urbanization and the shift to a nuclear family. Just as important is the developing body of knowledge that demonstrates that a high-quality child care program does not have a negative effect on young children, and that daily separation of mother from child during working hours is not comparable to a total separation such as family break up or death. Those who advocate for and provide expanded child care services must increase their concern for the adequacy of child care services and for the quality of facilities, programs, and staff.

Many people and agencies provide many types of child care in many places. Professional child care is primarily found in centers, although family day care may also have a professional component.

Child care centers may receive federal funds if they serve low-income families who are eligible for cash assistance under Title XX of the Social Security Act. The state receives support funds based on the proportion of the population that is eligible for Title XX under one of the following categories:

1. **Income maintenance.** The parent receives a public assistance check such as Aid to Families with Dependent Children (AFDC).
2. **Supplemental Security Income (SSI).** The parent receives a supplement to Social Security income; for instance, a widowed parent of young children can obtain SSI.
3. **Income Eligible.** The family is eligible for services if the family's gross income is below a figure set by the state.
4. **Group Eligibility.** Members of some groups are automatically eligible, including migrant workers and children, regardless of income, who are under protective care of the state.

Not only are many more child care programs available today than in decades past, but the sponsorship of these programs is more varied. Formerly, the majority of child care programs catered to needy families and were sponsored by community and philanthropic agencies, with a minority of centers privately owned, often by the persons who operated them. Today, most centers operate for profit, often as part of a chain of corporately owned or franchised centers. Children from all social strata are served in these centers.

Head Start

Head Start is a comprehensive child development program that provides education, health, nutrition, and social services to low-income children.

Both the nursery school and the Montessori school were originally designed to serve young children from poor families. As both of these programs were established in the United States, they primarily served children from affluent families, though social service agencies serving the poor did sponsor some of these schools. Most programs were not supported by public funds, in part because most Americans believed that young children were best educated at home by their parents. This situation changed dramatically when the federal government created Project Head Start.

In 1965 President Lyndon B. Johnson declared his War on Poverty, creating Community Action Programs to serve poor communities. One of these programs was Project Head Start, a comprehensive child development program to serve children before they entered public school. The original Head Start program recruited four- and five-year-old children, before they entered school, for an eight-week experience (at a time when most five-year-olds did not attend kindergarten). Realizing that the goals of the program could not be achieved in two months, educators expanded the program to operate throughout the school year. Head Start is now administered by the Administration for Children, Youth, and Families (ACYF) in the Department of Health and Human Services. Head Start has served over 10.9 million children and their families. Although Head Start is financed by the federal government, each community contributes to the support of its local program, which may be administered by a local community action agency or a public school system.

In 1975, performance standards were established to guarantee that every Head Start program maintains the essential services to meet goals for each of these components:

1. **Education.** Head Start's educational program must meet each child's individual needs. It also addresses the needs as well as the ethnic and cultural characteristics of the community served.
2. **Health.** Head Start focuses on early identification of health problems. Since many low-income preschool children have never seen a doctor or dentist, a comprehensive health care program is provided for every child, including medical, dental, mental health, and nutritional services.
   A. *Medical and Dental.* Children are given a complete physical examination, including vision and hearing tests, identification of disabilities, immunizations, and a dental check up. Follow-up care is provided for children with identified problems.
   B. *Nutrition.* Many children who enter Head Start may not have received nourishing meals at home. Children are provided with a minimum of one hot meal and a snack daily, which meet at least one-third of their daily nutritional needs.
   C. *Mental Health.* The program is attentive to the mental health and psychological services that children of low-income families need.
3. **Parent Involvement.** Parents are considered to be most influential in the child's development. The program involves parents in parent education, program planning, and operation of facilities. Many parents serve on policy councils and committees to provide input on administrative and managerial decisions.
4. **Social Services.** Head Start assists families to assess their needs and then provides services, including community outreach, referrals, family needs assessments, information on available resources, recruitment and enrollment of children, and emergency assistance and/or crisis intervention.
5. **Service to Children with Disabilities.** Following the 1972 Congressional mandate, at least 10 percent of Head Start enrollment in each state must be available for children with disabilities.

Head Start has had a striking influence on child development and child care services, on the development of state and local services for young children and their families, and on training programs for those who work in early childhood programs. The program assisted more than 548,00 children in 1990, about 27 percent of eligible children. Almost 36 percent of its staff are parents of current or former Head Start children. Unfortunately, although funds for the program have increased since its beginning, the limited budget provided by the federal government has meant that the majority of eligible young children cannot be enrolled.

More than 90 percent of all Head Start families have incomes below the poverty line. One of the program's most distinctive and important attributes is that it assists children and families to receive a range of services. In 1985–1986, for instance, 95 percent of Head Start families received social services from Head Start and through referrals to other agencies. In addition, 98 percent of the children who were enrolled for 90 days or more received medical examinations and essential treatment, and 98 percent completed all required immunizations. In 1989 about 14 percent of Head Start children nationwide had physical, emotional, or mental impairments (Children's Defense Fund, 1991).

The social context in which Head Start functioned during the 1980s made serving poor children's needs more complex. The rates of family poverty, homelessness, and substance abuse increased during this decade, along with an increase in the number of families headed by young, single mothers. In 1989–1990, more than 75 percent of Head Start families had annual incomes of less than $9,000, and more than half were headed by single mothers (Children's Defense Fund, 1991).

Early Childhood Special Education

The education of young children with disabilities began in the eighteenth century. The earliest pioneer of special education was probably Jacob-Rodrigues Periere, a contemporary of Rousseau, who developed a method of teaching language to deaf-mute people (Boyd, 1914). Jean-Marc-Gaspard Itard built upon Periere's work as he tried to educate Victor, the "Wild Boy of Aveyron," in the early 1800s (Lane, 1976). Itard's methods were adopted by Edouard Seguin, who created a systematic approach to sensory education (Talbot, 1964). In developing her approach to educating mentally defective children, as they were then called, Montessori built on the work of Sequin as well as on the work of Froebel (Spodek, 1991). In spite of this long history, the education of young children with disabilities was a small, poorly supported field that educated few children until recently. The field had its greatest growth in the 1970s, primarily due to the enactment of Public Law 94-142, the Education for All Handicapped Children Act, which provided federal funds to states and local education agencies for the education of handicapped children and young adults between the ages of 3 and 21. Public Law 94-142 and laws passed in individual states have created a network of programs that serve preschool children with disabilities. PL 94-142 was amended by Public Law 99-457.

PL 99-457, signed into law on October 8, 1986, reauthorized programs under PL 94-142 for students with disabilities ages 5 to 18. This law also requires the development of early intervention services for preschoolers with disabilities, ages three to five, and for infants and toddlers, from birth through age two. PL 99-457 made four broad legislative changes in regard to children with disabilities who are under school age:

1. It extended all rights and protections of PL 94-142 (EHA, Part B) to preschool (three- to five-year-old) children with disabilities by the 1990–1991 school year.
2. It provided a dramatic increase in federal financial support for preschool special education services (Sec. 619 funds) and for incentives for states to develop early intervention programs for infants and toddlers with disabilities and for their parents (Part H).
3. It established federal policy for early intervention programs for infants and toddlers (birth through age two) who have disabilities or are at risk and a new state grant program (EHA, Part H) supporting early intervention services for these young children and their parents who meet eligibility criteria established by each state.
4. It required that every state have an *Interagency Coordinating Council* composed of representatives of agencies that serve young children, families, and individuals who are handicapped (such as health, welfare, social service, and education agencies). This Interagency Coordinating Council is responsible for developing the state's early childhood education plan and for overseeing the development of a statewide system of services for handicapped children from birth through age five. It is also responsible for the organization of interagency agreements, appropriate state policies, and cooperative activities and services across relevant agencies.

Both PL 94-142 and PL 99-457 were extended through the Education of the Handicapped Act Amendments of 1990 (Public Law 101-476), which changed the name of the Education of the Handicapped Act to the **Individuals with Disabilities Education Act**. In 1992, PL 102-119 extended PL 99-457.

The **Individuals with Disabilities Education Act (IDEA)** and its amendments provide the basis for the education of all young children with disabilities. An earlier version of this act was the Education of the Handicapped Act (PL 94-142).

Programs for At-Risk Children

Educators have become increasingly aware of young children who present a probability of school failure or other developmental problems. Some of these children are identified during screening for disabilities, but often they are not disabled. These children, identified as being at risk of future academic failure, are increasingly being served by prekindergarten programs, often in public schools.

Children at *biological risk* have prenatal, perinatal, or postnatal biological histories that signal potential problems. Maternal diabetes, infection with German measles during pregnancy, complications during labor, prematurity, low birth weight, or the accidental ingestion by the child of toxic substances all render a child at risk for developing a disability. Children at *environmental risk* are biologically or genetically normal but have had adverse experiences early in life. Risk factors often occur in combination, interacting to increase the chances of delayed or aberrant development.

One of the most effective treatments for children at risk is placement in a high-quality early intervention program. The program should stress individualized education, language and cognitive stimulation, and opportunities for social interaction with adults and with peers. An estimated 2.5 million children under the age of six in the United States are at risk.

THE CONTEMPORARY SCENE

If we look at early childhood education today, we find a very robust field. Kindergarten has become a part of the normal school experience of the vast majority of children. Children below kindergarten age are increasingly being enrolled in early childhood programs. The greatest growth has been in the area of child care, with many children needing and being provided with full-day care.

Early childhood programs are also serving an increasingly diverse population. There are programs for young children with disabilities where none existed a few years ago. Children with disabilities are also being served at younger and younger ages. Children with other needs, including children at risk of future educational failure who are not considered disabled, as well as children from diverse language and cultural backgrounds, are also being served. Unfortunately, although early childhood programs and services have increased markedly during this generation, not all children who need early childhood educational programs are being served. The growth in the field, however, is based on increasing needs in our society and on the evidence that early childhood education programs can have pervasive and long-lasting effects on the children in greatest need.

LASTING EFFECTS OF EARLY CHILDHOOD EDUCATION

For many years early childhood educators have been driven by a belief that what they do with young children makes a difference in the children's current and future lives. Over the last two decades there has been increasing evidence to support this belief.

One of the more interesting studies focused on the effects of first-grade teachers on students' subsequent adult status. Longitudinal data as well as independent measures and estimates of characteristics and achievement were collected on a group of 60 children from a disadvantaged urban neighborhood. The study supported the hypothesis that "a good first grade teacher can provide children with such a head start that the effects, in terms of academic self-concept and achievement, will continue to be felt later in life" (Pederson, Faucher, & Eaton, 1978).

Positive, long-lasting results have also been shown for preschool programs. A number of university-sponsored early education programs were developed for poor and minority children during the early 1960s. Many of their students demonstrated immediate gains on academic and intelligence tests. More recently, the Consortium for Longitudinal Studies has followed up the children in these programs. Irving Lazar and Richard Darlington (1982) reported on the work of the Consortium in relation to six of these programs. The areas in which early education had lasting effects were the children's school competence, developed abilities, and attitudes, and family outcomes. Children from these programs were retained in grade or assigned to special education less often than children who did not receive early intervention. These children also performed better on tests of achievement and intelligence, although they did not sustain their higher scores on IQ tests in later years. The children who graduated from these programs showed more positive attitudes toward school and gave more achievement-oriented responses in interviews than did children who did not participate in such programs. In addition, their mothers were more satisfied with their school performance and seemed to exert more pressure on them to achieve.

These reported effects relate to special programs implemented in controlled settings. Similar results have been found in Head Start programs. Raymond C. Collins (1983) reported on the Head Start Evaluation, Synthesis, and Utilization Project:

> The data show clearly that Head Start programs have grown more effective over the years. Effect sizes calculated for children who attended Head Start since 1970 are nearly twice the size of cognitive gains reported for children who attended Head Start in the start up years 1965–69. Other specific findings pertaining to cognitive development are:
>
> - Children make immediate gains in basic cognitive competence, school readiness and achievement.
> - Head Starters generally outperform other low income children into elementary school (but continue to score below norms on middle class tests).
> - Head Start children usually perform better than non-Head Starters on real work indicators of school success (less likely to be retained in grade; avoiding inappropriate placement in special education; reduced drop out rates).
> - Head Start children sometimes maintain superiority on achievement test scores into later school years.
> - Head Start improves language development, especially for bilingual and handicapped children.
> - The children who appear to benefit the most from Head Start are the most needy (children from families whose mothers had a

10th grade education or less; children of single-parent families; and children with low initial I.Q. at the beginning of Head Start).
- Children in classes of mixed minority enrollment (26%–89% minority) averaged gains nearly twice as high as those in classes where minority enrollment ranges 90–100%.

Results of the Head Start Synthesis Project to date validate to a considerable extent in a Head Start context similar findings to those revealed in other contemporary child care research.*

Much of the early research on child care was designed to determine if placement in these programs had negative effects on children compared to home care. Later studies attempted to identify elements in child care programs that are associated with positive effects. A review of this research by Bettye M. Caldwell and Marjorie Freyer (1982) demonstrated the positive effects of good child care in both large-scale and small-scale studies. As a result of their review, these educators suggest that child care programs should be small, that attachment to parents is not impaired by early child care, that staff turnover in centers may be less debilitating than was feared, that the health of infants can be maintained in child care programs, that the effects of prohibitions and controls by teachers on children in child care programs need to be considered, that research offers little curriculum guidance for child care programs, and that parental involvement takes many forms and remains elusive and difficult to attain in many day care programs.

A more recent review of research on child care (Howes & Hamilton, 1993) concluded that child care quality seems more important than either the form of child care or the child's age at entry in predicting children's development. It also suggests that quality in child care is linked to the adults providing the care. Children develop more social and cognitivie competence in settings where caregivers function well in teaching and nurturing roles. Teachers' effectiveness is related to their levels of education and specialized training as well as to setting characteristics, including salaries and adult-child ratios. Essentially, these studies suggest that we know that good child care can enhance children's development. In spite of this knowledge, child care in America is less than ideal. Perhaps it is time for us to put the knowledge we have gained from research into more forceful action.

CURRENT CONCERNS

Educators cannot take increased public acceptance of early childhood education for granted. While high-quality programs have been shown to have positive effects, lack of availability of such programs remains a

**Source:* Raymond C. Collins, "Headstart: An Update on Program Effects." *Newsletter of the Society for Research in Child Development*, Summer, 1983, p. 2. Reprinted with permission.

problem. Good education for young children is expensive. Retaining competent teachers requires paying adequate salaries and benefits. Programs should remain small and child-staff ratios low. Physical facilities, furniture, equipment, and supplies are also expensive. As long as preschool programs must depend on tuition payments alone, or on low fees for purchase of service, quality will remain elusive.

All states have licensing standards that define minimum acceptable levels for child care; nursery schools are often included in these standards. Similar state standards often apply to public schools. Standards of quality in early childhood education remain low, in part because of the nature of the states' regulatory powers and because of pressures to maintain low standards or to exempt some centers from compliance. In addition, standards for early childhood staff outside the public schools remain low.

In 1985, NAEYC established the National Academy of Early Childhood programs to accredit early childhood programs. The Academy uses criteria for accreditation that are higher than those found in state licensing standards. The accreditation process includes a self-study of the program by its personnel. Using the self-study materials, areas of strength as well as those that need improvement can be determined. The results of the self-study, a program description, is submitted to the academy. If the description suggests that the program is worthy of accreditation, a visit is made by academy staff to validate the study. A report of the validation visit and the program description will then be submitted to the Academy Commission. If considered worthy, the program will be accredited for a period of three years, after which follow-up reports must be submitted for reaccreditation (National Association for the Education of Young Children, 1991). Such efforts can influence the field by providing criteria to determine quality of programs that go beyond the minimum standards of regulation. Parents enrolling their children are given assurance that an accredited program is of high-quality.

Financial support for maintaining high-quality programs, however, continues to be elusive. Only when services for young children are adequately funded and teachers of young children are given higher status, higher salaries, and better working conditions will the relative lack of high-quality programs be properly addressed.

While the increased evidence of positive child outcomes for high-quality early childhood programs gives members of the field cause for elation, the fact that we are not serving all children well gives us cause for concern. Among those children not being adequately served are abused and neglected children, homeless children, children with AIDS, and children suffering the effects of substance abuse.

Abused and Neglected Children

Child abuse has become a national problem that social agencies, hospitals, child care centers, and schools are doing what they can to identify, treat, and prevent. Child abuse includes physical, psychological, and sexual abuse, as well as neglect. The number of children in our society who are abused is difficult to determine, but experts agree that it is greater than many people would expect. Statistics indicate that one million incidents of abuse occur each year, although only one case out of four is reported.

Public Law 93-247, the Child Abuse Prevention and Treatment Act, defines child abuse and neglect as "The physical or mental injury, sexual abuse, negligent treatment or maltreatment of a child under the age of eighteen by a person who is responsible for the child's welfare" (United States Statutes at Large, 1976, p. 5).

Educators have become more sensitive to physical and sexual child abuse. While they cannot always prevent it, most states require that teachers and other professionals report cases in which they suspect such abuse. Child and family agencies then have the responsibility to investigate the case and protect the child if necessary.

Emotional abuse is just as injurious as physical abuse and neglect. In emotional abuse, adults (including parents, teachers, and caregivers) deprive children of their self-esteem and self-image. Adults destroy children's self-esteem when they continually criticize, belittle, scream and nag at, and threaten children as well as when they intentionally and severely restrict children's opportunities. Emotional abuse is hard to record, so that emotionally abused children are typically left in the abusive situation.

Homeless Children

The National Coalition for the Homeless calculates that between 500,000 and 750,000 children and youth live in homeless families or on their own. Homeless children are neglected and overlooked. Approximately 40 percent of homeless children do not attend school. Those who do attend school encounter numerous difficulties regarding their previous school problems, such having failed a grade, and concerning school attendance, such as long trips to attend school (Solarz, 1988). When they attend child care centers, these children often display a number of problem behaviors, including short attention spans, weak impulse control, withdrawal, aggression, speech delays, and regressive behaviors. They are at risk for health problems. Homelessness has serious mental, physical, and educational repercussions for children, such as causing developmental delays and high levels of stress.

Children with AIDS

Acquired immune deficiency syndrome (AIDS) is a relatively new disease, first described in 1981 and labelled in 1982. It is caused by the human immunodeficiency virus (HIV), which damages the immune system, making the individual susceptible to disease and infection. Children and adults who are infected with HIV may contract AIDS or acquire symptoms not ordinarily connected with AIDS that are referred to as AIDS-related complex (ARC).

Children with AIDS may suffer when they contract infections, such as pneumonia and central nervous system disorders. Children who are born with the HIV virus may have facial or cranial abnormalities. The Centers for Disease Control estimated that 1,908 children below 13 years of age had contracted AIDS by November 1989 and that in 71 percent of these cases the infected mothers had transmitted the disease to their fetus or infant during the perinatal period. A pregnant mother who has AIDS transmits the HIV antibodies to the fetus, although the actual virus is transmitted only 40 percent of the time as the blood is fused at birth or by the appearance of the HIV virus on the cervix. Children do not make their antibodies until they are 15 months old; therefore, the HIV virus in infants cannot be identified until the infants reach that age.

The American Academy of Pediatrics Task Force on Pediatric AIDS (1988) has provided the following guidelines for controlling HIV infection in programs for young children:

1. HIV-infected children must be allowed to enter group programs if their health, neurological development, behavior, and immune status permit. Qualified individuals who have expertise on HIV infections and AIDS, including the child's physician, should independently make these decisions, considering both the efficacy of program participation for the infected children and whether the child poses any possible hazard to others. According to the task force, although "Most infected children, particularly those too young to walk, pose no threat to others, HIV-infected children who persistently bite others or who have oozing skin lesions may theoretically transmit the virus, although such has not been conclusively demonstrated" (p. 806). Apparently, biting does not carry HIV infection from an infected biter to the child who is bitten unless the biter has a bloody mouth. The rule is that blood must be transferred to transmit the virus; however, bites rarely extract blood.
2. It is not necessary to screen children for the presence of HIV antibodies before they enter the early childhood program.
3. The children's parents do not have the right to know which children in the class are infected with HIV. Teachers must know that a child has immunodeficiency, regardless of cause, in order to take precautions in protecting the child from infections.
4. Appropriate alternative placements for individual children may be provided by programs offering services for children who have HIV infection, although separate programs are not imperative to control infection and must not be employed to segregate children.
5. Since it is difficult to identify children who have been infected with HIV or other infectious agents, precautions such as the following must be taken to reduce the risk of infection:

- Immediately clean soiled surfaces with disinfectant made of one tablespoon of bleach added to one quart of water, prepared daily.
- Blood spills require a solution of one portion of bleach to 10 portions of water.
- Use disposable towels and tissues for cleaning and throw them away properly.
- Use disposable gloves to avoid exposure of mucous membranes or any open skin lesion to blood or blood-contaminated body fluid.
- Good hygiene is the best approach to stopping the spread of all kinds of infections, including HIV. Staff and children must wash their hands correctly and often with running water and liquid soap, and dispose of the towels or tissues immediately after using them.

Children Suffering the Effects of Substance Abuse

Early childhood programs are beginning to encounter children suffering the effects of their parents' abuse of substances such as cocaine, both during pregnancy and afterward. At present, little is known about the long-term effects of maternal cocaine abuse on children. A recent Social Policy Report of the Society for Research on Child Development has summarized what is known and made recommendations for social policy.

Prenatal cocaine exposure has been associated with increased probabilities of premature birth, low birth weight, and small head circumference. It may also be linked to risk of physical malformation, symptoms of drug withdrawal, and difficulties in orientation. It may have long-term adverse effects on intellectual, social, and psychological functioning. Language, social-emotional, and intellectual development may be affected in the long term, yet more research is needed to identify the particular consequences of maternal cocaine abuse. Children of addicted mothers may face environmental risks, including poverty, maternal depression, and, possibly, physical and emotional neglect (Hawley & Disney, 1992).

Local, state, and federal programs, many of which focus on preventing or treating maternal addiction, have been developed to address these problems. Unfortunately, few programs deal with the developmental and educational needs of the child. Teachers and social service practitioners report serious learning and behavioral problems in these children. The extent to which these children will suffer long-term effects is unclear. These children should be assessed and receive treatment as children with disabilities. Teachers should deal with the behavioral and educational symptoms in the classroom and work with whatever social programs are available to provide help for parents of these children.

Summary

The field of early childhood education serves children in many different institutions: preschools, child care centers, nursery schools, kindergartens, and primary classes. The history of these institutions covers several centuries. Understanding the history of the field gives one a sense of how far we have come in recent years.

Today early childhood education is serving increased numbers of children with increasingly diverse backgrounds in increasingly diverse programs. While early childhood programs have proved successful, and high-quality programs have a long-lasting influence on children's education and development, there are still children in our society whose needs we are not adequately meeting. They represent the challenge to the field, today and in the future.

References

American Academy of Pediatrics Task Force on Pediatric AIDS (1988, November). Pediatric guidelines for infection control of human immunodeficiency virus (acquired immunodeficiency virus) in hospitals, medical offices, schools, and other settings. *Pediatrics, 82,* 801–807.

Boyd, W. (1914). *From Locke to Montessori.* London: Harrup & Co.

Caldwell, B. M., & Freyer, M. (1982) Day care and early education. In B. Spodek (Ed.), *Handbook of research in early childhood education.* New York: Free Press.

Children's Defense Fund (1991). *The state of America's children,* 1991. Washington, DC: Author.

Collins, R. C. (Summer, 1983). Headstart: An update on program effects. *Newsletter of the Society for Research in Child Development.*

Comenius, J. A. (1657). *The great didactic.* Amsterdam: de Greer Family.

Comenius, J. A. (1887). *Orbis Pictus.* Syracuse, NY: C. W. Bardeen. (Originally published in 1658.)

Davis, M. D. (1933). *Nursery schools: Their development and current practices in the United States.* Washington, DC: U.S. Government Printing Office.

Deasey, D. (1978). *Education under eight.* New York: St. Martin's Press.

Finkelstein, B., & Vandell, K. (1984). The schooling of American childhood: The emergence of learning communities. In M. L. S. Heininger, K. Calvert, B. Finkelstein, K. Vandell, A. S. MacLeod, & H. Green (Eds.), *A century of childhood 1820–1920.* Rochester, NY: The Margaret Woodbury Strong Museum.

Fisher, L. (1908). Report of the Commissioner of Education, as quoted in N. Vanderwalker, *The kindergarten in American education.* New York: Macmillan.

Forest, I. (1927). *Preschool education: A historical and critical study.* New York: Macmillan.

Gardner, D. E. M. (n.d.). *Education under eight.* London: Longmans, Green & Co.

Hawley, T. L., & Disney, E. R. (1992). *Crack's children: The consequences of maternal cocaine abuse.* Social Policy Report, Society for Research in Child Development, 6(4), 1–22.

Hill, P. S. (1913). Second report. In International Kindergarten Union. *The Kindergarten: Reports of the Committee of Nineteen on the Theory and Practice of the Kindergarten.* Boston: Houghton Mifflin.

Howes, C. & Hamilton, C. E. (1993). Child care for young children. In B. Spodek (Ed.), *Handbook of research on the eduction of young children* (pp. 322–336). New York: Macmillan.

Hymes, J. L., Jr. (1972). The Kaiser answer: Child services centers. In S. J. Braun & E. P. Edwards (Eds.), *History and theory of early childhood education* (pp. 169-179). Worthington, OH: Charles A. Jones.

Kramer, R. (1988). *Maria Montessori: A biography.* Reading, MA: Addison-Wesley.

Lane, H. (1976). *The wild boy of Aveyron.* Cambridge: Harvard University Press.

Lazar, I., & Darlington, R. (1982). Lasting effects of early education: A report from the Consortium for Longitudinal Studies. *Monographs of the Society for Research in Child Development,* Serial No. 195, 47, Nos. 2–3.

May, D., & Vinovskis, M. A. (1977). A ray of millennial light: Early education and social reform in the infant school movement in Massachusetts, 1826–1840. In T. Harevan (Ed.), *Family and kin in urban communities, 1700–1930* (pp. 62–99). New York: New Viewpoints.

Monroe, W. S. (Ed.) (1908). *Comenius' school of infancy.* Boston: Heath.

National Association for the Education of Young Children (1991). *Accreditation criteria and procedures of the National Academy of Early Childhood Programs* (rev. ed.). Washington, DC: NAEYC.

Nohle, E. (1924). *Report on the United States Commission of Education (1897–1898),* I, 24–25. As reported in C. S. Parker & A. Temple, *Unified kindergarten and first-grade teaching.* Chicago: Department of Education, University of Chicago.

Osborn, D. K. (1991). *Early childhood education in historical perspective* (3rd ed.). Athens, GA: Education Associates.

Peabody, E. (1874). *Record of Mr. Alcott's school exemplifying the principles and methods of moral culture* (3rd ed., revised). Boston: Roberts Brothers.

Pederson, E., Faucher, T. A., & Eaton, W. W. (1978). A new perspective on the effects of first-grade teachers on children's subsequent adult status. *Harvard Educational Review, 48,* 1–31.

Rousseau, J. J. (1911). (B. Foxley, trans.). *Emile.* London: J. M. Dent. (Original work published in 1762).

Silber, K. (1965). *Pestalozzi: The man and his work.* New York: Schocken.

Solarz, A. L. (1988). Homelessness: Implications for children and youth. *Social Policy Report.* Washington, DC: Society for Research in Child Development..

Snyder, A. (1972). *Dauntless women in childhood education.* Washington, DC: Association for Childhood Education International.

Snyder, T. D., & Hoffman, C. M. (1992). *Digest of educational statistics* (1991). Washington, DC: National Center for Educational Statistics.

Spodek, B. (1991). Early childhood education and cultural definitions of knowledge. In B. Spodek & O. N. Saracho (Eds.), *Issues in early childhood curriculum: Yearbook in early childhood education* (Vol. 2). New York: Teachers College Press.

Steinfels, M. O. (1973). *Who's minding the children? The history and politics of day care in America.* New York: Simon and Schuster.

Strickland, C. E. (1982). Paths not taken: Seminal models of early childhood education in Jacksonian America. In B. Spodek (Ed.), *Handbook of research in early childhood education* (pp. 321–340). New York: Free Press.

Swart, H. W. (1967). *Margarethe Meyer Schurz: A biography.* Watertown, WI: Watertown Historical Society.

Talbot, M. E. (1964). *Edouard Sequin: A study of an educational approach to the treatment of mentally defective children.* New York: Teachers College Press.

Taylor, C. W. (1968). *Parents and children learn together.* New York: Teachers College Press.

United States Department of Health and Human Services (1990). *Head Start: A child development program.* Washington, DC: Administration of Children, Youth, and Families.

United States Statutes at Large. (1976). Vol. P. 88 part 1. Washington, DC: U.S. Government Printing Office.

Willer, B., Hofferth, S. L., Kisker, E. E., Divine-Hawkins, P., Farquhar, E., & Glantz, F. B. (1991). *The demand and supply of child care in 1990.* Washington DC: National Association for the Education of Young Children.

3

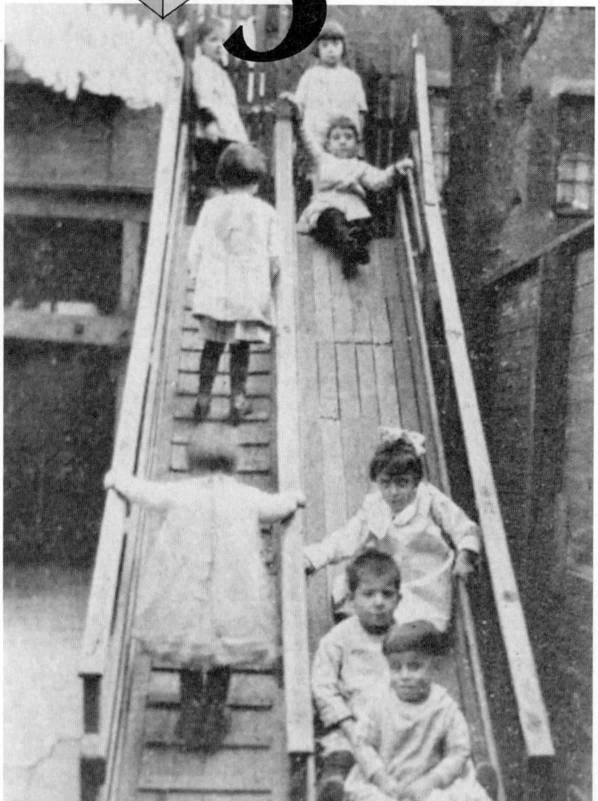

Developmental Theories and Early Childhood Education

CHAPTER OVERVIEW

This chapter presents:

- Developmental theories that have made contributions to early childhood education
- General characteristics of young children (birth through eight years), including physical, cognitive, language, emotional, and social development, and the development of values
- Individual differences among children and differences among identifiable groups of children

INTRODUCTION

Since its beginning, the field of child development has been closely entwined with early childhood education. Concepts and theories in child development have influenced early childhood educational practice and how we talk about it. This chapter will present the concepts and theories that have had the greatest influence on the field of early childhood education and their implications.

Theory refers to a systematic statement of principles related to observed phenomena and their relationships. A theory is a scheme for organizing and interpreting data. A theory of child development looks at children's growth and behavior and interprets them. It indicates which elements in the child's genetic makeup and/or in environmental conditions influence development and behavior and how those elements are related.

The theories discussed in this chapter include maturationist theory, developed by such theorists as G. Stanley Hall and Arnold Gesell; behavioral theory, developed by such theorists as Edward L. Thorndike and B. F. Skinner; psychodynamic theory, developed by such theorists as Sigmund Freud and Erik Erikson; constructivist theory, developed by such theorists as Jean Piaget, Lev S. Vygotsky, and Jerome Bruner; and ecological theory, developed by such theorists as Urie Bronfenbrenner. Each theory interprets the meaning of children's development and behavior. While the theories are grouped together into schools of thought, there are variations within each school.

MATURATIONIST THEORY

Maturationist theory suggests that the course of human development is primarily genetically determined.

Maturationist theory suggests that the course of human development is primarily genetically determined. Changes in the human organism occur as internal mechanisms guide development in a systematic way, independent, to a great extent, of environmental influences. While environmental conditions can thwart natural developmental patterns, the theory suggests that they cannot change those patterns.

The genetically timed natural maturation of the child's system occurs as a process of unfolding. Maturationist theory suggests that special efforts to elicit desired behaviors before they occur naturally are unnecessary and may even be harmful. Children who are pressured to achieve beyond their present maturational level may develop ineffectively and experience a diminished sense of worth and self-confidence. When a child does not mature as expected, however, intervention may be necessary. Murray Thomas (1992) believes that intervention to modify a child's characteristic is acceptable when (1) the characteristic is considered unsatisfactory, (2) the child's level of maturation permits the desired progression, and (3) elements in the child's environment fail to alter the objectionable characteristic naturally.

G. Stanley Hall, who is considered the father of the child study movement, brought his point of view to bear on both psychology and education. Arnold Gesell continued Hall's work on maturationist theory, applying modern research techniques to its evolution.

G. Stanley Hall, father of the child study movement

G. Stanley Hall (1844–1924) G. Stanley Hall completed his doctorate at Harvard University, where he studied with psychologist William James. He then went to Germany to study with Wilhelm Wundt, the pioneer of experimental psychology. When he returned to the United States, Hall applied his knowledge of experimental psychology to the study of children's development and to the application of developmental principles in education.

Hall's work in child study reflected the view that development was based in heredity. What a child was to become was determined by his or her genetic makeup. Hall also developed the basic method of child study: observation. Because there were no trained child psychologists in the United States at that time, Hall enlisted the work of persons interested in children to do his observations for him. These persons, primarily parents and teachers, were to observe children in their natural surroundings, rather than in laboratories.

Hall's work reflected Darwin's theory of evolution. Hall believed that each individual in the human race went through a developmental sequence that paralleled the development of the species. This developmental principal is often articulated in the phrase, **"ontology recapitulates phylogeny."** Hall felt that children needed to be freed from the primitive aspects of their evolutionary sequence in order to function as mature modern human beings and viewed the natural activities of childhood as the mechanism by which children achieved this freedom.

Ontology recapitulates phylogeny
means that each individual goes through a developmental sequence that parallels that of the species.

Hall's enduring contribution was his focus on the scientific study of childhood. Hall collected large amounts of information about children in an attempt to characterize children at different stages of life. Hall's method, collecting survey data about children from teachers who were not trained in observation techniques, would not be considered scientific today. However, with this work, he broke new ground in the study of childhood and established the basis for a more scientific study of childhood as well as for the application of child development principles in education. In many ways, Hall can be considered the founder of the child-centered approach to education, the view that education should respond to the nature of childhood, rather than children conforming to established forms of education (Strickland & Burgess, 1965).

Arnold Gesell (1890–1961) Arnold Gesell was a student of G. Stanley Hall and continued Hall's work in a more systematic way. For about forty years, Gesell studied the development of children in the Yale University Clinic for Child Development. He observed and measured large numbers of children in different domains: physical development, motor development, language development, intellectual development, personal and social development, and the like. Gesell created detailed descriptions of infants and children from birth through age 10. He described the development of children by identifying the typical characteristics of children of a

Arnold Gesell expanded on maturationist theory

particular age level. From these characteristics he created norms for children by age, which he took to be representative of the normal development of children.

Gesell's developmental theory was a simple one that focused on the importance of maturation in the child's development. While he did not espouse an evolutionary conception of development as did Hall, Gesell did believe that a child's development is genetically determined. While Gesell acknowledged that a person's personality, developmental rate, and abilities are individual and unique, he paid little attention to individual differences in his description of levels of development. He did stress the need to respect each child's basic inborn individuality.

Gesell and his colleagues, Frances L. Ilg and Louise B. Ames, developed an collection of tests, assessment strategies, and observation methods. They collected information about children's school and home behaviors in the Yale clinic and in parent interviews. The information allowed them to delineate *maturity traits* and developmental steps, called **growth gradients,** for the typical child, in 10 major areas:

Gesell's **growth gradients** were identifiable maturational traits and developmental steps.

1. motor characteristics (bodily activity, eyes and hands),
2. personal hygiene (eating, sleeping, eliminating, bathing, dressing, health, somatic complaints, tensional outlets),
3. emotional expression (affective attitudes, assertion, anger, crying, and related behavior),
4. fears and dreams,
5. self and sex,
6. interpersonal relations (mother-child, father-child, child-child, siblings, family, grandparents, groupings in play, manners),
7. play and pastimes (general interests, reading, music, radio, television, movies),

8. school life (adjustment to school, classroom demeanor, reading, writing, arithmetic),
9. ethical sense (blaming and making alibis; response to direction, punishment, and praise; responsiveness to reason; sense of good and bad, truth, and property), and
10. philosophic outlook (time, space, language and thought, death, deity).

Gesell asserted that development was determined by nature from within the organism, while the environment played a secondary role in altering behavior. Gesell believed that education should be responsive to each child's developmental pattern. Since education cannot influence development, it should provide a match between what a child is asked to do and what that child is capable of doing. Gesell advocated that children be permitted to develop at their own pace, both at home and at school. Pressuring or restricting the child, he suggested, would merely generate negativism and reduce constructiveness (Thomas, 1992).

Influence of Maturationist Theory

The maturationist point of view in child development has had a significant influence on early childhood education over the years, especially in nursery school and kindergarten. The maturationist view supports the notion of "child-centered" education. Since the environment has little impact on an individual's development, attempting to extend children's abilities beyond their native capacity can only cause frustration and be harmful to children. The idea of matching experience to children's present abilities, one interpretation of "developmentally appropriate educational practice," can be seen as humane. Unfortunately, it also creates self-fulfilling prophesies. If children are considered to be below average and so, out of kindness, are not provided with challenging educational experiences, then they will not learn more than they already know.

Kindergartens and nursery schools that followed a maturationist view of development, as proposed by Gesell and his colleagues, were to support development without placing undue pressures on young children. Teachers were told to follow the children in developing programs for them, building on their "needs and interests." Thus, programs were to be safe and comfortable, rather than challenging.

The maturationist point of view also led to a conception of readiness for learning. If a child was judged to be incapable of learning something, the teacher was to wait until the child matured further. This notion of readiness was especially evident in the area of reading instruction. For years, the conventional wisdom was that children were not ready to read until they had reached a mental age of six years and six months. Teachers would test for readiness but would not do anything to help children become ready.

The maturationist approach to learning in the early years is quite different from the interventionist approaches that early childhood educators have recently taken with many children. Programs for young children with disabilities or children who are judged to be at risk of future educational failure assume that, while some young children reach a level at which they can meet learning expectations without specific interventions, some children need more help. Many children are routinely offered experiences, formally or informally, that allow them to be successful in learning. Other children may not be offered such experiences, or may have disabilities or developmental delays that limit their ability to profit from such experiences. Special programs can be developed for such children to help them to be successful in school. Without such programs, their learning and their development would be limited.

The maturationist point of view is still found in some schools where children are tested to determine their developmental level on entrance to kindergarten. Using such devices as the *Gesell Test*, school authorities may judge that a child is "not ready" for kindergarten and advise parents to withhold the child from school for a year to allow the child to mature. Both the policy and the test have been severely criticized (see Meisels, 1989). In a sense such a procedure runs counter to the approaches taken with special populations noted above.

BEHAVIORAL THEORY

Behavioral theory has been a major theoretical influence in psychology for about a century. While essentially a theory of learning, it has been used as a theory of development as well. Unlike the maturationists, behaviorists believe that, except for physical maturation, the greatest influences on human development are in the environment. From the behaviorist perspective, what individuals learn is incorporated into their thinking and elaborated over time so that it ultimately influences development. Four great pioneers have helped develop behavioral theory: Ivan Pavlov, John B. Watson, Edward L. Thorndike, and B. F. Skinner.

Ivan Pavlov (1849–1936) Ivan Pavlov discovered the principle of conditioning while studying animals in Russia. He found that dogs salivated in response to food and that, when a bell was rung at the same time that food was presented, the dogs also salivated in response to the sound of the bell alone. The dogs had associated the ringing of the bell with the food and responded to it in the same way. Associating a new stimulus with a stimulus that elicited a natural response became the basis for what has been called *respondent* or *classical conditioning*. The principle is that an animal or human being associates a new stimulus to the original one and responds in a similar manner as to the original stimulus.

John B. Watson (1878–1959) John B. Watson of the United States applied the principle of respondent conditioning to child development and learning. Watson wanted to develop a scientific way of studying how people act under different environmental conditions. He coined the term *behaviorism* to identify a way of studying learning by observing behavior rather than by speculating about the inner structure of the mind. Watson believed that by controlling and manipulating the environment, one can influence an individual's learning and development. He developed a technology based on theories of respondent conditioning. The technology was designed to allow the developmental psychologist to control environmental conditions and thus control conditioning.

Edward L. Thorndike (1874–1949) Edward L. Thorndike was also concerned with the scientific study of learning. He attempted to explain the process by which stimuli are associated with responses. He developed a set of laws to explain this process. Most central to the process was the **law of effect.** This law stated that a response is strengthened if it is followed by a pleasurable effect and weakened if followed by an unpleasant effect. The **law of exercise** stated that the more frequently a stimulus-response bond is experienced, the longer it will be retained. The **law of readiness** suggested that learning is more effective when the nervous system is predisposed to action.

Thorndike's **law of effect** stated that a response was strengthened or weakened by its consequences.

His **law of exercise** stated that the more frequently a stimulus-response bond is presented, the longer it is retained.

His **law of readiness** stated that learning is more effective when the nervous system is predisposed to act.

Thorndike's law of effect was a precursor to the concept of reinforcement that became the basis for Skinner's approach to behaviorism. Thorndike's concern for children's natural tendency to develop habits also influenced kindergarten educators. Good habits, Thorndike felt, should be supported in the early years, while poor habits should be inhibited so the child will not have to unlearn them. Habit training became an important element of the kindergarten curriculum in the first quarter of the twentieth century.

Burrhus Frederic (B. F.) Skinner (1904–1990) B. F. Skinner contributed to learning psychology and developmental theory through his skillful and controversial practical application of learning theory to educational, personal adjustment, and social problems. Skinner believed that an understanding of learning comes from direct observation of changes in children's behavior related to changes in their environment (Bower, 1988). His contributions included creating and refining learning devices such as teaching machines and programmed textbooks in the mid–1950s and generating, in the late 1960s, Skinnerian doctrine, on which behavior modification was based. He also proposed a plan for social control through operant conditioning in the 1970s. Teaching machines and programmed texts presented material to be learned in small steps so that errors would be eliminated as much as possible. The teaching machine was a mechanical device to present materials to the learner and to reinforce the learner. The

B. F. Skinner studied learning based on operant conditioning

programmed text used the same principles to present material in printed form. Computers today may serve the same function as teaching machines, but in a more sophisticated form.

In **operant conditioning** an individual is encouraged to repeat a response when it is reinforced.

Skinner contends that most behavior is the result of **operant conditioning**, in which rewards or reinforcers encourage individuals to repeat their actions when they encounter situations similar to the ones that previously brought rewards. In contrast, if individuals experience painful or simply neutral consequences, they will be less likely to repeat their actions in the future. Rewards reinforce an act, whereas nonrewarding acts will be dropped or *extinguished* completely. Behaviorists refer to a reward as a reinforcer. A *positive reinforcer* stimulates an individual to repeat an act each time a similar situation occurs. Positive reinforcers provide some degree of pleasure to the learner. *Negative reinforcement* is not punishment but the removal of an unpleasant stimulus from the environment. Behaviorists view punishment, which consists of creating an unpleasant situation, as not particularly effective in increasing learning.

Skinner tested the effect of different kinds of reinforcement schedules on behavior. *Continuous reinforcement* rewards individuals each time they exhibit a desired behavior, whereas *intermittent reinforcement* rewards individuals some of the times they exhibit a desired behavior. Different schedules of intermittent reinforcement generate different results.

Skinner's theory has distinct implications for the field of child development. Skinner's behaviorist perspective on child development suggests that development is a function not only of physiological maturation, but also of increasingly complex learning. Changes in the growing individual's learning occur as a result of the consequences that have followed the behavior she or he has attempted. Skinner suggests that parents and teachers can promote children's learning by (1) getting children to attempt desirable behaviors and (2) organizing consequences that will encourage desirable behavior through positive reinforcement and extinguish undesirable behavior through punishment. Skinner believed that an individual's genetic and environmental history can be understood by studying environmental conditions and the individual's observable responses.

An individual's development results from the integration of all learning that occurs throughout life. Skinner argued that the environment rather than individual heredity develops human behavior. Selections of adaptive characteristics for the species are made naturally, individual behaviors are reinforced and altered by their consequences, and each individual's behavior is determined by external circumstances that promote cultural practices (Bower, 1988). Children can be provided with an environment that will elicit appropriate, desirable behaviors. These behaviors can surface and be maintained when they are purposely reinforced. Children expand their range of behaviors throughout their development, although specific stages are not related to specific kinds of behavior.

Influence of Behaviorism

Behaviorism had an influence on early childhood education in the 1920s and 1930s. Habit training, a concept developed by E. L. Thorndike, was seen as a goal of kindergarten education. The influence of behaviorism on the field has waned since that time, however, though the focus on observing behavior in children has remained important. Behaviorism has had a significant influence on the fields of special education and early childhood special education. Particularly in working with children with severe mental disabilities, special educators have used the theory to develop training programs for children. Increasingly, however, constructivist approaches are being used in early childhood special education programs.

PSYCHODYNAMIC THEORY

Psychodynamic theory has had a pervasive influence on child development theory as well as on early childhood education. Psychodynamic theory deals with personality. It developed out of clinical practice rather than in the research laboratory. Psychoanalysis, which deals with the personality problems of adults, has helped patients understand the influences that their childhood had on their developing personalities. In the process, psychoanalysis provided some significant insights about childhood and later came to be used in the study of child development.

Sigmund Freud (1856–1939) Sigmund Freud, an Austrian neurologist, treated several patients who had a variety of mystifying ailments, such as paralysis of the hand or arches and blurred vision, that had not been encountered in traditional physiological practice. While the patients'

Sigmund Freud, the father of psychoanalysis

symptoms indicated that nerve tissue was damaged, analysis revealed that their nervous systems were intact.

In **psychoanalysis** individuals talk about their past history as well as their present condition.

Sigmund Freud developed a form of treatment he called **psychoanalysis,** in which patients talked about their past histories and present conditions. Freud used such techniques as dream analysis and free association to help patients confront their unconscious fears and conflicts. Out of the case studies of his patients, Freud developed psychoanalytic theory, which has extensively influenced the thinking of psychologists, psychiatrists, and psychoanalysts. While his work was basically with adults, Freud concentrated heavily on memories of childhood experiences. His theory emphasized the fundamental role of early childhood experiences in the development of the individual's personality.

Freud's understanding of child development has inspired several important areas of contemporary child psychology, including child psychiatry, counseling for children and adolescents, nursery school teaching methods, and research in child development. A number of psychologists, educators, and social workers, including those who reject most psychoanalytic theory, have accepted several ideas from Freudian theory.

Freud developed a theory of development that says that individuals go through a series of psychosexual stages. Successfully moving through these stages, the individual develops a healthy personality. However, if conflicts arise, an individual may be fixated in a particular stage. In that case, the adult will unconsciously be dealing with needs related to an earlier period of development, thereby acting in a seemingly irrational manner. Freud viewed these stages of psychosexual development as universal: because they reflected human needs, they were embedded in development in all cultures.

Freud's work was influential throughout Europe and the United States. As psychoanalysts studied his theory, many of them modified the original theory and sought influences on development in the culture as

Table 3.1

Freud's Psychosexual Stages

Age	Stage	Characteristics
0–1 year	oral	Mouth and upper digestive tract is the center of sensual stimulation and pleasure.
1–3 years	anal	Anus and lower digestive tract is focal, pleasure in withholding or eliminating feces.
3–6 years	phallic	Pleasure focused in genital area, creation of Oedipal or Electra attachment, identification with parents.
6–12 years	latency	Focus on industriousness, suppression of sexual interest.
12 years and up	genital	Development of mature sexual interests.

well as in the individual. One of the most influential of these psychoanalysts was Erik Erikson.

Erik Erikson (b.1902) Erik Erikson extended Freud's concepts of personality development, emphasizing child development. He converted Freud's theory of development in psychosexual stages into psychosocial stages, believing that individuals develop throughout their lives through interactions with their social environment. Growth evolves through a series of stages (Erikson, 1968). Each of Erikson's stages depicts a distinctive crisis (see Table 3.2). Individuals attempt to settle one crisis before shifting to the next stage. They cannot remedy the crisis in a new stage

Erik Erikson viewed development as psychosocial in nature

Table 3.2

Erikson's Psychosocial Stages of Development

Age	Stage	Characteristics
0–1½ years	trust vs. mistrust	Reliance on caregiver: predictability leads to trust in environment, or lack of care leads to basic mistrust
1½–3 years	autonomy vs. shame and doubt	Environment encourages independence, pride, and sense of self-worth; or doubt and lack of self-esteem result from over-control
3–6 years	initiative vs. guilt	Ability to learn and to enjoy mastery; or fear of failure and of punishment leads to guilt
6 years–puberty	industry vs. inferiority	Valuing work, skill, and competence; or feelings of inadequacy and inferiority.
Adolescence	identity vs. role confusion	Development of individuality, or confusion related to self
Young adulthood	intimacy vs. isolation	Commitment to personal relationships, or withdrawal from others and self-absorption.
Middle age	generativity vs. stagnation	Care of next generation, widening interests; or self-indulgence
Old age	identity vs. despair	Understanding the meaning of one's existence, or disappointment with life and fear of death.

unless they have found solutions to earlier crises. Each stage relates to the effectiveness of the ego. The stages begin at birth and continue to develop throughout the individual's life (Erikson, 1963).

One interesting difference between Freud's stages and Erikson's stages of development is that Freud considered development to be complete by the end of adolescence, whereas Erikson recognizes development to be continuous throughout an individual's life. Erikson's stages are based on a series of social rather than sexual conflicts, which all individuals must master to attain maturity (Erikson, 1982). Conflicts are based on the individual's culture and place in history.

Influence of Psychodynamic Theory

The work of both Freud and Erikson has had significant implications for early childhood education. Both theorists viewed early childhood as important. Both perceived that young children needed to resolve a set of conflicts if they were to become mentally healthy adults. Both Freud's and Erikson's work suggests an active role for early childhood educators. In Freud's theory, teachers can create a mentally healthy environment in which children can express their deepest feelings without fear of criticism. In Erikson's theory, teachers can guide children to develop competencies to strengthen their egos. While the role of the teacher is different in each of these theories, both consider the teacher to be an important individual in children's lives.

CONSTRUCTIVIST THEORY

Constructivist theory is a dialectical solution to the opposition between rationalism and empiricism. Both of these points of view are ways of understanding how individuals come to know about the world. The rationalist sees reason (that is, the mind) as the source of knowledge, while the empiricist sees experience as the source of knowledge. The constructivist sees the individual as creating knowledge by acting on (or thinking about) information gained from experience. Even the youngest children have some understanding of what the world is like. This understanding helps them interpret the information they receive, while new information may also modify their understanding, in an active process that continues throughout each individual's life.

Constructivist theory views the individual as creating his own knowledge by processing information gained from experience.

While constructivist research and construction of theory on the development of the intellect have been going on for some time, these ideas began to have an impact on the fields of child development and education in America only in the 1960s. The works of several theorists, such as Jean Piaget, Lev. S. Vygotsky, and Jerome S. Bruner, were pivotal in developing constructivist views of intellectual development in children. Presently, constructivist theory is an important aspect of American psychology and education, although research continues and theories are being modified.

Jean Piaget (1896–1980) Jean Piaget was one of the pioneers of constructivist theories of cognitive development. Piaget gathered information on the ways children of various ages solve reasoning problems, communicate their dreams, make moral judgments, and conduct other mental activities. Piaget suggested that a child's system of thought develops through a series of stages common to all children in all cultures. In Piaget's model, young children are very self-centered; they interpret events solely from their own viewpoint. Normal adults, on the other hand, understand that different people may interpret events from different perspectives.

Piaget's study of intelligence suggested that he could integrate his biological and epistemological interests to study people's efforts to understand reality. Studying how children create and validate knowledge could provide an understanding of human knowledge. Piaget felt that logic and philosophy could contribe to this understanding. Apparently, Piaget had identified the problems to which he was to devote himself for the next thirty years (Gray, 1981).

Jean Piaget, a pioneer in constructivist theory

A **schema** is a mental construct respresenting a set of understandings.

In **assimilation,** individuals internalize information that is consistent with their existing knowledge.

In **accommodation,** individuals modify their existing concepts to account for new information.

Equilibrium is the balance between assimilation and accommodation.

According to Piaget, a child makes sense of the world by developing *schemata.* A **schema** (plural, schemata) is an integrated way of thinking about elements in the world. For the infant, a schema is a pattern of actions that are repeated in comparable situations. For example, when infants see a bottle, a rattle, or the edge of the crib, they may grasp it. This impulse to grasp in response to a perception represents a schema. As the child matures and develops language, schemata become more abstract.

The process of creating and modifying schemata includes two types of actions: *assimilation* and *accommodation*. In **assimilation**, as children encounter a problem in meeting their needs, they examine their repertoire of schemata to solve the problem. Matching environmental stimuli to their existing knowledge requires that children recalculate the event to correspond to the pattern of their repertoire of schemata. Piaget believes that "To assimilate an object to a schema means conferring to that object one or several meanings" (Piaget, Jonckheere, & Mandelbrot, 1958, p. 59).

Accommodation may occur if the new situation fails to correspond to the child's repertoire of schemata. This lack of correspondence will result in one of two consequences: (1) the incident is not assimilated at all, or (2) the dissatisfaction causes the child to modify an existing schema, that is, to accomodate it. According to Piaget (1963), "New objects which present themselves to consciousness do not have their own qualities which can be isolated . . . they are vague, nebulous, because inassimilable, and thus they create a discomfort from which there emerges sooner or later a new differentiation of the schemas of assimilation" (p. 141).

As children's cognitive patterns unfold and they interact with their environment, an instinctual balance occurs between the processes of assimilation and accommodation. This balance, or **equilibrium**, remains until new information causes the process to begin again. A child adapts to the environment through functions of assimilation and accommodation; thus, within the child's biological-mental self a process of *organiza-*

tion integrates all schemata that are properly adapted to each other. Piaget (1963) believes that

> It is sufficiently well known that every intellectual operation is always related to all the others and that its own elements are controlled by the same law. Every schema is thus coordinated with all the other schemata and itself constitutes a totality with differentiated parts. Every act of intelligence presupposes a system of mutual implications and interconnected meanings. (p. 7)

Piaget's theory has achieved popularity because it was perceived as being a response to the reigning theory of behaviorism. Piaget studied children in school and expressed his results in relation to biology, the history of ideas, and science in general (Mehler & Bertoncini, 1988).

Young children's play behavior reflects Piaget's concept of *equilibration*. In play, children assimilate new information and accommodate it to their intellectual structures. Mental activity and its parallel physical activity are basic, as children construct their systems of knowledge in more and more adult ways and become effective, competent, thinking grown-ups.

Piaget classified four primary stages of cognitive development: (1) the sensorimotor stage (birth to two years), (2) the preoperational stage (two to seven years), (3) the concrete operational stage (seven to eleven years), and (4) the formal operational stage (from eleven or twelve through adulthood). Children advance through these levels in a normal sequence but at their own developmental rate, which is determined by their experiences and their own maturing abilities.

Table 3.3

Piaget's Intellectual Stages of Development

Age	Stage	Characteristics
Birth to $1\frac{1}{2}$ or 2 years	sensorimotor	Children develop schemata based on sensory input and bodily motion.
2–7 years	preoperational	Children develop language and other symbolic representations. Intuitive thought is not systematic or sustained.
7–11 years	concrete operational	Children deal with logical processes, but deal with only one form of classification at a time; logical thought requires actual physical objects or events.
11 years +	formal operational	Children reason logically, formulate and test hypotheses, think abstractly.

Piaget's theory suggests an active role for early childhood education. Teachers should avoid telling children what they must know, either directly or indirectly. Rather, teachers should plan activities that provide children with the opportunity to think about activities related to manipulating concrete materials and to generate conceptual skills. Teachers also must raise questions, creating a degree of cognitive conflict, and propose issues that compel children to think in more mature ways.

This approach represents a major shift in theories about what schools do for young children. It has proved to be popular with early childhood educators, partly because it views young children as intellectually competent, though to a limited degree. While young children are able to process information and develop concepts, Piagetian theory suggests that their development should be encouraged through indirect means. Rather than telling children what we want them to know, we need to provide them with experiences that allow them to construct knowledge. In the early childhood years, these experiences cannot be abstract, but should include manipulation of concrete materials and direct experiences on which children can later reflect. Play and the arts have an important function in children's construction of knowledge.

Piagetian theory also has been especially useful in supporting the use of manipulative materials in teaching mathematics to young children. Constance Kamii has done extensive research on how children construct mathematical knowledge. Other mathematics educators have used the theory as well.

Lev Semenovich Vygotsky (1896–1934) Lev Semenovich Vygotsky was another theorist in constructivist psychology. Vygotsky was originally a teacher of literature. As a young scholar (1915–1922), he focused on artistic creation (Vygotsky, 1971), though later his work focused on developmental psychology, education, and psychopathology.

Lev S. Vygotsky, whose work is becoming increasingly influencial

Table 3.4

Vygotsky's Cultural Stages of Development

Stage I	Thinking in unorganized congeries or heaps. During this period the child puts things in groups (and may assign the group a label) on the basis of chance links in the child's perception.
Stage II	Thinking in complexes. Individual objects are united in the child's mind not only by subjective impressions but also by bonds that actually exist among the objects. This is a step away from egocentric thinking and toward objectivity. In a complex, the bonds between components are to some degree concrete and factual rather than abstract and logical.
Stage III	Thinking in concepts. In this final major stage, synthesizing and analyzing converge to make conceptual thinking possible. (Thomas, 1992, pp. 335–336)

Vygotsky distinguished between two kinds of development: natural and cultural. **Natural development** is the result of maturation. **Cultural development** relates to language and reasoning ability. Thus, an individual's thinking patterns are products of the activities practiced in the culture in which the individual grows up. Moreover, advanced modes of thought (conceptual thinking) need to be verbally communicated to children; thus, language is an essential tool in determining a person's ability to learn to think. Children's informal and formal education, using a language medium, determines their conceptual thinking level. If children experience a language climate of direct speech and mass communication media that is dominated by simplistic or "primitive" language, then their thinking will be simplistic or primitive. On the other hand, if the children's language environment includes varied and complex concepts, the children's thinking will be diverse and intricate, provided that their initial biological equipment (the senses, central nervous system, and so on) is not disabled.

Vygotsky distinguished between **natural development** and **cultural development.** Natural development results from maturation. Cultural development is related to language and reasoning ability.

Vygotsky proposed three stages of cultural development. Each of these stages is broken up into substages (Thomas, 1992). Vygotsky sees children developing through their **zone of proximal development,** or the point at which they can function independently. In this zone, children use supports provided by more mature thinkers. These supports are a form of scaffolding that allows children to function and learn new competencies. These competencies are then integrated within the children's

The **Zone of Proximal Development (ZPD)** is the point beyond which an individual cannot function alone, but where the individual can function when supports are provided.

Jerome Bruner has influenced education for more than three decades

repertoires. Thus, in this conception, learning leads to development rather than following it.

Vygotsky's theories have attracted a great deal of attention recently, especially among child development and education specialists who accept a constructivist view of cognitive development but are critical of Piagetian theory. Vygotsky's model has been especially applied to language and literacy education (see, for example, Mason & Sinha, 1993).

Jerome Bruner (b.1915) Jerome Bruner also studied the relationship between thought and language. He identified three representational systems:

1. **Enactive mode.** Individuals represent information through actions and manipulation (for example, tying a shoe).
2. **Iconic mode.** Individuals employ perceptual organization and imagery to represent information (for example, thinking of someone's face).
3. **Symbolic mode.** Individuals use language or symbols to represent information.

Bruner believes that cognition proceeds from the *enactive* through the *iconic* and ultimately to the *symbolic* mode of representation. A young infant represents the world *enactively*. Children physically do what they think. The only way infants can express the thought that they want a rattle is to grasp it. Similarly, infants suck an object to express the thought of hunger.

The two- or three-year-old child is typically at the *iconic* level. Children represent an action using some type of sensory image. Images may take many forms: visual, auditory, tactile, or kinesthetic (Pylyshun, 1973). In this level of representation, children can "image" a person who is absent, a previously performed action, or an event they have just witnessed.

The five- or six-year-old child is typically at the *symbolic* level. Language increasingly augments the range of possible experiences children can represent and assists them to manipulate and transform the experiences. Children learn the communicative nature of language at the same time they are learning to use language as an instrument of thought and action (Bruner, 1983). Understanding is developed through the same stages as representation in intellectual development: understanding by doing, by visualizing, and eventually by representing ideas symbolically.

Bruner has shifted recently to a more Vygotskian position in his understanding of child development. He sees young children as working at making sense of the world with the help of more mature thinkers. He accepts that learning influences development and that intellectual development takes place within a child's cultural context (Bruner, 1990).

Influence of Constructivist Theory

Constructivist theory has significantly influenced early childhood education. Piagetian theory has been used extensively in the areas of science and mathematics education for young children. More recently, Vygotsky's work has influenced reading and language education, especially in programs of emergent literacy. Bruner's work also continues to influence the field.

ECOLOGICAL THEORY

Ecological theory in child development focuses on the environment's influence in children's lives and development. This theory assumes that both obvious and subtle environmental factors directly influence children's growth and development. Children's environments vary in a variety of ways. The influences of such variations are intertwined with children's normal developmental pattern, making their effect difficult to understand. Ecological theory uses information about children's environments to describe, organize, and clarify the effects of environmental variations.

Ecological theory views the whole child as an integrated organism influenced by the environment.

The ecological theory of child development considers the whole child as an integrated organism influenced by environmental elements. Development progresses in small steps that build up to construct the personality through the child's experiences. According to the holistic or field theories, a new stimulus or experience adds a new ingredient to the child's knowledge. Thus, every meaningful new experience can alter the relationship of many or all of the existing elements that contribute to the personality, affecting the formation of the child's individuality (Thomas, 1992). The prime advocate of ecological theory in child development is Urie Bronfenbrenner.

Urie Bronfenbrenner (b.1917) Urie Bronfenbrenner conceives of the ecology of human development as a way to understand how the active, growing human being relates to the environment. He strives to understand the relationship between the immediate settings in which children develop and the larger contexts of those settings. Bronfenbrenner focuses on children's interpretations of their surroundings and how those interpretations change. For example, in a given setting (such as school, home, or a gathering with peers), with its physical and material characteristics, children experience a pattern of activities, roles, and interpersonal relationships. Activities are people's actions; roles are the actions society demands based on the individual's position (such as parent, infant, sibling, teacher, friend, coach, and so on). Interpersonal relationships include people's verbal and nonverbal responses to each other. Children's development is influenced by their perception or interpretation of those activities, roles, and interpersonal relationships. According to Bronfenbrenner (1979),

1. The phenomenological (internally interpreted or experienced) environment dominates the real environment in guiding behavior.
2. It is folly to try to understand a child's action solely from the objective qualities of an environment without learning what those qualities mean for the child in that setting.
3. It is important to discover how the objects, people and events in the situation affect the child's motivations.
4. It is essential to recognize the influence on behavior of "unreal" elements that arise from the child's imagination, fantasy, and idiosyncratic interpretations. (pp. 24–25)

Teachers, in interpreting children's behavior, must understand the children's perception of the activities, roles, and interpersonal relations manifest in that setting. Thus, one segment of the environment can have an impact on the entire configuration as the child constructs a new meaning. Obviously, teachers can design educational segments to influence children's perceptions of environments in relation to themselves.

Influence of Ecological Theory

While Bronfenbrenner's work has not had direct application in the development of the early childhood curriculum, it has influenced concern for social policy in the field. The influence of the classroom on the young child, many educators believe, cannot be separated from the influence of the family or from the context in which both the classroom and the family exist. Home, school, community, and culture are all linked to each other. Often, the only way to positively influence a child's development is to seek improvements in the community and society and to use the support provided by various social agencies.

NATURE AND NURTURE IN CHILDREN'S DEVELOPMENT

The concepts that have been set forth by these developmental theorists are different from each other in a number of ways. One difference relates to the areas of development each theory addresses. Some theories deal with all areas of development, while others address only one or two types of development, for example, intellectual development or social-emotional development.

Another way the theories differ is in the degree to which they view the individual's genetic makeup (nature) or the experiences of growing up (nurture) as most important in a child's development. Some theorists, such as Gesell, suggest that an individual's development is primarily determined by nature; while a poor environment might limit any individual's ultimate development, environment is not the prime inflluence on development. Others, such as Bruner and Vygotsky, suggest that a child's experiences determine to a great extent what the individual finally becomes, especially in regard to cultural development. Most child development specialists believe that both these influences are important and that environmental influences should never be ignored. Although the family serves as the major environmental influence on the young child, early childhood education is also important, as is the social context in which the child is reared.

Developmental theory and research provide a picture of normal, average development in children. Most children differ from the average. Norms allow teachers to anticipate what children will be like, but these early judgments need to be modified for each child in the class.

DEVELOPMENTAL AREAS

The discussion of child development theories presented here has focused on the theories that have influenced early childhood education in the past and continue to influence the field today. While a broad description of developmental theories has been presented here, this chapter did not attempt to provide a detailed overview of the child development knowledge early childhood teachers need. For more detailed information, we suggest that readers refer to the following texts:

Berk, L. E. (1994). *Child development* (3rd ed.). Boston: Allyn and Bacon.

Schickedanz, J. A., et al. (1993). *Understanding children* (2nd ed.). Mountain View, CA: Mayfield.

Seifert, K. & Hoffung, R. (1991). *Child and adolescent development* (2nd ed.). New York: Houghton Mifflin.

Spodek, B. (Ed.) (1993). *Handbook of research on the education of young children.* New York: Macmillan. (See especially Section 1: Early Childhood Education and Child Development.)

Cognitive Development

Young children develop their thinking and reasoning skills as they acquire language. Language allows children to convert the information they gain into abstractions so they can organize it into concepts or schema and store it for later use in a variety of situations. Cognitive development influences children's thinking, feelings, and behavior (Seifert & Hoffnung, 1991). Children should learn by physically manipulating materials (Kamii, 1985; Piaget, 1963) and integrating these experiences to real life experiences.

Language Development

Language development proceeds at a remarkable pace in children's early years. Children who are one-and-a-half years old understand around 25 words; by age six, most children accumulate a vocabulary of more than 1,800 words. Young children add nearly 600 words to their vocabulary each year and make outstanding progress in semantics and grammar (Corrigan, 1983; Helms & Turner, 1986). They learn basic spoken language in their early years and employ their developing speech skills to engage in conversations, continuous questions, dialogues, songs, or chants. Most children enjoy experimenting with manipulating language in rhythm and cadence activities (Helms & Turner, 1986; Schwartz, 1981).

Physical Development

Physical development transforms young children's muscles and general body build, changing their body proportions and physical skills. For instance, the toddler's round, babylike contours grow in spurts and become slender, so that the toddler's physical size and abilities increase. During the preschool years, children's bodies change in many ways. When they enter preschool, young children usually have all 20 of their baby teeth. Then they start to lose their teeth. Permanent teeth usually surface at age six (Spock & Rothenberg, 1985). The children's muscle and skeletal systems continue to develop. The head and brain reach their adult size. The connectivity and transmission of nerve impulses, which are essential for complex brain performance and motor control, increase (Helms & Turner, 1986; Malina, 1982, Schmidt, 1982). This physical evolution facilitates the child's participation in many different types of physical activities. In addition to physical development, other factors determine the overall course of development and the eventual expression of physical change.

Emotional Development

Children's emotional development has an impact on the other areas of development. Children's emotional stages are manifested in their overt behavior, physiological responses, and feelings. Emotions are difficult to explain. Often the reasons for children's manifestations of anger, fear, hostility, resentment, jealousy, and frustration can be inferred from the situations which provoked their behavior.

Young children's emotional development is influenced by their environment. Children are what they can do, sense, understand, imagine, feel, and choose (Whitesell & Harter, 1989). Theories of emotional development recognize that emotional expressions undergo a developmental change with age. For example, infants' emotional expressions are global. They become more graded, subtle, and complex after the first year of life (Demos, 1986). Control of facial expressive behavior develops during the preschool years (Cole, 1985). Each facial expression represents a different internal experience. However, the meaning of a smile differs for infants and for adults. Social learning processes become very important during the first two years of life.

Social Development

Social development is the mechanism through which children learn how they are expected to behave. From birth, children are expected to follow a set of standards reflecting the values of their family and society. Parents communicate their culture, religion, gender, and educational and ethnic backgrounds to their children. Children duplicate adult behavioral patterns and adapt social expectations to their own personality (Gordon & Browne, 1989).

This process, referred to as **socialization,** requires that children learn appropriate behavior in a variety of situations. At an early age, children learn to distinguish between each environment's expectations (Gordon & Browne, 1989). Beginning in the early years, children identify with others according to the quality of their interactions and the amount of time they spend with each other. Collaboration and dialogue are generated very early as children understand the notions of friendship in their interactions with their peers. Competition complicates friendship (Hartup, Laursen, Stewart, & Eastenson, 1988).

Socialization
is the process by which individuals learn appropriate behavior for varying situations.

Young children are socially vulnerable and physically dependent on others, particularly when they have different senses of self in multiple settings, such as family, school, and peer groups (Reid, Landesman, Treder, & Jaccard, 1989). During infancy, children's attachments and relationships in their widening worlds (Bretherton & Waters, 1985; Cauce, 1986) are crucial. They need a good social support network to promote their emotional adjustment, life satisfaction, and mental and physical health (Cohen & Wills, 1985). This need continues throughout early childhood.

REGULARITIES AND IRREGULARITIES IN YOUNG CHILDREN'S DEVELOPMENT

Teachers tend to treat all children as about average in their development. Although this might be a reasonable approach most of the time, on some occasions it is totally inappropriate. Many children differ from the average in profound and significant ways. Early childhood programs need to be designed to respond to the differences found among children in a class, not just to the average of the class. Both individual and group differences should be considered in developing an early childhood education program. Group differences generally include differences in language, culture, and social class. Individual differences include differences in development that lead to a range of exceptionalities, including giftedness.

Cultural Differences

Culture includes a set of attitudes and behaviors that have been learned and shared by a group of people. Each society develops specific values, languages, and cultural norms that are meaningful to the group. American society has been characterized by cultural pluralism, with a number of subgroups, each having their own culture, sharing in the culture of the nation. The **cultural pluralism** that characterizes our nation means that the values, attitudes, and behaviors children acquire as they interact with the persons closest to them may be different from those of other people they will meet throughout their lives. Our society requires that we help children learn to develop the flexibility they need to understand and accept cultural differences.

Cultural pluralism reflects the various cultural subgroups that make up American society.

Banks (1993) has suggested that much of the research in cultural awareness has grown out of a series of studies and a research paradigm developed by Kenneth and Mamie Clark. They studied African-American children, ages three to seven. Their study confirmed that young children are aware of racial differences and that African-American children often inaccurately identify themselves by race. There has been considerable research since the Clarks' studies and not all of the Clarks' findings have been confirmed. Debate still rages on the issues they raised.

The contexts and cultures in which children are raised promote their cognitive development. Some research suggests that specific cognitive skills may develop as a function of different contexts and cultures. This suggests that children in one culture might develop strong social skills, while children in another culture might develop strong intellectual skills. Studies of culture and cognition contribute to our understanding of cognitive development.

Early childhood education programs socialize children by exposing them to the dominant values, customs, and habits of the culture. This exposure creates a cultural frame of reference that will become part of the children and serve as a vital force in determining their behavior. Educators need a clear perspective on the role of culture in education and child development. Many of the children in our schools come from families that have a culture different from the dominant one. Teachers must be sensitive to the cultural roots of the children in their classes as well as those of others in our society. Teachers should keep in mind that though there are some cultural values we all accept, there are others that we must respect as being important to others, even though we may not accept them personally. Teachers need to use a variety of resources, including children, parents, and experts on culture, to help the children share their different cultures in the classroom. This approach communicates respect for cultural difference and shows that every culture is valued. Resources that can be particularly helpful in fulfilling our obligation to help children understand diverse cultural groups include

Derman-Sparks, L. (1991). *The anti-bias curriculum: Tools for empowering young children*. Washington, DC: National Association for the Education of Young Children.

Ramsey, P. (1987). *Teaching and learning in a diverse world: Multicultural education for young children*. New York: Teachers College Press.

Saracho, O. N., & Spodek, B. (Eds.) (1983). *Understanding the multicultural experience in early childhood education*. Washington, DC: National Association for the Education of Young Children.

Language Differences

Just as children's cultures differ, so may their dominant languages differ. As a matter of fact, language and culture are closely tied together. Some language differences are differences in dialect. The grammar of children from areas of the United States such as rural New England, Appalachia, and parts of the South (for example, where Creole and Black English are spoken) will be strikingly different from standard formal American English. Although children from these areas may not speak standard English, they may have achieved competence in their own dialects.

Groups of people who primarily speak a language other than English may incorporate rules of the first language into standard English. These children may come from Native American tribes or immigrant families. They may speak French, Chinese, or Spanish as their first language. Migrant children, regardless of their ethnic group, also speak differently since they move from place to place, being exposed to a variety of language patterns and meanings. Teachers should take these differences in language into account as they plan a program. In addition, teachers need to take care not to demean or embarrass children who not speak standard English. Teachers can provide opportunities in the classroom for children to share diverse languages and heritages and can provide meaningful learning experiences that enable children to learn to speak standard English.

Social-Class Differences

For several decades research has examined social-class differences in intellectual and academic skills between low-income and middle-income children. Some psychologists, including Hunt (1961), have asserted that these differences are not genetically determined and that changes in the environment could increase intellectual development. Since development is most easily influenced in a child's early years, Hunt suggested that preschool enrichment, preferably initiated at age two, be used as an effective "antidote" or compensation to enhance cognitive growth in low-income children.

A number of experimental early childhood education programs in the 1960s led to the creation of Project Head Start, an early childhood program for low-income children (see Chapter 2). Head Start has been characterized as a comprehensive child development program, providing health, nutrition, and social services along with education. Parent involvement is an important part of the program, extending children's learning beyond the classroom and ensuring that the program is responsive to the needs of the children, their parents, and their community.

Exceptional Children

With the passage of PL 94-142 and PL 99-457, most early childhood programs have assumed responsibility for educating children with disabilities in regular classes. These children deviate in one or more ways from other children; they may have behavior disorders, learning or developmental disabilities, mental retardation, visual or hearing impairment, communication disorders, and/or physical health impairments. Often these children have more than one disability, complicating diagnosis and remediation. Educators must take both children's disabilities and their strengths into account when designing or modifying an educational program. They must understand each child's total developmental condition.

Teachers who work with children with disabilities often require special assistance. While children with severe disabilities may need to be educated in segregated settings, increasingly, these children are being included in the regular class program so they can be educated in the least restrictive environment possible. The responsibility to identify children with disabilities and to provide appropriate education in the classroom is a public one, though children, especially those below kindergarten age, may be enrolled in nonpublic school programs. The classroom teacher is the primary provider of programs for these children. However, special education teachers, psychologists, parents, and others provide help and serve together as a team.

All children, regardless of whether they have identified disabilities, have special educational needs that require individualized educational programs. However, some groups of children have specific educational needs that require the modification of teaching techniques. *Dealing with Individual Differences in the Early Childhood Classroom* (Spodek & Saracho, 1994) is a rich source of material for teachers who work with young children.

SUMMARY

Since the beginning of the child study movement, the fields of child development and early childhood education have been closely related. Child development theories have informed early childhood curriculum practices. Child development research has also given us a clear picture of what children are like at various ages. This knowledge has helped teachers establish expectations for how children will function and what they will accomplish at a particular age.

Developmental norms are generalized statements about development in all children. These norms are usually helpful, though they can also be harmful. Because a norm represents an average of everyone's characteristics, it cannot accurately describe any single child. While children are alike in many ways, each child at any age will be different from all other children in important ways. Teachers must look at individual children and see how each one differs from the average before planning a program and establishing expectations.

REFERENCES

Bower, B. (1988). Skinner boxing. *Science News, 129*(8), 92–94.

Banks, J. A. (1993). Multicultural education for young children: Racial and ethnic attitudes and their modification. In B. Spodek (Ed.), *Handbook of research on the education of young children* (pp. 236–250). New York: Macmillan.

Bretherton, I., & Waters, E. (1985). Growing points of attachment: Theory and research. *Monographs of the Society for Research in Child Development, 50* (1–2, Serial No. 209).

Bronfenbrenner, U. (1979). *The ecology of human development*. Cambridge: Harvard University Press.

Bruner, J. S. (1966). *Toward a theory of instruction*. Cambridge: Harvard University Press.

Bruner, J. S. (1983). Play, thought, and language. *Peabody Journal of Education, 60*(3), 60–69.

Bruner, J. S. (1990). *Acts of meaning*. Cambridge: Harvard University Press.

Cauce, A. M. (1986). Social networks and social competence: Exploring the effects of early adolescent friendships. *American Journal of Community Psychology, 14*, 607–628.

Cohen, S., & Wills, T. A. (1985). Stress, social support, and the buffering hypotheses. *Psychological Bulletin, 98*, 310–357.

Cole, P. M. (1985). Display rules and the socialization of affective displays. In G. Zivin (Ed.), *The development of expressive behaviors: Biology-environment interactions* (pp. 269–290). Orlando: Academic Press.

Corrigan, R. (1983). The development of representational skills. In *Levels and transactions in children's development*. New directions for child development, no. 21. San Francisco: Jossey-Bass.

Demos, V. (1986). Crying in early infancy: An illustration of the motivation function of affect. In T. B. Brazelton & M. Yogman (Eds.), *Affect and early infancy* (pp. 39–73). New York: Ablex.

Erikson, E. H. (1963). *Childhood and society*. New York: Norton.

Erikson, E. H. (1968). *Identity: Youth and crisis.* New York: Norton.

Erikson, E. (1982). *The life cycle completed: A review.* New York: Norton.

Gordon, A. M., & Browne, K. W. (1989). *Beginnings and beyond: Foundations of early childhood education.* Albany, NY: Delmar.

Gray, E. M. (1981). Jean Piaget et sa recherche: Search and research. *New Universities Quarterly, 36*(1), 13–26.

Hartup, W. W., Laursen, B., Stewart, M. I., & Eastenson, A. (1988). Conflict and the friendship relations of young children. *Child Development, 59*(6), 1590–1600.

Helms, D. B., & Turner, J. S. (1986). *Exploring child behavior*. Monterey, CA: Brooks/Cole.

Hunt, J. McV. (1961). *Intelligence and experience.* New York: Ronald.

Kamii, C. (1985). *Young children reinvent arithmetic: Implications of Piagetian theory*. New York: Teachers College Press.

Malina, R. M. (1982). Motor development in the early years. In S. G. Moore & C. R. Cooper (Eds.), *The young child: Reviews of research*. Vol 3. Washington, DC: National Association for the Education of Young Children.

Mason, J., & Sinha, S. (1993). Emergent literacy in the early childhood years. In B. Spodek (Ed.), *Handbook of research on the education of young children.* New York: Macmillan.

Mehler, J., & Bertoncini, J. (1988). Development—A question of properties, no change? *International Social Science Journal, 40*(1), 121–135.

Meisels, S. J. (1989) *Developmental screening in early childhood: A guide* (3rd ed.). Washington, DC: National Association for the Education of Young Children.

Piaget, J. (1962). *Play, dreams, and imitation in children.* New York: Norton.

Piaget, J. (1963). *The origins of intelligence in children.* New York: Norton.

Piaget, J., Jonckheere, A., & Mandelbrot, B. (1958). *La lecture de l'experience*. Etudes d'Epistemologie Genetique V. Paris: Presses Universitaires de France.

Pylyshun, Z. W. (1973). What the mind's eye tells the mind's brain: A critique of mental imagery. *Psychological Bulletin, 80*, 1–24.

Pylyshun, Z. W. (1981). The imagery debate: Analogue media versus tacit knowledge. *Psychological Review, 88*, 16–45.

Reid, M., Landesman, S., Treder, R., & Jaccard, J. (1989). "My family and friends": Six- to twelve-year-old children's perceptions of social support. *Child Development, 60*(4), 896–910.

Schmidt, R. (1982). *Motor control and learning: A behavioral emphasis*. Champaign, IL: Human Kinetics.

Schwartz, J. I. (1981). Children's experiments with language. *Young Children, 36*(5), 16–26.

Seifert, K. L., & Hoffnung, R. J. (1991). *Child and adolescent development.* (2nd ed.). Boston: Houghton Mifflin.

Skinner, B. F. (1984). The shame of American education. *American Psychologists, 39*(9), 947–954.

Spock, B. J., & Rothenberg, M. B. (1985). *Baby and child care.* New York: Pocket Books.

Spodek, B. & Saracho, O. N. (1994). *Dealing with individual differences in the early childhood classroom.* White Plains, NY: Longman.

Strickland, C. E., & Burgess, C. (1965). *Health, growth and heredity: G. Stanley Hall on natural education.* New York: Teachers College Press.

Thomas, R. M. (1992). *Comparing theories of development* (3rd ed.). Belmont, CA: Wadsworth.

Vygotsky, L. S. (1962). *Thought and language.* Cambridge: MIT Press.

Vygotsky, L. S. (1971). *Psychology of art.* Cambridge: MIT Press.

Whitesell, N. R., & Harter, S. (1989). Children's reports of conflict between simultaneous opposite-valence emotions. *Child Development, 60*(3), 673–682.

4

Early Childhood Curriculum

CHAPTER OVERVIEW

This chapter presents:

- Different conceptions of curriculum
- Issues related to early childhood curriculum
- Educationally appropriate early childhood practices
- Ways to develop an anti-bias, multicultural early childhood curriculum

INTRODUCTION

Schools for young children are expressly designed to achieve specific goals. The expectation is that young children will be somehow different as a result of their early childhood education experience than they would have been without that experience. School personnel fill the day with activities designed to achieve this goal. The **curriculum** may be defined as the organized experiences designed to provide formal and informal opportunities for learning to children in a school setting. How does one develop a curriculum? This chapter discusses various conceptions of the early childhood curriculum, the sources of a curriculum and its appropriate goals, issues in the curriculum, early childhood curriculum models based on knowledge and development, educationally appropriate early childhood practices, and anti-bias and multicultural curricula.

The **curriculum** is the organized learning experiences provided to children in school.

CONCEPTIONS OF CURRICULUM

Both educational theories and child development theories have been used in formulating the curriculum of early childhood education. As noted in Chapter 2, in the 1890s the child study movement, under the leadership of G. Stanley Hall, initiated the close affiliation between early childhood education and child development. The acceptance of child development as a scientific discipline and the progressive education movement, concentrating on the child's reconstruction of knowledge, facilitated the interaction of the two fields (Weber, 1984). This reliance on theory was a major departure in early childhood curriculum development from earlier conceptions. While Froebel, in his creation of a kindergarten curriculum, envisioned the child as a growing, changing individual, no developmental theory undergirded his concept of a kindergarten curriculum (Spodek, 1988).

Developmental Theories and the Early Childhood Curriculum

Kohlberg and Mayer (1972) suggested that educational programs are related to particular points of view about human development. They categorized these points of view into three ideologies: *romantic, cultural transmission*, and *progressive*. The *romantic* ideology, based on works by Rousseau, Froebel, Gesell, and Freud, sees maturation and education as the unfolding of inner virtues and abilities. Concern with readiness for kindergarten or for beginning reading instruction often reflects this ideology. Teachers and parents are often advised to wait until the child is "ready" before beginning instruction.

The *cultural transmission* ideology assumes that education involves transmitting knowledge, skills, values, and social and moral rules from one generation to the next. Behaviorism provides the psychological principles for educational technology in this stream of thought. Many approaches to elementary and secondary education reflect the cultural transmission ideology, since the main purpose of these programs is to transmit knowledge to the young.

The *progressive* ideology asserts that education assists children to reach higher developmental levels if they experience structured but natural interactions with the physical and social environment. This assertion suggests a strong relationship between human development and education, inaugurating the concept of the teacher as a child development specialist.

What is interesting in this analysis is that, although the educational and developmental theories are distinct, each is mutually supportive. Early childhood education theory and child development theory represent two distinct types of theory, although they are often discussed as if they were interchangeable. Developmental theories are universal; they apply to all children in all contexts. They are also minimalist, suggesting the minimal requirements needed for development. In contrast, educational theories are particular; they deal with specific learnings in specific contexts. They are also maximalist, addressing ways to optimize development and learning. Developmental theory also considers multiple influences that transform individuals, whereas educational theory focuses on only one influence—the school—on individuals (Fein & Schwartz, 1982). Each type of theory informs the other, but neither can be generated from the other.

Although a curriculum might be identified as being derived from a particular developmental theory, that is really not the case. Some curriculum developers labeled their programs "Piagetian." Yet if we analyze each program and compare each with the others, we find that each program bearing the same label is different from all the rest (see Forman & Fosnot, 1982, for an analysis of Piagetian curricula). These differences result because each program developer selects elements from a developmental theory as the focus of the curriculum. In addition, developers add more to a curriculum beyond what can be derived from developmental theory. As a matter of fact, developmental theory should be used as a resource for the early childhood curriculum, rather than its source (Spodek, 1973b). The starting place for an educational program "should be a value statement of what children ought to be and become" (Biber, 1984, p. 303).

Knowing about children's development is important for teachers. This knowledge guides teachers in understanding what young children are capable of learning, how they learn at a specific point in their development, and how teachers can test and modify their knowledge. However, knowledge of child development does not provide a guide to content, that is, it does not tell us what we want children to learn (Spodek & Saracho, 1990). The decision about what should be included in an early childhood program must come from other sources, including the community's culture, level of technology, and symbol systems.

Determining the Content of Early Childhood Education

We can identify the categories of knowledge taught in traditional American early childhood programs. However, this content for the most part is tacit; while it does exist, it is usually not discussed or studied. The day-to-day curriculum experiences introduced in early childhood programs relate to the American way of life. Young children learn knowledge through the books we read to them, the stories we tell, the songs we sing, the experiences we offer, and the loyalties we nurture among children and between children and adults.

A critical facet of all early childhood programs is language and literacy education. However, literacy skills are only one segment of the language learnings that young children need. Both bilingual and monolingual children must learn American language. Teachers present the rich oral and written traditions of children's literature and poetry, folk stories, and fairy tales.

Holidays are one way we define our peoplehood. The history and traditions of the United States are integrated in most of the holidays we celebrate with children in school (for example, Columbus Day, Thanksgiving, Presidents' Day, Martin Luther King Day) to inspire a feeling of peoplehood. Such celebrations assist all children, regardless of their cultural background and heritage, to experience a feeling of belonging to the culture of the United States without requiring them to deny their own culture. Children can be aware of their own forebears and yet celebrate the first New England Thanksgiving as if they were descendants of the Pilgrims, regardless of when they or their ancestors actually came to our shores (Spodek, 1982). Such components are integrated in the curriculum of early childhood programs, even if they are not clearly defined.

While the content of early childhood education programs should be developmentally appropriate, it should also reflect the values of our culture and the nature of the knowledge children need, in order to be educationally appropriate as well (Spodek, 1986). A number of early childhood educators are advocating that program content be defined more precisely. For example, Elkind (1988) advises early childhood teachers to introduce young children to the content, concepts, and classification of the different subject areas such as science, social studies, and history. Young children also need to learn different colors, shapes, and sizes, as well as matching, categorizing, discriminating, and arranging things based on their similarities and differences.

Elkind advises teachers to use projects to teach young children. Elkind's recommendations are comparable to those of the progressive kindergartens of the first quarter of the twentieth century (Weber, 1984). Children in these early kindergartens inquired into the world available to them, the "here and now," depicting that world in their play, in their building, in their art products, and in the stories and dialogues they shared. The world that children experienced was a natural one; therefore, to educate young children, subject knowledge was organized around themes, units, or projects rather than by subjects or categories.

Early childhood educators can present content-rich programs and at the same time socialize children into the school and into the culture while continuing to prepare children for later schooling. Programs can be responsive to children's developing understandings and abilities while emphasizing cultural knowledge and anticipating academic scholarship.

THE SOURCES OF EARLY CHILDHOOD CURRICULA

During the past three decades, many innovative programs have been proposed for the education of young children. Although some programs described as "new" are essentially modifications of existing practice, differences exist between innovative programs and traditional practice in nursery schools and kindergartens. The differences in the sources of these new curricula are even greater.

Children as a Source of Curricula

According to some theorists, early childhood curricula should originate from children themselves, so that education follows the needs and interests of young children. Both Friedrich Froebel and Maria Montessori, pioneers of early childhood education, used their observations of children as the main source of their curricula.

The kindergarten of Friedrich Froebel consisted of the ordered use of manipulative activities, or *Occupations*, and the use of songs and finger plays, his *Mother's Plays and Songs*. Froebel used these activities as they were revealed to him by the children themselves (Lilley, 1967). Similarly, Montessori observed the uses children made of the didactic materials provided them. She then abstracted from those uses the essential elements for learning and ordered them into the *Montessori Method*. These observations became the basis of Montessori's scientific pedagogy (Montessori, 1964). Froebel's analysis of child behavior was more mystical than scientific.

The use of "natural" childhood activities as the source of curricula is a romantic ideal that can be traced as far back as Jean-Jacques Rousseau. The ideal of the unsocialized savage whose best instincts are destroyed by the surrounding culture is echoed by some contemporary critics who bemoan the "disappearance of childhood." Unfortunately, there is nothing natural about any school—even a preschool—and its activities cannot be directly derived from the natural activities of children. Play activities provided to children in educational settings are modified by teachers, who allow certain kinds of play to take place, disallow other activities, and intervene directly and indirectly to make play more educational. Selecting a room's furniture, materials, and equipment is one form of intervention; suggesting an activity is another. All schools are cultural contrivances to *do* things *to* children—to change them.

Looking at the curricula derived from observations of children, we become aware of the selectivity of both the observations and their uses. When one observes an object, one defines certain attributes as critical, providing a focus for observing and describing. Other attributes are overlooked because they are considered less crucial. The purpose of the observation determines what one will see.

In analyzing the arguments about the natural activity of childhood as a source of the curriculum, we become aware that the purposes of the observer determine what the observer sees. One educator may see a set of potentials while another sees only deficits; one may see only the intellectual behavior of the child, another only the emotional or social behavior. One educator may view a particular child as a problem solver, while another may see that child as responding to external rewards. The definition of the natural child becomes a product of the theoretical scheme that determines which observations of a complex organism should be attended to and which discarded.

Few contemporary educators can fail to see the contrived nature of both the Froebelian kindergarten and the Montessori school. If we are to understand the curricula developed by Montessori, Froebel, or any other educational developer, we must go beyond simple natural observation and identify the basis for selecting the observations and the conceptual framework used to give meaning to these observations in developing educational experiences for children.

Developmental Theory as a Source of Curricula

A second source of curricula used by early childhood educators has been child development theory. One such theory, derived from Arnold Gesell's research, considers child development as primarily maturational.

The developmental norms produced by Gesell and his colleagues are based on many observations of children of various ages. On the basis of these norms, children have been grouped by age and provided with experiences that are considered appropriate for their age level.

Arguments derived from Gesellian theory have been used to exclude activities thought to be inappropriate and to insure inclusion of appropriate experiences in the school life of children. However, age norms do not adequately describe the range of heights, weights, skills, abilities, or other attributes of children at any age. Nor do these attributes remain constant at all times for all persons in all cultures. Average heights and weights of children have increased in the last fifty years and vary from one geographic area to another, as the result more of environmental differences than of natural differences. Other attributes of childhood vary as a result of the cultural and physical environment. What a child is at any level of development is to some extent a result of what a culture says that child ought to be.

Psychoanalytic theory, which is concerned primarily with personality, has also been used to formulate curricula for young children. Interpretations of the work of Sigmund Freud, Carl Jung, and Erik Erikson led to an emphasis on expressive activities, dramatic play, and group interactions. When carried to excess, educational practices based on these theories resembled child therapy. With the increased emphasis on ego development in later years, however, psychoanalytic thinkers became concerned less with catharsis and more with the personal competencies required to build an integrated self, and many of the excesses eventually disappeared.

Piagetian theory has also been used as the basis of early childhood curricula. George E. Forman and Catherine T. Fosnot (1982) defined four propositions that underlie Piaget's constructivist theory: (1) a view of knowledge as a construction of our own inference making; (2) a belief in the individual's internal self-regulating mechanism; (3) a view of knowledge as resulting from an individual's actions, including both activity and reflection; and (4) a view that knowledge results from conflict resolution. These authors then analyzed six Piagetian early childhood programs in relation to these propositions. Each program focused on the propositions differently and interpreted them in various prescriptions for activities. Thus, each program both selected from among the elements of the theory and freely interpreted the theory.

Such an analysis raises the question of whether any early childhood program can be purely based in developmental theory. In translating theory to practice, program developers discard some elements of the theory and add others. Thus, even when programs are rooted in the same developmental framework, they can differ from each other in essential and significant ways. Is child development theory, Piagetian or otherwise, a legitimate source of educational curricula for young children? Child development theory has been popular in early childhood education for many years. However, it may not be appropriate as the prime source of curricula. Child development is a descriptive science; it can tell us *what is*. Education deals with *what ought to be*. Creating educational experiences involves choices and preferences that cannot be rationalized by recourse to child development theory.

In their discussion of developmental theories and early childhood education, Greta Fein and Pamela Schwartz (1982) suggest that developmental theory provides a rich source of information about the intricacies of human growth. While this information is necessary, it is not sufficient for generating practice. What may be needed, however, is a theory of practice (Bronfenbrenner, 1979). Such a theory would include statements about how controllable resources would be obtained and allocated, and allow for the creation of concepts of educational environments.

Learning Theory as a Source of Curricula

Just as child development theory has been identified by program developers as a source of curricula, so have learning theories. Developmental theory deals with change in the human being over long periods of time. Learning theory attempts to account for short-term change. The recourse to learning theory as a source of curricula has been manifest in several different ways.

The "conduct curriculum" developed in the early childhood program at Teachers College under the leadership of Patty Smith Hill (1923) shows the influence of Edward L. Thorndike's school of behaviorism. Kindergarten was a place for habit training to take place. Lists of appropriate habits and recommended stimuli for five-year-olds were developed for kindergarten teachers at this time.

Today the theories of behaviorist B. F. Skinner are having similar influence. Skinner's learning theory contains six major concepts:

1. **Operant conditioning**. Operations or responses that occur normally can be reinforced.
2. **Reinforcement**. A stimulus that increases the rate at which an operation occurs, such as food, toys, money, tokens, or praise is called a reinforcer.
3. **Immediate reinforcement**. There should be a minimum delay in time between the operant behavior and its reinforcement.
4. **Discriminated stimuli**. Behaviors that should occur under specific circumstances are reinforced only under those circumstances.
5. **Extinction**. A response can be decreased by its failure to be reinforced.
6. **Shaping**. Complex behaviors can be analyzed into simple components, which can be built into the complex behavior (Bugelski, 1971).

Behavioral learning theory has been used as a basis for developing teaching methods in early childhood education. It has been used as a technology—a method of teaching—especially with individuals who have difficulty learning independently. Some have suggested that behaviorism can be applied to any content (Bijou, 1977). Several problems have been identified with this approach, however. Children seem to have some difficulty in transferring what they learn in school situations to other situations. In addition, it is difficult to teach higher-order learning processes, such as problem solving or creativity, using this approach.

"Third force," or phenomenological, psychologists, view behaviorism as too mechanistic and simplistic to provide an adequate framework for understanding complex human processes. They suggest an alternate approach in dealing with human learning. Donald Snygg and Arthur Combs (1965), for example, view the process of education and of learning as a process of change in the individual's phenomenology. How individuals behave, they suggest, is a function of the individuals' understanding of a situation. The meanings of behavior and of situations become the focal point of learning. Meanings vary from person to person and cannot always be fully verbalized. The goals of learning are also individual. What individuals learn depends upon their goals and needs, which cannot always be manipulated externally.

In phenomenological psychology, the *self* plays an important role. How persons view themselves affects their behavior and what they learn. Children who view themselves as competent will be more ready to learn and will learn more than those who think of themselves as incompetent. Phenomenologists suggest that the school should concern itself with developing adequate self-concepts in its pupils.

Phenomenological psychology leads to a different set of instructional strategies in classrooms than does behavioral psychology. Complex learning situations are used intact, with children being helped to develop their own meanings; their behavior is not shaped, nor are specific behavioral goals predetermined. Instead, the teacher is concerned with moving children in the direction of appropriate behavior within a wide range of acceptable behavior. Such an approach allows a greater degree of freedom for children, enabling them to select alternatives and develop personal responsibility for their learning and growth.

Psychological theory focusing on behavior and behavior modification has determined the structure of a number of curricula in early childhood education. While short-term change is easily observed and evaluated, it is hard to study the long-term effects of these curricula. In the final analysis, such programs may be based as much on faith as are any of the more traditional programs. The description of a program in psychological terminology and the great emphasis on evaluating effectiveness without analyzing ultimate goals may, in the long run, obscure the ultimate consequences of these programs.

Nor can phenomenological psychology help us to determine what should be taught to children. At best, learning theory can help educators develop new instructional methodologies and analyze and assess established methodologies. This, in itself, is no small role.

One other facet of psychology that is often used for formulating curricula is psychological testing and evaluation. Many programs in early childhood education, for example, have been justified as ways of increasing intelligence, and one way of judging the intelligence of children is through the administration and scoring of intelligence tests. Such tests consist of items that purport to sample a broad range of intellectual behaviors in children. As a sample, each item achieves validity by representing many other kinds of behaviors that might have been elicited from among the total number of intelligent behaviors.

Since the effectiveness of educational programs can be demonstrated by students' achievement of higher scores on intelligence tests, tasks taken from or related to intelligence tests easily become the content of the program. Justifications for this approach to curriculum development often suggest that since test items are samples of intelligent behavior, having children practice these behaviors allows them to practice behaving in an intelligent manner.

There are a number of problems with using test items as the source of a curriculum. Most standardized tests are **norm referenced.** They sample a range of outcomes and judge each test taker's knowledge of the items compared to others' knowledge. When test items are used as the source of curriculum, the test becomes **criterion referenced** rather than norm referenced, since the items no longer represent the larger area of knowledge they are supposed to sample. Each item becomes a goal in itself, even though the worth of each specific piece of knowledge has not been validated. In a sense this outcome distorts both the testing process and the curriculum development process. (For a full discussion of the impact of the use of tests in this way, see Shepard, 1991.)

Norm-referenced tests are scored in relation to the scores of others taking the test.

Criterion-referenced tests are scored in relation to mastery of the material being assessed

Such distortions of psychological testing and curriculum development are not limited to the area of intelligence testing. Distortions take place in language development, in academic achievement, or in any other area in which samples of behavior are mistaken for the total range of behaviors they represent. The small number of items on a test that determine a difference in age or grade placement make this form of justification all too attractive in determining short-term intervention techniques for young children.

Organized Knowledge as a Source of Curricula

More than three decades ago, Jerome Bruner (1960) suggested that the organized fields of knowledge should become the basis of educational curricula for children at all levels. The "structure of the disciplines," Bruner argued, could provide a vehicle to insure that school learning would be intellectually significant. Key ideas in each area of knowledge would be revisited in increasingly sophisticated ways as children moved through their academic careers. These key ideas could be taught in an intellectually honest way at every level of development. *New Directions in the Kindergarten* (Robison & Spodek, 1965) provides an example of how this proposal could be translated into early childhood programs in science, social science, and mathematics.

The proposal to develop school curricula based on the structure of knowledge was attractive, and a number of curriculum development projects were organized along these lines. As work in these projects continued, a number of problems became evident. Scholars identified many different structures of knowledge, and some disciplines, such as social science, did not seem unified. Another problem was that identifying intellectual structures did not help to determine what school experiences would help children attain significant understanding in a field. The strategies for understanding the sciences did not seem to help in understanding the arts and the humanities. Fewer projects dealing with these areas of school learning were mounted.

The relationship between the conceptual structures of mature disciplines and children's less mature understanding is more complicated than was originally thought. Issues dealing with relevance to children, individual learning rates and style, and personal interests complicated what had once seemed a simple task. Although the content of the disciplines—the areas of knowledge—could help to determine the significance of school content, that content by itself was inadequate for determining school curricula at any level, and especially at the early childhood level.

School Content as a Source of Curricula

Another source for developing early childhood programs has been the content of later schooling. "Readiness," for example, is considered important because it prepares children for instruction. Readiness skills have no importance in themselves, but they and certain other kinds of learning prepare children for later school expectations.

This justification is to be found in the Bereiter-Engelmann Program (1966). Its content (reading, language, and mathematics) is determined by what is required of children in primary grades. The program also prepares children to behave appropriately in their later school life. Whether such preparation will benefit students later is debatable. The pressures of later life and schooling are sometimes heaped upon children in anticipation of what is to come.

One of the few long-range studies of the effects of education, the *Eight-Year Study* (Aiken, 1942) of progressive high schools, demonstrated that children from open schools did better than those from more restrictive schools when they went to college. While this was a study of older children, it raises questions about the desirability of providing children with rigid early schooling as preparation for rigid later schooling. In addition, later school learning is not a goal in and of itself, but a means to a goal. Using the later school curriculum to determine the content of early childhood programs only delays decisions about curriculum content. As it is, too little concern is given to the proper source of curricula.

Evaluating Sources of Curricula

Neither test items nor school content can be viewed as proper sources of any curriculum. Using either represents circular thinking that supports existing practice because it exists. School content is devised to achieve societal aims. To support school content as an end in itself is to deny the purposes of schooling and to legitimize activity solely on the basis of tradition. Similarly, test items are designed to help judge educational achievement; to use them to determine curriculum content is to distort both the educational process and the evaluation process. Rather, test items should be determined by educational practices.

Using children themselves to determine educational programs might also be questioned. Since what we see in children is determined by prior conceptions, we should make those assumptions explicit by defining the developmental theories and learning theories to which we adhere when we observe children's behavior. Learning theory, developmental theory, and concepts of organized knowledge and ways of knowing are all sources of curricula, but they can function properly only within the context of human values.

Schools at all levels help children learn the behaviors required to function in society. They also help children lead personally satisfying lives. To the extent that schools help to define the "good life" and the "good society," they are moral enterprises. The values growing out of this enterprise determine how we use our knowledge of human development, human learning, or the structures of knowledge in determining educational experiences for young children.

In addition to child development theory or learning theory, school programs are derived from beliefs about social purpose and forms of knowledge. All schools, including those for young children, are designed to serve social purposes. These purposes can be identified by studying the cultural values, levels of technology, forms of social organization, and symbol systems of the school's community.

Cultural values tell us what is important for an individual to know, and thus help us judge the worth of educational content. Our society is based upon such values as liberty, justice, equality, and the dignity of the individual. Valuing individual dignity causes us to consider the way we treat children in school and the nature of the materials we use. Individuals or groups should not be demeaned. In one interpretation, our concern for equality leads us to treat all children as if they were alike and to demand the same language learning for each; in another interpretation, we support diverse programs for different children, including bilingual-bicultural education. Valuing cooperation, competition, or independence can also directly influence the kinds of materials we provide young children and the forms of behavior we reward or restrict.

A society's level of technology determines to a great extent what forms and levels of knowledge an individual must acquire to cope with community life and to be productive. The change from teaching "nature study" to teaching "natural science" during the twentieth century is an example of how changing school content responds to changing levels of technology.

Forms of social organization also have their impact on school programs. In the primary grades, for example, we study families, communities, and community workers, making children aware of roles and structures in their communities. Cultural symbols, which allow us to share ideas and feelings, also inform curriculum development. Consequently, language instruction is a basic part of all school programs. Other symbols are taught as well; music, art, and movement provide nondiscursive symbolic forms. Our flag is another type of symbol; even the clothes we wear can take on symbolic meanings.

These are but a few examples of how our culture sets requirements for what is taught in school. These cultural imperatives become so much a part of our thinking that we seldom identify them explicitly. Cultural options, sometimes referred to as "stylistic differences," also exist.

FORMS OF KNOWLEDGE

Human development theory can tell us what children can learn. The cultural context of schools can tell us what children ought to learn. However, the content of school programs must be abstracted from existing forms of human knowledge. A number of attempts have been made over the years to identify the various forms of knowledge that can be used as the basis for school curricula.

During the colonial period, primary schools were mainly concerned with teaching literacy. Literacy was the foundation of education, since the ability to read gave the individual direct access to the Bible. Schools at all levels were taught or supervised by ministers. When Thomas Jefferson attended the College of William and Mary, all but one of the faculty members were ordained ministers. Since the Middle Ages, Western society has seen the Bible as the source of knowledge. When theories or observations were not consistent with the teachings of the Bible, they were considered erroneous. Thus, when Galileo began charting the skies and determined that the sun rather than the earth was the center of the universe, he was considered to be in error because his theory ran counter to the view of the universe presented in the Bible.

During the Enlightenment, it became more generally accepted that there were other views of the world besides those presented in the Bible and other ways of validating knowledge besides recourse to the Scriptures. During this Age of Reason, rationalism and empiricism evolved, and with these developments came changes in early childhood curricula.

Rationalism provided the epistemological basis for the Froebelian kindergarten. Rationalism held that truths were composed of self-evident premises that were not derived from experience but were held to be logically and undeniably true. Froebel's view of the world suggested that the key premise was the unity of humanity, God, and nature. This and related ideas were presented to children through a set of symbolic materials and activities: the *Gifts*, the *Occupations*, and the *Mother's Songs and Plays*. The kindergarten curriculum presented ideas to children through continued contact with their symbolic representations. The ideas themselves were never tested in the program, nor was there a concern with helping children understand objective reality except as that reality expressed those ideas.

Empiricism saw sense perception as the central means to knowledge. One came to know the world as a result of one's experiences, which provide information through the senses. To become more knowledgeable, one must have a greater number and variety of experiences and a greater sensitivity to the external world.

The development of the Montessori method reflected the belief that human knowledge results from experiences. Montessori education is sensory education. Children are trained through manipulative materials that isolate particular attributes of experiences, helping children to become aware of resulting sensory experiences and to learn to order them. Children discriminate between and order objects by their color, size, weight, and shape.

Sensory elements, however, do not account for the process of generating meanings from information—that is, the creation of knowledge. While the colors or shapes of an object are inherent in the object itself, the ways in which we classify objects are independent of the objects and of our sensory experiences with them. The structure we apply to our experiences gives them meaning.

More recently, early childhood programs have been based on the research and theory of Jean Piaget. Piaget viewed knowledge as resulting from something more than a person's experience. Children or adults construct knowledge by applying mental processes. The mental structures created by the individual interact with sensory information to create knowledge. Knowledge is neither simply the accumulation of sensory experiences nor the expression of innate ideas; rather, it is a human creation that uses sensory data—information resulting from experiences—to create ideas that can be tested against additional experience and discarded, elaborated, modified, or affirmed.

Constance Kamii (1973) has used a Piagetian framework to identify five forms of cognitive knowledge as objectives of early childhood education:

1. **Physical knowledge** about the observable properties and physical actions of things;
2. **Logico-mathematical knowledge** about the relation between and among objects, such as classification, order, and number;
3. **The structuring of time and space,** which must be created using reasoning although time and space are observable in external reality;

4. **Social knowledge** of conventions, structured from people's feedback; and
5. **Representation,** or the development of symbols and signs that can stand for objects.

Kamii and Rheta DeVries have used this scheme to design activities to teach logico-mathematical knowledge (1982) and physical knowledge (1993) to children.

In the framework above, one may know many things about, for example, a table. A child may determine if the table has a hard or soft, smooth or rough surface, if the table is high or low, and if its top is round or rectangular. These are elements of physical knowledge directly accessible through the child's senses. The child can then place this table into a previously constructed category of objects called "table," containing similar objects that may actually look different in many ways. The child can also distinguish this table from objects that are not tables. The child can count the tables in a room and order them by size, by height, or by some other attribute. These are forms of logico-mathematical knowledge. The child can identify where the table stands in relation to other objects in the room and recall whether the table was covered with a cloth last night, thus placing the table in a structure of time and place.

The child learns that it is permissible to place things on, write on, and eat from the table, but not to sit on it or jab a sharp knife into it. These learnings are not directly accessible through sensory experience, nor are they the result of logical processes. They are matters of social knowledge, common as they may seem, and must be communicated to the child, directly or indirectly. Finally, the child may represent the table by drawing a picture of it, creating a model of it, or writing the word *table*.

These various forms of knowledge deal with the same object, but each is derived and verified in a particular way. This Piagetian framework is limited to cognitive knowledge; however, an early childhood curriculum that deals only with the intellectual realm is too narrow. A concept of knowledge must go beyond cognitive knowledge. Other concepts of knowledge, developed by philosophers of education, should prove useful to early childhood educators (for example, Phenix, 1964; Hirst & Peters, 1970). Some of these have been elaborated elsewhere (Spodek, 1977).

Our views of the school's role, of the relationship between individuals and their development, of society's demands, and of the sources of knowledge can be used to identify goals for education. R. F. Dearden (1968), for example, has suggested that the goal of education is "personal autonomy based upon reason," which seems quite appropriate as one of the goals of early childhood education. He describes this autonomy as follows:

> There are two aspects to such an autonomy, the first of which is negative. This is independence of authorities, both of those who would

> dictate or prescribe what I am to believe and of those who would arbitrarily direct me in what I am to do. The complementary positive aspect is, first, that of testing the truth of things for myself, whether by experience or by a critical estimate of the testimony of others, and secondly, that of deliberating, forming intentions and choosing what I shall do according to a scale of values which I can myself appreciate. Both understanding and choice, or thought and action, are therefore to be independent of authority and based instead on reason. This is the ideal. (p. 46)

This concept of autonomy is relevant to the education of young children. Erikson's framework (1950) for human development includes the development of autonomy just after the development of trust. As the child's intelligence continues to develop, the basis for personal autonomy becomes more rational.

If we accept "personal autonomy based upon reason" as the goal of early childhood education, then psychological theory can help us determine ways of testing the effectiveness of a program in achieving this ideal. In addition, knowledge of developmental processes can help us order activities to serve an educational purpose at a particular level of child development. We can determine whether children can adequately cope with the degree of autonomy we provide. Developmental theory becomes a tool for analyzing the curriculum. The forms of knowledge also can help to determine whether the methods of teaching are consistent with what is being taught, and whether children can become not only independent learners, but independent verifiers of what they have come to know. The content of school programs must be recognized as a product of educators' imaginations, to be tested by psychological means, rather than as a natural consequence of children's behavior, adults' thinking, or institutional organization.

ESTABLISHING GOALS FOR EARLY CHILDHOOD EDUCATION

One of the prime goals of early childhood education, as of all education, is the development of knowledge in children. Knowledge, however, must be broadly defined and continually redefined as the sociocultural context changes. We should provide children with access not only to formal scholarly disciplines, but also to self-knowledge, that is, knowledge of what they can do, feel, and communicate to others. Values, aesthetic appreciations, attitudes, and predispositions are communally shared forms of knowledge that children must also learn, but they cannot be isolated by subject area. Knowledge of the culture's symbol system, both linguistic and otherwise, must also be developed in children.

The attainment of knowledge is a lifelong task. Although this task can begin in the early years, the goals of education can never be fully attained in these years. Therefore, teachers must identify *instrumental* goals as well as *terminal* goals. Instrumental goals are those that must necessarily be attained if terminal goals are to be achieved. For example, children might be taught to discriminate among and to name different colors and shapes in kindergarten. The names of colors and shapes are not significant except as labels. However, discrimination, categorization, and labeling are important cognitive processes. Once learned, these processes can be applied to many similar activities. Since the processes can be achieved through studying colors and shapes, the activity of sorting and naming has educational merit.

Sometimes we teach things to young children that they will have to unlearn later. Some early learnings are a necessary step to mature knowledge, even though they are inadequate for the mature scholar. Beginning reading instruction is a case in point. A mature reader does not associate sounds with words or use a large memorized sight vocabulary to gain meaning from the printed page. Such an approach would hinder the mature reader's progress in gaining meaning efficiently. But we can see no way for the young child to become a mature reader without learning a sight vocabulary and a set of letter-sound associations. These learnings constitute a transitional stage, and the child must be helped to discard them later. Our instrumental goals, although they might not look like our terminal goals, must be directly related to the terminal goals, psychologically if not logically.

MODELS OF EARLY CHILDHOOD CURRICULA

Within the last three decades a range of program alternatives have been developed for the education of young children. Many of these programs were to be found in the Planned Variations program of Project Head Start and Project Follow Through. The various curriculum models are described elsewhere (see Evans, 1975; Day & Parker, 1977; Spodek, 1973b; Roopnarine & Johnson, 1993). The discussion that follows will concern itself with ways of analyzing and comparing models.

Lawrence Kohlberg and Rochelle Mayer (1972) suggest that programs of education differ on the basis of their ideologies—value assumptions about what is ethically good or worthwhile and theoretical assumptions about how children learn or develop, as described earlier in this chapter. Underlying the romantic ideology is a conception of development as a process of unfolding, with education essentially being a support for development. The cultural transmission ideology is concerned with transmitting elements of the culture from the older generation to the younger generation, with little concern for maturation. In the progressive ideology, individuals create their own development by interacting with their environment.

Conceiving of educational programs as based in ideologies suggests that programs can have many different goals, yet be rooted in the same developmental or learning theory. For instance, the Behavior Analysis

Program of Project Follow Through, sponsored by the University of Kansas, is geared toward a set of rather narrow goals. It focuses essentially on social and classroom skills and on the core subjects of reading, mathematics, and handwriting (Bushel, 1973). In contrast, Sidney Bijou (1977), also operating from a behavior analysis framework, suggests goals for the development of abilities and knowledge including body management and control, physical health and safety, self-care, recreation and play, social behavior, aesthetic knowledge and abilities, everyday mechanical know-how, knowledge of how things work in the community, academic and preacademic subjects, and the methods and content of science. In Bijou's view, extending motivation involves the preservation and extension of ecological reinforcers, the development of attitudes and interests in people, and a positive attitude toward school. In the area of self-management skills, Bijou includes personal self-management techniques as well as problem-solving and decision-making skills.

Thus, in assessing early childhood education program models, one needs to know more than just the developmental theory associated with the model. One must know the basic assumptions underlying the model, including assumptions about the client, the educative process, the school, and the teacher. One needs to identify the long-range and short-range goals of the program and how the model handles the organization of time, space, and physical and human resources. If one is concerned with implementing a model, one should know whether the model has been imple-

CURRICULUM MODEL: THE COGNITIVE-ORIENTED CURRICULUM

The Cognitive-Oriented Curriculum was developed by the High/Scope Educational Research Foundation in Ypsilanti, Michigan. It is based on Piagetian theory and designed to allow children to develop meaningful representational abilities and to see relationships between objects and events. Four content areas have been established in this curriculum: classification, seriation, temporal relations, and spatial relations. Each content area has specific goals. Children are also helped to represent the ideas they encounter and to move through levels of representation.

Teachers are expected to plan the children's activities carefully, keeping the goals of the curriculum in mind. The classroom is organized into learning centers, with materials related to different activities provided in each. Children plan for their day when they arrive in school. They carry out their plans during a work period. At the end of this period, the children talk about what they did during the work period. Thus, verbalization relates to the children's activities and to the mental processes in which they engage. The teacher uses specific techniques of verbal stimulation with small groups of children. Dramatic play and field trips are an important part of the program.

High/Scope provides an elaborate staff development process to train teachers to use the model. The model has also been extended into the primary grades.

Source: D. P. Weikart, L. Rogers, C. Adcock & D. McClelland, *The Cognitive Oriented Curriculum* (Washington, DC: National Association for the Education of Young Children, 1971).

CURRICULUM MODEL: THE BANK STREET APPROACH

The Bank Street approach is rooted in three sources: (1) the psychodynamic theories of Sigmund Freud, Anna Freud, and Erik Erikson; (2) the theories of such cognitive developmentalists as Jean Piaget and Heinz Werner; and (3) the philosophies of such educators as John Dewey, Susan Isaacs, and Lucy Sprague Mitchell. It views development as a series of changes in the ways persons organize, experience, and cope with the world; it assumes a stage theory of development, with education helping children move from one stage to the next. It sees the role of the teacher as one of helping children to consolidate their understandings while challenging them in ways that promote growth. It considers the development of a sense of self as important to the child and sees this sense of self as resulting from interactions with other people. Growth, it assumes, is the result of conflict within oneself and with others.

In the Bank Street approach, development is the goal of education; competence is central to that development. Another goal is the development of autonomy and individuality. Social relatedness and connectedness is a third goal of the program. Creativity constitutes its fourth goal. Finally, the fifth goal is the integration of experience to help the child connect the self with the world. The curriculum is based on principles of child development and on children's needs and interests. Children are offered firsthand experiences that they use to build concepts. Play is an integral part of the learning process. Content areas, such as language and literacy, science, mathematics, art, music, and movement, are provided through these firsthand, integrated experiences.

Source: A. Mitchell & J. Davis, *Explorations with Young Children: A Curriculum Guide from the Bank Street College of Education*. (Mt. Ranier, MD: Gryphon House, 1992).

mented before and how effective it was. Practical issues regarding cost, what staff and materials are required, and the availability of support services can also affect a decision about a program's worth (Spodek, 1973a).

It is not surprising that different programs of early childhood education lead to different learning outcomes, since their goals are so diverse. When assessed in terms of academic achievement alone, some programs seem more effective than others. However, these differences are not just a matter of one program teaching *more* than another, but of programs focusing on different goals.

Different programs have different impacts on children. One must select a program not only because it works, but because what it achieves is worthy. Early childhood programs represent ethical principles. Our choice of goals and the means to achieve them should come from an awareness of the options available and from our judgment of the goals we consider appropriate for young children. We can then match goals with curriculum methods.

Teachers often select educational activities. Later chapters in this book look at the various subject areas, presenting a summary of the knowledge available about each area and a sample of strategies for teaching children that grows out of the basic summary. The discussions are organized by subject areas because educators have traditionally used this convenient way of talking about program content. Though the framework is handy, the reader should continually be on the lookout for ways of crossing subject lines, of integrating content through activities, and of seeking relationships with children's interests and experiences.

Developmentally Appropriate Practices

Because of the increased involvement of public schools in the education of young children, the National Association for the Education of Young Children (NAEYC) was concerned that many individuals without early childhood backgrounds were designing programs for young children. In 1984, the association established a commission to identify guidelines for appropriate educational practices for young children. After the commission report was submitted in 1985, NAEYC published a position statement on "Good Teaching Practices for 4- and 5-Year-Olds." This was later elaborated into the "NAEYC Position Statement on Developmentally Appropriate Practices for Early Childhood Programs Serving Children from Birth Through Age 8" (Bredekamp, 1987). This statement is included in Appendix B, at the end of this book.

Developmental appropriateness includes age appropriateness and individual appropriateness. Appropriate activities in early childhood education are child initiated, child directed, and teacher supported.

A number of educators have been concerned that this concept of developmentally appropriate practice is inadequate for judging early childhood programs. Age appropriateness is too often related to maturational approaches to education. While the notion of individual appropriateness might allow the concept to be applied to children who differ from the norm, including those with disabilities, with gifts, and from linguistic and cultural minorities, it still is inadequate. A judgment about the appropriateness of early childhood practices, as noted earlier, must also include an understanding of the cultural and knowledge domains to which children must relate. Thus, educational appropriateness is a more valuable category than developmental appropriateness in evaluating early childhood practices.

Educationally Appropriate Practices

The number of early childhood programs has increased in response to the growing demand for out-of-home care and education during the early years. In addition, the characteristics of the programs have changed to meet the needs of different age groups. For instance, children of all ages, including infants, are enrolled in early childhood programs. The length of the program day for all ages of children has extended in response to employed families' need for extended hours of care. Similarly, program sponsorship has become more diverse. The public schools are playing a larger role in providing prekindergarten programs

NAEYC CURRICULUM GUIDELINES

A. Developmentally appropriate curriculum provides for all areas of a child's development: physical, emotional, social, and cognitive through an integrated approach.
B. Appropriate curriculum planning is based on teachers' observations and recordings of each child's special interests and developmental progress.
C. Curriculum planning emphasizes learning as an interactive process. Teachers prepare the environment for children to learn through active exploration and interaction with adults, other children, and materials.
D. Learning activities and materials should be concrete, real, and relevant to the lives of young children.
E. Programs provide for a wider range of developmental interests and abilities than the chronological age range of the group would suggest. Adults are prepared to meet the needs of children who exhibit unusual interests and skills outside the normal developmental range.
F. Teachers provide a variety of activities and materials; teachers increase the difficulty, complexity, and challenge of an activity as children are involved with it and as children develop understanding and skills.
G. Adults provide opportunities for children to choose from among a variety of activities, materials, and equipment; and time to explore through active involvement. Adults facilitate children's engagement with materials and activities and extend the child's learning by asking questions or making suggestions that stimulate children's thinking.
H. Multicultural and nonsexist experiences, materials, and equipment should be provided for children of all ages.
I. Adults provide a balance of rest and active movement for children throughout the program day.
J. Outdoor experiences should be provided for children of all ages. (Bredekamp, 1987 pp. 6–11)

or before- and after-school child care. Corporations are also becoming more visible sponsors of child care programs (Spodek & Saracho, 1990).

While educators still seem to be concerned with developing innovative approaches to early childhood education, there has been a change in how these innovations are created. Early childhood educators are less concerned than in the past with creating new curriculum models. Such models are difficult to conceptualize, implement with integrity, and disseminate. Instead, educators now focus on identifying appropriate educational practices for young children and then adapting these practices to educational settings (Spodek & Brown, 1993).

Programs have changed to respond to social, economic, and political forces; however, these changes have not always taken into account the basic developmental needs of young children, which remain constant. Unfortunately, the trend for formal instruction in early childhood programs to concentrate on academic skills continues to increase. This trend is based on misconceptions about early learning (Elkind, 1986).

The trend toward early academics contradicts developmentally appropriate guidelines in teaching young children. Programs should be custom-made to meet the needs of children, rather than expecting children to accommodate to the requirements of a specific program. NAEYC (Bredekamp, 1987) has suggested curriculum guidelines for developing appropriate practice in early childhood programs for children from birth through age eight. These guidelines are presented in the box on page 110.

Important to these components is sensitivity to how young children mature. Thus a teacher's choice of certain activities and materials should be based in the knowledge that the young child's primary modes of learning are language and play, which are, respectively, the symbolic representation and the reconstruction of the world the child experiences. A central part of the teacher's role is to present experiences and materials that expand children's knowledge of the world and how that knowledge can be symbolized (Molnar, 1989).

Such guidelines relating to developmental appropriateness alone obscure the quest for the answer to the question: "What does the early childhood teacher teach and how well is it taught?" They imply that *what* one teaches young children is irrelevant, except to the extent that it nurtures development. Seldom is a program's evaluation based upon children's achievement or learning outcomes, except when that achievement is conceived of as having an impact on development.

However, enhancing children's knowledge may be equally important as enhancing their development, and possibly a better goal for early childhood education. Developmental theory and educational theory differ significantly. One can inform the other, but one cannot be derived from the other (Fein and Schwartz, 1982). Developmental theory can be a resource for early childhood curricula, but not a source (Spodek, 1973a). As a matter of fact, evidence on the long-term effects of early childhood programs questions the impact of early childhood education on the developmental process, while supporting its value for improving educational processes. In studies of the long-term effects of early childhood education, IQ gains, which are indices of developmental impact, faded by about third grade, while the impact on school achievement was sustained through high school (Lazar & Darlington, 1982).

As we look at early childhood education, we need to separate the content of education—what we teach—from the process of education—how we teach. The process of educating young children is closely related to their level of development. Knowledge of child development can help us understand what young children are capable of knowing, how children come to know what they know at a particular stage in their development, and how they validate their knowledge. But the content of what we want these children to know comes from our knowledge not only of what children are capable of knowing at a particular level, but also of what our culture thinks is important for children to know. An example of a concern for content can be found in the development of multicultural programs in early childhood education.

Anti-Bias, Multicultural Curricula

Individuals differ from each other in many ways. American society reflects a variety of cultures, languages, and values, making a multicultural perspective essential. This variety has been present in the United States since its beginning, but in recent years the number of cultures represented has increased. More and more students from different ethnic backgrounds are enrolling in the schools. Therefore, multicultural education is becoming more apparent in schools throughout the country. Multiculturalism requires that people learn about other cultures as well as their own. To achieve this goal, multicultural education must become a school requirement.

Louise Derman-Sparks and her associates developed *The Anti-Bias Curriculum* (1989). This curriculum suggests ways to combat bias related to gender, race, disability, age, and culture. It provides suggestions for materials and activities to achieve this goal and discusses ways in which teachers can help children learn about differences among human beings in a positive way. The authors suggest that children notice differences related to gender, age, race, disability, and culture, and begin to develop attitudes towards these differences, at a very early age. For this reason, they believe that educators must take the initiative in helping children form positive attitudes, rather than ignoring issues of bias and stereotyping.

The authors of the *Anti-Bias Curriculum* emphasize that their curriculum is meant to be integrated into all aspects of teaching and learning. This curriculum stresses the values that are taught to young children. Derman-Sparks and her colleagues include a discussion of classroom holiday activities and what children might learn from these activities. They also urge teachers to help children find ways to work together to change things they think are unfair.

Tsai (1991) suggests the following guidelines for developing an early childhood curriculum with a multicultural perspective:

1. Multiculturalism embodies an overall perspective rather than a specific curriculum. It should be integrated into children's everyday experience and infused into every area of the curriculum. Both the arrangement of the physical environment and the design of the activities should reflect cultural diversity. In sum, it should be a natural part of daily learning (Mock, 1986).
2. The multicultural curriculum should reflect each child's unique cultural life pattern. This will allow all children and their parents to feel proud of their culture and also enrich life experiences of other children.
3. Multiculturalism should reflect a commitment to preserve and extend cultural alternatives and broaden the school's cultural base (Mock, 1986). This commitment should be long lasting and not burn out after a fit of enthusiasm.

To implement a multicultural curriculum, teachers should

1. Create a classroom atmosphere conducive to the recognition of cultural diversity. The physical environment should include picture books, posters, music, toys, props for dramatic play, and other teaching aids that reflect many cultures.
2. Use parents or other adults of different ethnic groups as resources and experts. Invite them to join discussions on the themes and activities that best depict their life and should therefore be included in the program. Parents can also help to gather materials and resources for the curriculum.
3. Scan the teaching plan for the whole semester or year to find ways to integrate multicultural activities into a variety of units. The activities should be balanced so that every area of the curriculum has some activities reflecting other cultures. These activities should be designed to complement the total program and facilitate intergroup relations (New York Education Department, 1987).

Multicultural education is essential to help students learn to understand, accept, and value persons from cultures other than their own. Appreciation for other cultures should result from a program that encourages the attitudes and values that students need to gain. The multicultural curriculum helps students to learn values and attitudes of cultures that are different from their own.

SUMMARY

In developing early childhood education programs for children in contemporary American society, educators must reexamine their assumptions. The knowledge base of the field must become more precise. Early childhood programs must be appropriate for today's children.

Parents and teachers must understand the dichotomy between a socialization program and an academic one. Socialization is a continuous procedure, in the society at large and in each social institution or social group. Young children need socialization experiences that include learning the student role, the importance of academic learning, and basic literacy and mathematical skills. Socialization does not mean learning to follow teachers' directions and to be quiet and submissive, but should signify becoming an independent pursuer of knowledge and a creative thinker (Spodek & Saracho, 1990).

Early childhood programs can be improved if educators make the curriculum precise and justify its content. The early childhood curriculum must assist young children to socialize, equip them for later school learning, and teach them content that is important to them. Early childhood programs must be evaluated on their developmental appropriateness and their educational worth, keeping in mind the needs of the children taught and of the communities served. Only public content can be evaluated concerning its effectiveness, worth, and practicality (Spodek & Saracho, 1990).

REFERENCES

Aiken, W. M. (1942). *The story of the eight-year study.* New York: McGraw-Hill.

Bereiter, C., & Engelmann, S. (1966) *Teaching disadvantaged children in the preschool.* Englewood Cliffs, NJ: Prentice Hall.

Biber, B. (1984). *Early education and psychological development.* New Haven: Yale University Press.

Bijou, S. W. (1977). Behavior analysis applied to early childhood education. In B. Spodek & H. J. Walberg (Eds.), *Early childhood education: Issues and insights* (pp. 138–156). Berkeley: McCutchan.

Bredekamp, S. (1987). *Developmentally appropriate practice in early childhood programs serving children from birth through age 8* (Expanded ed.). Washington, DC: National Association for the Education of Young Children.

Bronfenbrenner, U. (1979). *The ecology of human development.* Cambridge: Harvard University Press.

Bruner, J. S. (1960). *The process of education.* Cambridge: Harvard University Press.

Bugelski, B. R. (1971). *Psychology of learning applied to teaching* (2nd ed.). Indianapolis: Bobbs-Merrill.

Bushel, D., Jr. (1973). The behavior analysis classroom. In B. Spodek (Ed.), *Early childhood education* (pp. 163–175). Englewood Cliffs, NJ: Prentice Hall.

Day, M. C., and Parker, R. K. (Eds.) (1977). *The preschool in action: Exploring early childhood programs* (2nd ed.). Boston: Allyn and Bacon.

Dearden, R. F. (1968). *The philosophy of primary education.* Boston: Routledge & Kegan Paul.

Derman-Sparks, L., & the A.B.C. Task Force (1989). *The anti-bias curriculum.* Washington, DC: National Association for the Education of Young Children.

Elkind, D. (1986, May). Formal education and early childhood education: An essential difference. *Phi Delta Kappan,* pp. 631–636.

Elkind, D. (1988). Early childhood education on its own terms. In S. L. Kagan & E. Zigler (Eds.), *Early schooling: The national debate* (pp. 98–115). New Haven: Yale University Press.

Erikson, E. H. (1963). *Childhood and society* (2nd ed.). New York: W. W. Norton.

Evans, E. D. (1975). *Contemporary influences in early childhood education* (2nd ed.). New York: Holt, Rinehart & Winston.

Fein, G., & Schwartz, P. M. (1982). Developmental theories in early education. In B. Spodek (Ed.), *Handbook of research in early childhood education* (pp. 82–104). New York: Free Press.

Forman, G., & Fosnot, C. (1982). The uses of Piaget's constructivism in early childhood education programs. In B. Spodek (Ed.), *Handbook of research in early childhood education* (pp.185–211). New York: Free Press.

Hill, P. S., et al. (1923). *A conduct curriculum for kindergarten and first grade.* New York: Scribners.

Hirst, P. H., & Peters, R. S. (1970). *The logic of education.* Boston: Routledge & Kegan Paul.

Kamii, C. (1973). A sketch of a Piaget-derived preschool curriculum developed by the Ypsilanti early education program. In B. Spodek (Ed.), *Early childhood education.* (pp. 209–229). Englewood Cliffs, NJ: Prentice Hall.

Kamii, C., & DeVries, R. (1982). *Numbers in preschool and kindergarten.* Washington, DC: National Association for the Education of Young Children.

Kamii, C., & DeVries, R. (1993). *Physical knowledge in preschool education.* New York: Teachers College Press.

Kohlberg, L., & Mayer, R. (1972). Development as the aim of education. *Harvard Educational Review, 42*, 449–496.

Lazar, I., & Darlington, R. (1982). Lasting effects of early education. *Monographs of the Society for Research in Child Development, 47* (2-3, Serial No. 195).

Lilley, I. M. (1967). *Friedrich Froebel: A selection from his writings*. Cambridge: Cambridge University Press.

Mitchell, A., & Davis, J. (1992). *Explorations with young children: A curriculum guide from the Bank Street College of Education*. Mt. Ranier, MD: Gryphon House.

Mitchell, A., Seligson, M., & Marx, F. (1989). *Early childhood programs and the public schools: Between promise and practice*. Dover, MA: Auburn House.

Mock, K. (1986). Integrating multiculturalism in early childhood education from theory to practice. In R. J. Samuda & S. L. Kong (Eds.). *Multicultural education programmes and methods*. Toronto: University of Toronto Press.

Montessori, M. (1964). *The Montessori method*. Cambridge, MA: Robert Bentley.

New York Education Department (1987). *A multicultural early childhood resource guide*. ERIC Document Reproduction Service No. ED 280924.

Phenix, P. (1964). *Realms of meaning*. New York: McGraw-Hill.

Robison, H. F., & Spodek, B. (1965). *New directions in the kindergarten*. New York: Teachers College Press.

Roopnarine, J. L., & Johnson, J. E. (1993). *Approaches to early childhood education* (2nd ed.). Columbus, OH: Merrill.

Sarason, S. (1982). *The culture of the school and the process of change*. Boston: Allyn and Bacon.

Shepard, L. (1991). The influence of standardized tests on the early childhood curriculum, teachers, and children. In B. Spodek & O. N. Saracho (Eds.), *Issues in early childhood curriculum: Yearbook in early childhood education*, Vol. 2 (pp. 166–189). New York: Teachers College Press.

Snygg, D., & Combs, A. (1965). *Individual behavior*. New York: Harper & Row.

Spodek, B. (1973a). What are the sources of early childhood curriculum? In B. Spodek (Ed.), *Early childhood education* (pp. 81–91). Englewood Cliffs, NJ: Prentice Hall.

Spodek, B. (Ed.) (1973b). *Early childhood education*. Englewood Cliffs, NJ: Prentice Hall.

Spodek, B. (Ed.) (1977). *Teaching practices: Re-examining assumptions*. Washington, DC: National Association for the Education of Young Children.

Spodek, B. (1982). Early childhood education: A synoptic view. In N. Nir-Janiv, B. Spodek, & D. Steg (Eds.), *Early childhood education: An international perspective* (pp. 1–13). New York: Plenum.

Spodek, B. (1986). Development, values and knowledge in the kindergarten curriculum. In B. Spodek (Ed.), *Today's kindergarten: Exploring its knowledge base, extending its curriculum* (pp. 32–47). New York: Teachers College Press.

Spodek, B. (1988). *Early childhood curriculum and the definition of knowledge*. Paper presented at the 1988 meeting of the American Educational Research Association, New Orleans, April.

Spodek, B., & Brown, P. C. (1993). Early childhood curriculum. In B. Spodek (Ed.), *Handbook of research on the education of young children* (pp. 91–104). New York: Macmillan.

Spodek, B., & Saracho, O. N. (1990). Early childhood curriculum construction and classroom practice. *Early Child Development and Care, 61*, 1–9.

Tsai, M. (1991). Integrating multicultural perspectives into early childhood education. In B. Spodek (Ed.). *Educationally appropriate kindergarten practices* (pp. 74–96). Washington, DC: National Education Association.

Weber, E. (1984). *Ideas influencing early childhood education*. New York: Teachers College Press.

Weikart, D. P., Rogers, L., Adcock, C., & McClelland, D. (1971). *The cognitive oriented curriculum*. Washington, DC: National Association for the Education of Young Children.

5

Dealing with Individual Differences

CHAPTER OVERVIEW

This chapter presents:

- Sources of differences among young children (development, environment, culture)
- Characteristics of populations of children with special needs (handicapped, at risk, multilingual/multicultural)
- Ways to deal with diverse children in the regular classroom

INTRODUCTION

The last two decades have seen a major expansion of educational opportunities for all young children. Most dramatic has been the expansion of services for young children with special needs. We have moved from a situation in which, for example, many children with disabilities were excluded from school, to the point at which schools are reaching out to identify and serve children with disabilities in the earliest years. In addition, instead of serving these children in predominantly segregated settings, schools are including children with disabilities in a great variety of settings. Many children with disabilities are being educated along with their nondisabled peers in regular classes.

The momentum to educate children with disabilities began even before the passage of PL 90-538, the Handicapped Children's Early Education Program, in 1968. A more concentrated effort, however, began quite recently, with the passage of PL 94-142, the Education of the Handicapped Act, in 1975, and its extension, PL 99-457, the Amendments to the Education of the Handicapped Act, in 1986. These acts were reauthorized under PL 101-476 and PL 102-119, the Individuals with Disabilities Education Act and its amendments. These acts are important because they extend public responsibility for the education of children with disabilities downward from school entrance age to birth.

PL 99-457 and PL 102-119 require significantly different services for infants and toddlers than they do for preschoolers (children between the ages of three and five). Part B of each of these acts, which deals with preschoolers, is of most immediate concern for teachers of children ages three to eight, since these parts require that children of this age with disabilities be served in group programs. In addition, these laws require that such children be included in regular early childhood programs, both public and nonpublic, to the greatest possible extent.

At present, all teachers of children in their early years are potentially teachers of some children with disabilities. This is true in all public school programs as well as in Head Start programs and in many other preschool programs. Most teachers today are required to serve a wider range of children, including those with disabilities, those who are gifted, and those who are at risk of future educational failure, than had been the case in the past. This chapter provides a review of issues related to the inclusion of these children and discusses identifying these children, planning for their education in regular classrooms, and modifying programs and settings to better serve them.

SOURCES OF DIFFERENCES

Too often teachers treat all children as average. This treatment is inappropriate for most children. While in some ways all children are alike, each child is also unique. Early childhood education programs must be designed to respond to the individual needs of children. The differences we find in children in any classroom are related to developmental, environmental, social-class, cultural, and/or linguistic differences.

Developmental Differences

Children differ in their developmental characteristics. They mature at different rates and have different sets of strengths and weaknesses as well as different styles of learning. Some differences seem to be related to children's internal mechanisms. Other differences result from children's interactions with their environment. Children learn different things from their environments, and this learning influences their developmental patterns.

Environmental Differences

Environment has a major effect on children's development and learning. Early experiences have a lasting impact, whether they contain positive, stimulating experiences or early trauma and deprivation (Peterson, 1987). The quality of the environment is especially important for children with special needs, because it defines the degree to which their needs become a disability. Environmental factors affect the extent which a disability interferes with a child's development and the degree to which children with disabilities can succeed with ordinary learning activities (Peterson, 1987).

Social-Class Differences

Social class has been identified as a major influence on development and on children's success or failure in school. Generally, children with low socioeconomic status are disadvantaged in a number of ways. They may not receive basic health services, and the conditions under which they live may create developmental problems. In addition, they may lack experiences that schools assume all children have and that support the development of language and literacy learning. Project Head Start was created in the 1960s as a comprehensive child development program to allow low-income children to develop more fully and, ultimately, to succeed in school and in society. In addition to educational opportunities, the program offers health, nutrition, and social services to young children. Parent involvement is a critical component of the program, promoting children's learning outside of the classroom and assuring that the program meets the needs of the children's parents and community.

Other programs have been developed by state and local schools and are sponsored by state and federal funds, such as state at-risk programs and federal Chapter I programs. Other programs may also be available for children who are living in poverty. Not all differences among children, however, are the result of socioeconomic differences.

Cultural Differences

Culture is reflected individuals' life style, including the language they use, the food they eat, the way they dress, the social patterns they manifest, and other indications of ethnicity (Saracho & Hancock, 1983). Geography, history, architecture, religion, folk medicine, diet, art, music, dance, and socialization practices all contain cultural elements. The cultural contexts in which children are reared promote differences in children's development. Differences in cognitive ability are affected by the individual's culture and context (Greenfield & Lave, 1982; Scribner, 1984; Stigler, 1984).

American society is pluralistic. It contains many subcultures that, while sharing many cultural elements, are also distinct from one another. This diversity has led to the suggestion that our school programs reflect this cultural pluralism. Living in a multicultural society demands that children develop flexibility in understanding and accepting cultural differences. Children need not only to assimilate and understand their own particular culture, but also to understand the cultures of others, in order to function well in our society. In addition, increased ease of transportation and communication places all of us in close contact with people from the diverse cultures of the world.

Linguistic Differences

One of the prime elements through which cultural differences are expressed is language. Many children in our society have a dominant language that is not standard English. They may employ words, grammar, and speech patterns that differ from the standard accepted pattern; while they speak English, they may speak it in some dialect. The grammar of children from rural New England, Appalachia, and southern parts of the United States (who may speak Creole or Black English) will be remarkably different from standard formal American English. Children from these areas may not speak standard formal American English, but they may be competent in their own dialect. In addition, a number of children who speak many different languages and come from many different cultural backgrounds enter school speaking a native language other than English. They may speak French, Russian, Chinese, Spanish, or a host of other languages. They may be recent immigrants to America, or they may live in communities that have continued to speak a language other than English. Many of these children will have to learn English as a second language.

MULTILINGUAL/MULTICULTURAL EDUCATION

Multilingualism and multiculturalism exist throughout the world wherever countries include individuals and regions with different languages and cultural heritages. The presence of people with different cultures and languages can be viewed as a rich resource for everyone or as a danger to some individual's culture and language, thus leading to conflict. We have always had speakers of many different languages from many different cultures living in America, from the time of the first colonization by Europeans. Thus, the phenomenon is not new. Through the years there have been different responses to multilingualism and multiculturalism, and different responsibilities have been assigned to the school. We have moved away from a "melting pot" mentality, in which all children are expected to speak only one language and express only one style of living, and have accepted the possibility that children in our schools may be different from one another in both language and culture.

Multicultural education is neither a distinctive phenomenon nor a contemporary reformation. For a number of years, bilingual education, the forerunner of multicultural education, has been integrated into public schools in the United States. It also characterizes education in many other countries (Saracho & Spodek, 1983).

Young children's socialization into the larger society is an appropriate goal in early childhood education. The family is the prime socializing agent, but the school has the responsibility to help children learn concepts, behaviors, and interactions that differ from those they learn at home but that reflect the larger society. Differences can exist between the familiar home situation and the more impersonal school setting, where children are required to function successfully. For many children the switch from home to school is difficult, representing a major break in cultural patterns. Children may perceive the language patterns, social interactions, and manifestations of values and culture of their schools as unusual (Saracho & Spodek, 1983).

When children first enter school, they may encounter a language and a culture that differ from the ones in their homes. They realize that the standard language of instruction in the school is not their native language and culture, and they respond in a variety of ways by

1. becoming confused,
2. denying their language and culture,
3. adapting to the new and/or different customs in the new language and culture, or
4. making the transition back and forth from one language and culture to the other (Saracho, 1986).

Teachers can use differences in language and culture as a foundation for learning. Although the teacher's language may be more formal than the one used at home, children do not usually find it totally unfamiliar. The values of the school may be somewhat different, but they should reflect the values of the home. The home and school should develop a partnership to enable young children to make the transition from one social environment to the other with relative ease and little sense of displacement (Saracho & Spodek, 1983).

Most children with a bilingual/multicultural background have some knowledge of the culture of the classroom. However, if their knowledge is limited, the teacher faces challenges. These children may be learning the culture of the school at the same time that they are becoming aware of the culture of the community if they have no or limited English, the challenge is even greater. Relatively few early childhood teachers are bilingual themselves, and even if they speak a second language, it might not be the same language as that spoken by a particular child in class. Thus, problems of communication can occur. In addition, the problem of instruction arises. These children will need to learn English. They also need to learn all the other content areas of the school. Many schools in which children who do not speak English are regularly present seek teachers who speak the predominant non–English language or hire aides or assistants who are fluent in the language. They may design bilingual education programs to teach children in their native language until they gain adequate competence in English. Children who do not speak English when they enter school may very well continue not to speak it long after they have mastered English adequately. Teachers must be sensitive to the needs of these children and support them as they learn the language and become a part of the school culture.

Teachers should also communicate that they value the cultures of the children in their classes, even if those cultures differ from their own. School lunches and snacks should reflect the tastes of all the children. Various celebrations can be an opportunity to enrich the lives of all children, rather than a grudging acceptance of a child who is different. In time, all children need to become aware of the many cultures in our society. They must value the knowledge and understanding that every child brings to school.

EARLY CHILDHOOD SPECIAL EDUCATION

As noted in Chapter 2, early childhood education throughout its history has been concerned with the education of all children, including those with disabilities and those whose environments put them at risk of school failure. Early childhood special education (ECSE) as a distinct field is relatively new, however.

ECSE originated as a result of developments in three related fields: special education as applied to school-age children with disabilities, regular early childhood education, and compensatory education, such as Head Start (McCollum & Maude, 1993). The most pivotal legislation for children with disabilities was signed into law by President Ford in 1975: PL 94-142, also known as the Education for the Handicapped Act (EHA). Its amendment, the Education for All Handicapped Children Act of 1986, PL 99-457, was reauthorized in 1991. Each of these acts contributed federal funds to state and local agencies for the education of individuals with disabilities, ages three to 21 (Hanson & Lynch, 1989; Peterson, 1987; Shonkoff & Meisels, 1990).

Public Law 94-142 requires that public schools educate all children with disabilities between the ages of three and 21. However, if a state does not educate normal children between the ages of three and five and between 18 and 21, then the state has no responsibility to educate children with disabilities of those ages. Public Law 99-457 requires all children with disabilities between the ages of three and five to be educated in schools. It also requires states to develop programs to serve children with disabilities from birth through age two, primarily through family-based programs. Unfortunately, these services are still provided in mainly segregated settings since there are no prekindergarten children with disabilities in the public schools. However, Head Start programs reserve at least 10 percent of their placements for children with disabilities, and other early childhood programs also enroll some children with disabilities, receiving needed services from the public schools.

Integrating Children with and without Disabilities

Mainstreaming or inclusion refers to the integration of children with disabilities with other children in regular classes.

The integration of all children, whether they have disabilities or not, in common educational settings—a procedure sometimes called **mainstreaming** or **inclusion**—has a sound rationale. Legal decisions have supported such a move, identifying the right of children with disabilities to a free public education, their right to be educated in the least restrictive educational setting, and the right of their parents to review educational decisions related to them. Educational research has also supported the move to mainstream most such children, since they can benefit from instruction in the normal classroom. Evidence shows that there is usually no academic advantage to placing children with mild and moderate disabilities in segregated educational settings. In addition, the social behavior of these children more closely approximates those of their nondisabled peers when they are integrated than when they are segregated. Children without disabilities also benefit from such a placement by developing increased understanding of and sensitivity to individual differences without any loss in academic achievement (Spodek & Saracho, 1994).

Least Restrictive Educational Setting

Not all children with disabilities are best served in a regular classroom, and those placed in regular classes may need help beyond what is offered to children without disabilities. The criterion for placing children with disabilities is to offer the least restrictive educational setting that will provide the type and level of services those children need. For most children, this criterion suggests placement in a regular classroom. Some children, however, may need to be placed in much more segregated settings. Evelyn Deno (1970) has identified a hierarchy of possible placements, ranging from maximum integration to maximum segregation:

1. Regular classroom assignment, possibly with classroom modification and supportive services provided;
2. Regular classroom assignment plus supplementary instructional services, such as a resource room or itinerant teacher;
3. Part-time special classes with the remainder of the day spent in a regular class or resource room;
4. Full-time special class with children segregated into a separate class in a conventional school;
5. Special day school;
6. Homebound instruction; or
7. Institutional or residential assignment.

Each succeeding level of placement provides a more segregated and less normal educational environment for the child. Most children with disabilities can be educated in normal settings with the classroom teacher providing help directly, often with additional support. Relatively few children need the more restrictive settings that are lower on the list.

Whatever the educational setting, an effort should be made to provide the child with as normal an educational experience as possible. One of the purposes of education for children with disabilities is to help them cope as well as possible with everyday circumstances, interact as well as possible with a variety of people, and live their lives as normally as possible. Given these goals, the school is expected to design educational experiences that enable these children to develop coping skills. Contact with a variety of children becomes important; but even in circumstances in which the child is educationally segregated, the educator is expected to make that learning situation as close to normal as possible.

Table 5.1

Changing Concepts in Early Childhood Special Education

Old Concepts	New and Emerging Concepts
1. Education is a privilege for those who can profit from it.	1. Education is a right for *all* children and is a means for preparing them to meet the demands of their environment, to learn, and to live as fulfilling, productive lives as possible.
2. Education consists of academic instruction in reading, writing, arithmetic, and in topic areas relating to the arts and sciences.	2. Education encompasses whatever skills a child needs to allow optimal functioning in our society and environment. For some children, this may mean instruction in skills as basic as walking, eating, talking, and attention, or in motor functions hampered by a disability.
3. Children must be "ready" to begin formal education and should wait to enter public school programs if basic social, self-help, cognitive, and language skills have not been mastered.	3. Children become "ready" through learning, experience, and training. The lack of prerequisite skills signals even more clearly a child's need for education and training and not the need to wait longer.
4. If children do not fit into the curricular offerings or respond readily to the teaching methods used in the classroom, they should be removed and placed elsewhere. (Underlying this concept is the notation that the system should be created to fit the child.)	4. Educators fit curriculum and instructional methods to the needs of their students. Teachers and specialists should make the necessary instructional and environmental adaptations (within reason) to help a child learn before considering removal from the regular classroom.
5. Children with disabilities should be placed in special classrooms, where they will not disrupt the learning of normal children and can be together with others of their own kind.	5. Children with disabilities should remain with their peers in the educational mainstream whenever possible unless their best interests clearly are better served elsewhere. If removed from the regular educational setting, it should be only for the time needed to deliver the special services. These children should not be isolated from normal peers or the mainstream of society in which we ultimately want them to be participating, functional members.
6. A child's failure to learn is attributable to that individual's disabilities and incapacities or limitations. Schools do not fail—only students fail.	6. All children are capable of learning. A child's failure to learn reflects the failure of teachers and specialists to select appropriate learning activities, to break down instructional tasks into small, sequential steps that facilitate learning, and to monitor the child's progress in ways that allow unsuccessful learning strategies to be identified and revised. (pp. 104–105)

Early Childhood Special Education Programs

Most early childhood special education (ECSE) programs offer services without categorizing children on the basis of disability. Children in these programs usually have a variety of special needs, including language delays, motor impairments, and developmental delays. Programs may separate children by age, or several age levels may be included in the same group.

ECSE programs may be home based, center based, or a combination of these. The programs may be housed in public schools, hospitals, universities, child-care settings, community preschools, churches, and private agencies. For children ages three and above, the children are the prime recipients of ECSE program services, although usually others receive some service, including parents, siblings, extended family members, and child-care providers. Children younger than three usually are served in a family-oriented program.

Some elements of ECSE programs differ based on their philosophies, especially since programs may differ in the ways they combine philosophies derived from both early childhood education and special education. Peterson (1987) compares several recent changes in special education. These comparisons are listed in Table 5.1.

IDENTIFYING CHILDREN WITH SPECIAL NEEDS

All children have special educational needs and should be dealt with in a personal manner. Groups of children with particular characteristics for whom education in the regular classroom requires special adjustments include those who are educationally or developmentally at risk, those who are gifted, and those with disabilities. The following sections describe the characteristics of these groups of children and suggest general classroom modifications for their education.

Children At Risk

Children at risk are those who have not been identified as having disabilities, but who may be developing problems because of exposure to adverse genetic, biological, or environmental factors. While many children who show evidence of risk factors never develop problems, others do contract disabilities. The term **at risk** suggests that these children have been subjected to various prenatal (before birth), perinatal (at birth), or postnatal (after birth) factors that substantially increase their chances for developing a problem.

Children at risk are typically grouped into three categories: (1) those at *established risk*, (2) those at *biological risk*, and (3) those at *environmental risk* (Tjossem, 1976). Children at *established risk* have a diagnosed medical or genetic disorder for which the potential symptoms are well known

Children are considered to **at risk** when, because of biological or environmental factors, they have a probability of later failing in school and documented. Children with the genetic disorder Down's Syndrome, for example, are considered at established risk because this disorder is known to produce mental retardation, deviant growth patterns, and classic physical characteristics, termed stigmata, especially in facial features.

Children at *biological risk* have prenatal, perinatal, or postnatal biological histories that signal potential problems. Maternal diabetes, infection with German measles during pregnancy, complications during labor, prematurity, low birth weight, or the accidental ingestion by the child of toxic substances are all biological factors that render a child at risk for developing a disability.

Children at *environmental risk* are biologically or genetically normal but are classified as at risk because of adverse early life experiences. Children who are homeless or those who are living in poverty are considered to be at environmental risk. These categories of children at risk are not mutually exclusive. Risk factors often occur in combination, interacting to increase the chances of delayed or aberrant development. A child who is identified as being at risk due to biological factors may also be at risk because of environmental factors.

It is estimated that over 2.5 million children under age six in the United States are at risk. Parents and teachers should be aware of the factors that put a child at risk of developing disabilities. The early identification and treatment of these children can bring many conditions under control, preventing adverse outcomes or diminishing their severity. The most effective treatment for children at risk is placement as early as possible in a high-quality intervention program that stresses individualized educational planning, language and cognitive stimulation, and opportunities for social interaction with adults and peers.

Gifted Children

Children are considered **gifted** when they are capable of a high level of performance in one or many areas.

Educators have become increasingly interested in identifying and serving young children who have special gifts and talents. Among the reasons for this interest are the following: (1) the **gifted** and the talented represent the brightest and the best among us, so that, in an increasingly competitive world, it is in our country's best interest to nurture their special skills; (2) gifted and talented children, like other children, have a right to develop their skills fully, and this development can best be achieved by providing services early in life; (3) early identification and appropriate programming can help establish lifelong positive attitudes and habits toward learning; and (4) early identification will help parents ensure that their gifted child receives the most appropriate education.

Educators have provided various definitions of giftedness, but no single definition pleases all. One of the most popular and widely quoted definitions was offered by former U.S. Commissioner of Education Sidney Marland (1972):

> Gifted and talented children are those identified by professionally qualified persons who, by virtue of outstanding abilities, are capable of high performance. These are children who require differentiated educational programs and services beyond those normally provided by the regular program in order to realize their contribution to self and society. Children capable of high performance include those with demonstrated achievement and/or potential ability in any of the following areas: (1) general intellectual ability; (2) specific academic aptitude; (3) creative or productive thinking; (4) leadership ability; (5) the visual and performing arts; and (6) psychomotor ability. (p. 10)

While this definition recognizes children with a diversity of talents, most schools still place considerable emphasis on tests of intelligence and academic achievement to identify gifted children. Such tests are well-developed and proven instruments that measure abilities critical to school performance, but they are not the only way to identify children's gifts.

Identifying gifts and talents in preschool children is often difficult because children of this age are developing rapidly, and their daily performance can vary greatly. Several studies, however, have identified gifts and talents in young children. Karnes (1983) suggests that, as a group, intellectually gifted young children share a number of characteristics:

1. they tend to be socially and emotionally well adjusted,
2. they have longer attention spans and more well-developed vocabularies than their peers, and
3. they are better than other children at solving problems and engaging in abstract thinking.

State funding for gifted/talented programs nationwide has increased since 1977, but most school systems are just beginning to be concerned with the needs of primary-age students. Efforts to educate gifted and talented preschoolers are often limited to early admission to kindergarten. Occasionally these children will receive special educational services as well. During the primary years, one or more basic delivery models may be used to educate gifted and talented children (Gallagher, Weiss, Oglesby, & Thomas, 1983). The *enrichment classroom* involves a special program of study, beyond that normally offered in a regular classroom, for a group of gifted students under the guidance of a specially trained educator. The *consultant teacher model* provides special programming for gifted students in regular classrooms with the assistance of a specially trained consultant teacher. The *resource room pull-out program* involves taking the child out of the classroom for short periods to receive instruction from a specialist. *Community mentor programs* provide gifted children with opportunities to interact with adults who have special knowledge in particular area. *Independent study* allows gifted students to explore projects of special interest under the supervision of a qualified teacher. The *special class placement* option groups gifted children together for most of the class time. *Special schools* provide gifted students with special programs in a segregated facility. Each of these options is designed to provide gifted students with an opportunity to interact with each other and to receive an appropriate level of instruction. The curriculum in each program emphasizes the development of knowledge and the enhancement of creativity and of problem-solving skills.

CHILDREN WITH DISABILITIES

One of the first tasks required in working with children with disabilities is to find out who they are and where they are, as well as to determine the nature of their disability. Often the process of identification is the responsibility of someone other than a classroom teacher–a psychologist, social worker, or coordinator of special services. Nevertheless, teachers should be aware of the process and become involved to whatever extent is possible.

Since a large number of children below kindergarten age are not in public schools, one of the main problems in identifying children with disabilities of this age is finding them. Some children, particularly those with obvious disabilities, will be referred to the school for educational services by a pediatrician or by a social service agency that deals with children and families. The majority, and especially those with less obvious disabilities, will need to be identified through a voluntary preschool screening program. Schools often announce such programs through local media, notices sent home with students, community surveys, and house-to-house canvasses. These programs are voluntary. A parent must choose to bring a child for screening; there can be no coercion.

The purpose of preschool screening is to identify, in a quick, simple, and inexpensive way, children who may have disabilities. Screening should encompass all the major developmental areas, including speech and language development, intellectual development, social development, fine motor and gross motor development, and the development of self-help skills. The screening instruments should provide information about possible problems in specific areas of development. They should be simple to administer and not require too much time or too great a level of sophistication. If a potential disability is identified, then a more extensive diagnostic procedure can be used.

The diagnosis will identify a child's specific disabilities. These disabilities can be of many kinds. Typically they fall into the categories of learning disabilities, mental retardation, behavior disorders, sensory impairments, communication disorders, and physical or motor problems.

This section describes the learning and behavioral characteristics of young children with disabilities. For convenience, each type of disability is presented as a separate category, but categories are of limited use in planning for children, who must be viewed and treated as individuals. Seven categories that closely parallel those presented in PL 94-142 are discussed: learning disabilities, behavioral disorders, mental retardation, visual impairment, hearing impairment, communicative disorders, and physical and health impairments.

Children with Learning Disabilities

Children who are **learning disabled** include those with either neurological or functional impairments. Children suffering from hyperactivity; perceptual-motor impairment; emotional liability; impulsivity; specific learning disabilities in reading, spelling, arithmetic, or writing; disorders of speech and hearing; and neurological problems have all been included in this category.

Children who are **learning disabled** may have neurological or functional impairment.

In general, a clinical approach is used in teaching children with learning disabilities. It begins with (1) the diagnosis of the specific learning problem, followed by (2) the establishment of goals—often stated in behavioral terms—to ameliorate the learning problem and (3) the development of a program specifically aimed at the learning problem, and, finally (4) an assessment of the changes in the original problem to determine if the program has succeeded. The curriculum strategy may be to simplify the program and teach directly to the area of weakness.

Some educators suggest that rather than focusing on the difficulties of children with learning disabilities, we should try to capitalize on their strengths. A child's sense of success in one area can be generalized to other areas of accomplishment. Other educators suggest a broadly based program. They argue that the educational goals for these children should be no different from goals for normal children and that unnecessary narrowing of the curriculum, either toward a child's strengths or toward a child's weaknesses, is wrong. What might be varied, however, is the pace of instruction, allowing these children more time for learning when they need it.

Children with Mental Retardation

Individuals who are **mentally retarded** lack the capacity to learn what a normal child can. In contrast, children who are learning disabled show a discrepancy between their capacity and their actual learning achievement.

Children who are **mentally retarded** lack the capacity to learn at a normal pace.

Although the evaluation of capacity might be accurate for severely and profoundly retarded children, the accuracy of such judgments for children with mild and moderate retardation has been open to question. Achievement is assessed by observing what a person actually has done. No evaluation of capacity can be made that does not rely heavily on observed achievement. Intelligence tests use achievement to judge capacity. Their use assumes that every child has had an equal opportunity to achieve the learnings sampled on the test. Hence, it suggests that any difference found must be a difference in capacity. While we can determine what a child has or has not learned, we have difficulty determining why the learning has or has not occurred.

Children with severe and profound retardation are often identified early in life, through either physical abnormalities or the failure to develop normally. These children may not walk or talk when expected as a result of general developmental retardation. Children with milder retardation are often detected only when they begin school. Their failure to learn to read or to respond to other academic requirements can lead to a referral to a psychologist and subsequent diagnosis of retardation.

Young children who are mentally retarded are generally categorized as educable, trainable, or severely and profoundly mentally retarded. The vast majority of these children score between 50 and 80 on tests of intelligence, suggesting a rate of intellectual development about one-half to three-fourths that of the normal child. These children usually have interests similar to normal children of the same mental age. It is generally believed that most mild forms of retardation can be ameliorated, especially if an intervention program is begun early in life.

Children with Behavior Disorders

Children with **behavior disorders** include those with a wide range of functional problems.

A number of emotional disturbances, behavioral disorders, and socioemotional problems can be identified in young children. Children with **behavior disorders** include children who withdraw totally from reality, such as those who are schizophrenic or autistic, or who withdraw less excessively, such as those who daydream or live in a world of fantasy. Some children manifest antisocial aggression through acting-out behavior or delinquency, the latter being a legal rather than a psychological or educational construct. The causes of the various emotional problems in children are not definitely known. Some theories suggest that the causes are primarily neurological or physiological, others that they are basically a function of family relations or problems of upbringing, and still others that they are situationally determined.

The treatment of these problems are equally varied: drug therapy, family counseling, psychotherapy for the child and/or the family, behavior modification techniques, and other forms of developmental or psychoeducational treatments. For the teacher who must respond to the child's behavior in the classroom, suggestions include helping the child adjust to the school setting or modifying the setting to be more responsive to the child's needs. Different theories suggest different teaching strategies. A teacher adhering to one theoretical viewpoint, for example, might welcome a show of adverse behavior and allow children to act out their conflicts in class as a form of therapeutic catharsis. A teacher with a different viewpoint might wish to change the child's behavior so that incidents of acting out are lessened and more desirable social behaviors are manifested in the class.

The child might be removed from class and put into a special environment that is more manageable in order to decrease the manifestations of negative behavior. The child may then be eased back into the classroom, where the teacher can learn behavior management techniques to sustain the change. If the teacher is not careful to modify those elements in the classroom that set off the negative behavior in the first place, the child may revert to the original condition.

Often the child stays in class, and help is provided to the teacher. The teacher learns to understand the child and the causes of the child's behavior in order to work more successfully with that child. The teacher might analyze and change the classroom environment to support the more positive aspects of the child's behavior. A crisis-intervention teacher or resource-room teacher could be made available to provide additional help on a long-term basis when the need arises.

Children with Sensory Problems

A number of children are considered exceptional because of a disability in sensory channels. These include children who are deaf or hard of hearing and blind or partially sighted. Either condition can exist from birth or occur at any point in the child's life due to accident or illness. The educational consequences of these problems differ, depending on when they begin. The ability to hear both themselves and others is important in children's language development. Deafness does not limit the language development of children who become deaf after they have established basic language patterns. Although children blind from birth may be unaware of certain basic concepts, such as color, this disability does not seem to have the same profound effects on development as does deafness.

Children Who Are Visually Impaired Children with visual impairments are usually categorized as either blind or partially sighted. Children who are blind are generally identified in infancy, but children who are partially sighted may not be identified until much later. The greater the degree to which the child can respond to visual stimuli, the higher the probability that the problem will not be detected until the child enters school.

Children who are **visually impaired** may be blind or partially sighted.

The teacher should help the child who is blind or partially sighted to use the sensory channels available to gain the maximum information possible from the environment. A child with a sensory disability can use existing senses to a much greater extent than can normal children to compensate for the disability. These children can develop thinking skills by mentally operating on available sense experiences. Many of the standard materials of the nursery and kindergarten, such as blocks, puzzles, and manipulative materials, are well suited for visually impaired children. The teacher should help these children to use materials optimally and should acquire and develop other appropriate materials as needed.

Children who are visually impaired can be helped to become independent in self-care skills and to move about their environment. They can learn to use climbing apparatus, ride tricycles and wagons, dig in sand, and move about the classroom and the outdoor play area. They will need some assistance, especially in the beginning. The teacher should be careful to orient such children to the physical environment, and to make no changes in the organization of the room without reorienting them. Rails and ropes might be set up in appropriate places to help mobility. Self-help training might have to be provided in each situation. As these children move into the primary grades they will, of course, have difficulty in reading. If the impairment is not great, large-print books and magnifiers can enable these children to read normally. If the problem is more profound, Braille reading and writing should be taught. A blind child can continue in a regular classroom for part of the day if Braille instruction is provided by an itinerant teacher or a resource-room teacher. The classroom teacher can probably provide arithmetic instruction with some modification of the normal program, but reading and writing instruction will require a special teacher.

Children who are **hearing impaired** may be deaf or may have limited hearing in all or part of the sound spectrum.

Children Who Are Hearing Impaired The educational problems of children who are hearing impaired can be profound. They may not only have problems in communicating, which is important from both a social and educational point of view, but their competence in many language-based activities may be limited. If the children have some residual hearing, they should be fitted with hearing aids. The teacher should modify the room to limit their difficulties. Care can be taken to diminish unnecessary and confusing noises by covering the floor of the block building area with indoor-outdoor carpeting, for example. In addition, the teacher should speak face-to-face with hearing-impaired children, allow them to sit close by when stories are read, and support their production of speech even when they have difficulties.

Children who are deaf must develop communication skills. Some educators of the deaf advocate speech reading or lipreading; others advocate the use of sign language or the manual alphabet. Still others prefer a combination of the two approaches. Whatever the approach used in the school, it will probably require the availability of a resource or consultant teacher in addition to the classroom teacher. Because deaf children must develop skills in communicating with nonimpaired children and adults, even part-time placement in a regular class should be considered as a way of providing them with skills to live as normal a life as possible.

Children with Communication Disorders

Children with **communications disorders** may have articulation problems, voice problems, stuttering, or language disorders.

Many young children have **communication disorders,** including articulation problems, voice problems, stuttering, and language disorders. The majority of young children's communication problems are articulation problems: sound substitution, sound omission, and sound distortion (including lisping and baby talk). Many of these problems are not evident at later ages; they may be problems of delayed development that disappear in time. However, some disorders require additional help, and separating the two sets of problems is difficult.

One of the more serious speech problems is aphasia, the partial or total failure of speech to develop. Some speech disorders are the result of other developmental problems, such as cleft palate or cerebral palsy.

The classroom teacher can do a number of things to help children who have speech and language problems and to enhance their language development. These children need to be allowed time to produce speech communications and to be rewarded for their efforts, even though their achievements may not seem great. The teacher should keep them from becoming too self-conscious or too defeatist in their attempts to communicate with others. With aphasic children, there is probably little that a classroom teacher can do to help. The teacher should recommend the help of physicians and speech clinicians.

Children with Physical or Motor Disabilities

Young children can have many different **physical or motor disabilities** that can create difficulties for them in working within the expectations of the school. Children who are ambulatory can often be accommodated in schools, fitting well into regular classes if appropriate accommodations are made. These include children with cerebral palsy; those who suffer from a complex neuromuscular condition due to brain injury prior to or at birth; children with epilepsy; children with other chronic illnesses such as rheumatic fever, congenital heart defects, or cystic fibrosis; and children with congenital malformations of the heart, hip, or spinal column.

Children with **physical or motor disabilities** may suffer from a range of physcial and health disorders.

The teacher should analyze the classroom and modify it as needed to allow these children to function as competently and independently as possible. The teacher might also have to design learning experiences and movement activities so that they are within the capabilities of these children.

While each of the exceptionalities discussed in this chapter has been presented separately, special needs do not always occur in isolation from one another. Many times teachers are faced with children with multiple disabilities. For the classroom teacher, a label for a child is less important than a descriptive statement of this child's educational strengths and weaknesses and of the disabling or strengthening aspects of the child's development that must be considered in designing an individual program.

Once the child with a disability is identified, the degree of disability and the extent to which educational programs will have to be modified must be determined. An in-depth evaluation, including reports from a psychologist, physical therapist, audiologist, occupational therapist, speech and language therapist, health professional, or special educator, should become the basis for a specific educational program designed for each child with a disability. Such a plan is called an **Individualized Educational Program (IEP).**

An **Individualized Educational Program (IEP)** is an educational plan designed for a particular individual who has a disability.

Figure 5-1 Stages in Developing an IEP

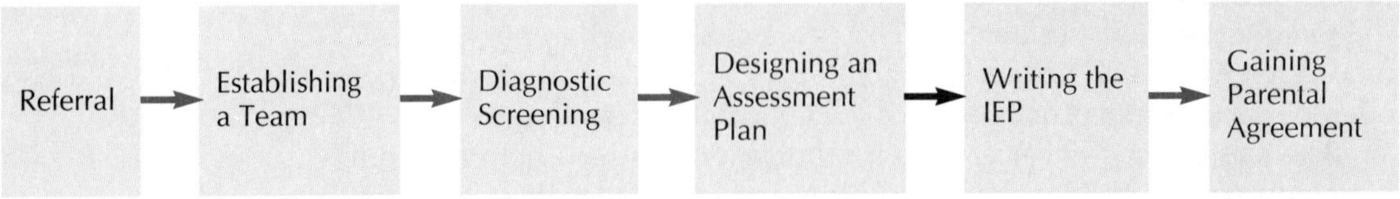

DEVELOPING AN INDIVIDUALIZED EDUCATIONAL PROGRAM

An Individualized Educational Program (IEP) is a written statement of the objectives, content, implementation procedures, and evaluation of a child's educational program. IEPs are required by law to show that children with disabilities receive an appropriate education. An IEP is developed by a multidisciplinary team composed of specialists, who inform the process from their own particular expertise; the classroom teacher, who has a sense of the child's educational performance; a coordinator; and the child's parent(s) or guardian(s). If the child's parents cannot attend an IEP meeting, they must be informed of the process and agree to all actions recommended for the child. If parents do not agree with the team's recommendations, then due-process appeal procedures must be available. For children below age three, an Individual Family Service Plan (IFSP) is typically prepared, since the family is the focus of programs for these children.

Included in the IEP should be statements of the child's present level of performance, of annual goals, and of the short-term objectives that are expected to lead to the achievement of the annual goals. Also included should be a statement of special education and related services that will be

OUTLINE FOR AN INDIVIDUALIZED EDUCATIONAL PLAN

- Present level of performance
- Annual goals
- Short-term objectives
- Evaluation criteria
- Projected date of mastery
- Special materials, strategies, and/or techniques

provided for the child, with descriptions of how often and where these services will be provided, along with a statement of the extent to which the child will participate in the regular classroom program. The criteria by which progress toward the goals will be evaluated should be noted; and finally, a justification for the child's educational program should be included.

When children with disabilities are educated in an integrated classroom, the primary responsibility for their education may rest with the classroom teacher. In this case, support services are usually provided, often through a resource or consultant teacher. Others may be involved periodically in providing special services to children with disabilities, including special education teachers, speech and language specialists, and physical therapists. Depending on the nature of the services, they might be provided in the classroom or outside it. The organization of the services to be provided, as well as a description of the services and the person who will provide them, should also be noted in the child's IEP.

ORGANIZING FOR AN INTEGRATED CLASS

When children with disabilities are integrated into a classroom, a great deal of attention must be given to the organization of classroom resources. Teachers should analyze traffic patterns to ensure free movement for all children. They should take care that no unnecessary obstacles are present. They may need to modify storage arrangements and arrange the classroom so that visual, auditory, and physical clutter is as limited as possible. They must sometimes provide new furniture, such as a table high enough for a child in a wheelchair to use, or a tape recorder to be used primarily by a child with a disability. The environment should be safe for all children.

The environment may need to be simplified and safety rules established and enforced. Sometimes simple things, such as putting crutch tips on the tables to keep them from sliding or making sure blocks are kept out of traffic areas, can significantly improve the safety of the class. Once the room arrangement is established, it is often best to make as few changes as possible in that arrangement. Changes can upset a behaviorally disordered child or make movement more difficult for a child with a visual disability.

If the room is organized to allow for a wide range of individual differences among children, then the teacher will not have too much difficulty in integrating a child with a disability into the program. Different children will be able to function at different levels within the classroom, and what one child does will be less likely to interfere with what others are doing. Activity centers such as those described in Chapter 6 help support individualization of instruction and allow a variety of activities to take place in a classroom at the same time.

In addition to modifying the resources available in the classroom, the teacher should procure additional instructional material. Teachers need to ensure that materials they select are both compatible with the program goals of the classroom and appropriate to the child's age, interests, and abilities. Cautions about safety, cost effectiveness, and freedom from stereotyping that are considered in evaluating all materials should also be considered in relation to special education materials.

MODIFYING THE PROGRAM

Many instructional strategies used with normal children are just as effective when used with children with disabilities. In many cases, for example in the case of physical disability, the disability does not affect the child's ability to learn. Such children will have problems with movement education, however, as well as in using many of the resources of the school. Other conditions, such as learning disabilities and mental retardation, may directly affect the learning process or, in the case of behavior disorders, the ability to function under normal conditions in the social setting of the classroom. Teachers should meet with special education resource persons to plan jointly for each child's learning experiences both inside and outside the classroom.

From the initial identification, the classroom teacher must become a part of a team who pool their knowledge and skills to find the most appropriate educational experiences for children with disabilities. Such teams usually include resource-room teachers. These may be individuals who work with only a single disability group, such as children with behavior disorders or cerebral palsy, who have the same instructional needs. In other schools, resource-room teachers may work with children with a range of disabilities but of a particular age group. Similar specialists may be available for preschools from the local school district, special education district, or public health district. These specialists may come to the preschool periodically to serve the children with disabilities enrolled there and to act as resource consultants to the teacher. Together with the classroom teacher, these individuals can plan a well-rounded set of educational experiences tailored to the specific needs and abilities of the individual child.

On many occasions the regular classroom program will have to be modified to meet the needs of the child with disabilities. Often the approach used in making such modifications is to plan prescriptively (Laycock, 1980). This approach requires that information be gathered initially about the skills and content that the child with disabilities has or has not mastered in each learning area. Such an assessment might include using many of the procedures discussed earlier in this chapter for the initial diagnosis. Based on this assessment, a series of instructional objectives might be specified for each area of school learning. If the learning needs are complex, the teacher might use task analysis to break down some of the more complex objectives into objectives that are more easily achieved, which can be integrated later. A set of instructional or lesson plans would then be developed, aimed at achieving these objectives.

Among the instructional techniques that could be used in these lessons are verbal instructions, telling children in as simple a way as possible what they must do, or modeling, demonstrating a skill and then having the child imitate the demonstration. Manual guidance might also be used, in which the teacher physically helps the child to move through the tasks to be learned. A set of prompts or cues that elicit particular actions on the part of the child might also serve instructional purposes, although in time these prompts should be lessened or faded.

Whatever skills are taught to children, the children should have ample opportunities to practice them to increase their proficiency. While some of this practice might be in isolation, ultimately the child should be given the opportunity to practice the skills learned in situations similar to those in which those skills will have to be used.

Because of the particular needs of children with disabilities, it is not always possible for them to learn things informally. Many times more formal and systematic approaches will be necessary. The degree of formality, and just how systematic the learning will have to be, depends on the nature of the disability as well as on the nature of the task to be learned. One of the guiding principles of mainstreaming is that the learning activities provided to children should be as close as possible to those offered normal children and should be provided in a way that allows for the maximum integration of children with and without disabilities.

DEALING WITH INDIVIDUAL DIFFERENCES

Teaching exceptional children is a highly specialized field. Programs are specifically designed to train teachers of children who are deaf, children who are gifted, children who are emotionally disturbed, and children with other specific exceptionalities. Each program provides teachers with special knowledge and skills. While regular classroom teachers may have to deal with children in many of these categories of exceptionality, they could hardly be expected to gain the knowledge of all these fields.

How, then, can teachers learn to cope with the many problems they face? Perhaps it is unfair to ask teachers to be prepared to work with children with a variety of exceptionalities while maintaining a full classroom as before. Special help should be provided to classroom teachers as exceptional children are integrated into their classes. Resource personnel, crisis-intervention teachers, and consultants have been recommended to help classroom teachers better understand and educate exceptional children, as well as to demonstrate specific techniques as required. Children may also be taken out of the classroom for periods of time for those aspects of the program which are beyond the capability of the regular teacher or beyond the range of regular classroom activities. Additional supplies and equipment might also have to be supplied. Consideration must also be given to reducing the number of children in a classroom when exceptional children are introduced.

In addition, there are some things a regular classroom teacher must learn. A general understanding of the nature of exceptionalities in children as well as a knowledge of the growth and development of normal children is a desirable, even necessary, component. In addition, the teacher should know some of the basic techniques of education for exceptional children. This requirement should create no problem, for these basic instructional strategies are little different from the strategies suggested for normal children. Useful resources in dealing with children with a wide range of individual differences include

Safford, P. L. (1989). *Integrated teaching in early childhood.* White Plains, NY: Longman.

Spodek, B., & Saracho, O. N. (1994). *Dealing with individual differences in the early childhood classroom.* White Plains, NY: Longman.

There are differences in specific content and methods, however. Here the teacher must learn to rely on outside experts, consultants, resource-room teachers, and clinicians who will join in designing and implementing programs for exceptional children.

In addition, certain personal characteristics are helpful. The teacher needs concern and caring for children without unnecessary sympathy and pity, flexibility in dealing with educational goals and methods, willingness to try new techniques and to remain tentative in approving tried and true techniques, willingness to communicate problems and to share concerns with others, the ability to function in a cooperative relationship, undying optimism and faith in the utility of education, and the ability to accept some degree of failure as well as success. Somehow the requirements for teaching special children are the same as those for teaching all children . . . only more.

Summary

Teachers of young children are increasingly being confronted with a wide range of individual differences in their classes. These include children from different cultural and linguistic groups, children who are gifted, children who might be at risk of future educational failure, and children with disabilities. The teacher should understand the strengths and problems of each child and modify the program to serve each child best. Even in a group setting, programs for children in their early years should be individualized. This need for individualization should be reflected in the plans that teachers make.

REFERENCES

Deno, E. (1970). Special education as developmental capital. *Exceptional Children, 37*, 229–237.

Gallagher, J., Weiss, P., Oglesby, K., & Thomas, T. (1983). *The status of gifted/talented education: United States survey of needs, practices and policies.* Los Angeles: National/State Leadership Training Institute on the Gifted and Talented.

Greenfield, P. M., & Lave, J. (1982). Cognitive aspects of informal education. In D. A. Wagner & H. W. Stevenson (Eds.), *Cultural perspectives in child development* (pp. 181–207). San Francisco: W. H. Freeman.

Hanson, M. J., & Lynch, E. W. (1989). *Early intervention: Implementing child and family services for infants and toddlers who are at-risk or disabled.* Austin, TX: Pro-Ed.

Karnes, M. B. (1983). The challenge. In M. B. Karnes (Ed.), *The underserved: Our young gifted children.* Reston, VA: Council for Exceptional Children.

Laycock, V. K. (1980). Prescriptive programming in the mainstream. In J. W. Schifarie, R. M. Anderson, & S. J. Odle (Eds.), *Implementing learning in the least restrictive environment: Handicapped children in the mainstream* (pp. 285–319). Baltimore: University Park Press.

Marland, S. (1972). *Education of the gifted and talented.* A report to the Congress of the United States by the U.S. Commissioner of Education. Washington, DC: U.S. Government Printing Office.

McCollum, J. A., & Maude, S. P. (1993). Portrait of a changing field: Policy and practice in early childhood special education. In B. Spodek (Ed.), *Handbook of research in early childhood education* (pp. 352–371) New York: Macmillan.

Peterson, N. (1987). *Early intervention for handicapped and at-risk children: An introduction to early childhood special education.* Denver: Love.

Saracho, O. N. (1986). Teaching second language literacy with computers. In D. Hainline (Ed.), *New developments in language CAI* (pp. 53–68). Beckenham, Kent: Croom Helm.

Saracho, O. N., & Hancock, F. M. (1983). Mexican-American culture. In O. N. Saracho & B. Spodek (Eds.), *Understanding the multicultural experience in early childhood education* (pp. 3–15). Washington, DC: National Association for the Education of Young Children.

Saracho, O. N., & Spodek, B. (Eds.). (1983). Preface. *Understanding the multicultural experience in early childhood education.* Washington, DC: National Association for the Education of Young Children.

Scribner, S. (1984). Studying working intelligence. In B. Rogoff & J. Lave (Eds.), *Everyday cognition* (pp. 9–40). Cambridge: Harvard University Press.

Shonkoff, J. P., & Meisels, S. J. (1990). Early childhood intervention: The evolution of a concept. In S. J. Meisels & J. P. Shonkoff (Eds.), *Handbook of early childhood intervention* (pp. 3–32). Cambridge: Cambridge University Press.

Spodek, B., & Saracho, O. N. (1994). *Dealing with individual differences in the early childhood classroom.* White Plains, NY: Longman.

Stigler, J. W. (1984). "Mental abacus": The effect of abacus training on Chinese children's mental calculation. *Cognitive Psychology, 16*, 145–176.

Tjossem, T. M. (1976). *Intervention strategies for high risk infants and young children.* Baltimore: University Park Press.

U.S. Office of Education. (1977). *Education of handicapped children.* (Federal Register, August 23, 1977). Washington, DC: Department of Health, Education, and Welfare.

6

Organizing for Instruction

CHAPTER OVERVIEW

This chapter presents:

- Planning for instruction
- Organizing children for instruction
- Developing a daily schedule
- Arranging the room to support learning
- Developing units or projects
- Moving from one activity or place to another

INTRODUCTION

Once teachers determine the goals and content of the program they design for their children, they must then create a setting for teaching. Teachers organize the school year into some meaningful sequence, create a daily activity schedule, arrange the children into manageable groups, and organize the room so that children can make the best use of space, materials, and equipment.

In their early years, children's autonomy is a goal rather than an established fact. We wish them to become independent, knowing full well that they will continue to be dependent upon adults well beyond the primary grades. The development of autonomy is nurtured by teaching children to assume responsibility while providing them with security and the guidance of a knowledgeable adult.

PLANNING

Teachers need to engage in both long- and short-range planning. Long-range planning helps them view the entire school year's activities, enabling them to build new activities on children's prior experiences. Short-range planning deals with the many details of day-to-day teaching. Short-term objectives are the anticipated outcomes of specific activities and should be related to long-term goals.

Planning begins before the children enter school. Teachers think about what the school year should be like and gather supplies, materials, and equipment to turn that image into a reality. Some supplies must be ordered well in advance of their use. Anticipating the need for materials and supplies gives teachers flexibility in using them. Teachers should find out what specific learning opportunities each child is ready for and provide opportunities to help each one use resources for learning. Finally, every child must be helped to become a responsible member of the class, learning to become a part of the group, gaining satisfaction and security from membership in it, and responding to its demands without submerging personal wishes. To do so, children must develop self-control and ways of dealing appropriately with their needs and feelings.

Long-Range Planning

In developing long-range plans, teachers identify threads that will tie the various elements of the program together throughout the year. Activities can be organized into units or projects reflecting particular themes or can be focused on developing sets of specific skills. As teachers develop goals for their classes, they must also decide the degree to which each child will be expected to achieve these goals. Our knowledge of individual differences in children tells us that not all children in a class will achieve all the established goals to the same extent, in the same period of time.

Long-range plans help give a program flexibility. As the children move through the program, teachers can modify their plans to take advantage of unanticipated learning opportunities while insuring a degree of program continuity. Without prior thought and preparation, teachers cannot integrate day-to-day learning activities with each other.

Too many educators think of long-range curriculum planning as a linear process. Teachers begin their planning by defining each long-range goal and then identifying the prerequisites needed to achieve that goal. These prerequisites then become a set of more approachable goals, and the curriculum becomes a series of orderly steps towards a goal. The assumption of such planning is that if a child adheres to these steps without any serious deviation, the ultimate goal will be achieved.

An example of this form of curriculum planning is found in the design of the program *Science—A Process Approach* (see Chapter 13). While such planning helps the teacher see the relationship between current and future activities and between immediate and long-range goals, it has disadvantages. Programs designed this way are excessively rigid. The only individual difference among children that is accounted for is the pace of learning—differences in learning styles or interests are disregarded.

Rebecca Corwin, George Hein, and Diane Levin (1976) have suggested curriculum webs as a form of nonlinear curriculum construction. The idea of curriculum webs has received increased attention in the past few years (see Spodek, 1991; Workman & Anziano, 1993). A single interest,

Figure 6–1 Curriculum Web for Grocery Store

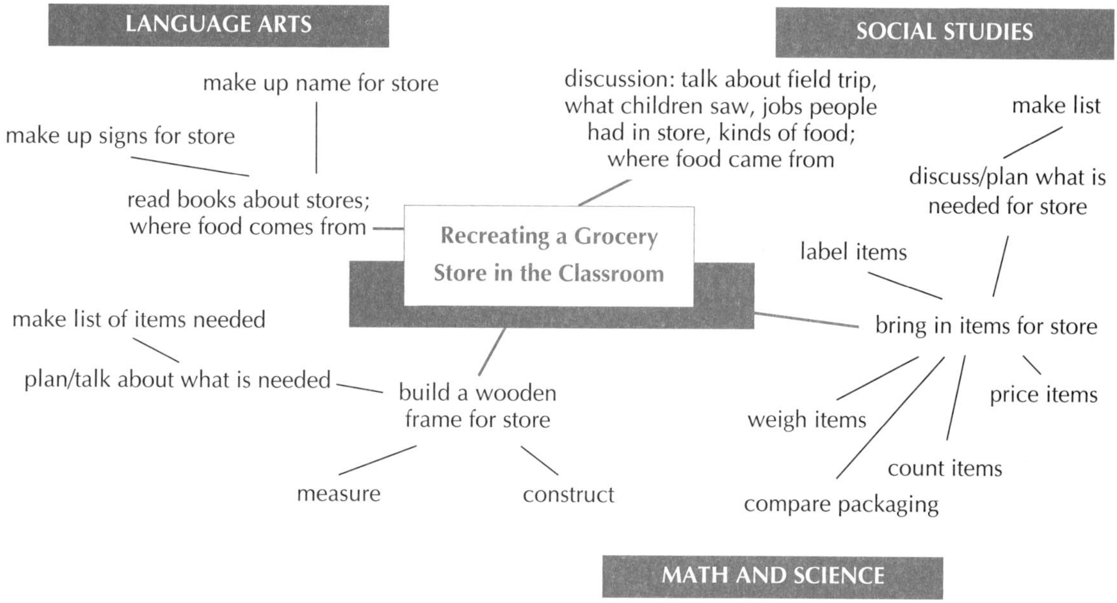

Source: Educationally Appropriate Kindergarten Practices, copyright 1991, National Association Professional Library. Reprinted with permission.

experience, or activity may take the children's learning in many different directions, leading to a range of activities in science, mathematics, and the arts as the program moves from the original experience. In a curriculum web various curriculum areas—language arts, mathematics, science, social studies, and art—are woven into the study through the activities the children engage in over a period of weeks.

Using a **curriculum web**, teachers can integrate various learning activities. They can move in a different direction when it seems appropriate without losing a sense of purpose for the activities. Webs can help a teacher design learning approaches that integrate various curriculum areas in special ways for each group of children. Children are often able to cope with advanced learning in this fashion without ever having achieved the necessary prerequisites required in more linear approaches. Teachers who are sure of program goals can be flexible in planning and in responding to children's interests and concerns, straying from the path as needed. A digression may lead to a new set of goals or may end up as a short cut to previously established goals. An example of the use of curriculum webs is presented in Figure 6–1, which was designed for a unit on the grocery store.

A **curriculum web** is a form of nonlinear programming that allows children's learning to go off in various directions from a single interest.

No matter what the overall program, teachers can modify it to be responsive to the needs and interests of individual children. No two children are alike—and no two classes are alike. No textbook author or curriculum development specialist has personal knowledge of the children in any one class. Only the teacher, knowing the children—their strengths and weaknesses, their backgrounds, and the school environment—can modify the program to fit them.

Developing year-long plans allows teachers to think through the program in advance and gather the necessary resources to carry it through. Films, filmstrips, videocassettes, new books, and supplies may have to be ordered in advance. Trips need advance planning. It is always easier to cancel a trip, postpone a visit, or decide not to use a film than to want to carry out an activity and find schedules filled or materials unavailable.

Short-Range Planning

Teachers must also organize classroom work on a daily, weekly, or periodic basis. In short-term planning, teachers consider the program's daily balance and the relationships they can establish among different subject areas. For instance, children can write sentence stories that correspond to

CURRICULUM GUIDE CHECKLIST

- ____ setting
- ____ age group/grade
- ____ philosophy (based on theory and history)
- ____ goals (long-range and short-range)
- ____ workable plan (flow chart, units, subject areas, etc.)
- ____ management system
  - ____ play
  - ____ schedule
  - ____ bulletin boards
  - ____ floor plan
  - ____ learning centers
  - ____ snack
  - ____ diverse grouping
  - ____ ways of guiding children
  - ____ ways of organizing adults
- ____ balanced curriculum
  - ____ art
  - ____ music
  - ____ movement
  - ____ language arts
  - ____ reading
  - ____ science
  - ____ mathematics
  - ____ social studies
- ____ working with parents
  - ____ parent involvement
  - ____ parent education
  - ____ parent conferences
  - ____ parent newsletters
- ____ evaluation
  - ____ children
  - ____ setting
  - ____ teacher

number facts or that tell about measuring experiences, thus integrating mathematics with language activities. Stories from a book can be acted out in pantomime or with puppets. Science experiences often require quantification. The possible ways of relating learning areas to one another are endless. Each allows the teacher to extend the children's experience beyond the obvious.

Some educators suggest that each detail in an instructional program be carefully planned in advance and that teachers stick to those plans. Unfortunately, this rigidity can limit activities. If the activities are varied enough and if children can differentiate their own roles in each activity, they will find areas of the program that are related to their needs and that will help them grow. Self-selection within carefully prepared alternatives is an important part of early childhood education. Adequate planning can help to ensure that legitimate learning activities are available and that each alternative provides a reasonable way of achieving educational goals. See the Curriculum Guide Checklist on the previous page.

DEVELOPING ACTIVITIES

The unit of instruction in nursery school and kindergarten is the activity. Instruction in elementary schools is organized into *lessons*, each of which has a formal beginning, middle, and end. **Activities** may be open-ended, coming to no neatly packaged conclusion, but possibly being revisited at some later time. Activities are not teacher-dominated. The teacher may plan the activity, make materials available, provide time, and even influence the direction of the activity, but children carry the activity forward and, in the final analysis, determine its content. Each activity may have

Activities are open-ended curriculum structures that provide children with learning opportunities.

STEPS IN INSTRUCTIONAL PLANNING

1. **Set goals and develop a rationale for instruction.** Goals are general statements of purpose which take into account (a) learners' needs, (b) society's view of the function of schooling, and (c) content to be learned. Teachers need to consider the basic reasons for teaching what they select to teach.
2. **Define objectives.** Goals are crucial to the planning process, but they are broad. Objectives indicate ways that goals can be met in specific situations that guide specific instructional decisions. Objectives can be written in several ways. Action words such as *write*, *choose*, *touch*, *say*, *cut*, and *mark* are helpful in writing objectives. Objectives should be clear enough to help the teacher develop teaching and evaluation strategies.
3. **Construct a way to evaluate learning.** (See Chapter 9.)
4. **Organize the content into activities, lessons, units, and/or projects.**
5. **Design activities or lessons.** The unit is divided into lessons or activities that are reasonable segments of the plan (Gunter, Estes, & Schwab, 1990).

no relationship to any other activity or, more often, be part of a series of interrelated activities. The teacher can relate block construction, music, and story activities to a single theme on the same day, or have a series of activities that continue from day to day, with each being an elaboration of the previous one. Activities may be organized into units or projects. In such planning, basic concepts and ideas can recur in different activities, providing continuity of learning over time.

The teacher should plan a program so that children are involved in the many different areas of the curriculum. The room must be organized so that each activity has the necessary space, materials, and equipment available when needed, and so that several activities can take place simultaneously without interfering with each other.

ARRANGING THE ROOM

Schools for young children are housed in many kinds of facilities. Some facilities were designed to function as early childhood classrooms, but others were never intended for young children. Sometimes, classrooms originally designed for older children are used for kindergarten or prekindergarten classes. In addition, church buildings, community centers, homes, or stores have become schools for young children. Sometimes a dual arrangement develops in churches and community centers, with a preschool using space for one part of the day or week and another activity being housed there at another time. Each arrangement creates different problems for the classroom teacher.

Yet administrators and teachers have been able to modify the physical spaces in which they teach. Suspended ceilings can be installed at reasonable expense, if the ceiling is too high, to improve lighting and acoustics. A loft can be built to allow an area for dramatic play or to provide some private space for children. Even painting the wall a brighter shade, hanging curtains on the windows, painting a mural, or creating an attractive wall display changes the nature of the physical space.

Teachers should think carefully about how the program can be better served by changing allocated space. If all children are expected to be involved in the same activity at the same time, room arrangements are of less concern than if individual and small group activities are to be nurtured in the classroom. In an individualized program, for example, the room should be arranged so that the children can work without constant teacher supervision and so that they will not interfere with each other's activities.

Organizing Physical Space

Basic space requirements for classrooms are often prescribed by law. Many states require a minimum of 35 square feet of classroom space per child in a preschool. The same minimum figure is sometimes suggested for space in a primary classroom. Many experts, however, recommend

Teachers arrange their rooms to optimize their resources.

that as much as 100 square feet per child be available. In addition, from 50 to 200 square feet of outdoor space per child should be provided for the program. There is some evidence that too little space interferes with children's social interactions (Ladd & Coleman, 1993). The indoor space should be well lighted, well ventilated, and well heated when necessary. Water should be easily available in the classroom. Ideally, there should be easy access from the classroom to the outdoor play area and to toilet facilities. If the classroom has a door leading directly to a play yard or terrace, the program can flow easily between indoors and outdoors.

Teachers need to check the physical arrangements of their rooms to ensure that they are safe. Furniture and equipment should have no sharp edges or protrusions that could harm children. Traffic patterns should be designed to avoid collisions. Climbing equipment should be installed over soft surfaces. When children with disabilities are present in a class, additional modifications may need to be made in the physical environment. Furniture might have to be rearranged or crutch tips placed on the legs of tables so they will not slip. In addition, teachers and children should establish and enforce safety rules for functioning in the classroom.

Most primary classrooms have somewhat informal seating arrangements, with chairs and desks or tables grouped together in horizontal rows or in a semicircle. Additional chairs may be arranged in a corner for reading instruction and an easel or a table for art work placed in the back of the room. There may be shelves and closets for storage of books and materials, and a display area for science or nature study. This type of room arrangement supports a classroom in which the basic mode of instruction is verbal, and in which children are expected to function as a whole class or in small groups under the teacher's supervision. Constructions for social studies and children's experiments require other kinds of space and other materials. A teacher who wishes to individualize instruction and provide for self-pacing will also find such an arrangement restrictive. Just as schedules reflect the kind of program a teacher wishes to develop, so does the arrangement of the room.

An activity-oriented primary classroom, in which individuals and small groups engage in different activities simultaneously, would benefit from a room arrangement closely resembling that of a preschool or kindergarten. A library center is a critical resource in the primary classroom. In addition, centers for activities in mathematics, science, social studies, language arts, and other areas could be developed.

Because there is so much variety among school facilities and groups of children, it is difficult to suggest an ideal room arrangement. However, there are criteria teachers can use to judge the balance provided in the room and the degree to which the physical design supports the educational design. Adequate separation between activity areas is important so that children's work will not be interfered with; both physical and visual boundaries work. Also, noisy and quiet, and messy and neat activities should be separated.

Elizabeth Jones (1979) has identified five dimensions that can be used to analyze a physical setting. They can be used in planning the physical facility and in selecting equipment and furniture. The dimensions are

Soft—hard
Open—closed
Simple—complex
Intrusion—seclusion
High mobility—low mobility

Soft areas are places where children can relax to read, listen, talk, or play quietly. Softness can be created by providing a small area rug, some pillows, a stuffed animal, an upholstered or a rocking chair, or even curtains. Other areas in the room are characterized by hardness. *Hard* floor and table surfaces facilitate the cleanup of messy materials and can take the punishment of children's work. Outdoors, grassy areas are soft, and paved surfaces are hard.

Most early childhood classrooms are fairly *open*. The room allows for easy access to materials through open shelf arrangements, although teachers will store some things in closed areas away from children. A balance of open-ended and closed-ended instructional materials for the children is provided. *Closed* materials, such as picture puzzles, have constrained goals and modes of relationship between their parts; *open* materials, such as clay, provide unlimited alternatives in their goals and modes of relationship. In addition, both *simple* and *complex* learning materials should be provided. *Simple* materials have one obvious use and no subparts; *complex* materials allow for manipulation and improvisation, with many subparts.

Some areas of the room should be *secluded* to allow for cozy spaces as well as for activities that need to be separated from the group bustle. Other areas should encourage the *intrusion* of teacher and children, such as when a teacher joins a dramatic play activity for a short period. As activities in the classroom encourage both high and low degrees of movement, the arrangement should support *high* and *low mobility*. Sitting quietly during a discussion is encouraged when the space is confined by physical limits set by a rug or furniture. Similarly, large, open spaces encourage large motor activities. Traffic patterns and the mobility required by different activities should be analyzed for this purpose.

Ideally, the indoor space should be designed to support flexible educational programs. Surfaces should be treated with acoustical materials wherever possible. Floors can be carpeted or covered with resilient tiles. Walls should be pleasantly but unobtrusively colored and should provide adequate display space, including bulletin boards and a chalkboard. Shades or blinds that both reduce glare and darken the room completely can be provided for windows. A drinking fountain and a sink to be used for activity and cleaning purposes limit the number of trips the children make down the hall. Bathrooms should be adjacent or close to the classroom.

A classroom should also have enough storage and locker facilities to hold children's coats, boots, extra clothing, and personal belongings, as well as for the teacher's needs. In addition, considerable and varied storage space should be provided for materials and equipment. Large wheel toys, paper, and art supplies all need different kinds of storage facilities.

Activity Centers

The terms *learning center*, *interest center*, and **activity centers** are often used interchangeably. These centers actually are what the labels indicate: areas with a variety of materials to support children's learning activities. Each center should be designed to provide activities that are based on children's interests and that support valuable learning. The activities provided should reflect children's developmental levels and experiential backgrounds, allowing children to learn at their own pace about the world around them by manipulating objects, building, immersing themselves in dialogue, and assuming different roles.

An **activity center** is an area of the classroom where materials based on a subject area or topic are provided to support children's learning.

Many early childhood classrooms are organized into centers, each of which supports some portion of the program. The centers can expand or contract with the needs of the program, though most are available regularly throughout the activity period. Activity centers allow rooms to become child centered rather than teacher centered. They help programs become more individualized and allow children's classroom participation to become more active and independent (Blake, 1977; Patillo & Vaughan, 1992). These centers should be used carefully, for too much dependence on self-contained centers can lead to a fragmented program.

The following learning interest and activity centers are suggested for three- to five-year-old children:

- **Dramatic Play Center** This center contains activities relating to various play themes. These could include housekeeping, a store, a restaurant, or any other activity reflecting the children's social life. When the home is represented, activities should reflect those engaged in by all members of a family. A dramatic play center many include the traditional housekeeping theme or support other themes relating to various aspects of adult and community life. Judith Bender (1971) suggests collecting materials for dramatic play in "prop boxes," each supporting one theme. A prop box for automobile repair play would contain discarded, cleaned auto parts, tools, and other materials. The teacher can create a camping box, a beautician's box, or various other boxes.

- **Block Center** The block center offers opportunities to construct houses, stores, schools, and transportation systems. Props are added to enhance play: a traffic light to control the movement of cars, toy farm animals and people to help simulate a farm, or toy airplanes to allow for the construction of an airport.
- **Puzzle and Game Center** Puzzles and games should be provided at different levels of difficulty, so that children can be directed to a choice they can successfully complete. Puzzles can be coded with colors or shapes to organize them by level or area of skill. Both commercial and teacher-made games that are suitable to the children's interests and levels of skill can be included.
- **Library Center** This center should be located in a quiet part of the room away from traffic. Books should be displayed so that children may easily select ones they want to look at. The books displayed for the day may relate to the topic being studied. Carpets or rugs and soft chairs or pillows, along with paintings and flowers, can make the place comfortable and attractive to the children.
- **Mathematics Center** This center should contain materials that allow the children to engage in solving mathematical problems. Counting rods, geoboards, containers for measurement, and felt figures for comparing may be utilized. Task cards, which pose problems for the children to solve, might also be included. A suggested task for using a scale might be, "How many nuts balance one apple? Write the number."
- **Science Center** This center could allow children to engage in simple experiments, observe natural phenomena, or care for a pet. Games for classifying or categorizing objects from the natural environment, such as seeds, seashells, leaves, insects, or foods, can also be provided.
- **Sand and Water Centers** These centers are appropriate for outside, but can be used inside if a table is placed in an area where the floor is of appropriate material.
- **Listening Center** This center could contain a record player and a cassette tape recorder. If headphones are available, then listening to

records will be less disturbing to the other children in the class. Commercial and teacher-made tapes of stories and songs, along with books, encourage children to listen and interact with what they hear.

- **Sound and Music Center** This center should contain simple musical instruments and other materials that can be used to emit sounds. Sand blocks, drums, or bells can help the children develop an appreciation for sounds and rhythm.
- **Art Center** An easel, a large table, paints, paper, paste, clay, and similar materials are basic. Appropriate and ample storage space should be provided. Children need easy access to materials and should be able to put them away and clean up independently.
- **Carpentry Center** This center should contain a heavy wooden table or workbench, some good 8– to 10–ounce hammers, a hand drill, a miter box, a backsaw or short crosscut saw, C-clamps, soft wood, and common nails. This center should be located where it can be supervised at all times.
- **Puppet Center** A simple stage and numerous commercial, teacher-made, and child-made puppets provide an opportunity for creativity and language development. A puppet center may be set up periodically for use by children.
- **Physical Education Center** A balance beam, hopscotch mats, Hula-Hoops, jump ropes, beanbag games, and balls are equipment that can be used. If the classroom does not have adequate space, other inside space, such as a multipurpose room, or a patio or playground area should be available.
- **Cooking Center** This center may also be set up temporarily as needed. It allows children to make their own snacks as well as to engage in special cooking projects. The center should include a low table, where children can prepare nutritious foods, and the tools children may need.

A classroom that is planned for learning invites children to engage in activities that are interesting and educationally valid. Appendix C, at the end of the chapter, presents ideas for organizing centers.

Activity centers that are well planned and provide many things for children to do prevent many discipline problems and permit the teaching staff to know children as unique individuals. Children should be able to select from a variety of activities and to move from one activity to another as they wish. Children need to learn through firsthand experiences, in ways that are natural for them. The daily schedule should provide a large block of time (between 30 minutes and an hour) for center activities. Equipment and supplies should be organized so that children can reach them without adult help and return them to their proper places after using them.

Figure 6–2 Floor Plan of an Early Childhood Classroom

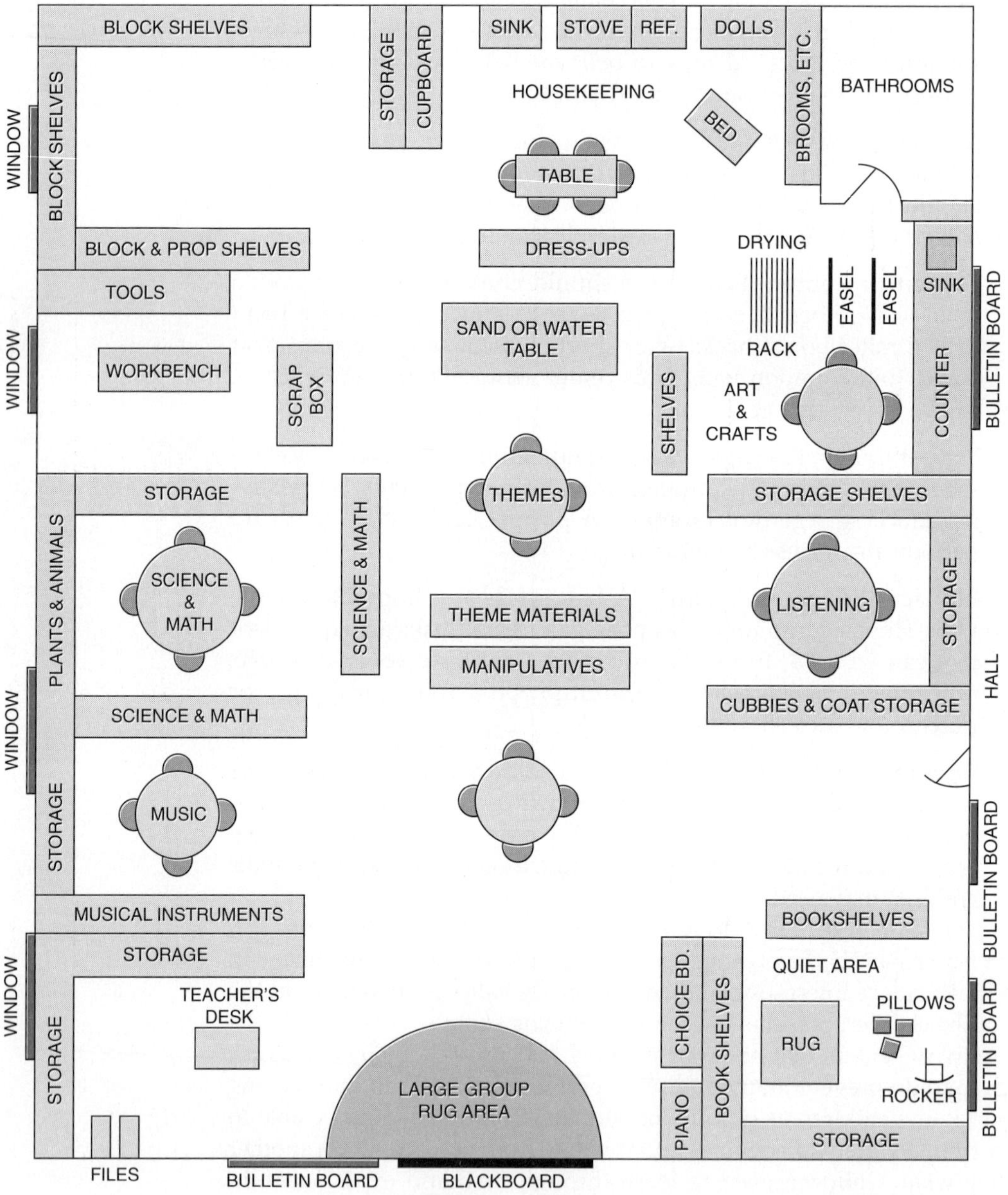

Source: B. Spodek, O. N. Saracho, and M. D. Davis (1991). *Foundations of Early Childhood Education,* (2nd ed.), Boston: Allyn & Bacon.

Activity centers need to be balanced. In setting up areas in the classroom, the teacher should separate noisy centers from quiet centers. It is difficult for children in the library to concentrate if the music center is next to this area and children are playing instruments. In addition, the art center should be close to the water area to avoid dripping water from one side of the room to the other. If water is not available in the classroom, then the art center should be near the door, because this part of the room is closest to available water. Figure 6.2 is a diagram of activity centers.

The following suggestions will help teachers plan and organize learning interest and activity centers:

1. Although the activity period is one in which children engage in self-selected activities, the teacher needs to design centers that will draw children into learning activities and provide ideas to the children.
2. Teacher planning and room arrangement should consider the children's muscle development and coordination, social maturity, language skills, interests, and needs.
3. Plenty of space, time, and equipment should be provided for uninterrupted play. Through involvement in play activities, children experiment with social relationships with others their age. They should have opportunities for physical and intellectual development, language practice, and critical thinking. Well-planned activities provide varied learning experiences of a concrete and sensory nature.
4. Many experiences should be available each day during center time. Children should be able to move freely from one activity to another, depending upon their interests and attention span.
5. The activity period should provide a balance between quiet and vigorous activities, and between individual and group activities. Teachers should provide for dramatic play, block play, science and mathematics learning with manipulative materials, and work in the creative arts. Frequently, the teacher will include experiences with music and books. Children should not be limited to the experiences set out for that day. Those experiences serve only as beginnings, as invitations to involvement. Teachers should respond to learning opportunities that occur spontaneously.
6. The teacher should be available to the children during the activity period. Children's play reveals interests, abilities, and needs. At times it is advisable for teachers to step in, to increase the potential of or encourage play. At times the teacher will temporarily take a role in play; perhaps the teacher's words of guidance will help the children grow toward self-discipline. Perhaps the teacher will see the need to provide new play materials. Many activities (such as carpentry) require adult supervision for safety's sake.

Activity Centers in Primary Classes

Activity centers in the primary grades are often organized by subject, for example, a mathematics center, a language arts center, a social studies center, and a science center. Activity centers related to themes or projects that appeal to children's interests are also useful. An environmental studies center, a transportation center, or a center that focuses on any topic could be created in a classroom. Such a center would be available for the children as long as the theme holds their interest.

A center should include materials to be used by individuals and small groups, with boundaries clearly defined for the use of those materials. Centers should be easily supervised, and their contents should support independent study and activity. Activity cards can provide direction to children without the teacher continually being present. Sometimes activities can evolve out of planning conferences.

A science activity center, for example, should be a place that has reasonable access to water. It could have a display area for plants and animals and shelves that hold magnifying glasses, magnets, containers of various sizes, and a variety of measuring devices. These might be grouped and placed in shallow trays for continued orderly arrangement. The materials in the center should be changed from time to time as different areas of science are investigated. Seasonal changes might suggest changes in materials. Open-ended questions can title displays, such as "Which materials sink and which float?"

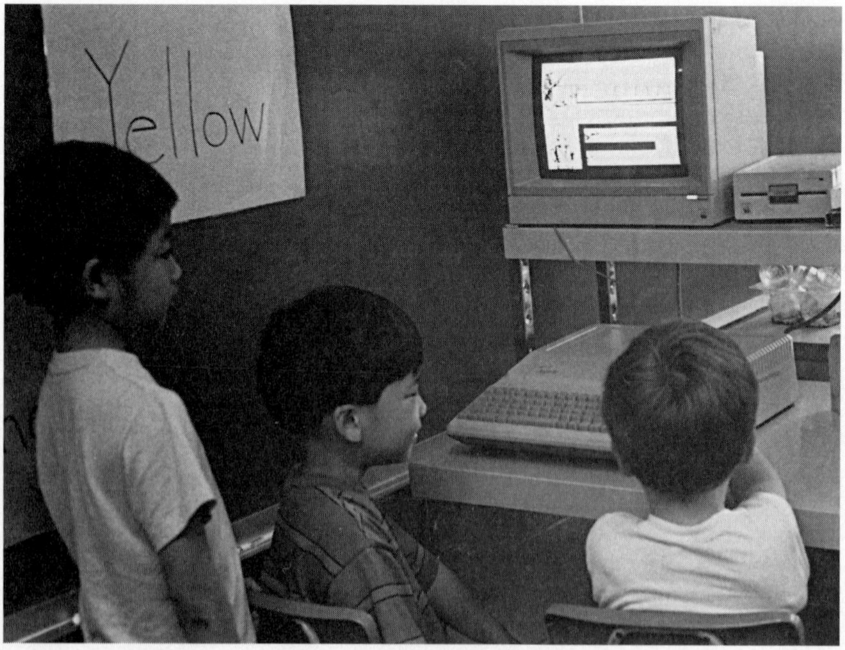

Computers can be used by small groups of children working together.

A reading center would have books on shelves or racks with their titles clearly visible, as well as comfortable places to read. A rug, some pillows, a soft chair, and straight chairs around a table might complement the library shelves. The books would be of different levels of difficulty and about different topics, including both fiction and nonfiction. Such a center could be augmented by a listening station, a cassette recorder or phonograph equipped with headsets, and a filmstrip or slide viewer.

Planning with Children for Work in Centers

In order to have a well-organized classroom plan that works, the teacher must provide children with a systematic way of working within the plan. Children and teachers need to plan together for self-selection of learning interest and activity centers. The teacher can hold a large group session to let the children know what is available and how many children can be at each center at a time. A planning board can be placed in a central location to let children know which centers are available. The board also lets the teacher know where the children are located. For example, the planning board can have a picture for each area. In each area, hooks can be placed with pictures or a number of how many children can use each area. Children can have markers with their names or symbols to hang on the planning board. If there is only room enough for four children in the blockbuilding area, the planning board should have only four hooks representing that area. Each area can have its own planning board, and a large planning board that shows all the areas can be placed in a particular place in the room to show where everybody is.

OUTDOOR SPACE

The outdoor play area needs to be planned as carefully as the indoor area. Outdoor areas pose some special problems. Activities are influenced by climate and weather. Additional maintenance problems exist as well. Outdoor areas also tend to support large-muscle activities, which might present special challenges for children with physical disabilities.

Outdoor play spaces should have both paved surfaces and grassy areas, if possible. The pavement allows children to use tricycles or other wheel toys. In addition, blockbuilding is more satisfying on a flat surface. A covered terrace or patio is desirable as part of the outdoor area so that children can be outdoors even when it rains. This space will allow some typical indoor activities to take place outdoors as well. There should be an area for digging; a dirt area will suffice, but a sandbox or pit large enough for a group of children to play in is desirable. A sand pit can be built right into the ground, with provisions for drainage and a cover to keep the sand clean and usable. A garden should be set aside for the children's use.

Provisions should be made for large-muscle activities and for dramatic play. Permanently installed equipment of wood, steel, concrete, and fiberglass, as well as portable equipment such as packing crates, boards, and ladders are useful. Very young children may be offered simple equipment; as they become more competent, more sophisticated and challenging equipment can be introduced. Adequate storage space in the outdoor area, such as a shed in the play yard or a locker at the door leading to the play area, should be available.

The prevailing climate will determine what kinds of activities will be offered children outdoors, and, in turn, how the outdoor play area should be designed. Other considerations include the problems of vandalism and the uses that will be made of the area when school is not in session. The outdoor area should be considered an extension of the classroom, providing opportunity for exciting learning experiences.

Frost and Klein (1979) suggest that children's playgrounds should be carefully planned, even before schools are built, to preserve the natural terrain. Permanent equipment such as fences, storage facilities, waterlines, water fountains, hard-surfaced areas, and shade structures should be installed. The **playground** should then be **zoned** to enhance the range and arrangement of equipment, taking into account such factors as (1) the need for complex multifunction structure, (2) the provision of varied equipment to allow a variety of forms of play, (3) the arrangement of equipment to allow cross-structured play, (4) the creation of zones that can be integrated, and (5) the creation of zones that allow for movement across zones. Spaces should also be provided for creative arts and natural activities. In addition, safety, maintenance, and supervision must be considered.

Playground zones allow organized spaces that support different kinds of activities

EQUIPMENT AND SUPPLIES

While educational supply houses are the source of much of the equipment needed in activity centers, some equipment can be purchased locally in hardware stores, supermarkets, and discount stores. This alternative is often less expensive, since there is no cost for packaging and shipping. Teachers who buy locally should be aware of school policy regarding purchases and the possibility of not paying a local sales tax. However, local purchases do take time, and the teacher must judge whether the hours spent offset the money saved. Many schools maintain a petty cash fund to help teachers make small purchases, such as cake mixes for a cooking experience or nails for the woodworking area.

Instructional kits for early childhood education contain complete sets of materials and teacher manuals packaged for classroom use. Kits are available for teaching mathematics, reading, language skills, cognitive skills, and human relations skills, as well as many other areas of learning. The entire program of a class could be taught through kits.

Some kits can be useful to teachers. They make materials that would be difficult to assemble available and insure proper instruction by structuring activities and giving directions to teachers. They are often well

Primary classes can be organized into activity centers.

conceived and well designed; some are even field-tested to determine their effectiveness. Other kits, however, lack imagination, contain closed-ended activities, are overpriced for the materials provided, contain stereotypes, or provide little evidence that they will teach what they promise. In fact, there are good kits and poor ones, closed-ended and open-ended ones, kits that nurture the children's learning and those that exploit children and provide too narrow a range of activities. Teachers should assess each kit as they would assess any set of materials provided in the classroom.

Some schools have expensive pieces of equipment, such as easels, lockers, climbing apparatus, or storage facilities, contributed or built by parents or members of the community. Parents or other adults who are willing to build equipment may be able to borrow or rent power tools locally. Local sewing centers will often lend sewing machines to allow parents to make doll clothes, sheets for resting cots, or curtains. Bringing the parents together for such a project has other advantages, for as they meet and work together, they will be knit into a group. They will also have an investment in the school. Care must be taken that parents do not feel exploited by such work sessions, however.

Many useful learning materials do not have to be bought. The teacher can salvage material that would otherwise be thrown away or even involve children and their parents in this process. Beans or pebbles can be used for counting as easily as can carefully designed mathematics material. Cast-off clothes make excellent additions to a dramatic play area. The chassis of a discarded radio, a broken alarm clock, castoffs from repair shops, buttons, egg cartons, and numerous other materials are useful in an early childhood classroom.

Figure 6–3 Bulletin Board Display for Manipulative Center

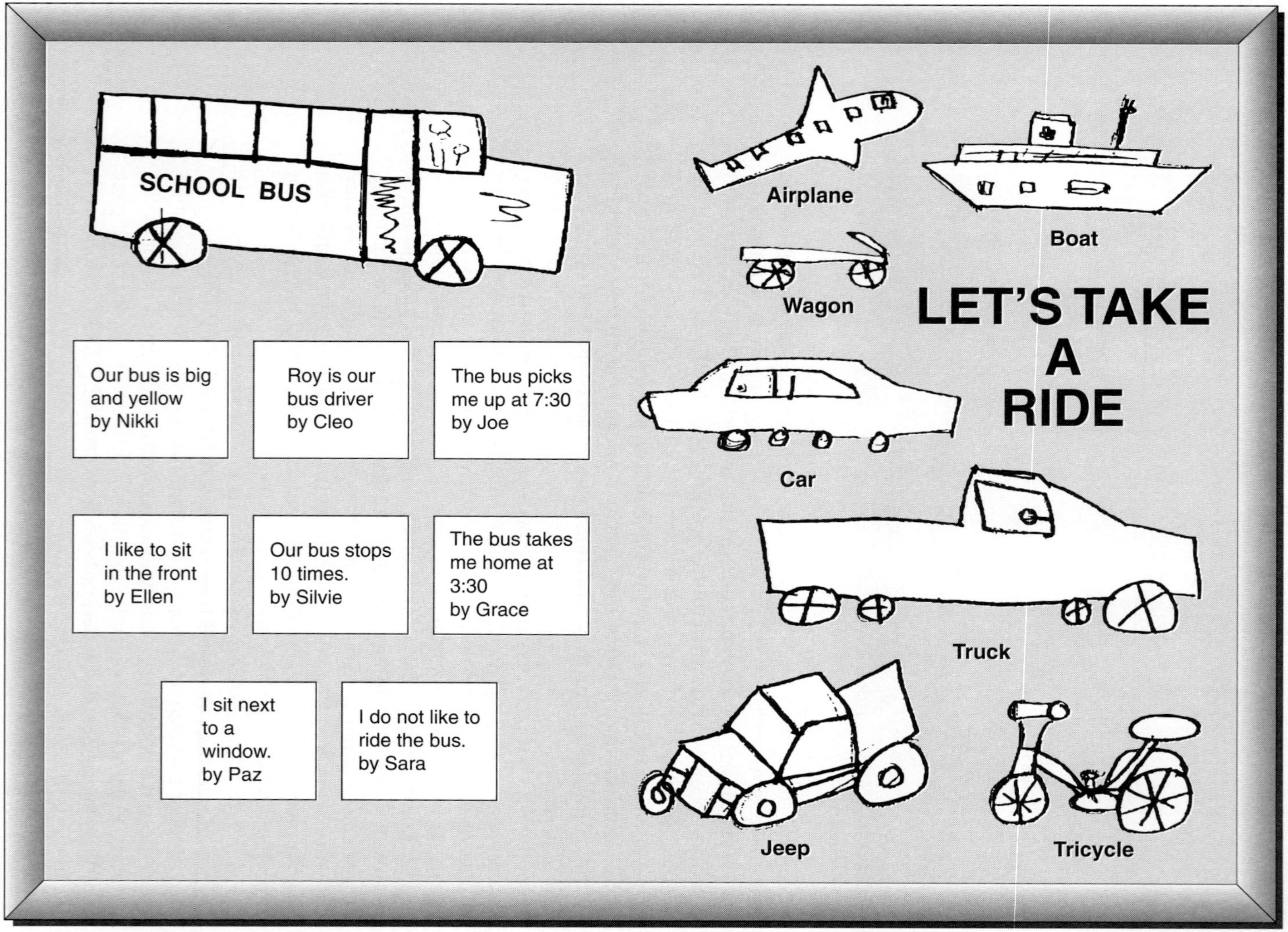

Instructional resources can help children visualize and understand ideas more clearly. They can include the following:

1. **Models, collections, and museums** can be used to help children understand concrete objects. For example, the Toledo Art Museum's Discovery Boxes include pictures, books, and objects related to a topic.
2. **Films, slides, filmstrips, and videocassettes** can contribute to the children's understanding. However, teachers should always preview the materials before using them in the classroom. They should also evaluate the value and appropriateness of materials in relation to their length, their difficulty, and the number of concepts that are taught. Slides and filmstrips make it possible for teachers to ask questions or discuss concepts of interest to them. However, teachers must be careful that these discussions are not so long that both teacher and children go off on a tangent or that children become bored.
3. **Computers and computer programs** are becoming increasingly familiar to young children. An increasing amount of discovery-oriented software, including simulations and games that are appropriate to early childhood classes, is available. Logo and other mathematics-oriented programs are available for young children. Simple word-processing programs are also being increasingly used to teach children writing skills. A computer center in a classroom can make these programs available to young children. Clements (1991) provides the following suggestions for teaching in a computer environment:
   - Introduce computer work gradually, one or two programs at a time.
   - Encourage children to work at computers in pairs.
   - Initially provide a great deal of support and guidance, gradually increasing self-directed and cooperative learning but continuing to provide guidance.
   - Teach children to cooperate effectively.
   - Be aware of the developmental limitations of the children.
   - Monitor student interactions to ensure the active participation of all.
   - Avoid quizzing or offering help before children request it.
   - Provide adequate preparation and follow-up for computer activities as for other activities. Plan carefully.
4. **Bulletin boards and displays** should reflect the children's current interests.
5. **Resource persons** can be invited to show pictures or other materials that are developmentally appropriate in teaching children about a specific topic. Resource people can teach a song, play a musical instrument, or share items from their trip or some relevant information.

Criteria for Selecting Equipment and Supplies

In selecting equipment and supplies, teachers may use a number of criteria. The following should be considered:

- **Cost** The amount of money spent for an object is an important consideration. Price alone, however, is often a false yardstick. Some less expensive items are not as satisfactory for their intended purpose as are more expensive items. Often the more expensive item will last longer and, in the final analysis, cost less. In any event, the cost of an item has to be balanced with the benefits provided.
- **Relationship to the School Program** Educational equipment illustrated in catalogues may be more fascinating to the adult than to the child. Items may be interesting but unrelated to the program. Teachers should select materials and equipment that will be interesting to children and help further the educational goals of the program.
- **Appropriateness for the Children** Learning materials should be matched to the interests, ages, and learning abilities of a particular group of children. The specific strengths and needs of individual children should be considered in selecting material.
- **Quality and Durability** There are many elements to consider in judging the quality of a piece of equipment. Equipment adequate for home use is often inappropriate for school. While design is important, the way a design is executed is equally important. The kind and quality of materials used—the care with which the equipment is fabricated, the way pieces are joined, the type of finish applied—help to determine quality.
- **Safety** Because young children are vulnerable to accidents, this criterion is of special concern. School equipment should not have sharp edges or protrusions. Finishes should be nontoxic as well as durable. For very young children, materials should be too large to be swallowed. If the equipment is for climbing, it must be strong enough to take the children's weight without collapsing, and have steps close enough together so that children can manage them easily. While most equipment and materials designed for young children meet safety requirements, this is not universally true. Caution is important.
- **Flexibility of Use** Since both budget and space are often limited, teachers should consider equipment that can be used in a variety of ways and situations. Such equipment will be stored less often and used in more ways. In the dramatic play area, equipment that has few details can often be used most flexibly, for the child's imagination turns a simple box into a rocket ship or a covered wagon. Of course, equipment designed for specific purposes should not be overlooked.

Many educational supply houses throughout the United States manufacture and/or sell equipment and supplies for early childhood education. These firms often have regional offices. Their catalogues or displays at conferences can help teachers select proper equipment and materials for their classrooms. Some traditional textbook publishers have also developed kits containing other kinds of materials in addition to books.

Most teachers have difficulty in selecting appropriate materials and equipment and deciding which manufacturer offers the highest quality at the most moderate price. Unfortunately, there are no *Consumer Reports* for this kind of equipment. It is helpful to ask the advice of teachers who have had some experience with specific equipment.

A number of guides to selecting equipment for early childhood education are available. These include lists in textbooks and pamphlets. Some useful, though somewhat dated, lists are found in the following material:

Association for Childhood Education International. (1976). *Selecting educational equipment for school and home*. Washington, DC: Association for Childhood Education International.

Evans, A. M.. How to equip and supply your prekindergarten classrooms. In J. L. Frost (Ed.), *Early childhood education rediscovered* (pp. 567–576). New York: Holt, Rinehart & Winston.

Although each classroom has specific needs, it is helpful to know what materials and equipment are generally used in classrooms.

- **Furniture** Furniture for an early childhood classroom should be movable and durable, scaled to the children's size. Tables and chairs should be of varying heights since children in any age group vary in size. Tables of different shapes might also be included for many purposes. The same tables can be used for both art work and eating. Special tables might be designated for use in the doll corner, the housekeeping area, and the library area, and for display purposes. Trapezoidal tables are quite flexible in that they can be grouped and arranged to create many different shapes. If chairs and tables are stackable, they can be stored in a corner of the room when not in use.

A teacher might wish to have some furniture for personal use: a desk, a couple of chairs, and a file cabinet. If work space is provided adjacent to the classroom, classroom space need not be used. Alternatively, an unobtrusive portion of the room can be set aside for the teacher's planning materials, records, personal supplies, and first-aid kit.

If young children stay in school for the full day, they need cots for rest. Lightweight cots that stack for easy storage can be purchased. These are not necessary for children in a half-day program. In kindergarten a time for informal quiet activity is advantageous.

SCHEDULING

A **daily schedule** allocates time for different learning activities.

A **schedule** allocates time for each day's activities. Children learn to anticipate future events through the regularity of daily occurrences. In the nursery school and kindergarten, time is alloted for various activities. Primary-grade learning may be organized into time periods by subject. Early childhood teachers provide large blocks of time for activities. The range of alternatives available for the children during the activity periods supports a degree of individuality and allows teachers to plan a different outcomes for different children.

Flexibility is necessary in any schedule. On one day, conversations with children may stretch to forty-five minutes, although only twenty have been scheduled; on other days, five minutes may seem too long. A teacher might wish to devote a whole day to a craft project, such as building a bus for a transportation unit, and simply not include a story or music activity. Balance over a long time needs to be considered. Children do not have to be involved in every area of the school curriculum every day.

SAMPLE SHEDULES

Preprimary Half-Day Class (Morning)

8:30–9:00	Arrival
	(Teacher greets children at door)
9:00–9:15	Check roll, collect milk money, etc.
9:15–9:30	Sharing time
9:30–10:30	Activity centers
10:30–10:45	Snack
10:45–11:15	Outdoor play
11:15–11:35	Story or music time
1:35–11:45	Getting ready to go home
11:45–12:00	Children leave for home

Preprimary Half-Day Class (Afternoon)

12:45–1:00	Arrival
	(Teacher greets children at door)
1:00–1:15	Check roll, collect milk money, etc.
1:15–1:30	Sharing time
1:30–2:15	Activity centers
2:15–2:30	Snack
2:30–3:00	Outdoor play
3:00–3:15	Story or music time
3:15–3:30	Getting ready to go home
3:30	Children leave for home

Preprimary Full-Day Class

8:30–9:00	Arrival
	(Teacher greets children at door)
9:00–9:15	Check roll, collect milk money, etc.
9:15–9:30	Sharing time
9:30–10:30	Activity centers
10:30–10:45	Snack
10:45–11:15	Outdoor play
11:15–11:35	Story or music time
11:35–11:45	Transition time
	(Children wash hands, get coats and belongings to go to lunch.)
11:45–12:00	Children go to the lunchroom
12:00–1:00	Lunch
1:00–1:30	Quiet activities
1:30–2:15	Large group activities
	(music, movement)
2:15–2:30	Snack
2:30–2:45	Storytelling
2:45–3:00	Getting ready to go home
3:00	Children leave for home

Teachers need to provide learning materials to children.

An alternative to scheduling time into periods would use some variation of the integrated day, which allows children to move through their activities at their own pace. Teachers concerned with individualizing instruction and developing autonomy in the children can plan many program strands to operate at the same time so that children can move from one curriculum area to another at their own pace. Thus, the organization of the school day may look like an extended activity period. Such an organization limits the amount of waiting children do in class, because they make optimal use of their school time in individual learning opportunities. Such organization could also be an aid to integrating school subject matter, for artificial time barriers could be lessened considerably or done away with entirely. The following are some sample schedules that teachers might use. These schedules provide structure to the day. As teachers feel comfortable with their classes, they can reduce the degree of structure in their daily schedule.

A more open structure might have the children coming into class and taking their own attendance, possibly by placing name tags on an attendance board. They may then go right into activities. Rather than having a snack period, snacks can be put out at a side table for children to take as they feel the need. Rather than have discussion or story time for the whole class, the teacher or an aide might take a small group into the library corner during the activity. There would still be a period for outdoor play and a time when the whole class would come together, but this would be for specific purposes, rather than as a ritual.

Much of the success of open scheduling rests on preparing the children to function autonomously. Some teachers may prefer to retain a structured portion of the day in addition to providing some time for independent activity. A period for independent activities might include opportunities for independent reading, project work, craft activities, and individual

Young children can help set up for snack.

research, as well as opportunities to complete elective assignments in various interest areas. Teachers should work with children in joint planning before the activities begin and in evaluation sessions afterward.

Transitions

While teachers generally plan carefully for the content of activity periods, problems often occur between these periods. Demanding that children clean up, line up, move from one area to another, or wait can create difficulties. Some children finish their cleanup well ahead of others, and some are naturally less patient than others. Often, one class's schedule must depend on the movement of other classes, which may be late.

Elizabeth Hirsch (n.d.) suggests that a number of factors contribute to difficulties around transition time including boredom, the absence of a future orientation, and fear of failure on the part of some children, as well as insistence on conformity and failure to define tasks clearly on the part of some teachers. Anticipating the problems of transition periods and planning for them can ease potential difficulties. The teacher can quickly learn which children will have problems during transitions and give them particular support. Making a game of cleanup makes it seem less overwhelming. Giving children specific directions and seeing that the requirements of the transition are not beyond their capabilities also help. A store of short games, stories, poems, and finger plays fills unanticipated periods of waiting. Most importantly, the teacher's sense of calm and order will help the children overcome problems that do arise.

ORGANIZING PEOPLE

Placing fifteen, twenty, or more children of like age into a single room for many hours each day creates conflict between the needs of the individuals and those of the group. We expect young children to give up the natural rhythm of their daily activity when they enter school. We demand that they all come to the school at the same time, sit in place for the same period of time, take care of bodily functions at prescribed periods, eat and play together at specific periods, and learn at more or less the same pace. We expect all children to "behave properly" irrespective of their earlier patterns of behavior or the particular expectations of their own outside world. Some degree of conformity is necessary for a child to get on in the world and is a form of acculturation, but how much conformity is really necessary is an open question.

Many educators have looked for ways to lessen the inherent conflict between the individual and the group in school. Some children learn faster than others and are more competent in certain areas. Children have different styles and interests and need different kinds of learning supports. Many techniques have been used to cope with this conflict. One technique is to provide a broad range of activities for children to choose among. A portion of the day may be assigned to an indoor or outdoor activity period during which children may select from structured or unstructured tasks and may change tasks. Only during short periods of the day are they required to be with the group—for "routine" activities, such as snacks or rest, or for large-group activities like music, storytelling, or discussion.

Grouping Children

Children are organized by ages and grades in prekindergartens, kindergartens, and primary classes, although some educators advocate mixed-age groupings. In kindergarten and prekindergarten classes, children are grouped in the class according to activity, with a combination of whole-class, small-group, and individual activities taking place daily. In primary classes, however, children are organized into groups for academic work, as well. Traditionally, the criterion for assigning children to classes and groups has been academic achievement or the level of their skills. Although this procedure might be comfortable for teachers, who work with the whole class, it presents certain problems for children. Narrowing the range of differences in one area of behavior, such as academic achievement, may have no effect on the range of differences in other areas. In addition, the placement of a child in a homogeneously grouped classroom creates an expectation of performance that may become a self-fulfilling prophecy. A child assigned to a slow class often performs according to what is expected of that group.

While homogeneous grouping is advocated by some teachers and parents, there is no evidence that it increases children's learning in any appreciable way. With the mainstreaming of children with special needs into regular classes, the presence of a broad range of educational abilities in each class has become the norm.

Instructional Grouping One way of dealing with individual differences at the primary level is to group children for instruction. Organizing a classroom into three reading groups, each representing a limited range of performance levels, is typical. The teacher can work with one group at a time, listening to children read, holding phonics lessons, or engaging them in other tasks, while other children are engaged in a seatwork activity. Using a team approach or individualizing instruction may limit the seatwork needed, since more than one instructional group can be dealt with at one time.

Individualized Instruction Individualized instruction often keeps the goals of education constant but allows children to move through the same tasks at different paces. Work is broken down into small steps and children are given individual instructional tasks based on their performance on diagnostic tests. They complete worksheets, are tested, and, upon evidence of successful attainment, move on to the next set of tasks. All children move through the same series of tasks, but at their own pace. Opportunities are provided for children to skip sets of tasks if they show competence in the area.

In this approach only the pace is individualized. An activity-oriented class individualizes other aspects of instruction. The classroom can become a workshop, allowing children to pursue different enterprises. Both the means and the goals are different for each child. Teachers can give children opportunities to express their interests and modify their programs accordingly.

Multi-Age Grouping

Another way of dealing with individual differences in the classroom is to do away with the age-grade organization of the school. When the differences in any one classroom increase, the teacher cannot have the same expectations for all children. In addition, less formal methods of instruction are possible and greater individualization may result. Children can help and teach one another, age-grade expectations are lessened, and the children's own capabilities become the basis for judgments about programs.

William Schrankler (1976) has identified several advantages of family grouping, as multi-age grouping is sometimes called. The multi-age class represents a microsociety that provides an enriched intellectual community for young children. It eliminates age-grade lines and thus allows for cross-age tutoring. It also lengthens the time period for teacher-parent and teacher-child interactions beyond a single term or year. In studying children in multi-age and single-age classes, Schrankler found that a positive relationship existed between multi-age grouping and such affective factors as children's self-esteem and positive attitude toward school. There were no differences in academic achievement between children in the two types of classes.

Multi-age grouping, like the other organizational schemes discussed above, presents the possibility for increased individualization. What teachers do with this potential becomes the crucial factor in supporting children's learning. Unfortunately, in some cases, multi-age grouping has meant replacing one criterion for grouping (age) with another (possibly reading achievement), with no change in classroom practice. In the multiage approach, the individual differences in the classroom can be viewed as an asset. If children are considered learning resources, then increasing the age range of children in a classroom can increase the range of learning resources available.

Methods of dealing with individual differences can be combined in any number of ways to improve the match of instructional techniques to children. Each arrangement requires a different way of thinking through the classroom organization. The layout of the physical facilities can enhance or thwart small-group activities. The availability of materials and equipment is also a concern. The teacher does not need a full set of textbooks in an individualized program. On the other hand, a greater variety of materials and equipment must be available for the children to use independently.

Organizing Adults

Adults play many roles in the education of young children. School principals and center directors assume primarily administrative responsibilities, although they may do some teaching. Head teachers, teacher-directors, and classroom teachers assume primary responsibility for classroom planning and teaching. Teacher aides, assistants, and volunteers may also be involved in teaching as well as in supportive activities. Volunteers might be either resource persons who are invited into the classroom briefly or part of the regular teaching staff, as is the case in many cooperative nursery schools. In addition, new roles are being defined for persons in early childhood education, such as the early childhood educator, which Almy (1975) defined as a highly qualified early childhood professional with an advanced degree and considerable experience and expertise.

Others in the school community also contribute to the education of young children; each leaves an imprint. Cooks, custodians, bus drivers, and others all influence the education of children. While teachers cannot be responsible for or supervise all the encounters children have with school personnel, they need to be aware of these encounters, using them to integrate learnings from many sources. Teachers must coordinate the use of volunteers, train them, and provide them with an orientation to the school.

Parents participating in a nursery school must be made aware of the school's philosophy, routines, techniques of teaching, and methods of classroom management. Teachers should define the parents' roles and responsibilities and explain the reasons for the classroom's organization; practice sessions for parents might help to create consistent performance.

Some educators advocate differentiated staffing patterns as a way of using and rewarding teachers with different skills and expertise. Prekindergarten classes have traditionally used differentiated staffing, with teachers working alongside teacher aides and teaching assistants. More recently it has been suggested that some teachers also be identified as master teachers or teacher mentors, whose roles would include helping other teachers as well as working with children. Such a differentiated pattern, according to Clinton Boutwell, Dean Berry, and Robert Lungren (1973), has five characteristics: (1) a formal system of shared decision making, (2) formal provisions for self-renewal, (3) performance-based organizational roles, (4) formal provisions for professional self-regulation, and (5) a flexible use of human and physical resources. Teams created this way lessen teachers' isolation and lead to flexible teaching arrangements.

Team teaching is a difficult and tenuous agreement. Successfully merging two personalities, teaching styles, and philosophies into one classroom with one group of children can be difficult. Teams that teach together every day spend more time together than most married couples (Thornton, 1990); therefore, teachers have to work together to solve whatever differences may arise in order to be able to achieve the program's educational goals. Team teaching does provide the opportunity to model cooperative behavior to young children. Successful team teaching requires sincere communication, trust, and the ability to work out differences on the part of both teachers.

Preprimary classes that use a head and an assistant teacher in each classroom represent one type of team. Using teaching aides in kindergarten or primary classrooms allows two individuals to work together and facilitates splitting the classroom in various ways, so that adults can attend to several individuals or groups at any one time.

More extensive teams can be created by merging classes of children into larger instructional units. Some activities, such as watching a video presentation, require little teacher supervision, so that a teacher might have responsibility for more children than would normally be found in a self-contained classroom during these activities. Other learning situations might be better organized as small-group activities, independent activities, or conferences. Members of a teaching team have greater opportunities to work with individuals and small groups and to specialize than do independent teachers.

The teachers in a team do not have to be equal in competence or responsibility. A master teacher and a fledgling teacher can learn from each other. Part-time teachers can be incorporated into the team, adding additional skills. Team teaching eliminates the problem of teacher isolation, for each teacher constantly interacts with others.

In creating a large instructional group, consisting of two or more classes, educators must take care that the group does not become so large as to overwhelm the individual child. There is the danger of creating a mass in which strong relational bonds between adult and child and between child and child are submerged. Large groups also tend to be handled in a more bureaucratic fashion than do small ones. Although there are no reliable rules about the optimal size of a group, some school systems and licensing agencies have established guidelines. Judgments about group size should take into account educational goals, available facilities, teacher competency, and the programs's basic philosophy of education, in addition to the absolute number and ages of children involved (Spodek, 1972).

Teachers who wish to support independent learning must provide a classroom that allows children to behave freely and reasonably. In a classroom with activity centers, children can move into areas that support a particular activity rather than being constrained to a single desk for most of the day. The test of a good room arrangement is the degree to which it helps children achieve the goals of the program. Teachers should experiment with room settings and modify them regularly so they support a dynamic learning situation.

SUMMARY

Organizing for instruction requires that teachers engage in both long-range and short-range planning. While plans may change as teachers work with children, such planning allows for greatest flexibility. In planning, teachers must consider the availability and use of various resources, including space, physical resources (furniture, equipment, and supplies), time (both calendar and clock time), and people, both adults and children.

REFERENCES

Almy, M. (1975). *The early childhood educator at work.* New York: McGraw-Hill.

Bender, J. (1971). Have you ever thought of a prop box? *Young Children, 26,* 164–169.

Blake, H. E. (1977). *Creating a learning-centered classroom.* New York: Hart.

Boutwell, C. E., Berry, D. R., & Lungren, R. E. (1973). Differentiated staffing: Problems and prospects. In M. Scoby & A. J. Fiorino (Eds.), *Differentiated staffing* (pp. 9–22).Washington, DC: Association for Supervision and Curriculum Development.

Clements, D. H. (1991). Current technology and the early childhood curriculum. In B. Spodek & O. N. Saracho (Eds.), *Issues in early childhood curriculum: Yearbook in early childhood education* (Vol. 2). (pp. 251–275). New York: Teachers College Press.

Corwin, R., Hein, G. E., & Levin, D. (1976). Weaving curriculum webs: The structure of nonlinear curriculum. *Childhood Education, 52,* 248–251.

Frost, J. L., & Klein, B. L. (1979). *Children's play and playgrounds.* Boston: Allyn & Bacon.

Gunter, M. A., Estes, T. H., & Schwab, H. H. (1990). *Instruction: A models approach.* Boston: Allyn & Bacon.

Hirsch, E. S. (n.d.). *Transition periods: Stumbling blocks of education.* New York: Early Childhood Education Council of New York City.

Jones, E. (1979). *Dimensions of teaching-learning environments.* Pasadena: Pacific Oaks College.

Ladd, G. W., & Coleman, C. C. (1993). Young children's peer relations: Forms, features and functions. In B. Spodek (Ed.), *Handbook of research on the education of young children* (pp. 57–76). New York: Macmillan.

Patillo, J., & Vaughan, E. (1992). *Learning centers for child-centered classrooms.* Washington, DC: National Education Association.

Schrankler, W. (1976). Family grouping and the affective domain. *Elementary School Journal, 76,* 432–439.

Spodek, B. (1972). Staffing patterns in early childhood education. In I. J. Gordon (Ed.), *Early childhood education.* 71st yearbook of the National Society for the Study of Education. (pp. 339–366). Chicago: University of Chicago Press.

Spodek, B. (Ed.). (1991). *Educationally appropriate kindergarten practices.* Washington, DC: National Education Association.

Thornton, J. R. (1990). Team teaching: A relationship based on trust and communication. *Young Children, 45*(5), 40–43.

Workman, S., & Anziano, M. C. (1993). Curriculum webs: Weaving connections from children to teachers. *Young Children, 48*(2), 4–9.

7

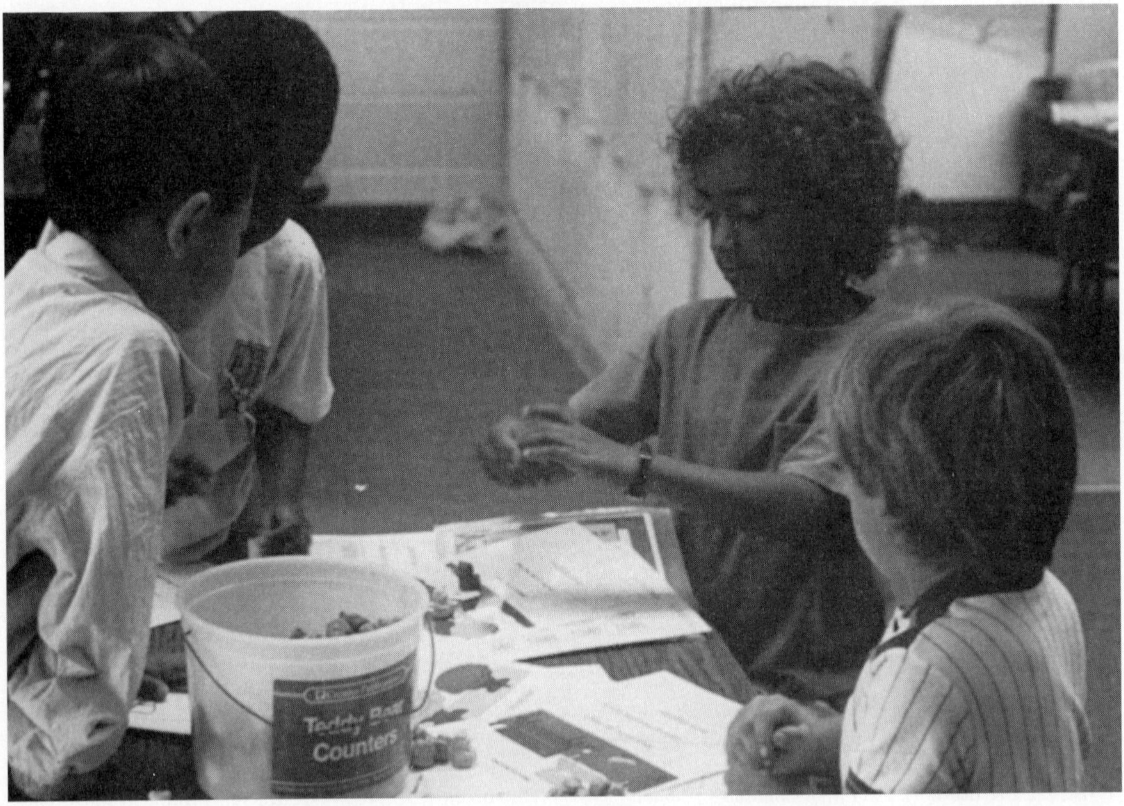

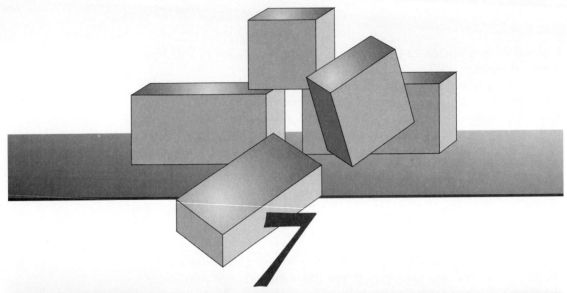

Creating a Positive Social Environment

CHAPTER OVERVIEW

This chapter presents:

- The importance of social integration to a child's development
- Strategies to promote peer friendships and social interaction in the classroom
- Ways for teachers and children to promote a positive classroom climate
- Techniques to manage behavior problems of young children in the classroom

INTRODUCTION

The development of social competence is an important goal of early childhood education. This goal has taken on increasing importance as more and more children enroll in early childhood classes and as these young children spend an increasing portion of their day in school.

Children are first socialized in the family. They develop relationships with parents and siblings. They learn their role in the family and how to function as a member of that social group. Entrance to school presents a major shift in the lives of young children. They become a part of a larger group. They take on a new set of roles. They have to learn to cope with the demands of a varied set of relationships. Thus, children must learn a new set of understandings and competencies. They need to learn the student role and what it takes to be effective in school. They need to get along with peers and learn how to build and maintain friendships. They need to respond to a new set of authority figures. This chapter will present ideas about helping children develop social competence in school, including building positive relations with peers, and about creating an effective classroom management system, both important elements in creating a positive social environment.

SOCIAL COMPETENCE

Social competence is a basic human ability. Social competence includes being able to function in a variety of social settings and having the skills and understanding to build friendships with peers. These abilities are important elements of a young child's life.

Although there have been many studies on training children in social skills, no consensus exists on the definition of social skills or social competence. Recent definitions highlight social interactions and differentiate between the terms *social skills* and *social competence*. **Social competence** relates to a person's total social performance. It focuses on the "social importance, effectiveness, and functional utility of performance" (Kratochwill & French, 1984, p. 332). **Social skills** refer to behaviors that lead to peer acceptance or popularity or that correlate consistently with peer acceptance or popularity. **Social skills training** refers to an intervention designed to improve such behaviors (Hughes & Sullivan, 1988). Role-playing, pairing more competent with less competent children, and using stories all can help children to develop social competence.

Social competence is a person's total social performance.

Social skills are behaviors that lead to social acceptance.

Social skills training refers to the intervention designed to improve social behaviors.

Developing positive social interactions in the early years is extremely important for children. The types of relationships they develop during this period will affect their later academic performance, their feelings about themselves, their attitudes toward others, and the social patterns they will adopt. Teachers can prevent behavior problems before they arise and support optimum social growth by identifying and helping socially unskilled children.

Several scholars have documented the importance of peer relations to children's cognitive development. Piaget (1965), for example, has asserted that peer interactions improve the cognitive development of preschoolers, providing them with alternative perspectives in problem-solving situations. Rubenstein and Howes (1979) found that the play of toddlers is more complex when they play with others. Guralnick (1981) noted that social interaction with other children improves communication skills as children adjust the complexity of their language to fit the cognitive level of the listener. Hartup (1983) demonstrated that peer exchanges teach children to share, to respond appropriately to aggression, and to develop appropriate sex-role behaviors. Murray (1972) and Perret-Clements (1980) showed that gains in cognitive skills result from social exchanges with more competent peers.

Gary Ladd and Cynthia Coleman (1993) reviewed the research on young children's peer relationships. They concluded that young children are capable of building peer relationships, or friendships, in which they mutually adjust their interactions with the children they prefer. In a preschool classroom, Ladd and Coleman assert, differences already emerge between children who are well liked and those who have difficulty in developing and sustaining friendships. Ladd and Coleman also note that friendships among children support their social development. Children with low social status, that is, those who are not regularly chosen as playmates by others, report higher levels of loneliness and dissatisfaction. There is also evidence that the social problems of young children are linked to problems of social adjustment in later childhood and adolescence.

Ladd and Coleman (1993) suggest that teachers can help children develop social competence. One thing teachers can do is to provide opportunities for children to interact with their peers. Teachers can help children to communicate better with their peers and to develop prosocial behaviors while diminishing antisocial behaviors, such as fighting and arguing.

STRATEGIES FOR PROMOTING PEER INTERACTION

Social skills are an essential component of the curriculum for young children. Young children should be helped to develop social competence over time and in different settings.

1. **Social interaction is reciprocal.** Social interaction involves social exchanges among individuals; training to improve young children's interaction requires providing a socially competent model, either an adult or another child. Children should observe and try to emulate the model. Teachers can provide encouragement. Children should practice newly acquired social skills in different situations so that the skill is generalized. Continued encouragement should be provided so the skill is maintained (Simpson, 1987).
2. **Young children need more than mere exposure to socially adequate models.** Young children need to learn to interact with other children to the point that their social initiations and responses persist without the teacher's prompting. Whatever social skill training is offered needs to be provided in a natural context.
3. **Young children need to learn behaviors that peers will naturally reinforce.** Adaptive, desirable target behaviors must be selected to contribute to the development of social competence and to prompt reinforcing peer responses (McConnell, 1987).

Example of Activities to Develop Social Competence

1. Introduce a puppet that children like, possibly a boy puppet for a male child or a girl puppet for a female child. It can be a sock puppet, stick puppet, or any other puppet that is easy to handle. Children would enjoy a puppet from the Smurfs family (a popular cartoon among children). Encourage the children to interact

with classmates using their puppet. Children will loosen up because they feel the puppet is doing the talking rather than they themselves. Once the children feel confident, they will interact by themselves without the puppet.

2. Cut a large shape from a poster board. Cut a circle in the middle large enough for a child's head. Encourage the children to put their heads through the hole and talk to other children. The more children participate in this activity, the less withdrawn they will become. Soon they will not need this prop to interact with other children.
3. Set up role-playing situations. Suggest social situations children can relate to, such as playing on a teeter-totter. Have them role-play the situation to solve a problem. Discuss the different solutions to the problem and write an experience story.
4. Read or tell stories about children who need friends, especially children who are somehow different from others. Allow children to discuss the story and share similar experiences of their own.

Social skill instruction must take place in natural settings, but strategies must be carefully planned to improve social skills. Teachers must realize that problems in social acceptance do occur and know how to ameliorate perceived difficulties before they become insurmountable (Sabornie, 1985).

Social skill training strategies can be either adult directed or peer directed. Teachers should strive to use a combination of these strategies in their classrooms.

Some learning strategies promote peer interactions.

Adult-Directed Strategies

Adult-directed strategies include reinforcement, modeling, verbal instructions, coaching, developmental play, incidental teaching, and using a classroom manager.

Reinforcement Teachers can provide verbal praise or give children attention following a social exchange. Each is an effective technique for promoting positive social interaction. Children can be encouraged to share, smile at their peers, begin an interaction, respond to someone else's interaction, or extend or sustain an existing interaction.

Reinforcement is a consequence of a behavior that leads to the recurrence of the behavior.

Example of Reinforcement

Albert goes to the manipulative area and takes all of the colored cubes. Later the teacher observes Albert sharing the colored cubes with Willie. The teacher can make a positive comment to Albert to reinforce his behavior, saying, "I'm so proud of Albert for sharing the colored cubes with Willie. Albert is going to find out that sharing can make the game more fun, because two children playing is more fun than playing alone."

Teachers must be careful that the praise or attention does not disrupt or interfere with ongoing social exchanges. In addition, the reinforcement should be given periodically and in a varied manner to sustain its effects. Teachers should also be aware that constant or indiscriminate attention or praise may not be reinforcing.

Modeling Modeling means showing someone how to do something. Modeling can enhance children's social abilities. Often, a teacher needs only to show a child how to behave in a social situation, such as initiating a social interaction ("Let's play in the doll area") or sustaining an ongoing interaction ("Let's build a block house, only this time with two kitchens"). Children's peers can also serve as models and may be more effective.

Modeling is a way of demonstrating a behavior.

Example of Modeling

Ms. Owen has noted that Richard has difficulty putting the blocks away at cleanup time. At times, he grabs blocks from another child who is also helping to clean up the block area. Ms. Owen kneels down next to Richard and begins picking up blocks alongside him, placing them in the appropriate place on the shelf. As she does so, she says to Richard, "See, there is work for each of us to do at cleanup time. But maybe it would be good to do it together. I will hand each block to you and you can put them on the shelf. That way we can work together and get cleaned up faster." They continue to clean up together.

Teachers can model appropriate behavior. However, teachers sometimes inadvertently model inappropriate behavior. For example, a teacher in a hurry might kick a toy aside to get it out of the way. Children observe this behavior and may imitate the teacher. Therefore, the teacher should instead take time to put the toy in its proper place in order to provide a good model for children.

Verbal instruction is telling a person what to do.

Verbal Instructions Verbal instructions involve offering suggestions, telling, or explaining to children what is expected of them in various social situations. Verbal instructions are most often used together with other techniques, such as positive reinforcement or modeling.

Coaching includes teaching a person a skill, and then having the person practice and later use the skill in a realistic situation.

Coaching Social coaching can teach interaction skills and reduce disruptive behavior, such as aggression. Coaching has been used with aggressive as well as with normal children. Coaching includes three components: (1) children are taught strategies for playing with others through verbal discussion and role-playing; (2) they are then given opportunities to rehearse these skills with peers; and (3) later, they use the strategies in natural social situations and report back about how effective the strategies are (Ladd, 1981). Spodek and Saracho (1994) provide the following suggestion:

Example of Coaching

Ellen is having difficulty working with others. Mr. Vargas assigned Ellen to set the table with Joanna. As they work together, Mr. Vargas says to Ellen, "Why don't you and Joanna share the work? You could bring the cups from the kitchen, then you and Joanna can match cups to chairs." He continually suggests ways for Ellen and Joanna to cooperate in doing their task.

Developmental play is a form of dramatic play that helps children deal with emotional conflicts.

Developmental Play Developmental play is similar in many ways to play therapy, although the level of interpretation is not as deep. In addition, developmental play can occur in groups. To conduct a developmental play session, the teacher sets up different kinds of toys, such as small dolls and dollhouse furniture or puppets, that allow children to create miniature dramatic play situations. The children can then discuss the play, describing what happened and how they felt. Weekly play sessions, extended over time, can help children develop attachments to the teacher and to other children that can assist them in developing more trustful and productive relationships with others.

Example of Developmental Play

Ms. Santos brings three boys together in a corner of the room. She brings out a set of puppets and discusses the hypothetical problem of a boy who has come to school angry and is fighting with the other children. She asks the boys to have their puppets act this out, with one puppet representing the angry boy and the other puppets other children in the class. After a few minutes she stops the play and asks the children how they felt. She then asks them how they might help the angry boy feel better.

Incidental Teaching Social skills can be taught incidentally during naturally occurring events in the course of the day. Though incidental, this kind of teaching can be systematic. Teachers should be sensitive to the need to support social learning and provide varying kinds of support "on the fly" while focusing on other teaching tasks.

Example of Incidental Teaching

During snack or lunch time, the teacher may positively reinforce Mary for sharing with her friends. The teacher may say, "Good for Mary. By cutting the apple four times, she has enough pieces for herself, David, Susan, and Sally."

Using a Classroom Manager Using a classroom manager (Sainato, Maneady, & Shook, 1987) involves selecting an unpopular child as class leader or manager during popular and visible classroom activities. Each child can serve as a manager, and, on occasion, teachers might use co-managers, pairing up children to work cooperatively on certain activities.

Teachers can observe young children to identify those who they feel need help with their social skills. They can then assess the children's sociability. Once teachers learn the degree to which a young child is socially withdrawn, they can use the strategies discussed earlier to help such a child develop social skills. Teachers should practice these strategies until they feel comfortable with them. Each will be effective with some children, but not with others.

Peer-Directed Strategies

Peer modeling has been widely used to teach social skills to children. Two types of models are used: (1) live models, with children observing the behaviors of their socially adept peers in the classroom, and (2) symbolic models, with children observing the social behaviors of children in a videotape or film. Live models should be children who are popular and who enjoy high social status in the classroom to increase the chances that other children will watch and imitate the model. Teachers should call children's attention to the model's behavior and publicly reinforce what the model is doing. Teachers should also employ more than one model.

To use peer-directed social skills training, teachers show a child or group of children how to engage their socially less skillful peers in social interactions. Children, rather than adults, become training agents, in a process that more closely resembles the natural process of acquiring social skills. Peer tutors for social skill training should be volunteers who attend school regularly, who already display positive social behavior toward other children, and who can follow adult directions. Peer-directed interventions include working in close proximity with a less adept child, prompting and reinforcing, getting other children to initiate social encounters, and accepting the initiation of another, as well as serving as models.

Placing a socially competent child next to a child with social problems and asking him or her to play with the target child should be linked with encouraging the target child to play with others and showing that child how to play. This *proximity strategy* facilitates the natural transmission of social skills.

Socially skillful children can learn to *prompt and reinforce* the social behaviors of others. Prompts may consist of invitations ("Come play with me"), and reinforcement may consist of praise after the interaction ("Thank you, I enjoyed playing with you"). Prompts and reinforcement are more effective when used jointly.

Socially competent children can be taught to direct social overtures to other children, asking a child to play, giving a child a toy, offering physical assistance, or suggesting a play idea. Teachers can rehearse the children in various *initiation strategies* and support them in being persistent in their efforts to engage the other children in social interactions. Social tutors can also be trained to *accept the initiation of others*, responding appropriately to social overtures from a child who has been prompted to initiate an interaction.

ESTABLISHING A CLIMATE CONDUCIVE TO SOCIAL INTEGRATION

Two factors play an important role in establishing a classroom conducive to social integration: teacher influence and peer influence.

Teacher Influence

Teachers are the most important factor in determining how children feel about school, themselves, and each other, and how much progress they make. Teachers also influence the extent to which children of diverse abilities accept each other. Brophy and Putnam (1979) have identified a number of attributes of effective teachers. They should be liked by their students and be cheerful, friendly, emotionally mature, sincere, and well adjusted. They should be able to stay calm in a crisis, listen to children without becoming authoritarian or defensive, avoid conflicts, and maintain a problem-solving orientation in their classrooms. Such teachers can use a variety of techniques to effectively manage their classes.

The impact of teachers' behavior on their classes has been demonstrated in a number of studies (Walberg, 1986; Rosenshine & Stevens, 1986). The characteristics of teachers that are conducive to a healthy social atmosphere in the classroom include positive self-concept, positive behavior, understanding, and knowledge about behavior problems and their solutions.

Teachers' Self-Concept While most research has focused on the relationship between children's self-concept and development, some writers (such as Clark & Peterson, 1986) have directed their attention toward the relationship of teachers' self-concept to children's social development. Jersild (1965) noted that teachers' personal problems can interfere with their classroom performance and influence their pupils. Combs (1965) found that effective teachers are distinguished by their positive attitudes toward themselves and others. He noted the importance of fostering positive self-concepts among teachers and asserted that teachers with a positive attitude toward themselves and others can enhance the self-concept of their pupils. Moreover, teachers with positive self-concepts promote a positive classroom atmosphere, while those with negative self-concepts promote negative feelings among pupils (Karnes & Lee, 1979).

Teachers' Positive Behavior Just as the children's social skills are important, so are teachers' social skills. Not only are these skills useful in working with students, but they have an overall influence in the classroom. If teachers are positive and enthusiastic, their students will be positive and enthusiastic. Negative teacher attitudes and behavior often make children passive, withdrawn, and even fearful. In addition, teachers' expectations can influence students' academic achievement and social behavior. If a teacher has low expectations for a child, these expectations may result in a self-fulfilling prophecy: the student may perform poorly (Rosenthal & Jacobson, 1968; Brophy & Good, 1986).

Teachers' behavior and expectations also influence the children's self-esteem. Through interactions with significant persons in their lives—family members, peers, and teachers—children begin to reflect the extent to which they are valued as people (Maccoby, 1980). Adults who demonstrate warmth, respect, empathy, and acceptance are far more likely to nurture positive self-images in children than are adults who demonstrate negative expectations (Gecas, Colonico, & Thomas, 1974). Positive attitudes and expectations for all children, but especially for those who have developmental differences from normal children, must be combined with praise, support, and encouragement. By emphasizing children's good points, teachers can build their students' confidence and persistence in completing difficult learning tasks.

Teachers' Understanding Teachers must be sensitive to differences in their students' abilities and to conflicts or misunderstandings that can result from these differences. The negative stereotypes and prejudices that even young children can develop are dangerous in the classroom. Teachers communicate important messages to students about attitudes toward individual differences. Students quickly learn whether teachers favor high-achieving students or feel respect or disdain for those who have special problems. Teachers' attitudes also set a tone for child-child relationships (Macmillan, Jones, & Meyers, 1976).

By gathering information in school and in the children's homes, teachers can gain a better understanding of their children and of the differences that exist among them. They can use this knowledge to design appropriate programs for all children.

An accepting atmosphere promotes integration and the social growth of the entire class. It will also provide children with a model for understanding individual differences.

GATHERING INFORMATION TO BETTER UNDERSTAND CHILDREN IN THE CLASSROOM

Teachers can gather information by recording diagnostic notes. They can keep a log of their diagnostic hypotheses and the instructional decisions they make based on their regular interaction with the students. Teachers can jot down their thoughts on questions such as the following:

- What strengths and weaknesses do I see?
- What problems do I see that can be addressed next?
- What strategy should I use?
- Can I try it?
- Did it work?
- What's my next idea?

Teachers can then save copies of the student's work or any documents on which they base their hypotheses, developing a portfolio of the child's work. When they use information other than written work, they can jot notes about the interaction and their hypothesis in whatever way is meaningful and easy for them. When teachers are ready to design a program, they can go back and amend these notes to make better sense of them.

This process helps teachers to be systematic about what good teachers do—making hypotheses about what students need and adjusting their lessons accordingly.

Knowledge of Behavior Problems Behavior problems can arise even in the most carefully planned social environment. Teachers must be able to recognize and cope with such problems. Children with diverse needs may act in ways that interfere with, prohibit, or compete with school-related activities and useful social and work skills. To maintain a positive social climate, classroom teachers must know what type of problem behaviors to expect and how to deal with them. Alternative approaches to discipline are presented later in this chapter.

Peer Influence

Young children learn from each other to see themselves as leaders, as followers, or as isolated. When children are accepted and liked by peers, they become confident and self-assured and so achieve better in school. On the other hand, uncertain or partial acceptance makes them anxious and causes self-doubt. Those who are completely rejected can experience trauma, act aggressively, or withdraw into apathy or fantasy.

The degree to which children are influenced by their peers depends on their age, maturity, social skills, ethnic background, and any disability they might have. For instance, preschool children are usually not as influenced by their peer group as are older children. Home and adult praise are more important to them than is peer approval. Beginning in the primary years, peer influence increases (Winkler, 1975).

Considering the impact that children's peers have on their social and academic development, teachers must learn to understand and use the social environment of the classsroom to promote the children's learning of social skills in a natural context. Teachers can increase the chances for healthy social interaction among children by being sensitive to peer norms and values and by making children aware of differing abilities.

Peer Norms and Values A system of norms and values that defines what will be accepted and admired exists in any class. Children want to be popular and accepted by their peers. If they perceive that such activities as participating in class, cooperating with the teacher, or accepting differences in others are approved, they will conform to these standards. Peer support for these behaviors can be effective in motivating individual children.

Teachers can explain the importance of cooperation and sharing, helping children understand that all individuals, however different their abilities and personalities, deserve the respect of all. Teachers should model appropriate social responses and reinforce children for appropriate behavior.

Knowledge of Differing Abilities All teachers require information about the abilities and backgrounds of the children with whom they work. Children need to know the specific effects that children who are different from them will have on their classmates and on themselves. Children will be curious about individual differences and may have misconceptions about those who are different, possibly perceiving, for instance, a child who speaks a different language as being retarded. To support an integrated environment, children must learn about one another.

Several strategies exist for helping children learn about the differing abilities and backgrounds of their peers. Teachers can develop units that emphasize the cultures of children in the classroom and the abilities of children who are gifted or who have disabilities, or devote learning centers to such topics. These centers may teach children about different languages (such as Spanish or French), show examples of different forms of communication (such as signing, Braille, or communication boards), or display books that address the needs of children of different cultures or those who are exceptional.

One of the most effective strategies for teaching children about each other is classroom discussion. Teachers may invite a resource person to speak about a topic, or a discussion may begin spontaneously as the result of an incident that occurs in the class. Discussions convey accurate information and impressions. In conducting classroom discussions, teachers should help the students who are the focus of discussion to feel comfortable about being the center of attention. Respect for the students should be maintained at all times, and problems or concerns should be dealt with in a direct yet sensitive manner.

Simulations can also increase children's knowledge of their peers. Students can assume the role of a student who is different from themselves. For example, a child without a disability might spend a day or a portion of a day in a wheelchair. Puppetry is another form of simulation. Puppets representing children with disabilities, for example, can be an effective tool for changing the attitudes of young children toward their peers. In planning such activities, teachers should emphasize the similarities as well as the differences that exist among children.

CLASSROOM MANAGEMENT

For most children today, entrance into the kindergarten or primary grades is not their first school beginning. For others, the first school day may be their first experience away from home, and the teacher may represent the first authority figure other than parents to whom they have had to relate. In any event, the beginning of school is always fraught with some fear, for children may not yet know exactly what to expect. School beginnings, therefore, require special consideration.

Beginning School: Preschool–Kindergarten Level

The child's introduction to school often begins months prior to the first school day. Many schools provide a spring visit for children who will enter that fall. New children may be brought into the classroom individually or in small groups, either when the class is in session or after school. They view the physical layout and explore the materials and equipment, most of which will be there when they return in fall. Most of all, they have a chance to meet the staff. The teacher in charge of the class when they visit will probably be their teacher. This orientation also gives parents a chance to find out about the school's expectations and routines, allowing them to prepare their child for entrance to school.

Teachers like to gather information about their new children's backgrounds and needs. Conferences with parents are helpful but cannot always be arranged. A student information form (see Figure 7–1), filled out by parents and returned before or when school begins, provides needed information.

Most children begin the school year in the fall. Having all the children come to class at the same time creates several problems. All the children are ignorant of the resources available and the procedures they are to follow. In addition, they each have individual reactions to this new experience. Some children find the new school setting stimulating and exhilarating and, rising to the challenge, immediately plunge into exploration. Other children find the newness of the situation frightening and refuse to have contact with people or things. Some families move often while their children are still young. If a child has recently moved to the community, adjustment problems may be compounded, as the child deals with additional uncertainty. Similarly, a child who is bused from his or her own neighborhood to a strange, possibly hostile, school and neighborhood, may have additional problems.

Teachers must deal with all these reactions in the first days of school, although children could also be introduced to the class at other times of the year. New teachers find the first day more anxiety-provoking than do experienced teachers who are firmly entrenched in a familiar situation. But to all teachers, the sense of novelty and uncertainty about a new set of children and a new class continues to produce anxiety, possibly generating feelings in the teacher that closely parallel those of the children.

Many teachers find that the transition is eased for them as well as for the children if the school term begins with some form of staggered enrollment, with only a part of the group being at school at any one time during the first week. Starting the school year with a small group each day allows teachers to give each child additional attention. It also lessens each child's need to work each day in a large group of unfamiliar children. Teachers may have only one-third of the class attend each day. The three groups may alternate days of attendance at first, or the children may come cumulatively, with the second third joining the first third on the second day of class and the third group joining the whole on the third day. The former plan creates a situation in which no one child attends more days than any other child. But children who come to school on the first day and then are kept out for the next two may feel strange when they return.

Figure 7–1 Student Information Form

Name of child ______________________________ Sex ______________

Name used at home ________________________ Date of birth__________

Does your child have any health problems that need special attention in school?

____

____

Does your child suffer from allergies? (Please list) __________________________

____

Is your child toilet trained?	Yes _____	No _____
Is your child likely to have accidents?	Yes _____	No _____
Does your child need help in toileting?	Yes _____	No _____
Does your child need help in dressing?	Yes _____	No _____

Does your child have any needs which the teacher should be aware? (Please specify) ____

____

____

Has your child previously attended nursery school? _______________________

Has your child had experience away from parents? ________________________

Have there been separation problems? (Describe) __________________________

____

____

Does your child have any favorite activities? (Describe) ____________________

____

____

Are there discipline problems at home? (Describe) _________________________

____

What methods of behavior control are used at home? _____________________

____

Problems of induction are lessened in a nongraded setting. With only a part of the class beginning school or joining the class each year, most children are already familiar with the teacher, room, and school and do not require a formal introduction. The more experienced children can help orient the younger and newer ones, thus simplifying matters for the teacher.

Children do not naturally know how to behave in school, nor do they enter school aware of the rules and regulations. While some parents make a conscious effort to help their children realistically and positively anticipate the beginning of school, others do not. Teachers must make a conscious effort to acquaint children with unfamiliar routines and procedures and to teach them appropriate behavior. Going through a typical schedule, perhaps in simplified form, is helpful during these first days. At each transition and before each set of new routines, teachers can talk to the children and tell them what to anticipate next, demonstrating such routines as cleaning up after a work period or getting ready for dismissal. Teachers may need to repeat these demonstrations until the children master routines and feel comfortable. Keeping a degree of consistency in the schedule helps children learn a routine and adds a degree of predictability to the school day. Once established, routine is a base from which to operate rather than a system to be slavishly followed.

In addition to being aware of the children's reactions to the new school situation, teachers must be sensitive to parents' reactions. Some parents wish to leave their child immediately, thus freeing themselves for independent pursuits. Some feel guilt at the sense of freedom and relief they may be experiencing. Others react hesitantly to "giving up" their child. At times, parents may feel that their child's entry into school is a sign of their own aging, a hard realization for many in our society to face. Thus, teachers should not forget the parents in these early days. In some schools, the parents are expected to leave their children outside the door on the first day and immediately depart. In other schools, parents bring the new children to school the first day and stay with them if possible. Children need not feel that they have been abandoned or that school is entirely separate from home, for parents can provide a transition. The teacher may begin separation by having parents leave for a short period for a cup of coffee. Usually children can be weaned from their parents relatively quickly.

Beginning School: Primary Grades

Primary-grade teachers may not have to deal with problems of separation. Generally, primary children have been to school before and have some idea of what to expect; however, they may have many concerns similar to those of preprimary children. As early as possible, teachers should establish classroom routines and organize school life, posting a daily schedule and adhering to it as much as possible. They should also introduce the procedures of group life. Ways of getting the teacher's attention, using materials in the classroom, gaining access to the bathroom, and moving to the outdoor area, lunchroom, or other places in the school should be presented, explained, discussed, and practiced. In addition, children need to learn what resources are available and how they can be used. Even though children may have been in school before, each teacher has some different routines. If operating procedures are clearly communicated to the children, there is a greater chance that the children will follow them.

In addition to acquainting children with school procedure, teachers must get to know them and establish positive relations with each one. Teachers should also become familiar with the children's records, which describe academic progress and other aspects of school experience. The entries in these vital records must be interpreted, for not all teachers have the same expectations of children or the same interpretations of their behavior. Being aware of the expectations of the child's former teacher can allow better use of records.

Academic work can be assessed in a variety of ways. Teachers probably should give informal inventories or tests in reading and mathematics. Children may also do some writing in class so that teachers can ascertain their writing skill and ability to communicate. Group discussions and short conferences allow teachers to make judgments about the children's oral language abilities and to gather information about their social abilities, interests in school, abilities to handle conflict and deal with frustration, and many other important things. A number of formal and informal evaluation techniques are discussed in Chapter 9. These early assessments should be only tentative judgments, for children change as they become familiar with new people and new surroundings. It would be unfortunate to create expectations based only upon information gathered in the first few days of school.

Just as the teacher is testing the children in the first few days, children also test the teacher. Teachers and children participate in a series of interactions that allow them to establish balanced relationships that may last for the entire school year. Each child finds his or her place in the classroom social structure, establishing and identifying a set of personal relationships with the other children and the teacher. Although friendships and animosities may be carried over from earlier years, the fact that most children are in a new class with a new teacher means that a fresh set of balances must be created each fall.

Organizing the Children

Teachers can organize the classroom to reflect the children's interests and work needs. Children need places to call their own. Nursery and kindergarten children usually have a cubby or locker, ostensibly to keep their wraps, but also to provide a private place since they have no assigned work space. Primary children may be assigned lockers or have only a hook for clothes. In most primary classes, each child has a desk at which to spend most of the day and work. In an activity-oriented program, individual desks may be eliminated, and children may work in many areas, moving around the room as needed. Though personal desks are unnecessary, every child needs a place for personal treasures: a drawer in a cabinet, part of a shelf, or even a plastic stacking vegetable bin.

Children need to assume responsibility both for their own space and for the rest of the room, seeing that things are neat and uncluttered. Early in the year, teachers should try to instill a sense of responsibility in the children. Every time they use an area or a piece of equipment, they should clean up the area and replace the equipment so that others may find and use it.

Rooms should be properly designed to enable children to operate independently in this fashion. Equipment and materials should have designated places; shelves should be clearly labeled with the names of the things that belong there. If children cannot read, teachers can substitute pictures or symbols on these labels. Shelves should be uncluttered, and there should not be too much equipment in the room.

Crayons and pencils can be placed in open-topped boxes, paper stacked in neat piles, small jars of paste put on shelves, and small objects like beads or pegs stored in covered containers. There should be racks for drying paintings and a place where clay work can dry undisturbed until it is ready for firing, painting, or taking home.

Finally, teachers must make sure that the children know how to use and care for the materials. Children may pick up proper habits from the teacher or peers, but unless a conscious effort is made to teach them, they may never learn some of the skills that lead to individual responsibility.

Children can also assume responsibilities for general care of the room. Every child need not be responsible for every part of the cleanup chore—the group can share responsibility. Sharing, they can set tables and clean up after lunch and snacks, prepare a room for rest, clean scraps of paper from the floor, and care for animals, fish, or plants. Teachers may assign these tasks on a rotating basis, possibly by setting up a work chart (Figure 7-2) and changing jobs weekly. Children enjoy this kind of work, since it allows them to show their developing competencies.

Preparing for Special Activities

While classroom routines are important, teachers and children should feel free to depart from routines when appropriate. Teachers can prepare children for occasions on which the class departs from routine, such as a special visitor, a pet in the class, the extension of an activity that takes a long time, or a field trip. Preparing the children requires involving them in planning for special activities.

Figure 7–2 Work Chart

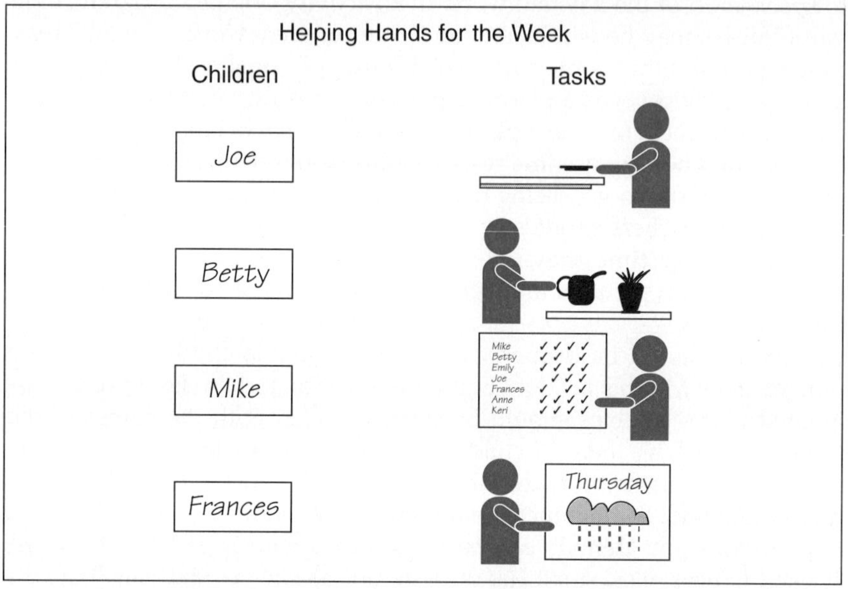

Most teachers believe in pupil-teacher planning. There are decisions that young children can legitimately make. Whether the arithmetic lesson will be held in the morning or the afternoon is not an important decision that should be shared with the children, since the consequences are minor, but children can make important decisions about the distribution of resources or preparation for special events.

The visit of a resource person might be such a special event. Though the teacher might make the arrangements and extend the original invitation, the children can be involved in planning for the visit, writing letters of invitation, and extending their appreciation.

In planning with children, teachers should talk about the purposes of the visit and how the children can best use the resources the visitor will provide. If the visitor is coming to talk about an occupation, the children may wish to ask questions about responsibilities, equipment, and other aspects of the job. Asking appropriate questions requires that children have a basis for judging the value of questions, so they may need to do research and discuss their questions prior to the visitor's arrival.

If the visitor is to perform, the teacher may help the children plan an appropriate room arrangement. The children might also wish to invite pupils from another class to share the experience. This planning helps children begin to anticipate future contingencies and makes use of their ideas in providing adequately for future events. Children cannot always be involved in these plans, and when involved they may not always make major contributions, but the act of planning and thinking about the future is important.

Children can also contribute ideas to planning a field trip. Pupil-teacher planning includes helping children anticipate what will happen on the trip and how they will use it, for a trip is not a time-filling excursion, but a means for collecting primary source data to be used in school studies. If the children are to gain maximum benefit from the trip, they should be helped to focus on its significant aspects. Prior knowledge about what they will see is helpful, as is more general knowledge about the topic of the trip. They may do research on the topic by themselves, or the teacher may present information from books or films and filmstrips. Children can help to formulate questions that the field trip might answer.

What constitutes appropriate behavior on a field trip varies, for what is appropriate in one setting is not appropriate in another. Children walking through a business office or factory where people are working need to behave in quite a different way than they do in a park or a field. Similarly, traveling on a school bus requires different kinds of behavior than does walking through a city street or using public transportation systems. In setting codes of behavior, teachers should communicate to the children not only the limits of acceptable behavior, but the reasons for these limits. Within the limits, the children should be able to set their own behavior patterns.

DISCIPLINE

Establishing discipline in the classroom forces teachers to deal with a dilemma, which is reflected in a continuum. On the continuum from freedom to control, strict authority is at one end of the continuum and sheer indulgence at the other end. The strict control end presents a classroom that is highly restrictive, while the sheer indulgence end presents a class that is highly permissive (Osborn & Osborn, 1989). A good early childhood program allows children a high degree of freedom while maintaining a degree of teacher control. In order to provide freedom in the classroom without chaos, teachers must set up a guidance system that uses positive discipline strategies (Marion, 1990).

Setting rules for appropriate behavior is no different at school than it is at home. However, the rules for appropriate behavior in school are different from those found in most homes. There are more children in a class than will be found in a home. There is also a specific educational function that would make some behaviors unacceptable that would be acceptable in a home. Thus, children entering school for the first time are not sure what behavior is considered appropriate. In addition, very young children have often not yet learned to control their desires. If they want a toy they might take it, even though another child is using it. They may also react immediately and physically to being hurt or frustrated. An occasional tantrum by a nursery-age child is not necessarily a sign of emotional disturbance.

Children learn proper behavior in school settings gradually. Proper behavior should be a goal to be achieved through extended experience rather than an immediate expectation. Teachers should plan to teach proper behavior as they teach other skills.

The form of discipline used on a child influences what kind of person the child becomes. Teachers who continually set limits and tell children how to behave without explanation are teaching that proper behavior is rooted in the commands of authority. On the other hand, children who are given no limits may learn that inner desires alone determine proper behavior. Ultimately, we wish to develop autonomous individuals who realize that there are reasons for order and limits. We want them to become flexible in their behavior, responding to each situation differently. The development of disciplined behavior requires the use of intellectual abilities. Children must use their intellect to understand the social as well as the physical world and to realize that acceptable patterns of behavior have an understandable regularity and reason.

John Holt (1972) distinguishes among three different types of discipline. According to Holt, children encounter the discipline of nature—how things work—when they fix or build things, learn a skill, or play a musical instrument. They learn this discipline through feedback from reality. They learn the discipline of society—how adults behave in the cul-

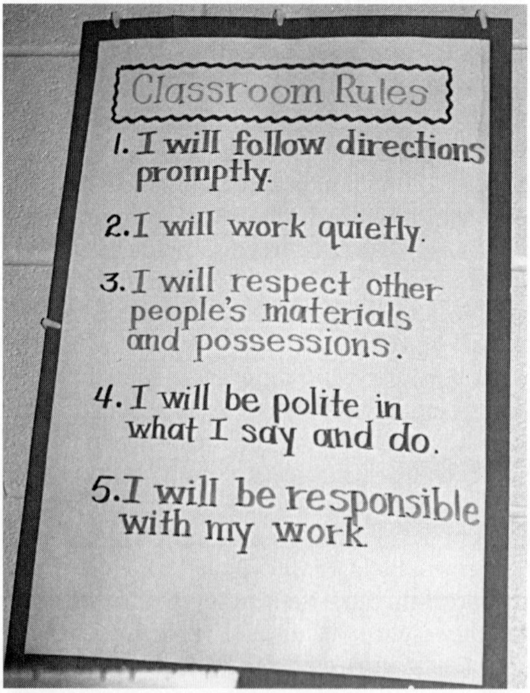

Posting class rules helps children know what is expected of them.

ture—through feedback in social settings. Adults impose the third type of discipline—coercion—to protect children from the unanticipated consequences of their actions. While some coercive discipline is necessary, coercion for its own sake is improper.

In developing an approach to discipline based on reason, teachers may follow several guidelines:

1. **Children should know what behaviors are expected of them.** Children's improper behavior may be a result of ignorance. Instructions will have to be repeated many times in many contexts before they are understood.
2. **Children need to be told why rules are in effect.** Even if they cannot fully understand, children should be given the reasons for rules. Most rules for school behavior are reasonable. Children can begin to see the reason for lining up at a slide or limiting the amount of time a child can ride on a bicycle. They can understand why they should behave differently in a crowded lunchroom than in their own classroom and why rules are promulgated for behaving certain ways in class, other ways in the hall, and still others on a school bus.
3. **Children should have opportunities to observe and practice proper behavior.** Children need demonstrations; they learn by imitating. They must also have opportunities to practice proper behavior, with feedback from the teacher.
4. **The behavior expected of children ought to be possible for them.** Children are not miniature adults and should not be expected to behave like adults. Teachers should develop reasonable expectations of child behavior. Young children, for example, cannot be expected to sit quietly or pay attention for long periods of time. As they mature, they develop longer attention spans and the ability to remain still for increasingly longer periods.
5. **Children cannot be expected to behave properly at all times.** Nobody is perfect, including adults. We do not expect adults always to be on their best behavior. The same is true for children. They should not be expected to conform to standards of model behavior at all times any more than adults should.
6. **Teachers should behave with consistency.** Teachers' behavior communicates a message to the children about what is acceptable and appropriate and what is not. If teachers vacillate or accept certain kinds of behaviors one time and reject or punish the same behaviors another time, they confuse children and blur their goals. Though teachers cannot always behave consistently, they should aim for this goal.

A number of distinct approaches have been suggested by educators and psychologists to improve children's behavior. These include behavior modification techniques, modeling techniques derived from social learning theory, psychodynamic approaches, redirecting children's activities, and an ecological approach. Sometimes a teacher can combine several of these approaches in a classroom.

Behavior Modification is a systematic approach to changing children's behavior using a system of reinforcements.

Behavior Modification

A number of psychologists have suggested systematic ways to modify the behavior of children, based on the application of behavioral theory. These techniques are proposed for all kinds of behavior problems, including academic as well as discipline problems. The overall strategy is that teachers first study the problem empirically and then, through the systematic application of reinforcers and punishment tied directly to the valued behavior, work on the problem until it is eliminated.

Charles and Clifford Masden (1974) have identified four steps in this process: pinpoint, record, consequate, and evaluate. To pinpoint is to identify the specific problem behavior and to define the goal of the intervention strategy in terms of observable behavior. The teacher should observe the conditions under which the problem behavior is occurring, and its frequency, and record these observations. Next, the teacher should develop a systematic program for controlling the target behavior by means of external reinforcers. To consequate, the teacher can offer a system of rewards contingent on the child's manifesting the target behavior. If the target is to reduce a negative behavior, manifestations of that behavior may be ignored, and alternative behaviors reinforced. Reinforcers can include social rewards, such as statements of approval or a pat on the back, or material rewards, such as food treats or toys. The opportunity to participate in valued activities can also become contingent on proper behavior. Sometimes tokens, to be exchanged later for rewards, are used as reinforcers. To evaluate, the teacher should allow the program to operate for a reasonable time to determine its success. If the child does not develop the desired behavior, the teacher should develop and try a new program.

For example, a teacher might use this program with a child who does not seem to be willing to clean up after activities. The teacher might observe that at each cleanup time the child takes a piece of equipment into a corner of the room and plays with it. The teacher might then decide to help the child clean up, giving an opportunity to play with a special toy on condition that the child help. If the child then does help, the teacher gives the child the toy. On occasions when the child does not help, the teacher might withhold all toys. After a while, the teacher tries to get the child to clean up with only an occasional offer of special toys, finally fading the use of the toys completely.

A large number of successful experiences with behavior modification have been reported in laboratory situations, homes, and classrooms. The technique, however, continues to be controversial. Some feel that the focus on behavior leads to a concern for symptoms rather than causes.

Others object to the use of rewards, equating it with bribery. Still others feel that this technique places the control of behavior outside the individual and does not help children learn to judge what is proper behavior, thus limiting autonomy. While advocates of this approach have countered these arguments, the controversy continues.

Modeling

Modeling techniques, based on social learning theory, involve learning by watching someone perform. This concept was discussed briefly earlier in this chapter. All of us learn some proper behaviors by watching and emulating others. When we are in a strange social situation, we may look to a person who seems socially accepted to get cues to proper behavior, and then emulate this person while trying to abstract rules for the situation.

Modeling can teach both behaviors we value and those we do not. Teachers should be careful not to inadvertently model behaviors they do not want children to emulate. By providing a model of good social behavior, teachers can get the entire class to behave in appropriate ways. The model should be someone who has status in the group, whether a child or the teacher, so that children wish to emulate that person's behavior. Providing cues for proper behavior is helpful to signal the behavior that should be modeled. Rewarding the target behavior in children will reinforce it and increase the probability of their maintaining it (Bandura, 1978).

As in behavior modification, the focus of this technique is on the behavior rather than on the reasons for behaving. Modeling manipulates children less, and, since the child ultimately decides whether to imitate the target behavior, allows for more autonomy than does behavior modification.

Psychodynamic Approaches

Psychodynamic approaches to discipline focus on the causes of behavior. Psychodynamic theorists often view behavior as a manifestation of developmental conflict or needs. Since conflict is seen as a necessary part of growth, neither conflict nor negative behavior is to be avoided. Instead, teachers should provide children with the means to work out these conflicts or manifest their feelings in socially acceptable ways. Sometimes catharsis is suggested: children are encouraged to show their feelings, channeling hostility into dramatic play or pounding clay or a punching bag. Serious problems might be handled by a therapist, but day-to-day conflict can be handled by a teacher at school. Teachers can also deal with behavior problems or developmental conflicts in indirect ways, modifying situations that might lead to conflict, for example, in anticipation of problems that might arise.

The human development curricula and affective curricula discussed in Chapter 15 attempt to help children deal with their feelings and become more sensitive in interpersonal relations. These programs are designed to improve classroom behavior by indirect means. To varying extents these programs are an application of psychodynamic theories.

The work of Rudolph Dreikurs has attracted its share of advocates in the field of early childhood education. Dreikurs (1968) considers that children misbehave for one of four reasons: to gain attention, to display power, to gain revenge, and to display a deficiency in order to seek special attention or to be exempted from some expectation. Dreikurs proposes that parents and teachers respond to children's misbehavior by using **logical consequences** rather than punishment. These consequences, which are set by the authority figure, are different from punishment in that logical consequences express the reality of the social order, are intrinsically related to the misbehavior, involve no moral judgment on the part of the implementor, and are concerned only with present occurrences (Dreikurs & Grey, 1968).

Logical consequences are consequences that children face as a result of misbehavior.

A logical consequence would be for a child to miss a valued activity because of dawdling or to clean up an area where the child deliberately created a mess. The key to these actions in changing behavior is that teachers realize the reasons for children's misbehavior and, rather than letting them achieve their goal, demonstrate why the behavior is both inappropriate for the situation and ineffective in achieving the desired result. The child is also told, if possible, why the particular consequence has been selected. The use of logical consequences might seem appropriate to what have been called social discipline situations; it is not suggested for dangerous physical situations.

Redirection

One traditional approach to young children's misbehavior, derived from teachers' experience rather than from theory, is redirection. The basic ploy is to take children's attention from difficult situations and focus on situations that provide immediate satisfactions. A child who is fighting with another over a fire truck, for example, might be steered to the woodworking area. To make redirection possible, teachers need to know which activities have high appeal for the children and to have alternatives available.

Although redirection may avoid conflict, conflict cannot be completely avoided, nor is conflict necessarily bad. Some situations will lead to conflict in any classroom: the opposition of individual needs or the clash of strong personalities. Teachers should help children develop acceptable means of dealing with conflict: compromise and use of verbal skills to negotiate problems, rather than use of physical coercion in influencing persons. Teachers continually have to step in to resolve conflicts among children. Unfortunately, they may have to use some forms of arbitrary coercion and even physical restraint; however, they should not use physical punishment. Ultimately, any system of discipline should move from the teacher controlling the child's behavior to the child becoming autonomous. The success of a teacher's discipline can be judged by the degree of autonomy found in the class.

Ecological Approach

An intriguing alternative to these approaches to discipline can be extrapolated from an article by Susan Swap (1974) dealing with emotionally disturbed children. Swap's thesis is that the disturbance resides not in the children, but in the interaction between the children and their environment. This argument seems related to Lilly's (1970) suggestion that educators focus on exceptional school situations rather than on exceptional children.

Swap says that many emotionally disturbed children misbehave because they are resolving conflicts associated with early development stages while most of their peers have successfully resolved these same developmental conflicts earlier. The resolution of these conflicts may be aided or thwarted by environmental conditions in the child's educational setting. Often, because the setting was designed for more emotionally mature children, the conflict is irritated by conflict with the environment. By understanding the child's conflict level and modifying the environment to help in conflict resolution, the teacher can effectively limit disturbances in the classroom. Elements in the school environment that can be modified include the physical setting, the educational requirements placed on the child, and the nature of teacher-child interactions.

We know that young children are confronted with rapid developmental change that can produce personal conflict. We also know that children develop unevenly; for instance, some children may be more mature in their language development than in motor development at a particular time. In addition, in any one class there will be children at many developmental levels. Teachers must become careful observers of children's behavior and skillful judges of developmental levels. Rather than attempting to modify the child to fit the setting, teachers can work to modify the setting to fit the child. By modifying academic requirements, creating varied space in the classroom, and using different kinds of educational materials and degrees of structure in the program, they can limit the number of conflicts between the child and the school setting.

Some children require formal structure; others do better in open settings. Some learn mathematics best with manipulative materials, but later those materials may hamper learning. Some children do best in large groups of peers, while others prefer seclusion. Some require challenge, while others need security. No one program or set of teacher behaviors best fits all children. A flexible teacher in a flexible environment can match the demands and requirements of the setting to the needs of the child, and thus lessen discipline problems.

The acceptance of individual differences in children requires that teachers become aware of each child's developmental level and the conditions that enhance or thwart learning, whether academic or social. From a behavioral point of view, they must set up events that lead to particular behaviors and use the natural reinforcers in the environment.

In addition to being aware of individual differences among children, teachers must be aware of the influences children have on each other's behavior, as well as of the sense of control they convey to students. Jacob Kounin's (1970) early studies of the "ripple effect" in classrooms demonstrated how teachers' ways of correcting a single child's behavior in class influences the behavior of other children in the room. This seems especially true with young children.

Kounin also found that a teacher's awareness of classroom processes is communicated to children and contributes to the effectiveness of classroom management. Teachers with "eyes in the backs of their heads," those who are able to attend to many activities at once and who are aware of the many things happening in a class, seem most effective in managing group activities. Similarly, alert teachers manage the flow of classroom activities, pacing them to maintain momentum and watching for the need for transitions (Kounin, 1970).

By managing the flow of activities and matching environmental conditions to each child's developmental level, teachers can improve educational conditions for all children. Thus, a classroom's organization for instruction, discussed in Chapter 6, is a major tool for improving classroom discipline.

Other Approaches

Other approaches to discipline can also be found in schools. The *Glasser Model* has been popular in some schools. William Glasser (1969) views discipline as a problem of making choices. Good choices lead to good behavior, while bad choices lead to misbehavior. Teachers should help children make good choices, while accepting no excuses for bad choices, so that reasonable consequences always follow behavior. Classrooms must have rules for behavior that are enforced. Teachers can use classroom meetings to deal with problems children have with rules, identifying suitable alternatives to bad behavior and dealing with problems that arise.

Assertive discipline is a discipline process in which teachers use assertive response styles, set limits, and follow through.

Another approach found in schools is **assertive discipline.** This approach suggests that teachers should insist on proper behavior in students and should maintain adequate classroom discipline. Both teachers and children have rights in the classroom that are met when teachers clearly communicate expectations to children and follow up with appropriate but fair action when necessary. Lee and Marlene Canter (1976) suggest that teachers can incorporate the principles of assertive discipline in their teaching repertoire. They identify five steps teachers should take:

1. Teachers should recognize and remove roadblocks to assertive discipline.
2. Teachers should practice using assertive response styles.
3. Teachers should learn to set limits.
4. Teachers should learn to follow through on limits.
5. Teachers should implement a system of positive assertion.

A number of these approaches to discipline have elements in common. One important element is that classroom rules should be clear. Another is that teachers should be consistent in applying rules. In addition, teachers should provide consequences for behaviors. All of these elements require that the children sense that the teacher is the authority in the class, though the teacher should not behave in an authoritarian manner.

In the final analysis, classroom teachers must realize that learning "proper behavior" is as much a goal as is learning to read or to express oneself through art. Children are not born with a sense of what constitutes appropriate behavior; they must learn it. In addition, what might be good behavior in one setting is not necessarily good behavior in another. Parents might want their children to act in an assertive manner and tell their children to stand up for their rights. The teacher might consider these same children aggressive or even combative. Such differences might stem from differences in values and goals or from a distortion that arises when children place too much stress on a parent's goal. Other children might be lacking in social skills and find that socially inappropriate behavior is the only means available to gain the attention of other children or adults. Still other children may simply be unaware of the rules for appropriate behavior in school. Each of these situations requires a different response as well as a different approach to teaching appropriate behavior.

All children behave inappropriately at times. Teachers also find that they are not as effective with some children as with others. Too often, teachers feel that their ability to control a class at all times is crucial to their ability to teach, and that any failure in dealing with a child or a group means failure as a teacher. They need to realize that teachers are not infallible, and that they, like all other professionals, need help from others: other teachers, a principal, a school counselor, a psychologist, or a social worker. Teachers should use all these resources.

SUMMARY

The social development of children in their early years has significant consequences for years to come. In order to support young children's social development, teachers need to create a positive social climate in their classroom. They have to help children learn to function well within the limits of school expectations and to develop strong positive relationships with their peers. Most importantly, teachers need to be able to respond positively to children's behavior and help them learn to function appropriately in class.

REFERENCES

Bandura, A. (1971). Psychotherapy based on modeling principles. In A. Bergin & S. L. Garfield (Eds.), *Handbook of psychotherapy and behavior change* (pp. 653–708). New York: Wiley.

Brophy, J. E., & Good, T. L. (1986). Teacher behavior and student achievement. In M. C. Wittrock (Ed.), *Handbook of research on teaching* (3rd ed.) (pp. 328–375). New York: Macmillan.

Brophy, J. E., & Putnam, J. G. (1979). Classroom management in the elementary grades. In D. L. Duke (Ed.), *Classroom management.* 78th Yearbook of the National Society for Education, Part 2 (pp. 182–216). Chicago: University of Chicago Press.

Canter, L., & Canter, M. (1976). *Assertive discipline: A take-charge approach for today's educator.* Seal Beach, CA: Canter & Associates.

Clark, C., & Peterson, D. (1986). Teachers' thought processes. In M. C. Wittrock (Ed.), *Handbook of research on teaching* (3rd ed.) (pp. 255–296). New York: Macmillan.

Combs, A. W. (1965). *The professional education of teachers: A perceptual view of teacher preparation.* Boston: Allyn & Bacon.

Crouch, P. L. (1980). *Parent version of the social behavior assessment.* Unpublished rating scale. Ames, IA: Iowa State University.

Dreikurs, R. (1968). *Psychology in the classroom* (2nd ed.). New York: Harper & Row.

Dreikurs, R., & Grey, L. (1968). *Logical consequences: A handbook of discipline.* New York: Meredith Press.

Gecas, V., Colonico, J. M., & Thomas, D. L. (1974). The development of self-concept in the child: Mirror theory versus model theory. *Journal of Social Psychology, 92,* 466–482.

Glasser, W. (1969). *Schools without failure.* New York: Harper & Row.

Guralnick, M. J. (1981). Peer influences on development of communicative competence. In P. Strain (Ed.), *The utilization of peers as behavior change agents* (pp. 31-68). New York: Plenum.

Hartup, W. W. (1983). Peer relations. In P. H. Mussen (Ed.), *Handbook of child psychology.* Volume 4, *Socialization, personality, and social development* (pp. 103–196). New York: Wiley.

Holt, J. (1972). Discipline: The most perplexive subject of all. *Teacher, 90*(1), 54–56.

Hughes, J. N., & Sullivan, K. A. (1988). Outcome assessment in social skills training with children. *Journal of School Psychology, 26,* 167–183.

Jersild, A. T. (1965). Voice of the self. *NEA Journal, 54,* 23–25.

Karnes, M. B., & Lee, R. C. (1979). *Early childhood education: What research says to teachers.* Reston, VA: Council for Exceptional Children.

Kounin, J. (1970). *Discipline and group management in classrooms.* New York: Holt, Rinehart & Winston.

Kratochwill, T. R., & French, D. C. (1984). Social skills training for withdrawn children. *School Psychology Review, 13,* 331–338.

Ladd, G. W. (1981). Effectiveness of a social learning method for enhancing children's social interactions and peer acceptance. *Child Development, 52,* 171–178.

Ladd, G. W., & Coleman, C. C. (1993). Young children's peer relationships: Forms, features, and functions. In B. Spodek (Ed.), *Handbook of research on the education of young children* (pp. 57–66). New York: Macmillan.

Lilly, S. M. (1970). Special education: A tempest in a teapot. *Exceptional Children, 37,* 43–45.

Maccoby, E. E. (1980), *Social development, psychological growth and the parent-child relationship.* New York: Harcourt Brace Jovanovich.

Macmillan, D. L., Jones, R. L., & Meyers, C. E. (1976). Mainstreaming the mildly retarded: Some questions, cautions and guidelines. *Mental Retardation, 14,* 3–10.

Marion, M. (1990). *Guidance of young children.* Columbus, OH: Merrill.

Masden, C. H., Jr., & Masden, C. K. (1974). *Teaching/discipline: A positive approach for educa-*

tional development (2nd ed.). Boston: Allyn & Bacon.

McConnell, S. R. (1987). Entrapment effects and the generalization and maintenance of social skills training for elementary school students with behavioral disorders. *Behavioral Disorders, 12,* 252–263.

Mercer, J. (1979). *System of multicultural pluralistic assessment: Technical manual.* New York: Psychological Corporation.

Miller, L. C. (1977). *School behavior checklist manual.* Los Angeles: Western Psychological Services.

Murray, F. (1972). The acquisition of conservation through social interaction. *Developmental Psychology, 6,* 1–6.

Nelson, C. M. (1988). Social skills training for handicapped students. *Teaching Exceptional Children, 20*(4), 19–23.

Osborn, D. K., & Osborn, J. D. (1989). *Discipline and classroom management.* Athens, GA: Daye Press.

Perret-Clements, A. N. (1980). *Social interaction and cognitive development in children.* European Monographs in Social Psychology, No. 19. London: Academic Press.

Piaget, J. (1965). *The language and thought of the child.* London: Routledge and Kegan Paul.

Rosenshine, B., & Stevens, R. (1986). Teaching functions. In M. C. Wittrock (Ed.), *Handbook of research on teaching* (3rd ed.) (pp. 376–391). New York: Macmillan.

Rosenthal, R., & Jacobson, L. (1968). *Pygmalion in the classroom.* New York: Holt, Rinehart & Winston.

Rubenstein, J. L., & Howes, C. (1979). Caregiving and infant behavior in day care and in homes. *Developmental Psychology, 15,* 1–24.

Sabornie, E. J. (1985). Social mainstreaming of handicapped students: Facing an unpleasant reality. *Remedial and Special Education, 6*(2), 12–16.

Sainato, D. M., Maneady, L., & Shook, G. (1987). *The effects of a classroom manager role on the social status and social interaction patterns of withdrawn kindergarten students.* Unpublished manuscript, Pittsburgh: University of Pittsburgh.

Simpson, R. L. (1987). Social interactions of behaviorally disordered children and youth: Where are we and where do we need to go? *Behavioral Disorders, 12*(3), 292–299.

Spodek, B., & Saracho, O. N. (1994). *Dealing with individual differences in the early childhood classroom.* White Plains, NY: Longman.

Swap, S. M. (1974). Disturbing classroom behaviors: A developmental and ecological view. *Exceptional Children, 41,* 163–172.

Walberg, H. J. (1986). Syntheses of research on teaching. In M. C. Wittrock (Ed.), *Handbook of research on teaching* (3rd ed.) (pp. 214–229). New York: Macmillan.

Winkler, D. R. (1975). Educational achievement and school peer group composition. *Journal of Human Resources, 10,* 189–204.

8

Working with Parents

CHAPTER OVERVIEW

This chapter presents:

- Conceptions of parent participation
- The roles of parents in early childhood education
- Levels of parent participation
- Techniques for working with parents
- Family-centered early childhood education

INTRODUCTION

The close relationship between programs for young children and their parents reflects an understanding of the close bond between parents and their young children. Because parents have a greater impact on the life of their children than do any educational programs, educators have learned to use this relationship to extend their programs.

John Amos Comenius, Johann Heinrich Pestalozzi, and Friedrich Froebel all believed in the importance of the mother's role in the education of the young. As kindergartens were established in the United States, mothers' classes were instituted to carry out Froebel's philosophy. In some kindergartens, the mothers' clubs were concerned with teaching about child study and about the theory and practice of kindergarten education. In others a concern for "Americanizing" the child's family was also evident.

The importance early kindergarten educators placed on involving mothers in their children's education significantly affected American education. The National Congress of Mothers grew out of a convocation of women connected with these kindergarten mothers' classes in the 1890s. This group eventually became the National Congress of Parents and Teachers, an organization that is well known in school circles today.

Nursery schools were also viewed as an important influence in augmenting and improving parent-child relationships. Margaret and Rachel McMillan emphasized placing nursery schools close to children's homes, allowing parents to observe nursery school practices, and establishing a good working relationship between parents and teachers. The pioneers of nursery education hoped that the parents themselves would ultimately become responsible for the education of their young children in nursery schools.

As the nursery school was transplanted to the United States, this close relationship between family and school continued. One of the first nursery schools established in the United States was a parent cooperative started by a group of twelve faculty wives at the University of Chicago in 1916. These parents wanted to secure "social education for their children, parent education for themselves and a little free time for Red Cross work" (Taylor, 1981, p. 294). Nursery schools are still organized by groups of parents and concerned community members.

CONCEPTIONS OF PARENT PARTICIPATION

Relationships between schools and parents are as varied as the kinds of schools that exist and the populations they serve. Child care centers operate quite differently in their relationship to families than do parent-cooperative nursery schools. Similarly, the primary grades of an elementary public school support a different relationship between home and school than do private nursery schools. Each type of early childhood program and each particular school designs its own approach to parent participation, choosing which activities should be its focus.

Parent involvement should be viewed broadly as a range of alternatives. Judging what is appropriate is best left to the discretion of the parent. Peterson (1987) offers a functional definition of parent involvement:

> Parent involvement or participation denotes a process through which parents are brought into contact with (a) the staff that has responsibility for giving service to the . . . child (and parent) for purposes of educational intervention, and (b) activities involving the child, which are created to inform parents and to facilitate parent roles with their own child. Involvement implies a variety of alternative activities that vary from program to program. Differences in the options available are affected by the unique features of a program, the geographical setting, the population of children and parents to be served, and the resources available. (pp. 434–435)

Parent involvement covers a range of possible services and activities that can be categorized under four broad kinds of involvement:

1. Things that professionals do for parents or give to them: services, information, emotional support, or advice.

2. Things that parents do for the program or professional staff: fund raising, dissemination, advocacy, or information gathering.
3. Things that parents do with their child as an extension of the program: teaching and tutoring the child at home or at school.
4. Things that parents and staff do together, working on a common activity relating to the program: planning, evaluating, working on joint projects; working together as trainer and trainee; discussing topics of common interest; or working as co-therapists with a child (Peterson, 1987).

These four broad types of parent involvement range from rather passive to very active roles for parents. Because parent needs vary so greatly, schools must judge which type of involvement is most desirable for their program.

The essential elements on which this involvement process should be built include:

- flexibility to allow changing levels and types of parent involvement over time;
- individualization to match the style and amount of involvement to meet parent, child, family, and program needs; and
- options to offer parents choices and the right of choice, in order to achieve constructive and meaningful outcomes.

Activities for parents should focus generally on one or more of the following goals:

1. **Personal contact and interaction** provide a means for achieving communication between parents and staff, among parents, and between parents and the ongoing service activities.
2. **Information sharing and exchange** provide a means for ongoing interaction and sharing as a vehicle for building staff-parent rapport, camaraderie, and a sense of mutual understanding.
3. **Social-emotional-personal support** builds a system of mutual cooperation between staff and parents, as well as among parents, and creates a support system parents can turn to for encouragement, understanding, counseling, and simple friendship.
4. **Coordination** creates a means for staff and parents to work hand-in-hand toward the same goals so that continuity is maintained between parents and staff in education and training of the young child. Coordination increases the chances of effective teamwork and reduces the risk that parents and staff will end up working against each other.
5. **Assistance** to parents provides a range of services that will facilitate parents in their roles, provide direct services to children, and aid families in ways that strengthen the overall family system.
6. **Education and training** provide information, specific training, or both, to parents to help them (1) gain an understanding of their

child and (2) acquire skills that will enable them to manage their child at home, provide appropriate care and support, and be effective teachers of their own child.

In developing a parent involvement program, teachers must be able to assume that they have the support of their school and its administration and that there are other persons in the school who are willing and able to help. They must also assume both that they have or can develop the skills necessary to carry out the program and that the parents for whom the program is designed are able and willing to become involved and to learn from their involvement.

Recently, concerns about parent programs have shifted from viewing parents as clients of educational institutions to viewing them as policy makers. The concern for community control of schools and parents' demands to have a voice in making educational policy at all levels must be understood as an extension of parents' responsibility for the education of their children.

The involvement of parents in the education of their children has educational and moral, as well as legal, justification. As children are primarily the responsibility of their parents, parents should be involved in determining educational decisions. Parental involvement is critical to the success of any educational program, and especially for programs designed for children with special educational needs (Brofenbrenner, 1974). When parents enter into partnership with the school, work with children can go beyond the classroom. Learning at school and at home can become supportive of each other.

Teachers' views of the role of parents in the education of their children vary widely. Some teachers deny the importance of family background to the education of their children, excluding families from school life. Others view children as totally shaped by their parents, seeing the parents within the child. In between are teachers who believe that information on family backgrounds allows them to communicate with and educate children more effectively (Lightfoot, 1978). Most early childhood teachers believe that an understanding of a child's home background is necessary to understand the child and that some involvement of parents in the child's education is necessary. In addition, research shows that parents create nurturing environments and that parent education behaviors affect children's functioning. Schaefer (1985) and Swick (1987a, 1988) also found that effective parents participate in more involvement activities than do less confident parents. According to White (1988), parental attributes and behaviors are related to productive involvement patterns such as high nurturing behaviors, supportive language activities, clear and consistent discipline, supportive parental attitudes, skill in designing home learning, and resourcefulness in using community supports. Studies also show that parental involvement influences the quality of children's characteristics such as positive self-image, sense of optimism, and productive orientation to social relationships (Swick, 1987b) and gains in language, motor skills, concepts, and problem solving (Pittman, 1987; Schaefer, 1985; Swick, 1987b).

Parents' Rights

Parents in our culture ostensibly have the right to rear their children in any way they see fit. Actually, however, parents' rights are significantly abridged. No parents have the right to inflict physical or emotional harm on their children. Parents must send their children to school for a certain period or provide a reasonable alternative. This requirement grows as much from the cultural need to maintain the social order as from the personal needs of children and their parents.

Thus, the "ownership" of children by parents is far from unencumbered by our society. In many schools, however, teachers feel that their right to determine what experiences to provide is inviolable. It is a "right" delegated to them by society by virtue of their special knowledge and preparation. Only recently have the rights of children begun to be recognized. Child advocacy groups have been established to protect these rights from incursion by parents or social institutions.

One of the larger issues confronting education today is the extent to which parents' wishes and demands should also constitute a legitimate set of restraints on teachers' actions. Parents have traditionally been kept out of decision-making roles in school. Parents who came to school to meet with teachers were to be informed, listened to, placated, and counseled. Seldom did teachers see parents as a source of decision making about classroom procedures.

Work with parents of children with disabilities takes on added importance. Since the passage of Public Law 94-142, the Education for All Handicapped Children Act, parents of these children must give consent before their child can be evaluated. They have the right to examine all records regarding the placement of their child as well as the right to participate in and approve the development of their child's Individualized Educational Program. In addition, they have the right to a due process hearing in relation to any complaint they may have regarding the education of their child. The requirements of this law were extended to younger children through its amendment, PL 99-457.

Relations between Teachers and Parents

Conflict has often characterized the relationships between schools and families and communities, especially in poor or minority communities. This conflict may be viewed as a response to school as a vehicle of oppression or an expression of liberation and interaction (Lightfoot, 1978). Whatever the view, schools must look for ways to transcend whatever conflict exists or use it in the best interests of children.

Many parents believe that schools are failing to provide their children with an appropriate education. They use students' lack of achievement in the academic areas and high dropout rates to justify their beliefs. Unfortunately, this attitude is based in the reality that students' educational achievement in the United States seems to have declined. Comparisons within the United States and between the United States and other nations should be questioned, however. Many standardized test scores suffer from what has been called the "Lake Wobegon Effect"—most children's test scores are above average. In addition, test scores from different nations may not be evaluating the same types of populations in the same way.

Just as parents may have misconceptions about teachers and schools, so teachers may have misconceptions about parents and families. Teachers may underestimate parents' skills. They may also underestimate the various kinds of stress in parents' lives. Home and family life can be a source of stress. In addition, parents' stress can be caused by

1. **Number of hours worked.** The more hours parents work, the more they experience problems.
2. **Lack of job autonomy.** Parents who have no control over the scheduling of their working hours experience conflict in balancing their job and family responsibilities.
3. **Job demands.** Parents who have demanding and hectic jobs usually have more stress than do those with less demanding jobs.
4. **Relationship with supervisor.** The parents' relationship with their supervisors helps determine their well-being (Galinksy, 1988).

Galinsky (1988) suggests the following ways for teachers to work effectively with parents:

1. **Understand your own expectations.** When a conflict occurs in teachers' relationships with parents, teachers should ask themselves what they are expecting and if those expectations are realistic.
2. **Understand the parents' point of view.** When teachers do not understand a parent's behavior, they should ask themselves, "How would I feel if this were happening to me?"
3. **Understand parent development.** Like children, parents also grow and develop, and teachers must understand this growth.
4. **Consider your own attitudes.** Teachers need to assess their feelings toward parents and then consciously make attempts to reach out to the parents they find most difficult.
5. **Accept diversity.** Parents may differ from teachers because of their culture, among other things. Teachers must find ways to accept parents who are different from them.

6. **Get support.** Teachers must have someone to turn to during conflicts. They need to search for their own sources of support, such as teachers in their own or other programs.
7. **Set appropriate limits to your role.** Teachers need to identify their roles in working with parents such as offering
   - childrearing information and advice,
   - emotional support,
   - role modeling, and
   - most importantly, referrals.
8. **Think about the words you use.** Language indicates the message. Teachers must be sure they use the appropriate language to communicate the right message.
9. **Provide a different expertise.** Teachers need to build an affiliation that reinforces parents' expertise. For example, a teacher describes this tactic:

   > I tell the parent what I've noticed at school and say, "Let's discuss it together." I ask what works at home so that I could try it at school or vice versa. There's give and take to my relationships with parents. (Galinsky, 1988, p. 11)

The content of a parent-teacher relationship can vary greatly. Teachers should be sensitive to the needs of parents and provide a variety of programming possibilities. Teachers may be concerned with communicating pupil progress to parents, sharing information, jointly solving problems, organizing parent meetings, developing parent education programs, supervising classroom participation, and providing professional consultation to policy-making groups. Each element of a parent program requires different skills and techniques from the teacher. Although teachers are not prepared as parent counselors and often lack the preparation to be parent educators, their position allows them to serve parents in a unique way. Within the limitations of their skills and roles, teachers should accept the challenge in each area.

LEVELS OF PARENT PARTICIPATION

Major variations exist in patterns of **parent participation.** For example, some parents relate to the entire program, while others relate mostly to the staff. Some parents make considerable contributions to group discussions, and some parents readily welcome ideas and activities, while others remain passive during discussions (Powell, 1986).

Parent participation requires parents to be actively involved in the functioning of the school or class.

Parent participation in classroom activities is an integral part of cooperative nursery school and Head Start programs. Parents can be invited into classes to read stories to children, provide tutoring services, help with instructional groups, help with classroom routines, and serve as resource persons, using their special knowledge and skill to enrich the program. They can often participate as teaching assistants as well.

In any educational program, information must be shared among parents and teachers. Parents can learn about their child's program and individual progress. Parents can also gain information about principles of child growth and development and learn specific things they can do to help their child. Teachers, too, need to have information about the child's background and home behavior to improve their understanding of that child's school behavior. This information can be used to build a better educational program for each child.

A range of approaches is available to help improve parent-child interactions. Some programs are designed to teach parents systematic, structured ways of working with their children (e.g., Becker, 1974; Linde & Kopp, 1974); others are designed to help parents develop insight into why their children behave the way they do (e.g., Ginott, 1971; Gordon, 1970). Still others provide experiences to support optimal interactions between parents and children (Gordon, Guinagh, & Jester, 1972; Sparling & Lewis, 1979). Another approach to parent involvement relates to having parents engage in activities related to their child's program. They may participate in advisory groups, act as aides in the classroom, or become involved in making materials for the program.

There are definite benefits to be derived from increased parent involvement. Parents can provide a pool of talent, often untapped, for the class. Many parents have special skills or knowledge related to their employment, hobbies, or special backgrounds and interests. Parents can also supplement resources provided by the schools by donating materials such as wrapping paper, scraps of cloth, egg cartons, paper tubes, and

Parents can serve in many ways in an early childhood classroom.

other items found in the home. These can be used in a variety of classroom projects.

Parents can be aides and helpers in the classroom, either on a regular basis or for specific projects or excursions. More adults in the classroom means more individual attention for children. In the classroom parents can help with working on projects, cleaning up, observing, and tutoring children with special needs. Providing experiences with more and varied adults may help children who need to develop skills in interpersonal relations, which may be especially important to some children with disabilities.

Parents' involvement in the program should initiate their participation in decision making. In making decisions, they are able to request more information and suggestions about children in general and specifically about their own child from staff members.

After they have been active and productive for a period of time, some parents show that they have some difficulty with the program by such actions as suddenly isolating themselves or withdrawing from the program, complaining about trivial issues (for instance, that their child gets too much paint on his or her clothes). Parents may complain to the teacher or appear distant and hostile, while the school staff may become frustrated with parents who feel everything is wrong with the program. In order to help parents establish realistic expectations of themselves, their children, and program staff, teachers must continuously point out the children's strengths and the parents' skills.

Once parents know the program and feel good about it, they can become good public relations resources, providing information to the community at large about what is happening to children in school. They can also become effective advocates for the school program. In many cases parents have been directly responsible for altering policies and laws relating to children, especially children with disabilities, through their work with school boards, advisory councils, and state and federal legislatures (Lillie, 1974).

Careful supervision should be provided when parents participate in the classroom. Orientation meetings with participating parents can lessen possible confusion. Parents need to know about the daily schedule of activities and the rules and patterns of behavior expected of children in different areas of the classroom and the school. They also need to be told their specific responsibilities. The development of a parent manual containing this information is helpful if a number of parents work in the program.

Teachers should supervise parents who participate in the program, keeping track of their behavior and possibly making notes to be used in evaluative conferences later. Parents and teachers should periodically review the work that both have done. Teachers should give ample praise and support, as well as careful criticism and advice for improving practice. As parents continue their work with a teacher, their areas of responsibility and amount of freedom can often increase.

DEVELOPING TECHNIQUES FOR WORKING WITH PARENTS

Working with parents requires that teachers develop long-range plans, interview and guidance skills, and the ability to work with small and large groups. Teachers must also develop skills in evaluating and recording the results of encounters with parents.

Planning

Teachers must be clear about the purposes of parent contacts, know about resources, and be able to think through the consequences of parent activities. Most important is the need to match the parent activity to its specific purposes.

If teachers wish to refer a parent for help to a social agency, they must be able to communicate that need without being threatening. They should have available the names and addresses of social agencies and know how to apply to them. If teachers wish to enlist parents in helping with a child's behavior problem in class, they should have observational records of the child's behavior available.

Planning a parent program on a full-year basis allows teachers to create a balance of different kinds of parent contacts. Meetings can be scheduled so they don't interfere with school operations or family traditions. In addition, teachers can anticipate the needs of the parent programs and prepare for them. If conferences are to be held, examples of children's work or behavior records relating to school performance should be gathered.

In planning group meetings, teachers should think through the content of the program, make arrangements for needed speakers or films, and assign responsibility for specific tasks such as hosting or cleaning up to insure that the meeting runs smoothly.

Planning requires providing appropriate space. A large meeting may require a school auditorium or multipurpose room. A class mothers' meeting might be held in a classroom after school with some rearrangement of the furniture. A conference with individual parents is best held in a quiet place that is free of interruptions. A parents' work session, using woodwork tools or sewing machines, requires special facilities and adequate space. Just allocating space for a parent bulletin board or a display of books requires the teacher to plan.

Sharing Information

There are a variety of ways of sharing information with parents. No one form of sharing information about individual children is totally satisfactory in all ways. The more specific and descriptive a report, the more time it takes to complete. Teachers are often caught in a dilemma about which form to use. Compromises often need to be made. A combination of different types of individual reports may provide the best balance.

One part of evaluation is the report to parents of their child's progress in school. Report cards, letters, and individual conferences are discussed more fully in Chapter 9. In reporting, teachers should be sure that parents understand the goals of the program and the way their child's progress is being assessed. Avoiding negative reporting can be dangerous; parents should be informed regularly and frankly.

A *descriptive letter* is one way of sharing information with parents about their child. Letters can communicate the qualitative aspects of a child's work better than can report cards or checklists, since they can describe activities more fully. Such a letter can detail a child's learning style and pattern of interaction with other children, as well as the books the child has read or the materials the child has used. Descriptions of specific incidents can be included. To save time, some teachers duplicate a letter describing activities of the whole class and supplement this letter with a few paragraphs specific to each child.

Report cards and *individual letters* to parents share specific information with individuals. *Newsletters* can be used to share information of general interest to all parents. They can describe incidents and activities of the entire class that would be interesting to all parents.

A newsletter might be sent home at the end of each semester, each quarter, or each month. How often it is sent depends on how much time a teacher can devote to its production as well as on how much help is available. Newsletters can describe special events (such as a field trip or the visit of a resource person) as well as ongoing activities of special interest (such as a cooking experience in a nutrition unit). They can include articles highlighting a particular staff member, describing his or her academic background and professional experience as well as personal information related to family, hobbies, or travel. Short vignettes describing individual children's products or activities can also be included, with care being taken to mention each child at some time during the year. Notices of community or school activities, reports on articles or books that might be of interest to parents, information about community resources, and requests for materials or help for the classroom might round out the content of a newsletter (see the sample newsletter on the following two pages for examples of the kind of material than can be presented in a newsletter).

Reporting pupil progress is usually one-way communication, with teachers telling parents about their child's performance in face-to-face conferences or in writing. Parents and teachers both have information about the child that would be useful to exchange—information not necessarily related to pupil progress, such as the child's level of involvement in activities or the child's range of social interactions. Teachers often elicit useful information about children through the applications that many nursery schools and kindergartens require prior to admission. Data on children's health and developmental background are required in this form, an example of which is presented in Chapter 7.

HAPPI-LEARNING NURSERY SCHOOL NEWSLETTER

November 1993

SPECIAL NOTICES

Wednesday, December 12
Book Fair. Your child will be bringing home a list of books that he/she picked out. Money for the books will be due Friday.

Thursday, December 13
Parents Association Meeting in the Yellow Room at 7:30 PM. Refreshments will be served.

Thursday, December 20
Chaperones needed. We still need parents to chaperone the trip to the ***Howard Science Center.*** If you are interested, please notify Ms. De la Rosa or Ms. Vanmeter at (301) 474-2124.

QUOTABLE QUOTES

Whitney: Yo, Holmes, I'm talking to David.
Patrick: I'm sick as a dog.
Jenny: We went on a walk today. We were looking for signs of winter, but I only saw one **STOP** sign.

If you wish to share something your child said, write it down and send it to school with your child.

GOALS FOR THIS WEEK

1. Understand the nutrition pyramid
2. Know where foods come from
3. Develop a sense of independence
4. Cooperate (share and work together)
5. Classify and sort
6. Count and add
7. Nutrition

THIS WEEK

We are working on a theme of food. We shall be covering the Nutrition Pyramid, and other exciting topics. There are some things you can work on at home with your child:

1. Let your child help you prepare a meal or perhaps a simple dessert. Talk with your child about the ingredients and what happens when you mix them.
2. On a trip to the supermarket this week, point out the different kinds of foods you see. Group them according to the pyramid.
3. Let your child help you pack his/her lunch. Talk about nutrition, as well as responsibility.
4. Point out the different containers and wrappers that food producers use.
5. On Wednesday of this week, during circle time, we shall have sharing time to talk about students' favorite foods. If their favorite is nonperishable, send it to school with them.

As always, thanks for your continued support and for working with your child at home. Education is so much more effective when it is continuous.

IMPORTANT DATES

- There will be no school on Friday, December 7, because of a state conference of the Mid-State Association for the Education of Young Children (MSAEYC).
- The December staff development meeting is on Wednesday, December 12. On that day, the afternoon children will attend in the morning and the morning children will not attend at all. On that day, as on September 30, children will eat lunch at 11:30 AM followed by dismissal at 12:30 PM. No breakfast will be served that day.

OTHER ITEMS OF INTEREST

Campbell Soup Company is offering a special bonus for labels removed from their selected products and collected by December 20. Please save and send in the following:

1. The front of the label from canned foods: **Franco-American, V-8,** and **Prego.**
2. Proof of purchase seals from **Pepperidge Farm Products** (newly added to the list), **V-8** juice boxes, **Prego** frozen foods, and **Swanson** frozen foods.
3. Quality Pledge panel from **Mrs. Paul's** products.
4. Lids from **Vlasic** pickles.

We have a good start with 650 labels. Keep sending in front labels and proofs of purchase from **all Campbell food products.** We need at least 2,000 for a tape recorder, to be ordered the end of February.

Thank you.

◆ ◆ ◆ ◆ ◆ ◆ ◆ ◆ ◆ ◆ ◆ ◆ ◆

The **Parent Discussion Group** will meet on December 10 at 9:45 AM. Please try to attend. We think you will find this a very worthwhile experience. Looking ahead, plan for December activities in school.

◆ ◆ ◆ ◆ ◆ ◆ ◆ ◆ ◆ ◆ ◆ ◆ ◆

The third in a series of community awareness forums designed to answer your questions on future development issues will be held on Tuesday, December 11, at Bowie City Hall in the multipurpose room from 7:30 PM until 9:00 PM. The subject being discussed is: Recreation in Bowie—Reviews and Previews. For further information, call (301) 262-0920.

◆ ◆ ◆ ◆ ◆ ◆ ◆ ◆ ◆ ◆ ◆ ◆ ◆

◆ ◆ ◆ ◆ ◆ ◆ ◆ ◆ ◆ ◆ ◆ ◆ ◆

There will be a Family Play Day sponsored by Let's Play to Grow on Saturday, December 8, from 12:00 NOON until 4:00 PM at the Carter Grounds at 16th and Colorado Avenue N.W. in Washington, D.C. You should wear comfortable clothing and tennis shoes. Please RSVP by calling Mrs. Spodek, (202) 628-3630.

◆ ◆ ◆ ◆ ◆ ◆ ◆ ◆ ◆ ◆ ◆ ◆ ◆

It is school regulation that parents send a note to the school explaining why children have been absent. Please make every effort to keep the school informed of absences.

◆ ◆ ◆ ◆ ◆ ◆ ◆ ◆ ◆ ◆ ◆ ◆ ◆

Please label your child's coats and hats with his or her name. There have been instances when these items have become mixed up on the buses.

◆ ◆ ◆ ◆ ◆ ◆ ◆ ◆ ◆ ◆ ◆ ◆ ◆

SPEECH HINT

Talk to your child often about what you are doing, about what she or he is doing, about what you are pointing out to her or him. You can get your child's attention by

1. getting on his or her level,
2. getting close to him or her,
3. establishing eye contact,
4. using an enthusiastic tone of voice,
5. calling his or her name, and
6. using gestures as you talk.

Providing examples of children's work helps to focus a parent conference.

GUIDELINES FOR PARENT–TEACHER CONFERENCES

Prepare in advance.

Be familiar with all relevant information about the child and the family and collect representative samples of the child's work.

Prepare the parents.

Send a note to the parent with the announcement of and general information about the conference. Describe your goals for the conference and suggest things for parents to think about before the meeting. This preparation makes parents feel less apprehensive concerning the conference.

Create an appropriate conference setting.

Set the room environment so that parents feel comfortable. For example, providing a low table with adult-size furniture is better and more comfortable for the parents than is confronting a teacher sitting behind a desk. At the conference, teachers should try to

- make the parents feel relaxed, comfortable, and wanted;
- communicate with parents using their language rather than educational jargon;
- underscore the child's positive qualities; and
- give parents precise suggestions on how to help their child at home.

Follow up and follow through after the conference.

Immediately after the parents' departure, carefully record the conference, including the suggestions that were made and questions raised. Teachers should immediately follow up on any questions that need to be answered or any commitments they made to parents, such as making referrals to other sources; scheduling other conferences; making a telephone call, a home visit, or a written report; or writing an informal note to parents.

Provide an evaluation form.

Ask for suggestions about conference format and informal daily chats with parents. (Allen, 1990; Bjorklund & Burger, 1987)

Table 8–1

Parents' Progress Report

Developmental Objectives	Progress	Notes
Social-Emotional Areas: Growth in children's sense of autonomy, initiative, and confidence—characteristics that make children feel good about themselves and affect their ability to relate well to other children as well as to adults—is a vital task during the preschool years. Children also need to grow in their ability to cope with fears and frustration and to show persistence in completing tasks.		
Cognitive Areas: Developing children's thinking processes during the preschool years involves coming up with interesting ideas, pursuing problems and questions, putting ideas or objects into relationships, and expressing ideas in a variety of ways. Children learn through active interaction with their environment.		
Physical Area: Physical aspects of growth provide children with an awareness of their bodies in space, how their bodies move, and the effects of these movements on the environment. Children also need opportunities to build small- and large-muscle coordination.		

(Bjorklund & Burger, 1987)

Parent–Teacher Conferences Communication with parents is essential in an early childhood program. Parents need and want to know about their child from the school's perspective. Simultaneously, the school gains from the parents' input. It allows teachers to know more about their children and make more informed decisions. Parent-teacher conferences are an essential component of the communication process. The success of conferences provides a foundation for high-quality early childhood programs.

Individual conferences at the beginning of and during the school year allow parents and teachers to share information about children and ask specific questions relating to important areas of behavior. What is significant for one child may be irrelevant to the teacher's understanding of another child.

Teachers use conferences to report to parents on their child's progress. A report such as that presented in Table 8–1 could provide a good basis for a conference. Teachers can note children's progress in each of the developmental areas presented. They can also jot down brief notes in the left-hand column that would provide the basis for the conference.

A sharing conference is particularly useful if the teacher has problems with a child. The information provided by a parent may help explain the change in a child's behavior. Similarly, parents may elicit information from the teacher that will help them deal with the child at home. If the teacher and parent are both concerned primarily with the child's welfare, information-sharing conferences may provide the beginning of a mutually beneficial relationship. Such conferences can easily lead to joint problem-solving sessions.

Joint Problem-Solving Conferences In many families, children may have had few contacts with other children of the same age before they entered school. Sometimes the parents will have made few demands of their children or not had the opportunity to compare them with other children at a similar developmental stage. If, in addition, the family has had few contacts with a pediatrician, the parents may suddenly see problems or abnormalities that have existed but have not been evident to them.

The entrance into school, with its new demands on the child, may suddenly bring forth a series of behavior problems. Hearing losses, poor vision, or other problems may also appear as new pressures are placed upon the child. At times, a change in the family situation—divorce, the arrival of a new baby, or moving to a new community—may also cause problems. Sharing information, pooling ideas for dealing with the problems, and developing a consistent way of handling the child both at home and at school may go a long way in providing solutions to difficult problems. Teachers may play a crucial role in helping parents deal with these problems, for quite often teachers are the only professionals with whom parents have regular contact.

A PLAN FOR BETTER CONFERENCES

1. Be open-minded (don't assume or leap to conclusions) and be realistic.
2. Listen to parents.
3. Show your concern! Express your delight!
4. Be prepared with accessible, factual records (tests, sample papers, written anecdotes, and so on).
5. Discuss reasonable expectations.
6. Define the problem (if there is one).
7. Agree on a plan of action that involves everyone. "How can we best meet the needs of this child?"
8. Follow up on the plan. When? Where? How?
9. If you're informing parents of test scores, remember to tell them that tests are only one aspect of the educational picture. Tests compare one child's progress with that of other children of the same age and/or grade. Emotional growth, attitudes toward learning, motivation, peer relationships, special talents, and self-image are also important. Show parents copies of the test(s).
10. Remember to use your resource people (if you need them).
11. Let the student in on the positive points, the negative points, and the game plan.

Teachers are not psychologists, social workers, or guidance counselors; they are child development specialists in only the broadest sense. Yet teachers must find ways to help parents become aware of problems and deal with them. Sometimes a friendly conversation over a cup of coffee will suffice; at other times a series of conferences leading to referral to an appropriate agency may be necessary. Teachers must be careful not to overstep the bounds of the educator's role. Often they should refer a problem to someone better qualified. Teachers should become familiar with the agencies that serve children and their families in the community and with the procedures used to seek the help of each agency. Many schools have ancillary personnel—guidance workers or family coordinators—who can help parents and teachers deal with problems.

Although referral is a significant contribution teachers can make, the importance of the personal support they can provide should not be underestimated.

Interviewing Interviews with parents allow teachers to both gather and offer information. Teachers should put parents at ease in a conference, providing coffee or speaking first about general school matters to establish rapport. They should not spend too much time in preliminaries, however.

Teachers often use an interview outline to make sure they elicit the information they want and cover all points in a conference. Such an outline should be used flexibly to insure that the purposes of the conference are met.

Teachers must learn how to listen to parents, being sensitive to their feelings as well as to the information they communicate. Teachers should listen responsively, reacting to messages when appropriate and helping parents work toward realistic solutions of problems regarding their children.

Although it is sometimes easy to give advice, a teacher's counsel must be particularly meaningful and relevant to each specific situation. If a child should be read to at home, the teacher should help the parents find the sources of books or make books available. The teacher should also help them learn some of the reading techniques that will eventually benefit the child.

Home Visits A home visit has many advantages. A conference in the home may allow parents to talk more freely than at school. In addition, teachers can learn about the home environment and so perhaps understand the child better. Home visits may also be more convenient for parents who are not able to come to the classroom during school hours.

If a home visit is to be effective, the parents should feel that they are inviting the teacher into their home. Forcing a visit on an unwilling family may cause hostility. The teacher might propose a number of dates and times so the visit can take place at a mutually convenient time. A teacher who visits the home without warning is acting unfairly. Such an action can destroy the hope of establishing a working relationship.

The purpose of a home visit is similar to that of a conference: sharing information and working on problems. Teachers should be careful to achieve these purposes while establishing friendly social relations.

Informal Contacts There are many opportunities for informal contacts with parents: the child's arrival or departure from school, the meetings of the parents' association, and the invitation to a parent to accompany the class on a field trip. Teachers should convey a feeling of friendliness and mutual concern for the children in these sessions. Holding parents at a distance or talking down to them can destroy the relationship that the rest of the parent program is attempting to build.

These occasions also allow teachers to hold mini-conferences—short informal sessions in which minor problems can be dealt with or information elicited easily. Teachers should encourage these exchanges, while being careful not to become too involved with the parents when they need to be working with children.

Parent Meetings

Often teachers must deal with parents in groups rather than individually. Teachers may be called on to plan and direct parent meetings or be seen as a resource person for meetings parents themselves plan and execute.

The first contact between parents and teachers is often the orientation meeting that takes place before the children enter school. This meeting provides an opportunity to communicate about what school will be like for parents and for their children. If parents have never had a child in school before, this type of information is important. Such a meeting may also be used to provide parents with information about the school's expectations of them and their children.

Teachers should be careful to communicate the fact that the school is a friendly place that welcomes parents as well as children (assuming that this is true). Teachers should allow time for informal chatter and opportunities for parents to become acquainted with each other. If information is printed in a simple brochure or leaflet, more of the meeting time can be devoted to establishing relationships and less to lecturing. It is a waste of meeting time to read materials to parents that they could easily read themselves.

During the school year, teachers may want to call other meetings to talk about the program, show some of the children's work, and answer parents' questions about what their children are doing. Because such meetings deal directly with their children, parents are usually happy to attend them. Care must be taken to schedule meetings at times when most parents can attend. Teachers may need to provide an informal babysitting arrangement or to allow the children to come to the meetings in order to insure attendance.

Most schools have a formal parent or parent-teacher association that attempts to organize all the parents in the school. It plans regular meetings and social events throughout the school year. Though the responsibility for such meetings is often in the hands of the parent officers, teachers may be asked to speak at meetings or to act as resource persons.

Teachers' attendance at these meetings is important in building close ties with families. A brief word to a parent on such an occasion can frequently do more to establish good relationships than can a lengthy conference.

Parent Education Programs

The importance of parent involvement in the education of young children has been underscored in the many research and development programs designed since the 1960s for children of poor and minority group backgrounds. The Head Start and Follow Through programs that resulted from this work, as well as other federally funded programs, have mandated parent involvement as an integral element. This involvement often takes the form of parent education, in which parents are helped to deepen their understanding of child development and to develop new skills for educating and rearing their children. Parents also help in classrooms, and they have been brought into the decision-making process through parent advisory boards and other mechanisms that give parents a voice in determining their children's educational programs and in selecting staff.

Many schools provide formal or informal parent education programs varying from highly organized courses that teach about child growth and development, childrearing practices, and homemaking skills, to informal club activities whose content is determined by the parents themselves. Still other programs may focus on group process and parent interaction rather than on any substantive content. Recently, there has been a striking increase in the number of programs that attempt to help parents handle the responsibility of their childrearing tasks efficiently. Program techniques vary from discussion groups to drop-in centers to home-based interventions (Powell, 1986).

Honig (1982) has suggested a Parents' "Bill of Rights" that could provide the basis for parent education programs. These include the right to

- knowledge about child development—both emotional and cognitive;
- observation skills for more effective parenting;
- alternative strategies for problem prevention and discipline;
- knowledge about how to use a home for learning experiences for children;
- language tools and story-reading skills; and
- awareness of being the most important early childhood teachers of their children (p. 427).

Some parent-cooperative nursery schools require that parents enroll in a parent education program as a prerequisite for the child's enrollment. Nursery schools in settlement houses, at-risk prekindergartens, parent-child centers, and Head Start programs often include a strong parent edu-

ALTERNATIVE PARENT PROGRAMS

Program A seeks to	Program B seeks to
1. Highlight family and community	1. Instruct parents on ways to inspire their children's cognitive development
2. Prescribe specific skills and styles relating to children	2. Help parents determine what is best for them
3. Disseminate child development information to parents	3. Foster supportive relationships among program participants
4. Provide a great deal of structure	4. Allow parents to select activities they wish to pursue.
5. Present staff as child development experts	5. Adhere to a self-help model with staff in nondirective facilitator roles

cation component in their program. Sometimes parents will spend many hours in classes. A parent library can be a strong addition to a program.

The parent education and support programs vary in each early childhood program. For example, Powell (1986) contrasts these programs. His contrast appears in the box on this page. Differences also exist in the roles of professionals, assistants, or volunteers; length of program (weeks versus years); and setting (center- versus home-based).

Many parent education programs teach specific parental skills that will support children's intellectual and language learning in the school. A program may portray model parental behavior, such as including children in discussions, conveying to them the meanings of parental action, reading simple stories aloud, and providing instructional activities and material in the home. The specific techniques are often taught directly to parents, who then practice them under supervision. Sometimes kits of materials are lent to parents to use with children at home. Working with babies may be stressed as much as is working with preschoolers; ultimately all the children in a family will be affected by what the parent learns.

Many parent education programs are based in homes rather than in schools, with parent educators working directly in the homes of their clients. These programs usually make provision for pretraining and orientation of parent educators as well as for orientation of parents. The educators generally provide specific guidance to parents and often demonstrate activities with the child as the parents observe. Programs for low-income parents often rely heavily on paraprofessionals as trainers, while programs for parents of children with disabilities may use primarily professionals. Parent educators are generally responsible for evaluating the children's progress and often consult in regard to activities for the children (Levitt & Cohen, 1976). In addition to these common elements, many differences exist among parent education programs that parallel the differences in approach to the education of young children discussed in Chapter 3.

Parent Support Systems

Social support for parents is important in linking home and school. A social network refers to an individual's circle of intimate peers, or that group of friends, family, or workmates who are meaningful to the individual (Hall & Wellman, 1985). Network support varies directly with network size; larger networks are more supportive (Hall & Wellman, 1985; Vaux, 1988). Network density affects how well the individual is able to use the network's support; usually more dense, or close-knit, networks, as compared to less dense networks, are more effective (Gottlieb & Pancer, 1988). Less homogeneous networks facilitate complex problem-solving tasks such as job searches (Granovetter, 1974).

The relationships between types of social support and parenting behavior suggests that emotional support promotes parents' ability to be accessible and responsive to their children, regardless of their current life situation. When parents are confronted by stress (for instance, the transition to parenthood, a developmentally at-risk child, or a temperamentally difficult infant), informational support directly related to that specific stressor can promote performance, coping, and problem solving (Stevens, 1991).

Social support systems influence parenting behavior through exchanges of informational support, emotional support, and perhaps tangible aid or assistance. Network members influence the childrearing beliefs and strategies of parents through modeling, reinforcement, and direct teaching. These mechanisms influence the parenting behavior of young parents (Stevens, 1988; Stevens and Bakeman; 1990). In modeling, which may or may not be deliberate, one caregiver shows the other ways to work with the infant. Reinforcement provides praise, which may or may not be verbal, or some reward, such a food, a trip, or an activity. In direct teaching, one caregiver tells the other about something, pointing out a behavior, an event, or a phenomenon and telling the other about its significance.

Coaching, interpreting, and evaluating are three other strategies individuals use to teach others (Stevens, 1991). Coaching is direct and may be intrusive, but usually communicates about adult's behavior, urging another adult to do something or to behave in a certain way. Interpreting is usually indirect, often less intrusive but no less instructive, and usually comments on the child's behavior. Evaluating is also indirect, but usually comments on an element of the physical atmosphere, rather than on either the adult's or the child's behavior. All of these strategies can transmit knowledge about children and about parenting.

Family-Centered Early Childhood Programs

Recently, family support programs and family-centered early childhood programs have emerged, in which the primary clients are adults and parents of young children (Kagan, Powell, Weissbourd, & Zigler, 1987; Galinsky & Weissbourd, 1992). These community-based programs educate and support parents in their role as socializers and caregivers. These programs empower parents and promote their interdependence, rather than increasing their helplessness and dependence (Weissbourd & Kagan, 1989), through parent education and support groups, home visitation, drop-in services, hotlines and warmlines (where response is not immediate), information and referral, lending libraries, health and nutrition services, and child care when parents participate at the center. Family support programs have become an important component in state-supported early childhood programs in Minnesota, Missouri, South Carolina, Kentucky, Maryland, Connecticut, and Oklahoma (Weiss, 1990).

Weissbourd and Kagan (1989) note that four principles underlie service delivery in these programs:

1. The long-range goal of programs is prevention instead of treatment.
2. The family, including parents and children, is the primary client.
3. Service delivery considers each parent's developmental characteristics.
4. Social support is considered a universal benefit to individuals, particularly during life transitions, such as transition to parenthood, child's transition into school, transition for the new parent back to the world of work.

Family Fair

One approach to promoting mutual knowledge and communication is the Family Fair, which includes a variety of formats such as large-group presentations and small workshop centers (Kerr & Darling, 1988). Special large-group presentations are scheduled to offer parents information on topics of specific interest to them. Topics may vary from coping with family stress, improving family communication, and fostering successful school experiences to providing activities for children outside of school.

The core of the Family Fair is exhibits and activities based on the families' interests. A variety of centers allows families to chose activities they want to participate in. Including several family members in the centers can reinforce the families' attendance and involvement. Parents and grandparents can engage in clogging or square dancing, quilting, crocheting, or wood carving. They can assist in the management of the centers to provide an essential communication bond with other families. The centers can also exhibit the children's achievements in relation to each center's themes.

Family Fair workshop centers can integrate a variety of interest areas, offering activities, demonstrations, and information of interest to parents and children. The emphasis in the use of these centers would be on family enjoyment, togetherness, and education. Each center will offer the families suggestions and ideas for activities that can be conducted at home to facilitate family closeness. The number of centers used depends on the size of the building and the available resources. The following are some alternatives:

- The *Family Recreation Center* offers families the chance to enjoy equipment such as balls of different sizes and purposes, jumpropes, tumbling mats, walking boards, hula hoops, bean bags, a parachute, and an obstacle course.
- The *Reading Center* includes a selection of books and magazines suitable for different age levels. Examples of books, stories, and poems written by area children could be exhibited. A librarian may have several storytelling sessions that absorb the listeners in a hands-on experience.
- The *Toy Factory Center* can provide families a chance to construct toys together, including puppets or kites. Examples of toys would be on display and materials for making the toys would be provided.
- The *Family Support Service Center* could offer opportunities for local organizations to communicate their purposes and services as they relate to the families:
  (1) The Red Cross could display information on programs for family members and illustrate basic first-aid procedures such as mouth-to-mouth resuscitation, minor burn care, and the Heimlich maneuver.
  (2) The community mental health agency and the YMCA could talk and exhibit materials about their family services and programs.
  (3) The local drug and alcohol program could dispense and discuss information on its support and treatment opportunities and give presentations on the different forms of substance abuse.

Other types of centers can include a book fair, where inexpensive books are sold to parents; a center on nutrition for a healthy family; and a game room. Creative approaches can assist in making this method a distinctive experience for the whole family. Bergstrom and Burbon (1981) suggest using community-based learning centers in a variety of settings that support parents in the education of their children. Centers can be located in museums, libraries, local schools, or businesses. Possible options include lending libraries for books, toys, and games; work areas where parents make educational toys and games from recycled, inexpensive, easily available materials; information and referral services and workshops; courses; and lectures. In Melbourne, Sydney, Canberra, and Adelaide, Australia, Reverse Garbage Centers have been created. Individuals and organizations pay a small fee to become members and purchase a wide range of industrial and commercial waste to make toys, collages, mobiles, and many other constructions. Educators must promote integrative family education programs, since the home is the most dynamic learning center. Educators and interested groups must work together to strengthen and support lifelong programs in family living.

Parent Policy Boards

Parent advisory committees are established to have parents help policies for a program.

With the establishment of **parent advisory committees,** including those in Head Start programs and in community schools, the relationship between parents and teachers is changing in many communities. Parents and other community members are becoming more involved in important areas of decision making relating to school policy and classroom practice.

As this change comes about, teachers need to view their roles in relation to parents and community members in a somewhat different light and to develop both skills in working with parents and alternative perceptions of what constitutes a viable parent-teacher relationship.

Traditionally the boundary of power between teachers, parents, and community has been determined by the kinds of decisions that need to be made. Parent and/or community agents have been responsible for policy decisions, and teachers and administrators for decisions relating to policy implementation. These lines, however, are often blurred, for implementation can affect policies considerably, and policy decisions often require professional knowledge of probable consequences.

The most difficult part of teachers' relationship with parents may be in developing educational and administrative policy for schools. Sometimes teachers feel they are better prepared than are parents to make decisions, because they have a greater amount of specialized knowledge. In addition, teachers have a vested interest in the decisions made about school practices.

Both parents and teachers may come to board meetings with their own particular difficulties. Some parents may view teachers with distrust. Teachers, on the other hand, may have difficulty communicating with persons who do not share their personal and professional vocabulary.

Teachers' effectiveness with boards is based on mutual trust. This trust grows out of a series of encounters in which teachers demonstrate trust for the board; it is facilitated by a show of competence and a concern for children. Keeping lines of communication open, listening to parents, and keeping the sources of decisions public also help teachers gain trust.

Ultimately, the role of teachers is to help parents make decisions. Teachers should educate parents, seeing that they have appropriate information on which to base their decisions. Further, teachers must help parents anticipate the consequences of their decisions.

Working with Groups

Large groups are not as useful as small ones for discussions and interactions. Small-group sessions require the teacher to use group leadership techniques. As leaders, teachers convene groups and chair discussions, being sensitive to group needs and allowing members to become responsible for the group's actions. Teachers should not impose their will on a group nor allow the discussion to move too aimlessly for long periods of time. A teacher must become a democratic leader, responsive and flexible, while maintaining authority, to best use the group process.

Sometimes a hands-on approach is useful for working with parent groups. Engaging parents in workshop activities utilizes nonverbal as well as verbal forms of learning. Teachers can lead parents into activities parallel to the children's to help them understand the learning potential of the activities. "Open science" or "hands-on math" is often not well understood by parents unless they have experienced these forms of learning. Similarly, parents might consider play activities or craft activities useless unless they can realize that the outcomes of these activities are valuable learnings for their children. Sylvia Newman (1971) describes a set of workshops and auxiliary activities that she instituted in a school program to help parents understand its content and to develop ways of extending the children's school learning in the home.

Large-group meetings are practical for telling things to people. While the same speakers or films used for large groups can be used for small groups as well, often using a large-group meeting is more efficient.

A group convened by a teacher frequently develops its own independent life. Parents may undertake projects for the education of the group's members or as a service to the school. Changes in the nature of the group sometimes require more time than a teacher can possibly give; in this event, finding another leader may help, either from the group or from outside. The teacher may then continue working with the parent group as an advisor. Teachers can feel legitimate pride when groups they have started become autonomous as a result of their leadership.

The group process is a powerful force. Groups can be helpful and supportive, or aggressive and oppressive. Teachers should use the group process carefully, ever cautious of any limitations in their skills in working with groups.

Using Public Relations Techniques

Most ways of working with parents involve face-to-face relations, but other types of relationships with family and community should also be established. A good school should have a strong program of public relations. Because the school belongs to the parents and the community, it must communicate what happens in school. A good public relations program ensures that parents and others in the community feel welcome in the school. This program should go beyond the annual "Open School Week."

Displays help in telling the community what children are doing. Art work, the results of projects, or tapes of children's songs and stories can be tastefully organized and used to tell about children's school experiences.

Local merchants will often make space available and provide other kinds of support, and local news media can tell the school's story to the public. Field trips, holiday celebrations, and other special events are often considered newsworthy by local media.

Teachers can carry on their own public relations activities through newsletters, notes sent home, and invitations to parents to participate in special events.

While good public relations are important to a school, teachers should be careful that their parent programs do not become nothing but public relations programs. When parents are invited to school, where their opinions and advice as members of advisory committees and boards are solicited, they expect that their ideas will be considered worthy, that their contributions will be respected, and that they will be heard and responded to. At times, however, schools have established parent boards and advisory committees, often in order to meet requirements of state and federal programs, without making use of the products of these groups. Under these circumstances, parents may feel that, although they are involved in school activities, they are powerless. What seemed to them a program of parent involvement has become instead a program of public relations. Such programs of public relations, however, can be counterproductive and lead to frustration and even anger on the part of parents.

SUSTAINING PROGRAM INVOLVEMENT

It is important to find ways to sustain parent participation in education and support programs. Powell (1986) suggests that programs offering a variety of services are most effective. Fredericks (1988) offers the following suggestions to increase parents' participation in the classroom:

1. Let parents know that you are expecting the best year ever for their child.
2. Communicate your expectation of positive parental involvement throughout the year.
3. Make parents aware that you will be working *with* them to ensure the best academic achievement for their offspring.
4. Inform parents that this will be an exciting year filled with new discoveries and new possibilities—and that they have a very active role in those proceedings (p. 33).

WORKING WITH PARENTS: A TWO-WAY STREET

Communication and cooperation between parents and teachers must be a two-way street. Each shares information and learns from the other for the benefit of the children (Siperstein & Bak, 1988). Orville Brim (1965) has identified the primary goals of outstanding parent education programs: making the parents more conscious of their how they function, making them more autonomous and creative, improving their independent judgment, and increasing the rationality of their performance as parents. These goals are appropriate for early childhood education. Just as teachers wish children to become more autonomous, more creative, more aware, and more rational in their judgments and performance, they wish these things also for parents. The differences in developmental levels of adults and children require that these general goals be manifest in different ways and in relation to different social roles. To support parent autonomy, rationality, creativity, and competence, teachers must have a helping relationship with parents, rather than a prescribing one.

Too often teachers feel that a parent program is an opportunity to do something to parents to change them. In a good parent program, parents should also have an opportunity to influence teachers and possibly to change the school. A strong parent program can open new avenues of communication. When there is no information there can be little criticism; as parents become more knowledgeable about the school, they will offer more criticism—which one hopes will be largely constructive.

Actually, parents' judgments can be considered another source of information about the effectiveness of the program. Parent reactions should be considered along with other data in making school decisions, and teachers should also be receptive to parents' ideas and criticisms. Changes should not be instituted merely as a way of placating parents, however—teachers should feel strong enough in their professional role to be able to justify their acts in school and to stand by programs they believe to be sound professional practices.

Future Directions

The major task for those who plan parent programs in the future should be to make program content and structure correspond to the parents' needs and characteristics. In addition, the manner in which parents change must be understood. For example, teachers need to know how parents cope with information that conflicts with their own ideas about their child and about child development so that they can help parents to alter their beliefs and behaviors and reinforce their receptivity to innovative ideas.

Parent education and support programs are an increasingly prominent segment of the early childhood field and have been in American society's best interest. The increasing number of programs must be guided by an informed interest in and a committed search for the characteristics of quality programs (Powell, 1986).

Summary

Working with parents is an important part of education at any level. It is especially important, however, in working with children in their early years. Teachers need to develop an understanding of the parents of their children and of the family situation. They need to develop a variety of techniques to work with parents in ways that serve different purposes. Most importantly, they must understand that the education of young children cannot be considered in isolation. In order to be successful in working with children, teachers need the active cooperation of parents.

REFERENCES

Allen, P. (1990). Working with parents: Parent-teacher conferences. *Day Care and Early Education, 17*(4), 33–37.

Becker, W. C. (1974). *Parents are teachers.* Champaign, IL: Research Press.

Bergstrom, J., & Burbon, J. (1981). Parents as educators: Innovative options to involve educators, parents and the community. *Australian Journal of Early Childhood Education, 6*(1), 16–23.

Bjorklund, G., & Burger, C. (1987). Making conferences work for parents, teachers, and children. *Young Children, 42*(2), 26–31.

Brim, O. G., Jr. (1965). *Education for child rearing.* New York: Free Press.

Bronfenbrenner, U. (1974). *A report on longitudinal evaluations of preschool programs: Is early intervention effective?* Washington, DC: U.S. Department of Health, Education, and Welfare.

Fredericks, A. D. (1988). Parent talk: a most wonderful world. *Teaching K–8, 19*(1), 32–34.

Galinksy, E. (1988). Parents and teacher-caregivers: Sources of tension, sources of support. *Young Children, 43*(3), 4–12.

Galinsky, E., & Weissbourd, B. (1992). Family centered child care. In B. Spodek & O. N. Saracho (Eds.), *Issues in child care: Yearbook in early childhood education,* Vol. 3 (pp. 47–65). New York: Teachers College Press.

Ginott, H. (1971). *Between parent and child.* New York: Avon.

Gordon, I. J., Guinagh, B., & Jester, R. E. (1972). *Child learning through child play.* New York: St. Martin's Press.

Gordon, T. (1970). *Parent effectiveness training.* New York: Wyden.

Gottlieb, B. H., & Pancer, S. M. (1988). Social networks and the transition to parenthood. In G. Y. Michaels & W. Goldberg (Eds.), *The transition to parenthood: Current theory and research* (pp. 235–269). Cambridge: Cambridge University Press.

Granovetter, M. (1974). *Getting a job.* Cambridge, MA: Harvard University Press.

Hall, A., & Wellman, B. (1985). Social networks and social support. In S. Cohen & S. L. Syme (Eds.), *Social support and health* (pp. 23–42). Orlando, FL: Academic Press.

Honig, A. S. (1979). *Parent involvement in early childhood education* (Rev. ed.). Washington, DC: National Association for the Education of Young Children.

Honig, A. S. (1982). Parent involvement in early childhood education. In B. Spodek (Ed.), *Handbook of research in early childhood education* (pp. 426–455). New York: Free Press.

Kagan, S. L., Powell, D. R., Weissbourd, B., & Zigler, E. F. (Eds.) (1987). *America's family support programs.* New Haven: Yale University Press.

Kerr, J. H., & Darling, C. A. (1988). A "Family Fair" approach to family life education. *Childhood Education, 60*(1), 1–6.

Levitt, E., & Cohen, S. (1976). Educating parents of children with special needs—Approaches and issues. *Young Children, 31,* 263–272.

Lightfoot, S. L. (1978). *Worlds apart: Relationship between families and schools.* New York: Basic Books.

Lillie, D. (1974). Dimensions in parent programs: An overview. In I. J. Grimm (Ed.), *Training parents to teach: Four models.* Chapel Hill, NC: Technical Assistance Development Systems.

Linde, T. F., & Kopp, T. (1973). *Training retarded babied and preschoolers.* Springfield, IL: Charles C. Thomas.

Newman, S. (1971). *Guidelines to parent-teacher cooperation in early childhood education.* Brooklyn, NY: Book-Lab.

Peterson, N. L. (1987). *Early intervention for handicapped children and at-risk children: An introduction to early childhood special education.* Denver: Love.

Pittman, F. (1987). *Turning points: Treating families in transition and crisis.* New York: Norton.

Powell, D. R. (1986). Parent education and support programs. *Young Children, 41*(3), 47–53.

Schaefer, E. (1985). Parent and child correlates of parental modernity. In I. Sigel (Ed.), *Parental belief systems: The psychological consequences for children* (pp. 287–318). Hillsdale, NJ: Erlbaum.

Siperstein, G. N., & Bak, J. J. (1988). Improving social skills. *Exceptional Parent, 18*(2), 18–22.

Sparling, J., & Lewis, I. (1979). *Learning for the first three years.* New York: St. Martin's Press.

Stevens, J. H., Jr. (1988). Social support, locus of control, and parenting in three low-income groups: Black adults, white adults and black teenagers. *Child Development, 59,* 635–642.

Stevens, J. H., Jr. (1991). Informal social support and parenting: Understanding the mechanisms of support. In B. Spodek & O. N. Saracho (Eds.) *Issues in early childhood curriculum: Yearbook in early childhood education,* Vol. 2 (pp. 152–165). New York: Teachers' College Press.

Stevens, J. H., Jr., & Bakeman, R. (1990, March). Continuity in parenting among black teen mothers and grandmothers. Paper presented at the biennial meeting of the Society for Research on Adolescence, Atlanta, GA.

Swick, K. J. (1987a). *Perspectives on understanding and working with families.* Champaign, IL: Stipes.

Swick, K. J. (1987b). Teacher reports on parental efficacy/involvement relationships. *Instructional Psychology, 14,* 125–132.

Swick, K. J. (1988). Reviews of research: Parental efficacy and involvement. *Childhood Education, 65*(1), 37–42.

Taylor, K. W. (1981). *Parents and children learn together.* New York: Teachers College Press.

Vaux, A. (1988). *Social support: Theory, research, and intervention.* New York: Praeger.

Weiss, H. B. (1990). State family support and education programs: Lessons from the pioneers. *American Journal of Orthopsychiatry, 59,* 32–48.

Weissbourd, B., & Kagan, S. L. (1989). Family support programs: Catalysts for change. *American Journal of Orthopsychiatry, 59,* 20–31.

White, B. (1988). *Educating infants and toddlers.* Lexington, MA: Lexington Books.

Yogman, M., & Brazelton, T. (Eds.) *Stresses and supports for families.* Boston: Harvard University Press.

Zarling, C. L., Hirsch, B. J., & Landry, S. (1988). Maternal social networks and mother-infant interactions in full term and very low birthweight, preterm infants. *Child Development, 59,* 178–185.

9

Evaluating Early Childhood Education

CHAPTER OVERVIEW

This chapter presents:

- Ways to collect information to evaluate young children
- Ways to select standardized tests to assess young children in different developmental and learning areas (such as cognitive, emotional, social, physical, and personality areas)
- Ways to determine the validity and reliability of standardized tests for young children
- Methods of observing young children in the early childhood classroom
- Approaches to developing an evaluation plan
- Ways to record and interpret the results of evaluation
- Methods of reporting children's progress to parents

INTRODUCTION

Teachers continually make decisions about the selection of programs, program elements, and program materials. These decisions are related to judgments about the children's ability to profit from these programs and about the effects of these programs on them. Each decision requires that teachers be involved in the process of evaluation: collecting information, making judgments based on this information, and developing ways to record and communicate the results of these evaluations.

The process of evaluation needs to be considered separately from that of instruction, although the two are interrelated. Evaluation includes both description and judgment of school programs and of children's attainment. Central to this process is a consideration of the goals of education and whether they are achieved.

Whether program goals have been achieved can sometimes be assessed only over a period of years. Studies of long-term outcomes have followed children through high school to determine the long-term effects of early educational programs.

Long-term evaluation is helpful for policy makers. However, it has limited use for classroom teachers. Teachers must act immediately, evaluating immediate past actions in order to plan immediate future actions—short-term goals. Teachers expect that long-term goals will be met if the related short-term goals are continually achieved. Evaluation of short-term goals can be based on observation of children's actions, analysis of their products, or some form of testing.

Many programs state goals in terms of specific behaviors that are immediately identifiable. Indeed, some psychologists feel that behavioral objectives based on the requirements of later schooling are the only legitimate goals of education in the early years. Behavioral goals are attractive because their attainment is easily judged. Often a criterion to be attained is stated, thus defining the judgments even more clearly. Information about attainment can be used to modify the program and improve its effectiveness. The availability of evaluation results is an attractive aspect of the use of behavioral goals (see Mager, 1975).

While the use of instructional objectives as the criterion for judgment might be appropriate for evaluating some learning activities, it can be a hindrance in evaluating others. Teachers often engage children in classroom activities, especially in play, music, and art, and in field trips, without a clear conception of what each child should learn. Expressive objectives that describe educational encounters might be more appropriate for evaluating these activities. Expressive objectives allow the teacher to examine the quality and relevance of a learning experience for a child without undue concern for its particular outcome (Eisner, 1981).

Much discussion of evaluation centers totally around evaluating pupil achievement, but teachers are responsible for evaluating other aspects of the program as well. These aspects include program models, program materials, and the implementation of the program in the classroom.

EVALUATING PROGRAMS

Teachers are often involved in selecting or modifying the programs they present to children. Especially in the current era of school reform, all programs are being assessed to determine if they are achieving the goals we want for our children. District-wide committees, which include teachers, are often established to evaluate the school system's goals and the degree to which those goals are being achieved. Some states are establishing initiatives in which teachers and administrators work together to design innovative approaches to education that serve the needs of local children. Primary-school teachers may be asked to join curriculum committees to determine the school program in a particular subject area or to select a series of textbooks.

Even at the preschool level, teachers may select from various programs. Some programs stress academic achievement, and some stress social relations, while others try to achieve a combination of goals.

One way to select a program is to determine the program's value base and match it with the value preferences of the teachers who must implement it. Another way of selecting programs is to determine if they are developmentally appropriate. The National Association for the Education of Young Children issued a set of guidelines for *Developmentally Appropriate Practices in Early Childhood Programs Serving Children from Birth through Age 8* (Bredekamp, 1987). The guidelines provide teachers with criteria to use in judging programs and provide examples of appropriate and inappropriate practices.

While these guidelines have been attractive to some educators, others have criticized them (Spodek & Brown, 1993). Some educators suggest that the developmental dimension is only one of several that should be used in judging programs. Others feel that adherence to these guidelines will limit diversity in early childhood programs. The cultural dimension and the knowledge dimension should also be used (Spodek, 1991).

Any approach to evaluating programs has dangers built in. What is considered worthy by one school or set of teachers may not considered worthy by another. Teachers, however, must make judgements about the programs they provide for the children in their classes, and they should be aware of the underlying bases for these judgments.

Often teachers' decisions about programs, especially in the primary grades, consist of selecting a textbook series in a single subject area. Teachers and curriculum committees may be swayed by book salespersons, special interest groups, or popular articles. They may adopt programs because they are familiar or have been adopted by someone else.

Robert Hillerich (1974) believes that teachers selecting a reading program need first to determine the philosophy and emphasis they desire. They must develop guidelines so they know what to look for in a reading program. The entire staff should be involved, in a consensus decision rather than a majority vote. Hillerich presents an evaluation form showing what a group could use to evaluate a reading program for kindergarten through second grade (see Figure 9–1).

Arthur Nichols and Anna Ochoa (1971) developed criteria for selecting social studies textbooks for the primary grades. They believe that teachers must evaluate both the knowledge component and the intellectual component of these books. In looking at the knowledge component, teachers should judge how social issues are handled, whether information is objectively presented, whether an interdisciplinary conceptual base is used, and whether the most recent scholarly findings are reflected in the material. The intellectual component refers to the ways in which the book encourages the development of intellectual skills. Teachers need to determine if the book can serve as a basis for inquiry, if higher-order questions

Figure 9–1 Evaluation of Reading Program: Kindergarten–Grade 2

Evaluating teacher ______________________ Grade ________

3 = Very good; 2 = Good; 1 = Poor; 0 = Omitted

		Name of program			
Teacher edition	Philosophy clear (introduction)				
	Specific direction for skill teaching				
	Ease of use				
	Provision for individual differences				
Content	Interest appeal to children				
	Variety of types of reading				
Format	Physically clear and attractive				
Illustrations	Aesthetic appeal				
ADEQUACY OF SKILL DEVELOPMENT					
Readiness deals with letters and sounds in words, not just with general language development.					
Skills are learned through use, not just through memorizing rules.					
Child is shown how the skill is used in reading.					
Reading includes use of context, emphasis on reading for meaning.					
Suggested questions for disscussion cover the inferential and critical as well as literal levels.					
Readiness for comprehension and study skills begins with these skills at the listening level.					
The child is taught a definite system for attacking an unknown word (mark *Yes* or *No* in each column).					
What is the system? (Put a check in proper columns.)					
Guess from context only.					
Remember the word from the introduction.					
Apply a rule or rules.					
Sound out the word.					
Use context and consonant-sound associations.					

Source: From Robert L. Hillerich, "So You're Evaluating Reading Programs," *Elementary School Journal,* 1974, *75*(3), 179. Reprinted by permission of the University of Chicago Press.

are asked, if the book could serve as a basis for decision making, and if the knowledge presented is related to the children's lives.

The Social Science Education Consortium (SSEC) has developed a system for analyzing social science curricula that describes program attributes using the following categories:

1. **Descriptive characteristics,** the "nuts and bolts" of the curriculum;
2. **Rationale and objectives,** why the program was created and what the anticipated outcomes are;
3. **Antecedent conditions,** the particular conditions under which the program might be successful;
4. **Content,** the specific changes intended in the knowledge, attitudes, and behavior of the students;
5. **Instructional theory and teaching strategies,** the underlying learning theory and teaching strategies and their relationship; and
6. **Overall judgments,** evaluative judgments about the materials.

These broad categories are further broken down in subcategories for analysis. The category of antecedent conditions, for example, includes subcategories relating to pupil characteristics, teaching capabilities, community requirements, school requirements, and the articulation of requirements (Stevens & Fetsko, 1968).

A program is a promise of learning activities to be. Teachers must see that the promise is fulfilled. Program implementation can differ significantly from program intent. By assessing the classroom program, teachers will be able to judge the quality of implementation. In addition to the classroom setting, the interpersonal environment, including the teacher's behavior, must also be assessed.

One of the most comprehensive approaches to evaluating preschool and kindergarten classes is the use of the *Accreditation Criteria and Procedures of the National Academy of Early Childhood Programs* (National Association for the Education of Young Children, 1991). The academy, a division of the National Association for the Education of Young Children, accredits early childhood programs to provide evidence that programs are of high quality.

The accreditation process consists of three steps. The first step is a self-study that staff and parents conduct to determine the degree to which the program meets the academy's criteria. If necessary, the program is expected to make changes to meet the criteria. In the second step, trained validators visit the program to verify the self-study. Finally, a three-person commission considers the information collected and makes a decision regarding the accreditation.

The self-study requires that the staff and parents look at the program's curriculum, the interactions between children and staff and between staff and parents, the qualifications of the staff, any staff development program that exists, the administration of the program, its staffing pattern, the physical setting, the way in which health and safety concerns are met, the food and nutrition services provided, and the forms of evaluation used by the program.

Such a self-study is comprehensive, and, while no teacher would be responsible for the entire self-study, teachers do participate in it. Such participation helps teachers become aware of the strengths and problems in the program. The self-study should lead to program improvement based on knowledge of what is actually happening in the program.

EVALUATING SETTINGS

A number of observational schemes are available to monitor and assess classroom practices. Most of these are designed for research purposes and require an outside observer. However, there are some simple techniques that teachers can use to gather information about their own classrooms. They can provide limited but reliable information that can be used to improve educational opportunities for children. Three examples of such techniques follow.

Chapter 6 refers to classroom dimensions identified by Elizabeth Jones (1979). Using the dimensions of hard/soft, open/closed, simple/complex, intrusion/seclusion, and high mobility/low mobility, a teacher can describe the physical dimensions of a classroom and determine if the classroom approximates the setting the teacher desires to create for children. After recording the classroom dimensions, the teacher can modify the room systematically to make it closer to the ideal.

In addition to the *Accreditation Criteria and Procedures of the National Academy of Early Childhood Programs* (National Association for the Education of Young Children, 1991), noted above, other observation instruments have been used to assess the quality of early childhood education settings. Thelma Harms and Richard Clifford (1980) have developed the *Early Childhood Rating Scale*, which is the most widely used scale for evaluating preschool settings. Their scale is composed of seven separate subscales: personal care routines of children, furnishings and displays for children, language and reasoning experiences, fine and gross motor activities, creative activities, social development, and adult needs. The teacher can observe the setting, then rate each of the 37 items on the scale, scoring them from 1 (inadequate) to 7 (excellent). Criteria and standards for each score are provided. Space is also provided on the scoring sheets for teachers to add comments. By adding the scores on all items in each of the seven subscales, teachers can develop a profile of the setting. Identifying strengths and weaknesses can suggest ways to modify the setting. Subsequent observations with the rating scale can help determine whether changes have led to improvements.

Janice J. Beaty (1992) developed the *Checklist of Classroom Competencies*, which is a preassessment tool with 23 performance areas. The first 13 check-

CHECKLIST OF CLASSROOM COMPETENCIES

_____ 1. Provide classroom areas.
_____ 2. Organize block-building areas.
_____ 3. Organize book area.
_____ 4. Organize dramatic play area.
_____ 5. Locate gross motor activities and equipment.
_____ 6. Arrange manipulative materials.
_____ 7. Have art materials for immediate use.
_____ 8. Arrange music equipment and activities.
_____ 9. Include science/math corner.
_____ 10. Arrange sand and water activities.
_____ 11. Provide woodworking activities.
_____ 12. Include cooking activities.
_____ 13. Provide general room conditions.
_____ 14. Provide in the daily schedule for
  - _____ Alternating active and quiet activities,
  - _____ Appropriate transitions between activities,
  - _____ Both indoor and outdoor play,
  - _____ Both gross and fine motor activities,
  - _____ A balance between teacher-directed and child-initiated activities,
  - _____ A sequence of activities that is clear to children,
  - _____ A means of handling routines that is clear to children,
  - _____ A quiet or rest time,
  - _____ A time to look at books and make individual choices,
  - _____ A story-reading time,
  - _____ A breakfast and/or mid-morning snack,
  - _____ A family-style noon meal,
  - _____ Individual and small-group activities,
  - _____ Opportunity for children to talk alone with an adult each day,
  - _____ Regular field trips.

_____ 15. Demonstrate personal participation.
_____ 16. Provide outdoor playground.
_____ 17. Promote physical coordination by providing equipment and opportunities both inside and outside.
_____ 18. Promote children's listening skills.
_____ 19. Promote clear and articulate language production.
_____ 20. Promote adult-child communication.
_____ 21. Promote child-child communication.
_____ 22. Promote recognition of symbols.
_____ 23. Encourage children to explore, experiment, question, and build concepts. (Beaty, 1992)

list items relate to room arrangement, while the last 10 items are related to a variety of areas such as scheduling, motor skills, and language skills.

EVALUATING MATERIALS

To select a set of curriculum materials, teachers must understand the purpose and function of the materials. Before selecting a set of materials, teachers must carefully and thoroughly analyze the materials available. The results of the analysis offer the basis for making sound judgments about each product's quality and appropriateness.

Teachers should analyze each part of a set of curriculum materials individually and in relation to each other. Materials can be analyzed by first making an inventory of dimensions such as publication and cost information, physical properties of the materials, content of materials, and their instructional strategies. Specifically, the following can be included:

1. Examine the authors' reputations, affiliations, and professional backgrounds as well as the role each author played in developing the materials. A qualified author should have had major input in developing the material.
2. Be sure the curriculum materials are up to date. Materials that are more than three years old may not be up to date. Some older books and educational materials may reflect sex, race, and age biases.
3. Consider the cost of the materials in relation to durability, practicality, aesthetic qualities, and usability by the children.
4. Determine if the materials were field tested. The location, purposes, and student population should be similar to those of the teacher making the selection. Also important are the carefulness and thoroughness of the testing.
5. Determine the amount of preparation teachers must have prior to using the materials.
6. Analyze the critical reviews the curriculum materials have received. These can be found in a professional, school, or public library. The librarian can be an excellent resource person in helping teachers locate most of these sources.

   Check:
   - **Professional Journals** Reviews often are published in professional journals such as *The Mathematics Teacher* or *Curriculum Review.*
   - ***School Library Journal*** This is a special professional journal for librarians. Reviews are published monthly from September through May. *SLJ* reviews books written for students at all levels.
   - **Media Review** If teachers wish to know whether there are published reviews of a particular curriculum product, *Media Review Digest (MRD)* is available as an index to reviews, evalu-

ations, and descriptions of all forms of nonbook media for all levels. *MRD* is published annually, with a semiannual supplement. A useful feature of *MRD* is that it provides a brief digest of the reviews available for each curriculum product.

- **Booklist** This publication appears twice monthly from September through July, and once in August. It contains reviews of books, films, filmstrips, and sound recording for all grade levels.
- **Curriculum Review** This publication appears five times annually. It contains reviews of textbooks and supplementary materials in all areas and levels (K–12) of the curriculum. Subject areas such as language arts, mathematics, science, and social studies are usually covered in each issue.
- **Previews** This publication appears every month from September through May. It contains reviews of videocassettes, 16mm films, filmstrips, slides, kits, and sound recordings.

In evaluating instructional materials, teachers can collect a range of information to help them make curriculum decisions. Teachers need to determine the effectiveness of the curriculum materials. Saracho (1987, 1988) suggests that teachers analyze the match between their goals and the purposes of the materials. They should also examine the materials' views of human development. If these views are not made explicit, teachers can infer the underlying theories of learning and development. Teachers can then compare these views with their own, asking whether these materials will meet their educational goals and enhance their philosophy of child development. These procedures help the teacher to identify components that need to be revised, added, or deleted.

EVALUATING TEACHING

A number of techniques have been used to analyze and assess teacher behavior. Generally, they require that observations be collected by an observer or through videotaping. The teacher can then analyze the records of these observations alone or with another person.

Probably most practical way for teachers to evaluate their teaching is to observe or recall classroom incidents and analyze them in relation to pupils' responses. Teachers might sit alone at noon or at the end of the school day and write what they can recall of an event of the day. For example, a teacher wishing to focus on a discussion session could try to write questions and comments as accurately as possible, analyzing those questions:

- Did I use open-ended questions, requiring divergent responses from children, or closed-ended questions, demanding a single convergent response?

- Did the questions elicit answers requiring higher-order thought processes, like analysis or criticism, or lower-order thought processes, like recall?
- Did my responses to children tease out additional information or did they limit discussion?
- Were my comments supportive of the children's contributions or did they "cut" children?
- Were my responses personal or stereotyped?

Using such an analysis, teachers can determine whether their behaviors are consistent with their intentions. In this way, teachers can begin to develop self-awareness and analyze all areas of their teaching and their relationships with all the children. With continued self-reflection, teachers can become more sensitive to children's needs and more aware of how to serve them appropriately.

Peer review might also be used, with teachers helping each other observe and describe their classroom practices and discussing these practices. Some school systems identify *mentor teachers* to work with new teachers. These mentors support new teachers, socializing them into the school culture. They also provide resources that new teachers might not be able to access. In addition, these mentor teachers are concerned with improving the performance of teachers by evaluating them.

EVALUATING CHILDREN

Teachers evaluate children in order to make four kinds of decisions about them. *Instructional decisions* are concerned with curriculum planning and effective learning. *Guidance decisions* allow children to make educational choices and to increase self-understanding. *Administrative decisions* relate to issues of selection of materials and the classification and placement of children. *Research decisions* may also be made (Mehrens & Lehmann, 1991). These relate to studying the educational process.

William L. and Laura D. Goodwin (1993) raise four issues about measurement and evaluation. The first issue is related to the overall value of measurement to American society. A number of professional associations, including the National Association for the Education of Young Children, have raised serious concerns about the increasing use of **standardized tests** on young children. While some form of assessment is important as an indicator of the effectiveness of programs, standardized tests may be the wrong instrument for this purpose.

Standardized tests are tests that are given to all individuals in the same way. These tests are usually norm referenced.

The second issue relates to the fairness of the tests used. Test bias has been a serious concern, for example. Some tests may penalize certain children because their background is not reflected in the test items. In addition, standardized tests are not valid for assessing learning in all curricula since a standarized test may not reflect the program in a particular class or school.

A third concern relates to the influence of tests on early childhood education programs. Shepard (1991), for example, suggests that tests help to determine what the curriculum will be and that standardized tests, in particular, influence school programs by narrowing their scope.

Goodwin and Goodwin's fourth issue relates to the measurement needs of teachers as opposed to those of researchers. Since teachers and researchers use tests for different purposes, what may be a satisfactory standardized test for the needs of one group may not be adequate or appropriate for the other.

Teachers need to find ways to evaluate the work children do in their classes. Since teachers cannot observe everything that children do, they look for ways to sample their behavior and generalize from the samples they collect. Teachers can use a variety of techniques to gather an adequate sample, including direct observation, checklists and rating scales, and formal and informal tests. The information gathered through these techniques must be judged, and both the information and the judgment recorded and communicated to others.

All evaluation involves some form of observation, either controlled, as in a test, or uncontrolled, as in a natural setting. Each kind of information gathered offers teachers different insights into the children. Often teachers combine information collected in different ways to make an evaluation.

No matter what method teachers use to collect information about children, they must be concerned with the validity, reliability, and practicality of the technique. **Validity** refers to the degree to which the evaluation technique assesses what it claims to assess. If an academic achievement test relies too heavily on children's ability to read and follow elaborate written directions, then the test may assess reading skills and mask the other academic abilities of children who have difficulty with reading. As noted earlier, an assessment device that is considered valid for one purpose may lose its validity when used for another purpose. Thus, a screening test may serve well for identifying potential disabilities in children. If, however, it is used as a readiness instrument, it can no longer be considered valid.

Validity
refers to the degree to which an evaluation technique assesses what it claims to assess.

Reliability refers to the consistency of a measure—the degree to which a child's score might vary from day to day on a test, or to which observations may vary depending on who is using an observation scale. **Practicality** refers to the ability of the teacher to use a specific technique under normal circumstances. Techniques that require high levels of training or a great deal of time to administer may be impractical for classroom teachers (Goodwin & Driscoll, 1980).

Reliability
is the degree to which a measure is consistent in its outcome.

Practicality
reflects the ease with which an evaluation technique can be used

Screening Young Children

Schools begin to evaluate children well before they enter school. As preschool programs for children with disabilities have been mandated, procedures to identify and screen such children have been established.

Screening Instruments Teachers Might Use

ABC Inventory. (1965). Muskegon, MI: Research Concepts.
Comprehensive Identification Process. (1970). Bensenville, IL: Scholastic Testing Service.
Cooperative Preschool Inventory. (1970). Princeton, NJ: Educational Testing Service.
Denver Developmental Screening Test. (1970). Denver, CO: Ladoca Project and Publishing, Inc.
Developmental Indicators for the Assessment of Learning. (1975). Highland Park, IL: DIAL, Inc.
Metropolitan Readiness Test. (1976). Atlanta, GA: Psychological Corp.

Screening procedures are designed to determine if a child has a disability.

These **screening procedures** can use paraprofessionals and volunteers as well as trained professionals. Parents are invited to bring their children into centers for screening of visual and auditory acuity, speech articulation, and social-emotional, cognitive, and physical difficulties. As problems are identified, specific in-depth evaluations are made. The results of these procedures are discussed with parents, and services to help children are then offered. The goal of such early identification is to help children with disabilities by providing early intervention and thus to improve their chances of being successfully integrated into regular school classes later (Spodek & Saracho, 1994).

Teachers continue to screen children for disabilities through the school years. Teachers in preschool, kindergarten, and primary classes need to be especially alert to possible disabilities in their children, since not all children have gone through the screening process and some disabilities show up only later in the child's life.

Testing Young Children

The scores on **norm-referenced tests** are determined by comparison with scores of a representative group of persons who took the test.

Despite the cautions that have been raised about testing young children (see Kamii, 1990; Shepard, 1991), children continue to be tested in their early years with both standardized and nonstandardized tests. Standardized tests are administered in the same way to all children so that the tests will be comparable whenever and wherever they are administered. Types of standardized tests include (1) *norm-referenced*, and (2) *criterion-referenced* tests. **Norm-referenced tests** compare performance among all those who are assessed. Performance may be assessed for a wide range of educational goals. A norm-referenced test is usually a standardized test. The performance of children on such a test theoretically is comparable with the scores of all other children. Actually test-makers select a norming sample of children that is supposed to be representative

Figure 9–2 Assessment Instruments for Young Children

Instrument	Age Level	Purpose
Caldwell Preschool Inventory	3 to 6 years	Assessing abilities in a variety of areas
Denver Developmental Screening Test (DDST)	2 weeks to 6 years	Diagnosing developmental delays in adaptive, motor, language, and personal-social areas
Engleman's Basic Concept Inventory	preschool & kindergarten	Assessing basic concepts and awareness of patterns, using repetition and completion of statements
Gessell Developmental Schedules (GDS)	4 weeks to 6 years	Diagnosing the maturity of the young child's adaptive, motor, language, and personal-social development
Illinois Test of Psycholinguistic Abilities	2 to 10 years	Assessing auditory, visual, verbal, and memory abilities
Metropolitan Readiness Tests (MRT)	kindergarten & first grade	Assessing educational abilities such as listening, matching, and copying, as well as understanding the alphabet, numbers, words meanings, and totals (Drawing a person is optional.)
Peabody Picture Vocabulary Test (PPVT)	$2\frac{1}{2}$ to 18 years	Assessing vocabulary through matching a word to one of four pictures
Stanford-Binet Intelligence Scale	2 years and older	Assessing individual intelligence
Wechsler Preschool and Primary Scale of Intelligence (WPPSI)	4 to 6 years	Assessing intelligence in fourteen areas of verbal and perceptual performance

of all those who will take the test. This sample's scores become the norm against which all other tests scores are compared. **Criterion-referenced tests** are constructed to evaluate a person's performance level in relation to well-defined criteria. Most teacher-made classroom tests are criterion-referenced. The criterion is the learning that students are supposed to have gained from classroom activities. The teacher will select a sample of items for a test to determine to what extent students have learned what they were expected to learn. Scores on such a test in one class cannot be compared with those from another class (Baker, 1988).

The scores on **criterion-referenced tests** are determined by comparison to a standard of performance.

In addition to these categories, the tests usually given to children in the early years of schooling can be categorized as developmental, intelligence, readiness, or achievement tests. Although readiness and achievement tests can be criterion-referenced, the vast majority of the tests used on young children are norm-referenced. The fact that a norming group is used allows these tests to be developmentally appropriate. Figure 9–2 provides examples of standardized instruments appropriate for young children, describing their age levels and purposes.

Developmental tests are used to assess an individual's degree of maturation.

Developmental Tests Developmental tests are used to determine an individual's degree of maturation. Observation of a child's physical characteristics, such as body proportions or development of the wrist bone, can be used to assess physical maturation. Most tests, however, consist of items that require children's performance. *School Readiness* by Frances L. Ilg, Louise Bates Ames, and their colleagues (1978) contains a series of tasks for children to perform. From an analysis of children's performance on these tasks, educators can judge their developmental maturity. Some schools have suggested that this developmental maturity can be used to determine whether a child is mature enough to profit from school instruction. As a result, the test has been used to determine whether children should be allowed to enter kindergarten. The tasks described in many of Jean Piaget's studies have also been considered as developmental tests, though these have been used primarily to determine levels of intellectual development.

Developmental tests assess maturity, not school readiness. To use a developmental test as a school test is a distortion of the original nature of the test. For instance, the Gesell Test, though used in many school systems, has been seriously questioned as to both its validity and reliability, since the assessment may be incorrect as often as it is correct (Graue & Shepard, 1993). Most developmental theories, as noted in Chapter 3, suggest that development is much more than maturation. Providing early experiences to children allows adults to nurture development. This principle is the basis of Head Start and other programs for at-risk students as well as of early intervention programs for children with disabilities. To deny a child educational experiences because of a judgment of immaturity, even if that assessment was accurate, is to thwart the child's possible development. Human development is highly plastic, and children's experiences tend to modify their development. Rather than exclusion, children need differentiated educational opportunities.

All tests have a degree of error to them. Actually, test scores are reported as a number on a scale; this number is the midpoint of many possible scores a child might have received. When testing large groups of children, these errors tend to cancel each other out. This is not the case, however, when an individual's score is noted. Thus, to take a single test score as absolute and to make decisions about a child based on that score is to compound the error.

Intelligence tests contain tasks that all persons in a society are supposed to have equal opportunity to learn. Thus, they purport to measure inherent ability.

Intelligence Tests Intelligence tests contain sets of tasks that require using learned skills for adequate performance at specific levels. The assumption underlying such tests is that if all children have equal opportunities to learn certain skills, the differences in levels of performance are the results of differences in inherent ability. However, not all children have the same opportunities to learn the skills sampled in intelligence tests. These tests generally seem to favor children of white, middle-class background and less adequately sample the inherent abilities of minority-group children.

Intelligence tests were originally designed to predict the academic achievement of children. Most intelligence tests can predict academic performance well when there is no significant change in children's educational circumstances. Evidence suggests that when these circumstances are changed, the predictive ability of intelligence tests does not hold up as well. Moving children with low IQ levels from an educationally dull to an educationally stimulating environment may not only increase educational performance but also lead to increases in scores on intelligence tests.

Significant decisions about a child's education are often based on intelligence test scores. Children can be penalized for not being able to score well because they have been denied the opportunity to learn those things sampled in the test. Careless use of intelligence tests can perpetuate unequal educational practices in schools.

Readiness Tests Most readiness tests assess the child's ability to profit from instruction. These tests are actually early achievement tests. If an analysis is made of specific items a child has answered correctly or incorrectly, these tests may also be used for diagnostic purposes.

Readiness tests are used to determine an individual's ability to profit from instruction.

In addition to using formal tests, teachers can also use a range of informal techniques to determining readiness. An informal assessment of reading readiness could collect information on children's language ability and their desire to learn to read, as well as the information on the readiness checklist presented in Chapter 11. Classroom observations can produce information about readiness, since any information about children's present achievement also provides information about their predisposition for further learning.

Achievement Tests Achievement tests assess a child's or a class's accomplishments in academic learning. Such tests are designed for administration in the primary grades or beyond. They are available for different curricular areas, and teachers may select a full battery of tests or administer only a single subtest. In using a single subtest, however, the teacher must be aware that any norming qualities of the test are lost, since no one part of the test is the equivalent of the entire test.

Achievement tests assess a child's academic accomplishments.

Achievement tests sample not the total curriculum offerings of the school, but only academic skills. Teachers need to insure that inappropriate use of test results does not distort the program offerings. Teachers also need to be sure that the use of achievement tests, which do not reflect the entire curriculum, does not result in a distortion of the curriculum. When test scores are made public and when teachers and schools are evaluated by their children's test scores, then teachers may "teach to the test," focusing on those elements of the program included in the test to the exclusion of other valuable topics or subjects.

Achievement tests, like intelligence tests, are standardized using a norm group including children from rural and urban areas, different socioeconomic levels, and different geographic areas. Since scores are averaged to create a grade-level norm, half the test scores fall above the norm and half below. Within the standardizing population, differences exist in average test scores of subgroups identifiable by geographic area, degree of urbanization, and socioeconomic status.

Norms are descriptive of a particular population at a particular time. They need not set expectations. Every group can exceed the norms on almost every achievement test under optimal learning conditions. One of the goals of teachers should be to create the best possible conditions for learning and for assessment.

Although standardized tests are useful, many times nonstandardized criterion-referenced tests are more appropriate. Teachers should develop many formal and informal techniques to sample children's learning systematically. Nonstandardized methods can also provide process data that can be used to improve instruction. A number of children might get the same mathematics item wrong on a particular test. One child might have computed wrongly, another might not have understood the concept involved, and a third might simply have been careless. Analyzing the errors children make on tests might suggest different activities for different children. If evaluation is used as a diagnostic tool in planning, this type of data becomes invaluable. Nonstandardized means of collecting data include teacher-developed tests, observational techniques, checklists, rating scales, sociometric techniques, and collections of children's products. Cryan (1986) provides the following advice:

> Observe, interact, take notes and write goals for learning. Use your own collected information as the true picture of the child's performance. Measure specific behaviors when necessary to diagnose entering ability or when transitions to more complex material require it. And above all, reduce both your and the child's anxiety level by keeping the extent of "testing" to an absolute minimum. Finally, guard against what Goodlad calls "CMD" (chronic measurement disease): preoccupation with pulling up plants to look at them before the roots take hold. Remember, learning will develop its roots if the conditions provided for learning and the kinds of learning supported are as important as what is being taught. (p. 350)

OBSERVATION TECHNIQUES

A test is a form of observation in which everyone is observed in the same way for the same thing. As such, tests mask individual differences in children's performance. Often teachers wish to know about how children function in nonstandard, naturally occurring situations. For this purpose, they must use observation techniques. This section deals with two kinds of observation techniques: direct and indirect. Anecdotal records, time samples, and event samples are forms of direct observation. Teachers record what they observe at the time. Checklists may be direct observations if teachers check off what is being observed. Rating scales, semantic differentials, and checklists, at times, are indirect forms of observation, since teachers made judgments on what they have observed in the past.

PROCEDURES FOR CLASSROOM OBSERVATIONS

1. Observations must record pertinent information, such as date, time of day, time intervals, place of observation, and other information that might have a specific bearing on the situation—weather, unpleasant surroundings, and incidental events.
2. In a planned observation, teachers must place themselves in a location where they do not interfere with classroom activities but can see everything that goes on in the classroom.
3. A shorthand recording system should be developed to record quickly and clearly the actions in the classroom. For instance, a circle with an X on the side records a child's location on a round table.
4. The ending time of an observation must be recorded. (Saracho, 1988)

Anecdotal Records

Anecdotal records are narrative descriptions of children's behavior.

Teachers may take time at the end of the day to record significant occurrences. They can note what happened to individual children or what individual problems arose. Such anecdotal records are helpful in thinking through a school day and in planning for future activities, but memory is selective. People remember the extraordinary, rather than the normal, so teachers may record unrepresentative pictures of children's behavior. The use of running records—on-the-spot observations of occurrences—is far superior in recreating a true picture of the day. Teachers should learn techniques for taking running records (see, for example, Cohen & Stern, 1983).

Anecdotal records must extensively describe actions, reactions, quotes, and personal cues, such as postures, gestures, and facial expressions. The observer must record behavior completely in its situation, which includes people, things, and the demands of the physical environment. Individuals react as whole persons with thoughts, feelings, and physical activity. In categorizing the observations, the teacher can record the frequency of each situation to keep track of behavioral patterns (Saracho, 1988).

Teachers who feel that they are overwhelmed with classroom events and that they do not have time to observe and to record any observations can use videotaped protocols that illustrate a variety of actions. Students from higher grades in the school or volunteers may use a video camcorder to videotape events. Later the teacher can view the videotape during conference time and record the events using the observation procedures suggested above.

The teacher and a colleague can view the tape together to identify, record, and discuss the episodes. This procedure can help the teacher understand the situation objectively. Also, the teacher can cite specific examples to support hypotheses.

Observing and recording children's actions is time consuming. One way to become more efficient in collecting this kind of information is to sample behavior systematically. Two approaches used in early childhood education are time sampling and event sampling (Genishi, 1982).

Time Sampling

Time sampling notes behaviors that occur at uniform time intervals.

In **time sampling,** teachers focus on selected behaviors, noting their occurrence at uniform time intervals, which could range from several seconds to five to ten minutes or longer. If a category system is selected in which a tally mark or symbol is used to record the presence of a particular type of behavior on a special observation form, then little time is spent in recording. A teacher might be concerned with the type of social play in which children engage. Periodically the teacher would scan the class and place a mark next to each child's name, **S** for solitary play, when the child plays alone; **P** for parallel play, when the child plays alongside other children but does not interact; and **C** for cooperative play, when the child engages in interactive play with other children. As noted in Figure 9–3, teachers can also use time samples to determine the dependency behavior of children. In this example, the teacher will observe the child and then, at one minute intervals, note whether the child functions as an onlooder, a follower, or a leader. By adding the tally marks in each category, the teacher can make an assessment of the child on this dimension of behavior.

Figure 9–3 ***Time Sampling***

Date: 11/14/93 Time: 10:00 AM

Activity: Block Play

Age Group: Three-Year-Olds

Dependency Behaviors ____________

Time Intervals

	1 minute	2 minutes	3 minutes
Onlooker	✔		
Follower		✔	
Leader			✔

Event Sampling

Teachers can use **event sampling** to collect information on the frequency with which a particular behavior occurs. Such an observation system need not be based on time intervals. Teachers who want to determine the amount of aggressive behavior manifested by certain children, for instance, might place a tally mark next to each child's name each time they see aggressive behavior (hitting or pushing, for example) in that child. At the end of the day, they can add the tally marks for each child to get a sense of each child's aggressiveness.

Event sampling notes the occurrence of a particular behavior.

Direct observation of children's behavior has the advantage of giving teachers clues about the process of their learning. A careful recording of the interactions between a child and other children or between a child and a set of instructional materials can provide the basis for judgments about how the child is thinking or feeling. The results of such observations can be compared over time to judge changes in behavior for individual children.

Checklists and Rating Scales

Checklists and rating scales allow teachers to assess children's behavior or performance. While they do not provide descriptions of behavior, they allow a summary judgment, based on continued observation, to be recorded simply.

Checklists generally include a series of descriptive statements about children's performance. Figure 9–4 presents examples of items on a checklist. These include lists of items, behaviors, or characteristics that help teachers assess whether a given child has those behaviors or charac-

Checklists include descriptive statements about children that allow teachers to note whether a trait exists or not.

Figure 9–4 Examples of Checklists

Check off the presence or absence of the characteristic. The child

_____1. paints in the art area

_____2. sings songs with others

_____3. saws wood in the woodworking area

Circle a "yes" to indicate the presence of each characteristic or a "no" to indicate its absence. The child

yes no 1. moves confidently during movement activities

yes no 2. freely selects different activities in the play areas

Emergent Reading Skills

yes no 1. has auditory skills

yes no 2. has visual skills

yes no 3. understands left-to-right progression

yes no 4. looks at pictures

Figure 9–5 Skills Rating Scale

Name of child ____________________ Date __________

	Rating	Comments
Self-Care Skills		
Zippers clothes		
Matches shoes to correct foot		
Ties laces		
Puts on snowsuit alone		
Washes hands properly		
Cleanup Skills		
Washes paint brushes clean		
Sponges tables clean		
Puts materials back in proper order		
Sweeps floor if needed		
Puts apron away properly		
Social Skills		
Shows leadership abilities		
Participates in group activities		
Takes turns		
Follows classroom rules		
Physical Skills		
Can walk a balance beam		
Can hop		
Can skip		
Climbs well		
Can draw a straight line		
Can use scissors well		
Can use a paint brush		
Can hammer a nail in straight		
Can saw a straight cut		

Rate each child on a scale from 1 to 5

5 Shows high level of performance consistently
4 Shows good performance, not consistent
3 Shows fair performance, inconsistent
2 Performs poorly, erratic
1 Cannot perform

Figure 9–6 ***Examples of Semantic Differential Scales***

good	–·–·–·–·–·–·–·–·–·–·–·–·–·–·–·–·–·–	bad
big	–·–·–·–·–·–·–·–·–·–·–·–·–·–·–·–·–·–	small
likes	–·–·–·–·–·–·–·–·–·–·–·–·–·–·–·–·–·–	dislikes

teristics. The teacher checks those statements that characterize the child, ignoring those that do not (Saracho, 1983). For example, using a reading checklist, the teacher, after marking the items related to emergent literacy that characterize a particular child, can judge the child to be ready to begin formal reading instruction, or determine whether the child needs particular readiness skills first.

Rating scales allow teachers to record judgments about children's behaviors or characteristizations.

Rating scales also allow teachers to record judgments about children's characteristics or behaviors and to make qualitative judgments. Rating scales have equally distanced units, points, numbers, or descriptive statements along a continuum to help teachers assess specific traits. An uneven number of intervals (three or five) leaves a neutral midpoint. The largest number may be the highest score, while the smallest number is the lowest score (Saracho, 1983). The skills scale allows the teacher to identify both the skills the child has and the degree of proficiency shown in each skill. In using such a scale, care must be taken that the rating on each item is well thought out and does not result from a halo effect.

A **semantic differential scale** allows teachers to estimate a child's behavior or trait in relation to opposing characterizations.

In using **semantic differential scales,** teachers make an estimate of a child's behavior or characteristics on a scale between two opposite adjectives such as good versus bad, big versus small, likes versus dislikes. Each set of adjectives is divided by seven points. Teachers examine each set to assesses that characteristic. They indicate their judgment by marking the point along the line that best describes the characteristics being appraised. The closer to the end of the continuum the point appears, the more that adjective describes the child's characteristic (Saracho, 1983).

Selecting Observation Techniques

In selecting a recording technique, teachers should establish the purpose of their observation and choose the technique that will present the most realistic picture of the situation. They can keep a log or diary about the class to record salient situations of the day. Charts and checklists can serve as reminders of activities and materials that were used throughout the day in the classroom. Checklists are inventories of what teachers feel must be observed in the classroom. Checklists can also help record the absence or presence as well as the frequency or number of certain elements such as behaviors, materials, or situations. Teachers must consider what they are looking for and the reason for recording the behavior (Saracho, 1988).

SELECTING THE APPROPRIATE OBSERVATION TECHNIQUES

Technique	Description
Anecdotal record	Narrative form recording specific behaviors or incidents
Checklist	Recording the presence or absence of materials, behaviors, etc. It serves as an inventory of materials or behaviors necessary to achieve the teacher's educational goals
Rating scale	Recording in a continuum the child's degree of development, performance, interest, or scaled behaviors
Semantic differential scale	Recording a judgment on a continuum between two opposites

A number of excellent resources describe the various observation techniques. Teachers may read these alone or in groups. It helps to practice a technique before attempting it in a class. If several teachers work on a technique together, they can judge each other's accuracy and become more capable.

Teachers can write reports after they gather information. These reports can help teachers further plan for the classroom or individual child as well as for parent conferences. The following suggestions are helpful in writing reports based on observations:

1. Sketch rough notes after observing an event.
2. Then return to the observation form and read it to remember any forgotten details.
3. The report can consist of three sections: (1) background comments (such as pre-observation impressions, sketches, and comments) that can add to the reader's perceptions of the situation, (2) detailed description of the report, and (3) summary (Saracho, 1988).

Sociometric Techniques

Teachers can use sociometric techniques to assess children's social behavior. Children can be asked a set of questions to elicit their choice of friends. Such questions as "Whom would you like to play with outside?" "Whom would you like to have sit near you at snack time?" or "Whom would you like to invite home after school?" might be used at the nursery or kindergarten levels. Appropriate questions for older children can be developed as well. The children's responses to the questions can be plotted on a chart, which will then show which children are more and less popular and what groups of friendships exist in the class.

Books on Observation

Almy, M., & Genishi, C. (1979). *Ways of studying children* (rev. ed.). New York: Teachers College Press.

Beaty, J. J. (1986). *Observing the development of the young child*. Columbus, OH: Merrill.

Bentzen, W. R. (1985). *Seeing young children: A guide to observing and recording behavior*. Albany, NY: Delmar.

Boehm, A. E., & Weinberg, R. A. (1977). *The classroom observer: Developing observations skills in early childhood settings* (2nd ed.). New York: Teachers College Press.

Cartwright, C. A., & Cartwright, G. P. (1984). *Developing observation skills*. New York: McGraw-Hill.

Cohen, D. H., & Stern, V. (1983). *Observing and recording the behavior of young children* (2nd ed.). New York: Teachers College Press.

Irwin, D. M., & Bushnell, M. M. (1980). *Observational strategies for child study*. New York: Holt, Rinehart & Winston.

Stallings, J. (1977). *Learning to look: A handbook of observation and teaching models*. Belmont, CA: Wadsworth.

Sociometric techniques are less reliable for children than for adults; best friends can easily change from day to day. Teachers need to collect a number of such observations over a period of time, looking for evidence of stable relationships and shifts that might occur as a result of program changes. They can then arrange groupings or enhance the social status of children who may be socially at risk.

Portfolios

Portfolios are collections of children's work.

Another way of sampling children's learning is to systematically collect the products of their work. For children in prekindergarten and kindergarten programs, this would include the drawings and paintings they make, the stories they dictate, and samples of other kinds of work. For children in primary grades, a portfolio would also include samples of their written work, including stories, reports of investigations in science and social studies, and mathematics work. The material should be collected systematically and labeled with the child's name, the date, and the context in which the material was produced. The materials are placed together in a folder so that teachers can see children's progress throughout the year in various areas of the curriculum. Teachers should use part of a file cabinet or a closet to keep the material. Such a cumulative collection allows teachers to review progress and judge children's work at any point in time.

To be most useful, the collection of children's products must be systematic. The great temptation is to allow young children to carry each product home so that parents can see the work their children are doing. Unfortunately, sending everything home leaves the teacher without an important data source. A painting or a story should be periodically selected for each child to keep in school. If the children are told why materials are being collected, they will usually not resist.

Some products are hard to collect. A clay bowl will not store in a portfolio, and a child's block construction cannot be saved. A story that a child tells disappears immediately. Works of this kind can be described or collected on tape or film.

These collections are invaluable in assessing children's progress throughout the year and demonstrating it to parents. They also allow teachers to see the breadth of children's work in a way that no other form of evaluation allows. In addition, teachers can evaluate what each child has actually done, rather than depending on an indirect assessment, such as a test. In addition, when using a portfolio approach to evaluation, there is no separation between instruction and evaluation.

RECORDING THE RESULTS OF EVALUATION

Collecting data is only one step in the process of evaluation. Teachers must then interpret and judge data. Finally, plans for action should result from these interpretations.

Teachers use evaluation data to make decisions about children's programs. If the children have achieved the goals of a study unit, they can confidently move on to new work. If they have not, then the teacher should plan special activities or modify the program.

The information collected on each child can also provide the basis for differentiated educational activities. As teachers become aware of each child's skills, abilities, interests, and behavior patterns, programming can become more meaningful and closer to meeting the needs of particular children. Teachers can vary the pace and try other forms of programming.

The results of evaluation are often shared with others: future teachers, ancillary personnel, the school principal, and parents. The need for communication and for later reference requires that teachers use some record-keeping system. Many schools maintain cumulative record folders on children; teachers may supplement these with their own records. A good record-keeping system is one in which significant information may be found easily.

In addition to the cumulative record folder, teachers keep a variety of records on children that may not follow the children to later classes. Records of daily attendance are generally required, and new teachers should become familiar with the procedures in their schools. Some schools require that all absences be accounted for or that children submit a release from a physician before entering school after certain illnesses.

Even if a child is absent for a short time, it is wise for the teacher to contact the family. Such absences may signal family crisis. At times, families may even move from a community without notifying the school. Brief contact with the family helps the teacher understand the reasons for absence and may provide clues to help the child.

Teachers often have the children tally their participation in specific activities and may wish to transfer the results of the tally to a more compact form later. The results of teachers' observations are also an important record of children's activities. Most observations are short and can easily fit on one or two five-by-eight-inch cards. Organizing these in a card file allows the teacher to leaf through quickly to review information on the children.

Because teaching is a public trust, teachers are being called upon more and more frequently to justify their professional acts. Records are important not only for teachers' decision making but also as a way of justifying their decisions to others. Demands may come from supervisors or from the parents and the community the school serves. The public can require professionals to document the sources of their decisions and judgments, and teachers must be prepared to meet this requirement.

REPORTING TO PARENTS

Parents are interested in the progress of their children in school. The Family Education Rights and Privacy Act, Public Law 93-380 (1974), grants parents and their children rights in relation to children's school records. The law provides the following rights (Herndon, 1981):

1. **Right to Examine Records.** Parents have the right to examine their child's official records. They also have the right to have the records explained to them. A written request should be honored within 45 days. Parents can work with the school to make sure that the child's records are complete and accurate. Students who are over the age of 18 also have this right.
2. **Right to Privacy.** This law protects the privacy of the child's official record.

(More information on parents' and children's rights under this law can be obtained by writing to FERBA, 330 C Street, N. W., Room 4511, Switzer Building, Washington, D. C. 20202.)

Reports to parents represent only one part of the teacher's relationship, but they are important and require the utmost care and honesty.

An ideal report should be easy to complete, yet comprehensive. It should communicate clearly and unequivocally the child's behavior and learning in school without being burdensome to read or requiring parents to comprehend professional language.

However, it is difficult to communicate clearly when teachers and parents may have different referents for the same words or use different words to describe the same behavior. It is hard for teachers to be fully descriptive when they must complete thirty or more reports several times during the year. It is also difficult to pinpoint progress without seeming unnecessarily judgmental.

Most reporting systems are the result of compromise. They are not too difficult to administer, and they communicate reasonably clearly. Teachers seem unsatisfied with almost all reporting systems; perhaps there is no ideal system. Most schools tend to use report cards, descriptive letters to parents, or parent conferences as ways of reporting; often these are used in some combination.

Reporting Systems

Report Cards Report cards are relatively simple to complete and communicate fairly well to parents. A report card may contain lines representing various areas of pupil achievement, such as reading and writing. Schools sometimes also include certain behavior characteristics or study habits.

Symbols are often used to report a child's achievement, such as letter grades A to D or F, or U for unsatisfactory and S for satisfactory achievement. Additional symbols for improvement or high achievement can also be used.

Though assigning a letter grade can be relatively simple, determining exactly what it means can be difficult. If grade-level standards are used, then performance level is fairly well communicated by the report card. It does not show, however, if a child is working at his or her expected capacity, above it, or below it. If children are graded according to teachers' estimates of their capability, then the letter or symbol will mean something different for each child and the common base in communication breaks down.

Schools use a great variety of report cards for kindergarten and elementary grades. D. Keith Osborn and Janie D. Osborn (1989) analyzed report cards in terms of the methods of grading used, frequency of reporting, the format of the report cards, and their content. The report of their survey presents a great many samples of the kinds of report cards used.

Despite the limitations of report cards, both parents and teachers often state that they like to use them, possibly because of the security built by years of tradition. However, schools frequently find that they must augment this type of communication, sometimes with supplementary checklists.

Descriptive Letters A report card communicates a child's level of performance but not the qualitative aspects of school work. Teachers may use descriptive letters to tell more about the quality and content of the child's work, providing a fuller picture for parents. A descriptive letter might contain information about the child's learning style, about books the child has read and materials the child has used, or about the child's interactions with others. Some teachers write individual letters about each child; others duplicate a single letter telling the parents what the class as a whole has done during the year, supplementing this information with individual reports in conferences.

Parent Conferences The most communicative, but also the most time-consuming, means of reporting is the parent conference. In a conference, parents and teacher can sit face-to-face and discuss mutual concerns about the child. They can correct any misunderstandings instantly and provide immediate feedback.

Parent conferences should be planned carefully. Suggestions for planning and conducting parent conferences are provided in Chapter 8. Teachers can make a list of concerns as an outline of items to be covered in the conference. Parents bring up their concerns as well. Teacher records are invaluable in the conference. Teachers can share observations; refer to test results, ratings, and checklists; and show pupil products to parents to demonstrate growth over the school year. It is useful to keep a record of parent conferences, noting the topics discussed, the reactions of parents, and any procedures that should follow up the conference, such as additional observation or communication.

Parent conferences are often used at the nursery and kindergarten level because the lack of grade-level standards on which to base a grade symbol requires that descriptive reporting take place. Conferences can be equally useful at every level of education, however, and in many cases the best communication takes place through a combination of techniques.

Reporting is only one component of a system of evaluation. The major impact of teachers' evaluations is the improvement of the educational experience of each child. By knowing their children and the effects of classroom activities on each individual, teachers can continue activities that have proved successful, replace unsuccessful ones with new activities, and continue to extend the learning opportunities of the children. A realistic picture of classroom activities and their consequences can help provide continually richer educational opportunities to children during their early years in school.

SUMMARY

Evaluation is an important part of teaching at any level. Teachers of young children are concerned with evaluating programs, settings, materials, and children. A variety of techniques must be used in evaluating children, and teachers should not rely heavily on standardized tests.

Evaluation includes making judgments as well as collecting information. The judgments made must also be reported to others, including parents, administrators, and other teachers.

REFERENCES

Baker, E. L. (1988). Domain-referenced tests. In J. P. Keeves (Ed.), *Educational research, methodology, and measurement: An international handbook* (pp. 370–372). New York: Pergamon Press.

Beaty, J. J. (1992). *Skills for preschool teachers.* Columbus, OH: Merrill.

Bredekamp, S. (Ed.) (1987). *Developmentally appropriate practices in early childhood education programs serving children from birth through age 8* (expanded ed.). Washington, DC: National Association for the Education of Young Children.

Cohen, D. H., & Stern, V. (1983). *Observing and recording the behavior of young children* (2nd ed.). New York: Teachers College Press.

Cryan, J. (1986). Evaluation: Plague or promise. *Childhood Education, 62*(5), 350–356.

Eisner, E. W. (1981). On the differences between scientific and artistic approaches to qualitative research. *Educational Researcher, 10,* 5–9.

Genishi, C. (1982). Observational research methods for early childhood education. In B. Spodek (Ed.), *Handbook of research in early childhood education* (pp. 564–591). New York: Free Press.

Goodwin, W. L., & Driscoll, L. A. (1980). *Handbook for measurement and evaluation in early childhood education.* San Francisco: Jossey-Bass.

Goodwin, W. L., & Goodwin, L. D. (1993). Young children and measurement: Standardized and nonstandardized instruments in early childhood education. In B. Spodek (Ed.), *Handbook of research on the education of young children*(pp. 441–463). New York: Macmillan.

Graue, M. E., & Shepard, L. A. (1989). Predictive validity of the Gesell School Readiness Test. *Early Childhood Research Quarterly, 4,* 303–316.

Harms, T., & Clifford, R. (1980). *Early childhood environment rating scale.* New York: Teachers College Press.

Herndon, E. B. (1981). *Your child and testing.* Pueblo, CO: Consumer Information Center, National Institute of Education.

Hillerich, R. L. (1974). So you're evaluating reading programs. *Elementary School Journal, 75,* 172–182.

Ilg, F. L., Ames, L. B., Haines, J., & Gillespie, C. (1978). *School readiness* (Rev. ed.). New York: Harper & Row.

Jones, E. (1979). *Dimensions of teaching-learning environments.* Pasadena: Pacific Oaks College.

Kamii, C. (1990). *Achievement testing in the early grades: The games that grownups play.* Washington, DC: National Association for the Education of Young Children.

Mager, R. F. (1975). *Preparing instructional objectives* (Rev. ed.). Belmont, CA: Pitman Learning.

Mehrens, W. A., & Lehmann, I. J. (1991). *Measurement and evaluation in education and psychology* (4th ed.). New York: Holt, Rinehart & Winston.

National Association for the Education of Young Children (1991). *Accreditation criteria and procedures of the National Academy of Early Childhood Programs* (rev. ed.). Washington, DC: Author.

Nichols, A. S., & Ochoa, A. (1971). Evaluating textbooks for elementary social studies: Criteria for the seventies. *Social Education, 35,* 290ff.

Osborn, D. K., & Osborn, J. D. (1989). *An analysis of elementary and kindergarten report cards.* Athens, GA: Education Associates.

Saracho, O. N. (1983). Using observation techniques to plan in-service education. *Child Care Information Exchange, 29,* 14–16.

Saracho, O. N. (1986). The development of the Preschool Reading Attitudes Scale. *Child Study Journal, 16*(2), 113–124.

Saracho, O. N. (1987). An instructional evaluation study in early childhood education. *Studies in Educational Evaluation, 13,* 163–174.

Saracho, O. N. (1988). Assessing instructional materials in an early childhood teacher education curriculum: The search for impact. *Reading Improvement, 25*(1), 10–27.

Shepard, L. A. (1991). The influence of standardized tests on the early childhood curriculum, teachers, and children. In B. Spodek & O. N. Saracho (Eds.), *Issues in early childhood curriculum:*

Yearbook in early childhood education, Vol. 2 (pp. 166–189). New York: Teachers College Press.

Shepard, L. A., & Graue, M. E. (1993). The morass of school readiness screening: Research on test use and test validity. In B. Spodek (Ed), *Handbook of research on the education of young children* (pp, 293–305). New York: Macmillan.

Spodek, B. (1991). Early childhood education and cultural definitions of knowledge. In B. Spodek & O. N. Saracho (Eds.), *Issues in early childhood curriculum: Yearbook in early childhood education*, Vol. 2 (pp. 1–20). New York: Teachers College Press.

Spodek, B., & Brown, P. C. (1993). Curriculum alternatives in early childhood education. In B. Spodek (Ed.), *Handbook of research on the education of young children* (pp. 91–104). New York: Macmillan.

Spodek, B., & Saracho, O. N. (1994). *Dealing with individual differences in the early childhood classroom.* White Plains, NY: Longman.

Stevens, W. W., & Fetsko. W. (1968). A curriculum analysis system. *Social Science Education Consortium Newsletter*, No. 4, pp. 1–4.

Vincent, D. (1988). Norm-referenced assessment. In J. P. Keeves (Ed.), *Educational research, methodology,*

10

Child's Play as Education

CHAPTER OVERVIEW

This chapter presents:

- Definitions of play
- Classic and contemporary theories of play
- Different types of educational play, including dramatic play, manipulative play, physical play, and games
- The relationship between play and the early childhood curriculum
- Ways to guide educational play

INTRODUCTION

Play activities or their derivatives have always been part of early childhood educational programs. The original Froebelian kindergarten included the manipulation of Gifts, the use of craft activities or Occupations, and the involvement of children in the Mother's Plays and Songs, described in Chapter 2. Although these activities were not free, expressive forms of play, they involved manipulation and were derived from observations of the free play of German peasant children. Friedrich Froebel abstracted and systematized what he identified as the essential elements of play, to insure that they would be given to all children.

Maria Montessori, in developing her educational method, similarly abstracted the essential elements of the natural play of children, reconstructed them, and systematized them as an instructional method. Activities in these two educational methods were meant to achieve different instructional goals. Froebel wanted children to gain the spiritual meanings symbolized by the materials and the activities. Montessori, however, wanted children to gain both a greater understanding of the properties of the objects themselves and specific skills in observing and ordering materials. Both educators abstracted elements they considered educationally productive from the informal activities of children and eliminated many of the qualities of play from the educational method.

Only with the advent of the reform kindergarten movement and the modern nursery school movement in the first quarter of the twentieth century did the natural play of children become accepted as a vehicle for learning. These approaches to early childhood education made no attempt to abstract only the "educational" elements from play. Instead, children's natural play activities were supported and nurtured as being educationally significant in their own right, though play was not considered to be the only way children could learn.

In these newer early childhood education programs, equipment and materials were designed to support play in classrooms. Teachers used these materials and equipment to stimulate and elaborate play activities. Many of these materials and equipment can be seen in preschool or kindergarten classrooms today. Almost all preprimary classrooms have some sort of doll corner or housekeeping area. In these areas, miniature representations of kitchen equipment—pots, pans, and dishes—household furniture, dolls, cleaning equipment, plastic food, and similar items allow children to act out their representations of home life. The block area is another place where equipment designed to foster children's play can be found. In addition to the equipment in these areas, one might also find dress-up clothes, steering wheels, toy cars and trucks, and innumerable other devices that support play.

Because of increased concern about the educational consequences of early childhood programs, alternative approaches to educating young children have developed, and there have been numerous studies of the varying approaches, including their consequences. This chapter will review definitions and theories of play, as well as analyzing the ways teachers can use play to further educational objectives.

DEFINITIONS OF PLAY

Play
is hard to define, but in a sense it defines itself.

Many psychologists, philosophers, educators, and others have attempted to define **play.** Each new definition solves some of the problems with previous definitions, but problems still exist in distinguishing play from nonplay activities. While most of us intuitively know play when we see it, it is difficult to specify what helps us separate play from nonplay. We do not have clearly definable, observable, mutually agreed-upon criteria for determining whether an activity is play. An activity might be considered play in some settings at some times and nonplay in other settings at other times. One method students of play have used is to define play is to state what it is not. Helen B. Schwartzman (1978) suggests, "Play is not *work*; play is not *real*; play is not *serious*; play is not *productive*; and so forth. . . . [Yet] work can be playful while play can sometimes be experienced as work; and likewise, that players create worlds that are often more real, serious and productive than so-called real life" (pp. 4–5).

Eva Neumann (1971) attempted to create a unified definition of play by identifying elements that many definitions have in common. She categorized these elements as *criteria* for play, or characteristics that differentiate play from nonplay; *processes* of play, or its form and method; and *objectives* of play, or the goals toward which play is directed. Neumann suggested that no clear-cut lines separate work, or nonplay, from play. Activities are more work or more play depending on the absence or presence of these three elements of play.

J. Nina Leiberman (1977) has identified a quality of *playfulness* that characterizes play, including physical, social, and cognitive spontaneity; manifest joy; and a sense of humor. Leiberman related these qualities to divergent thinking and creativity. While these characteristics are often manifest in play activities, they are also manifest in nonplay activity. Thus, they cannot be used to discriminate between play and nonplay.

Catherine Garvey (1990) proposed the following definition of play:

1. Play is pleasurable, enjoyable. Even when not actually accompanied by signs of mirth, it is still positively valued by the players.
2. Play has no extrinsic goals. Its motivations are intrinsic and serve no other objective. In fact, it is more an enjoyment of means than an effort devoted to some particular end. In utilitarian terms, it is inherently unproductive.
3. Play is spontaneous and voluntary. It is not obligatory but is freely chosen by the players.
4. Play involves some active engagement on the part of the players.
5. Play has certain systematic relations to what is not play. (pp. 4–5)

While such a set of criteria may not incorporate every belief about play or be conceptually pure, it is probably as good a definition as educators need. Play, in a sense, defines itself. Clear-cut rules of definition may be more important to researchers studying play than to educators using play for a variety of purposes.

THEORIES OF PLAY

Elmer Mitchell and Bernard S. Mason (1948) have identified four classes of theories of play. These include the surplus energy theory, relaxation theory, pre-exercise theory, and recapitulation theory. J. Barnard Gilmore (1971) characterized these theories as classical theories and identified another set of theories, which he characterized as dynamic theories of play. The dynamic theories have been further elaborated by Michael J. Ellis (1973) and Greta G. Fein (1979). While the classical theories attempt to explain why children play, the dynamic theories concern themselves with the content of the play.

Classical Theories

Surplus Energy Theory This theory postulates that a quantity of energy is available to the individual and that the individual tends to expend that energy either through goal-directed activity (work) or through goalless activity (play). Play occurs at any time individuals have more energy available than they need to expend for work. According to this theory, the content of the play activity is not important, and one form of play could easily be substituted for another.

Relaxation Theory This theory postulates that play is used to replenish expended energy. After a period of fatiguing activity (work), the individual needs an opportunity to be involved in a relaxing activity (play) that will generate new energy. According to this theory, play occurs when individuals have little energy left rather than when they have too much energy. Again, one kind of play activity can be substituted for another as a replenishing device.

Pre-exercise Theory According to the pre-exercise theory, play is instinctive behavior. Children instinctively involve themselves in play activities that are, in essence, a form of some more mature behavior they will later have to assume. The content of play is therefore determined by the content of future adult activity. Play is seen as preparation for future life.

Recapitulation Theory This theory suggests that play must be understood, not in terms of the future activities of the individual, but in relation to past activities of the species. Play becomes a way of engaging in the activities of past generations so that individuals instinctively rid themselves of primitive and unnecessary instinctual skills that have been carried over through heredity. The stages of play correspond to the stages of development of the human race, going from the most ancient and primitive to the most modern and relatively sophisticated. By allowing individuals to rid themselves of primitive activities, play prepares them for modern work activities.

While the last two of the classical theories have been discredited, the first two of the classical theories of play—though not grounded in research—seem to have a common-sense ring of truth. Teachers often feel that a classroom full of children is less capable of serious learning on a Friday afternoon, for example, or on the day prior to the start of a vacation. They may postpone important lessons until the children return with greater stores of energy amassed during the play times of weekends and vacations. Similarly, after a period of inclement weather, when outdoor play has been denied, children seem to have an overabundance of energy. Teachers may look for ways to help them work off their surplus energy so that they can settle down to work.

It is interesting to note that the same activity—play—has been understood through the years from a series of opposing theories. Play responds to either too much or too little energy. Play can be either a form of pre-exercise for sophisticated action or the purging of primitive forms of action in the organism.

Dynamic Theories

The dynamic theories of play do not attempt to understand why children play; they simply accept the fact. Instead, these theories attempt to explain the content of play. The dynamic theories of children's play are grounded in constructivist theory or in psychodynamic theory.

Constructivist Theory Piaget believed that the development of the human intellect involves two related processes: *assimilation* and *accommodation*. Together these processes create an *equilibrium*, which represents the state of an individual's knowledge at a particular time. In the process of assimilation, individuals continually abstract information from the outside world and fit it into organized schemes representing what they already know. Individuals also accommodate to new knowledge by modifying their organizational schemes when the schemes are not consistent with new information. The consequence of these two processes is a state of equilibrium. According to Piaget, play is a way of manipulating the outside world so that it fits a person's present organizational schemes. As such, play serves a vital function in the child's developing intellect and remains, to some extent, always present in human behavior.

Greta G. Fein (1979) has used the constructivist theory of Lev. S. Vygotsky to understand the play of children. According to Vygotsky, children form mental structures through the use of tools and signs. Play, the creation of imaginary situations, grows out of the tension between the individual child and society. It liberates the child from the constraints of immediate reality and allows the child to control the existing situation. Children can use objects to stand for something other than what they really are. A broom can become a horse and a length of hose a gasoline pump. In play, meanings are freed from their related objects and actions so that children can engage in higher-order thought processes. Thus, pretend play serves a central role in children's acquisition of language and problem-solving abilities.

Vygotsky believed that development follows learning. From this point of view, development is dependent on the child's social and historical context. Children are able to accomplish tasks somewhat beyond their level of development if they are provided with support from more mature individuals. This level of development that is just beyond the child's level at any time is called the *zone of proximal development (ZPD)*. Vygotsky suggests that play represents children's functioning in the ZPD and thus aids development.

Psychodynamic Theory Freud considered play to be a cathartic activity that allows children to master difficult situations by ridding themselves of feelings they cannot handle. Children use fantasy play situations to act out adult roles, gaining a feeling of mastery that allows them to cope with real situations. Through play, children can act out personally painful occurrences and master the pain by coming to grips with it in the fantasy of the play situation. This same mastery in fantasy can help children cope with the affective elements of more positive life situations as well. Lois Murphy, in her book *The Widening World of Childhood* (1962), presents vivid descriptions of young children using play activities to cope with problems of living. A young child who returns from an emergency visit to the hospital, for example, might play "hospital" as a way of making sense of that experience.

Current psychodynamic theory sees play more as a coping mechanism than as catharsis. Play has been used as a form of psychotherapy for children who are not able to articulate their feelings or describe their experiences in words. Psychotherapists engage individual children in play interviews, using toys to help children dramatize their feelings and experiences. Play therapists are trained in interpreting the emotional meanings of children's play. While such therapists as Anna Freud and Melanie Klein took a purely psychoanalytic approach to play therapy, others, such as Virginia Axline, were more nondirective in their orientation (Hughes, 1991). Axline believed that therapists should develop a warm, friendly relationship with the children they treat, accepting and respecting the children completely. She saw the therapy situation as a permissive one in which children could lead their therapist and express themselves freely, while the therapist recognized the children's feelings and reflected those feelings back to the children. However, limits were set for even this situation (Axline, 1980). For example, children would not be allowed to be self-destructive. While there is a difference between education and therapy, the idea of learning about children by observing their play remains a part of the tradition of early childhood education.

Other Theories Michael J. Ellis (1973) characterizes as modern theories those that view play as a function of competence motivation and those that view play as an arousal-seeking device. Traditionally, psychological theories conceive of humanity as naturally passive. Thus human activity usually must be explained in terms of either external rewards and punishments or internal drives.

Arousal-seeking theory suggests that individuals continually seek stimuli to maintain an active information-procession mode.

The **arousal-seeking theory** suggests that human beings normally need to be continually involved in information-processing activities; hence their normal state is active. The absence of stimuli in individuals' environment leads to discomfort that causes them to increase the amount of perceptual information available, either by seeking additional stimulation externally or by creating it internally, possibly by daydreaming. Too much stimulation leads individuals to attend less to their environment. Play is seen as a vehicle by which children can seek and mediate the amount of external and internal stimulation available to create an optimal balance.

Competence motivation is the desire to engage in an activity as a result of the feeling of competence provided by success.

Robert White's (1959) theory of **competence motivation** suggests that people receive satisfaction from developing competencies, independent of whether they gain external rewards in the process. From this point of view, human activity can take place without external reinforcement. Play is one way in which children act on their environment, becoming more effective in their actions and receiving more personal satisfactions. The activity of playing is self-rewarding.

Studying play from a cognitive-affective framework, Jerome Singer (1973) considers the children's imaginative play to be an effort to organize their experiences while utilizing their motor and cognitive capacities. Children show interest, alertness, and joy as they become familiar with and master materials. Singer sees the play of children as a vehicle for exploring, achieving competence, and developing creativity.

The dynamic theories of play suggest that play activities have significant consequences for children's development. These consequences are consistent with the basic goals of early childhood education. Our concern as teachers should be with the content of play and how to move it in desired directions. From Freud we learn that the content of play is strongly affective; from Piaget we learn that it is strongly cognitive. Play can support learning in both these domains.

Play can also have an important socializing role, a third significant domain. According to George Herbert Mead (1934), children use play as a way of developing their concept of self—what they are. They develop self-concept by actually trying on the roles of those about them in dramatic play. The concept of the "generalized other," the view of the individual in a cultural context on which mature socialization is built, develops in the next stage as children play games. The games are based on rules and require, for children to perform them properly, that they internalize an understanding of the others' role behavior as well as their own.

Stages in Play Development All of children's behaviors change as the children grow, including play behavior. As early as 1932, Mildred Parten observed young children and identified a series of stages in their social play. At age three, children were either *unoccupied* (not playing), *solitary players* (playing alone), or *onlookers* (observing the play of other children). By age four, children engaged in *parallel play* (playing side by side with others), and by age five they were engaged in *associative* or *cooperative play* (engaging other children in their play). For Parten, parallel play was a bridge between solitary play and cooperative play, allowing children to adjust to social situations in play. Parten's study seemed to identify a series of play stages, with onlooker and solitary play reflective of immaturity and cooperative play signaling greater maturity. More recent studies, however, have shown that both older and younger children engage in solitary play, though older children use this type of play in a more constructive way than do younger children (Johnson & Ershler, 1981).

Piaget (1962) identified three stages in young children's play—*practice play*, *symbolic play*, and *games with rules*—that parallel three of the stages of intellectual development he identified: the stages of sensorimotor thought, preoperational thought, and concrete operational thought (see Chapter 3). Practice play includes the manipulative play of infants and toddlers. Symbolic play can be seen in the dramatic play of preschool and kindergarten children. During kindergarten and beyond, children shift from dramatic play, spending more time playing formal games.

Sarah Smilansky (1968) adapted Piaget's stages of play to study preschool children's dramatic play. She defined *functional play* as the routine or stereotyped use of play materials or as simple motor activity. She defined *constructive play* as sequential and purposive play that results in a finished product and *dramatic play* as thematic role-play that involves transforming situations or objects.

Kenneth Rubin, Terence Maioni, and Margaret Hornung (1976) combined the stages of Parten with those of Smilansky in studying the influence of intervention on children's play behavior. This combination provides a framework for studying the intellectual and social aspects of children's play. Teachers can observe their children at play to determine the level at which the children play in various settings. They can then intervene in that play by modifying the setting, adding material, raising questions of the children who are playing, or even stepping in momentarily to move the play along and then stepping out again. By again observing the children at play, they can determine the influence they have had on the children's play. Such intervention needs to be done with sensitivity, allowing the children to maintain control over the play so that it continues to truly be a play activity.

Gender Differences in Play Girls' play is different from boys' play. Some scholars have suggested that the differences reflect inherent differences between males and females. Others have suggested that the differences reflect differences in what boys and girls are taught and how they are treated. For example, a boy may be given a bat and ball to play with while a girl is given a doll. More and more, we are learning that boys and girls behave differently, even from birth. At the same time, we are becoming increasingly aware that the way we treat boys and girls and what we expect of them shapes their behavior so that the two groups become either more alike or more different.

The research on gender differences in children's play has concentrated on (1) toy selection, (2) fantasy play, (3) rough-and-tumble play, and (4) games with rules. Most of the research reflects one of two theoretical orientations. According to learning theory, children begin to learn to function in gender-appropriate ways even before they understand the concept of gender. According to cognitive development theory, children engage in gender-appropriate activities because these activities are consistent with their emerging gender concept (Hughes, 1991).

James E. Johnson, James E. Christie, and Thomas D. Yawkey (1987) reviewed the research on gender differences in young children's play. They noted that boys engage in more rough-and-tumble play and often appear more active than do girls. Boys are also more likely to engage in superhero play. On the other hand, girls are more likely to engage in constructive and table-toy play. They also show interest in a greater variety of toys and play materials. Girls tend to prefer playing in smaller groups and tend to have imaginary friends more often than do boys. Both boys and girls tend to choose playmates of the same gender.

These differences are differences in tendencies of behavior. There is a considerable amount of overlap in the play of boys and girls, and any one child may not reflect the tendencies of his or her gender. Segregating children in play areas by gender tends to create gender stereotypes among children and to highlight differences. Teachers should design play activities that allow each child the widest possible range of play alternatives and that try to eliminate whatever gender segregation might exist. Doing so will avoid teaching children sex-stereotyped behavior in the school context.

EDUCATIONAL USES OF PLAY

The theories of play discussed above are descriptive theories. They attempt to explain play as it exists. An understanding of these theories can allow us to extrapolate guides for action appropriate for use in teaching situations.

Educational play is a play activity through which children learn.

A productive distinction might be made between ***educational* play** and *noneducational* play (Spodek & Saracho, 1988). The difference is not in the activities or the degree of enjoyment that children receive, but rather in the purposes ascribed to the play by the persons responsible for the children's activities. Educational play has as its prime purpose the children's learning. Such play is still fun for children, for if it does not provide personal satisfaction, the activity stops being play. Educational play activities, however, serve an educational purpose while remaining personally satisfying. Thus, children in the housekeeping area of a classroom receive personal satisfaction from playing out the particular role they have chosen, from interacting with persons in other roles, and from using various play props in innovative ways. The educational value of this play is that it helps the children explore and understand role dimensions and interaction patterns, thereby supporting their further understanding of the social world and helping them to build a realistic sense of self.

As noted earlier in this chapter, there is no clear distinction between work and play. Rather, some activities are more work and others are more play. Doris Bergen (1988) developed a schema to show the relationships between types of play and types of learning. On the continuum from play to work, she identifies different degrees of play, from free play, to guided play, to directed play, to work disguised as play, to work. Associated with each is a different type of learning, from discovery learning, to guided discovery learning, to receptive learning, to rote learning, to drill-repetitive practice. Just as there is room in early childhood programs for all types of learning, in varying degrees, so there should be room for all types of activity—from free play through work. As children

Figure 10–1 The Schema of Play and Learning

Free play	Guided play	Directed play	Work disguised as play	Work
Discovery learning	Guided discovery learning	Reception learning	Rote learning	Drill-repetitive practice

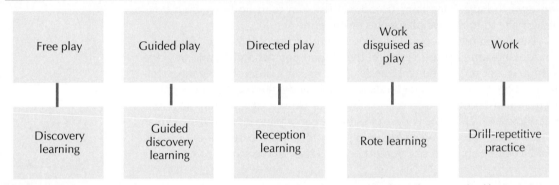

Source: Reprinted by permission of Doris Bergen. In *Play as a Medium for Learning and Development,* edited by Doris Bergen (Heinemann, A Division of Reed Publishing (USA) Inc., Portsmouth, NH), 1988, p. 171.

get older, teachers usually limit the amount of time assigned to free play in the classroom and increase the amount of directed play and work.

Educational play may take many forms. The key role of teachers here is in modifying the natural spontaneous play of children so that it has educational value while maintaining its qualities as play. Teachers also create less spontaneous educational play activities. Such play is evaluated not only according to the children's degree of involvement but also according to its effectiveness in achieving educational aims.

Manipulative play includes play in which children handle equipment or materials.

Most nursery school and kindergarten classes include four kinds of educational play: *manipulative play, physical play, dramatic play,* and *games.* In **manipulative play,** children handle relatively small pieces of equipment such as puzzles, counting rods, or peg sets. The actions are relatively self-contained; that is, there is no necessary interaction between the manipulative activity and other kinds of activities, nor is there a dramatic element to the play. Children can achieve the goals of manipulative play activities directly by handling the material. Using Montessori apparatus, although defined as "work" by Montessorians, is a good example of educational manipulative play. Children may be given a series of wooden cylinders and a case into which they fit. By comparing cylinders and attempting to fit them into the case, the children begin to learn to make size comparisons and to arrange items in a series. Manipulative play activities generally have fairly narrowly defined educational goals.

Physical play includes gross motor play activities.

Physical play involves children's large-muscle actions, such as running, jumping, or riding a tricycle. These activities help children increase their physical skills or learn to use them in new situations. Physical play can have a dramatic component, and teachers can elaborate the play either by making the physical activities more challenging or by providing social content to the play.

Dramatic play includes activities in which children act out a pretend role.

Dramatic play requires that the child pretend to act out a role, often in relationship to other children playing their roles in informal dramatic

Children can build fanciful creations with materials.

situations that may represent true-life situations. The housekeeping area (or doll corner) is the most readily observable setting for dramatic play. Here children act out the roles of family members in actions representing home situations. Teachers may set up other dramatic play situations to enable the children to play many roles. In addition to using dramatic play areas, children often manipulate small things that represent objects or characters. Informal puppet play allows children to act out roles. Building with unit blocks can also involve miniature dramatizations. To encourage this type of dramatic play, teachers must provide adequate accessories, enough time for children to go beyond manipulative building, and ideas of sources for dramatic themes.

Games are a different kind of play activity. They are highly structured and include specific rules to be followed. Children at the four- and five-year-old levels are beginning to move into a stage in which they can play games. Simple games or musical activities containing elements of games are quite appropriate. Children need to be taught the strategies of game playing. Teachers should guide the games, for the children may not be mature enough to maintain rules or understand rule-appropriate behavior.

Games
are structured play activities organized around specific rules.

Many educators accept play as a part of preschool or kindergarten classroom activities. Play has equally valid uses with primary grade children as with children at lower educational levels. The "messing about" of the science program (Hawkins, 1965) is a form of play, as are many of the newer materials-oriented programs in mathematics. Dramatic play is often a useful avenue of social studies education and a support for language learning. Appropriate play activities can be integrated in almost all areas of learning in the primary school.

The distinctions made here between different types of play are useful. However, they are not absolute. There can be manipulative qualities to dramatic play, for example, and dramatic qualities to physical play. The distinctions are useful in identifying the predominant qualities of play activities and in suggesting ways of supporting play in school.

Manipulative Play

A manipulative play center is desirable in prekindergarten or kindergarten classrooms. In the primary grades, manipulative materials are generally organized along subject-matter lines. A manipulative play center may have materials placed on open shelves, so they are readily accessible. A set of tables and chairs can also be included, but many of the materials can be just as easily used on the floor, preferably on a rug. The shelves can hold the types of materials discussed below.

Stacking and Nesting Toys Even younger preschoolers can use toys that contain parts to be ordered by size. These may be stacked on each other, threaded on a dowel, or nested in one another. Children learn to discriminate parts by size and to order these parts from the largest to the smallest. These materials are self-correcting, since children can easily see if they have put the parts in the right order.

Puzzles A wide variety of children's jigsaw puzzles is presently available, from puzzles that have just three or four pieces, each representing a single item, to rather complex puzzles made of two or three dozen pieces. Some of the simplest puzzles are formboards on which children put simple shapes, such as squares, circles, triangles, and trapezoids, into matching cut-out spaces. Picture puzzles are more complicated. The simplest ones have few pieces, and the pieces conform to the shape of the objects pictured. More complex ones have an increasing number of pieces, and the shape of the pieces may have nothing to do with the picture itself. Sturdy puzzles made out of wood or masonite will stand much use. It is a good idea to have a number of puzzles that vary in difficulty. If a puzzle rack is used for storage, the children can learn to carefully take out and replace puzzles, limiting the number of puzzle pieces that get lost. Marking the backs of each puzzle's pieces with a common symbol also helps children locate missing pieces. When losses do occur, teachers can shape substitutes out of wood putty, painting them to match the rest of the puzzle.

Teachers should organize the puzzles according to their difficulty and check the children periodically to see how they have progressed in their ability to complete puzzles. Although most children have had some experience in working with puzzles prior to school, some have not learned the appropriate skills. Teachers should not take these skills for granted, and a session or two at the beginning of the year explicitly showing all children how to complete puzzles may be useful.

Parquetry Blocks and Pegboards Parquetry blocks with wooden pieces of varying shapes and colors, and pegboard sets with pegs of different colors, are useful to teach children to distinguish among forms and colors and to remember those distinctions. Many of the skills children gain in using these materials lead to formal reading and mathematics instruction, since form discrimination is needed to distinguish letters and numbers from each other. Although children should have opportunities to manipulate these materials freely, teachers can make model cards for the children to replicate with the manipulative materials. These cards can be presented to children in order of difficulty to support mastery. Pegboard sets can also be equipped with elastic bands with which the children can create various shapes.

Construction Sets Small sets of constructive materials such as Lego, Tinker Toys, Lincoln Logs, or similar materials are useful. Children can use them to make fanciful creations or construct small buildings. A large variety of such construction materials is commercially available. Once children have built small structures, they can engage in miniature dramatic play with them.

Science Materials Plastic boxes containing sets of science materials can be included in the manipulative materials center. A battery, a bulb, and a couple of lengths of wire could constitute one set. A magnet with some small bits of material, some metallic and some not, could constitute another set. A plastic jar half filled with water, covered with a rubber membrane and containing a medicine dropper can be provided to allow children to explore what happens to the dropper when they press on the membrane and release it. A small basin of water along with some materials that float and some that sink, and a box of variously textured materials, can also be included for science exploration.

Mathematics Materials Counting rods; counting frames; simple measuring devices such as balances, primary rulers, and measuring cups and spoons; and materials to be measured or counted can all be incorporated into the manipulative materials center.

Montessori Materials Many Montessori didactic materials are ideally suited for the manipulative play center. They can be used independently by the children and are self-correcting in nature. Teachers need not use these materials as Montessori teachers would.

Locking Devices and Fastening Frames There are a number of commercially available boards that include different locking devices: hook and eye, barrel bolt, hasp, and the like. The parts to be locked may resemble small doors or windows that open and close. Teachers can make similar boards with materials assembled from a hardware store. These boards develop eye-hand coordination as well as teaching practical skills. Fastening frames with various fastening devices attached to pieces of cloth (zippers, buttons and buttonholes, snaps, shoelaces, and such) are

A galvanized tub can be used for water play.

also useful. Again, children develop not only eye-hand coordination but also skills they can use in dressing and undressing themselves.

Other Manipulative Materials A quick glance through an educational supply catalogue can provide further ideas for the manipulative center. Teachers might rummage through their own homes or through hardware stores to find materials that can be included in the classroom. Often some of the most stimulating and exciting materials for educational purposes result from the teacher's ingenuity.

Manipulative Play with Natural Materials While not generally included in the manipulative materials center, natural materials such as sand and water are important adjuncts to play. While specially designed sand-and-water tables are available commercially, a galvanized tub or a plastic wash basin can also be used. Children need freedom in using these materials but must also learn how to care for them and know the limitations for their use. A number of accessories, including containers, spoons, and shovels, should go with the water and sand. Wet sand can be molded in many shapes; dry sand can be sieved and run through funnels. Equipment for cleanup such as sponges, a floor brush, and a dustpan should be readily available for children to use.

Physical Play

Physical play generally requires much more space than does manipulative play. Much of children's outdoor play in early childhood classes falls into this category.

Outdoor Play The content of outdoor play depends as much on climate and weather conditions as on space and other considerations. In some regions, outdoor play consists mainly of sledding and building with snow during the bulk of the school year. In other areas, there are possibilities for free exploration and a wide use of materials, because the weather remains temperate during the school year. Teachers should vary outdoor play with the possibilities created by local conditions.

Outdoor space—both soft-surfaced and hard-surfaced areas—should be available and easily accessible to the classroom. The ground surface under any climbing equipment should allow children to fall or jump without being injured. Sand, tanbark, corncobs, pea gravel, or other appropriate materials should be provided. Some paved area should also be available for use with wheel toys. Teachers should have outdoor storage space for equipment, but they can also bring classroom materials outdoors.

Outdoor play activities and equipment should allow opportunities for climbing, running, jumping, riding on large pieces of equipment, and digging. Recent concern about playgrounds for young children has brought about the design of more complex pieces of equipment to support creative physical activities and social interaction in outdoor play. Some of these may be permanently installed and require little maintenance. In addition to permanent structures, other equipment should also be available, including

- sand pit for children's digging;
- playhouses and platforms;
- wheel toys, including tricycles, wagons, wheelbarrows, and boxes on casters;
- movable equipment for climbing, such as sawhorses, walking boards, barrels, packing crates, and ladders; and
- balls and jump ropes to be used for games.

VIGNETTE: PLAY, PRESCHOOL

The children run into the playground area. Emily and Elizabeth head immediately for the sandbox. They each grab a pail and shovel and sit down next to each other.

"Let's make mudcakes," says Elizabeth.

"OK," says Emily.

The girls work quietly, digging sand and filling their buckets. Soon Elizabeth gets up, walks over to the teacher, and asks, "Would you like a mudcake?"

"Oh, how wonderful!" the teacher answers, and pretends to taste the mudcake.

When Elizabeth returns to the sand, Emily is no longer there. In her place, Kristen is sitting in the middle of the sandbox.

"Kristen, move! You're in the way," says Elizabeth.

Kristen ignores Elizabeth and rubs her hands in the sand. Elizabeth looks over to the climbing apparatus, sees Emily, and runs towards her.

Indoor Play Many of the same physical play activities that are offered to children outdoors can be provided indoors as well. Sometimes these activities must be scaled down to the space available. In some schools a multipurpose room is available for vigorous play. In other situations, classes are limited to their own rooms. In any event, some physical play can take place indoors.

Teachers can often include some climbing apparatus in their classrooms. Boards, sawhorses, and ladders can be combined into rather elaborate, exciting edifices that require relatively little storage space and are fun for the children. Wheel toys can also be provided indoors for young children, but these should be smaller than the ones used outdoors—sturdy wooden trucks or boxes on casters rather than tricycles and wagons. In many cases schools have built playhouses with elevated platforms, ladders, staircases, slides, and other artifacts into small spaces in a classroom.

Dramatic Play

Dramatic play, or sociodramatic or pretend play, as it is also called, is a universal tendency of children between the ages of three and seven. It creates a microworld of social roles and relationships. Though dramatic play is universal, there are individual and group differences in the dramatic play of children, as Smilansky (1968) noted. Children can be helped to improve their dramatic play with relatively little investment of teachers'

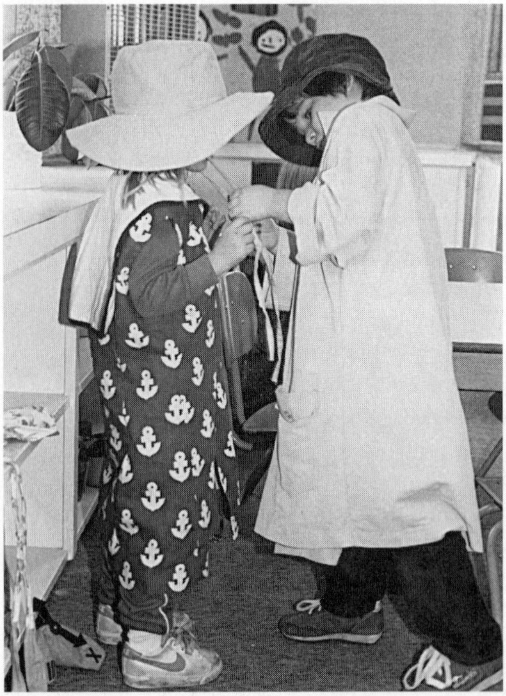

Dressing up helps children take on various roles in dramatic play.

time or effort. Teachers become facilitators of play, suggesting play themes, helping the children develop communication techniques, and demonstrating various play possibilities. Improving children's dramatic play has significant consequences in their social-emotional and cognitive development (Smilansky & Sheftaya, 1990).

In dramatic play children assume various adult roles, which unfold with a great deal of spontaneity. While children are generally acting out roles as they perceive and understand them, elements of fantasy may move the play far from reality. Children use objects to stand for something other than what they really are, so that a doll may stand for a baby, a stick for a horse, or a piece of hose for a gas pump. Children also develop their own scenarios in dramatic play. They set the stage, often using equipment to stand for whatever they wish. They plan the play activity, letting the plot and the dialogue evolve. Dramatic play is an important way in which young children express themselves. They test out their ideas and give expression to their feelings. They learn to work with others as they negotiate different social situations. Through dramatic play, children develop an understanding of the world around them and learn to cope with their environment.

Judith Bender (1971) has suggested setting up a number of "prop boxes" for the classroom. Each box would contain materials that would help children develop a particular dramatic play theme. The cardboard boxes in which stationery is shipped, or cardboard file boxes, can serve this purpose well. Each box should be labeled with the theme it supports, and materials and supplies in the collection should be listed on the out-

CONTENTS OF PROP BOXES

Restaurant: plastic dishes, tableware, napkins and napkin holder, trays, salt and pepper shakers, menus, ordering pads, pencils, sponges, towels, plastic food, cooking utensils, white apron, cash register, and telephone

Supermarket: empty food boxes and cans, wagon for shopping cart, play money, cash register, signs, and supermarket advertisements

Doctor's Office/Hospital: stethoscope, scale, gauze pads, bandages, adhesive tape, toy hypodermic syringe, white shirt or coat, and empty medicine containers

Hairdresser/Barber: mirror, comb, hairbrush, hair rollers, empty shampoo containers, empty hairspray cans, cloth to cover children's clothing, toy razor, and shaving brush

Construction Work: tools, such as hammers, saws, screwdrivers, wrenches, and pliers; tool box; paintbrushes; bucket; hard hat; painter's cap; overalls; and measuring tape

Airport: airline boarding passes, ticket envelopes, maps, pilot's caps, small suitcases, luggage tags, serving trays, steering wheel, and gauges

Post Office: envelopes, postcards, used stamps, rubber stamp and stamp pad, paper, pencils, play money, and empty milk cartons for mail boxes

side of the box. The appropriate prop box can be taken down and its contents used to encourage play. Once a box is used, the teacher should see that its contents are clean and replace any expendable materials that have been used before putting it back in storage. This way the material can be used immediately when the occasion arises.

In setting up an attractive dramatic play area, classroom teachers stimulate role-playing. If the materials reflect the home life of a family and little else, the play will generally remain in that realm. However, the total adult world, including work as well as family life, is the legitimate scope of school play.

For play situations to be educationally useful, they should be guided by teachers. This guidance requires that teachers be aware of and sensitive to children's play activities, that they have a sense of the goals of play, and that they be able to move into the play on occasion, making suggestions and even becoming players.

Most important, teachers are responsible for providing information that will move the play ahead; reading books or showing films and filmstrips often provides this information. Discussions, resource persons, and trips are all legitimate sources of new information for children's play, allowing the activity to shuttle between fantasy and reality in a wholesome way.

VIGNETTE: PLAY, KINDERGARTEN

Melanie and Jennifer are playing quietly together in the housekeeping area. Joshua and John are standing near the block area with large orange squares, pretending to be pizza delivery men. They walk over to Melanie and Jennifer and say, "Here are your pizzas," dropping them on the table nearby.

Melanie takes up one of the pizzas and pretends to taste it. "This is good," she says "I like pepperoni."

John and Joshua move off to another area of the room.

Block Play Falling somewhere between the categories of physical play and dramatic play is block play. Two basic kinds of blocks are used in early childhood education: the smaller unit blocks, which allow children to miniaturize their world, and the larger hollow blocks, which allow children to build large structures suitable as stages for dramatic play.

Unit blocks are solid, brick-like pieces of wood, generally made of hard wood. The basic unit is $5\frac{1}{2}$ inches by $2\frac{3}{4}$ inches by $1\frac{3}{8}$ inches. Double units and quadruple units are two and four times the length of the single unit block, and half units are one-half its length. Ramps, triangles, pillars, and boards are also part of a block set and are all scaled proportionately.

Children's block structures can be quite elaborate.

Because all blocks have the same proportions, children can build sturdy, elaborate structures that will stand up on their own.

Unit block structures are built on the floor. At first children will pile blocks up or build simple enclosures. As block play develops, children build more elaborate structures, sometimes taking days to complete them. These structures become representational; children add props, miniature people, animals, vehicles, signs, and the like as they use the blocks to represent places and to dramatize occurrences that might happen in those places.

Large hollow blocks are typically based on a unit of one square foot. The sides may be made of plywood or of solid wood with open ends. These sets usually include half units and double units as well as triangle ramps and boards. Because of the size and sturdiness of these blocks, children can use them to build large structures in which they can play. Hollow blocks can represent buildings, vehicles, or furniture. While large blocks made of cardboard are available, they are usually not as satisfactory as wooden ones. Their light weight makes structures less sturdy, and the blocks do not last as long.

Caroline Pratt and Jessie Stanton (1926) describe children going out into the neighborhood of the school and returning to symbolize their perceptions of it in block structures. Lucy Sprague Mitchell (1971) and Helen

Robison and Bernard Spodek (1965) provide examples of blocks being used to further young children's geographic understanding. Blocks can also be used to further science and mathematics learning. As children mature in their use of blocks, they move through various stages of block building, originally identified by Harriet Johnson (Hirsch, 1974) and modified by others. An awareness of these stages—beginning with just carrying blocks around and advancing to simple constructions and then to building elaborate structures that suggest dramatic content—is useful for teachers as an aid in guiding children's block building.

Blocks are expensive. They also take up a lot of space in the classroom. However, a great deal of learning can take place through the use of blocks, provided there is an adequate supply of them, there is space for building, and children are allowed to elaborate their block structures over several days. Teachers should also arrange the block area so that blocks are easy to take out and put back.

Games

A wide range of games can be used in early childhood classes. Some games are oriented only toward physical movement; others require little movement but a great deal of attention to problem solving. Different games can be used for different purposes.

In the nursery school and kindergarten years, games should be simple, with uncomplicated rules. Games at this level can include activities accompanied by singing and simple physical games in which children must follow a few directions. Lotto and other table games also have a place at this level. As the children move into the primary grades, more complicated physical activities requiring strict adherence to rules, and many of the traditional games of childhood, can be incorporated into the school day. In the classroom, teachers can use games to provide practice in the academic areas. Such games are often suggested in the teacher's manuals of textbook series and in teacher-oriented magazines such as *Early Childhood Education Today, Instructor,* or *Early Years.* Board games can also be used. Those that require evolving strategies and planning before making moves, such as checkers, can help children develop thinking skills.

In their book, *Group Games in Early Education* (1980), Rheta DeVries and Constance Kamii state that educationally useful games should

1. suggest something interesting and challenging for children to figure out how to do,
2. make it possible for children themselves to judge their success, and
3. permit all players to participate actively throughout the game. (p. 3)

DeVries and Kamii argue that group games can help children achieve the aims of early childhood education, including becoming more autonomous; developing the ability to decenter and coordinate different points of view; coming up with interesting ideas, problems, and questions; and putting things into relationships. Among the games these authors suggest are aiming games such as dodge ball; races; chasing games; hiding games; guessing games; card games such as Old Maid and Animal Rummy; and board games such as Candyland, Chutes and Ladders, and Lotto. Teachers should modify the games so that they are in harmony with the way the children think, and they should reduce adult power as much as possible while encouraging cooperation among children.

Group games also have a role in the outdoor activities of early childhood classes. Teachers will have to guide preschool children as they play games, but as children go through kindergarten into the primary grades, they become very good at playing games and very interested in them. Teachers should be careful to match the games they introduce to the developmental levels of their children. Ruth F. Bogdanoff and Elaine T. Dolch (1979) have provided a set of developmental guidelines for selecting games for various groups of children.

Although some games require specific equipment or sets of materials, many require little from the teacher other than direct instructions and supervision. Often a piece of chalk or a ball is all that is needed to keep children involved in playing a game for a long time.

PLAY AND THE EARLY CHILDHOOD CURRICULUM

While play is presented in this text in a separate chapter, it is considered in isolation only because of the need to discuss this important element in early childhood education. Play encourages learning in the arts, science, mathematics, social studies, and language and literacy. As a matter of fact, as Judith Van Horn and her associates (1993) have amply illustrated, play can be conceived as the center of the early childhood curriculum. It is important to note, however, how play can help to achieve the goals of early childhood education in the various subject areas.

Play and Language Learning

A number of researchers have documented the relationship between children's play ability before the primary grades and their ability to learn to read (for example, Gentile & Hoot, 1983; Pellegrini, 1980; Wolfgang & Sanders, 1981). Dramatic play is symbolic activity, as are reading and writing. Children use objects and people to stand for other things, just as they later use sounds and written symbols to stand for words that represent ideas. The symbolic learning children gain through play enhances their ability to deal with oral and written language. As children mature they tell stories, just as earlier they played out stories.

Teachers can enhance the language and literacy learning in dramatic play activities. Putting a telephone in a play setting encourages children to send verbal messages to each other. Including paper and pencil in a play setting helps children come to understand the purposes of reading and writing and allows children to begin to approximate writing even before they know written language. As children mature, teachers can set up a publishing center for dramatic play, focusing on children's production of written materials (Hartman, 1991)

Play and Mathematics Learning

Early childhood mathematics activities should include a great many hands-on experiences with manipulative materials. Thus, many of the materials provided to children in manipulative play can teach mathematics concepts. Sets of materials are commercially available that help children learn number concepts, count and match quantities, and discriminate shapes and sizes. Teachers can also create their own materials and games to achieve the same purposes.

Teachers can also enrich dramatic play areas to help children learn mathematics. In playing store or restaurant, children can count out or weigh merchandise. They can match plates, forks, and napkins to the number of customers. They can begin to explore ideas about money. Teachers can find many other opportunities for helping children to discover and use mathematics.

Play and Science Learning

A good portion of science learning can be play. David Hawkins (1965) identified one of the stages of science learning as "messing about with science materials." Children need first to explore the properties of things. Once this exploration is done, they can ask reasonable questions about the materials and phenomena they experience. Later they can seek ways to answer these questions. At a more formal level, this is what scientists do: observe materials and processes, play with ideas about materials and processes, generate hypotheses, and test these hypotheses. By having a playful attitude towards science learning, children may learn more about true science than if they learn specific science facts by rote.

Play and Social Learning

Dramatic play is an important vehicle for children to use to explore their understanding of the social world they see around them. They act out the roles and relationships they see at home, at school, and in the surrounding community. Dramatic play also allows children to develop social skills. They need to maintain friendships, negotiate meanings, and develop social skills to keep the play going. If they are not part of the original play group, they need to learn to negotiate entry into play situations. They also test out their ideas about the world with others and begin to validate their understanding by seeing if it is consistent with the understandings of others. By observing the dramatic play of children, teachers can learn about the understandings children have about the world and assess the children's social competence.

Play and the Creative Arts

The creative arts have much in common with children's play. Both are media that allow children to express their ideas and feelings. Both provide outlets for children's creativity. While assertions have been made about the relationship of these two areas of the curriculum (Eisenberg & Jalonga, 1993), there is little research evidence from which educators can draw curriculum implications. This area requires a considerable amount of study.

GUIDING EDUCATIONAL PLAY

If play is to be educational, teachers must take a primary role in setting the stage for play, in guiding its direction, and in modifying it. Sponseller's review of research on play and early education (1982) described several influences on children's play.

1. The physical factors of the play space affect social play, sex-role learning, and activity level and quality.
2. A child's interaction with parents affects the ability to play.
3. A child's interaction with peers influences social play, sex-role learning, and play level and quality, and assists with the decentering process.
4. A teacher's direct or indirect facilitation of play affects the type, quantity, and quality of play. It signals the appropriateness or inappropriateness of play in the school.
5. Training or experience in certain types of play can affect play behavior in the classroom, and it may improve the learning of academic skills, especially ones requiring higher cognitive processes. (p. 233)

Thus, while teachers cannot affect some of the influences on play, they do control other influences. In order to ensure that the play in a classroom leads to positive educational consequences, teachers must provide preparation, careful planning, and guidance. Teachers guide children's educational play as they plan for play and initiate play as well as in guiding during the play activity itself.

Planning for Educational Play

Although extremely satisfying play can erupt spontaneously in almost any class, adequate preparation greatly increases the chances that productive play will occur. Teachers should be aware of topics for play that are of interest to the children and have the potential to provide rich educational experience. Play activities revolving around various social roles can help children explore the functions of these roles and their limitations. Store play can help children understand economic principles. Block play can help them become aware of geographic relationships in their community. Playing at being a builder gives them practice in measurement skills.

In planning for play, teachers should provide the resources that will support play, including time for playing, areas set aside for particular kinds of play, adequate play material for each type of play, and the arrangements of groups of children who wish to engage in play. James F. Christie and Francis Wardle (1992) suggest that a period of at least 30 minutes be provided for play. This amount of time allows children to progress through preparatory activities and to elaborate dramatic play themes. If the room is organized into activity centers, then adequate space should be available for different kinds of play. Play props should be organized so that children can easily identify and select the materials they need in their play. The size of the play group may vary with the kind of activity, the amount of space available, and, possibly, the gender of the children playing. As noted earlier, girls tend to play in smaller groups than do boys.

Teachers should assess the learning potential of the play activity, then search for resources to help children gain information about topics related to the activity. Informational books, films, filmstrips, picture files, and recordings on the topic can be helpful. A search of the community might produce field trip possibilities or resource persons who can be brought into the classroom. Museums or educational resource centers may loan dioramas or other resource materials. Teachers may not use all the resources they have identified in the classroom or introduce everything to the children at one time. But a careful search will give teachers a choice of materials with which to provide enough information to stimulate play and to carry it forward.

In planning, teachers should also identify the play materials that will be used: articles of clothing for dramatic play, manipulative materials, and raw materials to allow the children to create their own props. Many of these things can be used from year to year; teachers often develop extensive collections of play materials over time. The materials teachers bring into class affect children's play activities. Singer (1973) suggests that both too much realism and not enough realism in children's toys can limit creative play. Because toys without definite structure, such as building blocks, are relatively nonspecific and flexible, they may lend themselves to long-term use better than do more structured toys. Unstructured materials can be mixed with more specific playthings to stimulate make-believe play.

Teachers should also think through the strategies they will use to stimulate play and the goals they want to achieve. An understanding of these goals can provide them with guidelines for the constant evaluation and guidance of play activities.

As well as planning for children's play, teachers should help children plan as well. They can ask key questions of children that provide verbal prompts, such as "How are you going to attach the sections of your block building?" or "What is your plan for figuring out this game?" This planning will help children take control of their activities and improve their sense of self-esteem and responsibility (Casey & Lippmann, 1991).

Initiating Play Activities

Simply setting out new materials in the classroom is often enough to start children's play. If teachers introduce new materials in two areas at the same time, they offer children choices, so that the whole class does not focus on just one exciting area and so that small group play can develop without undue coercion. The introduction of new materials and equipment frequently requires a certain amount of direction. Teachers may talk with their students about how the materials are used and their limitations. A short meeting prior to the introduction of the materials can prevent later problems .

In generating play activities, teachers can look for ways to stimulate the children's interests and imaginations. Teachers often stimulate interesting dramatic play activities by planning a field trip, showing a film or video, or reading a book related to the topic of play. The information children get from these experiences gives them ideas for using materials and suggests themes for play.

Guiding the Play of Children

Teachers should be aware of the processes of play and use the cues they get from their observations as the basis for supporting or modifying children's play. Useful techniques for guiding children's play can be identified by observing effective teachers and parents. Burton White and his colleagues (1973) described the role of effective mothers in their study of the influences of the environment on the development of competency in very young children:

> What they seem to do, often without knowing exactly why, is to perform excellently the functions of designer and consultant. By that I mean they design a physical world, mainly in the home, that is beautifully suited to nurturing the burgeoning curiosity of the one-to-three year old. It is full of small, manipulable, visually detailed objects, some of which were originally designed for young children (toys), others normally used for other purposes (plastic refrigerator containers, bottle caps, baby food jars and covers, shoes, magazines, television and radio knobs, etc.). It contains thing to climb, such as chairs, benches, sofas, and stairs. It has available materials to nurture more mature motor interests, such as tricycles, scooters, and structures with which to practice elementary gymnastics. It includes a rich variety of

> interesting things to look at, such as television, people, and the aforementioned types of physical objects. (p. 243)

Teachers are also designers and consultants, creating a world in which children can learn through play and modifying play opportunities to increase their educational value. Teachers, however, play a somewhat more active role in guiding educational play than did the mothers described in White's study.

Teachers can use a variety of techniques to guide children's play. Ann Spidell, in her study of preschool teachers' play interventions, or methods of guiding play, identified a number of these techniques. Teachers can observe how the children are playing, and then decide which is the most effective technique to use in that situation. Sometimes teachers can tell children what to do, talking with them and suggesting possibilities. If the play seems particularly productive, teachers can praise a child to encourage continuation of that play. Teachers might either add new materials to the play setting or withdraw some materials when their use no longer seems productive. They might ask the children what they need, suggest some things that would be useful, or simply put some things in the play area so that they will be available to the children. Teachers can also suggest roles for children in their dramatic play. Teachers may also join the play for a short time, taking on a role as a player, but being careful not to stay in the play too long. If teachers control the children's actions, the activity ceases to be play.

Observing the play of children sometimes shows the teacher that they lack some necessary information or are operating under certain misconceptions. Providing information by telling, or by having children read information books or look things up in resource books, can clear up these misconceptions. Sometimes a field trip or the visit of a resource person also provides significant information that will modify the play.

Sometimes teachers become active players for varying periods of time. In this way they can modify the direction of the play by introducing new elements as suggested below. They can also limit disruptive behavior. They provide a role model for the children by asking clarifying questions that allow the children to better understand the content of play and the meanings of certain behaviors. In becoming active players, teachers should not distort children's play; if they do, their involvement becomes a disruption, and the children may stop playing.

Sylvia Krown's (1974) report of a program for Israeli children includes delightful descriptions of how the children's play changed over time. In the beginning the activities were highly stereotyped, with children repeatedly engaging in the same play behavior. Two years later, the children had modified and enriched their play. Four basic strategies were used to stimulate children's play:

1. The teachers spent time "startling children out of vagueness into purposeful activity," sometimes inviting themselves into the play

activities for a period of time and then withdrawing (as in play tutoring, that is, teaching children how to play).
2. The teachers added new materials to the play situation as needed to move the activities along.
3. The teachers asked questions to stimulate more detailed observations to be used in play and to help children recall and associate past experiences.
4. Some teachers developed discussions to stimulate more detailed observations and play. They provided additional information to children through books, trips, and the like.

Thus the teachers influenced the play of children while still allowing them to maintain control over their play.

These strategies can be used by all teachers. "Startling children into purposeful activity" can be accomplished by interacting with the children in the context of the play while asking questions about the plot of the play. This technique can cause cognitive dissonance to extend both the play activities and the children's thinking about those activities. Cognitive dissonance, which results when children's observations are inconsistent with their expectations, can lead to higher-order thinking. Teachers' questioning techniques can help the children become more aware of what they already know and of how they can use that knowledge, comparing play situations to real situations and applying previously acquired knowledge to new situations. Teachers can also find many ways to provide children with additional information that feeds into current play structures and extends them. New materials, like new ideas, stimulate new play activities. A final form of play intervention is redirection. Often, when teachers find that children are unproductive or disruptive, they will move those children from the current play situation to a different activity area in the room. While this technique reduces disruptions in the class, it also limits the opportunities that children have for learning to resolve conflicts.

The decision of when to intervene or how far to go in extending children's play can only be made based on the particular situation. Teachers should base their judgments on their knowledge of children in general and of the particular children involved. They must assess the potential of a play situation for learning. Too much intervention can stop play or distort it; the absence of intervention can keep a play situation from realizing its potential. Teachers must continually strive to achieve an appropriate balance. This sensitive, provocative balance, together with design, consultation, and intervention, can help generate educational children's play. Learning can thus occur in the context of playfulness. The essence of good teaching lies in the ability to plan learning goals for children, to respond, to intervene without unnecessary interference and distortion, and to change direction when appropriate. Perhaps good teachers bring a quality of playfulness, as well as respect for children, to the classroom.

SUMMARY

Play has long been considered a key element in early childhood education programs. A number of theories have been expounded to describe how play functions in the lives of young children. Teachers of young children take the natural play tendencies of children and design settings that allow this play to be educational. In doing so, teachers take an active role in guiding children's play. The better teachers understand the play of children and the potential of different kinds of materials and equipment, the better play guidance they can provide. Most importantly, however, the children should always maintain ultimate control of their play.

REFERENCES

Axline, V. (1980). *Play therapy*. New York: Ballantine Books.

Bender, J. (1971). Have you ever thought of a prop box? *Young Children, 26*(3), 164–169.

Bergen, D. (1988). Using a schema for play and learning. In D. Bergen (Ed.), *Play as a medium for learning and development* (pp. 169–180). Portsmouth, NH: Heinemann.

Bogdonoff, R. F., & Dolch, E. T. (1979). Old games for young children: A link to our heritage. In L. Adams & B. Garlick (Eds.), *Ideas that work with children* (vol. 2, pp. 169–177). Washington DC: National Association for the Education of Young Children.

Casey, M. B., & Lippmann, M. (1991). Learning to plan through play. *Young Children, 46*(6), 52–58.

Christie, J. F., & Wardle, F. (1992). How much time is needed for play? *Young Children, 47*(3), 28–32.

DeVries, R., & Kamii, C. (1980). *Group games in early education: Implications of Piaget's theory*. Washington, DC: National Association for the Education of Young Children.

Eisenberg, J. P., & Jalonga, M. R. (1993). *Creative expression and play in the early childhood curriculum*. New York: Macmillan.

Ellis, M. J. (1973). *Why people play*. Englewood Cliffs, NJ: Prentice Hall.

Fein, G. G. (1979). Play and the acquisition of symbols. In L. G. Katz (Ed.), *Current topics in early childhood education* (Vol. 2). Norwood, NJ: Ablex.

Garvey, C. (1990). *Play* (enlarged ed.). Cambridge: Harvard University Press.

Gentile, L. M., & Hoot, J. L. (1983). Kindergarten play: The foundation of reading. *Reading Teacher, 36*, 436–439.

Gilmore, J. B. (1971). Play: A special behavior. In C. Herron & B. Sutton-Smith (Eds.), *Child's play*. New York: Wiley.

Hartman, J. A. (1991). Fostering emergent literacy in a publishing center. In B. Spodek (Ed.), *Educationally appropriate kindergarten practices* (pp. 52–73). Washington, DC: National Education Association.

Hawkins, D. (1965). Messing about in science. *Science and Children, 2*(5), 5–9.

Hirsch, E. S. (Ed.). (1974). *The block book*. Washington, DC: National Association for the Education of Young Children.

Hughes, F. P. (1991). *Children, play, and development*. Boston: Allyn and Bacon.

Johnson, J., & Erschler, J. (1981). Developmental trends in preschool play as a function of classroom setting and child gender. *Child Development, 52*, 95–104.

Johnson, J. E., Christie, J. F., & Yawkey, T. D. (1987). *Play and early childhood development*. Glenview, IL: Scott, Foresman.

Krown, S. (1974). *Threes and fours go to school*. Englewood Cliffs, NJ: Prentice Hall.

Leiberman, J .N. (1977). *Playfulness: Its relationships to imagination and creativity*. New York: Academic Press.

Mead, G. H. (1934). *Mind, self and society*. Chicago: University of Chicago Press.

Mitchell, E., & Mason, B. S. (1948). *The theory of play* (rev. ed.). Cranbury, NJ: A. S. Barnes.

Mitchell, L. S. (1971). *Young geographers*. New York: Bank Street College of Education. (Originally published in 1934.)

Murphy, L. (1962). *The widening world of childhood*. New York: Basic Books.

Neumann, E. A. (1971). *The elements of play*. New York: MSS Modular Publications.

Parten, M. B. (1932). Social participation among preschool children. *Journal of Abnormal and Social Psychology, 27*, 243–269.

Pellegrini, A. D. (1980). The relationship between kindergartners' play and achievement in prereading, language, and writing. *Psychology in the Schools, 17*, 530–535.

Piaget, J. (1962). *Play, dreams and imitation in childhood*. New York: Norton.

Pratt, C., & Stanton, J. (1926). *Before books*. New York: Adelphi.

Robison, H. F., & Spodek, B. (1965). *New directions in the kindergarten*. New York: Teachers College Press.

Rubin, K. H., Maioni, T. L., & Hornung, M. (1976). Free play behaviors of middle and lower class preschoolers: Parten and Piaget revisited. *Child Development, 47*, 414–419.

Schwartzman, H. B.(1978). *Transformations: The anthropology of play*. New York: Plenum.

Singer, J. L. (1973). *The child's world of make-believe*. New York: Academic Press.

Smilansky, S. (1968). *The effects of sociodramatic play on disadvantaged preschool children*. New York: Wiley.

Smilansky, S., & Sheftaya, L. (1990). *Facilitating play: A medium for cognitive, socio-emotional and academic development in young children*. Gaithersburg, MD: Psychosocial and Educational Publications.

Spidell, R. A. (1985). *Preschool teachers' interventions in children's play*. Unpublished doctoral dissertation, University of Illinois at Urbana-Champaign.

Spodek, B., & Saracho, O. N. (1988). The challenge of educational play. In D. Bergen (Ed.), *Play as a medium for learning and development* (pp. 9–22). Portsmouth, NH: Heinemann.

Sponseller, D. (1982). Play and early education. In B. Spodek (Ed.), *Handbook of research in early childhood education*. New York: Free Press.

Van Horn, J., Nourat, P., Scales, B., & Alward, K. (1993). *Play at the center of the early childhood curriculum*. New York: Macmillan.

Vygotsky, L. S. (1978). *Mind in society*. Cambridge: Harvard University Press.

White, B. L., Watts, J. C., with Barnett, I. C., Kaban, B. T., Marmor, J. R., & Shapiro, B. B. (1973). *Experience and environment: Major influences on the development of the young child* (Vol. 1). Englewood Cliffs, NJ: Prentice Hall.

White, R. F. (1959). Motivation reconsidered: The concept of competence. *Psychological Review, 66*, 297–333.

Wolfgang, C. H., & Sanders, T. S. (1981). Defending young children's play as the ladder to literacy. *Theory into Practice, 20*, 116–120.

11

Language and Literacy for Young Children I

CHAPTER OVERVIEW

This chapter presents:

- Early language development
- Language and dialect differences
- Goals of early childhood language learning
- The whole language approach
- Expressive oral language learning
- Receptive oral language learning
- Written language learning

INTRODUCTION

Language is one of the most precious possessions human beings have. Language understanding and language skills reflect each person's unique heritage. The richness, variety, and power of language explain our reality and raise our status above that of all other species. Language is composed of a shared set of symbols and experiences that assist us to internalize ideas and express our thoughts to others (Wishon, Brazee, & Eller, 1986).

Language is a code that allows us to represent ideas through a system of arbitrary signals, primarily vocal. As a system, it has a set of rules that determines which sounds can be combined into words and which words can be combined into sentences. Members of a community arbitrarily agree on the use of rules, sounds, and words so that utterances can be communicated and understood as representing knowledge, thus allowing the encoding and decoding of messages (Bloom & Lahey, 1978).

Children entering the early childhood classroom receive verbal messages from many sources. These messages give specific directions for actions, provide information about the world, and offer opportunities for enjoyment, aesthetic appreciation, and comfort. The children must act on the messages received, understanding and responding to them as appropriate. Children also send messages to others. They respond to teachers and attempt to influence the behavior of their peers, making their needs and wishes known to others and expressing the ideas and feelings they have developed. The continual verbal give-and-take of the active school day presents endless opportunities for speaking, listening, reading, and writing. These opportunities then become the basis for social interactions as well as for the development of cognitive processes.

EARLY LANGUAGE DEVELOPMENT

School does not provide children their first language learning situation. The role of the school is to extend and enrich language learning and to provide remediation if necessary. In entering school, children find themselves in an environment that often requires them to make themselves understood in ways that are not required at home. The communication demands made on children by both teachers and other children require an adjustment to an environment that is less responsive than those the children have previously experienced.

Most young children have learned to use appropriately the basic sentence forms of the language of their culture by the time they enter school. The basic acquisition of grammatical speech is complete by age three and a half, often before children enter preschool. By the time they enter first grade most children are competent performers in a language. They have probably mastered a listening and speaking vocabulary of about 2500 words and the basic rules for combining these words into complex sentences and phrases. By this time they have developed an intuitive sense of the structure of the language.

Through interaction with others, children learn language rules, for example, that adding *ed* to a verb places it in the past tense. The mistakes children make are often the result of applying rules to words that happen to be exceptions to those rules. Young children seldom misapply rules, however. A child may say, "He dided it" but will seldom add the *ed* to the end of a noun.

Individual children vary greatly in their language development. There are early talkers and late talkers, talkative children and quiet children. Some differences are a function of the way children react to a specific environment; others are developmental. Psychologists report that sex, class, position in family, and ethnic-group membership are all related to children's rate of language development. Differences reported by psychologists are usually differences in group trends; individuals may differ markedly from the norm of their group.

THEORIES OF LANGUAGE DEVELOPMENT

The study of language development in children has a long tradition that spans over a century. The earliest of these studies consisted of parents' diaries, which often focused on the beginning of new forms of vocalization in their children. The past three decades have generated many studies of child language development. The field has been spurred by the theories of Noam Chomsky and others and by social issues related to dialect differences and bilingualism. Much of the research on language acquisition is not directly relevant to classroom situations at the early childhood or later levels, since it deals with even younger children; also, few studies relate to the effects of changes in the environment on language acquisition. An understanding of the evolving theories, however, can help teachers understand the conflicting suggestions for educational practice that these theories generate.

Transformational grammar suggests that all sentences are transformations of key sentences in a language.

Noam Chomsky (1957) has proposed a **transformational grammar** as a way of understanding language. Children's mastery of language depends on their intuitive knowledge of this grammar. According to Chomsky, two levels of structure exist in language—a surface structure and a deep structure. The surface structure represents the pattern of words that are used; the deep structure represents the pattern of meanings underlying the words. Chomsky also differentiates between language competence and language performance. Competence is a person's knowledge of language; performance represents the use of that knowledge. Children's performance at any language task is only a partial indicator of their language competence.

Chomsky used transformational grammar to develop his model of language acquisition. Chomsky believed that language acquisition cannot be explained by modeling or repetition alone. Each utterance of an individual, including that of a very young child, is a unique sentence that may never have been articulated before in that particular way. Children do not merely repeat phrases and sentences that they hear. Rather, they use a set of rules to transform components of language that they hear to create their own peculiar messages. They continually test the language rules they have created, refining and elaborating their language competence and performance. Given a finite set of rules for grammar, any individual can construct an infinite number of sentences.

This view of language acquisition suggests that children have an active role as constructors of their own language within a cultural framework. The ideas and arguments that developed from the articulation of this theory have provided a basis for a great deal of current language research, much of it focusing on how children develop syntactical structures. Ursula Bellugi and Roger Brown's (1964) work, for example, focused on the process by which children develop syntax in language as a process of interaction between parent and child. Marcus, Pinker, Ullman, Hollander, Rosen, and Xu (1992) found that the more often a parent uses an irregular form of a verb, the less often the child overregularizes it.

Eric Lenneberg (1967) has developed a theory of the biological foundations of language that is compatible with the work of Chomsky. He analyzed knowledge of language development in human beings along with biological knowledge about human and nonhuman animals, synthesizing these two types of knowledge into a theory. He suggested that latent language structures are biologically determined and that they need to be actualized within a healthy setting through exposure to adult language behavior. The schedule for language development seems to follow a biologically programmed schedule. For example, the period of readiness for actualization of biological language potential through exposure to adult speech, Lenneberg suggested, is from two years to the early teens. In this period, children recreate the language mechanisms of the culture.

While Lenneberg's theories provide great opportunities for speculation, they give little guidance in how best to actualize language structures—the key role of language education. Education and child development specialists have developed research related to engineering the social setting to enhance language development. This research, which will be referred to later in this chapter, can be used to enhance language learning opportunities for young children.

B. F. Skinner (1957) has also developed a theory of language acquisition, based on behavioral principles. He believes that an infant's original vocalizations and babblings reinforce themselves. After a while, adults around the infant selectively reinforce sounds that are a part of the native language, thus strengthening those sounds while allowing the others to fade. Language forms are taught through imitation. Children learn grammar and proper word order as they distinguish sentences from nonsentences during listening. Thus speech is learned first, followed by grammar. Although Skinner's theory could explain repetition of language, it does not explain grammar-generating rules that have been observed by linguistic scientists. However, this behaviorist approach has been the basis for some language learning programs in schools.

Another view that is being tested to explain language acquisition in children sees language as an adjunct to cognitive processes. A number of developmental psychologists, including Jean Piaget and Lev Semenovich Vygotsky, have discussed the relationship between language and cognitive development. Marilyn Edmonds's (1976) research seems to indicate a direct relationship between stages of intellectual development and stages of language development in children. While most researchers agree that a relationship exists between language and cognition, the nature of that relationship remains open to further study.

How educators can best use the research in language development is not completely clear. Early researchers were concerned with normative studies, attempting to find the regularities in the development of language in children or attempting to discover how language is acquired by children at different age levels. Later researchers focused on the theoretical aspects of language development, studying the process of language acquisition or the factors that affect the development of language in children. One way in which educators have used our knowledge of language development has been to model approaches to language instruction on the natural development of language.

LANGUAGE AND DIALECT DIFFERENCES

Children learn the language they most often hear spoken by the significant adults around them. Most American children learn English; children in Japan learn Japanese just as easily. But the various forms of the English language spoken in American subcultures may differ markedly from one another. These differences are called **dialects.** The dialect prevalent in the schools and generally heard over radio and television has been called *Standard American English*. However, many children have been raised in environments in which different dialects prevail.

A **dialect** is a variation of a spoken language specific to a particular region or group of speakers.

Speech is oral language. Speech patterns may differ in many ways. There can be differences in the pronunciation of words or in speech inflections. Differences may exist in the labels ascribed to familiar things; what is called a "sack" in one area is called a "bag" elsewhere. There may also be syntactical differences among dialects, making understanding difficult because the structure of statements carries much of their meaning. For example, a child might say, "he be going," instead of "he is going." Teachers can provide experiences to help children understand that labels differ based on geographic region. It is not that we want children to learn various dialects of English, but that they should be aware of different dialects and realize that the dialects are all acceptable.

Bilingualism refers to the achievement of competence and performance in two languages (Gingras, 1983). Most bilingual speakers tend to be stronger in one language than in the other. The language first mastered in childhood is often referred to as the child's *native language* or *first language*. Some young children who enter school find that their home language and culture differ from the one that is used in school, in books, and by teachers. Such children will respond to the instructional situation at a variety of levels. Saracho (1986) identified four levels of response:

1. (lowest level) Students become confused when they experience a drastic difference between the two languages and cultures.
2. Students deny their language and culture, pretending that their language and culture is the same as the school's.

TEACHING SUGGESTION

Collect a set of pictures of familiar items that are frequently called different names according to geographic area. Students can talk to people who have lived in a different parts of the country to find out what these items are called in other regions. Make a chart of these pictures and label them with different names that children provide. For example:

bag	soda	couch
sack	pop	sofa

3. Students adopt those new or different customs in the culture that they perceive to be more advanced.
4. (highest level) Students can make the transition back and forth from one language and culture to another.

Culturally and linguistically different children have problems of functional language competence—the use of language for communication purposes—not just phonological or grammatical ones. Using language and reading in a meaningful context to teach culturally and linguistically different children is a promising area of practice. Presently, groups that wish to maintain the dominance of English in our culture are exerting pressure to teach Spanish-speaking and other bilingual children to read in their native language. However, limited empirical evidence is available to support this practice. More research on bilingualism and second-language learning is necessary to determine the best method to teach reading to these children.

Most studies of language acquisition focus on children's learning of their first language. Children seem to acquire their second language in much the same way as their first and appear to be able to keep the two languages apart. Children may, however, go through a silent period when initially introduced to a second language until they build competence. The pace of second-language acquisition varies among children. However, there does seem to be a consensus about the desirability of beginning second-language learning early, although just how early is not clear.

Dealing with Language Differences in the Classroom

The fact that many children enter school with a language background not shared by their teacher and significantly different from the language on which most school learning is based has many implications for programs and for teaching. Some educators suggest that differences in the language backgrounds of children are irrelevant in determining instructional goals. Since the school uses Standard English, teachers should teach Standard English, even if that means suppressing the child's language. Others suggest that the child's language is important and should be reflected in the school; teachers ought to teach not a single system of language, but the use of language appropriate to the situation in which it is used. Using Spanish in school would be justifiable if there were a number of Spanish-speaking children in the class. The African-American dialect prevalent in parts of the southern United States and in some northern cities could also be recognized as a valid and useful form of verbal communication.

Language serves many purposes. These purposes become the basis for establishing the goals of a language and literacy program in school. Speaking a dialect or using a particular style of language establishes an individual as a member of a specific group. To attempt to change this language system might have significant implications beyond learning the use of proper syntax. Language is associated with group identification as much as it is with communications.

As a preliminary step before beginning formal instruction in English, preschool teachers who have children in their classroom for whom English is not the native language might speak English simply and slowly, using frequently repeated syntactic patterns to help children assimilate new language patterns. Whether formal instruction in English should begin before or about the age of six is questionable (Gingras, 1983). When it is begun, Standard English might be taught using either naturalistic or synthetic methods.

Use of Naturalistic Methods

One way to teach Standard English is to imitate the natural processes of language acquisition by surrounding the child with people, both adults and children, who speak the majority dialect. Their natural interactions would help the child acquire this dialect.

Expatiation is the expansion of ideas in a child's utterances.

Courtney Cazden (1968) reported using a process known as **expatiation** in improving children's language. This process requires adults to react to children's utterances by expanding them ideationally rather than linguistically. An adult may respond to a child's remark, "Dog bark," by saying, "Yes, he's mad at the kitty." Marion Blank and Francis Solomon (1969) also used a naturalistic strategy in elaborating children's language. They suggested that a tutor, in a one-to-one relationship with a child, base instruction on the child's utterance but reflect open-ended questions that move beyond the child's original statements. This strategy allows the tutor to make judgments about the child's level of language development by listening to specific utterances. The tutor uses this information in framing the next question, in order to move the child along a developmental continuum. The program was designed not to teach language per se but to develop the linguistic base for thinking in children.

In the Tucson Early Education Model, developed for Mexican-American children, children are given opportunities to speak, and the language they bring to school is valued. Teachers respond in Standard English, acting as a model for the children. The model predicts that, through the interactions of adults and children, the children's language will be transformed. Arline Hobson (1973), working with this model, systematically utilizes elements found in natural adult-child interaction patterns that support language acquisition. These elements, according to Hobson, are

1. **Corrective feedback**—providing omissions, proper labels, proper word order, and appropriate vocabulary;
2. **Summary feedback**—gathering together ideas that have been expressed by the children, thus expanding the relationships among ideas;
3. **Elaboration and extension**—extending language and ideas beyond the immediate;

4. **Extending knowledge**—providing information beyond what is immediately available; and
5. **Reinforcing**—providing generous and specific reinforcement for generation of appropriate language.

Use of Synthetic Methods

Shari Nedler (1970) and Robert Reeback (1970) advocated the use of synthetic approaches to teach English to non-English-speaking children. Using their patterned drill approaches, a teacher states a sentence or asks a question, and the children must give the desired response.

Nedler (1975) has described the process of developing and testing several approaches to teaching English to non-English-speaking children. After experience with two synthetic approaches to teaching language, which did not have transferable outcomes that children could assimilate into their day-to-day verbal interactions, Nedler's group moved to a more naturalistic approach aimed at teaching English vocabulary and elements of syntactical structure.

The naturalistic and synthetic approaches to language instruction parallel the theories of language acquisition supported by the transformationalists, following Noam Chomsky, and the behaviorists, following B. F. Skinner. The transformationalists—who view children as active participants, generating rules to be tested and modified to create internal language structures—believe the school should provide opportunities for these language acts to occur, and feedback to allow children to test the rules they create. The behaviorists view language as being learned through direct instruction and through reinforcement of correct speech. They see the school as providing an opportunity for a more efficient, more systematic scheme of language instruction than can be provided in the home. By using explicit instructional strategies and manipulating rewards in the environment, teachers can help children move quickly through successive approximations toward mature language behavior. To do so, educators must clearly define the goals of language instruction as behaviors and determine the conditions for achieving these behaviors.

GOALS OF LANGUAGE LEARNING

Language arts programs in the early years have many goals. In general, the goals are as follows:

1. **The development of verbal communication skills.** Young children are constantly interacting with those around them, transmitting and receiving messages. Their ability to function in the world is determined to a great extent by their ability (1) to communicate their wants, needs, ideas, and feelings and (2) to receive and interpret similar communications from other persons. These two skills are in large part the goals of language arts programs. As children

mature, the communications sent and received are put into written as well as spoken forms—reading and writing become important skills. Reading and writing require extended knowledge of vocabulary and structural forms as well as skill in forming letters, words, sentences, and paragraphs.

2. **Development of a rich language repertoire.** Language is an extension of the person. To function effectively in the community, young children must have a sense of the shared meanings of words and of the structure of the language that allows them to be linguistically effective. They need to learn about the variety of styles and uses of language that are available. Chomsky's deep structure becomes important here, since understanding the deep structure of a language allows children to have the flexibility to create new utterances that are correct in that particular language. A language repertoire also serves as an aid to thinking. Since mature thought processes are so closely related to language both in structure and in content, growth in language will also support growth in thought.
3. **Development of an ability to use language to influence and be influenced.** Until children reach nursery school age, they are manipulated and manipulate others physically. As they enter school, the manipulation becomes more verbal; language, in this sense, is a tool. The teacher gives instructions in words. Children satisfy social needs by talking to other children. The give-and-take of human relationships becomes a function of language. Even in the dramatic play of children, verbal statements soon take the place of actual physical movements. All this suggests that the appropriate use of language is one of the most important social skills young children can learn.
4. **Developing personal satisfaction in and aesthetic appreciation of language.** Although most of the language arts program in the early school years is primarily utilitarian, aesthetics should not be excluded. The use of literature, poetry, creative dramatics, and other forms of expression can provide great personal satisfaction, aesthetic and emotional, for children.

WHOLE LANGUAGE AND NATURAL APPROACHES

Some writers (such as Holdaway, 1986; Smith, 1988) suggest that written language can, and should, be acquired just as naturally as is spoken language when the conditions for learning both forms of language are comparable. They promote the use of a natural or **whole language*** approach to written language acquisition.

Whole language is a unified approach to language learning in which reading, writing, speaking, and listening are viewed as part of an integrated whole and in which language is taught in a unified way.

*The term *whole language* is derived from the emphasis placed on performing "whole" language tasks rather than on acquiring subskills. Thus, it is believed that one learns to read by reading rather than by acquiring a series of component skills.

BASIC TENETS OF THE WHOLE LANGUAGE APPROACH

1. Children have a natural facility for learning language.
2. Reading and writing are natural extensions of linguistic development.
3. Speaking, listening, reading, and writing are language processes that are best acquired when learning activities stress their interrelatedness.
4. Children learn to read naturally if instructional practices are in keeping with their linguistic competencies and abilities.
5. Children's language development is best facilitated in a learning environment that provides them with varied opportunities to use spoken and written language for a wide range of personal, social, and academic purposes.
6. Language and language learning are social activities that occur best in situations that encourage discussion and sharing of ideas.
7. Students must have a choice in selecting materials and activities.
8. The teacher structures the learning environment to encourage and allow children to "teach themselves." Learning to read is more appropriately thought of as implicit language learning than the conscious learning of reading skills.
9. For the most part language instruction takes place in the context of activities. Only when the children demonstrate a need or a desire to acquire a skill is it taught in isolation (Fillion & Brause, 1987).

Whole language is a recent attempt to transform language and literacy education that has emerged in the past two decades. During this time, research in language and language learning (especially in written language learning) have been used to support the theoretical bases of whole language. Initially the whole language concept was launched based on research on the reading process. Educators concerned with this approach consolidated the movement under the name of whole language movement.

Whole language represents an evolution of an idea that reflects a holistic approach to children's learning to read. Current research on language development focuses on the importance of learning to read from an active, meaning-making stance that suggests that reading, like all language, should be taught in a natural context. The main idea in whole language is that reading and writing are learned by reading and writing rather than working through exercises or "make-believe" language skills. Children learn language by engaging in real meaningful language. Saracho (1993) identified essential principles of whole language:

1. Language is perceived as indivisible rather than as independent elements of writing, reading, or spelling. Students are the focus of instruction, and both teachers and learners develop and implement instruction. Students assume an active role in their instruction, making it meaningful to them. The key word in whole language is *meaning*.

2. In whole language beginning reading with letters and sounds is taught using real stories, poems, signs, and print from the children's environment.
3. Process, product, and content are merged. The product and events in which products are produced define the process, although the main concern is with the processes of reading, writing, and knowing.
4. Teachers and students guide their own educational lives. They have the ability to create curriculum and solve problems as they interact in a unique cultural and historical environment. Teaching and learning are related to the values of the larger community.

Different language educators define whole language in different ways. However, all the definitions include the idea that whole language is a set of beliefs and not a set of methods. Whole language views reading as a social activity that is embedded in a historical and cultural context and is related to psychological and linguistic processes (Bloome & Solsken, 1988).

Whole language advocates (Edelsky, 1990; Goodman, 1986) have described the following principles of children's language learning.

1. When children write, they develop spelling rules, invent spellings, and move toward standard spellings.
2. When children read stories and other texts that they feel are comprehensible and important, they acquire strategies to interpret print.
3. This procedure assists children to construct phonic rules and learn in different contexts. Direct teaching of phonics and vocabulary is counterproductive.

Whole language in the classroom integrates reading, writing, listening, and speaking: the interdependent language processes that occur naturally (Stahl & Miller, 1989). A whole language classroom resembles a home environment. Desks may be exchanged for large pillows, reading lofts, round tables and chairs, beanbag chairs, and old couches where children sit or lie to enjoy favorite books. Large carpeted areas for reading, discussing, or teaching enhance the whole language classroom. Children's compositions, dictations, and art work are displayed on ceilings, walls, floors, and windows as a natural "gallery" of the children's involvement in reading and writing. Typical whole language classrooms are noisy and busy. Ability groups are not used in whole language classrooms. Groups are composed of children who share a common need or interest. Students in whole language classrooms usually learn by engaging in learning activities in activity centers that focus on a single topic or theme. For example, centers of interest may include

1. A writing activity center with a number of different suggestions for children's compositions about a particular theme, based on their developmental level;
2. A social studies activity center that highlights an event of historical importance; or

3. A music activity center that includes several tapes and records of music.

Some educators (Goelman, Oberg, & Smith, 1984) criticize the whole language approach. They believe that even if writing and reading abilities can develop without direct instruction, research does not show that most children learn best with a whole language approach (Dickinson, 1987). Present research on the whole language approach provides descriptions of whole language classrooms (Smith-Burke, 1987)* without evaluating their effectiveness.

Some reading educators (including Harris & Sipay, 1990; Stahl & Miller, 1989) recommend the initial use of the whole language or language experience approach in early childhood classes followed by systematic instruction in word recognition or decoding. Initial use of the whole language approach allows children to understand the functional features of reading, such as concepts about print and the understanding that reading is a form of communication. After these concepts are secured, children must learn word recognition and decoding skills in order to comprehend text smoothly.

EXPRESSIVE ORAL LANGUAGE LEARNING

Language and literacy programs are concerned with both expressive and receptive language in both oral and written forms. Expressive language includes speaking and writing, while receptive language includes listening and reading.

There are many opportunities for oral language learning in the early years of school. Specific times are set aside for group discussion, story reading, and sharing, or "show and tell." Although such large-group activities may be suitable for teaching some receptive language skills, they are not efficient for teaching expressive skills, since each child spends too much time waiting for a turn in a large group. Teachers must develop alternate approaches to teaching expressive language skills. Some of these approaches require that teachers be sensitive to times when language learning can occur naturally in small groups or in individual interactions. These small settings are usually more appropriate for language learning than are whole-class settings.

The Activity Period

Most prekindergarten and kindergarten programs set aside a good portion of the day for an activity or work period. When primary grades are organized into activity centers that children use throughout a long period, these opportunities are also available. Some of the activities of the work period provide greater opportunities than others to support language learning.

*Jaggar and Harwood (1989) offer an extensive reading list on the whole language approach.

Dramatic play supports language learning.

Dramatic Play Dramatic play is an important area for language learning. Wagner (1988) provides a review of studies showing that drama improves oral language, including vocabulary development, as well as cognitive skills. Dramatic play involves children in role-playing with no predetermined script or plot. It might include family play in a housekeeping area or playing other roles reflecting a variety of social situations, as in supermarket play or garage play. In dramatic play, children can put into action their personal constructions of the adult world. The cognitive and affective meanings developed become intertwined in this play. Dramatic play is symbolic play. It requires the interaction of children in interlocking roles: they must communicate with one another to carry on the play. Language often substitutes for the actions of the play.

Although dramatic play is supported most often in prekindergarten and kindergarten classes, primary-grade children can develop similar play interactions. These interactions may be more narrowly focused, more closely guided, and related to specific learning situations. Often social studies activities include dramatic play incidents to encourage children to explore social roles.

Other Areas Although few activity areas are as productive for language learning as dramatic play, other areas do offer opportunities for language learning. The more mature levels of block building often involve verbal and social interaction. As children move beyond the manipulative stage of block building, a strong dramatic element takes over. This dramatic element may be used in much the same way as dramatic play to support language learning. Teachers can add to available opportunities, however, by holding intimate conversations with children.

Children who are shy and reticent in a large group will often speak more freely when alone with the teacher. Conversations can relate to the children's activities or to the materials they are using, allowing children to focus on something outside themselves and to refer to things immediately available. Teachers can use open-ended questions such as "Tell me what you have there," or "Are there other ways you could make something like it?" to elicit language expressions. These questions can be followed up to continue the conversation.

Conversations with children stimulate vocabulary development and help children learn about language taken out of context of the events that accompany it. Teachers can start by speaking about what children are doing, but they should also refer to objects and events that are not immediate in time and space. For example, if children are playing supermarket, teachers might ask about what the children have and how they are using it. They might then refer to supermarkets that children have visited on a class trip or with their parents. Such an understanding of "decontextualized" language influences children's development of abstract thinking and prepares them for formal instruction (Rogers, 1987).

Marion Blank (1973) designed a tutorial approach that emphasizes both language and cognitive goals. The tutorial is essentially a dialogue between a preschool child and a teacher. By asking questions about common occurrences and materials, teachers can extend children's language and thinking skills. Teachers attend to children's difficulties and help them deal with ideas on a more abstract level. Tutorial sessions are short but frequent in the Blank approach.

Teachers can set aside some time in the daily schedule to meet briefly with children who are having language difficulties. Teachers can plan brief dialogues relating to occurrences in the classroom and help children to think through and articulate their thoughts about those events. This form of interaction can help extend language and thinking skills.

Having the teacher immediately available as a respondent to the child makes these small verbal interactions very useful. If a teacher aide or volunteer is in the classroom, a great amount of teacher-child interaction can take place in an activity period, since two persons can be deployed to support verbal behavior.

Conversation is a cooperative endeavor and a social activity requiring a considerable trust in others. To promote dialogue in the classroom, teachers must provide a trusting and accepting environment that is naturally spontaneous. Children's ideas must be valued, honored, and complimented. Teachers must establish an open and accepting environment where children are not afraid of making mistakes. Conversations between young children and teachers are stimulated when teachers warmly and openly accept and respond to children's ideas (Rogers, 1987).

Discussion Sessions

Discussion sessions involving the entire class, as in sharing and "show and tell" periods, have many advantages. The sharing period generally

Discussions allow children to practice oral language skills.

requires that each child, in turn, speak to the entire class. Children may bring an object from home to show and discuss, or they may discuss something that has happened. If a child is reticent, the teacher can ask questions about the object. Other children can be encouraged to ask questions, comment, and make observations.

Teachers using this sharing period should avoid its inherent pitfalls. Rejecting objects or incidents from home may teach children that it is safer not to expose themselves in school, and thereby limit language learning possibilities. There is also the danger that limiting the length of each contribution, or having the children take turns or wait for their turn longer than they can bear, may have negative influences on language learning. The children should be learning to be listeners and speakers—skills not easily learned in a situation that supports the negative responses of "turning off" and "tuning out."

Several alternatives to the traditional sharing period can increase the benefits of this type of activity. One method is to limit the number of children who will speak at each session. Going through the class alphabetically and assigning five children per session, for example, can keep the sharing period to a reasonable limit. Asking that children bring items to class associated with a specific theme might also limit the range of items discussed and relate the discussion time to other learning in the classroom. Children can be asked to bring in something made of wood, something that is attracted by a magnet, something very old, or pictures of objects. The need to focus on some special area or class of object turns the home search for an object into a problem-solving activity for the child as well as the family. Haas (1986) suggests the use of pictures as the basis of discussions.

Another alternative is to make the sharing session a small-group activity. This would allow a degree of voluntarism to the child's involvement, a greater degree of participation among all the children, and far more interaction among children in the discussion. The children themselves might take turns asking about objects and events. The discussion session could also be changed to allow children to talk about what happened in school. If a sharing time is held at the end of the activity period, for example, the children can talk about what they made or did during that time.

Many other opportunities for discussions can be found. Informal discussions between the teacher and a child or group can take place on any occasion and should be regularly encouraged by the teacher. The more children express themselves verbally, and the greater the number of adult-child interactions that take place, the greater the opportunities for language learning in the classroom.

Activity PICTURE PLAY

MATERIALS

cardboard or large index cards
glue
magazine pictures
clear contact paper

STEPS

1. Look through old magazines to find colorful pictures of everyday objects, toys, animals, people, or clothing, and so forth.
2. Cut out and paste or glue the pictures onto a piece of cardboard or an index card. Label each one.
3. For durability cover each card with clear contact paper.

Now you have a set of picture cards with which to play innumerable games, depending on the age of the child. They can:

1. Look at the pictures.
2. Name each picture.
3. Name the colors in the picture.
4. Count the number of items in the picture.
5. Tell a story about the object in the picture.
6. Make a treasure hunt by hiding three or four picture clues under or behind various objects. Give the player the first card, which might be a picture of a telephone, and ask the player to look under the telephone for another picture. Under the telephone you will have placed a picture of a red book; under the book a picture of the refrigerator . . . and inside the refrigerator will be the treasure (an apple, a piece of cheese, or a glass of orange juice). The prize might be a small toy, a new box of crayons or a favorite toy or book hiding behind a pillow.

Creative Dramatics

Children can interpret the stories, poems, and songs they hear in a variety of ways. Creative drama focuses on a particular plot, such as a familiar story with a relatively simple plot line. The children can be assigned characters and make up their own dialogue. The creative aspect of the dramatic presentation lies in the interpretations of the children, the dialogue they develop, and the actions they assign to particular characters. Children can also base dramatic presentation on their own original stories, which provide them with a greater control of plot and character. Teachers should allow the content of the play to be the children's product. Teachers can provide a story that becomes familiar to the children through repeated telling, suggest actions and sequences, and refer to the original story as a source of dialogue and action. Often a suggestion such as "What happens next?" or "What did he say in response?" is the only guidance children need.

Creative dramatic presentations need no audience. Only a few props generally are needed. A pair of chairs can be made to represent an automobile, a table, a bridge, or a piece of carpeting an ocean. Odd pieces of drapery material, skirts, and floppy hats can be used for costumes. As children mature, dramatic presentations can become more elaborate, using more extensive stories and characterizations and more elaborate props and settings. The same story can often be dramatized in a variety of ways in a class. After interpreting a story in creative dramatics, the children can try it with puppets or flannelboard illustrations. They could also try acting out the story in pantomime—attempting to communicate with actions alone. Though not a verbal production, pantomime supports language learning in that it provides another means of communicating symbolically.

Creative dramatics is a good strategy for teaching concepts, social issues, or skills. Storytelling, puppetry, skits, and games are usually used. Creative drama consists of three basic building blocks: *imagination*, *movement*, and *improvisation* (Bontempo & Iannone, 1988).

1. **Imagination** is the basis of creative work. Children should be presented with experiences that require them to use their imagination. These activities assist children to become aware of their

Activity VISUALIZATION

Dim the lights and have the children close their eyes. Ask the children to imagine themselves (1) on top of the tallest house in their neighborhood; (2) looking at the other houses, people, and cars below; (3) floating in the air to get a better view of their town; and (4) flying next to an airplane. Depending on the children's attention span, provide directions for children to rise high enough to see rivers, mountains, other land and water forms, the world, and a space shuttle.

senses, feelings, and perceptions. Imagination gives children the ability to observe accepted facts and see them in new and different ways.

2. **Movement** requires children to use their bodies. Movement activities help children use their bodies through dance or pantomime. Children communicate their feelings, moods, and thoughts with their bodies as they gain confidence in their ability.

Activity

BECOMING A BUTTERFLY

Children use a sheet to become a caterpillar egg inside the sheet. Then they grow out of the egg, become a tiny caterpillar by covering themselves in the sheet, grow out of their skin a number of times, become the caterpillar in the chrysalis stage (cocoon), break out as a butterfly, and fly like a butterfly, using the sheet as wings.

3. **Improvisation** requires the use of speech and movement. The teacher or the children create a situation. When children have not had experience with improvisation, the teacher can introduce simple situations in which dialogue is used. For example, children can express their thoughts and feelings about such situations as when their mothers find that their room is a mess or their first day at school.

Activity

IMPROVISED PROBLEM SOLVING

The children return from outdoor play and find that their room is in a mess. Have children talk about how they feel when they cannot work with materials. Have them pantomime what they would do to clean up the room.

Puppets

Playing with puppets is a good way to get a shy child to vocalize, for the puppet becomes the center of attention rather than the child. A variety of excellent commercial hand puppets is available in supply houses, and teachers and children can also construct simple puppets.

Stick puppets can be made by pasting faces the children have drawn on paper to a flat stick. The children then hold and manipulate the puppets. Puppets can also be made out of paper bags on which a face has been drawn. If the mouth is drawn on both sides of the point at which the square bottom of the bag is folded, the mouth will open and close when the bag is held between finger and thumb, though such manipulations are not really necessary for young children. Puppets can also be made out of socks with buttons for eyes and a piece of felt for the mouth. Puppets can be improvised in many other ways. For very young children, a puppet stage is unnecessary, for even if the puppeteer is visible, as in Japanese puppet shows, the audience will focus on the puppets themselves. Puppet shows are best developed in small groups. In fact, an audience is not always necessary.

With older children, puppet making can become a more extensive craft activity with children using papier-maché or wood for the puppets' heads. Marionettes—puppets that move by the manipulation of strings—can also be used by children in the upper primary grades. As with creative dramatics, there is no age ceiling on the use of puppets, if their use is varied with the children's maturity.

Children's Storytelling

Young children should be encouraged to tell stories in class. These can be their original stories or stories they have heard. Teachers can ask leading questions or read part of a story and ask the children to complete it or to fill in portions. Children can also be encouraged to report on important events. They may return from a vacation or a trip and share their experiences with others. These reports may be given to a small group rather than to the entire class. On occasion teachers should write down such reports to be read back at a later time. Having children read the reports they have written to others allows them to see the value of written communication. Writing something down allows children to remember it as well as to communicate it exactly as it was recorded.

Teachers should take other dictation from children as well. Observing the process of dictating, recording, and reading back stories gives children an understanding of what reading and writing are, and the reasons for our concern for learning these skills. The phrase "writing is talk written down" comes to life in this process, which creates meaningful associations between children's verbal utterances and the books around them.

RECEPTIVE ORAL LANGUAGE LEARNING

As children mature, they spend less time in school speaking and acting and more time listening and watching. Children listen at different times for different purposes and with varying degrees of depth. Levels of listening have been classified as *marginal*, *appreciative*, *attentive*, and *analytic* (National Council of Teachers of English, 1954). Listening to sounds in the background can be characterized as marginal; listening to music or to a story is appreciative listening; attentive listening is listening for directions; analytic listening requires a more active role as individuals dissect and evaluate what they hear.

Teaching children to listen is worthwhile, but determining whether it has been achieved can be difficult. Children who are watching will usually provide visual clues of their attention: their eyes are focused and their faces turned toward the object being viewed. The child's ears do not give the same clues of attention. A child may be listening while looking away from the speaker, even while engaged in other activities. The only way we can actually tell whether children are listening attentively is to ask them questions that require them to reflect some element of what they have heard or to do something with what they have heard. Young children can be involved in the processes of appreciative, attentive, and analytic listening in schools. Storytelling and discussions about stories will help.

Telling Stories to Children

A large body of children's literature in English has developed in the last few decades. But reading books to children should never completely eliminate storytelling. Teachers can become familiar with stories from children's books in order to retell them in their own words. The repetitious language patterns and cumulative story events of predictable books and stories help children to make accurate predictions of meaning and to anticipate language patterns, plot, and sequence. Storytelling helps children develop sophisticated language patterns and motivates them to experiment with their own written and oral language (Nelson, 1989).

VIGNETTE: STORYTELLING, PRESCHOOL

The teacher sits with four children in the corner of the room. From a bag she brings out a gray puppet. "Do you know what this is?"

The children know immediately that it is an elephant. "But," the teacher asks, "what is different about this elephant from those you have seen in books or at the zoo?"

Karissa jumps up and says, "Its trunk is funny."

"That's right, Karissa," the teacher says. "Look. Its trunk is short. Don't elephants usually have long trunks? I have another animal that I would like to show you." The teacher brings a green animal out of her bag. "What do you think this little creature is?" she asks.

"It's a crocodile, like in Peter Pan," says Marsha.

"Wow, that's great," says the teacher. "Now, these two animals are puppets. I am going to need two of you to be my puppet holders during the story." She gives the elephant to Peter and the crocodile to Jill.

"I will tell you a story about how the elephant got its trunk. We said this elephant doesn't have a trunk. But the story I am about to tell you will explain how all the elephants got their trunks," the teacher says. The teacher begins the story about the elephant that asked too many questions. The one question that he asked more than any other was, "What does the crocodile eat for breakfast?"

"Peter," the teacher asks, "can you hold up your elephant and ask the question?"

Peter raises the elephant in the air and says in a loud voice, "What does the crocodile eat for breakfast?"

The teacher continues, "One day a bird told the elephant to go to the river and ask the crocodile what he eats for breakfast. So off he went. And what do you think he said when he found the crocodile?" The teacher continues, "This crocodile said, 'Come closer and I'll tell you.' Can you say that to the elephant, Jill?"

So Jill says, "Come closer and I'll tell you."

Peter moves the elephant close to the crocodile.

The teacher continues, "Well, the crocodile kept telling the elephant to come closer and closer until, guess what, he grabbed hold of the elephant's face and would not let go. Can you do that, Jill?"

Jill grabs the elephant. The children laugh and squirm. Peter pulls his elephant away.

The teacher says, "That's exactly what the elephant did. He pulled and pulled and pulled until finally the crocodile lost his grip. But guess what? When he got up on his feet and looked down, he had this long, long, long nose. Guess what we call that long, long, long nose?"

"A trunk!!" all the children shout.

"Do you think the elephant liked his trunk?" the teacher asks. "He did," she continues. "He liked it very much. He could spray water all over himself with it and catch bugs. He liked it so much that he went home to all the other elephants and told them to go down to the river and ask the crocodile what he eats for breakfast so they too could get a trunk."

The story told might be a fanciful, contemporary tale or a traditional story culled from folk literature. Stories may also grow out of the children's experiences. Trips or other experiences the children have had, or even an occurrence from the teacher's childhood experience, provide excellent resources for stories. Teachers often find that props or pictures help them dramatize a story. Simple figures for use on a flannelboard, simple objects, or pictures are commercially available.

Storytellers have left a valuable legacy of materials and techniques. Ruth Sawyer, in *The Way of the Storyteller*, discusses the history of folklore and the preparation of tales for telling stories, as well as presenting some of her favorite stories, such as "The Fairy Gold." Recordings of Ruth Sawyer reading Christmas stories from her book *Joy to the World* and of Frances Clarke Sayers telling some of Carl Sandburg's *Rootabaga Stories* and Hans Christian Andersen's stories are available from Weston Woods. Marie L. Shedlock's *The Art of the Storyteller* is an excellent resource for beginning storytellers.

Telling stories to children helps develop receptive language skills.

Reading to Children

Any prekindergarten or kindergarten class should have a good stock of well-written and well-illustrated books for children. Collections of stories, or anthologies, even when not illustrated, are also useful. Teachers can get help in selecting books from other teachers, supervisors, librarians, and local colleges and universities. In addition, several printed resources are available to help teachers select books.

Resources for Storytelling

Storybooks

Brown, M. (1939). *The noisy book.* New York: Harper.

Flack, M. (1932). *Ask Mr. Bear.* New York: Macmillan.

Holdsworth, W. (1968). *The gingerbread boy.* New York: Farrar Straus Giroux.

Izawa, T. (1968a). *Goldilocks and the three bears.* New York: Grosset & Dunlap.

Izawa, T. (1968b). *The little red hen.* New York: Grosset & Dunlap.

Johnson, C. (1955). *Harold and the purple crayon.* New York: Harper & Row.

McGovern, A. (1967). *Too much noise, Mr. Brown.* Boston: Houghton Mifflin.

Piper, W. (1954). *The little engine that could.* New York: Platt & Munk.

Seuss, Dr. (1970). *Mr. Brown can moo! Can you?* New York: Random House.

Slobodkina, E. (1947). *Caps for sale.* Reading, MA: Addison-Wesley. (Morrow, 1993)

Anthologies

Baker, A., & Greene, E. (1987). *Storytelling: Art and technique* (2nd ed.). New York: R. R. Bowker.

Bauer, C. F. (1977). *Handbook of storytellers.* Chicago: American Library Association.

Colwell, Eileen. (1962). *Tell me a story.* New York: Penguin. (Cullinan, 1989).

SOURCES OF CHILDREN'S BOOKS

Association for Childhood Education International. (1980). *Bibliography of books for children.* Washington, DC: Author.

Gillespie, J. T., & Gilbert, C. B. (1981). *Best books for children.* New York: R. R. Bowker.

Larrick, N. (1975). *A parent's guide to children's reading* (4th ed.). Garden City, NY: Doubleday.

Peterson, L. K., & Solt, M. L. (1982). *Newbery and Caldecott Medal and Honor books.* Boston: G. K. Hall.

Tway, E. (1980). *Reading ladders for human relations* (6th ed.). Washington, DC: American Council on Education.

White, M. L. (1981). *Adventuring with books.* Urbana, IL: National Council of Teachers of English.

In addition, each spring *Young Children* publishes a series of annotated bibliographies of outstanding new books for young children.

Teachers should carefully select books that are of interest to the children. Information books should be accurate and authoritative—accuracy of information may take precedence over literary style. Teachers might select a book to prepare children for a future study or because its theme concerns them. Books are also read simply for good fun.

Leland Jacobs (1972) has suggested that a classroom collection of books be balanced. The balance should be between contemporary works and classics, between realistic and fanciful literature, between fictional and informational material, between popular and precious reading matter, between expensive and inexpensive books, between periodicals and books, and between prose and poetry. No one type of children's literature should be selected to the exclusion of others.

Humorous books can lighten the classroom atmosphere, stimulate students, and develop reactive, thinking readers. Humor is an essential characteristic of most cultures and an effective social device. Humor in reading programs motivates children, balances the classroom atmosphere, encourages cooperation and discussion (Whitmer, 1986), and offers a vivacious environment. The interpretation of humor demands insight and thinking skills; humorous literature provides a tool to teach critical reading when integrated into the curriculum at all levels, including preschool (Whitmer, 1986).

Good children's literature has themes that concern young children. Books provide a way of learning about things outside the immediate time and place, thus expanding children's horizons. Persons different in manner and dress can be introduced to children through books. And certainly the world of whimsy and fantasy should be a part of children's literary experience.

Books can often help young children deal with the resolution of their own problems and conflicts; books may have a mentally healthful effect by showing children that the problems they encounter are not theirs alone. Some educators have suggested that teachers systematically use books and discussions to help children cope with the problems they encounter. Such an approach, called *bibliotherapy*, is seen as having preventative powers as well as therapeutic values in maintaining children's mental health.

It is important that teachers be familiar with the books they read to children. New teachers often find it helpful to take books home and practice reading them aloud. The stage should then be set for a pleasurable reading experience. An informal arrangement helps; seating the group informally on a rug so that each child has an undisturbed line of vision to the teacher is helpful. Chairs can also be informally arranged for reading—especially if a picture book is being read.

It is disturbing to have to interrupt a story constantly to admonish a child who is misbehaving or inattentive. Teachers sometimes place obstreperous children near them to forestall the need to interrupt. Making story listening a voluntary activity, with choices of other non-noise-producing activities available, is also useful. Often a child will begin to pay attention simply because it is not required.

Teachers generally read stories to children themselves, but it is beneficial to have an aide or a volunteer parent come to school and read. If more than one person is available, a story-reading time need not involve the entire class. Making the story-reading period more intimate is helpful in developing language learning. Children in the upper grades may be invited to read to the class, as may the better primary readers.

Books that depict children from minority groups in realistic ways are becoming increasingly available. Although such books are no substitute for an integrated classroom, they help majority culture members realize that people who may seem different are really not that different. Providing such books in school also shows minority-group children that members of their groups are worthy of being depicted in the national literature. Teachers should review the materials in their classroom to see that they are free of racial and sexual stereotypes. *Guidelines for Selecting*

RESOURCES FOR BOOKS DEALING WITH MINORITY CHILDREN

Harris, V. (1993). From the margin to the center of curricula: Multicultural children's literature. In B. Spodek & O. N. Saracho (Eds.), *Language and literacy in early childhood: Yearbook in early childhood education, Vol. 4*. New York: Teachers College Press.

Spodek, B., et al. (1976). *A black studies curriculum for early childhood education* (rev. ed.). Urbana, IL.: ERIC Clearinghouse for Early Childhood Education.

Interracial books for children bulletin (Council on Interracial Books for Children, 1841 Broadway, New York, NY 10023).

Bias-Free Textbooks and Storybooks (1980) by the Council on Interracial Books for Children should prove helpful.

Reading a story will often stimulate discussion. Teachers sometimes also like to ask questions to see if the children have understood the story. Although this is a good technique for ferreting out misconceptions, it can be overused. Teachers must take care that story-reading remains pleasant and does not become burdensome to children.

Big Books

Big Books are oversized versions of children's books that vary in size and shape. Hearing and seeing a Big Book read aloud is similar to the experience of sitting "down front" at the movie theater. The listener/watcher can become part of the action. Big Books can engage children to become active participants in their learning.

Big Books
are large, chart-sized versions of children's books that are used with groups of children.

Reading aloud from enlarged texts enhances children's enjoyment and understanding of literature, develops their oral vocabularies (receptive as well as expressive), fosters the concept of reading, develops prereading skills such as left-to-right progression, fosters an understanding of the conventions and jargon of print, gives children a sense of "book language," develops visual discrimination and letter and word recognition, and provides for activities that aid critical and creative thinking skills.

Making Big Books Several publishing companies provide stories in both Big Book and small versions. When a specific book is not available in Big Book size or is expensive, teachers may make their own Big Books. Students can

USING BIG BOOKS

1. **Read a book aloud to the class.** Read a story dramatically to the whole class, following the text with your hand or a pointer to ensure that the children see what is being read in a left-to-right progression and top-to-bottom. Stop at strategic points in the story to let the children predict what might happen next.
2. **Read the story again.** Read favorite stories again and again, teaching a variety of concepts such as prediction, conceptions of print, vocabulary, and so on.
3. **Encourage independent exploration and examination.** Have children read and reread stories in groups of two to four and then share and discuss the book. They may discuss the pictures or point out the words they recognize.
4. **Use a variety of instructional activities.** After reading a story several times, use such activities as choral or unison speaking or reading, predicting with pictures, sequencing and retelling with pictures, introducing innovations in the story, or writing string sentences (Cassady, 1988).

participate in the production process, stimulating their interest in reading and fostering a feeling of ownership and pride in their Big Book.

Children can also collaborate as authors of a shared big book (Trachtenburg & Ferruggia, 1989). First, the teacher reads the original story several times. To promote comprehension and motivate children to

GUIDELINES FOR READING BIG BOOKS*

1. **Set the environment.** Have children sit on the floor close to you so they can see the illustrations and print. The Big Book can be positioned on an easel to make it easier to turn the pages and point to the words as the book is being read. At times, a child may turn the pages.
2. **Introduce the story.** Provide a brief introduction. Discuss the front cover illustration, title, related past experiences, and other relevant information. For example, for Ezra Jack Keats's *The Snowy Day*, appropriate questions for the introduction may be: "What is snow like? How does it feel? Have you ever played in the snow? If not, what do you think it would be like to play in the snow?" The purpose of the introduction is to motivate children to listen to the story.
3. **Read the story.** First read the story for enjoyment and pleasure; successive readings can offer opportunities for learning to read. Teachers who have difficulty pointing to the words while reading with expression can postpone pointing until later readings. Some teachers prefer using a pointer to assist children in seeing exactly what is being read. When rereading the Big Book, point to the words and encourage children to participate. Children enjoy repeating a familiar refrain or chant or making simple hand actions or appropriate sound effects. When teachers point to the words, children can see that print follows certain conventions, and they begin to recognize words and sound-symbol relationships.
4. **Discuss.** After the initial reading, discuss the illustrations, characters, or favorite parts of the book. The discussion should have a natural flow. Discuss the author's proposed meaning and monitor the children's comprehension. Since the story will be read and discussed many times, the initial discussion should be brief and end before the children lose interest.
5. **Provide follow-up activities.** After initial or subsequent readings of the Big Book, implement appropriate follow-up activities, such as independent reading of the story, dramatization, art, music, and writing. Independent reading is an important activity because children become part of a reading community. Small versions of the Big Books can be made accessible for independent reading to encourage children to reread their favorite books as often as possible. Children learn to read by engaging in the reading act.
6. **Evaluate.** During and after reading, evaluate each student's progress.

(Meinback, 1991)

*Although these guidelines focus on Big Books, they can be adapted for other books.

Activity MAKING BIG BOOKS

STEPS

1. Select a favorite story.
2. Copy each page of text onto a blank piece of paper approximately 25 inches by 15 inches.
3. Write the text in print large enough for a group of children to see. Once the text is written, reread the story and discuss possible illustrations.
4. Illustrate the text. If groups of students are making the illustrations, the teacher should assist them.
5. Determine the correct sequence of illustrations by displaying them along a chalkboard, bulletin board, or clothesline.
6. A title page listing the names of the illustrators, a photograph of the class, the date of publication, and the name of the class as publishing company are a nice addition to the book.
7. The pages can be joined to make a Big Book, adding a cover and a title page. A heavy-duty stapler, metal rings, or heavy stitching (dental floss works well) are good for binding. The spine of the book can be strengthened with heavy book-binding tape.
8. Laminate the covers for durability and place a loan pocket on the inside of the back cover to encourage children to check out the book.
9. Provide children with opportunities to read and reread the story. (Meinbach, 1991)

read the book, the teacher can provide dramatizations and discussions. The children's participation in picture reading of the story can be tape recorded.

Library Areas

Children need opportunities to look at books themselves, to get the feel of books even before they learn to read them. A good library area has books attractively displayed and available for children. Martinez and Teale (1988) observed kindergarten children in the library corner and found that they had more advanced reading behaviors with familiar, predictable books. The children used the books in the library corner in many ways, browsing, silently studying, discussing a story or illustration, acting out, or listening to someone read. Apparently the library corner promoted voluntary reading habits.

Teachers should provide library areas that have a physical environment and materials to motivate enjoyable literacy experiences. The library area should be visible and inviting to anyone who enters the classroom. Privacy and physical definition can be provided by placing bookshelves, a

Children enjoy looking at books that are familiar to them.

piano, file cabinets, or freestanding bulletin boards on two or three sides of the area. The size of the library area will depend on the number of children and the size of the classroom. A throw rug and several pillows will provide a cozy and soft atmosphere. The area should also include a small table with chairs where children can look at books or create their own, a rocking chair where they can read comfortably, and headsets for listening to taped stories. When children listen to recorded stories on a headset, they can privately enjoy stories; but an oversize cardboard box, painted or covered with contact paper, can offer a secluded and cozy reading area as well.

Children can be involved in planning and designing the library area. The children and the teacher can continuously evaluate the area, set up rules for its use, and be responsible for keeping it neat and for naming it (for example, "Book Nook" or "Look at a Book").

Books may be laid on a shelf or placed in a rack so that children can easily see covers in order to select books that seem interesting. There ought to be a place where children can comfortably look through the books, examining the pictures, reading, and discussing the books with other children. A rocking chair, a table and chairs, a group of pillows on the floor, or even a small rug all make inviting settings for browsing through books. Of course, lighting must be adequate, and the area should be isolated to some degree. Children should also learn to care for books. When books are changed at frequent intervals, some new and exciting reading material is always available.

It is useful to allow children to take books home if possible. Particularly when a child has few books at home, the teacher should try to arrange to lend books. Inexpensive reprints of good children's books make the cost of this procedure reasonable. Parents should be encouraged

Figure 11–1 **Book Display**

to read to their children. Sometimes a simple instruction sheet sent home to parents is enough to help them read effectively to their children; in other situations, teachers might wish to devote a parent meeting to the specific skills of reading to children. Parents can also be encouraged to subscribe to an appropriate magazine for young children.

Children enjoy manipulating figures of story characters from favorite books on a flannelboard. Puppets also help children to act out favorite stories. Mobiles made from book jackets are very attractive. Attractive posters that encourage reading are available from several sources:

- Children's Book Council
  67 Irving Place
  New York, NY 10003
- American Library Association
  50 East Huran Street
  Chicago, IL 60611

Children also enjoy cuddling dolls or stuffed animals, especially if they relate to a favorite book. For example, a stuffed bear and/or doll with blond hair can be placed next to the book *Goldilocks and the Three Bears*, a stuffed pig can be placed next to *The Three Little Pigs*, and a stuffed rabbit can be placed next to *Peter Rabbit*. Children enjoy reading to dolls and stuffed animals or simply holding them as they look at books. Children can easily use viewmasters with story wheels, which are also a source of literature for young children.

The library area should also include materials that invite young children to create their own books, flannelboard stories, using felt characters, or stories that are told with pictures drawn on a roll of brown paper and rolled to simulate movies. Many magazines are also available for children today. They are current, aesthetically pleasing, and meaningful for curious children. Magazines can be included in a classroom library along with books and other materials. Appendix D at the end of this book lists some of the children's magazines that can be purchased for classrooms or school libraries. New or old children's magazines and newspapers are inexpensive and accessible to teachers. Many publishers and local magazine agencies will donate outdated periodicals to schools for the cost of mailing and shipping.

Poetry for Young Children

Children enjoy listening to poetry, for it combines the rhythmic flow of words with a concern for sounds. Teachers can introduce poems for young children ranging from Mother Goose rhymes and the poetry of A. A. Milne to the works of many contemporary poets. The repetitive quality of much of children's poetry will sometimes help the children learn the poems themselves. Poetry should be carefully selected and presented to children to make it appealing to them.

Sutherland and Arbuthnot (1991) suggest that humorous poems and narrative poems be used with children. Children have a strong preference for limericks, narrative, and rhymed verse, particularly rhymed story poems. Poetry's first and strongest appeal is its singing quality, the

Suggestions for Reading Poetry

1. Read poems aloud often.
2. Provide a variety of poems through different media, such as records, books, and tapes.
3. Select contemporary poetry as well as older material.
4. Select poems with comprehensible subject matter.
5. Select poems with action or humor.
6. Make several anthologies available to children.
7. Avoid singsong reading.
8. Try choral speaking.
9. Encourage children to write poetry.

(Sutherland & Arbuthnot, 1991)

melody and movement of the word patterns and the lines. Poetry should be heard and spoken just as music is heard.

Children who are in the process of learning to read should hear poems before they see them on the printed page. Children's reading abilities are dependent on their listening abilities in their initial efforts to read. Listening to poetry may give them greater pleasure than reading poetry.

Contemporary poets are more likely to provide poetry that is of interest to today's children than are most older poets, whose work may be better understood and more easily introduced when children reach junior or senior high school. Teachers should include contemporary poetry in their classrooms and attempt to find and invite a local poet to work with the children. Poets can read their own poetry to children, talk about how they write poems, and work with the children to help them become poets as well.

Often, reading poetry in a class will lead children to an interest in the sounds of words. Poems should be read aloud so that the rhyme and rhythm become more readily apparent. Rhyming and alliteration may fascinate some children who simply enjoy the sounds of the words and the way they feel on their tongues. Teachers should encourage play with words but be forewarned that young children can be terrible punsters.

Teachers of young children often use poems along with finger plays. These activities may lack literary value, but they are useful as time-fillers, and children enjoy them. Finger play has a venerable tradition in early childhood education, originating in Froebel's kindergarten.

Using Audio-Visual Aids

In most classrooms teachers are limited in the variety of listening activities they can provide for the children. If they read a story to all the children, then story time becomes a whole-class activity. Story reading should also be an intimate experience, as a teacher or other adult sits with one or two children and reads a story. In this setting, the adult can be more responsive to the children's reactions to stories, and story reading becomes an interactive experience. Many teachers have found that using audiovisual aids can extend their ability to provide receptive language activities under a variety of conditions and with smaller groups of children.

Cassette tape recordings of many children's stories are commercially available. In addition, teachers have found it helpful to make their own recordings of stories. Most children at the preprimary level can learn to handle a cassette tape recorder on their own. Providing children with a tape recording of a book along with the book itself allows them to listen to the story and look at the pictures at the same time. Recording an auditory signal for turning the page is helpful.

Many classes are equipped with *listening centers*, consisting of headphone attachments to a phonograph or tape recorder with multiple jacks so more than one child may listen at a time. Although some listening centers are designed with carrels to separate the children, such separations are unnecessary unless some children have severe attention problems. Listening to a story can and ought to be an experience children can share with others. The headsets are used primarily so that the sounds of the record do not interfere with other activities that may be occurring in the classroom.

Videotapes and sound filmstrips can also be used to extend children's receptive language experiences. A number of excellent children's stories are now available in these media, and rooms can be arranged and equipped to allow viewing by a single child or a large group. Creating a separate space by moving furniture around can provide the privacy needed for listening or viewing.

Using the Normal Occurrences of the Day

Teachers can find many opportunities to support language learning throughout the school day. Continual language instruction, however, requires a sensitivity to the potentials of learning in each situation.

A cooking activity might start with a planning discussion: "What needs to be done? How will we go about it? Who will do each task? What materials and equipment are necessary?" Questions can elicit responses from all the children. Recipes can be written on chart paper, using pictures of measures and ingredients. Rebuses can also help children understand the recipe, which they may have to read several times during planning and cooking. The teacher can review the entire cooking sequence at its termination and write a chart describing the experience.

In dramatic play situations, a telephone and note pad can be included among the props. Teachers can also make signs to be used by the children. In music, teachers might have children listen carefully to the words of a song and then talk about the sounds of the words as well as their meaning. Singing a repetitive verse can teach new words, or children can create their own verses. The need for finding rhymes will help the children learn to listen to the word endings and to compare the sounds of words. Teachers should explore each activity for its opportunities for language learning.

Other Language-Related Activities

Other opportunities exist for language learning in the classroom. In most classrooms, a number of manipulative materials are provided to support language learning. These materials can extend an understanding of specific language attributes.

Lotto games are a good example. In playing Lotto, children have to identify a picture, label it, and match it with another picture on a card; thus Lotto games can be used to teach names of categories of objects, names of objects, or names of actions, in addition to teaching visual matching skills. Sequence puzzles, in which the scenes from familiar stories must

Children can learn their letters by playing games such as alphabet lotto.

be placed in proper order, help children learn the sequence of events in a story. Then they may be asked to relate the story after they have put the pictures in order. Three-dimensional letters allow children to make up words and learn the letters without coping with the problem of forming the letters themselves. These tools also provide a tactile experience in perceiving the shape and form of letters. A number of reading-readiness games and materials can also be included here.

Many of the games in the manipulative material area can be used by children individually or in small groups. Once children have mastered the skills and rules needed for use of such materials, they can often work independently, with the teacher periodically checking on the accuracy of the activity. This independence allows children to use the manipulative materials many different times during the day.

Continued involvement in oral language activities—discussions, creative dramatic productions, and listening to stories and poems—has a direct connection with involvement in written language activities. There is less separation of the language arts in life than in school programs, which are too often segmented and compartmentalized. Reading and writing must go hand in hand with listening and speaking in the classroom.

WRITTEN LANGUAGE LEARNING

Primary teachers in particular are concerned with the mechanics as well as the expressive content of reading and writing. Much activity in the area of written language learning can be approached informally. However, teaching the skills of reading and writing requires some systematic approach to learning.

Writing

Most schools today teach young children to write in manuscript, a simple form of calligraphy using unconnected letters. The switch to cursive writing, in which all the letters in a word are connected, usually comes about the middle or end of second grade. Children often begin writing in kindergarten by learning to write their names. Sometimes they have learned this skill at home. It is helpful if kindergarten children learn to use manuscript rather than block printing to avoid an additional transition.

The beginning of writing letters actually starts even earlier. According to Vygotsky (1978), infants begin to develop writing. Its beginnings can be observed in the infant's actions, gestures, speech, play, and drawing, which are all forms of representation. Children's first undifferentiated marks on paper are indicatory signs, which become meaningful written language as children invent appropriate modes of representations for themselves. Saracho (1990) found the following levels of writing in three-year-olds:

- **Level 1: Aimless Scribbling.** Children attempt to write their name by moving the writing tool on the paper. Using their arms and hands to guide the pencil, they make longitudinal and circular motions. Many times they draw a picture instead of writing their name.
- **Level 2: Horizontal Movement.** The children' marks on paper have a considerable tendency toward the horizontal with some systematic up and down squiggling. They make hasty scribbling in an up-and-down motion progressing across the page. They attempt to imitate the adult's manner in rapid cursive writing.
- **Level 3: Separate Symbol Units.** Though horizontal movement (with greater regularity in the vertical strokes) still exists, children have a tendency to make discrete symbol units, some of which are almost recognizable as letters.
- **Level 4: Incorrect Written Letters.** Letters are written incorrectly. The waviness in imitation of adult cursive writing from Level 2 is almost absent. Most letter units are recognizable. Children have discovered separate letter units and have developed an interest in writing those letter symbols.
- **Level 5: Correct Spelling of First Name.** A mixture of correct and incorrect letters appear in words written at this level. Children can usually spell their first name correctly.

If children learn to hold and use crayons and paintbrushes properly, the transition from drawing to writing is simplified. Children can be provided with pencils in the kindergarten for both drawing and beginning writing. They can be helped to make the strokes necessary for manuscript writing: circles and horizontal, vertical, and slant strokes.

TEACHING SUGGESTION

Preparing Young Children for Creative Writing

1. **Interrupted Episode.** At a climatic point in a story or film, stop reading or viewing. Ask the children what happens next. Write down and discuss their responses. There is no one right response, but discuss which of the responses are plausible.
2. **Story Illustration.** When introducing a story, identify a character to which children should pay particular attention. Do not show children the illustrations, so that, at the end of the story, children can depict the character through drawings. Later, have children compare their illustrations with those of the book. Make a bulletin board with the children's drawings and the original illustration in the middle.
3. **Inkblot Writing.** Place a large sheet of newsprint on the floor. Add cornstarch or flour to ink to make it thick. Let the children throw the ink mixture onto the paper, and then fold the paper in half and reopen it. Ask the children to identify and describe the hidden pictures in the blob they have created.
4. **Mystery Box.** Make a fist-sized hole in the top of a shoe box and attach a toeless sock to the edge of the hole, or use a long sock over a coffee can. Place objects of various sizes, shapes, and textures in the box. The children will place their hand through the sock into the box and describe what they feel. Record their descriptions on a chart. Encourage children to review mystery box charts from previous sessions.

Teachers can use a variety of techniques to teach the formation of letters, including the use of templates and wooden or sandpaper letters. These materials let children feel the shape and form of letters. Children can form letters in sand or on a chalkboard before using paper and pencil. They can then copy letters the teacher writes or those printed in worksheets or exercise books, or they can write over letters the teacher has formed. Teachers may also give children models printed on paper placed under clear acetate sheets that children can write on with markers, so that the first writing is directly on the model. When such activities are provided, they should be provided only to those children who are interested and who can benefit from them rather than as a whole class assignment.

In many cases, children will be able to *use* writing long before they have perfected the ability to write each letter clearly, legibly, and without error. They should be encouraged to do so, since unnecessary attention to the mechanics of writing without any concern for its use may lead them to lose interest. Teachers should have children write words, sentences, and stories as early as possible. They should also prepare children who cannot yet read and write for creative writing. Writing activities should encourage creativity and divergent thinking in order to help children understand the creative dimension of writing done by others. Such activities can help children actively engage in the creative writing process.

Reading is related to writing. In writing, meaning is constructed by constructing texts, while in reading text is constructed through anticipating meanings (Morrow, 1993). Children test their ideas about language in learning to write and read. They test their ideas by

1. inventing and decorating letters, symbols, and words;
2. mixing drawing and writing;
3. inventing messages in various forms and shapes; and
4. continuing to use invented spelling after they master conventional forms.

Children's experiments with the written language makes reading possible. Morrow (1993) and others believe that early writing is acquired when

1. Children's literacy experiences are integrated into familiar situations and real-life experiences such as family and community memberships (Gundlach, McLane, Scott, & McNamee, 1985).
2. Children's early writing process moves from playfully making marks on paper to communicating messages on paper to making texts as artifacts.
3. Children learn the purpose of written language before they learn its forms (Gundlach, McLane, Scott, and McNamee, 1985; Taylor, 1983).
4. Children constantly invent and reinvent the forms of written language (Dyson, 1986: Parker, 1983).
5. Children's writing is integrated in self-initiated and self-directed social situations and interactions.
6. Children's writing is motivated by story making.
7. Children observe and participate in literacy events with more skilled writers.
8. Children work independently on the functions and forms of writing they have experienced through interactions with literate others.

According to Teale (1986), these exploratory activities make it possible for children's literacy to come to "complete fruition." Both reading and writing relate to children's evolving knowledge about language. Thus, children should have opportunities to initiate and practice writing.

With the introduction of computers into early childhood classes, especially at the primary level, children have a new writing tool. Once children master the keyboard, simple word processing programs allow them to focus on the content of what they write rather than on the mechanics. They can correct errors and revise content without rewriting completely—and the final product is always presentable.

Teachers who take dictation from children can move the children into writing. The children can begin by dictating a short story of only a few words that they can later copy. They might also illustrate the story on large sheets of paper. Copying short stories can be extended as stories become more elaborate. Groups of children can write stories, but individual children should be encouraged to write their own stories as soon as possible. Children should read the stories they write, either to the teacher

Writing conferences individualize expressive language teaching.

or to other children. The stories may also be sent home. It is helpful to collect the writings of each child in a book with the child's own covers and illustrations, so that children can show their progress in school and read their own works for pleasure. The volume can be displayed or put into the reading area for others to read as well.

Providing children with thin writing tablets at the beginning of the year gives them a sense of writing a book. Teachers should take care that these tablets not contain too many pages so that completing them will not seem an overwhelming task. Children should be encouraged to write as much as possible. They can write about experiences out of school as well as in: reporting incidents may help the children start to become writers. As time goes on, they can become more creative in the writing, composing fanciful tales and poetry.

Spelling is not important in the beginning and should not be stressed. Children should be encouraged to invent their own spellings, spelling words the way they hear them. When children know the names of some of the letters of the alphabet and are able to segment phonemes in spoken words, they can discover the alphabetic principle and begin to use letters to spell words by their individual sounds. Many five- and six-year-old children are able to do this, even before they learn to read. Children need to feel comfortable in writing; premature criticism can stifle their early attempts. The teacher or other children can correct the work later. Eventually children will develop the habit of proofreading their written work. It is helpful to provide them with primary dictionaries so that they can begin to look up the spellings of words. A file box and a set of cards, or a notebook with each page devoted to a single letter of the alphabet, can help them develop their own dictionaries or word lists. Children can put into their dictionary new words that they have learned to spell and

STAGES IN SPELLING

1. **Prephonemic Spelling.** The letters for a given word have no apparent relation to the sounds in the words. Letters appear to be used at random, for example, *LMOS* for *wind*.
2. **Early Phonemic Spelling.** Sounds in the given word are represented by letters, but fewer than half the sounds are represented. Typically, initial or initial and final sounds are represented by letters, for example, *WD* or *YD* for *wind*, *JAT* for *jumped*.
3. **Letter-Name Spelling.** Half or more of the sounds in a word are represented by letters. The relation between letters and sounds rests on the similarity between the letter's name and its sound, for example, *YTS* or *YUTS* for *once*, *JRPT* or *CHRP* for *chirped*, *LAT* for *late*, *STAD* for *stained*.
4. **Transitional Spelling.** More than half of the sounds in a word are represented, but here the relation between the letters and the sounds is not based on letter names but on common spelling conventions. Short vowels, consonants, blends, and digraphs are spelled correctly. Marker letters may appear but be used incorrectly. Errors occur in consonant doubling, inflectional ending, and unstressed syllables. Examples include *SETER* for *setter*, *FECHER* for *feature*, *STANED* for *stained*, *NACHURE* for *nature*, *BUTTEN* for *button*.
5. **Correct Spelling.** The entire word must be correct. If only a minor part is incorrect, the spelling is transitional.

define. They will soon begin to use each other as well as the teacher as resources for proper spelling.

Educators do not agree on when a systematic program of spelling construction ought to begin for children or on what such a program should be. In the past, many spelling programs provided lists or books of words for children to memorize. Sometimes pretests were given weekly and children periodically wrote the words they could not spell until they were retested at the end of the week. Often the length of the word was the criterion for determining its suitability for children, with young children being asked to learn shorter words. They were often helped to focus on the visual aspects of the word to enhance retention.

Research indicates that children consider patterns in spelling in relation to letters and sounds. Children learn to spell by expressing their own ideas of the way they think the patterns work. Many times in the process they make some bizarre-looking spellings. Children apparently go through a rough set of stages in spelling development. Gillet and Temple (1990) reviewed the research and have mapped out in detail the stage-bound set of discoveries by which many people learn to spell.

TEACHING SUGGESTION

Spontaneous Writing Activities

1. **Catalog Shopping.** Children can go through catalogs or store brochures, writing their names or initials next to the items they would order.
2. **Graffiti Bulletin Board.** Poster boards or bulletin boards can be used for children's messages. Children can post comments, illustrations, or cartoons with dialogues. Children might also record a story or message using a cassette recorder.
3. **Stationery Design.** Children can design their own stationery, using potato prints, for example, at the top or along the borders. The children can write their messages on this sta-

Grammar

Teachers of young children do not usually concern themselves with teaching formal grammar. In the early years they are concerned with having children become good users of language rather than scholars of the structure of the language.

One approach to teaching about grammar is to provide children with opportunities to play with the structures of language just as they play with the sounds of words. Children can be given simple sentences and asked to transform them in a variety of ways. Given a declarative sentence, children could be asked to state it as a question or as a command. They could add modifiers to noun or verb phrases, thus becoming more specific in their language use. They could also be asked to place words in different sequences to try to change the meaning of sentences or to become sensitive to grammatical and ungrammatical structures.

Teachers need to be aware of the beauty of language that can be found in the ways children express themselves. Often adults suppress the idiosyncratic phrases of young children because these expressions do not seem proper. Subcultural groups have expressions that have enriched our language, yet we often exclude such expressions from our schools. Teachers should support and cherish these differences rather than trying to eliminate them. The beauty of the language is enhanced when communication is a personal statement rather than a stereotyped series of phrases.

Reading

Instruction in reading and in writing should go hand in hand. Having the children write early is consistent with a number of methods of teaching reading reviewed in the next chapter. It can also help classroom teachers develop an integrated approach to the language arts in their classrooms.

Children should learn not only to read but also to want to read. Reading should become a meaningful and personally satisfying experience, which can happen only when children read because they want to rather than because they have to. If children are to become "hooked on books," books have to be introduced early in their reading experience. Children should have opportunities for free browsing and reading. They should be able to determine what they will read, when they will read, and for how long. Even preschool children need opportunities to look at and get the feel of books before being required to learn to read them. Once children develop reading skills, they should have many opportunities for independent study.

The books available in a classroom should range broadly in topics and reading levels. If a book is interesting, children will be able to read beyond their level as well as beneath it. Children need places to sit or stretch out and read undisturbed. Conversation should not be limited in a reading area, for a child who is truly interested in a book will want to share its contents with others. If the school has a library, it is important to schedule times for children to read or select books in it. However, a school library is a supplement, not a substitute, for a classroom library. Children need continual access to books. If they are reading independently, a record-keeping system will enable teacher and children to keep track of books they have read.

Children learn much by observing the behavior of teachers. Teachers who wish to teach children to enjoy reading must be readers themselves, able to communicate their enjoyment of reading. Reading stories to the class is one way of showing this enjoyment. Most important, the climate of the classroom and the values the teacher's behavior reflects will determine the nature of the language program. The same room with the same materials can be a dull setting or an exciting place with children eagerly learning, listening, reading, talking, and writing. It is what the teacher does with the materials at hand that makes the difference.

SUMMARY

In order to serve children best, teachers should see language as an integrated whole, including receptive and expressive, oral and written language. Thus, speaking, listening, writing, and reading are all intertwined. In preschools, teachers must focus on oral language, but they should also lay the foundation for children's successful learning in written language. They should help the children become not only competent in their use of oral and written language, but joyful participants in language activities as well.

REFERENCES

Bellugi, U., & Brown, R. (1964). The acquisition of language. *Monograph of the Society for Research in Child Development*, 29(2).

Blank, M. (1973). *Teaching learning in the preschool.* Columbus, OH: Merrill.

Blank, M., & Solomon, F. (1969). How shall disadvantaged children be taught? *Child Development, 40*, 47–63.

Bloom, L., & Lahey, M. (1978). *Language development and language disorders*. New York: Wiley.

Bloome, D., & Solsken, J. (1988, November). *Cultural and political agendas of literacy learning in two communities: Literacy is a verb*. Paper presented at the annual meeting of the American Anthropological Association, Phoenix, AZ.

Bontempo, B., & Iannone, R. (1988). Creative drama: A special kind of learning. *Teaching K–8, 18*(6), 57–59.

Cassady, J. K. (1988). Beginning reading big books. *Childhood Education, 65*(1), 18–23.

Cazden, C. (1968). Some implications of research in language development. In R. Hess & R. Bear (Eds.), *Early Education* (pp. 131–142). Chicago: Aldine.

Chomsky, C. (1971). Write now, read later. *Childhood Education, 47*, 296–299.

Chomsky, N. (1957). *Syntactic structure*. The Hague: Mouton.

Council on Interracial Books for Children. (1980). *Guidelines for selecting bias-free textbooks and storybooks*. New York: Author.

Cullinan, B. E. (1989). *Literature and the child*. Washington, DC: Harcourt Brace Jovanovich.

Dickinson, D. K. (1987). Oral language, literacy skills, and response to literature. In J. R. Squire (Ed.), *The dynamics of language learning: Research in reading and English* (pp. 147–183). Urbana, IL: ERIC/RCS.

Durkin, D. (1987). *Teaching young children to read*. Boston: Allyn and Bacon.

Dyson, A. A. (1986). Children's early interpretations of writing: Expanding research perspectives. In D. B. Yaden & S. Templeton (Eds.), *Metalinguistic awareness and beginning literacy* (pp. 201–218). Exeter, NH: Heinemann.

Edelsky, C. (1990). Whose agenda is this anyway? A response to McKenna, Robinson, and Miller. *Educational Researcher, 19*(8), 3–6.

Edmonds, M. H. (1976). New directions in theories of language acquisition. *Harvard Educational Review, 46*, 195–198.

Fillion, B., & Brause, R. S. (1987). Research into classroom practices: What have we learned and where are we going? In J. R. Squire (Ed.), *The dynamics of language learning: Research in reading and English* (pp. 201–225). Urbana, IL: ERIC/RCS.

Gillet, J. W., & Temple, C. (1990). *Understanding reading problems: Assessment and instruction*. Glenview, IL: Scott Foresman.

Gingras, R. C. (1983). Early childhood bilingualism. In O. N. Saracho & B. Spodek (Eds.), *Understanding the multicultural experience in early childhood education* (pp. 67–74). Washington, DC: National Association for the Education of Young Children.

Goelman, H., Oberg, A. O., & Smith, F. (Eds.). (1984). *Awakening to literacy*. London: Exeter.

Goodman, K. S. (1986). *What's whole in whole language?* Portsmouth, NH: Heinemann.

Goodman, Y. (1986). Children coming to know literacy. In W. H. Teale & E. Sulzby (Eds.), *Emergent literacy: Writing and reading*. Norwood, NJ: Ablex.

Gundlach, R., McLane, J., Scott, F., & McNamee, G. (1985). The social foundations of early writing development. In M. Farr (Ed.), *Advances in writing research, Vol. 1: Children's early writing development*. Norwood, NJ: Ablex.

Haas, C. B. (1986). Getting ready for school: Make your own board books. *Day Care and Early Education, 14*(1), 40–42.

Harris, A. J., & Sipay, E. R. (1990). *How to increase reading ability: A guide to developmental and remedial methods*. New York: Longman.

Hobson, A. B. (1973). *The natural method of language learning: Systematized*. Tucson: Arizona Center for Educational Research and Development.

Holdaway, D. (1986). The visual face of experience and language: A metalinguistic excursion. In D. B. Yaden & S. Templeton (Eds.), *Metalinguistic awareness and beginning literacy* (pp. 79–97). Portsmouth, NH: Heinemann.

Jacobs, L. B. (1972). Providing balanced contacts with literature for children. In L. B. Jacobs (Ed.), *Literature with children* (pp. 5–8). Washington, DC:

Association for Childhood Education International.

Jaggar, A. M., & Harwood, K. T. (1989). Suggested reading list: Whole language theory, practice and assessment. In G. S. Pinnell & M. L. Matlin (Eds.), *Teachers and research: Language learning in the classroom* (pp. 142–177). Newark, DE: International Reading Association.

Lenneberg, E. H. (1967). *Biological foundations of language.* New York: John Wiley.

Marcus, G. F., Pinker, S., Ullman, M., Hollander, M., Rosen, T. J., & Xu, F. (1992). Overregularization in language acquisition. *Monographs of the Society of Research in Child Development, 57*(4, Serial No. 228).

Martinez, M., & Teale, W. H. (1988). Reading in a kindergarten library classroom. *The Reading Teacher, 41*(6), 568–572.

Meinbach, A. M. (1991). *Sources and resources: Ideas and activities for teaching children's literature.* New York: Harper Collins.

Morrow, L. M. (1993). *Literacy development in the early years: Helping children read and write.* Englewood Cliffs, NJ: Prentice Hall.

National Council of Teachers of English. (1954). *Language arts for today's children.* New York: Appleton-Century-Crofts.

Nedler, S. E. (1970). Early education for Spanish-speaking Mexican-American children. Paper presented at the annual meeting of the American Educational Research Association.

Nedler, S. E. (1975). Explorations in teaching English as a second language. *Young Children, 30,* 480–485.

Nelson, O. (1989). Storytelling: Language experience for meaning making. *The Reading Teacher, 42*(6), 386–390.

Parker, R. (1983). Language development and learning to write. In R. Parker & F. Davis (Eds.), *Developing literacy: Young children's use of language.* Newark, DE: International Reading Association.

Pflaum, S. W. (1986). *The development of language and literacy in young children.* Columbus, OH: Merrill.

Reeback, R. T. (1970). *Teacher's manual to accompany the oral language program* (3rd ed.). Albuquerque, NM: Southwest Cooperative Educational Laboratory.

Rogers, D. L. (1987). Encouraging extended conversations with children. *Day Care and Early Education, 15*(1), 23–27.

Saracho, O. N. (1986). Teaching second language literacy with computers. In D. Hainline (Ed.), *New developments in language CAI* (pp. 53–68). Beckenham, Kent (London): Croom Helm.

Saracho, O. N. (1990). Developmental sequences in three-year-old children's writing. *Early Child Development and Care.*

Saracho, O. N. (1993). Literacy development: The whole language approach. In B. Spodek & O. N. Saracho (Eds.), *Language and literacy in early childhood education: Yearbook in early childhood education, Vol. 4.* New York: Teachers College Press.

Skinner, B. F. (1957). *Verbal behavior.* Englewood Cliffs, NJ: Prentice Hall.

Smilansky, S. (1968). *The effects of sociodramatic play on disadvantaged preschool children.* New York: Wiley.

Smith, F. (1988). *Understanding reading: A psycholinguistic analysis of reading and learning* (4th ed.). Hillsdale, NJ: Erlbaum.

Smith-Burke, M. T. (1987). Classroom practices and classroom interactions during reading instruction: What's going on? In J. R. Squire (Ed.), *The dynamics of language learning: Research in reading and English* (pp. 226–265). Urbana, IL: ERIC/RCS.

Stahl, S. A., & Miller, P. D. (1989). Whole language and language experience approaches for beginning reading: A quantitative research synthesis. *Review of Educational Research, 59*(1), 87–116.

Sutherland, Z., & Arbuthnot, M. H. (1991). *Children and books.* New York: Harper Collins.

Taylor, D. (1983). *Family literacy.* Exeter, NH: Heinemann.

Teale, W. (1986). The beginning of reading and writing: Written language development during the preschool and kindergarten years. In M. Sampson (Ed.), *The pursuit of literacy: Early reading and writing.* Dubuque, IA: Kendall/Hunt.

Thomas, J. L. (1987). Magazines to use with children in preschool and primary grades. *Young Children, 43*(1), 46–47.

Trachtenburg, P., & Ferruggia, A. (1989). Big books from little voices: Reaching high-risk beginning readers. *The Reading Teacher, 42*(4), 284–289.

Vygotsky, L. (1978). *Mind and society.* Cambridge: Harvard University Press. (Originally published in 1935).

Wagner, B. J. (1988). Research currents: Does classroom drama affect the arts of language? *Language Arts, 65,* 46–52.

Whitmer, J. E. (1986). Pickles will kill you: Using humorous literature to teach critical reading. *The Reading Teacher, 39*(6), 530–534.

Wishon, P. M., Brazee, P., & Eller, B. (1986). Facilitating oral language competence: The natural ingredients. *Childhood Education. 63*(2), 91–94.

12

Language and Literacy for Young Children II

CHAPTER OVERVIEW

This chapter presents:

- Definitions of reading
- The relationship of reading to language
- The reading process
- Approaches to teaching reading
- Approaches to teaching reading to at-risk students

INTRODUCTION

Reading is often considered the most important subject in the primary curriculum. Success in school is heavily dependent on the ability to read, not only in the elementary school, but at higher levels as well. While universal literacy has been the goal of public education in America for generations, this goal has never been totally achieved. The fact that some children complete schooling without having learned basic reading skills and that others have difficulty in learning to read has led to a wide range of recommendations and proposals concerning when to begin reading instruction, what instructional program to use, and how reading should relate to the entire early childhood education program.

Reading instruction is increasingly being seen as an integrated part of the language arts program. Recent research in cognitive development, language acquisition, early reading, and what children learn before school about books, print, and writing has changed ideas about early childhood instructional strategies and literacy development. Until recently, reading, writing, listening, and speaking were thought of as separate skills that should be taught independently. Teacher education programs have tended to separate courses in the teaching of reading from those in language arts. We now realize that literacy involves all of the communication skills and that each skill enhances the other as they are learned concurrently.

In presenting a discussion about reading in the early years, this chapter offers various definitions of reading and conceptions of the reading process as they relate to various reading programs. It discusses reading instruction in the context of other language arts activities. Finally, the chapter offers a conception of an early childhood reading program. In proposing an early childhood reading program, we must distinguish between reading as a mature process and learning to read. Just as a good bicycle rider does not attend to or do all the things a beginner must do, so a mature reader attends to different things and reads differently from the novice reader. An analysis of reading will help in understanding the goals of the reading program, though the differences between mature readers and beginning readers mean that the ways in which the goals of an early childhood program are achieved cannot be directly derived from this description.

DEFINING READING

Some of the controversy about reading instruction arises from the ways in which the reading process is defined. Some educators contend that reading is basically a decoding process—learning the relationship between written symbols and spoken sounds. Once these associations are learned, the child is a reader. Since young children already know a great deal about meanings and processes in oral language, beginning reading teachers need not worry about these meanings and processes. The goal of reading instruction, according to this point of view, is to provide children with the key letter-sound associations that will unlock the written code and allow children to relate what they see about the written language to what they know about the spoken language.

Although few will disagree that successful beginning readers must learn letter-sound associations, the reading process is more than "code cracking." Many experts extend their interpretations of the reading process to include much more. Some educators claim that reading is gaining meaning from the printed page. This definition suggests that interpreting the sounds associated with the letters is also a part of reading and should be included in any program of instruction. Deriving meaning from the printed word, rather than "code cracking," should be emphasized in any reading instructional program. Still other educators suggest that the reading process is really an extension of intellectual processes, for interpreting meaning is a significant part of reading also. Critical reading, problem solving, and other complex processes should also be included in any reading program.

Reading
is a process by which meaning is gained from the printed page.

Frank Smith (1988) sees **reading** as gaining meaning from the printed word. He identifies two ways of achieving comprehension in reading. The first, *immediate comprehension*, is accomplished by going directly from the visual features of writing to their meaning. The second, *mediated comprehension*, requires a prior identification of the sounds of words. Children need to sound out words to understand them, moving back and forth between oral and written language. The fluent reader reads primarily by way of immediate comprehension, using alternative sources of information to speed the process along. This information comes from word forms, syntactical structures, and the context of words. Only when difficulties arise does the fluent reader use mediated comprehension. Readers who have problems with immediate comprehension can use mediated comprehension.

Schema Theory

Psychologists and educators have always been concerned about reading comprehension. Teachers have assumed that reading instruction is based on common sense. Since they see reading as the process of relating written words to spoken words, they get children to sound out words in order to learn how to read. Garner (1987) describes several views of reading comprehension, such as a representative interactive model for text processing, in theoretical approaches to reading. Of those presented, *schema theory* is the most widely accepted view.

A **schema** is a repertoire of expectations that evolves as individuals reiterate experiences with objects and events. It is an abstract knowledge structure reserved in the memory system and used to interpret new information (McNeil, 1984). Incoming information that conforms to individuals' repertoire of expectations is encoded into the individuals' memory systems. Information that fails to conform to that set of expectations may not be encoded or may be distorted. The set of expectations that guides the encoding of information also guides the retrieval of information (Anderson, 1984).

A **schema** is a repertoire of expectations about objects or events.

An example of a schema is provided in a description of a ship christening. Individuals who have experienced or read about the way a ship is given a name have developed a set of expectations regarding the event. They expect a celebrity to be present, a new ship to be the major focus of the ceremony, a bottle of champagne to be broken on the ship's bow, and so on. These different *slots* are *instantiated* with specific information in the following passage:

> Queen Elizabeth participated in a long-delayed ceremony in Cyldebank, Scotland, yesterday. While there is still bitterness here following the protracted strike, on this occasion, a crowd of shipyard workers numbering in the hundreds joined dignitaries in cheering as the *HMS Pinafore* slipped into the water. (Anderson & Pearson, 1984, p. 260)

The conformity of new information in this passage to old information in the ship-christening schema is good (Anderson & Pearson, 1984). Queen Elizabeth fills in the celebrity slot while the *Pinafore* fills the new-ship slot. Although breaking the bottle of champagne on the ship's bow is not mentioned, a "default" inference can easily be made that it occurred, since it is an obvious element of the schema. Inferences such as these can take place at various points in the encoding and retrieving of information.

Reading as Thinking

Reading is an act of thinking and understanding, and learning to read is a constructive problem-solving process. Reading instruction should focus on children's own thinking about ways to approach, learn, and remember information in print (Mason, 1986). Readers interact with authors by inspecting texts in relation to their meanings, functions, and characteristics. Thus, they begin to communicate with the author. In order to become literate, children must feel the need to communicate, writing to share their meanings with others and reading to gain meaning from others.

Children who lack experience with the reading process may have problems in developing comprehension. If they have not been read to, for example, they may focus more on word calling than on the flow of meaning. Having a rich background of related experiences, such as having been read to and told stories, helps beginning readers associate reading with language and thinking processes.

As noted in Chapter 11, storybook reading is essential to young children's emerging literacy. When children look at books, they explore their contents in interaction with the text and with others. McIntyre (1990) examined the reading strategies young children use during their independent reading time. She found that when children read in the classroom library, they used different strategies to understand the text in books: (1) reading pictures with oral-like language; (2) reading pictures with textlike language; (3) saying the text from memory (reciting text almost verbatim); (4) reading the text from memory (reciting text almost verbatim with eyes focusing on print); (5) reading the text but skipping words; (6) reading the text; (7) repeated reading (repeating the reading of others); and (8) browsing. Obviously, the setting in which young children read and their natural developmental patterns influence their use of reading strategies.

Literacy requires representational skills. Children acquire these skills from infancy; they continue to develop these skills throughout life. Words written on a page require children to identify the meanings of symbols. The printed visual features of a text allow readers to interpret meaning. Most children who read fluently have good comprehension. They make sense of the printed page by using a number of different sources of information, such as word forms, syntactical structures, and the context of words. The fact that mature readers use redundant sources of information may explain why various programs stressing different reading skills may be equally successful in teaching beginning reading. Since each reading program offers more than one way to approach reading, there is more overlap than distinctiveness among programs.

The arguments about different reading programs have been presented as either/or alternatives. In reality, most reading programs differ only in the degree to which they emphasize either reading subskills or gaining meaning from the context of the passage and from the reader's language background; few programs exclude either approach. In fact, a number of reading specialists suggest synthesizing these alternatives as the basis for teaching reading.

As John Carroll (1978) notes, reading is a process of gaining meaning, and sometimes sound, from print by converting print into inner representations analogous to speech. This conversion of visual signals into sounds is the basis for mediated comprehension, as noted earlier. The written language, he suggests, is understood much as speech is understood. Readers use their knowledge of the letter representations of sounds, as well as their knowledge of vocabulary, of the way words are arranged in the language, and of the meaning of speech utterances in various situations, to gain meaning from print. Graphemic cues are used to reduce the uncertainty of intended meanings of words. According to Carroll, an awareness of the way language is segmented into phonemes, syllables, and words, as well as an ability to use these language units, is critical to learning to read, just as practice is critical to achieving reading competence.

THE RELATIONSHIP OF READING TO LANGUAGE

Language includes four modes of communication: speaking, listening, reading, and writing. Linguists study written language as a way of expressing oral language in visual symbols. Writers take oral language and encode it into a series of characters that can be decoded in order to ascertain their meaning.

There are many ways of encoding language. In the beginning of written communication, people used pictures to illustrate the things they wished to communicate. Some peoples eventually developed abstractions of these pictures, replacing them with a set of symbols, each symbol reflecting a single idea. The advantage of this ideographic approach was that the symbols could be combined to create representations of abstract ideas and actions. The traditional Chinese written language is composed of such ideographs. While the written symbols relate to the spoken language ideationally, they have no relationship to the sounds of the language. The advantage of such a written system is that it allows people to communicate across languages and dialects without sharing a common spoken language. The disadvantage lies in the large number of symbols people must learn to establish basic literacy, let alone the vast number a scholar would need.

In an alphabet system, such as our own, the written language uses symbols to represent sounds in the spoken language rather than objects or ideas. By mastering a set of 26 symbols and their multiple sound relationships, one can read any material in English, no matter how complex. The need to crack the code of letter-sound association, therefore, becomes obvious, for the written symbols carry no meaning except in relation to their oral counterparts. Some reading specialists suggest that one of the major problems in learning to read stems from the fact that a sound can be represented by more than one letter and that letters or combinations of letters can represent a multitude of sounds. Still, there is a high degree of correlation between the sound symbols and the visual symbols of our language.

Reading requires decoding written symbols. The written word in our language is derived from the spoken word, but this does not mean that readers must translate each word they read into a word they hear. Rather, once they have achieved skill in reading, individuals have two parallel forms of receptive language, oral and written, available to them. In the early years of schooling, children may have to move from the novel (for them) written symbol to the more familiar spoken symbol before they can achieve meaning. At this point, the meanings gained from written words are usually those the children have already learned as spoken words. Only as children approach maturity does their reading vocabulary outstrip their listening vocabulary. Few books developed for beginning reading instruction under any system contain a vocabulary that is beyond the listening vocabulary of the children for whom the books are designed.

The emphasis in beginning reading programs should be on children's understanding of whole concepts, rather than on such isolated reading skills as letter-sound relationships and decoding. Though children who are taught letter-sound relationships have been found to get off to a better start in learning to read than other children, there is evidence that teaching many phonic rules does not greatly help children learn to read, since most of these rules are irregular. Rather, only the most regular letter-sound relationships should be taught. Once children know those regular rules, the best way to refine and extend them is to give the children repeated opportunities to read. Teaching and learning the alphabet, letter-sound relationships, and decoding skills are only a very small part of reading instruction. The time spent on these skills should be minimal and the strategies for instruction appropriate for young children.

Defining the process of reading does not solve the issues inherent in reading instruction, though it is a necessary first step. The crucial issues relate to *how* children can best learn the reading process. Is meaningful or meaningless material best for teaching the code-cracking system? This is one question that even the proponents of "phonics only" or linguistic approaches to reading raise. Another relates to the appropriateness of using cues other than letter-sound associations in gaining meaning from the printed page. Yet other issues relate to the form, organization, and materials of instruction in reading. Some of these issues will be clarified by a description of the process of reading.

THE READING PROCESS

Even in its simplest form, the reading process involves a broad range of perceptual, associative, and cognitive elements. Though these processes may be analyzed and described separately, they are intertwined, so that people do not practice each one separately as they read. Nor is reading simply a matter of making a series of letter-sound associations. Preschool children can roam the aisles of a supermarket identifying and reciting labels of packages made familiar through television commercials. Although this might not be "reading," much early reading seems to mirror this process; in attempting to gain meaning from the written page, young children use a variety of approaches and clues.

Young children can learn a reasonable number of words without using any analytic techniques. The associative learning technique used in the "look-say" method has proved successful and is probably responsible for the fact that very young children can read product labels. The continually repeated association on television between the pictures of the prod-

ELEMENTS IN A READING INSTRUCTIONAL PROGRAM

1. The child must know the language that she or he is going to learn to read.
2. The child must learn to dissect spoken words into component sounds.
3. The child must learn to recognize and discriminate the letters of the alphabet in their various forms.
4. The child must learn the left-to-right principle by which words are spelled and put in order in continuous text.
5. The child must learn that there are patterns of highly probable correspondence between letters and sounds.
6. The child must learn to recognize printed words from whatever cues she or he can use.
7. The child must learn that printed words are signals for spoken words and that they have meanings analogous to those spoken words.
8. The child must learn to reason and think about what he reads.

Source: J. B. Carroll, "The Nature of the Reading Process," in D. V. Gunderson (Ed.), *Language and Reading* (Washington, DC: Center for Applied Linguistics, 1970), pp. 31–33.

ucts and their names helps children learn the words and recall them when they see the symbols.

Other techniques can be used for associating visual cues with the sounds of words, such as the shapes of beginning and ending letters. Using these visual cues, children can be helped to make the association between the written symbol and the spoken word. Children also learn to use a word's context as a clue to reading it. The structure of the language and the meaning of phrases have a degree of regularity that creates a fairly high chance that the use of context clues will be successful.

As children begin reading instruction they learn other techniques of word recognition. Structural analysis—breaking large words into their parts—is an important one. Phonetic analysis, one way children can identify letter-sound associations, is another important technique. Phonetic analysis is not the only method, however, that young children can use in learning to read, nor is it necessarily the first. Teachers should provide children with as many different ways of unlocking the mystery of the written word as they can use, for the synthesis of many skills makes a competent reader.

Word identification, although important, is just one part of beginning reading. Meanings must become evident to children. They must associate the written words with the spoken words and move quickly from reading symbols to reading ideas.

APPROACHES TO READING INSTRUCTION

Many different reading programs are available today, some quite similar to each other in approach. Programs may differ, however, in the stress they place on the teaching of letter-sound relationships, in how they relate reading instruction to the entire language arts program, and in their organization. Differences can also be found in the conceptions of the reading process on which the programs are based.

M. J. Adams, Richard Anderson, and Dolores Durkin (1978) have suggested that reading programs are based on one of three conceptions of the reading process. Some programs are *data driven*, some are *conceptually driven*, and others are *interactive*. In the data-driven programs, readers attend to the printed letters and develop expectations from the words they spell out. Readers build on these expectations as they deal with larger units, from words to phrases to sentences. These programs use a *bottom-up* process.

Different programs of reading instruction are related to different models of the reading process. For example, Philip Gough (1972) proposed a linear model of the reading process that can be considered data driven. Readers proceed from identifying letters to forming words from these letters, identifying words by sound. They then apply syntactic and semantic rules to these representations to derive meanings. The process is a linear one, and no stage can be bypassed. Gough's model of reading suggests a program of reading instruction that focuses primarily on teaching decoding strategies through phonics and structural anaylsis.

In conceptually driven programs, readers use their knowledge of the language to approach reading by testing hypotheses against what is printed. The context of a passage and the readers' knowledge of syntax provide important cues for developing hypotheses. This psycholinguistic approach to reading has been characterized as *top-down* processing. Kenneth Goodman (1968) has proposed a conceptually driven model of reading in which children go through three stages or proficiency levels. In this model, reading focuses heavily on deriving meaning directly from complex elements—phrases and sentences—with children filling in the meanings of those smaller elements they cannot decode. This model sees reading instruction as helping children make sense of written messages, even if they cannot identify and analyze all elements of the message.

The third conception of the reading process sees both top-down and bottom-up processing as occurring simultaneously. This process is *interactive*. In this view, readers depend as much on what they already know as on what the author has put in the text to gain meaning from the printed page. David Rumelhart (1976) has developed an interactive model that conceives of reading as utilizing both top-down and bottom-up processes. This model does not emphasize abstract letter or word recognition. Rather, perceptions of letters and words are dependent on the surrounding letters and words. Thus, knowledge of syntactical and semantic rules, by helping readers judge what letter or word they should perceive, drives word and letter identification. Interpretation of written symbols is determined by the context in which those symbols are embedded. Both conceptually driven and interactive conceptions of reading view the reading process as consisting of something more than decoding, while the data-driven conception sees reading as a process of changing written language into its oral counterpart, with meaning embedded in oral language. These latter two models of reading are consistent with whole language or language experience apporaches to reading.

The Whole Language Approach

The whole language, or language experience, approach conceives of reading, together with writing, speaking, and listening, as a unified whole of language experience in children's lives. The whole language approach allows children to learn reading in as natural a manner as they learn speech. The desire to learn to read grows from children's need to communicate in writing as well as in speech. Reading and writing go hand in hand in the classroom, with children often beginning by reading what they have written themselves. This approach makes use of children's understanding of oral language as well as of their awareness of print.

When children write, they develop spelling rules, invent spellings, and move toward standard spellings. What they learn about writing can be applied to their learning to read. When they read stories and other texts that are important to them, children acquire strategies to interpret print. Thus, children generate phonic rules and identify words and their meaning. They learn phonics and vocabulary indirectly (Goodman, 1986). Children learn to read

1. by engaging in reading. Teachers should encourage children to read whole, meaningful, relevant texts.
2. as they attempt to interpret text. The classroom environment must encourage children to take risks in reading even if they are not sure of what the text says.
3. if both teacher and children attempt to understand written language. In this way, the children will gain greater reading power.

Teachers who use the whole language approach should find out what children already know about reading and build on the children's existing knowledge and competence. Teachers must also create an environment that is rich in written materials and in the functional uses of the written language. Such a class would include many charts, posters, and signs that the teacher and children use. There would be a great variety of books available for children to read. Adults and children would engage in many literacy-oriented activities throughout the day. Play activities would provide the basis for developing literacy, and reading would be related to all school subjects as well as to the other language arts. The reading experiences provided would reflect a range of language functions (Goodman & Goodman, 1979). Reading for fun, for gathering information, and for recalling events would take place regularly.

The whole language approach works most effectively in a classroom that is filled with stimulating learning opportunities. As children involve themselves in classroom activities, they feel the need to communicate what they are doing. Early communication takes the form of speaking and listening; later, a natural transition to reading and writing takes place. Children first dictate stories about their experiences to the teacher, who writes them on experience charts; the children learn to read from these charts.

Children are also encouraged to write early. Soon they are writing their own stories rather than having the teacher do the writing. These stories become the content of the children's reading. Since the children have written the material, they seldom have difficulty with vocabulary, for they remember even difficult words that they generated themselves. The next transition is from reading their own writing to reading someone else's writing, and each child is encouraged to read other children's work as well as books available in the classroom. Stories and experience charts can also be written as a group endeavor.

The whole language approach requires the use of a wide range of instructional strategies. In writing activities, children usually need to plan, write, edit, and revise in peer conferences. Children daily read relevant materials such as trade books, newspapers, and other children's written materials. Children are responsible for their learning. Therefore, the curriculum is based on the children's interests. Teachers only instruct directly if individual children need to be taught particular reading skills (Smith-Burke, 1987). The whole language approach is child-centered and lightly structured. Many educators have criticized whole language advocates for their philosophy, because these critics believe that children need more than exposure to learn to read and write. Thus, they believe that some direct instruction is needed. Kenneth Goodman (1986) and other whole language advocates strongly believe that whole language is taught as a whole or not at all. There is no such thing as a partly whole language classroom.

Under ideal supportive conditions, writing and reading abilities may arise without direct instruction, but many children are not able to learn this way (Dickinson, 1987). Research on the whole language approach offers only classroom descriptions (Smith-Burke, 1987), not empirical studies on the approach's effectiveness. Researchers who have compared traditional and whole language approaches have found that whole language approaches and traditional basal reader programs are equally effective. Stahl and Miller (1989) reviewed 51 of these studies and discovered that the more rigorous and recent studies show that basal reader programs are more effective, particularly when used with children who are at risk of future educational failure. Whole language approaches seem to be effective in emergent literacy and beginning reading programs. Stahl and Miller (1989) and Harris and Sipay (1990) recommend that if the whole language approach is used, it should be followed by systematic instruction in word recognition and decoding. The whole language approach will help children understand the purposes of reading, teaching concepts about print and reading as communication. Then teachers should directly teach children word recognition and decoding skills so that they can smoothly comprehend text.

Patterns for Teaching Reading

In most primary classes, reading instruction is provided to groups of children, most often using a *basal* reading series. Other classes use an *individualized* approach to teach reading. These represent the two most popular patterns of organization for reading instruction.

The basal approach consists of teaching reading through a series of ordered reading textbooks. Along with the textbooks, and often available from the same publisher, come workbooks and other instructional aids, such as flash cards, pictures, films, filmstrips, and records. In most classrooms, children are divided into groups for instructional purposes based on reading ability: one group of high ability, another of low ability, and a third, usually the largest group, in the middle. This procedure limits the range of ability in each instructional unit.

Most basal reading programs are carefully designed, eclectic ones containing some balance of activities to promote both reading skill and comprehension. Such programs provide teachers with a detailed manual of instructions describing the content of the program and the activities to be used and may carefully prescribe how teachers should use textbooks and related activities. In addition, the books are carefully graded so that teachers need only take their class through the books and related exercises to carry out the program. Generally, all groups will go through the same reading program, but the pace of instruction will vary.

Basal reading programs are modified from edition to edition to mirror the changes that take place in reading instruction theory and in views of what should be taught. Today's basal readers are much more literature-based than were the readers of decades past. Changes in the content of basal readers also reflect the changing social scene. Many readers have begun to change their illustrations to reflect the multicultural nature of our society. The characters now reflect greater sexual and cultural diversity. Additional changes include new format designs for basal reader series, especially the use of smaller books and integrated teaching aids.

Most basal reading series begin by providing pupils with a limited sight vocabulary of words and names of characters in the stories. The vocabulary is carefully restricted and constantly repeated. As the program's sight vocabulary increases, a variety of word-recognition skills, including phonics and structural analysis, are introduced. There is, however, considerable variation in methodological emphasis and textbook content among basal reader series.

Individualized reading programs are designed to deal with the inherent problem of the inappropriate fit of instructional programs to the diverse needs of children in any group. In a single group of children there are differences in skills, learning styles, interests, and reading abilities. While ability grouping might limit the range of differences in one dimension, differences continue to exist in other dimensions. Individualizing reading instruction provides neither a single medium nor a single organizational framework for instruction. Instead, a great variety of books are provided for the children—both trade books and basal readers. Trade books vary in topics and level of difficulty, and so children select books themselves as they set their own learning pace.

Central to the organization of the individualized reading program is the pupil-teacher conference. Several times each week the teacher meets with each child in conference. The conference is used to review the child's progress in reading and to plan new work for the future. The teacher often asks the child to read aloud and asks questions about what the child has read to check on the child's degree of comprehension.

An individualized program requires an extensive amount of record keeping and planning. Teachers keep records on the books the children have read as well as on the content of the conferences. These records might include notes about children's progress in reading and problems that need to be dealt with. Planning consists of selecting and providing books, and then suggesting specific books for particular children.

If more than one child needs instruction in a particular set of reading skills, teachers may organize a group for instructional purposes. The group is convened for a particular task and may include children of different levels of reading ability who nevertheless have the same instructional need. When the instructional task is completed, the group may be disbanded. Practice in reading skills may also be provided through worksheets and other materials. Some teachers may begin a program of instruction with individual lessons, but more often such a program is designed to extend from some form of group instruction. As the children show competence in reading skills, they are allowed greater degrees of freedom in reading.

Computer-Assisted Instruction

In recent years, an increase in the availability of microcomputers in schools has led to the development of a number of projects in the use of computers in early childhood education.

Computer-assisted instruction (CAI) is any form of instruction that is delivered through computers.

Computer-assisted instruction (CAI) is a form of individualized instruction in which students interact with computers. CAI reading programs feature one of three forms of interaction: drill-and-practice, tutorial, and dialogic interaction. In drill-and-practice programs, exercises are presented on the screen to students, who type a response on the computer keyboard. The material offered to children in this approach is essentially similar to that in a workbook. The computer, however, gives students immediate feedback on the correctness of their responses and can store a record of errors for review by the teacher.

The tutorial mode of CAI allows the computer to present a concept or skill, offering tutorial assistance to help students understand the concepts and correct their responses. Such programs allow the computer to teach skills or concepts to children rather that just having them practice what they have already learned. The dialogic mode allows students and computers to explore a curriculum together. Dialogic programs allow children to interact with a computer program in a more sophisticated way. What is presented to the child at the computer is determined by the prior reponse. Such programs can teach higher-order thinking skills, such as approaches to problem solving. A vast array of information and potential responses must be programmed into a computer for it to function in a dialogic mode (Saracho, 1982).

Most CAI reading programs use the drill-and-practice mode. More modern approaches to CAI use problem-solving programs. These programs have a greater potential in helping children become readers (Clements & Nastasi, 1993). Word-processing programs have also been used effectively with kindergarten and primary-grade children.

Evaluating Approaches to Reading Instruction

Considering the number of possible approaches to beginning reading instruction and of programs available in each approach, it becomes difficult for teachers to decide which program to institute in their classrooms. In many school systems the individual teacher has little choice, for the decision has already been made by the administration or by a curriculum committee, which usually selects one reading program to be used in all classrooms.

Some teachers are involved in program selection procedures through their involvement in curriculum and textbook selection committees. All teachers can also supplement any program that has been adopted by adding other materials in their own classroom. In determining what program to adopt, selection should be made among alternatives, considering evidence of program effectiveness, practicality, content, and the willingness of teachers to use the program. Chapter 9 discusses how to evaluate programs.

The First Grade Reading Studies (Bond, 1966), a series of studies that evaluated various approaches to teaching reading based on their effectiveness, suggested that the best results come from programs that use a combination of approaches to teach beginning reading. Many primary teachers feel comfortable in planning a reading program around a basal reading series. They can add a supplementary program of phonic materials if such instruction is not part of the series's program. To round out the program, teachers can include elements of a whole language approach, such as having the children write stories and using experience charts and group stories for instructional purposes. Finally, teachers can devise ways of individualizing the program. The majority of teachers who are most comfortable using published instructional materials can implement such an integrated approach.

The combined approach should not be merely a basal reading program with a few chart stories used at the beginning and a few trade books available for children to read as time fillers. The range of classroom activities available at any time should be great. The combination program would not be a basal program, but would use basal reading materials.

BEGINNING A READING PROGRAM

A reading program begins long before children attempt to make sense out of their first preprimer. Reading is an extension of the language process, so that reading instruction begins in the infant's babbling stage. For most children, the first reading teachers are usually their parents, who help them develop language skills, provide an environment in which reading and writing occur, and motivate their children to learn to read.

Most schools, however, wait until the child is old enough to be enrolled in an institutional group program before beginning any kind of formal instruction. The age at which a formal reading program should begin is open to controversy, and it is doubtful that any single age limit would be appropriate for all children.

When should reading instruction begin? In the United States, the traditional age for beginning reading instruction is the sixth year. Some countries postpone reading instruction until age seven, while others begin at age five. Generally, the age at which children begin to learn to read is related to the age at which most children in the community enter primary school, though some reading instruction is often offered in kindergarten.

Many books on early childhood education and beginning reading instruction have stated that children cannot benefit from beginning reading instruction until they have achieved a mental age of six years and six months. This recommendation grew out of a study done in a Chicago suburb many years ago, which found that children in the Winnetka schools with a mean age of six years and six months benefited from reading instruction (Morpell & Washburne, 1931). A study conducted a short time later by Arthur Gates (1937), however, suggested that the necessary mental age for beginning reading instruction is not rigid but is related to the size of the group and the flexibility of the program.

When to begin reading instruction depends, to begin with, on children's maturity, level of intelligence, and language background and capability. The decision also depends on the particular program of reading instruction and the way it is organized. Younger children, for example, can probably be introduced earlier into a program that is flexible and responsive to each individual's abilities and skills than into one that expects all children to follow a single sequence of learning activities. Not all classroom situations or teachers can provide the individual attention or flexibility needed to support an early reading program. The question of when a child might begin formal reading instruction is best answered on an individual basis. Providing children with individual or small-group instruction when they seem most receptive to it is probably the best method of matching a program to the children's capability.

Teachers can assess the readiness of children to benefit from such instruction in a variety of ways. One way is to use reading-readiness tests. Although they correlate well with successful results on reading achievement tests in first grade for groups of children, these tests are not accurate enough to predict the success of any single child. Teachers may also make their own personal assessment of a child's readiness to read. Spache and Spache (1986) suggest that teachers observe their children for good vision, good speech, listening ability, social and emotional behavior, and interest in learning to read as indicators of readiness. Research reviewed by Schickedanz (1982) suggests that teachers might also wish to assess their children's knowledge of the features of print, of reading processes and functions, of the characteristics of words in print, and of phonemes, in order to provide some indication of their ability to profit from reading instruction. Teachers might select or develop checklists and rating scales, such as those described in Chapter 9, to help in the process. Leslie Morrow (1993) provides a list of developmental areas to assess and determine a child's ability to benefit from a formal reading program.

Lists of developmental areas that can help determine children's readiness to begin reading instruction go on and on. Often teachers assume that a child must master all behaviors on the list before entering formal reading instruction. There are sad stories of kindergarten teachers who have not promoted children who were not able to master skipping, trotting, or galloping. Parents have become frantic and children been brought to tears by teachers' insistence on mastery of motor skills. It still is not uncommon to see classes of kindergarten children undergoing skipping lessons to the teacher's cadence of "step-hop, step-hop, step-hop, step-

DEVELOPMENTAL AREAS IMPORTANT FOR BEGINNING READING INSTRUCTION

1. **Social and Emotional Development**: The child
   a. shares;
   b. cooperates with peers and adults;
   c. demonstrates confidence, self-control, and emotional stability;
   d. completes tasks;
   e. fulfills responsibilities.
2. **Physical Development**: The child
   a. demonstrates gross-motor control by being able to run, hop, skip, trot, gallop, jump, and walk a straight line;
   b. demonstrates eye-hand coordination;
   c. can write name, copy letters, draw a human figure;
   d. is generally healthy and vigorous;
   e shows no visual or auditory defect;
   f. has established dominance (hand, eye, foot).
3. **Cognitive Development**: The child
   a. demonstrates auditory discrimination by identifying familiar sounds, differentiating sounds, recognizing rhyming words, identifying initial and ending consonant sounds, and possessing an auditory memory;
   b. demonstrates visual discrimination by understanding left-to-right eye progression, recognizing likenesses and differences, identifying colors, shapes, letters, and words, possessing visual memory, and showing a sense of figure-ground perception.

Source: Leslie M. Morrow, *Literacy Development in the Early Years: Helping Children Read and Write* (Englewood Cliffs, NJ: Prentice Hall, 1993), pp. 70–71.

Providing opportunities for young children to explore books supports their emergent literacy.

hop." Educators have, however, become aware of the inadequacy of the maturation approach to readiness. Success in reading achievement is correlated not just with maturity, but with specific learned skills such as auditory and visual discrimination, familiarity with language and print, and knowledge of letter names. Children must learn these skills before being introduced to formal reading instruction. A purely maturational approach to reading readiness is wholly inadequate today.

DEVELOPING A PROGRAM OF EMERGENT LITERACY

Emergent literacy reflects a view that literacy develops slowly from the time children attain oral language competence.

The term "reading readiness" has been replaced by the phrase *emergent literacy*. Marie Clay (1966) first used this phrase to refer to early literacy. **Emergent literacy** describes the early stages in children's development toward literacy; emergent literacy precedes the conventional reading of print (Clay, 1979). The development of literacy begins early in life and continues every day in the home and the community. Children at every age have some degree of literacy skill, which develops into mature reading and writing (Teale, 1986). Proponents of emergent literacy consider a child's scribble marks on a page, though not even a letter is discernible, to be writing. However, children who can differentiate between scribbling and drawing definitely know the difference between writing and pictures. Giving the impression of reading, as when children narrate a familiar storybook as they look at the pictures and print, parallels that ability. Although such discrimination cannot be called reading in the conventional sense, the activity is regarded as legitimate literacy behavior (Morrow, 1993).

Researchers of early reading have suggested instructional strategies for literacy development in early childhood. Literacy integrates all of the communication skills: reading, writing, listening, and speaking. Each skill compliments the other, and all are learned concurrently. Thus, a dynamic relationship exists among the communication skills. Leslie Morrow (1993) has identified four conditions that encourage emergent literacy.

1. **Reading is acquired through socially interactive and emulative behavior.** Literacy is the result of children's involvement in reading activities mediated by literate others (Teale, 1982). Social interactions teach children the functions of reading and its conventions in society. Children also relate reading to enjoyment and satisfaction, thus developing a desire to participate in literacy activities. Social relationships internalize higher-order mental functions. Children favor participating in reading activities that enable them to interact with more literate others. Holdaway's (1979) theory of literacy development states that

> The way in which supportive adults are induced by affection and common sense to intervene in the development of their children proves upon close examination to employ the most sound principles of teaching. Rather than provide verbal instructions about how a skill should be carried out, the parent sets up an emulative model of the skill in operation and induces activity in the child which approximates towards use of the skill. The first attempts of the child are to do something that is like the skill he wishes to emulate. This activity is then "shaped" or refined by immediate rewards. . . . From this point of view, so-called "natural" learning is in fact supported by higher quality teaching intervention than is normally the case in the school setting. (p. 22)

Holdaway believes that this form of developmental teaching is appropriate for school-based literacy instruction. He based his model on observations of home environments where children have learned to read without direct instruction.

2. **Children acquire the ability to read as a result of life experiences.** Many children read early because they acquire competencies and literacy skills before starting school and without formal instruction. A literate environment develops literacy. Even three-year-old children can read common words (such as Burger King, McDonald's, Exxon, and Sugar Pops) in their environment (Hiebert, 1981; Mason, 1980; Saracho, 1984, 1985a, 1985b). Obviously, young children are aware of print, letters, and words and have the ability to identify familiar printed symbols. In a literate environment children discover the purpose, organization, and functions of print. Children's reading abilities should be developed by using their knowledge of and strengths in reading .

3. **Children acquire reading skills when they see a purpose and a need for the process.** Children need to know that reading, writing, and speaking are purposeful and useful. Young children first acquire information about reading and writing through their functional uses (Goodman, 1980; Heath, 1980, Mason, 1980). Functional written materials that children encounter daily include grocery lists, directions on packages, recipes, telephone messages, school notices, menus, mail, telephone numbers, and letters. Learning to read must be meaningful to the children.

4. **Being read to plays a role in the acquisition of reading.** Reading to children promotes their literacy skills, interest in books and reading, and sense of story structure. A well-structured story provides a *setting* (a beginning time, place, and introduction of characters), a *theme* (the main character's problem or goal), *plot episodes* (a series of events in which the main character tries to solve the problem or achieve the goal), and a *resolution* (the accomplishment of the goal or solving of the problem and an ending). Children who are aware of a story's structural elements can predict what will happen next in an unfamiliar story (Morrow, 1985).

Reading to Children

Researchers (Morrow, 1986; Saracho, 1985a, 1985b, 1987; Smith, 1978; Sulzby, 1985; Yaden, 1985) show that reading to children helps them develop literacy in many ways. Reading the same story to children over and over again is an important technique (Morrow, 1986; Sulzby, 1985; Yaden, 1985), because children acquire an understanding of the functions of print, of how print is used, and of what people are doing when they are reading (Smith, 1978). Storybook experiences teach children how to handle a book and its front-to-back progression; the idea that stories have a beginning, middle, and end; and the concept of authorship (Clay, 1979; Torvey & Kerber, 1986). Listening to stories helps children become aware of the functions, forms, and conventions of print, as well as developing their metacognitive knowledge about reading tasks and their interactions with teachers and parents (Mason, 1980). **Metacognition** is the individual's own awareness of the way learning occurs. Being aware of one's own intellectual processes allows an individual to become more competent in learning.

Metacognition is knowledge of the process of how one achieves knowledge.

Often children's comprehension skills improve as they assimilate and become familiar with vocabulary and syntactic structures in books that have been read to them. Children who have been read to frequently and early tend to learn to read earlier and more easily than others (Clark, 1984; Durkin, 1966; Hiebert, 1981; Schickedanz, 1978). Furthermore, reading to children at school or at home generally leads them to associate reading with pleasure (Saracho, 1987) and provides them with models for reading. In fact, when children begin to read on their own, they often chose books read to them earlier. After a four-year-old had heard *The Little Engine that Could* (Piper, 1954) read aloud, she said, "Show me where it says `I think I can, I think I can.' I want to see it in the book." She proceeded to search through the rest of the book, reading with great enthusiasm each time she found the line "I think I can, I think I can."

Formal reading instruction should be considered an extension of a program of emergent literacy that provides children with knowledge and skills to be used in formal reading instruction. Some children arrive at school already knowing what is necessary, having been taught by siblings, peers, or parents or having picked up this knowledge on their own. The

Teachers can provide their best work on phonics when working with small groups of children.

school must create a program of instruction to foster this readiness for those who lack it. All children, however, should be in an emergent literacy program that builds on their language strengths and serves their needs.

FORMAL READING INSTRUCTION

The move to formal reading instruction should be gradual, almost imperceptible. If the children have been writing stories and charts, they can easily begin to read simple short charts. Individual children or small groups can begin this activity as they become able to profit from reading instruction. Such a beginning will build on the language knowledge each child already possesses and will keep reading from seeming like an exotic skill. Charts can become longer and more elaborate as each child progresses. Teachers should have pupils write their own stories on smaller sheets of paper, rather than transcribing all stories onto large sheets. Teachers can also have children start to read books.

Developing Word-Recognition Skills

Many word-recognition skills can be introduced in conjunction with experience charts. Because the content of the chart is so close to the children's experience, teaching them to use context clues seems natural. Their intuitive knowledge of sentence structure and the fact that they have shared in the experience recorded on the chart make this an effective technique. Experience charts have the advantage that they extend beyond a limited vocabulary. Children's experiences and interests are so broad that they cannot be described with only a small number of words, so that children's writing will contain a sprinkling of fairly sophisticated, complex words, though not all children will have fully learned all these words.

Phonics is the relationship between letters and the sounds associated with them.

Independent of experience charts, teachers can provide more systematic instruction in reading subskills, including **phonics** and structural analysis. Many educators consider that phonics instruction is essential to help children learn to read and spell, but various psycholinguists doubt its value. Phonics instruction has been a source of controversy since the middle 1950s. Most teachers feel guilty if they do not teach the phonics skills in basal readers or spelling books, although mastery of phonics skills has not been shown to lead to ability to read a text (Manning, Manning, & Kamii, 1988). Children learn to spell words in their own way. Similar errors in spelling occur within age groups (see Chapter 11). Regardless of the evidence, the debate on teaching phonics to beginning readers and spellers endures. Little evidence emerges from the research on the consequences of phonics instruction.

A **basal reading series** is a set of books designed as a program of reading instruction.

Using a Basal Reading Series

Most teachers in the primary grades establish a reading program based on basal readers. Basal readers are a resource to be used in the teacher's program rather than as a program by themselves. Teachers should avoid slavish adherence to teachers' manuals and to the traditional grouping practices.

Teachers should take into consideration their pupils' abilities in planning the reading program. Bright children seem to do better in individualized programs, while slow readers seem to profit more from a basal reading approach. Bright children rapidly develop the basic techniques of reading and should be allowed the freedom to select books under the teacher's guidance. Children who need the help provided by basal readers, with their controlled vocabularies, should be given opportunities to use them. But even then, teachers should be flexible and use alternative resources.

When teachers use basal readers, they need not operate in the traditional "three-reading-groups-everybody-reads-aloud-today" fashion. They can provide opportunities for silent reading and use pupil-teacher conferences even when the reading program is not fully individualized. Task grouping can replace ability grouping. Task grouping, as noted in Chapter 6, is temporary grouping organized around specific concepts and skills that need to be taught to several children.

Nor should teachers follow a workbook step by step. Reading-readiness skills can best be taught by experience, as children learn to use their language skills by interacting with the human environment. Children differ in their educational needs and patterns of learning. Skill learning and practice ought to be a part of a beginning reading program, but children need not systematically go through a set of prescribed exercises. Spache and Spache (1986) suggest that instead of using a single workbook, teachers should order a few copies of a number of different workbooks and skill sheets. These can be organized into sets of related exercises for each skill area and placed in heavy acetate folders on which children can mark their answers, so that other children can use the same materials.

Children should have opportunities to discuss the books they have read.

Using a Classroom Library

A classroom library is vitally important. If children are to learn to read, they must learn not only the basic skills, but also the uses of reading. The more children read, the more they will master the rules for gaining meaning from the written page. Most reading is an intimate personal experience based upon a person's interests and need for knowledge. Classroom reading should reflect this fact. As soon as children have mastered a rudimentary vocabulary, they should be introduced to a variety of books. Fortunately, books are available that even first-grade children can read independently. Children who do not know all the words in a book can practice their developing word-recognition skills. Teachers should select books carefully, keeping a relatively small number in the room at any one time and changing the selection constantly throughout the year.

Using Reading in Other Subject Areas

While the appreciation of literature is an important aspect of a reading program, reading has other uses. Reading in specific subject areas for particular purposes helps increase the children's comprehension and helps them learn to use reading skills flexibly, reading differently for different purposes. Many information books are available in the various subject areas, written at a primary-grade level.

In addition, primary children can begin to use reference books. Encyclopedias, dictionaries, atlases, and other reference books are available in simplified children's forms. Using reference books requires that children learn techniques for seeking information. Alphabetization becomes important, since topics are often listed in alphabetical order. Children also need to learn to use the book's table of contents and index. Teachers can teach children to use information books by phrasing questions to guide their reading. At first these questions may be related to the specific content of the book. As the children develop skills in informational reading, more critical elements should be included in the questions so that children learn to read carefully and make judgments about what they have read. Often, asking children to read and compare material from two different sources on the same topic is helpful.

Teaching reading is not a simple activity. Many children do learn to read very easily, and some even learn to read without a teacher's aid. But a large number of children have difficulty learning to read. Teaching children to read requires more than simply presenting learning activities in some sequential order. Teachers must use children's current language competence and be aware of any disabilities that might inhibit learning. Most importantly, they have to sense the forces that would create a desire to read in a child. Children for whom the reading material is irrelevant, dull, or even insulting may not progress readily through the stages of reading instruction. Yet teachers often present suburban, middle-class-oriented materials to urban, working-class children and female-oriented material to boys. Teachers sometimes make unnecessary demands on children, for the sake of the reading method rather than of the reading process, and so create discomfort or confusion. Teachers sometimes ask children to read in a dialect or language that is foreign to them. This demand compounds the problems of learning to read, for children must assimilate a new language as well as a new coding system; the cues they have used before to unlock language may no longer have any power at all. Teachers must know not only methods of instruction but also their children—their competencies and their backgrounds. They must use special procedures with children who have special needs.

READING FOR AT-RISK STUDENTS

While most children learn to read in school, some children can be identified as having difficulty in learning to read. In the past, these children have typically been put through a standard reading program in the primary grades. If they failed to learn to read adequately, they would then be put into remedial reading programs. Too often, these children continued to fall further and further behind in their reading ability. Recently, a program designed to address the problems that these children have in their initial stages of reading has been implemented in schools. This program, called **Reading Recovery,** is an early intervention program. It is based on a theory of literacy learning developed by New Zealand psychologist Marie M. Clay. It has been adapted and tested for eight years in the United States (42 states) and Canada (4 provinces).

Reading Recovery is a program of supplementary reading instruction designed for children who are considered to be at risk of failing in normal instruction.

The Reading Recovery program supplements children's regular classroom reading instruction (Clay, 1985). Children in the Reading Recovery program are low-achieving readers who temporarily receive individual services. Initial identification of such children begins with observing them as they read, talk, and write using an observational survey composed of six individually applied instruments: letter identification, word test, concepts about print, writing vocabulary, dictation task, and running record of text reading. Information is obtained from all assessments to establish an initial point for both teacher and children. During the first 10 days of the Reading Recovery program, children engage in reading, writing, and language activities so the teacher can assess their knowledge. During this period, the teacher avoids presenting new learning until children feel fluent and flexible with what they already know. Teachers identify strengths that were not identified in the initial assessment. A representative activity is to collaboratively write books, with children supplying the words or letters they can write and teachers writing the rest. These assessments and the classroom teacher's estimate are considered as entry criteria for admitting children to the program. The observational procedures suggest a useful, systematic way to identify students' strengths. An independent assessor assists the teacher in evaluating the need for extra help or when to terminate it.

As long as children are in the Reading Recovery program, they participate in their own daily individual program of intensive reading and writing activities. A specially trained teacher provides daily individual reading instruction outside the classroom for 30 minutes. Individual instruction is maintained for a short period of time, between 12 and 20 weeks, depending on the children's progress. Once children's reading behavior indicates that they have acquired an independent system of strategies to enable them to read and write within the average range for the school or classroom, they no longer receive instruction from the Reading Recovery program. Reading Recovery 30-minute lessons include reading and writing activities: (1) rereading books that students have previously read; (2) reading a book that was new the previous day while the teacher takes a running record; (3) composing and then writing a brief story or message; (4) putting together a cut-up version of that same message; and (5) attempting, with support, to read a new book. The lessons also include teacher-child conversations. In the Reading Recovery program, teachers select the strategies that most productively assist children to engage in problem-solving work while maintaining comprehension and fluency (Pinnell, 1993).

SUMMARY

The concept of emergent literacy helps us see the relationship between language activities in preschool and kindergarten and formal reading programs in the primary grades. Learning to read should be a natural extension of other language activities in early childhood classes. Teachers should be sensitive to the strengths and needs in children's language abilities in order to individualize the approach they use to teach reading.

REFERENCES

Adams, M. J., Anderson, R. C., & Durkin, D. (1978). Beginning reading: Theory and practice. *Language Arts*, *55*(1), 19–25.

Anderson, R. C. (1984). Some reflections on the acquisition of knowledge. *Educational Researcher*, *13*, 5–10.

Anderson, R. C., & Pearson, P. D. (1984). A schema-theoretical view of basic processes in reading comprehension. In P. D. Pearson (Ed.), *Handbook of reading research* (pp. 255–259). New York: Longman.

Bond, G. (1966). First grade reading studies: An overview. *Elementary English*, *43*, 464–470.

Carroll, J. B. (1970). The nature of the reading process. In D. V. Gunderson (Ed.), *Language and reading*. Washington, DC: Center for Applied Linguistics.

Carroll, J. B. (1978). Psycholinguistics and the study of reading. In S. Pflaum-Connor (Ed.), *Aspects of reading education*. Berkeley, CA: McCutchan.

Clark, M. M. (1984). Literacy at home and at school: Insights from a study of young fluent readers. In H. Goelman, A. Oberg, & F. Smith (Eds.), *Awakening to literacy*. Exeter, NH: Heinemann.

Clay, M. M. (1966). *Emergent reading behavior*. Doctoral dissertation, University of Aukland.

Clay, M. M. (1979). *Reading: The patterning of complex behavior*. Exeter, NH: Heinemann.

Clay, M. M. (1985). *The early detection of reading difficulties*. Portsmouth, NH: Heinemann.

Clements, D. H., & Nastasi, B. K. (1993). Electronic media and early childhood education. In B. Spodek (Ed.), *Handbook of research in early childhood education*. New York: Macmillan.

Dickinson, D. K. (1987). Oral language, literacy skills, and response to literature. In J. R. Squire (Ed.), *The dynamics of language learning: Research in reading and English*. (pp. 147–183). Urbana, IL: ERIC/RCS.

Durkin, D. (1966). *Children who read early*. New York: Teachers College Press.

Garner, R. (1987). *Metacognition and reading comprehension*. Norwood, NJ: Ablex.

Gates, A. (1937). The necessary mental age for beginning reading. *Elementary School Journal*, *37*, 497–508.

Goodman, K. S. (1968). *The psycholinguistic nature of the reading process*. Detroit: Wayne State University Press.

Goodman, K. S. (1986). *What's whole in whole language?* Portsmouth, NH: Heinemann.

Goodman, K. S., & Goodman, Y. M. (1979). Learning to read is natural. In L. B. Resnick & P. A. Weaver (Eds.), *Theory and practice of early reading*, Vol. 1. Hillsdale, NJ: Erlbaum.

Goodman, Y. (1980). The roots of literacy. In M. Douglas (Ed.), *Claremont Reading Conference forty-fourth yearbook*. Claremont, CA: Claremont Reading Conference.

Goodman, Y. (1986). Children coming to know literacy. In W. H. Teale & E. Sulzby (Eds.), *Emergent literacy: Writing and reading*. Norwood, NJ: Ablex.

Gough, P. B. (1972). One second of reading. In J. F. Kavanaugh & I. G. Mattingly (Eds.), *Language by ear and eye*. Cambridge: MIT Press.

Harris, A. J., & Sipay, E. R. (1990). *How to increase reading ability: A guide to developmental and remedial methods*. New York: Longman.

Heath, S. B. (1980). The function and uses of literacy. *Journal of Communication*, *30*, 123–133.

Hiebert, E. H. (1981). Developmental patterns and interrelationships of preschool children's print awareness. *Reading Research Quarterly*, *16*, 236–260.

Holdaway, D. (1979). *The foundations of literacy*. Sydney: Ashton Scholastic.

Manning, M., Manning, G., & Kamii, C. (1988). Early phonics instruction: Its effect on literacy development. *Young Children*, *44*(1), 4–8.

Mason, J. (1980). When do children begin to read: An exploration of four-year-old children's letter and word reading competencies. *Reading Research Quarterly*, *15*, 203–227.

Mason, J. (1986). Kindergarten reading: A proposal for a problem-solving approach. In B. Spodek

(Ed.) ,*Today's kindergarten: Exploring the knowledge base, expanding the curriculum* (pp. 48–66). New York: Teachers College Press.

McIntyre, E. (1990). Young children's reading strategies as they read self-selected books in school. *Early Research Quarterly, 5*, 265–277.

McNeil, J. D. (1984). *Reading comprehension: New directions for classroom practice*. Glenview, IL: Scott Foresman.

Morpell, M. V., & Washburne, C. (1931). When should children begin to read? *Elementary School Journal, 31*, 496–503.

Morrow, L. M. (1985). Reading stories: A strategy for improving children's comprehension, concept of a story structure and oral language complexity. *Elementary School Journal, 85*, 647–661.

Morrow, L. M. (1986). Promoting responses to literature: Children's sense of story structure. Paper presented at the National Reading Conference, Austin, TX.

Morrow, L. M. (1993). *Literacy development in the early years: Helping children read and write*. Englewood Cliffs, NJ: Prentice Hall.

Pinnell, G. S. (1993). Literacy programs for at-risk children: Reading recovery. In B. Spodek & O. N. Saracho (Eds.), *Language and literacy in early childhood education: Yearbook in early childhood education*, Vol. 4. New York: Teachers College Press.

Rumelhart, D. E. (1976). *Toward an interactive model of reading*. San Diego: Center for Human Information Processing, University of California at San Diego.

Saracho, O. N. (1982). The effects of a computer-assisted instruction program in basic skills achievement and attitudes toward instruction of Spanish-speaking migrant children. *American Educational Research Journal, 19*(2), 201–219.

Saracho, O. N. (1984). Young children's conceptual factors of reading. *Early Child Development and Care, 15* (4), 305–314.

Saracho, O. N. (1985a). The impact of young children's print awareness in learning to read. *Early Child Development and Care, 21*(1), 1–10.

Saracho, O. N. (1985b). The roots of reading and writing. *New directions in reading research and practice*. 1985 Yearbook of the State of Maryland International Association, (pp. 81–87).

Saracho, O. N. (1987). Evaluating reading attitudes. *Day Care and Early Education, 14*, 23–25.

Schickedanz, J. A. (1978). "Please read that story again!" *Young Children, 33*(5), 48–55.

Schickedanz, J. A. (1982). The acquisition of written language in young children. In B. Spodek (Ed.), *Handbook of research in early childhood education*. New York: Free Press.

Smith, F. (1978). *Psycholinguistics and reading*. New York: Holt, Rinehart & Winston.

Smith, F. (1988). *Understanding reading*, New York: Holt, Rinehart & Winston.

Smith-Burke, M. T. (1987). Classroom practices and classroom interactions during reading instruction: What's going on? In J. R. Squire (Ed.), *The dynamics of language learning: Research in reading and English*. (pp. 226–265). Urbana, IL: ERIC/RCS.

Spache, G. D., & Spache, E. B. (1986). *Reading in the elementary school* (5th ed.). Boston: Allyn and Bacon.

Stahl, S. A., & Miller, P. D. (1989). Whole language and language experience approaches for beginning reading: A quantitative research synthesis. *Review of Educational Research, 59*(1), 87–116.

Sulzby, E. (1985). Children's emergent reading of favorite storybooks. *Reading Research Quarterly, 20*, 458–481.

Teale, W. (1982). Positive environments for learning to read: What studies of early readers tell us. *Language Arts, 55*, 922–932.

Teale, W. (1986). The beginning of reading and writing: Written language development during the preschool and kindergarten years. In M. Sampson (Ed.), *The pursuit of literacy: Early reading and writing*. Dubuque, IA: Kendall/Hunt.

Torvey, D. R., & Kerber, J. E. (Eds.) (1986). *Roles in literacy learning: A new perspective*. Newark, DE: International Reading Association.

Yaden, D. (1985). Preschoolers' spontaneous inquiries about print and books. Paper presented at the National Reading Conference, San Diego.

13

Science in the Early Years

CHAPTER OVERVIEW

This chapter presents:

- Conceptions of early childhood science education
- Contemporary views of early childhood science education
- Criteria for selecting science programs for preschool, kindergarten, and primary grades
- Ways to support science learning in the classroom
- Ways to integrate science with other curriculum areas

INTRODUCTION

Almost from the moment of birth, young children reach out to their surroundings in an attempt to gain information about the world through their senses. At first their understanding of the physical world is limited by their perceptual field. Things they do not perceive do not exist; things they perceive often seem to have no explanation. They make sense of the world through movement and sensation.

As children mature and their experience increases, they become aware of the existence of order in the world. Some cause-and-effect relationships soon become evident. Items previously dealt with as discrete phenomena are now classed with other similar items and treated accordingly. Children will even try to create order where none exists. They develop concepts, both physical and social, about the world; these concepts allow children to accumulate knowledge from experience and to develop new powers of understanding.

It is easy to see how early observers in the field of child development, such as G. Stanley Hall (see Chapter 2), conceived of children's intellectual development as following the pattern of the development of cultures; the parallels are striking. Early humans also viewed occurrences as discrete, attributing changes to magical powers beyond human understanding. Human society moved through a series of progressions whereby people could explain, understand, and to some extent deal with the world of people and things by developing concepts. These concepts treated whole classes of objects as equivalent. Generalizations could then be developed about regularities of relationships among concepts. Systems of knowledge could be created by relating concepts and generalizations to each other. The ability to create symbols allows us to retain abstract knowledge as well as to record what we know in writing.

Knowledge could be accumulated and transmitted from generation to generation. In time, knowledge systems became complex, and divisions were established to allow specialization of inquiry and an efficient system of knowledge storage and retrieval. This specialization has evolved into the *scholarly disciplines* as we know them today, with separations based on the subject, the basic sets of assumptions, and the agreed-upon ways of accumulating and verifying knowledge in each area.

One of the basic purposes of school is to transmit significant portions of knowledge to the young. This transmission allows each generation to grasp what previous generations already know about the world, so that they can deal effectively with it, building upon what is already known and, in time, accumulating greater knowledge.

School subjects—sciences, social studies, mathematics, and others—closely parallel the scholarly disciplines. Science, mathematics, and the social sciences are the results of intellectual processes by which the physical and social world has been explored. Science is an important method for exploring the world that deals with physical properties. It orders these properties, identifies relationships among them, and establishes theories that can be empirically tested to explain those relationships. These theories allow us to predict events and the consequences of acts, and thus to develop technology to harness natural phenomena. Philosophy, literature, and religion are a few of the other tools we have for knowing about the world. Unlike science, knowledge in these areas is personal, often not generalizable, knowledge that cannot be validated by recourse to public, empirical testing.

YOUNG CHILDREN AND SCIENCE LEARNING

One question that must be asked about offering science programs in early childhood education is whether young children are capable of developing science concepts, that is, whether science teaching in the early years is developmentally appropriate. Scientific inquiry is rather abstract, and developing scientific knowledge and using the scientific method might require mature thought.

Paul Hurd and James Gallagher (1968) have identified the ability to comprehend science as

1. the ability to grasp the central theme of a set of observations;
2. the ability to look at data from a variety of vantage points;

3. the ability to recognize the effect of changing one variable at a time;
4. the ability to discount irrelevancies and focus on the useful aspects of information;
5. the ability to formulate useful hypotheses and test them;
6. the ability to search for new evidence; and
7. the ability to reason logically from a model. A good imagination is also helpful. (pp. 5–6)

These skills represent a high order of intellectual development, derived from a long train of maturational stages and prior experiences. The ability to think scientifically requires nurturing from the early years on. The theories of Jean Piaget have provided one framework within which we can understand how children might generate science concepts; learning theory provided another. Models of curriculum development now evident in science programs parallel beliefs about what and how children can learn. Basic to this development in science education is the belief that schools should teach science as an intellectual activity.

A great deal of the research on children's development of science concepts has used the Piagetian framework. This framework suggests that children must be at the operational level of cognitive development in order to learn science (see Chapter 2). Ann C. Howe (1993) has reviewed this research and suggests that achieving the operational level of development is not decisive in the ability to learn science processes and concepts. However, the concepts presented to children should be consistent with what they are capable of learning. Instruction in science should be based on children's experiences and their ability to observe scientific processes in these experiences. This research suggests that science education in early childhood make heavy use of hands-on experiences and that children be able to test their understanding by working with objects and processes. Simply telling children about scientific phenomena is inadequate and may even lead to their developing misconceptions.

SCIENCE EDUCATION IN THE PAST

Science has been an important part of the elementary and early childhood curriculum since the beginning of the twentieth century. John Dewey (1956) was a strong proponent of including science in the education of young children, and the University of Chicago Laboratory School was an early center of such science education.

Elements of science education were found in earlier programs in early childhood education, though they were not identified as such. In Robert Owen's nineteenth-century infant school, children were taken out to the fields to observe nature. Specimens from nature and models of nature were also brought into the classroom for observation. Froebel's kindergarten included nature study—the observation of natural phenomena for the sake primarily of appreciation rather than of comprehension. Teachers provided a garden for the children to cultivate. Children cared for small animals. Teachers brought rocks and leaves into the classroom and arranged them on a table for the children to observe. They read nature stories and exhibited pictures to further children's learning. The primary purpose of these activities was to develop children's reverence for the outdoors and their appreciation of the wonders of nature. In urban schools, nature study was especially needed because city children had fewer opportunities for encounters with nature.

After the first quarter of the twentieth century, the study of science began to replace nature study in elementary and early childhood education. The inclusion of kindergartens in elementary schools may well have been one impetus for expanding the elementary school curriculum beyond the three Rs. Science education in its newer form became concerned less with appreciation and more with understanding scientific concepts and the scientific method, even at a rudimentary level. Elements of nature study are still found in early childhood classes today, when teachers display natural materials and read anthropomorphic nature stories.

Although teaching an appreciation of nature and providing opportunities to observe natural phenomena are worthwhile activities, they are not adequate as a science program. Teachers should develop activities that improve children's observational skills, for example. They should also teach children that an appreciation of nature requires an understanding of how to preserve nature and of the effects of technology on nature.

Knowing what science is allows teachers to use everyday occurrences in a classroom to build a science program. Careful observation, description and measurement, development and testing of hypotheses, acceptance of multiple explanations of happenings—this is the stuff of which science programs are made.

Actually, very little science was taught in the elementary schools until the 1960s (Howe, 1993). New science programs for young children were developed at that time as part of a broader move to reform the school curriculum. One stimulus to the change was the hypothesis voiced by Jerome Bruner (1960) that "any subject can be taught effectively in some intellectually honest form to any child at any stage of development" (p. 33). An intense period of curriculum development was spawned at that time, most of it focusing on children of kindergarten age and above. With the interest in Piagetian theory at this time, however, science learning in the prekindergarten period was also seen as legitimate. Young children would be able to approach scientific knowledge in an intuitive way, through concrete experiences.

Conceptions of Early Childhood Science Education

How science is taught depends to a great extent on how science is conceived. In modern society, science education is considered part of general education, since all persons ought to have some knowledge of science to use in their daily activities. They should have an understanding of the nature of scientific inquiry and the role of science in modern society. Thus, scientific literacy is an educational goal for all children.

Science as a System of Knowledge

Science is sometimes considered to be a body of knowledge about the physical world. In that view, a curriculum should contain those scientific facts most useful to children and adults, to be accumulated throughout a child's school career. The problem with this approach is that so many scientific facts continue to be accumulated that selecting the most significant ones is difficult. The number of facts an individual would have to learn and remember would make science education a formidable task. Teaching a body of scientific facts to children becomes a cumbersome, never-ending task of questionable ultimate value.

This approach to science teaching has generally been discarded in favor of a view of science as a set of organized concepts and generalizations. Scientific information can be organized into systematic sets of concepts. The concepts give meaning to the facts by allowing a person to relate pieces of information to a system of knowledge about the world.

Science is also conceived to be a method of generating and verifying knowledge. The methods scientists use in observing phenomena, testing hypotheses, controlling variables, and carefully reporting and replicating experiments are all part of the *structure* of science. Teaching this structure is the goal of the newer science programs.

The organizing of the content of science into a conceptual structure is not a completely new idea. Gerald Craig's (1927) research in science education in the 1920s was aimed at developing a unified science program for children based on generalizations that cut across the boundaries of separate scientific disciplines. This work led to the development of a conceptual scheme for education that is still in use today:

1. The universe is very large—*Space*
2. The earth is very old—*Time*
3. The universe is constantly changing—*Change*
4. Life is adapted to its environment—*Adaptation*
5. There are great variations in the universe—*Variety*
6. The interdependence of living things—*Interrelationships*
7. The interaction of forces—*Equilibrium and Balance*. (Craig, 1958; pp. 93–101)

Paul Brandwein and his associates (1966) developed a similar conceptual scheme for science teaching:

1. When energy changes from one form to another, the total amount of energy remains unchanged.

2. When matter changes from one form to another, the total amount of matter remains unchanged.
3. Living things are interdependent with one another and with their environment.
4. A living thing is the product of its heredity and its environment.
5. Living things are in constant change.
6. The universe is in constant change. (pp. 8–9)

Within this framework, Brandwein and his colleagues have designed an integrated science program for the kindergarten through the sixth grade.

Such conceptual schemes are useful in integrating information into meaningful concepts and generalizations. In addition, almost all scientific knowledge and information fits into a category, programs at different levels can be articulated with one another, and the entire content of science education for the school can be integrated by fitting each science experience into a concept and then determining the level at which it can best be taught. What is taught in the kindergarten can be related to what is taught in the third grade, with little danger of too much overlap in the content of instruction from grade to grade.

This approach is based on a conception of science primarily as a system of knowledge and information. Scientific concepts are taught through elements of knowledge that reflect these concepts. The concepts order this knowledge and allow it to be transfered to new situations. This process does not, however, allow us to test the concepts' truth or usefulness.

Other programs of science education have focused on the phenomena of science, the concepts of science, or the processes of scientific inquiry rather than on scientific knowledge. The American Association for the Advancement of Science (AAAS) has developed the program *Science—A Process Approach* (S–APA). The *Science Curriculum Improvement Study* (SCIS) was developed at the University of California under the direction of Dr. Robert Karplus. The *Elementary Science Study* (ESS) is a product of the Educational Development Center. Robert Karplus and Herbert Thier (1967) have characterized the differences in these three science curriculum projects as follows:

> . . . the units produced by the SCIS and the parts written by the AAAS form a complete and integrated curriculum, while the ESS is creating self-contained units that may be fashioned into a curriculum by local teaching groups. He will also find that there are significant differences in emphasis on the three elements—concepts, phenomena, processes—which make up the science course. Thus, the ESS stresses the child's involvement in the phenomena and is confident that he will thereby gain practice with processes and achieve understanding of valuable concepts even though these are not made explicit. The SCIS stresses the concepts and phenomena, with process learning an implicit by-product of the children's experimentation, discussion and analysis. The AAAS stresses the child's practice with the processes

> and uses the phenomena only as vehicles and the concepts as tools. An added difference is that the AAAS program attempts to appraise the children's progress more systematically and in greater detail than do the others. (p. 8)

Differences in programs reflect differences not only in content emphasis but also in ideas about how children learn and develop as well as about the nature and purpose of school. These programs have a number of common attributes. They all are based on modern conceptions of science, view of children as active learners, and require active participation in science experiences.

A brief sketch of the three science programs discussed by Karplus and Thier should help to illustrate the likenesses and differences among programs spawned by the curriculum reform movement. These science programs represent major innovations in how science curricula and their materials are developed. While earlier materials were based on what was thought to be of intrinsic interest to children, these curricula were based on theories of cognitive development or learning. Science—A Process Approach (S—APA), the Science Curriculum Improvement Study (SCIS), and the Elementary Science Study (ESS) are but three of many science programs available today. They are presented here because each is well conceived and developed, and each represents a distinct point of view about what science is and how children can best learn it.

Science—A Process Approach

The American Association for the Advancement of Science (1967), in its primary science curriculum *Science—A Process Approach* (S—APA), conceived of the processes of scientific inquiry as the elements of science that are most essential for children to learn:

1. observing,
2. using space-time relationships,
3. using numbers,
4. measuring,
5. classifying,
6. communicating,
7. predicting, and
8. inferring.

A principal aim of the program is to develop skill in the careful and systematic use of these processes in the primary grades as a necessary preliminary to undertaking more complex science learning in the later grades (p. 3). These more complex processes include formulating hypotheses, defining operations, controlling variables, experimenting, formulating models, and interpreting data.

Activities in the S—APA primary program were designed to teach children the eight processes listed above. Young children are to *observe* objects and identify their colors, shapes, and textures. They might observe weather phenomena, or the various parts of a plant, and then describe their observations. In the area of *space/time relationships,* children learn to identify two- and three-dimensional shapes and angles and deal with concepts of speed. *Number* work includes identifying and comparing sets, finding the sum of two numbers, and dealing with number relationships. Children explore *measures* of length, weight, area, and volume by making comparisons and using standard units of measurement. Specific experiences are provided to help children *classify* objects by visible attributes, moving from single stage to multistage classifications. *Communication* requires identifying and naming objects, using graphs, and describing experiments to others. Children learn to *make and test predictions*. They are also required to *draw inferences* from information and demonstrate how they may be tested.

The program is hierarchically structured, with simpler activities followed by more complicated ones. The program is linear, so that what a child needs to know for a particular activity has already been taught in earlier activities. In the area of observation, for example, early activities include identifying and naming attributes of an object—is it rough or smooth, large or small, or of primary or secondary colors? Later children are required to identify and name two or more characteristics of an object, such as roughness and smallness. Similarly, children learn to identify two-and three-dimensional shapes early. They are later asked to identify the two-dimensional shapes that are the components of three-dimensional ones.

This approach conceives of science education as teaching the processes used in scientific inquiry. These processes were identified through a task analysis of the scientist's role. While the facts of science and the level of technology used continually change, the basic processes of scientific inquiry remain relatively constant. In a sense, the developers of S—APA viewed science as what scientists do.

This method of teaching scientific processes leans heavily on learning theory. Readiness is identified as the achievement of prerequisite learning. On successful attainment of one level of skill development, children move up to the next. What children can learn is a function of what they already know. If they are unable to master a scientific process, then they need to master the prerequisite skills. The S—APA program has been designed to achieve specific observable behavioral goals. Identified in each lesson are the goals children are expected to achieve, specified in behavioral terms. Since teachers can directly observe these behaviors, immediate evaluation becomes possible.

Critics of this approach are concerned that while it does teach some of the basic processes in science, it omits other important ones, including thinking creatively about phenomena, inventing concepts, and developing divergent notions about aspects of the world. The lack of concern for children's stages of intellectual development has also been criticized.

Science—A Process Approach materials are available from the American Association for the Advancement of Science, Washington, DC 20005.

Science Curriculum Improvement Study

The *Science Curriculum Improvement Study* (SCIS) of the University of California conceived of science education as a way to help children form "a conceptual framework that permits them to perceive phenomena in a more meaningful way. This framework will also help them to integrate their inferences into generalizations of greater values than they would form if left to their own devices" (Karplus & Thier, 1967, pp. 20–21).

The topics of the SCIS program reflect basic concepts in science and a Piagetian conception of intellectual development. Level I in the program corresponds to the transition from preoperational to concrete operational thought; level II reflects concrete operational thought; level III reflects the transition from concrete operations to formal operations; level IV requires facility with formal operations. The materials, activities, and concepts the program offers are compatible with children's reasoning ability at each level, and science learning is seen as providing a bridge from personal exploration and interpretation of the world to an understanding of scientific concepts.

Units in the SCIS program are taught in a specific sequence. Each unit covers a number of topics and contains *invention* lessons and *discovery* lessons. Invention lessons allow the teacher to define new terms or concepts; discovery lessons permit the children to apply these new ideas. Optional activities are also provided. In each lesson children are given specific sets of materials and asked to experiment with them. All the children in the class are usually working on the same experiments, either individually or in small groups. Some lessons in the program are left completely open-ended; others may terminate in classroom discussions. Teachers are often advised to guide discussions with open-ended questions such as, "Tell us what happened in your experiment," or "How did the objects change?" A range of outcomes could be expected from any of the experiences provided, since different inferences might legitimately be made from any one set of experiences. Scientific concepts and an understanding of the processes of science, the goals of the program, are to be achieved cumulatively over long periods of time.

The *Science Curriculum Improvement Study* is available from Lawrence Hall of Science, University of California, Berkeley, CA 97420.

Elementary Science Study

The *Elementary Science Study* (ESS) provides a set of instructional units, each of which can be used at several grade levels. David Hawkins, former director of ESS, defines three phases of science instruction. In the first, children primarily "mess about," freely exploring materials and making their own discoveries in an unstructured environment.

In the second phase, the work is externally guided but still highly individualized through the use of "multiply programmed" materials—materials that contain written or pictorial guidance for the student but are designed to provide variety in the ordering of topics. Consequently, for almost any way children's learning may evolve, material is available to help them move along their way.

The third phase of science instruction moves children from concrete perception to abstract conceptualization. This phase of theorizing must be built upon experience and experimentation, but abstraction does not develop without special attention. The description of each of these phases represents central tendencies of the phase, but each phase includes activities reflecting the others (Hawkins, 1965).

The "messing about" phase can be illustrated in the directions for getting started provided in the *Teachers' Guide for Geo Blocks*. Children are provided with a set of blocks smaller than the traditional kindergarten unit blocks. These blocks are designed as units, so that a number of small blocks equal the size of a larger one. Many small blocks and fewer larger ones are provided, so that children are forced to develop equivalences. The blocks are used to build towers, ramps, three-dimensional maps, and other constructions. Specific problems are provided for the children to work through with the blocks. Teachers are asked to observe but not intervene in these early explorations, although they may make informal suggestions for elaborating the use of the blocks. Later, as the children move into the second phase of their work, teachers can ask questions to encourage more directed use of the blocks. Questions may deal with building, counting, shapes, slopes, grouping, surface area, and volume.

In addition to Geo Blocks, a number of other units have been prepared by ESS. Some of these are appropriate for young children, while others are designed for the intermediate grades. Units include *Small Things*, *Growing Seeds*, *Batteries and Bulbs*, *Mirror Cards*, and *Light and Shadows*, among others. The *Elementary Science Study* materials are available from Delta Education, Inc., P. O. Box M, Nashua, NH 03061.

While the S—APA and SCIS programs tend to support whole-class activity, the ESS units can be used by a small group. The ESS program also uses discovery techniques as an instructional strategy to a greater extent than do the others. Children are placed in direct contact with scientific phenomena with a minimum of structure provided by the teacher. Teachers play an active role in helping children build scientific concepts. In the first phase of the learning situation, that role relates to organizing the environment to facilitate children's discovery. In the second phase of the learning situation, teachers ask questions to create cognitive dissonance and to help children see the phenomena being observed in different ways. In the third phase, teachers provide greater structure to the learning situation and help children build theories to explain what they have observed.

SELECTING A SCIENCE PROGRAM

Science—A Process Approach, *Science Curriculum Improvement Study*, and *Elementary Science Study* represent only a few of the programs available in science education today. These programs generally contain up-to-date science content. They also provide for children's active participation in the learning process, so that science instruction goes well beyond rote memorization. Barbara Waters (1973) presents six different early childhood science programs for teachers to analyze in choosing a program. Though her book is over 20 years old, it is still a useful resource. In addition to programs generated as part of the curriculum reform movement, textbook publishers have developed a number of science programs for kindergarten and primary grades, often including teachers' manuals and kits of materials. Descriptions of these materials and other science materials for early childhood education are available in the National Science Resource Center's 1988 publication, *Science for Children: Resources for Teachers*.

The first decision in selecting a science program is to decide to include science in the classroom. Too often kindergarten and primary school teachers are so concerned with language and literacy instruction that they use all their classroom time for this program area. The art program may then be relegated to Friday afternoon; physical education becomes a way of helping to rid children of their excess energy; science and social studies may be offered only erratically and superficially. In addition, some teachers in prekindergarten programs are fearful of imposing on young children's thinking. They prefer a program based on children's play and advocate that all activities be child-initiated. An alternative is to pick up on the cues that children provide regarding their interests and match science and other activities to those interests. In addition, teachers are obliged to help children become interested in things they do not already know. Children's development, including their intellectual development, requires that adults and other children extend the children's understanding and challenge their ways of looking at the world.

Evidence has accumulated that current science programs can have an important impact on children's thinking and academic achievement. Increases in scores on IQ and achievement tests have been noted as a result of children's immersion in a science program. Mary Budd Rowe (1976), who summarized a number of studies detailing these positive gains, suggests that too often those children who can benefit most from science programs, including the poor and the disabled, are the ones who are denied them. If teachers could provide enriched educational opportunities for all children in these early years, perhaps these children would have fewer learning difficulties in the upper grades.

Once teachers opt to include a science program, they need to decide which one to use. Teachers might decide to be systematic in their teaching of science, using a well-conceived and well-designed program. Selection of such a program could be based on an analysis of what programs are available, their content emphasis (for example, whether they emphasize facts, concepts, or skills), and the requirements for teaching them, including the resources needed and the knowledge a teacher should possess to be successful with them. Teachers might also analyze the programs' assumptions about child learning and development and whether those assumptions are compatible with their own and the school's approach to early childhood education.

A science program should be compatible with the rest of the classroom curriculum. The S—APA program, for example, would fit into a more formal, behaviorally oriented classroom. The SCIS and ESS programs, derived from a constructivist view of cognitive development, could be implemented by teachers who support this view. None of these programs would fit into a textbook-oriented classroom where children are expected to read books, listen to lectures, and watch demonstrations for their science activities. These programs all require children to *do* science, to engage in inquiry-oriented, hands-on activities. The science program should also use a "minds-on" approach, as Eleanor Duckworth and her associates (1990) suggest, requiring children to think about what they do and to solve problems the teacher presents.

At the kindergarten and primary levels, a number of fully developed science programs are available that have the potential of providing significant science learning for young children. Often the program decision rests with a school system, which may adopt a single textbook series or program to insure continuity of learning through the grades. But even using a program someone else has adopted, teachers still have the discretion to adapt the program to their children's abilities. Preschool teachers have greater freedom in selecting or creating science programs. However, there are fewer resources available to help teachers at this level.

A Program for Kindergarten and Prekindergarten

Prekindergarten and kindergarten teachers have fewer guidelines to follow in selecting a science program than do elementary school teachers. Some teachers adapt experiences from science programs intended for older children to offer to their classes. However, such activities may be unrelated to each other, and the intended outcomes of the experiences may actually be beyond young children's capability. Other teachers continue to use a nature study approach, creating displays of leaves, rocks, small animals, or other science material in the classroom and talking to the children about weather and seasonal changes. Still others provide children with scientific labels for everyday phenomena.

Observing and appreciating nature is important, but by itself, it is not enough. The key to science education is helping children to do something with what they observe of the natural world and to think about what they do. The three science curriculum projects described above can provide

Categorizing objects by color, size, and shape develops an awareness of the attributes of objects.

guidelines for structuring a science program at the preschool level, since they all seem to have common prerequisites. Each program requires that children be able to make and describe observations of physical objects, categorize objects by certain attributes, and discriminate between groups of objects that fit into a category and those that do not. A significant program could be built around experiences that help children to observe, describe, and categorize physical phenomena. These activities could be balanced with others in which children freely explore scientific materials and their use in a variety of classroom experiences.

Exploring and Describing Attributes and Actions

Each person receives information about the external world through the five senses: sight, sound, touch, taste, and smell. This information can be identified and categorized. Visual properties of things can be differentiated in terms of size, shape, color, and other qualities. Sounds can be identified by pitch, intensity, quality, and regularity. Sounds can also be related to the things that produce them. Touch sensations can be described as hard or soft, rough or smooth, warm or cold, sharp or dull. The qualities of taste and smell, although not as precisely identifiable, can also be differentiated.

An approach to science education in the preschool based on exploring the attributes and actions of objects would be similar to the approach to physical knowledge advocated by Constance Kamii and Rheta DeVries (1978). It also may seem similar to the program of sensory education found in many Montessori programs. While the goals are the same, the difference is that science programs do not attempt to isolate any single attribute of objects and teach that attribute in a systematic way (see Chapter 2). Nor do special materials need to be purchased for such a program. In addition, language learning should go hand-in-hand with exploring and describing attributes.

Young children can go beyond just learning to use their five senses. They can learn to expand their powers of observation by using simple devices. A stethoscope, for example, can allow children to hear sounds they would not be able to hear with the ear alone. A magnifying glass will allow children to see things they could not see with the eye alone, or to see them larger. Carolyn Herman (1987) also suggests using a magnifying glass to help children explore the attributes of light. They can see how light bends through the double convex lens of a magnifying glass. They can experiment with a magnifying glass in many ways, seeing objects upside down and identifying how far from an object to hold the glass for proper focus. They can compare how things look with the eye alone, through a magnifying glass, and through a clear container of water, for example, a drinking glass or an aquarium.

VIGNETTE: SCIENCE, KINDERGARTEN

The teacher begins a large-group discussion about observing. "What does it mean to observe?" she asks.

Destinee answers, "It means to look at things."

Derek adds, "It means to touch things, too."

The teacher elaborates on these answers. "We can use all of our senses when we observe. We can touch, taste, smell, listen, and see." She then asks the students to work with their assigned partners on an observation activity. She hands each pair a brown lunch bag with various kinds of pasta inside. She explains that they are to observe the pasta in any way they think is appropriate.

One pair of students immediately calls out, "One looks like a bow tie."

The teacher responds affirmatively, and then asks the children to work quietly with their partners. After several minutes she calls the children's attention. "Please share with me and your class members what you have observed about your bag of pasta," she says.

The students are anxious to share. "All of our pasta was hard," says Tiffany.

"We had red pasta, green pasta, and yellow pasta," announces Jonathan.

The teacher asks, "Did any of you taste the pasta?"

One girl says, "Yes, we tried to eat our pasta, but it tasted yucky."

"What do you mean by 'yucky'?" asks the teacher.

"Well, it was kind of boring and didn't taste like anything," the girl replies.

"Did anyone smell the pasta?" asks the teacher.

No one responds. The teacher then asks them all to smell the pasta. She praises the children for being good observers, and then asks, "What would happen if we placed our pasta in hot water?"

One boy's hand shoots up, and he shouts, "It will turn into macaroni and cheese."

The teacher says, "You're on the right track. Tomorrow, we will put our pasta in hot water and observe what happens. We can taste the pasta. We can also smell it, touch it, and look at it. Maybe some of you will want to listen to it while it is cooking." The class then goes on to another activity.

For each sense there are manipulative activities and related language experiences that would help children identify, categorize, and differentiate experiences and begin to describe objects according to their sensory properties. This process is the beginning of scientific thought. Children must also learn descriptive language that allows them to symbolize and communicate their sense experiences.

Other cooking experiences can also be used to support science learning in young children. Books such as Jeanette B. Endres and Robert

Activity EXPLORING TASTE, TEXTURE, AND SMELL

Vary the traditional milk or juice and crackers by bringing in a variety of foods to taste at snack time. The children can eat these foods and talk about how they smell, taste, and feel. Fruits make excellent samples, as do many vegetables. Try to include vegetables that children seldom see in their natural form or eat raw, for example, carrots, jicama, potatoes, celery, turnips, and spinach. Try different fruits as well, such as kiwi, Asian pears, mangos, and the like. A variety of breads and crackers, including whole-grain breads, as well as many other foods can be included.

As the children taste these foods, have them talk about their sense experiences. Focus on taste, texture, and smell. You can categorize the foods in a variety of ways, such as sweet or salty, soft or hard, mushy or crisp. Make a chart for the bulletin board, arranging the foods according to category. The name of the category could be listed at the top of each column, and pictures of the foods can be pasted underneath. Some foods might appear in more than one category.

You might wish to cook some of these foods, especially the raw vegetables, to help children discover what happens when heat is applied. Cooked spinach looks different from raw spinach. Cooked carrots feel different from raw carrots. Even mixing foods together often makes significant differences in the way they look, taste, and feel. Sugar dissolved in water still tastes sweet, but no longer has a granular feel. Flour also changes consistency when mixed with a liquid. Foods can be used in an endless variety of ways. A chart describing changes can be made as a result of a discussion. Such a chart can be referred to in later discussions.

Rockwell's *Food, Nutrition, and the Young Child,* 3rd ed.; Mary T. Goodwin and Gerry Pollen's *Creative Food Experiences for Children*; and Nancy Wanamaker, Kristin Hearn, and Sherrill Richarz's *More Than Graham Crackers* provide useful ideas. Beverly Boals (1992) suggests setting up a permanent cooking center if the classroom is large enough. The cooking center should contain a table, chairs, a work space, and storage space. In addition to tasting and smelling ingredients, children should have the opportunity to observe various cooking processes and their effects on ingredients. Heating, cooling, and freezing all affect foods in observable ways, as do beating and combining foods. Adding rising agents such as yeast or baking powder will have a dramatic effect on a combination of flour, water, and other ingredients. Mathematics concepts can be presented to children as they measure ingredients for cooking. In addition to all this learning, cooking experiences provide excellent opportunities for talking about nutrition and what children need for healthy growth.

Children create generalizations as the result of their observations and descriptions, for example, that when food is heated, it changes. A generalization that seems wrong to the teacher but fits the children's observations should be accepted. The teacher can later provide experiences that complicate the observations in the hope that a new and more accurate generalization will be forthcoming.

Experiences with many materials help children become aware of the attributes of things. Providing similarly shaped objects of lead and of aluminum helps them differentiate between heavy and light objects. A touch board containing sandpaper, velvet, absorbent cotton, a piece of aluminum foil, and other such everyday items displays different textures. Setting up a "feeling box" containing an object hidden from view that children can touch helps focus on tactile perception. Teachers can talk about the colors and shapes of things, bringing in samples of primary colors and specific shapes and using everyday objects around the school. Block structures can be identified as larger or smaller, wider or narrower than other block structures.

Children can focus on the different elements of their perception in the free, unstructured activities of play situations, or in more structured activities specifically designed to help them learn a particular category or name for an attribute. Once they have learned several attributes, children can be helped to make finer and finer discriminations and to begin to categorize things by their attributes. The same objects can be used to teach different kinds of categorization. A box of buttons, for example, might be given to a group of children to be separated by color, by size, or by the material from which they are made.

Observing and describing the physical attributes of objects and organizing these observations in some meaningful way is just one part of an early childhood science program. Another part relates to observing and describing the actions of objects and the interaction of objects with each other under varying conditions.

Constance Kamii and Rheta DeVries (1978) use the term *physical knowledge* to distinguish between what they see as stereotyped science activities and activities designed to help children develop mental schema about scientific processes. Many science programs and science educators, such as the SCIS and ESS programs and the work of Eleanor Duckworth (1987) and C. Chaille and L. Britain (1991), conceive of science education within a similar Piagetian framework. In their book *Physical Knowledge in Preschool Education* (1978), Kamii and DeVries describe activities that can be used with young children to help them develop an understanding of the actions of and interactions among objects. Providing children with rollers and flat boards allows them to experiment with activities related to balance and motion. Equipping a water play area with various sizes and shapes of bottles, cups, tubes, and funnels offers them opportunities to explore the properties of water as it is transferred from one container to another or as it flows through a tube. Other play activities teachers provide could allow children to explore additional aspects of the physical world as they develop descriptions and tentative explanations of what happens and as they test their ideas with each other, with the teacher, and against further encounters with similar phenomena.

Additional Science Activities An early childhood science program can go beyond the activities described above. Elements of nature study continue to serve the goals of early childhood education. Field trips to parks, wooded areas, and nature preserves are worthwhile, both as opportunities to learn and practice observation skills and as ways of helping young children learn to appreciate and develop a sense of wonder about nature. Books such as *Hug a Tree and Other Things to Do Outdoors with Young Children* (Rockwell, Sherwood, & Williams, 1983) provide excellent suggestions of activities for teachers to use with young children.

VIGNETTE: SCIENCE, PRESCHOOL

The teacher asks the children at the end of group time what they do at home to care for birds.

Lisa says, "My mommy puts sunflower seeds in the feeder almost every day."

Tommy answers, "My daddy says it's not good to feed the birds in our front yard because they make a mess."

Ryan notes, "We made a tree just for birds in our yard. We put peanut butter on the tree."

The teacher announces that the class will make special gifts for the birds today. He says, "I would like each of you to go to your working table. You will notice it is covered with newspaper today. Please be careful not to push the newspaper off the table."

As the children seat themselves, the teacher distributes a pine cone to each child. A piece of string is attached to the top of each pine cone. He says, "Each of you will be given a small cup of peanut butter, a small cup of bird seed, and a popsicle stick. The first thing you should do is spread the peanut butter all over the pine cone. Then you can sprinkle your cone with bird seed. It's just like sprinkles on an ice cream cone. The more seeds you get on the cone, the more the birds will like it."

The children chatter among themselves. They seem anxious to begin work on their project. As they work, they talk about where they will hang their bird feeders. The teacher reminds them to choose a safe place for the feeders, away from hungry cats and squirrels.

Even trips through the schoolyard and along the streets surrounding the school can provide opportunities to learn about and come to appreciate nature. A wide variety of plants grow unattended in many places, such as around fences and in cracks in sidewalks. These plants are worth studying. Bringing plants, rocks, and other elements of nature into the classroom for closer observation is also helpful. These might be placed on science tables for continued observation. A terrarium could be made with some of the material collected, using a jar or large glass container. If each

Activity A FIELDTRIP TO A NEIGHBORHOOD PLAYGROUND OR PARK

Take the children to a neighborhood playground or park where they can observe and collect materials. Give each child a paper bag to store and carry things the child collects. Select a focus for each trip; for example, one trip might focus on observing and collecting rocks while another might focus on leaves. Before leaving, discuss the purpose of the trip and how the children should behave as they go about their collecting. Also, set conditions and limits for collecting; for example, children should collect only rocks smaller than their fist or only one sample of each type of object. Thus, children might look for leaves that are shaped differently or that have different colors. They might select rocks of different sizes, shapes, textures, or colors.

On return to the classroom, have the children sort and arrange their samples by categories the class establishes together; for example, rocks could be organized by size, shape, texture, or color. They could also be ordered from the biggest to the smallest or from the smoothest to the roughest. If a child wishes to create a different category, accept the new category and have the child explain it to the class. The class should discuss what the children have collected. They might select from each child's material for a class display. The children could also engage in art projects with the materials they collect. They can trace leaves or make spatter prints with them. They can use small rocks in a collage or make a miniature rock garden with them. You might want to use a reference book to find the proper names of plants or rocks the children have collected.

Activity ECOLOGY IN THE CLASSROOM

Start a recycling program in the classroom. Find out what materials are collected in your community and how they are recycled. Place recycling containers in a convenient spot in the classroom. Have the children place materials for recycling (such as paper and glass containers) in these containers to be collected or sent for recycling periodically. You might want to take a field trip to a recycling center if there is one handy in your community.

Discuss with the children how they can reuse materials rather than discarding them. Newspapers can be painted on. Egg cartons can be cut and the pieces used for collage. Other materials can be collected to be used in art projects as well.

If your school has a garden, start a compost heap in a bin. Explain what happens when things are composted. Children can place leaves, plant cuttings, and food scraps in the compost bin, turning it every so often. After the materials have been composting for a while, have the children look at the materials and talk about what happens to the materials as they are composted. Use the compost in the garden when the class plants in spring.

child makes a terrarium with different materials (using sand instead of soil, for example) and if different terrariums are tended in different ways (some with more light than others, or with more or less moisture included, for example), children can observe the effects of different environmental conditions on plants.

Science should not remain abstract for the children. Rather, they should learn how science relates to what we do in our everyday lives. Cooking activities such as those described above provide excellent opportunities for children to learn about nutrition. Field trips around the neighborhood can provide a springboard for lessons about ecology. Children may not be able to understand all the principles behind the exhortation to eat a balanced diet or to protect their environment, but they can be helped to know which foods are more nutritious than others as well as to appreciate the importance of protecting the physical environment and keeping it clean.

Including Science Materials in Classroom Activities

Teachers should design play activities so that children can discover and use properties and relationships. Setting up a pulley system in the block area for the children to use in building will help them learn about force and how it can be increased or changed in direction. The children should be allowed to verbalize the experience in their own ways. It is less significant that they learn such terms as *friction*, *inertia*, or *mechanical advantage* than that they intuitively learn through experience that a pulley makes it easier to lift things.

A battery-operated doorbell and buzzer in the housekeeping area can stimulate dramatic play; as people come and go, children can see the effects of electricity and the need for a circuit in operating electrical devices. Battery-powered electric lights, complete with switches, could also be wired into a playhouse. A bulb, a battery, and a couple of lengths of wire can be provided in a box for the children's free manipulation and discovery. Magnets, magnifying glasses, and other items can be made available to children for "messing about" or for inclusion in their play.

Teachers can enhance science learning by asking children to explain what happened when they used these materials. Responses need not be formally accurate; children should reasonably explain their experience from their point of view. Teachers then know what the children understand and what confusions still exist. They must then determine whether to leave the adequate, though erroneous, explanation alone for a while or to engage the children in other experiences that will lead them to discover their errors. Often group discussions allow children the opportunity to test their perceptions and understandings against those of other children.

Children might also be given opportunities to grow plants from seeds, tubers, and cuttings. If the class does not have a garden, plants can be grown in window boxes or flowerpots. The children should be able to describe how things grow as well as what seemed to help them grow. They can measure growing plants weekly once they sprout and make a chart of their growth. Children should also be able to describe how they care for the plants. Fish and small animals, in fishbowls or cages, can also be provided.

In all science inquiry, children should be given opportunities to ask questions about what they see and to learn how to find the answers. Sometimes the questions are unanswerable. "What is electricity?" might

A classroom aquarium allows children to observe living things.

best be answered by, "I don't know, but we can see some of the things that electricity can do." It is better to answer questions honestly than to offer inaccurate or semimagical answers. Children need to become comfortable with the unknown.

In using everyday classroom activities to further the science program, teachers break down artificial barriers between subjects. Most of society's problems cannot be labeled "science problems" or "social science problems," but rather spill over into many areas. Ecological issues, for example, may have a biological base, but the tools to resolve them grow out of a knowledge of economics and politics also.

Science activities can enhance the language arts program. The observations and descriptions generated in science activities enable children to use words effectively. Their descriptions will become more accurate and vivid. Their vocabularies will increase, and they will use more adverbs and adjectives. Measurement used in science can benefit the mathematics program as well. Even drawing and modeling as ways of recording observations tie science to the arts. Both science and social studies units can provide themes to help integrate the early childhood program. Ecology and conservation are examples of areas in which social and scientific inquiry can converge.

SUPPORTING SCIENCE LEARNING IN THE CLASSROOM

Teachers must organize their classrooms so that science learning can take place in an identifiable area that has a degree of isolation. The science center should include or have nearby an enclosed storage space, such as a cabinet, in which science materials not currently in use can be kept. If these materials are readily available, teachers can use the children's cues to move into a science topic that interests them, thus exploiting their personal motivation for learning. If teachers do not have a variety of materials available, they may have to postpone an experience, allowing a critical moment for learning to pass right by.

In addition to storage, the science center should include some open shelf space that allows access to a variety of materials. Space should also be available for children to work on problems. If the center is relatively isolated, teachers can set up a problem and allow children to work on it individually or in small groups. Since scientific inquiry is an important goal of science instruction, most of the science work ought to be done by individuals or small groups.

Using Displays and Demonstrations

Simply having a display is inadequate for science education in the early years; the key to the effectiveness of a display is how it is used. Teachers should organize their displays for the children's use. For instance, bulletin boards can be organized to demonstrate a scientific concept. Leaves of the

A science display supports science learning.

same kind of tree as well as from different kinds of trees can be pinned up to show diversity of foliage. Pictures of a plant at different periods can demonstrate the process of growth. Objects of varying size can show the concept of *bigger than* or *smaller than*. Similarly, materials on a science table can be organized so that children can actually use them. The children might organize a group of rocks by texture, color, or form. They might look at objects through different types of lenses to discover how the apparent size of the objects changes. Children can discover the effects of magnets on both magnetic and nonmagnetic material. Displays can be organized in many ways. The crucial element is that children use the display in learning to develop modes of scientific thinking.

Effective displays are changed regularly. If the content of a display reflects the children's concern with particular areas of scientific inquiry, it can be changed to keep up with shifts in the focus of science learning in the classroom.

Actual experiments, in the traditional sense—including the use of laboratory controls—are seldom carried out in the classroom. Often little is to be gained from controlled experiments that cannot be gained from freer experiences with the same materials. Teachers often use demonstrations instead.

Demonstrations can be a way either of telling or of asking children about science. If the demonstration is followed only by an explanation, it is merely an illustration. Demonstrations lead to scientific inquiry when followed by questioning and discussion sessions. Teachers can stimulate such sessions by asking questions such as, "What happened? Why did it happen? How do you know? Did you see anything else happening? Can you think of other ways we can explain what happened? How can we tell that our explanation is correct?" If these questions are a part of honest inquiry, the children must have access to the information they need to test their conclusions. If they cannot directly observe a process, their responses may border on the magical rather than the scientific.

For example, a child who is told that the flame of a candle in a jar went out because it had used up all the oxygen has not been told anything useful, from a scientific point of view. The absence or presence of oxygen cannot be demonstrated to that child. The explanation must be accepted on faith, which is in itself unscientific. Teachers should avoid demonstrations in which the children cannot observe the phenomenon and must rely only on what teachers tell them.

Demonstrations are ways of helping children focus their observations so that they can better see a phenomenon. If children can perceive a thing or action, they can abstract ideas about the physical world from their observations and thus understand them. If children are not able to answer the questions the teacher asks, then the demonstration may not have served its purpose. It might have been beyond the children's understanding, or the ideas might have been presented in a confusing or obscure way.

Recording the Results of Inquiry

The processes and results of scientific inquiry should be recorded and communicated so that ideas can be retested and the results of various inquiries can be compared. Children in the upper primary classes can write with sufficient competence to begin to develop science notebooks that reflect their science activities. Teachers can devise many ways of helping younger children record their scientific activities. For instance, children can dictate materials into tape recorders or for the teacher to record on experience charts or in individual books; they can use paintings and drawings to record their experiences symbolically. Teachers should set aside time for discussion and recording, because the language and symbolic aspects of recording scientific observations are important for the children's continued learning.

The records developed for science activities provide one way of interrelating subject areas. Helping children draw objects accurately or use words that accurately represent an observation can help them become more creative artists or writers. As they gain mastery over ways of recording and representing observations and experiences, they become able to do more with the media they use. They also learn the uses of records so that the acts of reading and writing become more meaningful.

Taking Field Trips

In addition to using classroom resources for science activities, teachers should plan field trips outside the school. Some of these trips can be simple, like the trips to parks or playgrounds suggested above. Mark Jenness (1987) suggests taking schoolyard hikes that support the science program.

Recording the results of observation is part of science inquiry.

A child in the class, an older child, the teacher, or a parent can serve as secretary, recording data on what the children observe. A shape hike could be organized to help children explore the environment for things that are oval, spherical, square, crescent shaped, and the like. A touch hike will help children look for things that feel soft, hard, rough, smooth, bumpy, oily, or gritty. Hikes can be organized around themes of number, color, or sound. Once back at school, the children can review what they observed and go over their list, which could be posted on a bulletin board.

Other field trips might be more extensive. A trip to a farm or a park to look at the change of seasons is useful. Classes can visit farms, zoos, or animal shelters to look at animals. The kinds of trips a teacher plans depends in part on the resources available near the school. One type of resource that is developing around the United States is children's museums or children's exhibits in larger museums. Victor Danilov (1987) describes some of the museums in large cities, such the Field Museum of Natural History and the Museum of Science and Industry in Chicago, the Museum of Natural History in New York, and the National Museum of Natural History in Washington, DC. In addition, he describes museums for children in many communities, including the Exploratorium in San Francisco, the Boston Children's Museum, and the Children's Museum in Indianapolis. These museums have exhibits designed for children of all ages, many of them allowing children to explore scientific phenomena. Other, smaller communities also have museums with exhibits appropriate for young children. Museum curators are careful to see that, while their exhibits are entertaining, they are also educational (Ault, 1987). Class visits can be arranged to these museums, but they must be planned in advance.

INTEGRATING SCIENCE ACTIVITIES WITH OTHER CURRICULUM AREAS

Science activities are important in themselves. However, what children learn about science and how they do science can be related to other areas of the curriculum. Maryann Ziemer (1987) suggests that, because all things are related to each other in some way, activities in science can spin off into art, music, mathematics, literature, and other areas of the early childhood curriculum. The relationship between science and mathematics is readily apparent. Much of what children do in an early childhood science program requires that they deal with quantities. They need to count or measure things. They compare and contrast shapes of objects. But there are equally important relationships between science and other curriculum areas.

The area of language and literacy is very important to an early childhood science program. Children need to learn to describe and record what they observe, often keeping journals in which they record their observations and compare observations with those of other children. They learn to communicate the results of their activities to others. They learn to use language more precisely and develop a vocabulary of adverbs and adjectives—words that describe things. Children should also have available to them a variety of good science books that are appropriate to their reading level. The September, 1987, issue of *Young Children* provides an annotated list of science trade books for children. Marguerite C. Radencich and Gerry Bohning (1988) also recommend using natural science action books with children. These books, with their movable three-dimensional parts, help clarify particular science concepts and are also fun for children to use. Radencich and Bohning also provide an annotated book list that can help teachers select such books for their classes.

The arts can also be integrated with science. As children learn about music, they might inquire about what makes music. They can explore sounds, asking such questions as, "How are different sounds made? How are they transmitted? What happens if you pluck strings of different sizes or if you tap glasses that are the same size but have different amounts of water in them?" In the area of visual art, children can mix different colors of paint to come up with new colors and record their observations. They might also compare these observations with their observations of the effects of mixing different colored lights, derived by shining a flashlight through different colored lenses or sheets of plastic to see what colors of light they can make and how. As children learn about light, they can play with shadows, studying how to make longer and shorter shadows. They can go from this experimentation to making a shadow play, acting behind a large bedsheet or making puppets that they use behind the sheet. Paul Joslin (1988) describes several indoor and outdoor activities with shadows, including tracing children's shadows in the outdoor area at different times of the day or manipulating familiar objects behind a screen so that the children see only the shadows. He also suggests sending children home with a set of questions that would allow them to continue their explorations of shadows there. In addition, since children need to describe the observations they make in a science project, they can draw their descriptions in pictures as well as writing narratives.

Summary

This chapter has emphasized that science instruction requires children to actively inquire. Science is not a set of labels or concepts, but a way of conceiving of the world—a way of thinking about things. Thus, at every point in the science curriculum, children should have direct experiences with elements of the world. They should also actively think about their experiences, so that their thought processes about physical and natural phenomena will parallel their acquisition of scientific information. Classroom activities must thus be organized so that children can act on materials and experiences and arrive at their own conclusions. This active participation requires that most activities be organized for individuals and small groups. Teachers should not spend a great deal of time telling children about science, but should instead continuously provide them with opportunities to find out on their own.

In this approach, teachers must both be sensitive to the children's thought processes and observe what they do in class. The important element of science learning is not necessarily the product of scientific inquiry—the conclusions that children arrive at or the kinds of categories they develop—but rather the process by which they generate these conclusions and the reasons and methods they use to develop a set of categories. This approach should support a great deal of diversity in the classroom—diversity in achievement, goals, and activities.

A good early childhood science program requires more than a set of apparatus and some instructions for its use. It demands that a climate of inquiry pervade the class. Lazar Goldberg (1970) defined the characteristics of such a climate as

> anti-authoritarianism and democracy; high tolerance for dissent, argument, error and failure; regard to aesthetic reward; absence of fear and humiliating measures; emphasis on cooperation rather than competition; respect for manual as well as intellectual effort; and above all interesting and significant activity. It is not a climate where "anything goes." Rather it is one which is humane and reasonable. It is a climate in which children cultivate valid criteria for choosing among alternative beliefs. (pp. 14–15)

Such a climate can support the achievement of "autonomy based upon reason" (Dearden, 1968) in young children.

REFERENCES

American Association for the Advancement of Science. (1967). *Description of the program: Science—A process approach*. New York: Xerox Educational Division.

Ault, C. R., Jr. (1987). The museum as science teacher. *Science and Children, 25*(3), 8–11.

Boals, B. (1992). Cooking in the classroom. *Dimensions, 20*(2), 19–24.

Brandwein, P. F., Cooper, E. K., Blackwood, P. E., & Hone, E. B. (1966). *Concepts in science* (Grade I, Teacher's Edition). New York: Harcourt Brace Jovanovich.

Bruner, J. (1960). *The process of education*. Cambridge: Harvard University Press.

Chaille, C., & Britain, L. (1991). *The young child as scientist: A constructivist approach to early childhood education*. New York: Harper Collins.

Craig, G. S. (1927). *Certain techniques used in developing a course of study in science for the Horace Mann Elementary School*. New York: Bureau of Publications, Teachers College, Columbia University.

Craig, G. S. (1958). *Science and the elementary school teacher*. Lexington, MA: Ginn.

Danilov, V. J. (1987). Discovery rooms and kidspace: Museum exhibits for children. *Science and Children, 24*(4), 6–11.

Dearden, R. F. (1968). *The philosophy of primary education*. Boston: Routledge & Kegan Paul.

Dewey, J. (1956). *The child and the curriculum*. Chicago: University of Chicago Press.

Duckworth, E. (1987). *The having of wonderful ideas and other essays on teaching and learning*. New York: Teachers College Press.

Duckworth, E., Easley, J., Hawkins, D., & Henriques, A. (1990). *Science education: A minds-on approach for the elementary years*. Hillsdale, NJ: Erlbaum.

Endres, J. B., & Rockwell, R. (1990). *Food, nutition, and the young child* (3rd ed.). Columbus, OH: Merrill.

Goldberg, L. (1970). *Children and science*. New York: Scribner.

Goodwin, M. T., & Pollen, G. (1980). *Creative food experiences for children* (rev. ed.). Washington, DC: Center for Science in the Public Interest.

Hawkins, D. (1965). Messing about in science. *Science and Children, 2*(5), 5–9.

Herman, C. (1987). Through the magnifying glass. *Science and Children, 25*(3), 36–38.

Howe, A. C. (1993). Science in early childhood education. In B. Spodek (Ed.), *Handbook of research on the education of young children* (pp. 225–235). New York: Macmillan.

Hurd, P. D., & Gallagher, J. J. (1968). *New directions in elementary science teaching*. Belmont, CA: Wadsworth.

Jenness, M. (1987). Schoolyard hikes. *Science and Children, 24*(6), 23–25.

Joslin, P. (1988). The shadow knows. *Science and Children, 26*(2), 16–17.

Kamii, C., & DeVries, R. (1978). *Physical knowledge in preschool education*. Englewood Cliffs, NJ: Prentice Hall.

Karplus, R., & Thier, H. D. (1967). *A new look at elementary school science*. Skokie, IL: Rand McNally.

National Science Resource Center. (1988). *Science for children: Resources for teachers*. Washington, DC: National Academy Press.

Outstanding science trade books for children. (1987). *Young Children, 42*(6), 52–56.

Radencich, M. C., & Bohning, G. (1988). Pop up, pull down, push in, slide out. *Childhood Education, 64*, 157–161.

Rockwell, R. E., Sherwood, E. A., & Williams, R. A. (1983). *Hug a tree and other things to do outdoors with young children*. Mt. Ranier, MD: Gryphon House.

Rowe, M. B. (1976). Help is denied to those in need. *Science and Children, 12*, 323–325.

Wanamaker, N., Hearn, K. \
& Richarz, S. (1979). *More than graham crackers*. Washington, DC: National Association for the Education of Young Children

Waters, B. S. (1973). *Science can be elementary: Discovery-action programs for K–3*. New York: Citation Press.

Ziemer, M. (1987). Science and early childhood education. *Young Children, 42*(6), 44–51.

14

Mathematics for Young Children

CHAPTER OVERVIEW

This chapter presents:

- Views of what kinds of mathematics young children can learn
- Ways to teach mathematics using informal experiences
- Ways to teach various topics in mathematics using formal experiences
- Ways to develop mathematics understanding by using measuring activities
- Ways to integrate mathematics with other curriculum areas

INTRODUCTION

Just as children enter school having learned much about the spoken language and the physical world, so they come to school with a broad background of experiences in mathematics. Children have been living in a world of quantity. They have experienced *too small*, *too large*, and *all gone*. Their parents may have taught them to count before they enter nursery school, although parents may mistake saying number names in order for rational counting. Children probably also have an intuitive understanding of mathematical processes and how to solve mathematical problems.

Mathematics is a way of thinking about things and organizing experiences. It seeks order and looks for patterns. It requires reasoning and problem solving (Steen, 1990). Mathematical knowledge consists of both conceptual knowledge and procedural knowledge (Carpenter, 1986). Conceptual knowledge includes mathematical concepts and understandings. Procedural knowledge is knowledge of mathematical processes, or the ways of applying conceptual knowledge. Young children need to acquire both types of knowledge in learning mathematics.

YOUNG CHILDREN AND MATHEMATICS

Research in early childhood mathematics education has followed two lines of inquiry: information processing theory (see, for example, Price, 1989) and constructivist theory (see, for example, Baroody, 1987; Kamii,

1982). Information processing theory, as applied to early childhood mathematics, has focused on children's working memory and its limits and on how familiarity with information affects children's performance. Research in this area suggests that teachers of very young children should focus on counting, making numerals familiar to children so that they can better deal with higher-order processes. It also suggests that teachers should differentiate between four kinds of word problems: join problems, in which two quantities are joined together; separate problems, in which a single entry is separated into two; combine problems, in which a number of entities are combined; and compare problems, in which two entities are compared with each other. Children use different strategies to solve different kinds of problems (Price, 1989).

Research on mathematics education in a constructivist framework views children as constructing or "inventing" mathematics. They actively construct mathematical knowledge as they interact with the physical and social environment and think about those interactions. Children solve problems and come to understand the processes they use and why they use them. As a result of young children's mathematical actions on objects, they create a schema of the mathematical order they discover.

By the time children enter kindergarten, they have a great deal of procedural and conceptual knowledge about mathematics. Robert Rea and Robert Reys (1971) studied entering kindergartners' knowledge of geometry, numbers, money, and measurement. They identified a wide range of abilities. Nearly three-fourths of the children correctly identified the numerals *1, 2, 3, 4,* and *5,* and between 50 percent and 80 percent of the children were able to point correctly to the appropriate numeral when the number names *one* through *eight* were presented. When a sequence such as *1, 2, 3* or *5, 6, 7* was presented, about 90 percent of the children could provide the next number in the sequence. Over half the children were able to form groups of three and seven discs, count up to five items on a card, identify the number of items in a group up to eight, and point to the first and last item in a sequence when asked. About three-fourths of the children could also compare the number of items in two groups containing up to four items each.

Rea and Reys (1971) also found that the majority of the children could identify penny, nickel, and dime coins and distinguish between one, five, and ten dollar bills. More than half knew that a penny bought the least and a half-dollar the most of all coins, and that ten dollars bought the most of all the bills. The children also possessed a wide range of geometric knowledge.

Herbert Ginsberg (1980), in reviewing studies of young children's knowledge of arithmetic, also concluded that children have gained a considerable amount of knowledge of arithmetic before entering school. He found that preschool children are able to count and to solve simple addition problems. Thomas P. Carpenter (1986) has also indicated that many children use informal strategies to solve mathematical problems before they enter school. Ginsberg (1980) suggests that once in school, children do not always do arithmetic as teachers wish, preferring their own intuitive strategies to standard algorithms. However, the informal sense of number and mathematical processes that children bring to school can provide the basis for a sound mathematics program.

DECIDING WHAT AND HOW TO TEACH

The work of Jean Piaget (see Chapter 3) has been used to illuminate the capabilities of young children in mathematics more than in any other curriculum area, in part because mathematics operations are closely related to the formal mental operations Piaget and his colleagues identified.

The operations that can serve as the basis of an early childhood program have been characterized by Constance Kamii (1973) as **logico-mathematical** and **spatio-temporal knowledge.** Children structure these types of knowledge from their own actions and the logical sense of these actions, using the processes of assimilation and accomodation to achieve a new equilibrium of knowledge. Thus, the children themselves construct these types of knowledge. The three areas of logico-mathematical knowledge include *classification* (finding similarities and differences among objects as well as grouping and separating objects according to their similarities and differences), *seriation* (ordering things according to relative differences), and *number* (judging *same, more,* or *less,* and conserving quantity, or realizing that the amount of matter does not change when its shape changes). In relation to time and space, children need to structure time in sequence and to develop topological structures at the representational level, as will be discussed later. These are essentially the mental operations children need as they approach mathematics instruction in school. Kamii (1982, 1986) developed a series of studies describing how children make sense of the mathematical world.

Logical (or logico-) mathematic knowledge consists of processes used in operating on information.

Spatio-temporal knowledge consists of processes used in operating specifically on information related to space and time.

While many mathematics educators no longer strongly adhere to an orthodox Piagetian orientation to children's learning, the ideas that children should act on their environment through hands-on approaches to learning, that they should manipulate concrete materials in ways that are parallel to mental operations, and that they should learn to solve mathematical problems is still seen as good education. However, whether Piaget's stages of intellectual development represent good guidelines for what children may be capable of learning is being seriously questioned. Many children can learn to think in mathematical terms before they are capable of succeeding in conservation problems. At best, it may be that stages in intellectual development do exist, but that these stages are not universally related to all areas of knowledge. Rather, they are related to specific different domains of knowledge (Baroody, 1993). Thus individuals may be able to operate at an advanced level in an area in which they are highly competent, while being able to operate only at a lower level in areas in which they are less competent.

A decision about what to teach in early childhood mathematics programs cannot be derived from studies of intellectual development. Rather it must come from an understanding of the nature of the subject itself along with an understanding of what children are capable of learning in a specific educational context. In 1989, the National Council of Teachers of Mathematics issued *Curriculum and Evaluation Standards for School Mathematics*. This document calls for changes in the way mathematics is taught. It suggests that children need to learn to understand the procedures in mathematics rather than just memorizing them. It also suggests that teachers should use a problem-solving approach in teaching about mathematics. Especially at the primary level, it suggests, children should discuss the relationships among everyday occurrences, manipulative materials, pictorial representations, and mathematical ideas and symbols.

Building on this document and on an extensive review of research in early childhood mathematics education, Arthur Baroody (1993) suggests that the primary mathematics program emphasize the development of number sense, including the estimation of quantities, measurement, and computation. He suggests that the program should also work on two- and three-dimensional geometry, space, and measurement. In addition, it might include an informal introduction to probability and statistics.

Douglas E. Cruikshank, David L. Fitzgerald, and Linda R. Jensen (1980) suggest that a beginning mathematics program should focus on an understanding of the concept of number, as children explore the mathematical relationships among objects and among sets. Children must learn the meaning of *number* and the symbols for numbers. They should also be able to learn basic number facts and number operations. Children can also begin to understand concepts of space, including both topological and Euclidian geometry, and to apply number to space through measurement. Euclidean geometry is the geometry with which most people are most familiar. When we talk about shapes, such as circles, squares, and triangles, or when we talk about angles, we are using Euclidian geometry. Topological geometry deals with concepts such as proximity, separation, order, enclosure, and continuity. Children can also develop problem-solving skills. This set of mathematics topics for young children, like that suggested by Baroody, is in keeping with the studies of young children's mathematical capabilities.

As important as the topics to be covered in mathematics education is the method by which children will be expected to approach these topics. In an attempt to ensure that significant mathematical learning will take place in school, many elementary schools, kindergartens, and even preschools have adopted workbook-based and textbook-based programs. Unfortunately, these programs often give children an opportunity to approach mathematical concepts only through words or, at best, through words accompanied by pictures. Yet our knowledge of young children's thinking suggests that children must first have experiences with concrete objects before moving on to more abstract representations. Pictures are still abstract representations, though less abstract than either spoken or printed words. Depending solely on pictures and words to provide mathematical experiences places an added burden on young children.

In addition, most textbook-based programs isolate mathematics from children's experiences, making it difficult for children to apply what they already know about the quantitative world to a growing understanding of number, number relationships, and number operations. Constance Kamii (1982) has actually asserted that "worksheets are harmful for first graders' development of arithmetic" (p. 6). Most workbooks and worksheets are based on a drill-and-practice approach to teaching. Rather than helping children solve problems or understand mathematical processes, they focus on having children practice a process they may or may not understand, so that memorization takes the place of thinking.

Despite the criticisms that have been made of worksheets over the years, they are still popular in schools. Janet I. Stone (1987) believes they are popular because teachers feel that worksheets are more convenient than manipulative materials. They also help teachers demonstrate their accountability, because worksheets provide tangible evidence that children are doing productive work. In addition, using worksheets is a classroom management device, helping to create a quiet, controlled, structured environment. Stone suggests that worksheets can be turned into playsheets. Teachers can use them after exploratory activities that allow for manipulation of materials. Thus the worksheets become a device for children to record the work they do with manipulative materials.

The important point is that children should not learn mathematics through rote activities. Rather, teachers should help children learn to use their intuitive knowledge as a way of approaching more formal learnings. Teachers can develop textbook-based programs that use a hands-on approach and build on children's experiences. *Mathematics Their Way* (Baratta-Lorton, 1976) is such a program for the primary grades.

Rather than depending on workbooks and worksheets, teachers should seek out the problematic in the children's environment, helping children identify problems and seek ways to solve those problems. Kamii (1982) suggests that a great many situations that occur in the lives of preschool and kindergarten children can be used to help teach about numbers and number relationships. She also suggests that a variety of group games can be used with children to this end.

Organizing a mathematics center in one section of the classroom supports the regular use of manipulative materials and games for mathematics learning. Directions for using manipulative materials should be available so that individuals or small groups can engage in activities independent of the teacher. Richard Copeland (1976) provides suggestions for organizing and equipping a mathematics laboratory. Children can use a great variety of manipulative materials in games to gain experience with numbers, size, shapes, and the like. Various structured mathematics materials such as the Stern blocks, Cuisenaire rods, or Montessori mathematics material may be used. Puzzles using geometric inserts, peg sets, and sets of beads and strings can be used for counting, showing numbers, and patterning. The endless opportunities available in any classroom for counting, comparing, and measuring provide children with a wealth of opportunity to do mathematics.

Experiences with real things in their environment, if used appropriately, can keep children from feeling that mathematics is alien to their lives. It is disheartening to see some young children labeled incapable of understanding mathematics when they go to the store each day, order groceries for their families, pay the grocer, and count the change, being sure to check the transaction so that they are not cheated. Often it is the way mathematics is taught rather than the nature of mathematics that creates learning difficulties.

TEACHING BASIC MATHEMATICS CONCEPTS IN THE EARLY YEARS

While it is possible to order the range of mathematics learning for the early years and to assign grade placements for each topic, such an exercise is not productive, since interest in a topic and opportunity to make use of what is learned are as important as sequence in determining what to teach. Delbert W. Mueller (1985) suggests a strategy for defining the scope and sequence of a preprimary mathematics curriculum by

1. providing new mathematical experiences in a nonthreatening, nondirected, exploratory environment;
2. offering both directed and nondirected experiences using manipulative materials;
3. planning direct experiences that are matched to the children's level of intellectual experience; and
4. moving from the concrete to the pictorial to the symbolic level of presentation.

Children should learn to describe, classify, compare, order, equalize, join, and separate quantities. They should also focus on the attributes of objects, including color, shape, size, and mass.

Such a list would help teachers decide what to teach, but it does not provide guidance to a sequence for introducing topics. Teachers should keep these guidelines in their minds as they respond to the individual children in their class. They should note also that concepts are not learned in an all-or-none fashion. Starting with intuitive responses to the environment, children go through a series of successive approximations of mature concepts. Their first experiences with mathematics concepts should be informal. Providing continued experiences with an idea and how that idea might appear in different circumstances, and providing many different examples of that idea, helps children understand the concept in greater depth. Therefore, no age or grade placements are suggested for topics discussed in this chapter. Teachers must be sensitive to the children's level of understanding and to the prerequisites for understanding a particular concept.

Assessing children's levels of understanding is more difficult than assessing their ability to produce specific responses. One way of assessing their level of understanding is to see if they can use what they have learned in other situations. Teachers can gain important clues by listening carefully to children's responses to questions. Incorrect responses may be a result of inattention, but more often they reflect an inability to grasp concepts. Teachers can diagnose children's difficulties and either present activities that will clarify misconceptions or gear their teaching more closely to children's ability to understand.

INFORMAL INSTRUCTION

Children can learn a great deal about mathematics from informal activities. Informal activities need not be offered in an unsystematic way. Rather, teachers should plan systematically to incorporate mathematical ideas in a variety of activities.

Preschool children can learn to deal with quantities by comparing things and determining whether one object is bigger than, smaller than, longer than, or shorter than another object. They can also play with groups of one, two, or three objects, adding an object or taking one away, so that they see how the process of addition and subtraction works. They can learn to share out a quantity equally by dealing out candy, for example, giving each child one piece of candy in turn until there is no more left.

TEACHING SUGGESTION

Having Children Help with Routines

A number of classroom routines regularly require children to deal with quantity. Involve the children in them.

- **Snack time.** Arrange the tables at snack time so that a small number of children will be seated at each table. Set out napkins, cups, and other things needed for the snack. Have two children, in turn, set tables. Have them be sure that there is one napkin, one cup, and one of whatever else is needed for each place. Have them count the number of places at each table. Have the children check each other's work. After a while, vary the number of children at each table and have the children match the number of objects with the number of places. The same can be done for setting tables for lunch if lunch is part of the program.
- **Attendance.** Set up an attendance board with hooks for each child's tag. Set the hooks in two rows with hooks equally distant from each other. Make a tag for each child. At the beginning of the year the tag might have a picture of the child on it, or any other picture or symbol the child might recognize. After a while, write the children's names on the tags; later, change the tags so that only the children's names appear on them. As the children come into the class, have them take their own tags and place them on a hook. Have the girls place the tags in one row, and the boys in another. Ask such questions as "How many children are in school today? How many children are absent? Are there more girls or more boys present? How can you tell? Are more children present or absent from school?' The teacher might want to list these numbers on a chart each day. In time some of the children might be able to engage in these counting and comparing activities alone and report to the class. They will also be able to record the attendance on their own.
- **Preparing for activities.** Many activity centers need certain quantities of supplies each day. Have children help with these tasks, counting out, for example, the number of paint cans or of boxes of crayons that should be taken from the shelves and put on the table. Have children check each other's work to be sure that they have selected the proper amount.

They also understand that a whole is larger than any of its parts. A great many of these activities can be embedded in the routines of the classroom.

Cooking is a wonderful activity in which to practice informal mathematics, as well as integrate science to teach nutrition. Have the children help with any recipe to be cooked. They should be aware of the different measuring tools: cups, spoons, and the like. Children should learn to carefully fill cups and spoons, counting out the proper number they will need for the recipe. Besides food to be eaten, children can make playdough, fingerpaints, and other materials according to a recipe.

Formal Instruction

In addition to using the natural occurrences of the classroom, teachers should arrange experiences that are designed specifically to help children understand mathematics. The following are some of the topics that should be covered.

Grouping

In developing young children's concepts of quantity, teachers can begin by having children group things. They can group the pencils in a box, the red beads in a bead set, the pieces of a puzzle, containers of milk, or the children in a class. Such groups can be made up of dissimilar things, but it is less confusing for the children in the beginning to use objects with common elements.

Young children can also begin to compare the number of items in a group by matching the items with those in another group. In setting the table for snack time, children can compare the number of napkins with the number of straws laid out. In matching, they might discover that there are the same number of straws and napkins or, if the numbers are dissimilar, that they will need to even them out. The children need to learn the concepts of *more, fewer,* and *same* before they can determine *how many more* or *how many fewer* there are. Such a use of groups has practical application for the children, making the uses of mathematics obvious to them because they now have to modify their environment on the basis of increased mathematical knowledge (provide more napkins or more straws).

Children can also match objects from pictures and charts to learn one-to-one correspondence. However, they should have real objects to manipulate at first. With manipulative objects, they can line up two sets of objects, matching a member of one set with a member of the other, even before they can count.

Counting

Children often come into nursery school or kindergarten "knowing how to count." What too often passes for counting is the ability to recite the names of numbers in sequence without any understanding of the idea of the number that corresponds to a given name or numeral.

Using concrete materials helps children understand counting.

Young children need experiences that help them associate names or symbols with the numbers they represent. They see little connection between a physical representation of a number and the idea of a number. They can be helped to make these associations through the grouping experiences described above. At first, children can be given manipulative materials and asked to put together groups of two and three; later they can make groups of four or more. They can check whether they are correct most easily if they can match their sets with a model, either a picture of a group or another set of manipulative materials. Using the word for the number helps children associate what they hear or say with a particular quantity. As children begin to write—numerals as well as letters—they can begin to match the numerals they write with the correct number of objects in a set.

From this point, children begin to construct new groups by adding one more object to a group they have constructed. They can also construct different groups by taking one object away from a group they have constructed. These procedures allow the children to come to understand the mathematical operations of addition and subtraction. Children can also order groups in relation to the number of objects in each. Through a series of such experiences, children will learn that the numbers *one* to *ten* fit into a particular order from the smallest to the largest quantity. This understanding is the beginning of counting and understanding ordinal numbers. A

TASK CARD: Counting

Count the number of windows in the room.

How many can be opened?

How many must remain closed?

Are more windows open or closed?

variety of materials may be used to move children along, and a number line of numerals from 0 to 10 may help them in their final ordering.

The Number System

Once children begin to count beyond nine and to write these numerals, they must become aware of our numeration system. The children are already aware of the number named by each symbol or digit, zero through nine. (Children may have to learn the concept of *zero,* but it is important.) They must now learn that the numeration system has a base of ten and that the place of each digit in a numeral represents its value. Thus, children need to learn that the number value of a digit is determined not only by the value of the digit itself, but by the place of that digit in the whole number. Thus the digit 2 can stand for two, twenty, or two hundred.

Constance Kamii (1986) notes that first graders have no difficulty counting out the correct number of chips when they are shown the numeral 16, telling whether 16 is larger than 61, or remembering that 10 plus 10 equals 20. Yet they have difficulty with place value. She suggests that children have this difficulty because place value is not simply a matter of representing number. Children have to go through a process of constructing the number system, learning to count by tens in order to understand the decimal basis of the number system.

A variety of activities can be provided to children to help them learn the number system. Learning to substitute 10 unit elements (rods, beads, chips, or markers) for an element valued at 10 can help them develop this concept of equivalence. Then, working with columned paper or pocket charts, they can study the role of position in relation to value. The notation of two-place numerals can be presented at this time.

Three-place numerals and other ways of representing numbers would be taught next. One-place numerals are easily represented by

Using counting rods can teach children the equivalence of 10 ones to one 10.

squares and sets of squares lined up to 10 or by rods or sets of beads. Two-place numerals can be represented in like fashion, with one kind of rod representing the ones value and another kind of rod represent the 10s value. A set of 10 rods, each representing the 10s value, equals 100.

Larger numbers become rather cumbersome in concrete representation. The Montessori golden beads represent one thousand as a cube ten beads long, ten beads wide, and ten beads deep. Children soon become aware of the need for more efficient ways of representing numbers, especially large numbers, and so are ready to represent and read large numbers in the Arabic notation system.

Number Operations

Children can go from counting, comparing, and noting numbers to the basic operations on numbers: addition, subtraction, multiplication, and division. By counting up or down, children can develop the basics of addition and subtraction. For centuries people have used counting up and down as the basis for addition and subtraction, as evidenced in the use of the abacus. With this sophisticated yet simple device, a person can go through complicated mathematical procedures by counting beads. Similarly, beginning addition and subtraction problems can use the process of counting objects. Only later, when children have developed an understanding of the process, do they move to the use of shorter processes so that can be introduced to **algorithms.** After understanding is developed, practice activities can be offered to improve computational skills.

An **algorithm** is a specific calculation for solving a particular problem.

Children should be provided with many situations in which they can put together sets of objects to establish the facts of addition and to gain an intuitive understanding of the process. At this point, the process of addition can be formalized and the appropriate language of mathematics introduced. Too early an emphasis on the formal aspects of arithmetic may thwart the children's intuitive acquisition of concepts and operations. Continued practice with the operations will lead to their mastery.

Similar approaches can be used in teaching subtraction, beginning with the opportunities to actually take away members of a large group and see how many are left. The children can then count down on an abacus or similar device, moving objects over and then comparing larger sets with smaller ones. The proof of the correctness of response is immediately available.

VIGNETTE: MATH, PRIMARY GRADE

The students are sitting in a carpeted area near the chalkboard. The teacher announces that the lesson will be on subtraction. "What do we do when we subtract?" she asks.

"We take away," answers Louise.

The teacher writes a subtraction problem on the board: "6 – 3 = ___." She asks the children to solve the problem. After a few seconds, she asks

Brendan for the answer. After he gives the correct answer, she asks, "How did you think to solve that problem?"

Brendan explains, "I thought that 3 + 3 = 6."

"Good! Did everyone hear what Brendan said?" The teacher repeats Brendan's response. She then sends the children to their tables and distributes sets of linking cubes to each child. "Now," she explains, "I would like you to solve some problems using cubes." She turns on the overhead projector and writes "5 – 4 = ___."

As the children work independently, the teacher moves about the room, quietly helping those children who are having difficulty.

If children have already learned the concept of place value and understood the equivalence of one 10 to 10 ones, it becomes relatively simple to move from adding and subtracting one-place numbers to performing those operations on two-place numbers, since the readiness for this learning has already been developed.

Multiplication and division are usually introduced in the primary grades. These processes, too, can be approached by the use of manipulative materials and by recourse to prior mathematics learning. Children have probably already learned to count by twos, fives, and tens before multiplication is introduced. They have also learned to add. If they are asked to put together five groups of two blocks each, for example, they can visualize the process of multiplication. Concrete experiences such as these are helpful to begin with. Later the multiplication facts can be organized into tables.

Teaching division can begin with asking such questions as, "If I want to make groups of three out of this pile of twelve beans, how many groups will I have?" or "I want to give the same amount of pretzels to each of the five children here. I have ten pretzels. How many will each child receive?" Using real situations, involving the children in the manipulation of concrete objects, and having them act on their environment provide the basis for later mathematics learning.

Geometry

Almost from birth, children have been developing an understanding of spatial relationships. They are beginning to grasp the basic concepts of topological geometry in their intuitive constructions. Copeland (1984) suggests that this form of geometry might best be presented to children informally prior to Euclidian geometry, which is the familiar geometry of circles, squares, triangles, and angles. Among the basic topological concepts that can be taught are *proximity*, the distance of objects from each other; *separation*, the lack of nearness; *order*, the arrangement of objects in space; *enclosure* or surrounding; and *continuity*, the state of being continuous. Any number of experiences with blocks, beads, or other manipulative materials could be used to illustrate these concepts. Children separate blocks or beads as they move them away from each other. They often talk about objects or persons being far and near. The ongoing activities of the class provide opportunities for teaching these concepts if teachers are aware of them and make them explicit.

Copying the pattern of beads, blocks, or other manipulative materials, or placing objects in a pattern, can help children understand the concept of order. Dealing with the idea of *in* and *out* ("Put the crayons *in* the box; put the box *between* the other two on the shelf") can help children use the concept of surrounding or enclosing. Children should operate on materials, and teachers should ask them questions about objects' relationships to each other to help them formalize their understanding of these concepts.

Young children can also learn to identify and compare basic shapes: square, circle, and triangle. Rectangles and other shapes, more difficult to identify, can be introduced at whatever point children are able to compare the measurements of sides and angles. In identifying these shapes, the children learn to count sides and angles, or "corners." They can later compare sides, as well, so that they can differentiate between a square and a rectangle.

Later, as the children learn to measure, they will begin to compare perimeters and areas of different objects and shapes. Problems such as which shape of several has the greatest perimeter or how many of one type of object it takes to cover the top of a table (a problem in area) can be worked out by children who have been provided with the proper manipulative material and have learned how to set out to solve problems of this nature. Children can also learn to classify objects by shape and to find geometric shapes in familiar objects around them.

John A. Van de Walle (1988) suggests that teachers help kindergarten and elementary school children engage in problem solving through activities using materials of different sizes, shapes, and colors. Such activities will help children understand the geometric attributes of things. Commercial attribute blocks—sets of blocks of different shapes, sizes, and colors—or teacher-made attribute pieces made into squares, triangles, and rectangles of different sizes and colors could be used. Children can be asked to show which pieces are alike and which are different. They can learn to make or copy patterns in rows of attribute pieces. Geoboards

TASK CARD: Shapes

How many things can you find in the room that have circles in them? List them.

Draw a design using 10 squares.

How many different designs can you make?

TASK CARD: Area

Cover the top of your table with index cards.

How many index cards do you need?

could be used in similar ways. These boards are usually 12 inches square, with nails inserted at one-inch intervals. Children can make different geometric shapes by wrapping rubber bands around the nails. Children can be given pictures of shapes and asked to make their mirror images on the geoboard. Children can check their constructions by using an actual mirror. The concrete nature of geometry makes it a natural part of an early childhood program because children can handle things, ask questions, and test their ideas on elements of physical reality. Although proper vocabulary is important in teaching geometry to children, the language should be an outgrowth of experience. Otherwise, the content becomes abstract and, unfortunately, meaningless.

MEASUREMENT

One way to integrate mathematics learning and to make quantitative and spatial concepts meaningful is to use measurement. Measuring allows young children to use their developing mathematical knowledge in thinking about their immediate world. Young children can approach measurement simply and intuitively. Teaching children to measure begins with teaching them to compare things to each other. It then moves to comparing things to an informal standard. Finally, children learn formal measurement, comparing things and quantifying them in relation to established standards. Each kind of measurement has its unique set of problems.

Measuring Distance

Young children come up against problems of linear size early in life. For example, children may have to match the heights of two sides of a structure in the block area in order to fit a roof, or they may need to find a piece of wood that fits in a woodwork construction. Children may be given sets of wooden rods and ask to find the longer one or the shorter one, or two children may even to be asked to stand beside each other so a third child can judge who is taller. The words *tall, taller, short, shorter, long,* and *longer* can be taught in these contexts.

A somewhat higher order of linear comparison is reached in asking children to compare things that cannot be placed next to each other: the lengths of block structures on two sides of the block area or the heights of the sink and the woodwork bench. In this case, the children have to somehow record the measurements and compare the recording of one object

TASK CARD: Linear Measure

Measure the length of your desk.

Measure the length of the teacher's desk.

Which desk is longer? ________

Measure the heights of all the boys in the class.

List the boys in order of height, starting with the tallest.

with that of another. A length of wood might be marked to record the height of one block building and later moved to the other block building so children can make a visual comparison. After many such experiences, regular measuring devices can be introduced, such as rulers and yardsticks. As children learn to count, they can be taught the numbers on the ruler and the unit *inch*. Before they learn fractions, children can report a length as "between three and four inches long." After working with inches, children may be taught the concepts of *foot* and *yard*. Unfortunately, our measurement system is still not metric, and the relationships between various units of measure are irregular (for example, there are 12 inches in a foot, 3 feet in a yard, and 36 inches in a yard). Children may take some time to master these relationships.

Once children have learned to measure objects, there is no end to the amount of measuring they can do and, with these measurements, no end to the amount of practice in addition and subtraction that can result. Floors, walls, furniture, materials, and people are all objects to be measured. Children can compare the measurements and make spoken and written statements about them.

Measuring Weight

Weight is somewhat less directly perceivable than length. Placing an object in each hand and comparing weight is tricky, for the volume of the object distorts our perception. A pound of feathers, for example, does not *feel* as heavy as a pound of lead. External aids to judgment are necessary in teaching children about weight comparisons. A simple balance is a useful tool in helping young children make weight comparisons. A balance can be either purchased from an educational equipment company or made by using a length of wood, some string, and a couple of pie tins. If teachers make such a device they should be certain that the two pans do indeed balance when empty.

Again, the measurement of weight begins with comparing objects. When children place two objects in the balance pans, they make a visual judgment about which is heavier and which lighter by noting which pan

TASK CARD: Measuring Weight

Place a cup of rice in one pan of a balance and a cup of beans in the other.

Which is heavier?

Write about what you have learned.

Choose two things that look the same size and weigh them. Are they the same weight?

Now choose two things that seem to feel the same weight, but are different in size. Weigh them. Are they the same weight?

Which is easier to guess, equal weights or equal sizes?

Take your shoe and place it in the scale. Weigh it to the nearest ounce.

Record the weight. "My shoe weighs ____ ounces."

is lower. The next step is to make comparisons with arbitrary standards with which the weights of objects can be measured. These standards might be anything—large metal washers, fishing line sinkers, or rocks. Later, metal weights representing units of measure can be introduced—one-ounce weights, half-pound weights, and one-pound weights.

Young children find the relationships between units of weight complicated; they simply have to learn these relationships arbitrarily. It is helpful if the children first have the experience of direct comparison of weights before moving on to indirect comparison using units of measurement. A limitless number of objects in the environment of the school can be weighed. These weights can be added up, subtracted from one another, or compared. Statements about these activities are communicated orally and in writing. The language of measurement, including concepts such as *lighter than*, *heavier than*, and *the same weight as*, becomes important.

Measuring Volume

In learning to measure volume, children can be provided with containers of various sizes and shapes to fill, and they can transfer the contents from one container to another. Using containers of the same volume but different shapes will show children that volume is not simply a function of the height or width of a container. In time, containers of standard volumes should be introduced: one cup, half cup, pint, quart, and gallon. The sand table and water play area are excellent places to introduce measurement of volume.

Measuring the amount of liquid a container holds helps children understand volume.

TASK CARD: Measuring Volume

Use a one-cup measure, fill up a quart container.
How many cups does it take?

Metric Measurement

One of the complicating factors in teaching measurement is the movement in the United States toward use of the metric system. We are using more metric measurements while we continue to use the more familiar traditional units. States are presently mandating the teaching of the metric system in schools, while children continue to be confronted with pounds, feet, quarts, and Fahrenheit degrees of temperature in their everyday lives. They may not care that their milk was poured from a container that holds .95 liters, that the cottage cheese was scooped from a package weighing 227 grams, or that their parents must drive no faster than 104 kilometers per hour (one quart, one-half pound, and 65 miles per hour respectively). Although the interactions of the two systems during this interim period will require that people learn to convert from one system to the other, it is probably best to teach metric measurement directly, parallel to teaching measurement with traditional units.

When children engage in measuring activities using metric units, they need meter sticks rather than yard sticks, weights for the pan balance in grams rather than ounces, Celsius scale thermometers rather than Fahrenheit scale thermometers, and containers based on liters rather than on quarts and pints. Since units in the metric system are based on the decimal system, conversion from smaller to larger (as from millimeters to centimeters to meters) or vice versa is easier than in our present system with its irregular set of relationships. The fact that time units will not be going metric means that children will still have to learn complicated time units, but at least there will be no need for conversions here.

Measuring Time

Much attention in the early years is given to the measurement of time. Time is abstract, making it a difficult dimension for young children to measure. Actually we don't teach children to measure time. Rather we teach them to read the instruments that measure time. Early childhood teachers seem to do a lot of work with calendars and clocks.

There are two processes involved in learning to measure time that need to be addressed separately. One is reading clock faces and calendars; the other is measuring something that cannot be seen or felt. The passage of time is perceived subjectively. All of us have experienced periods of time that have dragged on interminably and others that have moved too quickly. Time is a difficult concept for children to grasp. Before entering school, they seldom have much awareness of time, except for the passage of day and night and the regularity of daily occurrences, including viewing television programs. They have experienced few expectations to be on time or to do things at a particular time. They have also experienced few cycles of seasonal change. With the beginning of school, children's lives suddenly become ordered in time, and time takes on increased psychological importance.

Many of the problems that children face in clock and calendar work stem from the fact that they are being asked to read fairly sophisticated material on the clock or the calendar without being taught the symbols and systems by which they are ordered. Other problems stem from the complicated relations of time segments to each other, as well as from the children's lack of knowledge of the benchmarks needed for the measurement of time. Often the only alternative left to the children is to memorize the material offered without ever really understanding it.

One of the ironies of modern technology is the availability of digital clocks and watches. Direct reading of hour and minutes may be easier with a digital clock, but the passage of time is more evident with an analog clock than with a digital clock. The movement of a hand over the face of a traditional clock or watch is a direct analogy to the movement of time. There is no such relationship in a digital watch face. Other-time measuring devices, like kitchen timers and sand-filled hourglasses (small three-minute egg timers using the hourglass principle) can also be brought into the class. While experiences with real clocks and timing devices are important, simulated clocks that allow children to set the time and see the relationship between the movements of the hour and minute hands are good devices for clarifying concepts and practicing clock reading.

OTHER TOPICS IN MATHEMATICS

A number of additional topics are usually touched on in a mathematics program for the early years. Although generally not treated as extensively as the ones described above, they are still important elements. Included are the study of fractions, the use of graphs and charts, and money.

Fractions

Once they understand whole numbers, young children can be helped to understand simple fractions as equal parts of a unit. Young children often have experience with fractions. They might have been given half a sandwich to eat or had a quarter of a dollar to spend. Based on these experiences and their intuitive sense, they can learn the meaning of one-half, one-fourth, and one-third. Their first understanding is of the number of parts of a unit, without concern for their equality. The teacher will find many opportunities to use fractions in the classroom: sharing snacks, giving out materials for craft work, and children's work in the block area or at the woodworking bench.

Understanding in this area, as in other areas, grows slowly in young children. A young child's concept of *half* comes from seeing objects divided into two parts. The fact that the parts must be equal to be considered halves is a part of the definition that comes later. Children's understanding, however, grows as a result of many encounters with their environment, beginning long before they are able to grasp complex, sophisticated meanings.

Nadine S. Bezuk (1988) suggests that a great deal of time be spent with fractions in the early childhood years. Children should learn to compare fractions, and learn the equivalents of different fractions (two quarters

Manipulative materials help children see fractions.

equals one half). If a good foundation is laid in the early years, children will have fewer problems in learning to do mathematical operations on fractions in later years. Bezuk recommends using the proper names for fractions, teaching the written symbols only after children fully understand the concept. She also recommends using manipulative materials that illustrate fractions and finding opportunities to see fractions in real situations: for instance, into how many equal pieces a pizza should be divided. Fraction problems can be introduced as word problems dealing with real-life situations. The topics to be covered about fractions should include (1) partitioning a unit into equal parts; (2) naming unit fractions, those that are part of a single whole such as three-fourths, and nonunit fractions, those that are larger than a single whole such as five-fourths; (3) comparing fractions; and (4) generating equivalent fractions.

Graphs and Charts

As children learn to communicate in writing, they may become aware that some things are communicated in ways other than through the use of words. Geography requires written communication of topographical information through maps. Quantitative information, similarly, might best be communicated using graphs and charts. A variety of graphic representations can be used in the early years. Use of graphs and charts might start simply with ways of comparing children in the class in just two columns, such as the number of boys versus girls, those who go home for lunch versus those who stay at school, or those who live in houses versus those who live in apartments. Beginning graphs can be three-dimensional representations. A line of building blocks or wooden cubes representing each group, with each block or cube standing for one person, can be used at first; later, two-dimensional representations can be added.

The children can then move on to more complicated graphs: of children's birthdays (by months), heights, weights, hair colors, or interests. Line graphs can be made of the morning temperature in the room or outdoors over a period of time, of the number of children absent each day, or of the number of cars passing the school in a five-minute interval. Creating such graphs requires collecting the information from which the

TASK CARD: Graphs

Make a graph using a unit block for each person.

Show the number of persons in the class who have a birthday during each month of the year.

Write a story about making your graph.

graphs will develop, often as a part of a more extensive study. Using graphs in this fashion demonstrates that they are a practical way of recording and communicating information.

Money

Another topic often included in the primary mathematics program is the study of money and money equivalence. Our monetary system is based on the unit of 10, as is our system of numeration. Once children have learned the relative value of coins and paper money, they need little new knowledge to develop skills of monetary computation. As a matter of fact, the use of real or play money is a helpful resource in teaching the numeration system itself to the very young. In early childhood education, the main concern is teaching children to recognize coins of different values and to exchange coins properly. Manipulations with real coins are necessary to some extent, although play money can be used. Opportunities for using coins in play, as in a mock supermarket, or in real situations, such as shopping trips, and experiences in purchasing, making, and selling objects are helpful.

VIGNETTE: MATH, KINDERGARTEN

The children are sitting in a circle around the teacher, who says, "We're going to continue talking about money. What did we say our fingers represented yesterday?"

Tommy raises five fingers and says, "Pennies."

The teacher affirms his answer, then raises her ten fingers and says, "Each one of my fingers is one penny. How many pennies do I have? Let's count." As she points to each finger, the students count, "One, two, three, four, five, six, seven, eight, nine, ten."

The teacher says, "I am going to ask you to use your fingers to show me how many pennies you have. Before you put up your fingers, I want you to figure it out in your lap. When I say, 'Show me,' then put your fingers up. Show me nine pennies, but first do it in your lap." After a few seconds, she says, "Now show me. . . . Good."

"This time show me five cents," the teacher says. "Figure it in your lap first. . . . Now show me. . . . Good."

"Now we are going to do magic with our fingers," says the teacher. "I will say the word *abracadabra* and change my five cents into a nickel." As the teacher says this, she makes her open hand into a fist. "This is a nickel. And how many pennies are in a nickel?" One by one, she unfolds her five fingers, while counting. "There are five pennies in a nickel."

"Now I would like you to show me ten cents. Think first, then figure it out in your lap. . . . Now show me," says the teacher. When the children show their ten cents, they have different ways of showing it. Brian shows two fists. Erin shows one fist and five fingers. Jessica shows ten fingers. The teacher asks each child to explain why each answer is correct.

INTEGRATING MATHEMATICS WITH OTHER CURRICULUM AREAS

Preschools and kindergartens are replete with opportunities for infusing mathematics learning into the day's activities. Children can tally attendance, making marks for each boy and girl and later grouping and adding them. Other routine activities hold similar promise. Setting up for snack time provides opportunities to see one-to-one relationships and to count. Work in the block area requires a mathematical sense, as do woodworking and crafts activities. Music, dance, and games all allow counting and matching. Dramatic play activities can offer other experiences: playing store or driving a bus includes using money, counting, and measuring.

As children move into the primary grades, less fanciful activities are available in the classroom. Most classrooms are full of things that can be compared, counted, added, weighed, and measured. Teachers should give children both the chance to involve themselves in these operations and direction in doing them. Task cards, or assignment cards, can help.

Task cards spell out simple problems or activities in which children can engage. These cards allow individualized instruction and provide many learning activities without constant teacher supervision. Specific tasks are written on each card in simple language. Pictures may be used instead, to allow children who cannot read to follow directions. Sometimes a rebus, a combination of words and pictures, serves the purpose. A small file box can contain a large number of assignment cards, numbered in order of difficulty and coded by topic, to be placed in various activity centers in the room. Activities related to measuring weight, linear measure, clock work, counting, writing equations, measuring volume, and geometry can all be taught through task cards. Examples of task cards have been presented throughout this chapter. Teachers can set up a chart for each area of assignment cards on which children can check off those they are using in order to simplify record keeping. Teachers should also devise ways to check the accuracy of completed assignments.

Some task cards may list closed-ended tasks, which have only one correct solution. Other tasks may be open-ended, with more than one solution that can be considered correct, allowing opportunities for creativity and discovery in mathematics. The key to developing good assignments is to analyze the environment in which the children live and work and the activities in which they and others around them engage. Teachers should look for areas in which children can practice and extend the mathematical skills and concepts they have gained in the more formal parts of the school program. Such assignments can also allow opportunities to relate mathematics tasks to other subjects. Thus, a child could use a graph for quantitative representation and then represent the idea in another way, writing a story or drawing a picture.

Integrating mathematics into various activities allows the children to grasp mathematical relationships in the world around them. They will gain new mathematical insights and be able to apply and practice the knowledge they have already acquired. Almost all areas of the early childhood program provide opportunities for children to group things and to count limited numbers of objects. In the block-building area, children can make comparisons and show one-to-one correspondence by matching two walls of a block construction. The woodwork area can provide experiences in comparing lengths of wood or counting nails, while art and crafts activities also allow for comparing the volume of clay being used or grouping the paper for collage by shape and other attributes. Sand tables and water play areas can be provided with a variety of containers so that children experience and compare different measures. Even the library area presents opportunities to teach mathematics, through counting either books or other types of literature.

One way of infusing mathematics into the program is through the creation of an integrated curriculum. Even without a fully integrated curriculum, ways can be found to integrate ideas from various curriculum areas. A number of educators have suggested ways to teach mathematics through children's literature. Marcus Ballenger and his colleagues (1984) suggest using counting books for teaching about numbers in preschools and kindergartens. They warn, however, that teachers need to assess the books to be sure that they use cardinal numbers correctly and numerals to express ordinal position properly. Illustrations should accurately depict the text and should be unambiguous. Also, the books that are used and the concepts presented in the books should be matched to the children's levels of understanding. Ann Harsh (1987) illustrates how these criteria could be used to assess other children's books, in addition to counting books, in terms of how they present mathematical concepts to children. Rosamund W. Tischler (1988) describes how picture storybooks can be a jumping-off point for mathematics activities. Games using manipulative materials, she suggests, can be developed from picture storybooks. She presents examples of the use of *Caps for Sale* (Slobodkina, 1984), *Corduroy* (Freeman, 1968) and *Frog and Toad Are Friends* (Lobel, 1970). Using such games, children can practice classifying, forming hypotheses, choosing mathematical strategies, and creating mathematical problems.

Blocks are another important area where mathematics can be taught. Besides being a manipulative material children can count and group (Singer, 1988), blocks are also a way to represent space. Thus, children explore concepts from topological geometry in block play (Reifel, 1984). In addition, both two-dimensional and three-dimensional space is represented in blockbuilding.

Although many opportunities exist for learning mathematics in the classroom, teachers cannot depend on natural occurrences as the only source of mathematics learning. They must provide activities specifically designed to promote mathematics learning. Such activities often depend on the use of special mathematics-oriented materials.

In the primary grades, one usually finds a dependence on mathematics textbooks and workbooks. If used flexibly, these books provide an excellent source of learning activities. Textbooks may offer teachers as well as children a guide to learning. The selection of a single textbook series can assure a degree of continuity of learning from grade to grade and provide a number of instructional and practice activities.

Mathematics instruction must go beyond the textbook, however. Manipulative materials help the children understand concepts and processes through practical, concrete application of the ideas they learn. A large number of these materials are commercially available. Many teacher-made materials should be included. Although the quantity and type of materials provided depends on the needs of the class, it is helpful to have a mathematics center in the classroom where mathematical material can be kept and used. The materials should be easily accessible and well organized so that cleanup is not cumbersome.

No matter how much material and supplies are provided, teachers remain the key to the success of the program. Teachers need to be knowledgeable in mathematics and methods of teaching mathematics, but they must also be sensitive to the children's needs. Within the framework of their knowledge, teachers are constantly planning activities, assessing progress, diagnosing difficulties, and providing additional sources of learning for some children while looking for enrichment activities for others. Teachers are the ones who make mathematics a vital and meaningful area of inquiry for young children.

SUMMARY

There is increasing concern that mathematics be taught in the early years. Young children develop an intuitive sense of number and mathematical operations through the many experiences they have in the world. Teachers should maintain an informal but systematic approach to mathematics instruction at first. They should make sure that children do not simply learn mathematical terms by rote, but that the children understand concepts and processes. The use of a hands-on approach to teaching mathematics, in which children manipulate concrete materials and think about what they do, is vital. While various topics need to be addressed in the mathematics program, teachers should look for opportunities throughout the curriculum to have children illustrate and practice their mathematics learning.

REFERENCES

Ballenger, M., Benham, N., & Hosticka, A. (1984). Children's counting books: Mathematical concept development. *Childhood Education, 61*(1), 30–35.

Baratta-Lorton, M. (1976). *Mathematics their way.* Menlo Park, CA: Addison-Wesley.

Baroody, A. J. (1987). *Children's mathematical thinking: A developmental framework for preschool, primary, and special education teachers.* New York: Teachers College Press.

Baroody, A. J. (1993). Fostering the mathematical learning of young children. In B. Spodek (Ed.), *Handbook of research on the education of young children* (pp. 151–175). New York: Macmillan.

Bezuk, N. S. (1988). Fractions in the early childhood mathematics curriculum. *Arithmetic Teacher, 35*(6), 56–60.

Carpenter, T. P. (1986). Conceptual knowledge as a foundation for procedural knowledge: Implications from research on the initial learning of arithmetic. In J. Heibert (Ed.), *Conceptual and procedural knowledge: The case of mathematics* (pp. 113–132). Hillsdale, NJ: Erlbaum.

Copeland, R. W. (1976). *Mathematics and the elementary teacher* (3rd ed.). Philadelphia: Saunders.

Copeland, R. W. (1985). *How children learn mathematics* (4th ed.) New York: Macmillan.

Cruikshank, D. E., Fitzgerald, D. L., & Jensen, L. R. (1980). *Young children learning mathematics.* Boston: Allyn and Bacon.

Freeman, D. (1968). *Corduroy.* New York: Viking Press.

Ginsberg, H. P. (1980). Children's surprising knowledge of arithmetic. *Arithmetic Teacher, 28*(1), 42–44.

Harsh, A. (1987). Teach mathematics with children's literature. *Young Children, 42*(6), 24–29.

Kamii, C. (1973). A sketch of a Piaget-derived preschool curriculum developed by the Ypsilanti Early Education Program. In B. Spodek (Ed.), *Early childhood education* (pp. 209–229). Englewood Cliffs, NJ: Prentice Hall.

Kamii, C. (1982). *Numbers in preschool and kindergarten.* Washington, DC: National Association for the Education of Young Children.

Kamii, C. (1986). Place value: An explanation of its difficulty and educational implications for the primary grades. *Journal of Research in Childhood Education, 1*(2), 75–86.

Lobel, A. (1970). *Frog and toad are friends.* New York: Harper & Row.

Mueller, D. W. (1985). Building a scope and sequence for early childhood mathematics. *Arithmetic Teacher, 33*(2), 8–11.

National Council of Teachers of Mathematics (1989). *Curriculum and evaluation standards for school mathematics.* Reston, VA: Author.

Price, G. G. (1989). Research in review: Mathematics in early childhood. *Young Children, 44*(4), 53–58.

Rea, R. E., & Reys, R. E. (1971). Competencies of entering kindergartners in geometry, number, money and measurements. *School Science and Mathematics, 71,* 389–402.

Reifel, S. (1984). Block construction: Children's developmental landmarks in representations of space. *Young Children, 40*(1), 61–67.

Singer, R. (1988). Estimation and counting in the block corner. *Arithmetic Teacher, 35*(5), 10–14.

Slobodkina, E. (1984). *Caps for sale.* New York: Scholastic.

Steen, L. A. (1990). *On the shoulders of giants: New approaches to numeracy.* Washington, DC: National Academy Press.

Stone, J. I. (1987). Early childhood math: Make it manipulative. *Young Children, 42*(6), 16–23.

Tischler, R. W. (1988). Mathematics from children's literature. *Arithmetic Teacher, 35*(6), 42–47.

Van de Walle, J. A. (1988). Strategy spotlight: Hands-on thinking activities for young children. *Arithmetic Teacher, 35*(6), 62–63.

15

Social Studies for Young Children

CHAPTER OVERVIEW

This chapter presents:

- Elements of a social studies program
- Approaches to early childhood social studies
- Ways to use resources in early childhood social studies
- Ways to integrate social studies with other curriculum areas
- Multicultural education

INTRODUCTION

Schools help young children understand themselves, the world around them, and their relationship to it. Children learn about themselves through feedback from the outside world as they test their powers on the physical and social world. They become aware of the context in which they live and strive to understand it, becoming more a part of that context as they define the boundaries between themselves and the surrounding world.

Young children develop knowledge and skills that are useful both for everyday life and as a prerequisite for future learning. Their approach to the physical world is direct; they test what they know about physical things by touching, listening, or viewing. Although children have direct contact with people and can observe their behavior directly, it is the *meaning* of behavior that is important rather than the observable behavior alone—and the meaning is not directly accessible. The products of social behavior and the contexts in which behavior takes place, however, are more accessible.

ELEMENTS OF A SOCIAL STUDIES PROGRAM

The National Council for the Social Studies (1983) has defined the social studies as an area of the curriculum that derives its goals from the nature of citizenship in a democratic society and from links to other societies, draws content from the social sciences and other disciplines, and reflects personal, social, and cultural experiences of students.

Sunal (1990) has identified the following characteristics in the social studies:

- They involve a search for patterns in our lives.
- They are a daily part of human activity.
- They involve both content and the process of learning.
- They are based on information.
- They require information processing.
- They require decision making and problem solving.
- They are concerned with the development and analysis of one's own values.

Thus, in the social studies we have a combination of content from academic disciplines, from social processes, and from individual responses to the human beings around us. We learn about our backgrounds through history, about the social groups to which we belong through anthropology and sociology, about the values we consider essential through philosophy and religion, about where we live and how we relate to our environment through geography, about how others influence and are influenced by us through political science, and about how we satisfy our basic needs and wants through economics.

In studying various social studies topics with young children, teachers must help children develop the intellectual processes that enable them to understand the world. Teachers should help children develop an understanding of social roles and institutions and find their places in society. Children must understand and develop a set of values that are consistent with those of the community. Teachers can also help children develop and understand their inner world as well as the world surrounding them.

Intellectual Processes

Physical knowledge is knowledge of the physical attributes of objects.

Social knowledge includes knowledge of social conventions, symbols, values, rituals, and myths.

Logico-mathematical knowledge consists of processes used in operating on information.

Using the Piagetian construct of knowledge as articulated by Kamii (1973) and presented in Chapter 4—including physical knowledge, social knowledge, logico-mathematical knowledge, and representation—one can identify the intellectual elements in a social studies program. **Physical knowledge** includes knowledge of physical elements in the world. This knowledge can probably best be gained by direct experience through field trips, observations, and interviews. Symbolic representations, including books, audiovisual materials, and simulations are also useful. **Social knowledge** includes the knowledge of social conventions, symbols, values, rituals, and myths. Social knowledge also includes knowledge of what is considered right or proper and what is taboo. Conventions of right and wrong can be told to children, directly or indirectly, but the reasons for determining what is right or proper must also be explained. **Logico-mathematical** knowledge requires that children use their thought processes to process information. Categorizing and ordering objects and events, observing and stating relationships, and putting things into the proper time/space context are included in logico-mathematical knowledge. Representing ideas and feelings is achieved through pictures, maps, charts, play activities, and stories (Spodek, 1974).

Socialization

Socialization—learning rules and values and finding one's role in society—is one of the prime goals of early childhood education. The social studies contribute to the socialization process, as do many other learning opportunities in the school day. In the classroom, teachers create conditions that help children learn the pupil role and that teach the rules, expectations, mores, and values of the school. Developing an awareness of the way the class is organized, the ways rules are made and enforced, the amount of freedom provided, the kinds of activities rewarded, and the rituals of daily life all contribute to this socialization. But there is more to socialization. At times group efforts are nurtured in the classroom; at other times, children are expected to work alone. They soon learn the need for sharing. They learn that physical conflict is frowned on and that there are other ways of resolving disputes. Children also learn that there are appropriate ways of interacting with and addressing teachers. The lessons of the socialization process are sprinkled throughout the entire program.

The social studies program can play an important part in helping children find their roles in the larger community. Children need to understand how society is organized. They need to learn the shared values, rituals, symbols, and myths of their society. The school's attention to holidays, to stories of historic figures and heroes, and to the reading of traditional stories and the singing of traditional songs all contribute to the process. Activities that allow children to inquire into social phenomena can help them better understand the organization of society and thus be better able to act out their roles in appropriate ways.

Values

All education is concerned with values. The basic social values that children should learn include concern for the worth of the individual, concepts of freedom and responsibility, the importance of democratic decision making, and concern for the safety of persons and property. These values cannot be taught as a separate subject, for they are communicated as much by the way teachers organize their classrooms and deal with individual children as through separate lessons. If children from minority groups are not respected and valued for the contribution they make in the classroom, then patriotic exercises have little meaning. If rules of behavior are arbitrarily set by the teacher, children learn not to value rational decision making as a basis for developing behavior controls. Children learn what to value from inferences they make about the behavior of significant adults in their lives, imitating adult behavior and assimilating the values

STAGES OF MORAL DEVELOPMENT

- **Stage 1: The punishment and obedience orientation.** The physical consequences of action determine its goodness or badness. Avoidance of punishment and unquestioning deference to power are valued in their own right.
- **Stage 2: The instrumental-relativist orientation.** Right action consists of that which instrumentally satisfies one's own needs and occasionally the needs of others.
- **Stage 3: The interpersonal concordance or "good boy-nice girl" orientation.** Good behavior is that which pleases or helps others and is approved by them. Behavior is frequently judged by intention—"he means well" becomes important for the first time. One earns approval by being "nice."
- **Stage 4: Authority and social order-maintaining orientation.** There is orientation toward authority, fixed rules, and the maintenance of the social order. Right behavior consists of doing one's duty, showing respect for authority, and maintaining the given social order for its own sake.
- **Stage 5: The social-contract legalistic orientation.** Right action tends to be defined in terms of general individual rights and standards (laws), which have been critically examined and agreed upon by society.
- **Stage 6: The universal ethical principle orientation.** Right is defined by a decision of conscience in accord with self-chosen ethical principles. These principles are abstract and ethical; they are not concrete moral rules like the Ten Commandments.

Source: E. Turiel, "Stage Transitions in Moral Development," in R. M. W. Travers (Ed.), *Second Handbook of Research on Teaching* (Chicago: Rand McNally, 1973), pp. 732–758.

they perceive. Children learn values constantly, not just in segmented subject-oriented periods. Teachers transmit their values to children all day long. The social system in the classroom and the school operates as an educative force that may be more powerful than any curriculum in developing values.

While many of these values are "caught" rather than "taught," teachers need to create situations in which they can be transmitted. Bernice Wolfson (1967) suggests that young children can learn values through role-playing, creative dramatics, literature, and art experiences. She concludes that value development is promoted by providing a wide variety of opportunities for individual selection of goals and activities and by allowing children to consider alternatives and possible consequences of acts and of their own feelings.

In addition to teaching values, schools have often been concerned with moral education—helping children distinguish right from wrong. While most Americans share a common moral code, the sources of morality are varied in our country. Families and religious institutions are also concerned with the moral education of children. Nor are educators at all sure how effective schools can be in teaching morals. However, in teaching specific morals, teachers can help children think about the moral judgments they make.

We must also be concerned with children's readiness to learn. Lawrence Kohlberg has identified three levels, with two stages at each level, of moral development in children (Kohlberg & Turiel, 1971). Kohlberg's framework provides a way of identifying how children judge moral dilemmas, considering their level of development. Most children in their early years operate at level two or three, that is, not beyond the early stage of the conventional level. These children can be helped to see what is proper behavior, but they will not understand why it is proper in terms of higher-order ethical principles. Discussions about the reasons for moral judgments might help teachers identify children's present level of development. Questioning children about the reasons for their actions might help move them up to the next level.

Self-Awareness

All programs, but especially those at the early childhood level, should concern themselves with affective development. Children can be helped to explore their self-concepts, deal with feelings about themselves and others, and develop appropriate means of expressing themselves and interacting with others. Such goals can be achieved through discussions, role-playing, storytelling, and other techniques by which children are stimulated to express their feelings or concerns with the teacher, alone, or in a group.

Children should learn ways of dealing with their emotions and develop a heightened awareness of themselves, but teachers should be cautioned not to go beyond their own capabilities in exposing feelings with which they themselves might have difficulty in coping. The key to success in these programs is to focus on educational outcomes rather than on cathartic effects. The educational outcomes with which teachers should be concerned are the children's awareness of the roles and relationships in their social setting and of the values of the culture, as well as an ability to think about moral issues in ways that are consistent with their levels of development.

APPROACHES TO TEACHING SOCIAL STUDIES

Over the years, many approaches to teaching social studies to young children have been used in schools. Some approaches have taken the ways in which basic human needs are met and organized the program around these needs. Young children learned how these needs were met in their home and community, while older children learned about how these needs were met in the wider society and in communities more remote in time and space. This "expanding communities" approach can still be seen in schools, where the kindergarten theme is the school and family, while the primary grades deal with the neighborhood and the municipality. In this approach, teachers deal with how people satisfy the need for food by taking a kindergarten class on a visit to a supermarket. Children can observe how people select and pay for food. Later, back at school, they can use dramatic play to act out what they have seen and make sense of it. As the children grow older, they can learn how food gets to the supermarket, where it comes from, and how it is raised. They also begin to learn history, seeing how people got their food in generations past or in the pioneer or colonial periods. Unfortunately, if a textbook approach was used in these programs, social processes remained remote, even for young children.

As educators become more aware of the nature of young children's learning processes, programs make greater use of children's experiences as the basis for knowledge. Some of these programs go back to the days of the progressive education era. Lucy Sprague Mitchell describes some of these in her book, *Young Geographers* (1971). Others are described in *Educationally Appropriate Kindergarten Practices* (Spodek, 1991). No matter what the topic, there is a need for immediate, firsthand experiences as the basis of what children will learn.

DECIDING WHAT AND HOW TO TEACH

When teachers make decisions about what to teach children, they need to assess what children are capable of learning, what they already know, and what society considers to be important for them to learn. Because the social studies are seen as composed of abstract knowledge, some people think that this area of the curriculum should be postponed to elementary school. Kindergarten and prekindergarten children have a limited ability to understand time. Since history is related to time, these critics suggest postponing history. Similarly, young children have difficulty with concepts of space: they are limited in their understanding of distance and direction and have problems representing things symbolically. Thus, it is suggested that geographic learnings be postponed as well. Despite the limits of young children's ability to understand the remote in time and space, however, such children can learn a great deal about social studies.

Identifying Goals of Instruction

The process of deciding what and how to teach in an early childhood social studies program involves setting goals, identifying topics, and developing instructional units or programs based on these goals and related to these topics. Teachers must gather materials and resources and plan and implement activities. They must also identify ways of judging the program's effects. Kindergarten and primary school teachers can adopt a total program from either a textbook publisher or a curriculum project. However, no one program serves all the purposes of social studies.

In many social studies curricula, the relationship of social studies to the social sciences has been emphasized. The goals of instruction are concerned with understanding basic concepts, generalizations, or conceptual schemes. Such a scheme might be identified for the social studies as an integrated field. Paul Brandwein (1970) has identified the following "cognitive scheme" in the social sciences:

1. Man is a product of heredity and environment.
2. Human behavior is shaped by the social environment.
3. The geographic features of the earth affect man's behavior.
4. Economic behavior depends upon the utilization of resources.
5. Political organizations (governments) resolve conflict and make interaction easier among people. (pp. T–16–17)

Other conceptual schemes have been developed that underlie a number of curriculum guides or programs in the social studies. Such schemes provide unity to a set of diverse activities. They also help teachers fit unplanned learning opportunities into the program. Children do not learn the scheme itself; it is a tool for teachers to use.

However, social studies goals cannot be conceived in terms of concept attainment alone. Hilda Taba (1967) identifies four categories of objectives: (1) basic knowledge; (2) thinking; (3) attitudes, feelings, and sensitivities; and (4) skills. Basic knowledge includes basic concepts, main ideas, and specific facts. Thinking includes concept formation, the inductive development of generalizations, and application of principles and knowledge. Attitudes, feelings, and sensitivities include the ability to identify with people in different cultures, self-security, open-mindedness, acceptance of change, tolerance of uncertainty and ambiguity, and responsiveness to democratic and human values. Skills include both academic skills, such as map reading, and research and social skills, such as the ability to work, plan, discuss, and develop ideas in groups.

Identifying Topics for Study

The number of topics for early childhood social studies programs has traditionally been limited. No topical themes are identified in the literature for prekindergarten social studies. At the kindergarten and primary levels, themes have usually revolved about the immediate environment of the children: home and family, the school (including the classroom), the neighborhood (stores, supermarkets, filling stations, and so on), and the community (community services, agencies, and workers), as well as transportation and communication. Sometimes comparative studies of communities are suggested, such as the urban community versus the rural or suburban community.

Recent curriculum guides, textbooks, and curriculum projects have widened topics for study by young children. These include family life in far-off countries such as Israel or Japan, broader comparative community study, and the study of concepts from the social sciences, such as *consumers* and *producers* and how they are related—derived from economics—or an understanding of *actions* and *interactions* among people—derived from sociology.

Teaching About History

Young children may have difficulty in dealing with history because they have difficulty dealing with concepts related to time. Sunal (1993) reviewed the literature on the relationship of young children's understanding of time to history. The research suggests that the language of time teachers use should be related to the developmental level of their children. Young children may use abstract terms for time without understanding them, a usage that may cause teachers to believe the children understand more than they

Activity

TEACHING ABOUT PERSONAL HISTORY USING A TIME LINE

Cut a piece of rope for each child, allowing one foot for every year of the child's age. Mark the rope by one-foot (one-year) segments, marking one end *birth* and the other end with the child's age. Send home notes asking the children's parents to send pictures or souvenirs (for example, photographs, first shoes, baby toys, and the like) depicting their child at different ages, with the ages noted on the souvenirs. Have the children attach the articles at the proper intervals on their rope. Have the children talk about what they were like or what they did at various ages. Discuss how each child has changed.

Activity

MAKING A LOCAL HISTORY MUSEUM

Have the children ask their parents if they have mementos of their earlier years or of their grandparents. These mementos could be articles of clothing, early radios or home appliances, or pictures of people and places. Using a bulletin board and tables, organize these objects by eras or by people. Have the children or their parents tell stories about these objects to be written up and displayed with the objects themselves.

Visit the local public library. See if it has collections of photographs or objects related to the community from different eras that you can borrow or copy. Display these objects, if possible, along with similar, more modern objects or photographs of contemporary scenes. See if a local historian can come to the class. Ask the librarians; they often know of such persons in the community. Have the children discuss the community as it is now and as it was long ago. Invite parents and other groups of children to your display.

in fact do. Children can distinguish between past and present by age four and come to understand the cyclical and sequential nature of events by age five or six. As a matter of fact, time concepts might best be taught in relation to history, rather than being a prerequisite to learning history. Thus, introducing young children to historical events and ideas may very well help children develop an understanding of important time concepts. Thus, as Vygotsky (see Chapter 3) noted, education can have a significant impact on young children's ability to move to new stages in intellectual development.

Teaching About Geography

Research on young children's understanding of space (Sunal, 1993) suggests that they can develop concepts of topological space, such as proximity, enclosure, continuity, separation, and order. They also begin to understand the relationship of things to each other in space. This knowledge may be the beginning of geographic understanding as children come to understand their surroundings concretely. They can learn about their surroundings and begin to interpret simple maps.

Lucy Sprague Mitchell (1971), many years ago, developed a program of teaching geography for children from the preschool through the elementary grades. Each element of geographic learning was presented. Mitchell viewed the world as a laboratory to help children develop geographic understanding. The children would go on field trips and then return to school to represent what they saw. She also used models of geographic area; lakes, islands, and peninsulas made of clay and placed in a pan or frame so that children could feel as well as see them. One of the most important tools she used in teaching about geography was the use of maps. Children learned to read as well as make maps. Maps were simple for the youngest children and more complicated for older children.

There are four key concepts related to maps and map-reading skills: (1) representation, (2) symbolization, (3) perspective, and (4) scale (Hatcher, 1983). Children learn many ways to represent things, including pictures and words. Maps are a form of representation, a special kind of picture of a place. Children can begin to represent places in three dimensions. A block structure, for example, can stand for a building, and a more elaborate arrangement of blocks can stand for a street, a grouping of buildings, or a neighborhood. Symbolization is also important in map making. Road maps, for example, use different kinds of lines to represent different kinds of roads. They also use symbols to represent cities, airports, rest areas, and the like. Water and land are symbolized in particular ways as well. What each symbol stands for is noted on a legend in one corner of the map. Children can be helped to note these symbols on their own representations, creating a set of symbols that they learn to use consistently on drawings of places or in block structures.

Helping young children understand the perspective of a map can be difficult at first. A map is like a picture seen from a bird's-eye view.

However, distant places do not seem smaller on a map, as they do in a picture. Kindergarten teachers can begin helping children learn about map making and map reading by having them do floor plans of their room. A floor plan is much like a map, but it depicts a much smaller area. Children can draw the objects in the room as if they were seeing the room from the ceiling. The children may start out by drawing the tables with the four legs jutting out from a rectangle in different directions; because they see the legs on the tables in their room, they expect that the legs should be represented in their floor plans. With some experience, the children will begin to understand the notion of perspective, and will begin to draw floor plans as they would look from the ceiling. Later, maps can be made of the school property, the neighborhood, and the like. The understanding of scale comes later for children. They will come to know that there is a constant relationship between the size of objects and their distance from each other on a map and the size of objects and their distance from each other in reality.

Teaching About Political Processes

Sunal (1993) notes that young children have been shown to be intuitive political thinkers. Many young children today are quite aware of the electoral process. They know something about candidates in local and national elections. They also know something of the voting process. Teachers can help children become politically socialized by taking advantages of such situations as elections in the community. When elections arise, teachers can talk about the offices and candidates, being careful to be nonpartisan in their discussions. Children can be involved in elections, as well. They can vote in mock elections for local and national offices.

Activity

HOLDING A CLASS ELECTION

Have the children vote on some element in the curriculum (for example, their favorite story of the ones read that week, their favorite song of those sung that week, or their favorite activity center). Talk with the children about the process: that each person makes only one choice and that each person's choice is noted as a vote, that each vote is tallied, and that the story or song with the largest number of votes is the winner. Primary-grade children can mark secret ballots that they insert into a ballot box. These ballots are then counted by a committee of children, and the results are announced in the class. Younger children might be asked to place blocks one atop the other in the pile labeled for their particular candidate. Young children will thus be able to see the results of their vote. Discuss the fact that while not everyone voted for the winner, the final result reflects the views of most of the children in class.

During local, state, or national elections, the children could hold mock elections in their class using similar techniques.

They can also elect class officers. Children can be helped to understand voting by participating in a variety of situations in which they vote and the votes of all the class are tallied.

Teaching About Economics

Research suggests that children as young as five can learn economic concepts and make decisions using them. As a matter of fact, when young children enter school they have already developed some knowledge of the social and personal world that is related to economics. Karen F. A. Fox (1978) suggests that children bring to school a "knapsack" of economic knowledge consisting of economic attitudes, unprocessed direct experiences, and cognitive capacities. These capacities place limits on young children's abilities to understand the abstract. Learning words and labels is not the same as developing understandings. Misconceptions may exist that should be clarified, but teachers can develop flexible programs that use children's unprocessed economic experiences.

Children come in contact with economic processes every day. They go with parents to stores to purchase commodities. They observe transactions and come to realize that each item has a price. They might have asked their parents for a toy only to be told that it costs too much. Their parents may be occupied as producers of goods or services, or they may be unemployed. Young children can understand these processes to some extent. But this understanding requires that the processes be pointed out to them and explored.

Some traditional activities related to community workers can be used to teach economic principles. Teachers can arrange for workers to visit the class. Visitors can be asked to talk about what they produce—goods or services—and how what they produce gets consumed. They can also show and possibly demonstrate the tools of their work and some of the materials they use. Teachers can provide books about the visitors' occupations in the library corner. Children might also be given the opportunity to act out the various occupations in the dramatic play area. Tools, materials, and clothing associated with the occupation could be collected in a prop box to be used at an appropriate time.

Sunal, Warash, and Strong (1988) describe an economics program that was developed in two preschools, one a university laboratory school and the other a rural program. Program activities revolved around four questions: (1) What goods and services shall be produced, (2) how shall they be produced, (3) how much shall be produced, and (4) who shall receive the goods and services? In the first part of the program, the children categorized pictures of goods by where they could be purchased. They identified their wants. They identified things that they or members of their families used, and they made the distinction between goods and services. The children then matched items and the jobs associated with them. They also investigated different occupations.

Activity

A VISIT TO A SUPERMARKET

Arrange to take the children on a field trip to the supermarket. Talk about the trip beforehand and discuss the important things children should look for and ask about: Where does the food come from? Why are certain foods sold in the store? How is the price of an item determined? What do the various people who work in the supermarket do? You might want to bring a camera and a tape recorder along to take pictures of the supermarket and to tape conversations to refer to later.

Once back at school, the children can talk about what they learned at the supermarket. They might wish to make a group mural or individual pictures of what they saw. Set up a play supermarket in the dramatic play area. Collect various food packages for display on shelves or tables. Children could be asked to price various items. Provide a counter with a toy cash register and play money for the children to use. Children can choose or be assigned various roles: checker, stock person, or customer. These roles can change over time as children continue to play their roles. After the play period, have the children tell what they did and why.

Teaching About Social Institutions, Roles, and Processes

Kathy R. Thornberg (1983) found that young children have some understanding of what comprises their family and their own role in that family. This knowledge varied with the age of the child but not with the child's sex or family size. This knowledge comes from children's own experiences in their own families. Thornberg suggests that the limits of young children's knowledge at the nursery, kindergarten, and first-grade level calls for a social studies program that is concrete and related to children's immediate lives.

Activity

A CLASSROOM BAKE SALE

Organize a bake sale with the children. The children can make cookies, brownies, or other treats that they can sell to other children in the school. Let the children keep track of what they pay for the ingredients. Using this information, the children should determine the price of each item. They can discuss whether they want to lose money, earn money, or break even on their sale. The sale could be advertised in the school with notices on bulletin boards, announcements over the school public address system (if there is one), or in other ways the children think up. Set a time for the sale and arrange the various roles: who will be salesperson, who will collect money, who will make change. If young children need help in the sale, parents or older children might be enlisted. After the sale, figure out with the children whether they made or lost money. If they made money, the children could decide how to spend it: for example, buy something for the class, have a party, or make a contribution to a charitable cause.

When children first arrive in school, teachers should explain the way the school is organized, who the different people are and what they do, and what the rules are. Children can take a field trip within the school to see its various parts and the adults who are involved: other classes and teachers; the school office, with its administrator and secretaries; the kitchen and the people who work there; and the various other people who staff the school, including those responsible for transportation and maintenance. It is important for the children to learn who these people are and what they do. Children also need to begin to learn the rules of the school and the reasons for them, though the children might not be told all the rules at one time.

Children will also meet children from families that are different from theirs: traditional families, extended families, single-parent families, blended families, and the like. There may also be children who live with foster parents. The children need to be helped to see that families are different, but that families serve the same functions and may work well despite the differences.

Children's prior experiences and concrete perceptions of the social world provide a foundation from which children create understanding. What they know about their immediate lives also provides a basis for understanding more remote aspects of social life. Through understanding themselves children can come to understand others. Children at the nursery school level, for example, can begin to deal with sociological concepts such as *self* or *group* as they explore themselves in relation to others in school and at home. Their understanding of these concepts will be different from that of primary-grade children. When children enter school, they begin to experience a new institution, the school, with its different roles. Instead of parents, children, and siblings, they meet teachers, fellow students, administrators, and others related to the school. They need to develop new relationships as they themselves learn the student role.

Goals for the social studies must be related to the overall goals of early childhood education. Instructional programs should be based on children's readiness. Children should be given material that is appropriate, in a way that is consistent with their specific levels of development. Teachers should use children's activities to explore concepts, rather than just having children read from a text or telling them about a concept. Concepts will be learned shallowly and by rote if teachers do not provide first-hand experiences for the children's inquiry. Especially when topics remote in time and space are offered to young children, teachers must ensure that the children have the requisite learning necessary to establish their own meanings and that they have access to appropriate data sources. A program focused on inquiry skills requires that opportunities be provided for collecting and acting on information. Concepts and generalizations abstracted from such inquiry can later be applied to more remote topics, in which there are few or no opportunities for direct collection of information.

A unit on families in a foreign country can provide meaningful study if the children have some understanding of family structures, roles, and relationships. This understanding might be achieved through studying families in the immediate environment. Teachers can alternate topics dealing with the immediate environment with related topics dealing with the remote in time and space, giving children an opportunity to apply concepts and generalizations to new situations and to broaden their already developed conceptual schemes. A broad range of resources should be available for this study, including books, audiovisual materials, and collections of artifacts and simulated materials.

Teaching for Social Competence

Social competence has been identified as one of the major goals of early childhood education. Social competence includes the behavior and thought processes that result in effective interpersonal relations. Four types of skills have been studied in relation to early childhood programs: situation-specific behavioral repertoires (for example, actions that build friendships), interpersonal problem solving, role-taking, and verbal self-direction and impulse control (Price, 1982). Programs have been developed by Shure and Spivack (1971, 1978) to teach interpersonal skills to four-year-old and five-year-old children by generating alternative social strategies for solving given problems and by helping children think of the consequences of their actions. Similar strategies could be used by teachers as they observe children who have particular social problems.

Early childhood programs often help children develop role-playing and fantasizing skills primarily through dramatic play activities. Educators believe that children's social competence will increase as they gain these role-taking skills. Through assuming another role, children are able to understand and appreciate the perspectives of others.

Children can also be helped to develop greater control over their impulses and their aggressive behavior through early childhood activities. Having children think aloud and verbalize what they intend to do helps children gain control over their impulses. By using this articulated "private speech," they come to know and understand their behavior and thus gain control over its aggressive aspects. Such strategies for teaching young children prosocial behavior have an appropriate place in the kindergarten and primary grades as well as in the preschool. (For further discussion of children's social competence, see Chapter 7.)

USING RESOURCES IN EARLY CHILDHOOD SOCIAL STUDIES

Once decisions about goals and topics are made, teachers must organize for instruction. Planning at this point includes deciding on classroom activities and identifying and organizing resources.

Teachers are the single most important resource in the classroom. They serve as models for values and behaviors. The type of questions teachers ask can either further inquiry or lead to stereotyped responses. In addition, teachers set up the classroom, deciding on the activities to be included and on the range of behavior they will permit. They use their knowledge of the children, the resources available, and the topic under study to further children's learning. Inquiry is important in early learning, but exposition still plays an important role. The teacher's role as teller—as source of information—is never to be underestimated.

Books also provide information not directly accessible to children. Children's nonfiction books are available that are well written, understandable, and accurate. Books of fiction also reflect the social world, often with greater insight than many nonfiction books. Children need to learn to use these important sources of information.

The oral tradition is important in social studies. Verbal descriptions offered by children and adults are useful sources of information. Group discussions help clarify ideas and provide teachers with feedback about the concepts and misconceptions the children might have. A group discussion cannot determine the truth of a child's statement. Having children check their assertions against those of others, however, can help them become less self-centered and more aware of the external criteria of truth.

Although language is the most often used symbol system in the social studies, nonverbal symbols are also used, providing a useful resource for children as both a source of data and a way of recording and communicating data. The most used nonverbal symbol systems are the map and the globe. Globes that represent the world in simple form should be introduced early in school. The globe is a more accurate representation of the world than is a flat map. Maps, however, are also important in the social studies. Children can learn to understand maps by developing their own maps of field trips and other experiences. Children might begin mapping with three-dimensional representation—using blocks—and later use pictures, and finally use pure symbolizations. They could even invent their own symbol systems as they move to higher levels of abstraction (Richards, 1976). Charts and graphs are other nonverbal symbols children must learn to use.

Using Concrete Materials

The concrete materials of the social studies are representations of social science phenomena, either artifacts out of which we must infer behavior, such as tools and toys, or symbolic representations. For instance, teachers may bring a map or a three-dimensional model into the classroom. Slides or a movie can help make the children familiar with geographical areas that they cannot visit and explore.

The earliest development of concrete materials for use by young children in social studies education was by Maria Montessori, who designed tactile globes and devised map puzzles. By playing with the map pieces, children became familiar with the names of countries and their boundaries. Each puzzle piece had a small knob attached to it to facilitate the children's handling. Similar geographic puzzles are available today.

With the development of the reform kindergarten movement in the United States during the first third of the twentieth century came the development of new educational materials. One of the most useful and flexible of these is building blocks (Hirsch, 1984). Two basic variations were developed. Patty Smith Hill devised a set of large floor blocks. Long blocks could be fastened to corner posts with pegs to create structures for children's dramatic play. These structures were large enough to allow children to play inside them and sturdy enough to take the occasional knocks of five-year-olds. Several variations of this type of block are available today, including hollow blocks, variplay sets, and Sta-Put blocks.

Unit blocks were developed by Caroline Pratt about the same time. The unit block, looking much like a length of two-by-four-inch lumber, is based on a specifc unit of measure. Each block is either the size of the unit or a multiple or fraction of that unit. Thus there are half-unit, quarter-unit, double-unit, and quadruple-unit blocks. Various shapes are added, such as columns, wedges, curves, and semicircles, to make a set. A good set of unit blocks is constructed of hardwood that will not splinter or wear excessively and is finished so that each block is in exact proportion to the unit. This consistency allows the children to construct complicated buildings that will stand securely for days.

Because unit blocks are much smaller than floor blocks, they cannot be used for dramatic play. With unit blocks, children miniaturize the world

Children can reconstruct familiar places with unit blocks.

and play with, not in, this miniature world. In the early stages of block play, young children are content to build abstract structural designs. This type of block building gives way to building individual structures and then to building large, elaborate, interrelated structures. These structures may represent either a fantasy world or the real world, depending on the guidance the child has received and on the child's present moods or needs. Block constructions can represent a home, a school, a shopping center, a neighborhood, a harbor area, or an airport provided that enough blocks, freedom of ideas, and time are available to the children.

Children can incorporate other materials in block construction. Miniature wooden or rubber people representing different family or community roles can be utilized, as can toy cars, trucks, boats, and airplanes. Traffic signs and street lights add to the reality of a construction. Signs written by teachers or children can identify places; strips of paper or plastic can represent streets or rivers. A ball of twine can help the children build a suspension bridge. Imaginative use of many everyday materials enhances the building and provides an outlet for the children's creativity. Blocks become arbitrary symbols to be used in representing portions of the world. Building with blocks, a form of concrete representation, provides a good transition to the children's use of maps and other forms of symbol learning in the classroom.

Other forms of concrete material can be used to make models of places. Cardboard cartons, papier-maché constructions, or other kinds of materials work well. Also available are commercial sets such as Kinder City, Playskool Village, Lincoln Logs, and Lego.

The dramatic play area, with its props, can encourage the exploration of family roles and relationships. Dress-up clothes and play props can suggest many situations; hats representing different occupations, in particular, are helpful. A ladder and a length of hose inspire children to work as firefighters. A table, a cash register, some paper sacks, and empty food containers suggest a supermarket. Sometimes an article does not even have to look like what it represents in play. A bicycle pump, for example, can be a gasoline pump in a service station or a firefighter's hose. If teachers are imaginative in the use of materials, the children will soon match, if not surpass, this imaginativeness in play.

Audio-Visual Representations

A variety of audiovisual representations can also provide resources for social studies teaching. Still photographs stimulate discussions and provide information. Sets of pictures for use in developing discussions are commercially available. Pictures should be large enough to be viewed by a group of children and contain enough detail without clutter so children can focus on what is important. Teachers can show pictures to children in a group discussion or place them on bulletin boards. If they use bulletin boards, teachers should take care that the arrangement helps the children see what is important. Pictures may also be combined with other display materials. Magnetic boards and flannelboards allow children or teachers to manipulate the materials and change the organization, thus allowing a more active use than simple picture displays provide. Commercial flannelboard and magnetic board materials can supplement what teachers develop.

Commercially produced pictures may not contain the specific elements needed to study a particular environment. These materials can be supplemented by locally developed and teacher-developed materials. Fortunately, audiovisual technology is at the point where much good material can be produced by persons having little technical skill. Instant cameras allow teachers to take still pictures that are immediately available. A variety of cameras with automatic features that are simple to use can help teachers produce high-quality color slides that can be projected on a screen or placed in a viewer. Even disposable cameras are available. Videotape cassettes can be made just as easily with a camcorder.

Sound recordings also provide a good resource for learning. Commercial recordings of songs and stories can be an authentic mirror of a culture. Children can supplement these materials with tape recordings of their own songs and stories. Children can recapture a field trip in their classroom if teachers have recorded sounds and taken pictures. On return from an airport visit, for example, children could listen to the announcements of flight arrivals and departures and the roar of the jet engines as a plane taxis to the runway and takes off. Tape recordings can also be made of visits by resource persons or of class discussions. Audio and visual resources combine very effectively.

Exhibits of materials are often useful in communicating information. Studying a service station, for example, might suggest an exhibit of things used and sold there or an exhibit about petroleum and petroleum products. The first exhibit might include containers for products sold for automobiles, collections of small spare automobile parts, road maps, and simple hand tools used by mechanics. The petroleum exhibit could include a chart of petroleum products and refining processes. Containers of crude oil, lubricating oil, diesel fuel, home heating oil, kerosene, petroleum jelly, and paint thinners could be brought into the room for exhibit. Care should be taken with these materials since they are flammable and dangerous if swallowed. Pictures of these products or their uses can be substituted if necessary. Teachers generally collect materials and arrange displays alone, but children and their parents can profitably be involved in this enterprise. Sometimes commercial sources provide display materials for school use. Teachers should make a survey of the resources available in their community. However, they must take care that commercially available materials are not distorted by advertising messages. In some areas, local museums lend displays of social studies materials to schools. Dioramas or artifacts may come in commercially available kits.

Using Community Resources

Teachers should look beyond the classroom for learning resources. Resource persons are often quite willing to come to school: representatives of community workers (such as a garbage collector or a firefighter) or persons with a particular skill or area of knowledge (a weaver or an anthropologist). A hobbyist, a visitor from a foreign country, a member of a particular ethnic group under study, or an older person who has first-hand historical knowledge might be of great interest. In using resource persons, teachers should be sure that both the children and the visitor know the purpose of the visit and that basic ground rules for participation are laid down. Children enjoy acting as hosts in their classrooms.

Field trips into the community must be properly planned. In addition to technical planning, teachers should make the children aware of the purpose and focus of the trip. Although chance occurrences can enhance a trip, leaving its organization to chance is not wise. Field trips need not be elaborate; often the simplest are the most meaningful. A walk to the corner to watch traffic control operations or a visit to a local supermarket can provide a fruitful experience. Even though children may have had the same experience outside of school, the focus and preparation provided by teachers can open new learning opportunities as new aspects of a familiar situation unfold.

Using Textbooks and Curriculum Guides

Social studies textbooks are available at the kindergarten and primary level. Often textbooks at this level take the form of workbooks with pictures for the earliest grades and become social studies readers at later grades. While many texts follow a story line, newer ones present social science materials directly to young children.

Textbooks can provide only a limited amount of information; they should not be the only resource used. Textbooks can provide common knowledge or pull together knowledge from a variety of sources. A good teachers' manual may also offer helpful suggestions for resources and instructional procedures. Rather than reading about concepts from a book, children should actively inquire about and develop concepts on their own. Teachers may not want to order a single set of textbooks for an entire class, but rather have available several copies of many textbooks for children's use.

Curriculum guides can help a teacher develop significant instructional activities. Curriculum guides vary in scope and organization. Some provide a generalized scheme of the subject matter area and are relatively suggestive; others are highly prescriptive, describing in detail the work that is to take place. Still another kind of guide takes the form of resource units containing outlines for study and information for planning activities. Often resource units contain more information than teachers can use at any one time, thereby allowing freedom and flexibility without imposing too great a need to seek out materials and instructional ideas.

In most states and large local school systems, curriculum guides and resources are developed and made available to teachers. Where such materials are not available, teachers must use their own resources. Teaching units are available commercially and can also be found in such magazines as *Early Childhood Education Today*, *Early Years*, and *Instructor*. Teachers should assess the worth of available units in terms of the significance of their goals, the practicability of the suggested activities, the availability of resources, and the applicability of the program to the particular class of children. At the preschool level, few resource units are available, and teachers must generally rely on their own ingenuity for developing classroom activities.

Ensuring Significance in the Use of Resources

Classroom activity can take place that does not produce learning or that causes children to learn the wrong things. Amassing resources and materials and providing children with activities does not insure learning. Although children's involvement is important, the achievement of instructional goals is the prime criterion by which we judge success. Teachers should select carefully from the resources available, using only those that help children achieve significant and worthwhile goals.

Teachers frequently use free and inexpensive materials because they are readily available, but they should judge the worth of materials as much by their benefits as by their cost. Criteria for selecting resources include the material's usefulness for achieving instructional objectives, its possible effectiveness compared to other resources, and its appropriateness to the maturity level and background of the particular children. In addition, teachers should consider the ease of use of the resources and the cost of the materials in relation to gains, in terms both of initial expense and of time and effort expended by children and teacher.

INTEGRATING SOCIAL STUDIES WITH OTHER CURRICULUM AREAS

Social studies programs often lose their distinctiveness as they merge with other portions of the program. In nursery school and kindergarten, portions of the social studies program should be integrated into a general activity period. Rosalind Charlesworth and Nancy Miller (1985) describe how basic skills can be integrated with socials studies. These basic skills are taught even while the social science concepts noted earlier in this chapter are approached. Charlesworth (1988) describes how children in preschool can learn about mathematics and science in a social studies unit. In working on a social studies unit, children can build with blocks, act out social roles, and look at pictures, while at the same time other children are busy in other curriculum areas. Even in the primary grades, social studies can integrate a wide range of learning, so that the school day is not made up of distinct, disparate activities. Other parts of the early childhood program have much to offer the social studies.

Social studies activities often include constructing models or dioramas. Many art and crafts activities can be related to social studies, providing children with opportunities to develop expressive skills. At the same time, the products become useful tools for social studies education. Drawing a picture of a supermarket, devising a decorative chart, or making Indian handicrafts are examples of how art activities can express social studies learning. Children can also use paintings, drawings, and constructions to tell what they have learned.

Music and literature of a culture can provide a key to understanding its symbol system and values. Ethnic music, songs, stories, and poetry have an important place in the social studies program. Good literature for children (and adults) provides insight into people, institutions, and social relationships that are hard to describe in straight exposition. Children can empathize with persons by sharing their feelings long before they can intellectually understand them.

The basic concepts of topological geometry, discussed in Chapter 14, are just the concepts necessary to understand geography and maps. Being able to locate places and to determine proximity and separation are needed in map reading.

Language arts provide an excellent resource for the social studies. Children can create dramatic presentations or puppet shows for social studies units. They can use dramatic play to act out roles and relationships, and tell or write stories that express the insights they have gained. They also need to develop command of language skills in order to be effective in gathering information and communicating the fruits of their learning to others.

MULTICULTURAL EDUCATION

As Herbert Zimiles (1991) has reminded us, teachers today are being urged to be mindful of the differences among the children they teach and to provide an education that is responsive to those differences. Increasingly, teachers are becoming aware of the differences in language and culture among the children they teach. School populations are becoming increasingly diverse, with more children in school who come from different linguistic and cultural backgrounds than had been experienced before.

The cultural and linguistic backgrounds of children are important in planning an appropriate education for them. These backgrounds are important not only because of the overt behaviors and reactions they

Participating in a Brazillian "carnival" helps foster multicultural education.

shape, but also because of the covert, unstated values, attitudes, and assumptions that result from one's cultural background (Garcia, 1991). These cultural differences suggest that teachers need to respond differently to children who come from different cultural backgrounds.

Because our society is becoming increasingly multicultural, all children, including those who live in relatively heterogeneous groups, need to learn about their own group within the larger social context. They also need to learn to respect and appreciate each other and to deal effectively with a wide variety of people. Thus teachers must provide a multicultural perspective in early childhood programs (Ramsey, 1992).

Although this book discusses multicultural education in the context of social studies, multicultural education should not be limited to that area. Rather, educators should enrich the entire curriculum with a multicultural orientation, selecting books, pictures, and other materials that reflect the multicultural reality of our nation and our world. Indeed, Louise Derman-Sparks and her associates (1989) have suggested that teachers offer an anti-bias curriculum in early childhood education, that is, a program that takes a proactive stance on issues of culture, class, gender, age, and individual identities. They argue that children notice differences among individuals and develop attitudes about those differences at an early age. They believe that early childhood educators should take the initiative in helping children form positive attitudes towards differences among people and in dealing effectively with stereotyping and bias from the beginning of the children's education.

Christine E. Sleeter and Carl A. Grant (1988) have identified five approaches to multicultural education. The first approach sees this as a way to help all children fit into the educational mainstream. Unfortunately this approach does not support a mutual accommodation between children and school regarding the differences that exist. A second approach has been labeled a human relations approach; it provides children with interpersonal skills to identify and reduce prejudice and stereotypes. This approach does not take into account our society's structural inequalities and assumes that social inequalities and conflicts of interest will be eliminated if people can learn to get along with each other.

The third approach Sleeter and Grant identified, the single-group studies approach, includes curriculum units on specific groups of people for specific parts of the school year. Such an approach adds these units to the existing curriculum without essentially changing the nature of children's school experiences. The fourth approach has been labeled multicultural education, in which the entire curriculum is modified to reflect a broad world view. This approach, if care is not taken, can be superficial, reflecting on obvious differences among cultural groups, such as food, holidays, and ethnic dress. It does not pay enough attention to basic social inequalities.

The fifth approach Sleeter and Grant identified is an activist one that focuses on social reconstruction goals. It aims to help children fight discrimination and attempts to eliminate inequalities in our society. This approach may be unrealistic in terms of what schools can do and of what young children are capable of learning and doing in school. Each approach to multicultural education has its strengths and weaknesses. Teachers may choose elements of each, being sensitive to the way in which the entire curriculum reflects a view of people and developing activities that help children learn in a positive way about people who are culturally different from each other. As an example of what young children are capable of learning, this chapter presents materials about Chinese culture.

There are other ways teachers can extend children's knowledge about cultures beyond those that are immediate to them. These techniques are important not only for developing multicultural understanding but also for providing a way in which children can develop an understanding of a broad range of social activities and social structures, whether they are directly accessible or remote. Teachers can be informed about multicultural experience using such resources as *The Anti-Bias Curriculum* (Derman-Sparks, 1989) and *Understanding the Multicultural Experience in Early Childhood Education* (Saracho & Spodek, 1983), both available from the National Association for the Education of Young Children. They can use resources from other associations, as well. For example, The Council on Interracial Books for Children (1841 Broadway, New York, NY 10023) has many resources regarding appropriate books for young children that positively represent different racial and cultural groups.

UNIT: CHINESE HOLIDAYS AND FESTIVALS

[Note: This unit can be developed as a whole, or portions of it can be used at appropriate times during the year.]

CHINESE NEW YEAR

The Chinese New Year, or Spring Festival, is the most important festival in Chinese culture. It is a time to celebrate the birth of the new year, the continuation of life, after surviving the past year.

> A long time ago, a monster named "Nien" (meaning "Year") lived deep in the mountains. He came to the village to prey on people, at the end of every year. The village people would hide in their houses or in some safe places at this time and came out again the next morning when "Nien" had left. People said "Kung Hsi" (congratulations) to each other for having survived the attack of "Nien."
>
> One time, when "Nien" came down to the village, someone was just putting some dried bamboo sticks into the cooking oven. Knowing that the monster was coming near, he ran away without extinguishing the fire. Unexpectedly, "Nien" was frightened away by the '"pi-pa" sound of bamboo cracking in the burning fire.
>
> After this, people used a similar strategy of making loud noises to drive "Nien" away each year. This is one version of the origin of Chinese New Year and the use of firecrackers.

The New Year celebration starts on the thirtieth day of the twelfth moon—New Year's Eve (the Chinese calendar is a lunar calendar). On that evening, family members return home for a family reunion and a splendid feast. Fish, if eaten that day, is not fully consumed, because the character "Yu," meaning fish, is pronounced the same as another "Yu," meaning "to leave something." Hence, fish is saved, meaning that this family has something to be stored every year. After dinner, the children bow to the elders in the family to show their respect. The adults then give them red envelopes containing money.

Since the New Year's season signifies a fresh start, the mood is festive. The home is thoroughly cleaned in preparation and no sweeping is done on New Year's Day, lest the family's good fortune be swept out the door with the dust. No work is done on New Year's Day. The food has been prepared the day before, so that one actually eats last year's food. This is a good omen, signifying one is not so destitute as to have to eat every bit of food as soon as it becomes available. Signs containing couplets to express good wishes and paper guards are pasted on the doors.

In rural China, people spend almost all their time tilling the land. The Chinese New Year season was the only time for them to visit relatives and friends. After a few days' rest, on the fourth or fifth day of the New Year, the sounds of firecrackers proclaim the resumption of business.

Activities

1. Planting Narcissus Flowers

The narcissus, which blossoms during the New Year season, is a traditional New Year flower. It is easy for children to plant because all one has to do is place the bulb in a bowl of water filled with pebbles to hold it in place. Growing the narcissus can be an interesting science lesson. Children can compare its attributes with other plants growing in the classroom.

Both the Chinese version of the narcissus story and its Greek version can be told at story time so that children can compare the two stories.

The Chinese Version of the Narcissus Story

> A long time ago, in a little village in southern China, there lived a widow and her only son,

UNIT: CHINESE HOLIDAYS AND FESTIVALS *(continued)*

A-long. Besides cultivating the land, A-long hunted to make a living.

One day, A-long was hunting early in the morning. The widow found that the rice pot was almost empty. At dusk, the widow washed the small amount of rice left, cooked it, and waited for her son to return home. She grew more and more worried about her son's safety and thought he must be very hungry after hunting all day.

It became darker and darker. The widow pricked up her ears to listen to the sounds of her son's footsteps. After a while, the sounds of footsteps were heard and came closer and clearer. Opening the door, instead of A-long, she found an old, shabbily clothed beggar. He looked weak and spoke to the widow in a tiny voice:

"I am so hungry. Would you please give me some rice or leftovers?"

The widow wanted to help the beggar. But, with only one bowl of rice left, what could she do? "Maybe A-long has killed a big boar today," she thought, and decided to give the only bowl of rice to the beggar.

The rice smelled so good with its rising steam. The old beggar seemed to have hungered for a long, long time for he ate the rice within a few seconds. Licking his mouth clean, he said, "Can I have some more? I am still hungry." Thinking of A-long, who still hadn't come home and who had no rice to eat now, the widow shed tears. The old beggar wondered why she cried. After being told by the widow, he felt sorry that he had eaten all their food. He left the widow's house and stood beside the pond nearby. Then, he bent down and spit all the rice he had just eaten into the pond. Then suddenly he disappeared.

After a while, A-long came home with a big, fat hare in his hand. The widow told him about the old beggar. A-long felt that what had happened was quite strange.

The next morning when A-long was ready to go hunting, he passed the pond and was startled by what was beside the pond. The barren land was now filled with white, fragrant, beautiful flowers. The widow came nearer to look and muttered, "Is the beggar a god in disguise? Are these flowers transformed by the rice spit from his mouth?"

They named the flowers "water-god" (narcissus). A-long did not go hunting any more. He planted narcissus, sold them, and led a far better life.

2. *Making Chinese New Year Cakes*

See recipe provided at end of unit.

3. *Window Paper Cutting*

Teachers and children can cut designs from red paper and paste them on the windows. Teachers might be able to find traditional Chinese New Year woodblock prints and window paper decorations to show children the authentic forms and to decorate the classroom. These can also be purchased from China Books and Periodicals (Mail Order Department, 2929 24th St., San Francisco, CA 94110).

4. *Spring Festival Signs*

Teachers can also decorate the classroom with signs (Chun Lien) that they make or they can ask parents to provide some authentic ones.

At New Year time, spring festival signs are pasted on the walls inside the house as well as on the outside of the door.

The most common spring festival sign is a square piece of red paper, with a character signifying "good luck" or "spring." Such signs are usually pasted upside down because "upside down" is pronounced exactly the same as the character "arrive." The upside-down sign expresses the hope that spring and good luck will arrive for the coming year.

UNIT: CHINESE HOLIDAYS AND FESTIVALS *(continued)*

LANTERN FESTIVAL

The fifteen day of the first moon is the Lantern festival.

Activities

1. *Cooking Yuan Shiau*

Yuan Shiau are small dumplings eaten on the Lantern Festival.

Recipe

Ingredients:

red bean or sesame paste
glutinous rice powder

(These can be bought in a Chinese food mart.)

Directions:

a. Take a small portion of red bean or sesame paste and roll it into a small ball.
b. Spread some glutinous rice powder in a pan.
c. Soak the small ball of red bean paste with water.
d. Put it into the pan and shake the pan till the ball is covered with glutinous rice powder.
e. Boil a pot of water and put Yuan Shiau into it.
f. Boil the Yuan Shiau until they float.

2. *Making Lanterns*

The traditional Chinese lantern is made of paper and thin bamboo sticks. The one described here is the kind that children in Taiwan make.

a. Take a can, clean it, and punch two holes on each side of the can. Be sure to watch children carefully for safety's sake.
b. Cross a piece of wire through the holes.
c. Fasten the wire on a chopstick, and place a candle into the can. (Setting up the candle in the can is a good topic for a problem-solving discussion.)

(Children can also make lanterns out of construction paper, but these should not be used with candles.)

The children can compare Chinese lanterns with pumpkin jack-ó-lanterns.

CHING MING OR GRAVE-SWEEPING FESTIVAL

This holiday often falls on April 5 or 6. On this day, Chinese visit the tombs of their ancestors to show respect to their memory.

April 4—Children's Day in Taiwan.

Usually, schools celebrate this holiday with a variety of special programs, such as talent shows, or contests with themes related to children. Parents generally buy gifts for their children on this day.

Dragon Boat Festival

This festival falls on the fifth day of the fifth moon. It is believed that the festival commemorates Chu Yuan, a loyal minister of the king of Chu who committed suicide in the Milo river because his remonstrations had been ignored.

On this day, people eat *tsung tzu* (made mainly of glutinous rice and meat), they make *hsiang pao* (see Figure 1), and they hold dragon boat races.

Activities

1. *Making Hsiang Pao*

Hsiang Pao is a small pouch containing incense. It is worn by children during this festival to avoid evil spirits. (See Figure 1.)

2. *Dragon Boat Race*

A small-scale dragon boat festival can be held in the classroom's water table.

a. If possible, show children pictures of a real dragon boat race in Taiwan or Hong Kong.
b. The children can make boats either by paper folding or from polystyrene foam.
c. Separate channels by rope.
d. Have the children discuss how they can move the boats.
e. Children can have a race by blowing the boats with straws to see which boat reaches the destination first.

(This activity can be added into projects whose theme is the wind, the boat, or water.)

UNIT: CHINESE HOLIDAYS AND FESTIVALS *(continued)*

Figure 15–1 Making Hsiang Pao

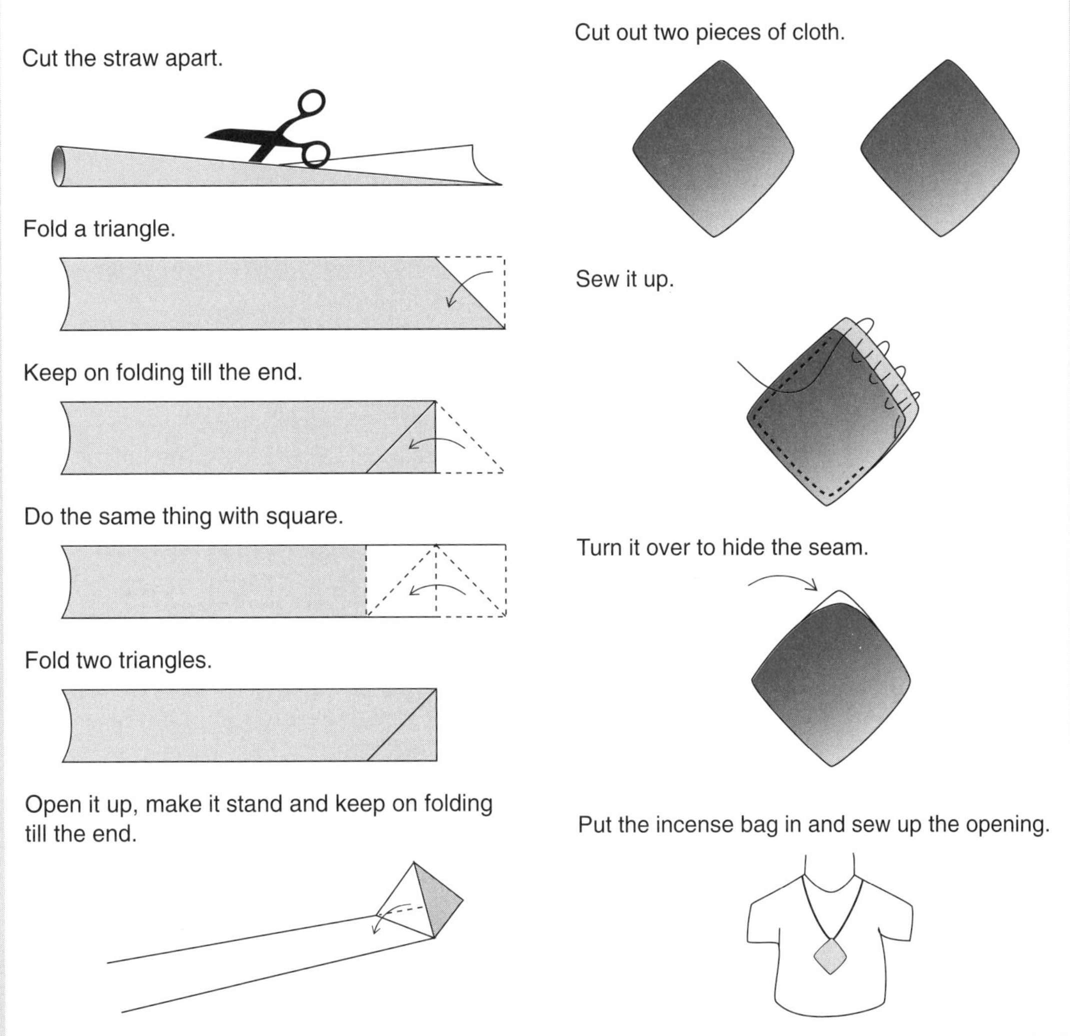

Cut the straw apart.
Fold a triangle.
Keep on folding till the end.
Do the same thing with square.
Fold two triangles.
Open it up, make it stand and keep on folding till the end.
Cut out two pieces of cloth.
Sew it up.
Turn it over to hide the seam.
Put the incense bag in and sew up the opening.

TEACHER'S DAY

Confucius is revered as the man who established the system of moral values that has guided the Chinese people from thousands of years ago to the present day in the Republic of China (Taiwan). Out of respect for him as a model teacher, his birthday, which falls on September 28th, is celebrated as Teacher's Day.

UNIT: CHINESE HOLIDAYS AND FESTIVALS *(continued)*

OTHER CHINESE ITEMS FOR THE CLASSROOM

In addition to integrating Chinese holidays and festivals into the early childhood curriculum, the following materials can be included in the classroom:

Snacks: Chinese cookies and desserts, such as pineapple cake, puffed rice cakes, soft flour cakes, tofu cakes, Ma Hua cookies, Chin Hua cookies or sesame peanut cookies. (These items can be bought in a Chinese food mart).

Block Area: Posters of Chinese architecture (both ancient and modern) can be hung on walls nearby.

Dramatic Play Area: Chinese dolls made of dough, Chinese puppets, paper dolls, Chinese flour people, Chinese opera props such as a whip, or masks of painted faces.

Clay: Chinese play dough.

Art Area: Chinese writing brush, works of calligraphy, and Chinese painting.

Reading Area: Books with Chinese as main characters. For example: Ian Wallace, *Ching Chiang And The Dragon's Dance* (New York: Atheneum, 1984); Diane Wolkstein, *White Wave* (New York: Crowell, 1979); Jane Yolen, *The Seeing Stick* (New York: Crowell, 1977); and Jane Yolen, *The Emperor and The Kite* (New York: World Publishing, 1967). Unfortunately, few books are available in English that depict modern Chinese.

Musical Instruments: Chinese bells, drums, Chinese flute. (These can be bought in stores in Chinatowns located in such cities as Chicago, Los Angeles, New York, and San Francisco. They may also be available in some local Chinese food stores.)

[Note: These materials are not just for display. They can be used within suitable unit themes or in appropriate, related activities. For example, a Chinese writing brush can be used by children to experience its feel, which is different from that of a pen. If teachers happen to talk about "written words" of different cultures, resource persons can be invited to demonstrate calligraphy in the classroom.]

Chinese Games and Activities

Games Chinese children play can be incorporated into the early childhood education curriculum. They are close to the life experiences of children everywhere. They appeal to children and are developmentally appropriate. In addition, they enhance the development of fine and gross motor skills, creativity, imagination, and cooperation, and are educationally worthwhile. The following activities and games can be allocated in a semester or integrated into any project as long as they match the theme of the project.

Paper Folding

Chinese people love and are very good at using different kinds of paper. A small piece of paper can be folded into a tiny boat, different kinds of hats, a jet plane, a crane, a frog, and other small animals. (See Figure 2.) This activity can enhance fine motor skills and foster children's patience. The products of paper folding can become props in the dramatic play area or can be used to decorate the classroom.

Playing with Rubber Bands

Using one or more rubber bands, children can "pull out" lots of patterns to amuse themselves. This activity enhances the fingers' fine motor development and encourages imagination. It is also appropriate for solitary play. Children can experience elasticity by manipulating the resilient rubber bands. Care needs to be taken in handling rubber bands so that children do not hurt themselves or others.

Many rubber bands can be strung together to form a long jump rope. One child holds each

UNIT: CHINESE HOLIDAYS AND FESTIVALS *(continued)*

Figure 15–2 Paper Folding

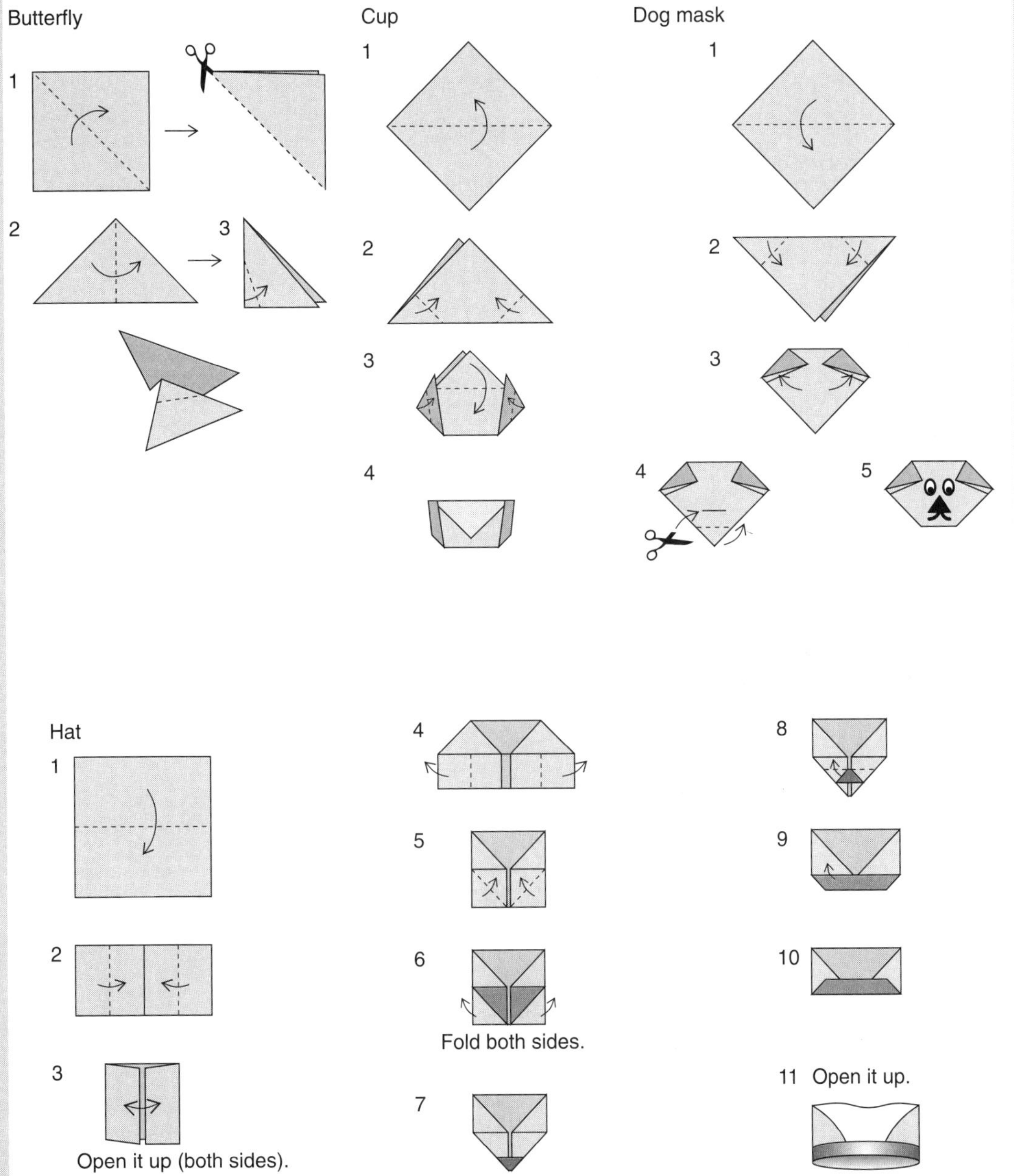

UNIT: CHINESE HOLIDAYS AND FESTIVALS *(continued)*

end of the rope while a third child tries to jump over the rope without touching it. The children holding the rope raise the height of the rope gradually, moving it up to the level of the third child's knees, waist, shoulders, mouth, nose, ears, and top of the head. (See Figure 3.)

Chinese Hopscotch

1. Draw a pattern on the ground as shown in Figure 4.
2. At the beginning, throw a marker (a pebble, a small stone, or a bottle cap) into square 1.

Figure 15–3 Playing with Rubber Bands

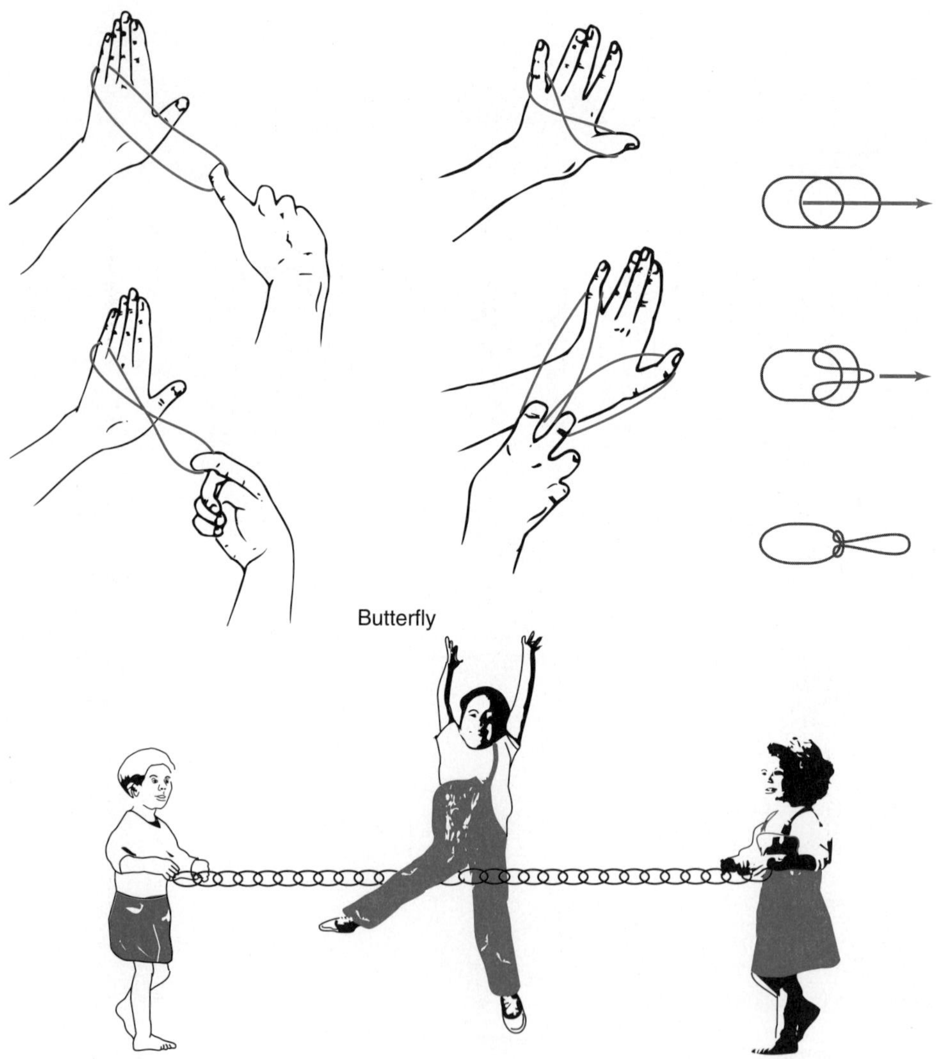

UNIT: CHINESE HOLIDAYS AND FESTIVALS *(continued)*

Figure 15–4 Hopscotch

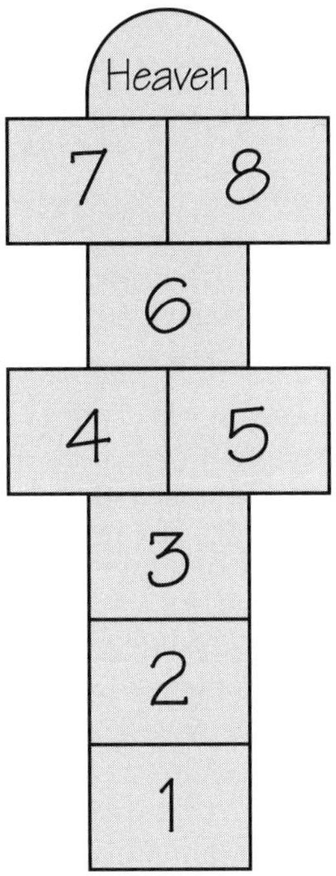

3. Players hop on one foot and kick the marker into square 2. Anyone who steps on a line or falls loses the turn and has to start all over again.
4. The first player to reach square 10 is the winner.
5. The winner then chooses a square for a private house and marks it. No one else can stop in the "privately owned house" except the owner. The player with the most private houses wins the game.

Shadow Figures

This activity can be included in topics related to light, shadow, or hands. The teacher can design hand shadows to illustrate or tell a story. (See Figure 5.) The room should be dark and a blank space on the wall available.

Figure 15–5 Shadow Figures

Mask Making

The Chinese people's daily life is closely related to nature. Many of the children's play materials are derived from nature.

1. Use large leaves and flowers to make masks. (It is very possible for spontaneous dramatic play to take place in a field.)
2. The teacher can introduce the names of different plants and their attributes.
3. When children find out that some flowers or leaves stick to their clothes while others do not, it might be a good time to introduce different textures of cloth after returning to the classroom.

Eagle Chases Chicks

This is an outdoor group game played in the yard or playground.

1. Ask a volunteer to be the eagle.
2. Ask one child to be the hen and other children to be chicks. The chicks line up behind the hen, holding their hands

UNIT: CHINESE HOLIDAYS AND FESTIVALS *(continued)*

tightly on the shoulder or around the waist of the one in front.

3. The game starts with the hungry eagle flying around everywhere to grab the chicks. The hen spreads out her hands as wings to protect her children. The chicks have to run to right or left according to the hen's gesture; at the same time, they have to hold tightly to one another. If a chick gets out the line, he or she will get caught. This activity reflects the themes that mothers will try every way possible to protect their children and children have to be cooperative in fighting against enemies. The game enhances gross motor development and facilitates cooperative learning.

Cooking

Baking Sweet Potatoes Baking sweet potatoes is a sweet childhood memory for many people who grew up in Taiwan. Since food is a topic dear to almost all children, exploring the taste of baked sweet potatoes might provide an excellent beginning for learning about cultural differences.

Making New Year's Cake

Recipe

Ingredients:

6 cups glutinous rice powder
2 cups sugar (either white or brown)
2 cups water
cellophane, 12 inches in diameter
bamboo basket for steaming food
(These can be bought in a Chinese food mart.)

Directions:

1. Stir sugar in water until completely dissolved.
2. Pour glutinous rice powder in mixture and stir it well.
3. Spread the cellophane in the bamboo basket.
4. Pour in the sugar and rice mixture and steam for two hours.

Many Chinese utensils are made of natural materials, such as bamboo. Many Chinese dessert are steamed in bamboo baskets so as to imbue the food with the refreshing smell of bamboo.

Teachers can introduce the Chinese way of making cakes, which is different from the Western way (steaming versus baking).

Chinese eat New Year's cake at New Year festivals. It is pronounced as *Nien* (year) *Gou* (cake). Eating New Year's cake symbolizes good luck because the pronunciation suggests being promoted higher and higher every year.

Source: M. L. Tsai, "Integrating Multicultural Perspectives into Early Childhood Education," in B. Spodek (Ed.), *Educationally Appropriate Kindergarten Practices* (Washington, DC: National Education Association, 1991), pp. 74–96.

Barbara Hatcher, Diane Pape, and R. Tim Nicosia (1988) suggest using group games to develop cultural awareness. Games such as London Bridge, Dragon's Tail, and In and Out the Window originated in different countries. Cynthia Sunal (1988) suggests studying other cultures through children's games and provides examples of children's games from Nigeria. Sources of other children's games include

Arnold, A. (1972). *The world book of children's games*. New York: World Publishing.

Watching a Japanese picture story box gives children a sense of another culture.

Gunfield, F. V. (1975). *Games of the world.* New York: Holt, Rinehart & Winston.
Prieto, M. (1973). *Play in Spanish: Spanish games and folksongs for children.* New York: John Day.
Schmidt, N. J., Twerefour, G. O., Kamanda, D. S. M., & Kennedy, J. (1975). *African children's games for American children.* Urbana: University of Illinois.
United Nations International Children's Fund (1981). *Games around the world.* New York: UNICEF.

A study of the families of the children in class (done carefully and with permission) can help children see the range of social structures within the community and the similarities and differences in the functions of family units. A study of community workers can help children understand what people do at work: whether they produce goods or services, for example. This study can help children to see the relationship between what workers do and what people want and need in a community. To the extent that the families and communities available to the school reflect multiculturalism, these resources are most useful. If such resources are not available, however, teachers will need to seek elsewhere.

For each topic, teachers must view social studies as a method of inquiry rather than as a body of information to pass on to children. Additional topics can also be used, such as a unit on Mexican-Americans or on African-Americans, taught within a framework of anthropology, that presents significant learnings from both a social science and a human relations point of view. A Black Studies curriculum has been developed with units in social studies, as well as language arts, art, and music, that could be easily integrated into a social studies program (Spodek, 1976). Studies of other ethnic groups are also worth including in the early childhood program. The United States is a multicultural nation. While the social studies program must deal with elements of the majority culture, elements of other cultures impact on children of both minority and majority groups and should be included. These elements provide opportunities for children to cope with a multicultural existence and to enjoy the benefits of this diversity.

SUMMARY

A social studies program in the early years might not help children learn the names of presidents in order or the capitals of countries throughout the world. It should, however, help them begin to understand social processes and develop skills in social inquiry. It should also help them gain a better understanding of themselves in relation to the social world in which they live. In addition, it should provide children with an understanding and appreciation of people from backgrounds and cultures that are different from their own. Linked with an understanding of the physical world, such knowledge helps children begin to make reasonable decisions about some of the things that happen to them.

REFERENCES

Brandwein, P. F., et al. (1970). *Principles and practices in the teaching of social sciences: Concepts and values*. New York: Harcourt Brace Jovanich.

Charlesworth, R. (1988). Integrating math with science and social studies: A unit example. *Day Care and Early Education, 15*(4), 28–31.

Charlesworth, R., & Miller, N. L. (1985). Social studies and basic skills in the early childhood classroom. *Social Studies, 76*(1), 34–37.

Derman-Sparks, L. and the A.B.C. Task Force (1989). *The Anti-bias curriculum: Tools for empowering young children*. Washington, DC: National Association for the Education of Young Children.

Fox, K. F. A. (1978). What children bring to school: The beginnings of economic education. *Social Education, 42*, 478–481.

Garcia, R. L. (1991). *Teaching in a pluralistic society* (2nd ed.). New York: Harper Collins.

Hatcher, B. (1983). Putting young cartographers "on the map." *Childhood Education, 59*, 311–315.

Hatcher, B., Pape, D., & Nicosia, R. T. (1988). Group games for global awareness. *Childhood Education, 65*(1), 8–13.

Hirsch, E. S. (Ed.). (1984). *The block book*. Washington, DC: National Association for the Education of Young Children.

Kamii, C. (1973). A sketch of a Piaget-derived preschool developed by the Ypsilanti early education program. In B. Spodek (Ed.), *Early childhood education*. Englewood Cliffs, NJ: Prentice Hall.

Kohlberg, L., & Tureil, E. (1971). Moral development and moral education. In G. Lesser (Ed.), *Psychology and educational practice* (pp. 410–465). Chicago: Scott, Foresman.

Mitchell, L. S. (1971). *Young geographers*. New York: Bank Street College of Education. (Originally published in 1934).

National Council for the Social Studies (1983). *Definition of the social studies*. Washington, DC: Author.

Price, G. G. (1982). Cognitive learning in early childhood education: Mathematics, science, and social studies. In B. Spodek (Ed.), *Handbook of research in early childhood education* (pp. 264–294). New York: Free Press.

Ramsey, P. G. (1992). Caring for children in a diverse world. In B. Spodek & O. N. Saracho (Eds.), *Issues in child care: Yearbook in early childhood education, Vol. 3*. New York: Teachers College Press.

Richards, B. (1976). Mapping: An introduction to symbols. *Young Children, 31*, 145–56.

Saracho, O. N., & Spodek, B. (Eds.). (1983). *Understanding the multicultural experience in early childhood education*. Washington, DC: National Association for the Education of Young Children.

Shure, M. B., & Spivack, G. (1971). *Solving interpersonal problems: A program for four-year-old nursery children*. Philadelphia: Department of Mental Health Sciences.

Shure, M. B., & Spivack, G. (1978). *A mental health program for kindergarten children*. Philadelphia: Department of Mental Health Sciences.

Sleeter, C. E., & Grant, C. A. (1988). *Making choices for multicultural education: Five approaches to race, class, and gender*. Columbus, OH: Merrill.

Spodek, B. (1974). Social studies for young children: Identifying intellectual goals. *Social Education, 38*, 40–45.

Spodek, B. (Ed.). (1991). *Educationally appropriate kindergarten practices*. Washington, DC: National Education Association.

Spodek, B., Andrews, P., Lee, M., Morris, J., Riley, J., & White, D. (1976). *A black studies curriculum for early childhood education* (rev. ed.). Urbana, IL: ERIC/EECE.

Sunal, C. S. (1988). Studying another culture through group games: Examples from Nigeria. *Social Studies, 79*, 232–238.

Sunal, C. S. (1990). *Early childhood social studies*. Columbus, OH: Merrill.

Sunal, C. S. (1993). Social studies in early childhood education. In B. Spodek (Ed.), *Handbook of research on the education of young children* (pp. 176-190). New York: Macmillan.

Sunal., C. S., Warash, B. G., & Strong, M. (1988). Buy! Sell! Produce! Economic education activities. *Day Care and Early Education, 15*(4), 12–15.

Taba, H. (1967). *Teachers' handbook for elementary social studies*. Reading, MA: Addison-Wesley.

Thornberg, K. R. (1983). Young children's understanding of familial concepts with implications for social studies units. *Social Education, 47*, 138–141.

Tsai, M. L. (1991). Integrating multicultural perspectives into early childhood education. In B. Spodek (Ed.), *Educationally appropriate kindergarten practices* (pp. 74–96). Washington, DC: National Education Association.

Turiel, E. (1973). Stage transition in moral development. In R. Travers (Ed.), *Second handbook of research on teaching* (pp. 732–758). Skokie, IL: Rand McNally.

Wolfson, B. J. (1967). Values and the primary school teacher. *Social Education, 31*, 37–38.

Zimiles, H. (1991). Diversity and change in young children: Some educational implications. In B. Spodek & O. N. Saracho (Eds.), *Issues in early childhood curriculum: Yearbook in early childhood education, Vol. 2*. New York: Teachers College Press.

16

The Expressive Arts for Young Children

CHAPTER OVERVIEW

This chapter presents:

- Concepts of creativity
- Developmental stages in art
- Arts and crafts in early childhood education
- Music in early childhood education
- Movement in early childhood education

INTRODUCTION

The expressive arts have traditionally held honored positions in early childhood education. The early Froebelian kindergartens included music and art activities in the *Occupations* and the *Mother's Songs and Plays*. Both were carefully patterned according to explicit directions and gave children opportunities to be actively involved in making and doing, though not in being creative.

The arts communicate the humanness in each one of us. They awaken learning because they touch the true inner being, the outlook of the self that is not body, the part that lies outside the domain of science—the spirit, the realm of dreams, caring, daring, and dedication. The arts, like the sciences, are symbolic systems that communicate meaning about the world (Fowler, 1989).

Individual expression is found in the art activities of many contemporary programs for young children. Classrooms in which every child is given exactly the same paper construction to do leave no room for the children's interpretation of reality or their outpouring of ideas and feelings. Used properly, though, music, movement, and art can serve as vehicles for creative expression and can enhance individuality and creativity.

There are those who believe that creativity flourishes only when children are given free rein with materials and that any requirement for their activity is an unnecessary and stifling imposition. Others feel that children left unbridled cannot develop the inner discipline and self-reflection necessary for creative activity. In reality, children can benefit from a variety of structures and degrees of adult intervention. Formal relationships between teachers and children do not necessarily lead to stereotyped activity. Involvement in a Froebelian kindergarten and training in the prescribed use of blocks—one of the Froebelian *Gifts*—had a major formative influence on Frank Lloyd Wright, one of the most creative American architects (Kaufman, 1989). Froebel (1782–1852) praised the importance of blocks for building activities and applied them as learning tools in his curriculum. He presented a series of toys or apparatus known as *Gifts*, which were arranged in ascending order. Blocks were used from the second *Gift* through the sixth. Since Froebel's initial teachings and writings in this area, the advantages and values inherent in blocks have been continuously valued by educators (Gelfer & Perkins, 1987).

The arts are to be valued in school as a way of using feelings, sensitivities, and understandings that require expression in a nonrational, often nonlinear form. Shaping the children's expression into two- or three-dimensional constructions, into sound patterns, or into the deliberate development of movement patterns extends their way of understanding the world in a manner not possible through the sciences or conventional verbal description. The arts express a personal way of knowing, but one that can be shared with others.

According to Nancy R. Smith (1983), children build basic concepts of the world of objects and how they work, and of their own effectiveness in this world, through their experiences. This world of materials lends itself to representation. Through representation, children create meanings. By age four or five the practice has matured into a beginning repertoire of concepts. Children become interested in favorite themes to authenticate their identity. During this phase, children initiate their reactions to and descriptions of the outer world in relation to their own identity. Universal themes emerge including families (animals, humans), homes (rooms, furniture), space, school, city life (buses, cars, street lights), natural phenomena (flowers, volcanoes, caves, tunnels), friends and pets, food (cookies, pizzas), and wonderful combinations of these themes (Neubert, 1991). Artistic representations have a narrative strand (the idea of the story), an emotional strand (the feelings communicated), and a compositional strand (the interest and unity created by the arrangement of elements). The aesthetic qualities of artistic work are rooted in the quality of the meanings and the organization of each strand and the whole.

Creativity

Creativity is the process of developing original, high-quality, genuinely significant products. In teaching young children, emphasis should be placed on developing and generating original ideas, the basis for creative potential. Teachers' acceptance of multiple ideas, without evaluation, will encourage children to generate more ideas or to move to the next phase of self-evaluation. As children develop the ability to evaluate themselves, concerns about quality and the creation of products become more meaningful. Although most teachers of young children know that the creative arts are a legitimate and crucial element of the curriculum, many depend on product-oriented activities instead of valuing the children's creative process (Edwards & Nabors, 1993). An emphasis on production alone, however, does not lead to creative products. Moran, Sawyers, and Moore (1988) found that explicit instructions for the use of structured materials reduce flexibility in four-year-old children.

Creativity is a basic component of problem solving. It is used to solve special kinds of problems, usually complex ones. Popular or conventional responses will not help solve these problems. Creativity requires flexible modification of thoughts. The Carnegie Report (1986) suggests that students need to possess these critical skills.

Mary L. Marksberry (1963) identifies three types of creative products: unique communications, plans or proposed sets of operations, and sets of abstract relations. Music, movement, and art activities generally produce creative products in the first category: a painting, a piece of sculpture, a musical selection, or a series of movements. Other areas of the curriculum, such as language arts—including children's own stories, poems, or special descriptive phrases—are unique communications. Personal interpretations of other people's works might also be considered unique communications. The other two types of creative products can also be found in early childhood programs. The techniques for learning science and social studies lead children to create plans and proposed sets of operations that often result in the creation of sets of abstract relations.

Teaching music, movement, and art cannot be understood only in terms of creativity, for in dealing with these expressions, one must deal with concepts of aesthetics as well. Young children must be surrounded by beautiful things to begin to appreciate and understand beauty. They also must learn to criticize their own work and that of others constructively to develop criteria of aesthetic appreciation. Such criticism need not be negative or sophisticated. As children experience the creative process themselves and share their expressions with others, and as they mature to the point that they can separate themselves from their products, they can learn to become critics and accept criticism themselves. Elwyn Richardson (1969) described how children developed sensitivity to aesthetic components as a result of the criticism of their art work. Such criticism heightened their appreciation of others' individuality and helped them develop more artistic approaches to materials.

The Creative Process

Gladys Andrews (1954) suggested that the creative process involves three phases: "(1) The child and his creative power, feelings, and imagination;

(2) the action or interaction of his experience; and (3) his outward form of expression" (p. 21). The experience of putting one's expressions in concrete form using words, paints, musical rhythms, or movement through space is the culmination of a chain of events. Each aspect of the creative process should be supported in the classroom. Children must be given opportunities to freely use their imaginations, with the products of imaginative thought accepted and cherished. Children must feel a degree of acceptance in a climate in which they are viewed as competent individuals, important and worthy.

Children should be provided with a broad range of experiences. Children who can see, hear, taste, smell, and touch a great variety of things have access to the raw material of creative expression. Jeannette F. Lacy (n.d.) suggests training children in visual literacy to enable them to look at, see, select, evaluate, record, correct, and restate their experiences. Children can be made aware of the examples of beauty in their natural environment and in the world of their personal vision and response. Lacy suggests helping children learn the elements of artistic composition—line, shape, color, value, and texture—through this training in visual literacy. Perhaps this idea could be generalized to other areas of personal sensation as well, to provide a broad basis for children's creative expression.

Sensory perceptions are meaningless, however, when provided in isolation. Giving children a set of color chips, a set of tone blocks, or a board covered with materials of various textures may help them become aware of sensory experiences or learn to name and categorize them, but the creative process may be thwarted if these isolated sensory explorations become the sum and substance of their education. Creativity grows out of experiencing the rich fabric of sensory images woven into the complexities of real life. Children who are taken to the docks of a seaport can not only perceive the visual images of ships, cargo, and machines but also have this experience heightened by the smell of salt water, the feel of damp air on their skin, and the sounds of sea gulls. They can then represent personally meaningful portions of the experience through art. Similarly, children who are allowed to sit for long periods of time watching the movement of a lonely insect in a field—seeing how it travels from place to place, how it eats and collects its food—have a perception of the natural world far richer than that provided through a book. Experiencing the world in its realistic state is an important part of the creative process.

The opportunity to interact with their environment is just as important for children as the opportunity to observe it. This interaction may be physical, as they talk to people or touch things. It can also be intellectual, an internal process that allows them to reflect on experience and abstract significant aspects for further study. They can compare recent experiences with ones remembered from an earlier time, comparing their perceptions and interactions with those of other people. The abstraction of personal meaning from the surrounding world provides the raw material from which creative expressions are derived, while the expressive act serves as a way to integrate these meanings into mental structures.

As children develop outward forms of expression, they learn to master media so that their expression is deliberate rather than accidental. This means teaching children to use the self—body for movement, hands for painting and modeling—to control the media. Paints and brushes become an extension of the person, as do musical instruments, words, and all the raw materials out of which we create artistic products.

The quality of the materials and tools provided in early childhood classes is important. Materials must extend rather than limit possibilities. A sturdy brush for painting is better than a string or a piece of sponge if it allows greater control of the expression. Modeling clay that is malleable and responsive is more useful than oil-based Plasticine because children have greater control over it. The attractiveness of the final product is not the criterion for success. The degree to which the product—painting, pot, movement pattern, or song theme—is a deliberate outgrowth of the children's intent and extends their ability to express themselves determines the success and worthiness of the activity.

Young children are to some extent stimulus bound. The use of a medium of expression becomes a significant experience that, in effect, transforms itself. Colors dripping into each other on a painting may elicit new forms and new colors that will stimulate opportunities not even present at first. These explorations should be supported, for through individual exploration of the medium, children develop control.

CHILDREN'S DEVELOPMENTAL STAGES IN ART

Improving artistic expression is not merely a matter of teaching children control. The stages of human development influence children's creations as much as anything else. A substantive difference exists between children and adults that cannot be explained on the basis of experiences alone. Every person goes through a series of metamorphoses in development so that each level is different in kind from the one preceding it and those following it. It is enticing to observe the development of young children's drawings. Young children's drawings instantaneously unfold from energetic scribbles to delightful, dramatic expressions of form and figure. In a four-year longitudinal preschool study, Clare (1988) found that scribble patterns are reflections of accidental motor activity and that a large drawing surface allows children to express their drawings in more detail because they can use their gross motor movements more effectively. Clare also found that some children tend to draw a graduated series of figures from small to large or vice versa. Children who do not include a torso in their human drawings have the capacity to do so but either choose not to or do not think of doing so.

Table 16.1

Children's Developmental Stages in Art

Stage	Age	Characteristics
Scribbling	2 to 4 years	• lacks control over motor activities • associates motions and marks • initiates complex motions • relates motions with creative experiences
Preschematic	4 to 7 years	• parallels actual drawing with representation • initiates an interest in representation
Schematic	7 to 9 years	• breakthrough in social independence • individual perception for people and their environment • restriction on the child's knowledge about the environment • represents unforeseen experience (Lowenfeld & Brittain, 1987)

Levels of artistic development have been identified as being similar to those of intellectual development (see Table 16–1). Victor Lowenfeld and W. Lambert Brittain (1987) describe a scheme of stages in the artistic development of children. The levels of development in early childhood include the *scribbling* stage (ages two to four), the *preschematic* stage (ages four to seven), and the *schematic* stage (ages seven to nine).

Between the ages of two and four, children in the scribbling stage have a kinesthetic experience through drawing. They move through longitudinal to circular motions, becoming more coordinated as they mature. Children first experiment with materials and then find likenesses in their drawings to objects in the real world, thus coming up with "names" to give the drawings.

Between the ages of four and seven, children in the preschematic stage discover the relationships between drawing, thinking, and reality. Although a continuous change occurs in the symbols children create as they continue to draw, children start out with an idea of the objects they want to represent. They begin to develop representational forms, although these may not be related in the picture as in reality. Objects in a picture may range all over the page, with no relationship to where they actually are in a scene. Children are also developing concepts about form and shape.

When children move to the schematic stage, between seven and nine, they begin to create realistic representations of people and things. They learn to use color and space realistically and to depict movement in pictures. The children then move on to more mature stages of artistic development.

Lowenfeld and Brittain's stages in art closely parallel Jean Piaget's stages of intellectual development. It is quite possible that artistic expression is related to the child's levels of perception conceptions, muscular control, and coordination. Children's artistic development is to some extent a function of general intellectual and physical development.

Geraldine Dimondstein (1974) suggests that the use of stages to explain changes in children's art products has tended to inhibit teachers' fresh perceptions of the specific qualities of an art product. It has also perpetuated the myth that teachers should leave children to grow through these stages rather than helping them to move from one stage to the next. These dangers grow from a conception of development as maturation. A conception of stages can help teachers establish tentative expectations for children. It can also help them interpret children's products and determine what are the best next steps for the children and how to help them to take those steps. Thus, an interactionist view of stages in artistic development can enhance assessment and future planning for increased learning.

What children do or how they develop does not predetermine how they should be taught or what the content of instruction ought to be. It does, however, establish a framework within which goals can be determined and expectations set. Knowledge of children's development in art also suggests directions for education, so that teachers can help children move from present stages to more mature stages. Children in nursery school, for example, should not be expected to create representational paintings and drawings. Nor should kindergarten children be expected to draw a room with all the objects shown in proper size and place relationship to one another.

The concept of stages of development in art by itself does not suggest that teachers ought to wait for children to mature. The role of teachers is to guide children to arrive at more mature ways of handling media and creating expressions. A knowledge of stages of development provides a series of benchmarks that teachers can use in directing children's learning. However, Patricia Tarr (1991) suggests that art educators tend to focus in teacher training and research on children five years of age and older, rather than on preschool-age children. Adults place greater value on the representational works of school-age children than on the marks created by children working at the preschematic stage. Tarr shows that attitudes toward children's preschematic art are reflected in the negative language used to describe this period of art making. Focusing on the product makes educators forget the creative process, so that they cannot see children's drawings as anything but irregular marks or forms created during their sensory-motor developmental level (Tarr, 1991).

Art as a Scholarly Discipline

Jessica Davis and Howard Gardner (1993) conceive of young children as artists. As artists, young children must develop the symbolic tools of literacy in the visual arts. They must also be able to "read" the aesthetic symbols of their culture. This need to develop literacy in aesthetic symbols is reflected in *Discipline-Based Art Education* (DBAE) for older children. This approach suggests that children should be educated in art production, art history, art criticism, and aesthetics (Smith, 1989). The notion of the discipline of art as a basis of early childhood programs is a relatively new approach. In general, the performance part of the arts has been integrated into early childhood programs. But helping children to learn the symbolic tools of artistic literacy as well as to be able to read the aesthetic symbols of their culture is an intriguing idea.

Building on children's intuitive knowledge, teachers can help young children attend to the qualities of their art work. They can also surround children with mature art, especially with works that parallel the works of the children. Teachers can also provide children with tools for art and help them become more competent in their control of those tools. These elements can be provided in a framework that is developmentally appropriate.

Discipline-Based Art Education consists of four components: art production, art history, art criticism, and aesthetics. Art production will be discussed later in this chapter. This section will present ideas related to art criticism, art history, and aesthetics.

Art Criticism

Young children begin art criticism before adults recognize the children's visual reactions. From the preschool years on, teachers' questioning can systematize young children's liberated conversations about art. Teachers

Table 16.2

Stages of Young Children's Art Criticism and Related Encouragement

Stage	Example of Encouragement
1. **Description:** Taking an inventory by listing all the literal qualities visible in a work of art.	"Pretend you're talking to me on the telephone. Can you name the things in this picture so that I"ll be able to recognize it?"
2. **Analysis:** Determining the relationships among qualities in an art work (line shape, space, color, texture, and balance).	"How do the colors get along? Are they quiet or noisy? Fighting or friendly?"
3. **Interpretation:** Responding to questions that focus children's attention on ideas, feelings, or moods communicated by the work of art.	"What happened just before or just after this scene?"
4. **Judgment:** Using information from previous stages to derive a conclusion.	"Which do you like the most: the story the art tells, the shapes and colors and designs in it, or the way it makes you feel when you look at it?" (Feldman, 1970; Cole & Schaefer, 1990)

can help children articulate their impressions of works of art. Children can learn to interpret lines, shapes, and clusters of marks so they can begin to read visual images in works of art. In order for effective criticism to occur, there must be a communicator (the artist); a medium (the artwork); and a receiver who accepts, interprets, and incorporates what is sent (the viewer), as well as a facilitator (the teacher) who guides the encounter between the work of art and the children (Cole & Schaefer, 1990).

In the critical process, a provocative dialogue must occur to help viewers scrutinize a work of art to examine everything about the art work even if they do not like the work. Four general stages of art criticism can be identified (Feldman, 1970). We can match these stages to ways of encouraging young children's art criticism (Cole & Schaefer, 1990).

Currently art museums are introducing very young children to the pleasures of enjoying and responding to works of art. They provide discussion with children about specific works of art and encourage young viewers to respond verbally to works of art.

Intellectually, art criticism initiates the process of logical and creative thinking. The procedure helps children to organize their thoughts. Children learn the pleasure of enjoying art. The combination of curiosity, emotional interest, and critical reflection is a highly charged experience. Children can look forward to discussing art works as they look forward to solving a new puzzle. Such discussions of art go beyond typical experiences in art appreciation (Cole & Schaefer, 1990).

Art History

Research suggests that children below the primary grades lack the understanding of time necessary to gain insights into formal history. There is evidence, however, that these children can learn some history if it is presented in a concrete manner (Sunal, 1993). Thus, if educators are to teach anything about art history to young children, they must present it in a concrete form. Good examples of such concrete presentations are found in the *Early Childhood Discovery Boxes* of the Toledo Museum of Art (Box 1013, Toledo, OH 43697). This museum has developed a set of self-contained activity boxes based on different art themes. Two of these discovery boxes deal with art history—one on ancient Egypt and the other on medieval Europe.

Each Discovery Box contains a teachers' guide, a set of art reproductions related to the theme, a set of costumes and props, a set of books, an audio cassette tape, and other resources. Through the resources provided, children learn about the time and culture of the works of art provided. Children can dress up and role-play activities of the period, for example, writing hieroglyphics, building tombs, or making jewelry of the period that they can wear. They then learn about the works of art of the period, using the museum reproductions as examples. Providing the context

Activity — STEPS IN DEVELOPING A SENSE OF ART HISTORY

1. **Match identical paintings.** Matching three identical pairs of simple subjects (for instance, two copies each of a hare by Durer, a chair by Van Gogh, and an abstract resembling a Tinkertoy by Miro) is an easy task for young children. As soon as children are able to match these identical paintings, add more pairs, one pair at a time (for instance, *A Girl with a Watering Can* by Renoir, and then *Pot of Geraniums* by Matisse). Increase the difficulty as children are able to master each task.
2. **Pair similar paintings by an artist.** Once children can match identical pairs, children can learn to pair companion drawings by the same artist. This task requires children to recognize a similarity in subject and style in two examples of a painter's work. For example, a child can pair two paintings of ballet dancers by Degas, two Audubon paintings of birds, and two Mondrian geometric designs. Difficulty is gradually increased.
3. **Group paintings by an artist.** Children group four paintings by three different artists. Begin with highly contrasting subjects such as four still lifes by Cezanne, four abstracts by Kandinsky, and four paintings of people by Goya. If children are successful with this task, print the artist's last name under one of his or her four paintings. Children can capture a visual impression to associate with the style of each artist.
4. **Learn about artists and their times.** At this point, challenge children based not on their age but on their level of experience. Beginning readers can learn to recognize the names of important artists and the titles of some of their most famous paintings. Further experience can help them to classify paintings based on the characteristics of some of the well-known art schools. Ultimately, they can organize postcard-size reproductions consecutively on a time line, acquiring a visual representation of the development of art through the centuries. (Wolf, 1990)

information and the props for dramatic play allows the children to gain information about art history in a developmentally appropriate way.

Postcard-size reproductions of art works can be used to teach children. Such reproductions are sized to a child's hand and are small and lightweight enough to be used in a variety of activities, such as matching, pairing, sorting, and placing in chronological order.

Aesthetics

Aesthetics
is the study of beauty.

Early childhood educators from Froebel through Montessori acknowledged the profound aesthetic appreciation of young children. **Aesthetics** is the awareness and appreciation of pleasant sensory experiences. Specifically, it is the ability to judge works of art critically, based on criteria defined by a culture. Feeney and Moravcik (1987) define aesthetics as the love of beauty, as well as criteria for evaluating beauty and individual taste. Aesthetic perception includes the ability to react to the uniqueness, the singular quality of things—to benefit from the integrity of individual objects and to decline the cliché and the stereotype.

Feeney and Moravcik (1987) believe young children are able to acquire aesthetic experience and develop the foundation for a lifetime of enjoyment of art. Young children can develop their aesthetic sense when they have opportunities to create and appreciate beauty. Gilliat (1983) emphasizes that teachers must provide direct opportunities for art appreciation for this type of learning to occur. In observing classrooms to determine how they supported development of aesthetic appreciation in young children, Feeney and Moravcik (1987) found that classrooms were usually cluttered or decorated with "cute" commercial products; many consumer goods were unattractive and of poor quality. Apparently, teachers failed to encourage aesthetic sense. Feeney and Moravcik suggest that attention be paid to color, furnishings, storage, decoration, and the outdoor environment to create an aesthetically pleasing environment.

IDEAS TO ENHANCE AESTHETIC QUALITIES OF CLASSROOMS

1. **Color.** Bright colors overshadow a room and may detract from artistic and natural beauty. Soft, light, neutral colors for walls and ceilings should be selected. Learning centers should be color coordinated to help children to view them as a whole instead of as parts. A variety of patterns in any one place can be distracting and should be avoided.
2. **Furnishings.** Similar furniture should be clustered together. Colors must be natural and neutral to focus the children's attention on the learning materials on the shelves.
3. **Storage.** Materials on shelves should be rotated, with only a few materials available at any one time instead of having many materials crammed together. Materials can be stored in attractive containers. For example, storage tubes should be placed together on one shelf, and cardboard boxes should be painted or covered with plain colored paper.
4. **Decoration.** Children's work should be mounted before it is displayed. The work of fine artists should be displayed rather than garish, stereotyped posters. Children's and artists' works should be displayed at the children's eye level. Sculpture, plants, and items of natural beauty (such as shells, stones, and fish tanks) are displayed on top shelves, not teachers' materials. If teachers are short of storage space, they can create a teacher cubby consisting of a covered box or storage tub.
5. **Outdoor Environment.** Play structures should be designed and organized to reflect an extension of nature instead of an imposition on it. Natural materials, such as wood or hemp, should be used instead of painted metal, plastic, or fiberglass. Materials can be conserved when they are stored appropriately. Children, parents, and staff can help maintain a clean outdoor environment that is free of trash. A garden, rock arrangement, or other modest arrangements can be included to communicate that the outdoors merits attention and care. (Feeney and Moravcik, 1987)

Many early childhood educators have recognized the importance of beauty in the lives of young children. Aesthetic appreciation has been included in the revised curriculum for kindergarten education in Japan. Teachers can make children more sensitive to the beauty that surrounds them and help them understand the aesthetic elements in their culture by borrowing from Japanese kindergarten programs. Japanese kindergartens are often decorated with a large mural that may cover an entire wall. The mural is made by the teacher and includes a variety of material, including drawing, painting, and collage. The mural may reflect the season of the year or another theme. Often the mural includes many kinds of Japanese paper, reflecting a long tradition of paper making in Japan. Although there is no similar tradition of mural making in America, such murals could be incorporated into early childhood classrooms.

Another idea that could be adopted from Japan is the *tokonoma*, an alcove in the tatami room that is found in traditional Japanese homes and inns. The rooms themselves, their floors covered with straw mats or *tatamis*, are sparsely furnished. On one wall is usually a small alcove, the *tokonoma*, that is devoted to the display of something beautiful—a scroll, a flower arrangement, or a ceramic piece, for example. The display adds beauty to the surroundings. Kindergarten or prekindergarten teachers could establish their own *tokonoma*, or beauty area, just as they might have a science or nature display area. An art reproduction or a vase of flowers could be tastefully displayed in this area. Children can observe the display on their own, and teachers can engage them in discussions about the display and why it is considered beautiful. Infant schools in England used similar displays and discussions during the height of the informal education movement, when children's expression and aesthetics were valued in English schools.

ARTS AND CRAFTS

Arts and crafts activities are often considered less important in the primary grades than in the nursery school and kindergarten. Too often arts and crafts work is designed solely to insure that a finished product will be presentable and that each child will have something to take home. This practice makes for good public relations, for parents can see that their children are doing something in class. At times it is appropriate to have children make a product for the home, such as a Christmas or Mother's Day gift. However, concern for the image of the school should not take precedence over learning, for the goal of the school is not products but the children's growing mastery over materials. The children's completed works have significance only in that they provide teachers with insights into what the children have learned and what difficulties they still must master.

The most productive art media for young children are those that can be used at any age level. Paints, clay, drawing, and collage, for example, can be used by the three-year-old as well as by the mature artist. To promote the creative process in children's art, teachers should provide an abundant assortment of materials to encourage children's art work. Naomi Pile (1973) identifies the basic art materials as paint, clay, and drawing and collage material. These materials are basically formless and offer endless possibilities for change, mastery, surprise, and self-reflection. For small drawing paper, teachers should provide colored markers and pencils. They should provide large drawing paper for use with blunt instruments such as crayons and brushes (Clare, 1988). Teachers should not limit a medium to a particular age level. Nor should the children's prior experience with the material concern teachers, because in their developing competency, young children will continue to see in these media fresh possibilities that represent increased mastery and maturing artistic development. The materials, however, do need to be introduced in fresh ways through the years.

Two-Dimensional Art Work

Much of the art children do in early childhood programs involves using materials on a flat surface. Paints, crayons, and collage materials are used on a single plane, although collages can have depth as a result of overlaying various materials and textures. The children's concern is primarily with line, shape, and color.

Painting Painting is one of the mainstays of the early childhood program. In many classrooms, an easel is accessible to the children for a good part of the day. The top of a table or a bit of floor space is just as good. A level surface, as a matter of fact, will limit the amount of dripping that occurs during the painting. Teachers should organize the painting area so that cleanup is as simple as possible, having children spread papers under their paintings and making sponges and paper towels readily available. They should keep paints in containers that can be covered.

The teacher's role is not to provide models for children to copy but to encourage them to explore the media and to observe and guide their progress, providing new techniques consistent with the children's development and needs.

Finger Paints Though finger paints are often difficult for children to control, they offer children a kind of release not matched by other media. Children have direct contact with the medium. For finger painting, glossy nonabsorbent paper is available from school supply houses; glazed shelf paper may also be used. Sometimes the painting can be done on the plastic surface of a table. When children are finished painting, a print can be made by carefully placing a paper over the painting, pressing it down firmly all over, and carefully lifting it off.

Finger painting can be done on the plastic surface of a table.

Activity FINGER PAINT DESIGN

Children can create a design using finger paint and hang their painting to dry overnight. The next day, have the children trace their design on tag board, cut it out, and paste it on construction paper. The design does not have to be cut exactly the way the children drew it; therefore, this activity is appropriate for children with a range of physical skills.

Tempera Paints Tempera paints come in either powdered or liquid form. If powdered, they should be mixed thickly enough so that the colors will be rich and the paint opaque. For young children, the primary colors (red, blue, and yellow), along with black and white, are adequate; intermediate colors can be added later. Color mixing using a cookie sheet palette can lead to new discoveries. Young children can experiment with form and color, moving their arms to form shapes on paper. These experiments often have rhythm, balance, and interest. Many children appear to have an instinctive aesthetic sense, and their abstract paintings sometimes resemble works of art.

Although young children should be encouraged to explore and experiment, teachers can demonstrate simple techniques for controlling the medium: wiping the brush so that it is not overloaded with paint, cleaning brushes before using them for other colors, mixing colors in specific proportions to achieve desired results, and placing the right brush into the right container of paint. However, a color mixture that results from an improperly placed brush or an accidental drip can lead to exciting learning.

Activity MAGAZINE AND TEMPERA PICTURES

Wash styrofoam meat trays carefully with soap and water to remove any residue of the meat. After the trays have dried completely, children can paint the trays with tempera paint (using a second coat if necessary). Let the painted trays dry for at least a day. The next day, have the children cut out pictures from magazines and glue them on the painted trays. Attach yarn to the top of the tray for hanging.

Brushes should be large and rather stiff so they respond easily to movement. Several sizes should be available. Most of the painting in classrooms is done on unprinted newsprint. The standard size is 18-by-24-inch; paper of a different size, shape, or even texture will stimulate new ways of painting. The classified section of a newspaper or a piece of wrapping paper with a small design might also be used for painting.

Tempera painting is usually an individual activity. Even when two children are painting together at an easel, they are seldom interacting, for their work is separated. Children, however, enjoy painting side by side or in groups. A double easel or the floor supports painting as a group activity, as does mural painting.

Murals Children can paint murals on large sheets of brown wrapping paper, which many schools keep available. At first, young children's murals will actually be collections of individual paintings. There is usually little group planning, and teachers often find it useful to simply allocate space on different parts of the paper to different children. As the children mature and gain experience, they can begin to plan toward a unified product.

Activity CELLOPHANE MURAL

Tape colored cellophane to a windowpane that the children can reach. Have the children draw a mural of a story, the neighborhood, the zoo, or anything of interest to them using a variety of colors of tempera paint and brushes. Leave the mural on the window. The children will enjoy their mural as the light shines through the windows.

Wax Crayons Early childhood classrooms almost always contain wax crayons. Their use requires little teacher preparation, they seldom create much of a mess, and they are easily available. Large hexagonal or half-round crayons make bold, controllable strokes and will not roll off the table. Children may be given their own sets of crayons, or crayons may be kept in a class pool. Large sheets of manila paper are useful for coloring with crayons, but other kinds of paper can be used as well.

As the children learn to use crayons, they can also be encouraged to mix crayons with other media. A waxy crayon drawing provides a surface to which tempera paint will not adhere, so covering the surface with a single coat of paint allows the crayon drawing to stand out in interesting relief.

Colored Markers Children can use colored markers for drawing much as they would use crayons. The variety of colors available enhances children's drawings. Children need to learn to care for markers, covering them so they don't dry out. Teachers should provide only washable markers; the permanent ones can damage clothing.

Chalk Children can use colored or white chalk at a chalkboard. Chalk can also be used on paper; wetting the paper with water or buttermilk makes the colors show up more brilliantly, and spraying a fixative on the chalk drawings keeps them from rubbing off the paper.

Cutting, Tearing, and Pasting Paper Using paper to create interesting designs has long been a school activity. The Japanese art of origami involves creating three-dimensional forms by folding a piece of paper. Children can also create interesting two-dimensional designs. For very young children, teachers can cut pieces of colored paper in various shapes to be pasted on a background. As children develop competence in using scissors, they can create their own shapes.

VIGNETTE: ART, PRESCHOOL

The children are gathered in a circle as the teacher tells them that they are going to make a very special art project. She asks them to think about times that they have either been in church or seen churches. "What kind of special windows do churches sometimes have?" she asks. The students respond with many answers.

"My church has big windows," answers Todd.

"Mine has yellow ones that let the sun shine in on us, and it gets in my eyes," responds Mary.

The teacher listens to the answers that the children give and then asks if any of them have seen windows that have pictures or different colors. One girl raises her hand and says that she thinks they are called stained windows.

The teacher smiles and says, "That's exactly right, Amy. Many churches, especially older churches, have windows that are called stained glass windows because the panes of glass are different colors. Sometimes there are pictures in the windows. And sometimes you can look at the windows in different ways and see different pictures."

Mark interrupts the teacher, saying, "Yeah, my church has windows like that, and I see birds and flowers in them."

The teacher explains that the students are going to make their own stained glass windows out of tissue paper. Each one will be different. The teacher begins demonstrating how to make the stained glass windows, as the students sit in a circle around her.

"First, you will take a piece of tissue paper and fold it in half. After you fold it, open it up again, and make sure you can see where the fold is. Then take a long piece of yarn and dip it into this runny glue. I've added some water to my glue to make it a little runny so it will be easier to work with. Put the yarn in the glue and make sure to get the glue all over the yarn. Now, here comes the tricky part. You are going to bring the yarn out of the glue without making a disaster. Pull the yarn out of the glue by running it between your fingers to remove extra glue. See how I'm doing this. Once the yarn is out of the glue, place it in any design on your piece of tissue paper. Be careful to put the yarn on only one side of the tissue paper. Then quickly fold the tissue paper in half along the same crease line that you had before. Now I can hold my tissue paper up to the light and we can see what shapes and images I've created."

The teacher stands up and moves over to the window. She holds her stained glass project up to the window, pointing out the lines created by the yarn. "What do you see, boys and girls?" she asks.

Tiffany answers, "I like it that way. It looks like a duck."

Rodney disagrees, "Turn it upside down the other way. Now it looks like a plane."

"OK," the teacher announces, "I'm going to let my stained glass dry overnight, and tomorrow when we come in we'll be able to hang mine and the ones that you are about to make on the window."

She then instructs the students to quietly walk over to the art table and wait for the two assistants to help them get started on their windows.

Collages Using materials other than paper can increase the variety of textures, colors, and shapes in collages. Teachers can pick up many scavenged materials rather than ordering them from a supply house. A variety of materials, organized so that teachers and children can select them without too much difficulty, enhances an art program. Various kinds of special paper and cardboard; pieces of fabric of various sizes, shapes, colors, and textures; bits of rope and yarn; feathers; buttons; colored sawdust; metal foil; and almost any other kind of material can be shaped, cut, pasted, and otherwise included in a collage. Children should be offered a limited variety of these materials at any one time, but they can also be encouraged to think of new materials. Using varied materials means coming up with various ways to attach them to paper: rubber cement, white glue, staples, or cellophane tape.

Many kinds of materials can be used to make collages.

Printing Designs There are many ways of printing designs. Dipping an object with an interesting texture or shape into a shallow dish of tempera paint and pressing it firmly on a sheet of paper works well. Sponges, grainy ends of wooden boards, and vegetables such as carrots or potatoes are among the many materials that can be used. A design can be carved into these materials to enhance the printing. Teachers of very young children can create the designs and let the children print. Using different colors and patterns makes printing an interesting medium.

Three-Dimensional Constructions

In the early years, the three-dimensional media include woodworking, clay modeling, cardboard box constructions, and the creation of mobiles and stabiles.

Woodworking Children get a great deal of pleasure out of working with wood—the simple activity of hammering and sawing is often enough to satisfy very young children. Unfortunately, many teachers hesitate to include woodworking, usually because they lack experience with carpentry and tools. Hammers, saws, and other tools, if improperly used, can injure children, but young children can develop a respect for tools and learn to use them safely.

Glue can also be used to attach pieces of wood to each other or to other materials. If children have a wide choice of materials, they can easily create a boat from a large block of wood, with a smaller one on top for a cabin, or an airplane by gluing two narrow strips of wood at right angles—small pieces could also be glued in place for a tail, motor, and so on. Other things children can make with just wood and glue, without any tools, include a

Children can begin woodworking by making simple constructions.

small table and bench or chair for a doll, a small box for treasures, and innumerable other things. Even a classroom that is not equipped for any type of real carpentry can use this type of wood-with-glue-and-beautiful-junk activity as a variation during its art or activity period.

After the children have the idea that pieces of wood can go together to make things and have some experiences in selecting shapes and sizes of wood, they can acquire some simple skills with tools: driving one nail into crossed pieces of wood to make an airplane, drilling one hole to insert a piece of doweling for a smokestack or a mast on a boat, or making two cuts with a saw to produce a point for the bow of a boat.

Scrap wood is easy to find at almost any lumber yard, building supply store, or carpenter's or cabinetmaker's shop. Disposing of the scraps is usually one of their problems. They are usually willing to put scrap aside for teachers or to let them go through the scarp pile to find usable pieces. Teachers can find out when the lumberyard usually disposes of its rubbish and plan to go just beforehand in order to have a large selection. Teachers should select wood of all sizes and shapes, being sure it is clear, with no knots or blemishes, and finished, or planed down so there are no splinters. If children are going to be doing any hammering and sawing, the best wood is usually one-inch clear finished pine. Although one-inch boards, if finished, are actually only about three-fourths of an inch thick, they are still referred to as one-inch lumber. Other useful dimensions are one inch thick by two inches wide, one by four, one by six, two by four, and two by two. These come in varying lengths. In ordering lumber, one must give all three dimensions, in this order: thickness, width, and length (Pitcher, Feinburg, & Alexander, 1989).

A woodworking area should promote positive activities and avoid danger; it must be isolated to a certain degree from other activities. Tools and supplies should be stored so they are readily accessible and be in good order and in proper repair, with saws sharp and hammer handles firmly embedded in the heads. A number of accessories can be included as the children mature in their ability to use wood and tools. Lightweight but good-quality hammers and short crosscut saws should be provided. Sandpaper, block planes, rasps, and wood files help children smooth their woodwork. A brace and drill bits and hand drill are useful. Screwdrivers can be added as children learn to use screws as well as nails for fastening boards together. A woodworking vise, a workbench or saw horses, and C-clamps are useful, too.

Children usually begin by building simple constructions, often put together with nails and glue. As the projects are elaborated, teachers can add dowels, empty paper rolls, spools, and just about anything they and the children find useful. Woodworking projects can be painted with tempera and then covered with shellac or lacquer so the color will not run; enamel paint is harder to work with and to clean up.

Clay Modeling Clay is an excellent material for young children. It strengthens development of fine motor muscle control and promotes self-expression. Potter's clay is soft and malleable and can be used over and over. Clay of proper consistency can be stored in a plastic bag for an indefinite length of time. If it has dried out, water can be added to it; if it is too wet, it can be left to dry. Clay should be soft enough to work with and thick enough that it does not stick to the fingers. A grapefruit-sized piece of clay may be an appropriate size for children to work.

Young children enjoy manipulating clay. They knead it, pound it, roll it, flatten it, break it up, and push it all together again. Playing with the clay often takes precedence over creating something. Working with clay allows children to use their fingers and muscles in unusual ways. Very young children beat and pound the clay without any purpose. This play is similar to children's scribbling. Later, children make coils and balls, in a stage similar to controlled scribbling. Even later, the children will pick up chunks of clay, accompanying their action with noises, and name their chunk an airplane or say, "This is a car." At this point, children's thinking has matured to include imaginative thinking (Neubert, 1991).

Two- and three-year-old children can be gradually introduced to wooden clay tools and small objects to put on clay including shells, pods, and beads. Plastic and most metal tools should be avoided. Plastic will snap, break, and invisibly implant itself in the clay, cutting the children's hands; whereas metal cookie cutters will probably draw children into making patterns, inhibiting their creativity (Neubert, 1991). Later, children can learn to make pinch pots, pulling the clay into shapes and tearing off pieces. They can create figures, adding pieces of clay—heads, arms, and legs—to a rolled body to create people and animals. After a while, they can even learn to build pots, using the coil or slab method.

After children are through working with clay, they are often content to put it back into the crock. When they wish to save what they have made, however, the clay can be dried slowly and then painted. If a kiln is available in the school, seeing how the clay is transformed by heat is exciting for children. Teachers should make sure, however, that work to be fired in a kiln is sturdy and will not explode or come apart. If the children have worked over the clay for a while, it may not need to be wedged, that is, cut and pounded to eliminate air bubbles that might burst at high temperature. Pieces should not be too thick, and appendages should be securely attached. Teachers might wish to glaze some of the children's work.

In some classrooms, other modeling material such as Plasticine, an oil-based clay, is sometimes substituted for clay. Although Plasticine is not as responsive to modeling as is potter's clay, and the children's work cannot be preserved, Plasticine can be used again and again and will not dry out. Some teachers also use modeling dough, which can be purchased commercially or made out of simple household ingredients—salt, flour, and water.

Sculptures Simple constructions—houses, cash registers, rocket ships, or automobiles—can be made out of cardboard boxes and cartons that are cut up, pasted together, decorated with paper, and painted and colored. The skills the children have developed in two-dimensional work can be elaborated and used in endless constructions.

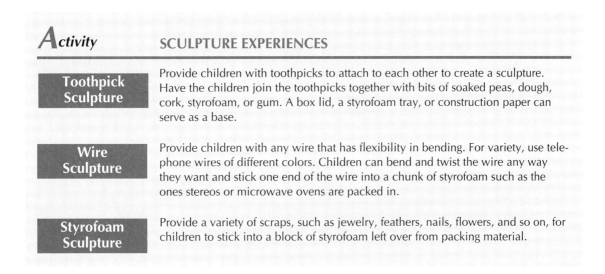

Activity SCULPTURE EXPERIENCES

Toothpick Sculpture

Provide children with toothpicks to attach to each other to create a sculpture. Have the children join the toothpicks together with bits of soaked peas, dough, cork, styrofoam, or gum. A box lid, a styrofoam tray, or construction paper can serve as a base.

Wire Sculpture

Provide children with any wire that has flexibility in bending. For variety, use telephone wires of different colors. Children can bend and twist the wire any way they want and stick one end of the wire into a chunk of styrofoam such as the ones stereos or microwave ovens are packed in.

Styrofoam Sculpture

Provide a variety of scraps, such as jewelry, feathers, nails, flowers, and so on, for children to stick into a block of styrofoam left over from packing material.

Mobiles and Stabiles Mobiles and stabiles are three-dimensional designs. Mobiles are designed to move; stabiles remain stationary. Both are created by combining a variety of materials in interesting fashions—dowels, tongue depressors, wire coat hangers, pipe cleaners, metal foil, yarn, balls, sponges, rubber bands, and so on. Bases for stabiles can be easily fashioned out of clay or styrofoam; mobiles are designed to hang and do not need a base.

Weaving Young children can weave on simple looms early in their school careers. *Loopers,* using cotton loops and simple metal looms, are a beginning. Teachers can also make simple looms out of squares of corrugated cardboard. Half-inch-deep slots in two opposite ends allow children to thread the loom; the yarn can then be woven back and forth until a square is completed. Simple looms can also be made by driving nails into the edges of wooden boxes or frames.

Sewing Children can begin to sew designs onto pieces of burlap with tapestry needles. In time, these designs can be combined with sewn pieces of felt or a similar fabric to create interesting pictures.

The classroom should be a place where children can explore material. Teachers can acknowledge accomplishment and provide criticism, but only in the spirit of guidance and to move children to further accomplishments. This work is the children's way of expressing themselves and so is personally important to them.

Music

As in art, children may go through stages in music. Frances Aronoff (1979) uses Jerome Bruner's conception of three modes of learning—*enactive, iconic,* and *symbolic*—in her framework of music education: "(1) the *enactive* through action and manipulation; (2) the *iconic* through perceptual organization and inquiry—aural, kinesthetic and visual; and (3) the *symbolic* through words and symbols" (p. 7). She suggests that the enactive and iconic modes are the ways in which young children know music. They respond readily to the elements of music through movement and play. Without using symbols, they are able to organize their perceptions of and responses to music, forming mental structures that become the basis for understanding, remembering, and creating music. This use of a Brunerian framework also suggests that the development of concepts in music is a function of general intellectual development. Other conceptions of musical development also exist (see Peery, 1993).

Aronoff defines the discipline of music as including concepts of music; concepts about music; a repertoire of songs, patterns, and qualities of sound; and musical skills. Skills include listening, singing, playing, moving, and reading and writing music. A music program in early childhood education, therefore, should provide children with opportunities to listen to music, to learn to understand its elements, to reproduce these elements through singing and playing instruments, and to relate bodily movement to musical expression. Creation of musical compositions or movements should also be included. The music program must relate to other parts of the curriculum, especially the language arts and social studies, to help children learn about the uses of music in various cultures. Such a program provides opportunities for children to deal critically with music, to learn to reproduce it, and to learn to express themselves through it. When teachers include a wealth of musical experiences in programs for young children, the children, in addition to learning about music, learn about language arts and other subjects (Wolf, 1992). Song lyrics possess qualities that assist children to relate oral and printed language (Barclay & Walwer, 1992).

The Pillsbury Foundation Studies of 1937–1938 (Zimmerman, 1985) identified four propositions that control young children's relationship to music:

1. Music is basically the discovery of sound.
2. Music must contain purposive action or involvement.
3. Music demands that social, environmental, and procedural conditions be considered.
4. Music should be spontaneous.

These propositions can provide guidelines for selecting and creating music activities for young children.

Though movement is often a child's initial reaction to music, it is usually neglected as an opportunity to participate in a variety of experiences (Stamp, 1992). Children, however, come to understand music through their movements. They respond to music with fast or slow, large or small, continuous or discontinuous movements. They respond physically to changes in pitch as well. Creative music and movement are noisy activities—a teacher cannot allow children to experiment with the sounds of a drum while a reading lesson is in progress. Specific times should be set aside and musical noise and movement controlled so that real learning can occur.

Many music and movement sessions are organized as large-group activities; children also need times to work alone or in small groups. During the activity period, a portion of the room can be set aside for movement. Musical instruments can be furnished for use by a few children; others can listen to a tape recorder or phonograph, possibly using headphones. The music that children create in their ongoing activities can be recorded or transcribed by the teacher. A multipurpose room, the play yard, an auditorium, or a gymnasium are often available for a portion of the day for such activities.

Music programs for the early years of school generally consist of singing, playing simple instruments, listening, and creative movement. Often creative movement involves children in mime and creative dramatics. Even when musical activities are the responsibility of a music teacher, the classroom teacher has some obligation. There are many opportunities in a school day that support music education and many ways to integrate music into children's learning.

Singing

Almost all children enjoy singing. They sing loudly, often with more energy than skill. Young children pick up songs they hear and repeat them to the best of their ability, sometimes repeating a phrase over and over, often mispronouncing or not completely learning the words. At times the pitch is off, but this seldom discourages young children in their continued singing. Teachers should capitalize on this enthusiasm. Greater adherence to melody and verse comes with experience and repetition. Young children have different levels of singing accuracy, the ability to clearly imitate a melody without assistance. Accuracy levels vary from not being able to imitate a melody at all to singing a song without any assistance and without any melodic errors (Raut, 1985). Children do not learn to sing a tune accuractely until they are about eight years old (McDonald, 1979).

Teachers need to perceive themselves as participants in order to be able to relax and concentrate on the musical activity rather than on themselves (Jalongo & Collins 1985). Thus, teachers should not be performers but should sing *with* children.

Robert Smith (1970) has designed a signing program to develop and improve children's vocal accuracy, range, and quality. Songs chosen to help this development, according to Smith, should continue to appeal to children after many repetitions; they should include melodic phrase repetition, repeated word phrases, and the appropriate vocal range for the children's stage of vocal development.

The piano and other instruments, such as the autoharp or guitar, can be played to accompany the children's singing. However, some music

Children enjoy singing in groups.

Activity HALLOWEEN SONG AND ART

SONG

TUNE: "Did You Ever See a Lassie?"

Once I had a pumpkin, A pumpkin, a pumpkin,
Oh, once I had a pumpkin, With no face at all,
With no eyes, With no nose,
And no mouth, And no teeth.
Oh, once I had a pumpkin, With no face at all.

So I made a Jack-o'-lantern, Jack-o'-lantern, Jack-o'-lantern,
So I made a Jack-o'-lantern, With a big funny face,
With big eyes, And big nose,
And big mouth, And big teeth.
So I made a Jack-o'-lantern, With a big funny face.

ART

Follow-Up Art Activities

1. Children can draw a pumpkin and a jack-o'-lantern. Provide black, yellow, and orange construction paper, scissors, paste, and crayons. Children can draw a pumpkin, cut it out, and paste it on black construction paper.
2. Cut one set of pumpkin and jack-o'-lantern features out of different colors of flannel for a flannelboard. Use this material to dramatize the song as it is sung.

educators feel that instrumental accompaniment is unnecessary for singing, even with young children. The Kodaly method suggests that human voices be used to accompany other human voices, leading to a program of unaccompanied singing and simple two-part singing for primary children. The Kodaly method offers a sequential system of sight-singing, leading to an understanding of musical notation.

Carl Orff, a German composer, has developed an approach to music education beginning with young children. The program's basic premise is that feeling precedes intellectual understanding. Specific musical lyrics invite children to link their imagination and enjoyment. Young children often memorize verse after verse of elaborate song lyrics such as "I Know an Old Lady Who Swallowed a Fly" and "Supercalifragilisticexpialidocious." The early focus is on rhythm—through the rhythm of speech and movement, children are encouraged to explore music. Lawrence Wheeler and Lois Raebeck (1977) describe how the Kodaly and Orff approaches can be used with elementary school children. They can be used with younger children as well. Teachers interested in these approaches to music education should realize, however, that special training is necessary to implement them with children.

A focus on rhythm and movement is certainly a possible approach to teaching music in the early years, one that has been suggested by early childhood educators in the past. Teachers who want to adopt and adapt

SONGBOOKS FOR YOUNG CHILDREN

Adams, P. (Illustrator). (1973). *There was an old lady.* Child's Play International.

Adams, P. (1975). *This old man.* Child's Play International.

Barbaresi, N. (Illustrator). (1985). *Frog went a-courtin'.* New York: Scholastic.

Brett, J. (Illustrator). (1990). *The twelve days of Christmas.* New York: Putnam.

Child, L. (1987). *Over the river and through the woods.* New York: Scholastic.

Dietz, B. W., & Parks, T. C. (1964). *Folk songs of China, Japan, and Korea.* New York: Harper & Row.

Fowke, E. (1969). *Sally go round the sun.* New York: Doubleday.

Glazer, T. (1973). Eye winker Tom tinker chin chopper: Fifty musical fingerplays. New York: Doubleday.

Griego, F. M. (1980). *Tortillas para mama.* New York: Holt, Rinehart & Winston.

Hazden, B. (1973). *Frere Jacques.* With illustrations by L. Obligado. Philadelphia: Lippincott.

Hoermann, D., & Bridges, D. (1988). *Catch a song.* Nashville, TN: Incentive Publications.

Jenkins, E. (1969). *The Ella Jenkins song book for children.* New York: Oak Publications.

Kennedy, J. (1983). *Teddy bear's picnic.* With illustrations by A. Day. San Marcos, CA: Green Tiger Press.

Kovalski, M. (1987). *The wheels on the bus.* Boston: Little, Brown.

Landeck, B. (1950). *Songs to grow on.* New York: Morrow.

Landeck, B. (1954). *More songs to grow on.* New York: Morrow.

Langstaff, N., & Langstaff, J. (1970). *Jim along, Josie.* New York: Harcourt Brace Jovanovich.

Palmer, H. (1971). *The Hap Palmer songbook.* Baldwin, NY: Educational Activities.

Raffi. (n. d.). *The Raffi singable songbook.* Toronto: Chappell.

Raffi. (1986). *The second Raffi songbook.* Toronto: Chappell.

Richards, M. H. (1985). *Let's do it again!* Portola Valley, CA: Richards Institute of Music Education and Research.

Rounds, G. (Illustrator). (1989). *Old MacDonald had a farm.* New York: Holiday House.

Seeger, R. C. (1948). *American folk songs for children.* New York: Doubleday.

Seeger, R. C. (1950). *Animal folk songs for children.* New York: Doubleday.

Sendak, M. (1975). *Maurice Sendak's Really Rosie: Starring the Nutshell Kids.* New York: Harper & Row.

Sharon, Lois, & Bram. (1985). *Mother Goose.* Boston: Atlantic Monthly Press.

Spier, P. (Illustrator). (1967). *London Bridge is falling down.* New York: Doubleday.

Westcott, N. (Illustrator). (1989). *The lady with the alligator purse.* Boston: Little, Brown.

Winn, M. (1966). *The fireside book of children's songs.* New York: Simon & Schuster.

Winn, M. (1970). *What shall we do and allee galloo!* New York: Harper & Row.

Wolcott, P. (1980). *Double-decker, double-decker, double-decker bus.* Reading, MA: Addison-Wesley.

Orff and Kodaly approaches might need specific training in music theory, performance, and music education. However, all teachers can help children develop rhythmic awareness. Listening to natural speech, poetry, rhymes, and jingles, children can learn to identify rhythmic patterns. They can clap out the rhythms they hear and improvise movement patterns to follow them. Musical instruments might also prove helpful.

Teachers who need help beyond these simple techniques can find resources. A number of music textbooks and books of children's songs are available. Teachers who cannot read music may be able to learn children's songs from records; some music textbooks have accompanying records.

Children's songs come in a great variety (Wolf, 1992). Many, of course, are written especially for children. Popular songs should also be welcome in class. The folk tradition is rich in children's songs, which include nursery rhymes. Many folk songs are simple, contain much repetition of musical phrases and words, and are easy for children to learn. Children should have opportunities to explore many kinds of music. Much contemporary music is rich in line, harmony, and meanings. Jazz, folk, and rock should be included in both singing and listening activities. Many of the ethnic traditions composing American culture provide musical resources as well; for example, the music of African-Americans, Spanish-speaking people, Native Americans, and people of various European heritages should be included in the repertoire of the class. Teachers should select songs they like that also meet Smith's criteria, outlined above, for repetition and vocal range. Songs can be selected to fit a particular area of study in the program, such as African songs for a program on African-American culture or holiday songs at appropriate times of the year.

Although most portions of the singing program are concerned with the recreation of musical experience, singing has creative aspects as well. Children can compose their own verses to familiar songs and write new

RECORDS AND TAPES FOR YOUNG CHILDREN

Fred Koch	(1989) *Did You Feed My Cow?* Lake Fluff, IL: Red Rover Records.
Hap Palmer	(1976) *Witches Brew.*
	(1978) *Seagulls.*
	(1982) *Walter Waltzing Worm.* Freeport, NY: Educational Activities.
Kathy Poelker	(1983) *Looking at My World.*
	(1985) *Amazing Musical Movements.* Wheeling, IL: Look at Me Productions.
Raffi	(1976) *Singable Songs.* (1979) *More Singable Songs.* (1980) *Baby Beluga.* (1982) *Corner Grocery Store.* (1985) *One Light, One Sun.* Ontario, Canada: Troubadour.
Sharon, Lois, and Bram	(1984) *Mainly Mother Goose.* Toronto, Ontario, Canada: Elephant Records.
Tonja Evetts Weimer	(1986) *Fingerplays and Action Chants.* Pittsburgh: Pearce-Evetts Productions. Volume 1, Animals; Volume 2, Family and Friends.

songs. Teachers can write these songs in musical notation and read them back to the children or use tape recorders to capture the children's creations.

Playing Musical Instruments

Early childhood classes should provide opportunities for children to play many musical instruments. Group playing is desirable at some times, but children also need to explore the use of musical instruments independently. They should not be required to beat out a particular rhythm, but should be given the freedom to experiment. Drums, tambourines, rhythm sticks, maracas, and tone blocks are all instruments simple enough for young children to use.

Some commercially made instruments should be provided, because many homemade instruments do not achieve a high quality of tone, but children can create their own instruments as well. These instruments can be as simple as shakers made out of milk containers or plastic boxes holding beans or sand; different objects in the box give different tones to the shaker. Sandpaper attached to wooden blocks and rubbed together makes a suitable instrument. Many objects found around the house or salvaged from the trash heap can also be fashioned into instruments—pot covers and automobile brake drums make percussion instruments, for example. All instruments, whether purchased or homemade, should be treated with respect.

Simple tonal instruments should be included along with rhythm instruments, although teachers should avoid those that must be placed in

Rhythm instruments can accompany singing.

the mouth to be played. Tone blocks in small sets, xylophones, marimbas, and tuned bells can be provided for the children. These instruments encourage exploration of tonal as well as rhythmic relationships, and the children often begin to play simple tunes by themselves.

Musical instruments can be used to accompany the children's singing or movement, to reproduce rhythmic or melodic patterns, or to create original compositions. They also provide an avenue for free musical exploration. Sometimes merely leaving an instrument on a table is enough to stimulate children to "mess about" with sound. Teachers can direct this type of activity by helping children extend beyond their simple explorations. Sometimes children can abstract patterns of sound from the world around them: the sound of running, the noise of the copying machine, and the sounds of activities in the streets. The rhythmic patterns of the names of people or objects or of the words in a story can also be reproduced on a percussion instrument. Children can also listen to songs, abstracting the meter or the accented beat and reproducing it. They should feel and reproduce changes in tempo. Individual explorations lead to group playing, with children playing in unison or even in turn, as a dialogue.

As children play instruments, they should attend to the range of sounds that can be made with each instrument. A drum struck with a hand sounds different from when it is struck with a stick. Struck in the center, it emits a different tone from when it is struck at the edge. Children can learn to create different effects using the same instrument.

As children move into the primary grades, they can begin to learn aspects of musical notation. They can clap out different note values or run, walk, and skip to different rhythms. They can even learn to follow the melody line of a song as the music rises and falls in pitch. Teachers can move a hand up and down or mark the chalkboard to illustrate changes in pitch.

Children should not be forced into a rigid pattern of music production. Activities with instruments should be a function of the children's interests and their willingness to try out new ideas in sound. Teachers should help young children explore and discover the richness of music through the use of instruments.

Listening to Music

Listening is the basic music skill. Children, listening to the world around them, abstract sounds as a way of knowing about the world. They can also listen for elements of music such as pitch, intensity, and rhythm, as well as for patterns and themes. Attentive listening helps children characterize music and determine its mood. In addition, listening is needed for singing or developing creative movement.

As children listen to music, they soon become aware of its various qualities. Some music is loud, some is soft; some is fast in tempo, some is slow; musical pitch rises and falls. Teachers can help children become aware of and characterize the elements, design, and texture of music. Children can also learn to distinguish the various musical instruments and identify their sounds. Differences between families of instruments—brass, woodwinds, strings, and percussion—can be noted first, and differences among the instruments in each family can come later. Records of musical pieces highlighting the various instruments are useful, as are pictures and charts of the instruments. Teachers might also be able to bring musicians to class to play for the children.

Children often listen to music actively in the early years, responding to rhythm and melody with bodily movement or by using musical instruments or their voices. Active listening can extend into creative expression. At other times, children are expected to listen to music more passively, attending to it the way they would attend to a story.

Teachers can develop discussions that enhance attentive listening and lead to critical listening. Children can talk about the feelings generated by music and the kinds of activities that might be evoked. They can also talk about the uses of music: for relaxation, to accompany dancing, to facilitate work, to set a mood, or to accompany a story. Teachers should help children explore their music preferences and help them discover which elements appeal to them most. Almost every aspect of the music program is built on the development of listening skills. If children are to learn to sing properly, they must accurately reproduce the pitch and rhythmic pattern of a song; thus, they must listen to and recall the song. Creative movement activities in which children respond to music require that they listen.

Although recorded music for children is plentiful, children should have opportunities to hear live musicians as well. Some teachers are talented enough to play for their classes. Parents or older children might be willing and able to perform. In some communities, local orchestras or ensembles perform in schools. Sometimes young children are considered too immature to be included in the audience, but they can profit from this experience. The one problem is that young children sometimes do not manifest "proper" audience behavior. Audience behavior can be taught: although children naturally move in response to music, they can learn that there are times when it is appropriate to sit quietly.

MOVEMENT

Movement education helps children gain an understanding of the structure of movement and improve their bodily skills and coordination. Children learn to adapt movements to different spaces, different tempos and speeds, different levels, various numbers of people, variations of force and intensity, and different shapes of small and large objects. Dance, gymnastics, and games are introduced in the early years to achieve these goals (Schurr, 1980). Basic movement education should use activities that integrate learnings in these three areas.

The movement program should be appropriate for young children. According to Eastman (1992), the following criteria should be addressed in selecting movement activities:

1. A variety of movement patterns must be provided.
2. They must be creative.
3. They should be fun.
4. They should encourage children to make decisions and solve problems.
5. They must emphasize safety and control.
6. They must be appropriate for the specific age of the children.

Children's exploration of the body's uses and the extension of the children's ability to express feelings and ideas with the body and with instruments are the goals of this portion of the program. Children in the early years are not being prepared to become musicians or artists any more than they are being prepared to become scientists and mathematicians. Learning to express themselves and to appreciate the expressions of others, and to find beauty in themselves and in their surroundings, are discoveries that can last throughout their lives.

Basic movement education is best seen in a developmental framework. David L. Gallahue (1989) has described the motor development of

Activity MOVEMENT LESSON PLAN

This lesson, whose theme is space and direction, will help children move through space, making high and low movements with body parts toward, away from, in front of, behind, around, through, and between objects.

Begin the lesson with a song. Action songs (such as "Hokey Pokey") are attention getters as well as a tool to get young children into more vigorous and complicated movements.

The second element of this lesson involves vigorous activities that reinforce the theme of space and direction. The activities should be selected to encourage problem solving. An obstacle course including hula hoops, a long bench, chairs, and a target game would highlight the theme. Obstacle courses are popular with young children and teachers because they bring many movement patterns together as well as enabling children to engage in problem-solving experiences under the appearance of fun.

The third element of the movement lesson is the game. The game selected should also reinforce the theme. Games should be simple in nature and scope and never competitive; the focus should be on personal challenge. Teachers can devise their own games, thus developing a movement experience that is suitable to their specific setting.

The final phase of the lesson is referred to as cooling down. Children play hard; therefore, a cooling-down period is essential. The cooling-down activity is beneficial both physiologically and behaviorally. The activities should be designed to calm children. Animal imitation, in which children mimic slow-moving animals, is suitable (Eastman, 1992).

children as moving through a series of phases, each divided into two or three stages. These stages parallel those described by other developmentalists. The first phase, the *reflexive movement phase,* begins in utero and extends through approximately the first year of life. The first part of this phase consists of the information-encoding stage. During this stage the infant gains information, nourishment, and protection through reflexive action. In the second, information-decoding stage, the infant develops voluntary control of skeletal movement and processes information gained from sensory stimuli.

The second phase, the *rudimentary movement phase,* overlaps the first phase and extends from birth through the second year. It, too, is divided into two stages. In the first, the reflex inhibition stage, reflexes are replaced by voluntary behavior in the children's movement repertoire. Though purposeful, these movements appear uncontrolled and unrefined. At about one year, the precontrol stage begins. At this point children show greater precision and control of their movements. They learn to maintain their equilibrium, manipulate objects, and move through their environment.

The third phase, or *fundamental movement phase,* extends from about age two through age seven, approximately the age span covered by educational programs discussed in this text. This phase is divided into three stages. During the first of these, the initial stage, children explore and experiment with their own movement capacities involving locomotor, stability, and manipulative movements. The integration of movement patterns is poor at this stage. Greater control and better coordination develops in the second, elementary stage. The third stage of this phase, the mature stage, is characterized by more mechanically efficient, controlled, and coordinated performance.

The fourth phase of movement development, the *sports-related phase,* lasts from age seven through age fourteen and beyond. This phase also consists of three stages: the general or transition stage, the specific stage, and the specialized stage. In this final phase of development, basic locomotor, manipulation, and stability skills are refined, combined, and elaborated. They are also applied to games, sports, dance, and other recreational activities. The initial stages of motor development are primarily influenced by maturation. However, Gallahue views development in the latter two phases as especially influenced by opportunity, motivation, and instruction.

A movement education program should be developmentally appropriate, fun, and stimulating, and contribute to comprehensive motor development in young children. Experiences with movement should include activities both with and without equipment as well as locomotor activities, manipulative rhythmics, and games. For example, themes such as holidays or transportation can be imaginative, stimulating, and fun. To participate in developmentally appropriate experiences in aerobic exercise, young children can follow the same sequence as do adults: warm-up, workout, and cool-down. However, children's physiology and attention span require that any activity be relatively short and vigorous in nature

THE IMPORTANCE OF MOVEMENT FOR YOUNG CHILDREN

1. To young children, movement means life. Not only do they experience life in their own movements but also they attribute life to all moving things.
2. Movement is, for young children, an important factor in self-discovery. The emerging concept of self is ego-enhancing as children call attention to their stunts and tricks.
3. Movement means discovery of the environment. Movement assists young children in achieving and maintaining their orientation in space. It is an important factor in their development of concepts of time, space, and direction.
4. What does movement mean to young children? It means freedom—freedom from the restrictions of narrow physical confinements and freedom to expand themselves through creative body expressions.
5. Movement means safety. In a basic sense it has survival value.
6. To young children, movement is a method of establishing contact and communication.
7. Not the least among the meanings of movement for young children is sheer enjoyment and sensuous pleasure. They run and scream with excitement as an expression of joy in just being alive.

(American Association for Health, Physical Education, and Recreation and National Association for the Education of Young Children, 1988).

and that it can be carried out with a minimum of directions (Fish, Fish, & Golding, 1989).

Physical Education-Oriented Movement

Movement activities should include developmental exercises, stunts, tumbling, and performing on small and large apparatus. At the nursery or kindergarten level, these activities are generally provided informally. Adequate space is needed both indoors and outdoors for running, jumping, walking, and crawling and for other large-muscle activities. Equipment should be available for jumping, grasping, and climbing on stairs, ladders, and ropes. Balance beams, hoops, rings, ropes, bicycles, scooters, and wagons all contribute to large-muscle skills at this level. As children move into primary grades, more formal activities might be introduced. An exploratory approach to gymnastics is wise in the primary grades.

Games must be played flexibly in nursery school since children are generally not able to follow game rules or goals for any length of time. In the primary grades, games that teach rudimentary skills can be introduced. The use of games in early childhood education is discussed in relation to all play activities in Chapter 10.

Movement education programs generally emphasize developing and refining fundamental movement patterns. Gallahue (1989) views the movement curriculum at the preschool and primary level as focusing on three categories of movement: stability, locomotion, and manipulation. In the area of stability, the program should help children develop axial

Activities

ENHANCING LOCOMOTOR, MANIPULATIVE, AND STABILITY SKILLS FOR FOUR- AND FIVE-YEAR-OLDS

MUSICAL HOOPS

(This is similar to musical chairs.)
Skills: running, hopping, and jumping
Equipment: 15–18 hoops, music
Formation: children standing inside hoops, 1–2 children per hoop
Procedure: When music starts, children move freely in and out of hoops. When it stops, children must be in a hoop. With each new start, remove 1–2 hoops until children have to share several hoops at the end of the game.

STICKY POPCORN BALL

Skill: jumping
Equipment: none
Formation: scattered
Procedure: Children begin "popping" by jumping and trying to stick to others. When a child makes contact with another, the two must pop together. The popcorn ball gradually gets larger.

BALLOON VOLLEYBALL

Skill: striking
Equipment: several 7- or 8-inch balloons, string
Formation: 2 equal groups scattered on opposite sides of string, which is strung about 3–4 feet high
Procedure: Children strike balloons up and across the string. Emphasize that children should work cooperatively to keep all the balloons up as long as possible.

MUSICAL SOCCER

Skills: kicking, trapping
Equipment: one ball per child, music
Formation: scattered with balls on floor at children's feet
Procedure: When music begins, children practice kicking balls. They should trap the balls when the music stops. This can be varied by asking what ways they use to stop the ball. For example, they could use their feet only, or they could vary the speed and direction of their kicking.

BEENBAGS AND HOOPS

Skill: throwing
Equipment: 6 hula hoops for every group of 6–8 children, 4 beanbags, tape
Formation: Tape 6 hoops in a line on the floor. Place numbers 1–6 consecutively in hoops. Children stand several feet away from first hoop.
Procedure: Children stand several feet away from first hoop and attempt to throw all four beanbags into it. The farthest hoop, number 6, should be the most difficult to hit. Other children can help retrieve. Children take turns.

DEVELOPMENTAL STUNTS: ANIMAL ANTICS

Bear walk: Children bend forward and place hands on floor about 12 inches ahead, keeping their knees straight. If possible, they walk forward.
Kangaroo jump: From a semi-squat position with arms folded over chest, children spring into the air and back to a squat position with their knees flexed.
Duck walk: Children sit down on their heels, place their hands on their knees, and waddle slowly forward.

Activities

ENHANCING LOCOMOTOR, MANIPULATIVE, AND STABILITY SKILLS FOR FOUR- AND FIVE-YEAR-OLDS *(continued)*

INDIVIDUAL STUNTS

Egg roll: In squat position with arms grasped around legs, children roll to one side, to the back, and to the other side. Then they try to return to starting position.

Stork stand: Children stand on one foot and grab the opposite foot in back. Then they try the other leg.

Coffee grinder: From a long sit position, children roll to one side, with their weight on one hand and one foot and their body straight. They pivot around in small increments. Repeat with other side.

PARTNER STUNTS

Wheelbarrow: One child bends at waist and puts both hands on the floor. The partner steps between the first child's feet and grasps the ankles. The partner lifts the first child's legs and walks forward. Switch positions.

Leap frog: Children assume squat position four to six feet apart. The "frog" puts both hands on each child's back in turn and leaps, with legs wide apart, over each child. After completing the line, the child joins the line and another begins. (Leap frog can be done with a partner or a group.)

Wring the dishrag: Partners of approximately equal height and weight face each other. They join hands and turn completely around by swinging their arms up and over their heads. Hands should remain joined as the children turn (Madsen, 1987).

Movement exploration is important to young children's development.

movements, as well as static and dynamic balance, that is, balance both when moving and when standing still. In the area of locomotion, the program should focus on such activities as walking, running, jumping, sliding, and climbing. The manipulation area would include activities related to such skills as catching, trapping, throwing, and kicking.

Robert Pancrazi and Victor Dauer (1981) suggest that preschool movement programs focus on (1) gross motor experiences that allow children to manage their bodies efficiently; (2) learning manipulative skills through handling such play objects as balls and beanbags; and (3) using floor apparatus such as boxes, boards, ladders, and planks that allow children to slide down, jump down, go through openings, and bounce. At the kindergarten and primary level, Pancrazi and Dauer say the program should focus heavily on movement experiences and body mechanics and on rhythmic activities. As children mature, increasing emphasis can be placed on apparatus, stunts, tumbling, and simple games, with fitness routines and sports skills introduced in the late primary grades.

VIGNETTE: PHYSICAL EDUCATION, KINDERGARTEN

The students enter the gymnasium and each child goes to a red mark on the floor. The teacher begins playing some lively music, saying, "I'd like all of you to jog in place on your red mark. Is a jog fast or slow?"

The students respond together, "Slow," and begin to jog in place for a few minutes. The teacher praises the children for following directions and for lifting their knees to the ceiling. "Now jog anywhere you want," he says. The students excitedly begin moving around the gymnasium. "Now, when I stop the music, I want you to find a red mark and stand on it."

After a few seconds, he stops the music, and the students rush to find a red mark.

The teacher continues with the lesson, tossing each child a beanbag. "Today we are going to use beanbags in class. I'd like you to stay on your red mark and do anything you want with the beanbag."

One girl places the beanbag on her head and slowly turns around and around. A boy throws the beanbag into the air above his head and tries to catch it.

"Now I'd like all of you to try the same thing," the teacher explains. "Raise the beanbag high above your head and see if you can drop it onto your red mark, like this." He demonstrates.

Excitedly, the students begin dropping their beanbags. The teacher calls attention to one girl named Christina. "I'd like all of you to watch Christina. She's doing a very good job." The class stops and watches.

The teacher then asks the students to try throwing the beanbag into the air and catching it. The students spend a few minutes with this activity before they move on to a few additional beanbag activities.

Dance-Oriented Movement

Gallahue's and Prancrazi and Dauer's approaches to movement education basically reflect a physical education orientation. Other educators emphasize a more creative, dance-oriented approach to movement education in the early years. This latter approach has been heavily influenced by the work of Rudolph Laban (1975), who analyzed and described basic body movements and developed an approach to movement education in England.

Bonnie Gilliom (1970), using the work of Laban and his followers, analyzed the structure of movement education. Through movement education, she states, children should experientially learn about

1. time, space, force, and flow as elements of movement;
2. the physical laws of motion and the principles of human movement which govern the human body's movement; and
3. the vast variety of creative and efficient movements which the human body is capable of producing through the manipulation of movement variables. (p. 6)

Gilliom has developed a series of units that focus on problems of movement. Teachers set up problems and guide children to develop creative ways of solving them. Much of the teaching is indirect, but verbal instructions and demonstrations are also used. Classroom teachers can create a variety of activities to enable children to explore their bodies and their abilities to move through space, using time, rhythm, force, and flow to create movement sequences.

While movement education is a worthy curriculum area in its own right, it has also been considered in relation to its contributions to other program areas. Lydia Gerhardt (1973) reports how young children orient themselves in space and use movement to understand concepts of space, time, length, shape, and direction. She also offers suggestions for enhancing the early childhood curriculum through movement. Concepts of topological geometry, geography, and the measurement of time, space, and weight can all be encountered through movement exploration. Such a use of movement suggests systematic ways in which motor patterns generated by children can be integrated into cognitive schema. Betty Rowen's book on movement education (1982) contains examples of strategies for using movement as an aid to learning about language, science, social studies, and number concepts.

Movement also helps children explore the structure of music. Movement and music have gone together since the beginning of time (Ludowise, 1985). The inclination to move to music can be used as an exciting means for children to learn about music by listening and doing.

The Eurythmics of Emile Jaques Dalcroze provided the basis for the music program developed by Aronoff (1979), mentioned earlier. This approach introduces children to formal concepts of music through movement activities. Although most teachers lack the specialized training of a

Activity — COMBINED MOVEMENT–MUSIC ACTIVITIES

BODY LANGUAGE

Purpose: Movement to a steady beat while developing a repertoire of movement for each part of the body

Materials: Hand drum or musical recording with a steady, even beat, such as Hap Palmer's "Mod Marches"

Directions: Children take their places, making sure they are far enough apart that no one can touch another. When the music plays, have the children move a pre-selected body part, such as their arms, to the beat. At a certain point, say, "Change," which is a cue for children to find a new way to move their arms. Encourage children to find three to four ways to move each part of the body, including arms, elbows, shoulders, head, eyes, legs, feet, torso, and hips.

DRUM MOVEMENT

Purpose: Introduce movement to the accented beat

Materials: Hand drum and mallet

Directions: Children can march to the beat of the drum as you play. The beat should be steady and even, although the first beat should be louder. On the accented beat, children should dip by bending their knees as they march. Help the children understand where the accented beat occurs, by chanting "strong" and "weak" as you play patterns of four ("STRONG, weak, weak, weak"), three ("STRONG, weak, weak"), and two ("STRONG, weak") beats. (Ludowise, 1986)

Dalcroze teacher or a dance instructor, they have many ways to encourage children to explore movement. The instinctive search for discovery and the drive to move and explore make children engage in creative dance. The quality of the children's learning experiences determines their pleasure in dance. Children should be introduced to fundamental elements of movement and age-appropriate elements of dance (body, articu-

Activity — MOVEMENT USING PHOTOGRAPHS OR PAINTINGS

PHOTOGRAPH

Snowy scene

Visual Impressions: cold, slippery, white, imprints in the snow made by people or other objects

Movement Associations: shivering, sliding, shapes to represent snow flakes and imprints in the snow

PAINTING

Starry Night by Vincent Van Gogh

Visual Impressions: sleeping village, pointed church steeple, towering cypress trees, swirling sky, golden moon, waves from the stars

Movement Associations: reclining shapes, pointed shapes that grow into towers, towers created by two or more children together, waving actions, swirling actions. (Nicholes, 1991)

lation, time, space, energy, and motion). They must be taught developmentally appropriate movement skills and progressions to become part of a progressive learning experience that provides appropriate challenges in creative movement.

Teachers can help children use movement to express ideas and feelings. Joan Russell (1987) has grouped the dimensions of movement thus used under four main headings: the body, the instrument of expression; effort, how the body moves; space and shape, where the body moves; and relationship, relationship of body parts to each other, of dancers to each other, and of groups to each other. Russell has built on the work of Rudolph Laban to develop a program of creative dance aimed at helping children develop competency in movement through a series of basic themes.

Dance that is appropriate for young children is usually referred to as *creative dance* or *creative movement*, which is an artistic form based on natural movement, although not all natural movement is dance. Stinson (1991) believes that dance is natural movement that becomes significant when attention is paid to it. Making movement into dance requires that the children create patterns. Everyday movement is automatic, but dance requires that we sense ourselves as completely as a baby who is taking its first tentative steps.

Activity SPACE MAPS

Have children find five pictures with interesting shape and motion possibilities from magazines and cut out the pictures. Have the children arrange their pictures and glue them onto construction paper. The paper symbolizes the dance space of their classroom; thus, the location of each picture determines where the children will perform the elements of the picture. Children draw a floor pattern (for instance, straight lines, scallops, or zigzags) to link each picture. Children then generate dance movements in relation to each picture. Challenge them to move through the floor patterns of their space map. Provide support when needed. Children can reveal their maps to each other and then perform the map dances, one or two children at a time. (Nicholes, 1991)

Activity WORKING IMAGES

BANANA BACK

Objective: To improve posture, a slouched back
Image: Banana back
Steps: Have children pull up and eliminate the banana's back.

HUGGABLE TEDDY BEAR

Objective: Arm placement
Image: Hugging a huge teddy bear
Steps: Have children hug a huge teddy bear that is so large they cannot get their arms halfway around. (Overby, 1991)

Dance helps children discover a new world of sensory awareness made possible though kinesthetic sense. Dance as a creative art includes both body and spirit, another dimension of the self. It requires not only body movement, but also an inner awareness of movement (Stinson 1991). Teachers who believe that children should go beyond movement to dance must facilitate this transformation. Stinson (1991) suggests the following:

1. Children can sense themselves moving and immobile if teachers lead them to practice the contrasts of making sound and making silence.
2. Children need to respond to signals such as complete silence or a sound made by the teacher's voice or body (such as pounding on the floor or slapping the legs).
3. Children need to appreciate and attend to the sensation of stillness by using their kinesthetic sense.
4. Children can listen to music with a magical quality to guide their movement.

Playing music on a phonograph or piano often stimulates children to move, and varying the pitch, intensity, and rhythm leads them to move in different ways. A drum beat also stimulates them. Movement can also be encouraged without any musical accompaniment by using descriptive phrases, or asking children to show a soft movement, a hard movement, high steps, or a close-to-the-ground movement—all allowing them freedom of expression within a framework established by the teacher.

Such experiences are often enhanced with simple props. Hoops or fine silk scarves affect children's motion, often enabling them to make more flowing movements. Asking them to move in ways that represent specific things can also extend their movements. Children can be a jet, a slithery snake, a boat, or a flower growing. Each object calls forth certain associations for children, which they should be able to interpret in their own way. Having the children all move in the same stereotyped way stifles rather than supports creative expression. Indeed, individual interpretation is essential in these rhythmic activities. The role of early childhood teachers is to elicit movement and to encourage new ways of using one's body rather than to teach specific forms and techniques.

However, there should be opportunities for other kinds of dance activities as well. Rhythmic games coupled with songs or chants are enjoyable and can be learned by young children. Such games as "Looby-Loo" or "Bluebird, Fly Through My Window" are simple to direct and so full of repetition that children can master them with ease. Many of these activities grow out of folk tradition, and teachers sometimes find that children know versions somewhat different from the one the teacher is using. This variation may occur when teachers introduce folk songs. These differences are interesting to study, for they represent a portion of the folk tradition in American society. It may be easier, however, for teachers to learn the local version than to teach a foreign version.

Play and party activities can give way to folk dancing, of American, European, or other origins. Children can learn the simple basic steps of folk or square dances and then do the patterns as called by the teacher. Records and books are available that provide music and directions for simple dances. More formal dances should probably be postponed until later in the children's school career.

SUMMARY

Art, music, and movement all have important places in the early childhood curriculum. These areas allow children to express themselves creatively in many ways. They also allow children to make sense of the world in a different way than language does. In order for children to function creatively in these areas, they must develop a control of themselves and an understanding of what each medium can do. Thus teachers must function actively in helping children become better skilled and gain greater knowledge in each of these areas. Discipline combined with freedom provides the basis for learning in the expressive arts.

REFERENCES

American Association for Health, Physical Education, and Recreation & National Association for the Education of Young Children (1988). *The significance of the young child's motor development.* Proceedings of a conference sponsored by the American Association for Health, Physical Education, and Recreation and National Association for the Education of Young Children.

Andrews, G. (1954). *Creative rhythmic movement for children.* Englewood Cliffs, NJ: Prentice Hall

Aronoff, F. W. (1979). *Music and young children* (expanded ed.). New York: Turning Wheel Press.

Barclay, K. D., & Walwer, L. (1992). Linking lyrics and literacy through song picture books. *Young Children, 47*(4), 76–85.

Burns, S. F. (1975). Children's Art: A vehicle for learning. *Young Children. 30*(3), 193–204 .

Carnegie Forum on Education and the Economy (1986). *A nation prepared: Teachers for the 21st century.* Washington, DC: Carnegie Forum on Education and the Economy.

Clare, S. M. (1988). The drawings of preschool children: A longitudinal case study and four experiments. *Studies in Art Education: A Journal of Issues and Research, 29*(4), 211–221.

Cole, E., & Schaefer, C. (1990). Can young children be art critics? *Young Children, 45*(2), 33–38.

Davis, J., & Gardner, H. (1993). The arts and early childhood education: A cognitive developmental portrait of the young child as artist. In B. Spodek (Ed.), *Handbook of research on the education of young children* (pp. 191–206). New York: Macmillan.

Day, B. (1988). *Early childhood education.* New York: Macmillan.

Dimondstein, G. (1974). *Exploring the arts with children.* New York: Macmillan.

Eastman, W. (1992). The values and purposes of human movement. *Day Care and Early Education, 19*(4), 21–24.

Edwards, L. C., & Nabors, M. L. (1993). The creative arts process: What it is and what it is not. *Young Children, 48*(3), 77–81.

Feeney, S., & Moravcik, E. (1987). A thing of beauty: Aesthetic development in young children. *Young Children, 42*(6), 7–13.

Feldman, E. (1970). *Becoming human through art*. Englewood Cliffs, NJ: Prentice Hall.

Fish, H. T., Fish, R. B., & Golding, L. A. (1989). *Starting out well*. Champaign, IL: Leisure Press.

Fowler, C. (1989). The arts are essential to education. *Educational Leadership, 47*(2), 60–63.

Gallahue, D. L. (1989). *Understanding motor development in children*. New York: Wiley.

Gelfer, J. I., & Perkins, P. G. (1987). Young children's acquisition of selected art concepts using the medium of blocks with teacher guidance. *Early Child Development and Care, 27*, 19–20.

Gerhardt, L. A. (1973). *Moving and knowing: The young child orients himself in space*. Englewood Cliffs, NJ: Prentice Hall.

Gilliat, M. T. (1983). Art appreciation: A guide for the classroom teacher. *Educational Horizons, 61*(2), 79–82.

Gilliom, B. C. (1970). *Basic movement for children*. Reading, MA: Addison-Wesley.

Kaufman, E. (1989). *Nine commentaries on Frank Lloyd Wright*. Cambridge, MA: MIT Press.

Jalongo, M. R., & Collins, M. (1985). Singing with young children. *Young Children, 40*(2), 17–22.

Joan, B., Haines, E., & Gerber, L. (1984). *Leading young children to music*. Columbus, OH: Merrill.

Laban, R. (1963). *Modern educational dance*. London: McDonald and Evans.

Lacy, J. F. (n.d.). *Young art: Nature and seeing*. New York: Van Nostrand Reinhold.

Lowenfeld, V., & Brittain, W. L. (1987). *Creative and mental growth* (8th ed.). New York: Macmillan.

Ludowise, K. D. (1986). Movement to music: Ten activities that foster creativity. *Childhood Education, 62*, 40–43.

Madsen, K. (1987, February). Children in motion. Paper presented at the Illinois State Kindergarten Conference. Oak Brook, IL.

Marksberry, M. L.(1963). *Foundation of creativity*. New York: Harper & Row.

McDonald, D. (1979). *Music in our lives: The early years*. Washington, DC: National Association for the Education of Young Children.

Moomaw, S. (1987). *Discovering music in early childhood*. Boston: Allyn and Bacon.

Moran, J. D., Sawyers, J. K., & Moore, A. J. (1988). The effects of structure in instructions and materials on preschoolers' creativity. *Home Economics Research Journal, 17*, 148–152.

Neubert, K. (1991). The care and feeding of clay. In L. Y. Overby, A. Richardson, & L. S. Hasko (Eds.), *Early childhood creative arts* (pp. 121–127). Reston, VA: American Alliance for Health, Physical Education, Recreation and Dance.

Nicholes, V. F. (1991). Creative dance for the primary child: A progressive approach. In L. Y. Overby, A. Richardson, & L. S. Hasko (Eds.), *Early childhood creative arts* (pp. 144–159). Reston, VA: American Alliance for Health, Physical Education, Recreation and Dance.

Overby, L. Y. (1991). Imagery use in children's dance. In L. Y. Overby, A. Richardson, & L. S. Hasko (Eds.), *Early childhood creative arts* (pp. 160–166). Reston, VA: American Alliance for Health, Physical Education, Recreation and Dance.

Pancrazi, R. P., & Dauer, V. P. (1981). *Movement in early childhood and primary education*. Minneapolis: Burgess.

Papalia, D. E., & Olds, S. W. (1987). *A child's word*. New York: McGraw-Hill.

Peery, J. C. (1993). Music in early childhood education. In B. Spodek (Ed.), *Handbook of research on the education of young children* (pp. 207–224). New York: Macmillan.

Pile, N. F. (1973). *Art experiences for young children*. New York: Macmillan.

Pitcher, E. G., Feinburg, S. G., & Alexander, D. A. (1989). *Helping young children learn*. Columbus, OH: Merrill.

Raut, S. (1985). Identifying the inaccurate singer in your classroom. *OMEA General Music Journal, 3*(2), 28–30.

Richardson, E. S. (1969). *In the early world*. Wellington, New Zealand: Council of Educational Research.

Rowen, B. (1982). *Learning through movement* (2nd ed.). New York: Teachers College Press.

Russell, J. (1987). *Creative dance in the primary school*. London: Macdonald and Evans.

Saracho, O. N. (1992). Preschool children's cognitive style and play and implications for creativity. *Creativity Research Journal, 5*(1), 35–47.

Schurr, E. L. (1980). *Movement experiences for children* (2nd ed.). Englewood Cliffs, NJ: Prentice Hall.

Smith, N. R. (1983). *Experience and art: Teaching children to paint.* New York: Teachers College Press.

Smith, R. A. (1989). *Discipline -Based Art Education: Origins, meanings, and development.* Urbana: University of Illinois Press.

Smith, R. B. (1970). *Music in the child's education.* New York: Ronald Press.

Stamp, L. N. (1992). Music time? All the time? *Day Care and Early Education, 19*(4), 4–6.

Stinson, S. W. (1991). Transforming movement into dance for young children. In L. Y. Overby, A. Richardson, & L. S. Hasko (Eds.), *Early childhood creative arts* (pp. 134–139). Reston, VA: American Alliance for Health, Physical Education, Recreation and Dance.

Sunal, S. S. (1993). Social studies in early childhood education. In B. Spodek (Ed.), *Handbook of research on the education of young children* (pp. 176–190). New York: Macmillan.

Swann, A. (1985). A naturalistic study of art making process in a preschool setting. Unpublished doctoral dissertation, Indiana University.

Tarr, P. (1991). More than movement: Scribbling reassessed. In L. Y. Overby, A. Richardson, & L. S. Hasko (Eds.), *Early childhood creative arts* (pp. 112–120). Reston, VA: American Alliance for Health, Physical Education, Recreation and Dance.

Wheeler, L., & Raebeck, L. (1977). *Orff and Kodaly adapted for the elementary school.* Dubuque, IA: William C. Brown.

Wolf, A. D. (1990). Art postcards–Another aspect of your aesthetics program? *Young Children, 45*(2), 39–43.

Wolf, J. (1992). Let's sing it again: Creating music with young children. *Young Children, 47*(2), 56–61.

Zimmerman, M. (1985). The state of the art in early childhood music and research. In J. Boswell (Ed.), *The young child and music: Contemporary principles in child development and music education* (pp. 65–78). Reston, VA: Music Educators National Conference.

17

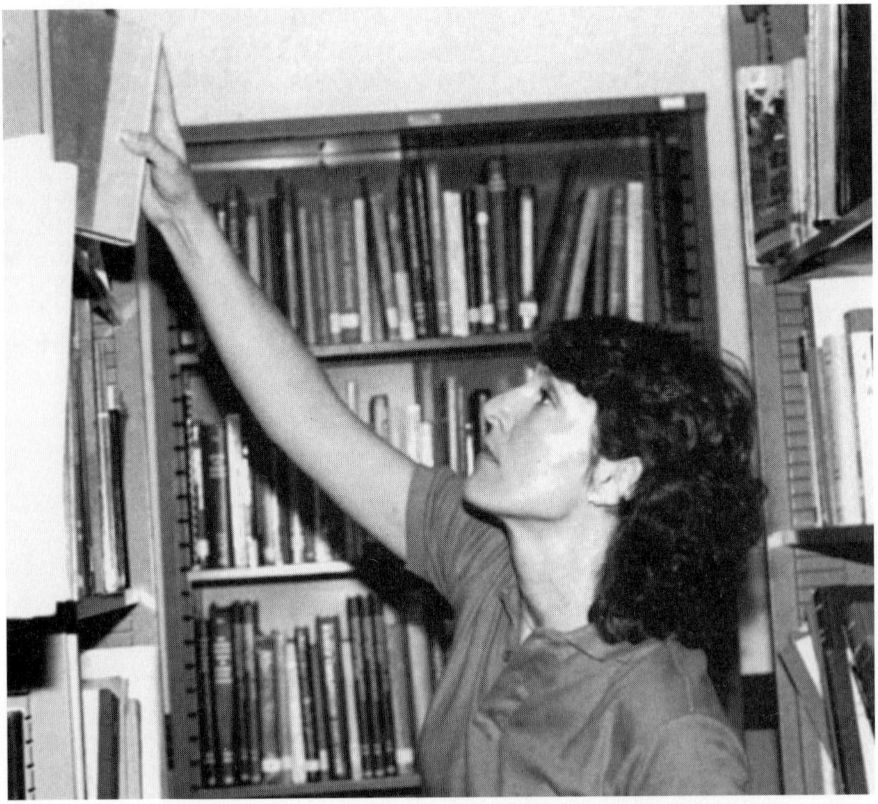

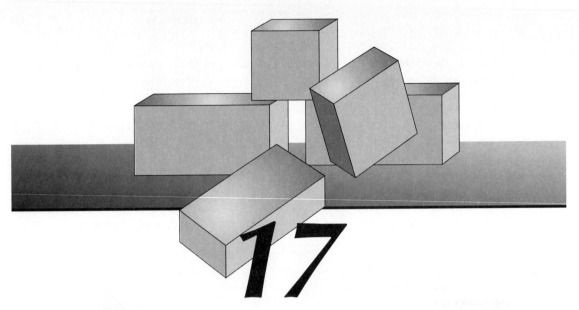

Resources for Teachers' Professional Development

CHAPTER OVERVIEW

This chapter presents:

- Ways for teachers to pursue their professional development
- Several types of in-service programs
- Information about professional organizations and publications in early childhood education
- Resources and information on various topics in early childhood education

INTRODUCTION

In recent years concern for professionalism in early childhood education has increased. This concern is expressed not only in the call for higher criteria for admission to practice in all early childhood programs, but also in the emphasis on the continued professional development of practitioners (Spodek, Saracho, & Peters, 1988).

A major defining attribute of a profession is that it requires entrants to undergo prolonged preparation. Although there are no standards by which to judge how long such training should be, Katz and Raths (1985) have identified several characteristics of the process of professional preparation itself:

1. The preparation is specialized, in order to ensure the acquisition of complex knowledge and techniques.
2. The preparation is cognitive in nature and difficult; there is a screening process, and some candidates can be expected to fail. Training is marked by optimum stress and sacrifice, resulting in dedication and commitment to the profession.
3. Candidates are required to master more knowledge than is likely to be applied and more than the student perceives to be necessary. In all professions, candidates are said to complain about these excesses and the apparent irrelevance of much of the knowledge they are expected to master.

4. Institutions responsible for professional preparation must be accredited or licensed. These institutions award certificates, diplomas, or degrees under the supervision of members of the profession.
5. All professional preparation institutions, very often in concert, provide systematic and regular continuing education for members (Katz & Raths, 1985).

What does it take to be an effective teacher of young children? To find out, researchers in the field have studied teachers and their teaching over the decades. The more we know about teaching, the better able we will be to improve teachers' effectiveness and thus influence the process of educating young children. Thus, teachers must not only learn more about what they teach young children, they must also learn more about the nature of teaching.

STAFF DEVELOPMENT

The first chapter of this book presented ideas about what one should know to become an early childhood teacher. This foundational knowledge is just the beginning. Teachers at any level must continue their professional development throughout their careers. Novice teachers usually discover that additional knowledge will help them to perform better in their classrooms. They usually express concern about such topics as discipline, curriculum ideas, learning centers, early literacy training, language development, and transitions.

To keep up with the latest information in the early childhood field, teachers must make education an ongoing part of their life. Many early childhood programs have in-service training built into their schedules. The school year should begin with a workshop for all teachers and aides and continue with on-site workshops in the various component areas such as curriculum, nutrition, health, mental health, and parent involvement (Beatty, 1992). Providing a workshop at the beginning of the year is not enough. An in-service program of some kind should be offered throughout the year.

Good staff development—designed to solve practical problems and to meet the needs of different types of teachers—is important for two reasons: it contributes to the quality of teaching and increases professional satisfaction.

In most schools for young children, teachers are isolated and unaware of what others are doing in the classroom. They rarely share ideas and resources. Some schools, however, find creative ways to support staff attendance at conferences and workshops, to provide released time to visit other programs, to reimburse tuition for college courses, and to stock their library with a variety of professional journals and curriculum guides (Jorde-Bloom, 1988). Opportunities for learning and reflection, and the personal growth that accompanies them, can even be seen as the hallmarks of a professional orientation.

Programs of staff development can enable teachers to evaluate their instructional practices and to master new skills. These programs provide opportunities for staff members to expand their knowledge and widen their repertoire of competencies. At the same time, such programs create a nonthreatening atmosphere in which staff members are encouraged to help each other.

Schools that encourage a climate of high professional growth also gear in-service staff development activities to individual experience and tie opportunities for professional advancement to a well-defined career ladder (Association of Teacher Educators, 1985). These programs encourage staff to stretch and develop their potential.

Teachers must feel good about themselves in order to function well in the classroom. An informal assessment can help teachers determine whether anything is wrong and how to improve their teaching. Teachers themselves are the best source of information because they reflect the reality they perceive and because their perception of their experience is what is important, since they act on their perceptions. Teachers can be asked to make a self-assessment and design a program for their own professional development.

Figure 17–1 Self-Assessment Form for Teachers

Teacher______________________________ Date__________

1. Strengths:

____

____

____

____

2. Needs:

____

____

____

____

3. Professional plan:

____

____

____

____

Paula Jorde-Bloom (1988) believes that a systematic method for measuring staff perceptions of the school's organizational climate can be extremely useful to

1. clarify staff members' feelings about work,
2. gauge personal and organizational efficiency and effectiveness,
3. help explain why and where things are going well,
4. identify where changes are needed,
5. increase staff involvement,
6. give direction about program priorities,
7. target areas for staff development,
8. improve overall morale and staff performance, and
9. help ensure the center stays healthy.

People's social needs make it important that they feel that others care about them and are concerned about their welfare. Emotional support is a potent force that promotes a positive work climate. Staff members' mutual support and trust in the educational setting can develop an *esprit de corps*. Open communication is needed to avoid misinterpretations.

An environment that promotes friendly, supportive relationships helps individuals acquire job satisfaction and self-fulfillment. Educational settings should have a unified team spirit, a strong sense of collegiality, a collective sense of efficacy, and an avoidance of social cliques. Interactions among individuals should be comfortable so that coworkers have the freedom to express their thoughts openly. Patterns of collegiality, which can vary based on the formal and informal structures of the setting and its needs, and expectations, are characteristic of effective early childhood education programs.

Schools usually offer the following staff development:

1. they organize in-service training programs;
2. they depend on professional organizations to offer the knowledge through conferences and publications;
3. they have teachers attend college or community courses; and
4. they allow teachers to acquire their own resources.

Teachers have the ultimate responsibility to improve their professional knowledge. They can attend in-service programs, enroll in a program at an institution of higher learning, participate in professional organizations, and use a variety of available educational resources. Teachers can develop professionally through a variety of **in-service programs** such as in-service meetings, teacher study groups, observing other teachers, mentoring and networking, using technology, and college or university courses (Spodek, Saracho, & Davis, 1991). Workshops are beneficial for viewing films or videotapes, listening to lectures, attending classes or study groups, or observing and recording other teachers' performance. Teachers can acquire the information they believe they need by identifying their strengths and needs in order to identify topics for their in-service

In-service teacher education programs are programs of continuing education designed to improve the performance of teachers in the field. They may be formal or informal. Some are sponsored by universities and lead to advanced degrees.

activities. Specialists can assist in identifying the resources available to meet the teachers' needs.

Some teachers may be sufficiently mature to discuss problems openly and to provide constructive feedback that is valuable in enhancing their professional competence. These teachers can cluster in interest groups, promoting professional development by inspiring other teachers to enlist in in-service activities. Teachers who profit from these sessions will be the best advertisers to motivate others to join this type of in-service. In addition to learning from each other, exchanging ideas, and testing a variety of teaching techniques, the group also provides teachers with encouragement and support.

Teacher Study Groups

A small, manageable set of problems (such as transitions, flexibility, or short-term planning) can be worked out in a teacher study group. The group should identify an area of study, appraise the strengths and needs of each participant in that area, make definite learning plans, and institute a strategy for accumulating feedback to help each member improve as a teacher. Participants in a teacher study group learn by discussing, exchanging ideas, viewing videotapes, highlighting their questioning techniques or how they pace discussions, or observing other teachers' practices.

Observing Teachers

Teachers can observe other teachers more objectively than they can assess their own behavior. When they engage in their own teaching, teachers may fail to notice many classroom events and behaviors, while a neutral observer might see them more objectively.

Teachers from the same school or from different schools can observe each other. Observers can learn new instructional routines, expanding their accumulated teaching skills. Some teachers may fear observers' opinions or feel that a conflict of educational philosophy might exist between themselves and their observer, which, in the interpretation of observations, could be demeaning. Teachers should be able to select the observers with whom they will be paired, so that both members of an observation team can share a consistent approach.

Teachers and aides working in the same classroom can also observe each other. The aide's qualifications (education and experience) are usually less than the teacher's. This means the pair is not equal, even if both members work together as a team, know the classroom situation, and have the same educational philosophy. However, their feedback can still be worthwhile to each other. Intermittent short observations (of perhaps 15 or 20 minutes) can be scheduled when one of them is free of other responsibilities. Observations can provide intense insight into the class, offering important information about classroom events as well as about individual children that the team can use to meet the children's unique developmental needs.

The teacher-aide team needs to know how its performance influences the children. The team's expectations of children and its teaching patterns can influence each team members' conviction. The observer's knowledge can suppress some of the preferences of a team member.

Teacher Mentors and Networks

Mentors and networks can be used to enrich communication and to provide a forum in which teachers can share practical knowledge about curriculum and about methods of organizing physical and social resources, teaching, evaluating the program, and working with parents.

More experienced teachers can become mentors for novices, taking the new teachers under their wings. Mentors customarily share their knowledge of practice and support new teachers who may feel insecure and need to justify their practice. Mentors also identify standard procedures in the school, help to organize the classroom, and provide new teachers with information concerning the staff, the children, the parents, and the community. Mentoring helps new teachers to make the transition into the profession and promotes the professional development of both novice and experienced teachers. Mentors need to have acquired personal maturity to become helpers to other professionals. They need to have achieved a level of development that Erik Erikson characterizes as supporting generativity (see Chapter 3).

After students graduate from teacher preparation programs and join the teaching profession, they frequently lose contact with their classmates, especially those who go into different professions or who transfer to different locations. Many graduates develop a network to cultivate relationships, communicate with each other, exchange ideas, and support each other emotionally when needed. Networking helps teachers in their professional development. They can explore or organize new networks to help them meet new challenges and perform a variety of roles.

College or University Courses

Institutions of higher learning often plan a set of courses that enable teachers to obtain an additional certificate or approval (such as a professional certificate, an advanced certificate, a teaching certificate as a reading specialist, or a certificate in teaching children with language or learning disabilities) or an advanced degree (for example, the M.A. or M.Ed.). Some early childhood programs require teachers to complete college courses on a regular basis. Early childhood programs may schedule their teachers' work so that teachers can attend a college or university. Programs may pay teachers' tuition or determine teachers' salaries according to their advanced education.

Technology

Teachers' professional development can be enhanced by the use of technology. Video recordings of experts in the field, teaching demonstrations, and other instructional situations can be used to share information. Video recordings of teachers can also be used to evaluate teachers and to gather information for research purposes. Teachers can use video cameras and video cassette recordings to view, evaluate, and improve their teaching. Some teachers may refuse to be videotaped, because they believe that videotaping will stifle their spontaneity or that their rights may be breached. This fear results from teachers' concerns that information about their performance that was collected to help them improve as teachers might be used as an evaluation of their performance. However, teachers are beginning to welcome being videotaped. Teachers' written permission must be secured before any videotape is recorded or made accessible to others. Teachers must have the right to decide who watches the tape and when to erase it. It is possible that the analysis of teachers' classroom instruction using videotapes may have to be suspended until teachers' rights are protected.

Computers can also be used to support teachers' professional development. E-mail (electronic mail) allows teachers to communicate through an electronic network. FREDMAIL (Free Educational Mail) is an electronic mail service that teachers can access without charge. They can communicate overnight with a vast number of teachers, raising questions on a bulletin board and getting answers from other teachers in the network or joining in projects with other teachers. A computer and a modem, which are available in many schools and in some teachers' homes, are all that is needed to join the network. Local colleges of education and education service centers can provide information on this service as well as a local telephone number to use.

INFORMATION RESOURCES

Information about early childhood education is important in teachers' development. Productive ideas and teaching come from teachers' awareness of emerging practices, products, sources of research and professional literature and information, and key organizations and agencies and their dissemination procedures. Various agencies disseminate information on useful resources such as aids to locate and retrieve information (including reference books), computerized information research systems, abstracts of professional publications, and resource people with specific areas of expertise.

Teachers should know which resources are available to meet their classroom requirements. Teachers with worthwhile resources at their fingertips are usually more efficient. According to Peterson (1987), "Individuals may not always have the answer to a problem at their fingertips or the information they need tucked away neatly in their heads. But if each of us knows where to find the information we need and how to retrieve it, our ability to perform efficiently and successfully in our jobs is enhanced tenfold" (p. 495).

Teachers should know how to obtain the available resources, which can be extremely useful to them. Teachers should know the following resources in early childhood education:

1. professional organizations;
2. professional literature, including journals, periodicals, government documents, and reports;
3. reference materials and bibliographic listings; and
4. information storage and retrieval systems.

Professional Organizations

Teachers can obtain many helpful resources from the following major professional organizations in early childhood education. Membership in these organizations often includes a subscription to an early childhood journal, with articles that discuss the latest ideas, findings, and issues in the field.

1. **National Association for the Education of Young Children (NAEYC)** (1509 16th Street, NW, Washington, DC, 20036). NAEYC is one of the strongest and largest organizations in early childhood education, with over 70,000 members, in almost 300 affiliated groups, who are concerned with the education and well-being of children under the age of eight. NAEYC offers professional development opportunities to help early childhood educators improve the quality of services they provide for young children. NAEYC publishes two journals, *Young Children* for practitioners and *Early Childhood Research Quarterly* for researchers, along with other publications, and organizes an annual conference. Its affiliates also hold conferences and workshops and publish a variety of material.

2. **Association for Childhood International (ACEI)** (11501 Georgia Avenue, Suite 315, Wheaton, MD 20902). ACEI promotes appropriate educational conditions, programs, and practices for children through the elementary grades. Its goal is to promote teachers' professional growth and disseminate information about school programs. ACEI includes individuals, local affiliate groups, and state and provincial associations. It publishes two journals, *Childhood Education* for practitioners and *Journal of Research in Childhood Education* for researchers, as well as other publications; it also holds an annual conference.

3. **World Organization for Early Education (*Organisation Mondial pour l'Education Prescolaire,* OMEP).** OMEP promotes the study and education of young children to help those who work with young children to become aware of young children's needs. It shares information on education, development, health and nutrition, playgrounds, and toys, in reference to young children all over the world. OMEP and UNESCO join

OTHER PROFESSIONAL ASSOCIATIONS

American Montessori Society, Inc., 150 Fifth Avenue, New York, NY 10010
Child Welfare League of America, Inc., 67 Irving Place, New York, NY 10010
Division of Early Childhood, Council for Exceptional Children, 1920 Association Drive, Reston, VA 22091
National Committee on Education of Migrant Children, 1501 Broadway, New York, NY 10016
Parent Cooperative Preschool International, 9111 Alton Parkway, Silver Springs, MD 20910
Southern Early Childhood Association (SECA), formerly Southern Association for Children Under Six (SACUS), Box 5403, Brady Station, Little Rock, AR 72205

efforts to work on projects of mutual concern. OMEP publishes a journal, *The International Journal of Early Childhood Education*, and holds a biennial international assembly. An active OMEP Committee exists in the United States. (OMEP National Committee, 1718 Connecticut Ave, NW, Washington, DC 20009).

NAEYC sponsors a large national conference held annually in a major U.S. city. The conferences offer early childhood professionals a wide variety of workshops and speakers who discuss everything from the latest early childhood research to the most effective curriculum materials. These conferences provide an unparalleled opportunity to meet other professionals as well as authors of early childhood textbooks and other respected persons in the field.

ACEI also sponsors a national study conference in the spring of each year. Every few years OMEP holds international conferences in different cities throughout the world. Its U.S. National Committee has an annual meeting in conjunction with the NAEYC annual conference.

Professional associations provide several means to help early childhood educators. Members of professional organizations receive early childhood publications and resource materials as well as attending conferences, workshops, and meetings to keep abreast in the field of early childhood education.

Professional Literature and Information

Resources in professional literature and information consist of journals and periodicals, government documents and reports, reference materials, and bibliographies, which help locate different kinds of materials and information.

Professional Journals and Periodicals A variety of professional journals provide readers with practical methods to assess and teach children, theoretical and philosophical issues, empirical research, or reviews of

PROFESSIONAL JOURNALS

Advances in Child Development and Behavior
Child Care Information Exchange
Child Care Quarterly
Developmental Psychology
Directive Teacher
Early Child Development and Care
Early Childhood Research Quarterly
Early Education and Development
Early Years (now published as *Teaching Pre-K–8*)
Education and Treatment of Children
Focus on Early Childhood
Infant Behavior Development
Infants and Young Children
Instructor
Journal of Experimental Child Psychology
Journal of Research in Childhood Education
Merrill Palmer Quarterly
Monographs of the Society for Research in Child Development
Early Childhood Education Today
Teaching Pre-K–8 (formerly *Early Years*)

research. These journals in the general areas of child development and early childhood education are published by both scholarly organizations and commercial publishers.

Journals related to young children's education are distributed by the following agencies and organizations. These organizations also issue non-periodical publications related to early childhood education.

American Education. Superintendent of Documents, U.S. Government Printing Office, Washington, DC 20402.

Child Development, *Child Development Abstracts*, and *Child Development Monographs*. Society for Research and Child Development, University of Chicago Press, Chicago, IL 60637.

Child Welfare. Child Welfare League of America, Inc., 44 East 23rd Street, New York, NY 10010.

Childhood Education. Association for Childhood Education International, 11501 Georgia Avenue, Suite 315, Wheaton, MD 20902. ACEI also publishes bulletins, leaflets, and books.

Children Today. Office of Human Development Services, Department of Health and Human Services, Room 356–G, 200 Independence Avenue, SW, Washington, DC 20201.

Day Care and Early Education. Human Sciences Press, 72 Fifth Avenue, New York, NY 10011.

Dimensions. Southern Early Childhood Association, Box 5403, Brady Station, Little Rock, AR 72215.

Journal of Home Economics. American Economics Associations, 2010 Massachusetts Avenue, NW, Washington, DC 20036.

National Parent-Teacher. National Congress of Teachers and Parents, 700 North Rush Street, Chicago, IL 60511. Study guides are also available.

Young Children. National Association for the Education of Young Children, 1509 16th St., NW, Washington, DC 20036.

Government Documents and Reports The United States government publishes documents on many topics (such as child development, child care, special education and children with disabilities, early intervention, and child abuse) in technical bulletins, annual reports on programs, reports on population data, investigative series, subject monographs, periodicals, handbooks, regulations on federal programs and services, congressional reports, and copies of federal laws. Government documents can be purchased from the Superintendent of Documents in Washington, DC, or read in many libraries. They are economical and provide a rich source of information.

The Government Printing Office classifies government publications in two of its sources: (1) *Monthly Catalog of United States Government Publications*, a series of reference volumes including index listings of available materials with brief abstracts and (2) *Subject Bibliography Index*.

The *Monthly Catalog of United States Government Publications*, a series of catalogs, can be located in most university libraries and some large public libraries. Monthly catalogs are published and assembled into both semiannual and yearly cumulative indexes. A series supplement, listing only periodical publications, is also published. Information is catalogued by (1) an author index and (2) a subject index at the back of each volume. The indexes mark the monthly catalog entry number for each government publication denoting the monthly catalog volume. An abstract summarizing each publication is also included. An abstract typically contains (1) the original document's call number, (2) the author, (3) the title, (4) the government publishing agency, (5) the price, and (6) ordering information. Publications can be ordered directly from the Government Printing Office in Washington, DC. The *Subject Bibliography Index* catalogs the government's publications according to single-subject areas (such as child welfare, children, day care, and persons with disabilities). Publications are listed in alphabetical order along with their federal number and price.

Reference Materials

Reference materials present comprehensive summaries on precise topics. Comprehensive summaries may be reviews of research or of theories of early childhood education or child development. Such resources are found in books and special publications such as the following:

1. ***Carmichael's Manual of Child Psychology* (1983), published by John Wiley & Sons.** P. H. Mussen edited two large volumes, which include a comprehensive summary of current philosophical and theoretical thought and reviews of research in the psychology of human development, including such areas as the biological bases of development, infancy and early experiences, cognitive development, and socialization in young children. Comprehensive summaries provide current knowledge in selected topic areas along with critical analyses of the literature in those areas.

2. ***Review of Child Development*, under the auspices of the Society for Research in Child Development (SRCD).** This series provides integrated reviews of literature on children's development, including, for example, the history of child development (Vol. 5), the development of deaf children (Vol. 5), child abuse (Vol. 5), the effectiveness of environment intervention programs (Vol. 3), programs for disadvantaged parents (Vol. 3), psychological testing of children (Vol. 2), and genetics and the development of intelligence (Vol. 4). Russell Sage Foundation of New York published volumes 1 and 2; University of Chicago Press published volumes 3 through 6.

3. ***Handbook of Research on the Education of Young Children*, published by Macmillan.** This handbook, published in 1993 and edited by Bernard Spodek, provides researchers, practitioners, and students with a comprehensive, critical review of theoretical and empirical research in early childhood education. It brings together knowledgeable reviews of research in developmental areas, of major curriculum areas in early childhood education, of topics related to public policy, and of research methodology.

4. **The *Yearbook of Early Childhood Education* series published by Teachers College Press.** Bernard Spodek and Olivia N. Saracho are editing a series of volumes that appear annually. Each yearbook presents empirical and theoretical research currently being generated to inform practice in the field of early childhood education. Key issues, including concerns about educational equity, multiculturalism, the needs of diverse populations of children and families, and the ethical dimensions of the field, are woven into each of the annual volumes. Scholarly, yet accessible, the series covers such relevant topics in early childhood education as kindergarten education, curriculum models, literacy, bilingual and special education, physical settings, play, child care, and many others.

Bibliographies of Resources on Specific Topics Professional literature also provides teachers with bibliographies, or lists of resources, on specific topics. Reference guides classify published materials under alphabetized topic categories to introduce teachers to primary sources of information or to representative examples of literature on a precise topic.

- *Bibliographical indexes* list periodicals and other published literature under an alphabetized subject listing. Author listings may also be provided.
- *Bibliographical abstracts* provide annotated references on publications in defined topic areas in specific professional fields, such as psychology or child development.
- *Service directories* list agencies that can provide information or some type of special service.

Bibliographical indexes and bibliographical abstracts can be found in university and college libraries. Community libraries often own smaller col-

SOURCES OF BIBLIOGRAPHIC REFERENCES

Child Development Abstracts and Bibliography
Current Index to Journals in Education (CIJE)
Dissertation Abstracts
Education Index
Psychology Abstracts
Research in Education (RIE)
Research Relating to Children

lections. Bibliographical reference works summarize literature in areas such as general education, child development and early education, psychology, and other related fields. Professionals can browse through these materials to learn their content and organization. Each abstract helps the reader identify articles related to a particular topic.

State or federal agencies, and local community organizations publish *service directories*, which typically list the agencies in a specific geographic area that offer specialized services to children, families, or other service agencies. Since such directories are not widely circulated, they usually are not available in the library. Typically, key state and federal agencies that provide services and funding for services, such as state departments of education or regional offices of child development, own these directories. The Educational Resources Information Center (ERIC) may support a way to secure information concerning the existing directories.

Information Storage and Retrieval Systems

Professional literature and information on specific topics can be found in search and retrieval systems, which assemble information to provide it to possible consumers in education and psychology. Information retrieval systems provide access to research literature, government and project reports, teaching materials and aids, and other media. Users provide descriptors, or precise definitions of a subject, to retrieve information from the computer bank. The location of the exact information is indicated to help teachers save time. Computer-based information retrieval systems include

- Educational Resources Information Center (ERIC),
- National Information Center for Educational Media (NICEM), and
- SpecialNet Communication Network

Other sources can also be used. The Educational Resource Information Center (ERIC), funded by the U.S. Office of Education, provides the most widely available print resources on educational topics.

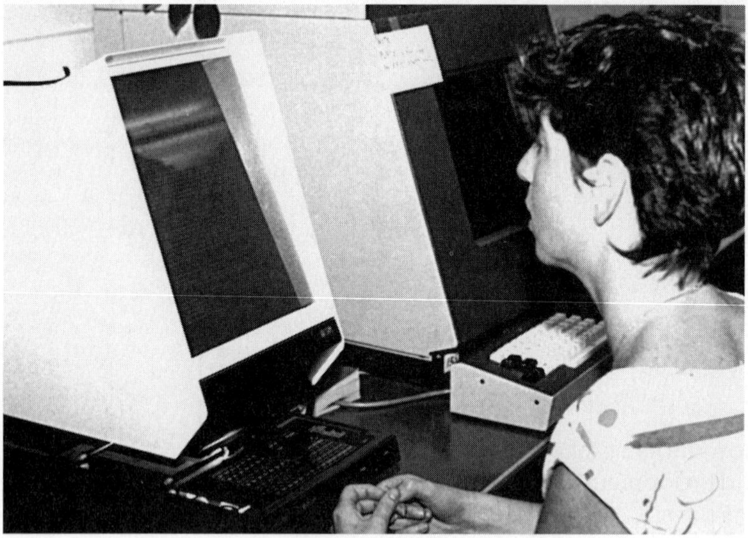

Teachers can access ERIC documents and other resources through computers and microfiche readers.

ERIC, an access system, collects a variety of information on education in both printed and audiovisual media. It is a network of 16 specialized clearinghouses, each in a precise subject area, which are found in the appropriate ERIC reference documents. ERIC clearinghouses are identified with key professional associations, government and private agencies, and training institutions, which help ERIC collect materials on new educational products and information.

ERIC's clearinghouses peruse the education field for precise subject areas (such as counseling and personnel services, science and mathematics, and levels of education—preschool, elementary, secondary, and higher education). The Clearinghouse on Elementary and Early Childhood Education, which is located at the University of Illinois College of Education, specializes in material on early childhood education.

There are 16 specialized clearinghouses throughout the country that are responsible for acquiring and handling materials in their specialized area. A central processing facility receives, enters, and indexes all documents into the ERIC system, a computerized collection of the newest documents and journal articles germane to the field. The ERIC Document Reproduction Service (EDRS) films documents onto microfiche to sell to consumers. *Current Index to Journals in Education* (CIJE) publishes monthly an extensive annotated bibliography, which covers over 700 major education periodicals. *Resources in Education* (RIE), published by the U.S. Government Printing Office, summarizes the materials in all 16 specialized ERIC clearinghouses. These materials are available through ERIC in hard copy or microfiche. The central ERIC management team, located in the National Institute of Education, sets ERIC policy and monitors the operation of the ERIC system.

In addition, ERIC provides the following user services:

- provides workshops at professional meetings to teach professionals to use its resource system;
- produces computer search reprints, which are documents of current high interest;
- responds to users' requests by conducting special computerized searches. The *Directory of ERIC Computer Services* identifies the locations at which computer searches can be run on special topics. Institutions, universities, and colleges that subscribe to ERIC offer these ERIC resources on CD-ROM in their own computer facilities.

Information can solicited from the proper ERIC Clearinghouse, which draws on the appropriate national database.

ERIC CLEARINGHOUSES

Adult, Career, and Vocational Education, Center for Vocational Education, Ohio State University, 1960 Kenny Road, Columbus, OH 43210–1090.

Counseling and Personnel Services, 2108 School of Education Building, East University and South University Streets, Ann Arbor, MI 48109–1259.

Early Childhood and Elementary Education (ERIC/EECE), University of Illinois, 804 West Pennsylvania Avenue, Urbana, IL 61801–4897.

Educational Management, University of Oregon, Eugene, OR 97403–5207.

Handicapped and Gifted Children, Council for Exceptional Children, 1920 Association Drive, Reston, VA 22091–1589.

Higher Education, George Washington University, One Dupont Circle, NW, Suite 630, Washington, DC 10036–1183.

Information Resources, School of Education, Syracuse University, 150 Marshall Avenue, Syracuse, NY 13244–2340.

Junior Colleges, University of California at Los Angeles, 405 Hilgard Avenue, Los Angeles, CA 90024–1564.

Language and Linguistics, Center for Applied Linguistics, 1118 22nd Street, NW, Washington, DC 20037–0037

Reading and Communication Skills, Indiana University, 2805 East 10th Street, Bloomington, IN 47408–2698.

Rural Education and Small Schools, Appalachia Educational Laboratory, 1031 Quarrier Street, P. O. Box 1348, Charleston, WV 25325–1348.

Science, Mathematics, and Environmental Education, Ohio State University, 1800 Cannon Drive, 1200 Chalmers Road, Columbus, OH 43212–1782.

Social Studies/Social Science Education, Indiana University, 2805 East 10th Street, Bloomington, IN 47408–2373

Teacher Education, American Association of Colleges of Teacher Education, One Dupont Circle, NW, Suite 610, Washington, DC 20036–2412.

Tests, Measurement, and Evaluation, American Institute for Research, 3333 K Street, NW, Washington, DC 20007.

Urban Education, Teachers College, Columbia University, Box 40, 525 West 120th Street, New York, NY 10027–9998.

SUMMARY

Early childhood education is continuously changing. Early childhood teachers must keep up to date to continue their self-education throughout their career. Teachers can learn more about themselves and their teaching as well as keeping up to date in the field in many ways. Staff meetings, invited speakers, films, or workshops can assist teachers to upgrade the quality of their teaching. Some early childhood programs facilitate professional development by funding staff members' attendance at community workshops; local, regional, and national conferences; and college and university courses. Educators can also exchange craft activities, songs, or action plays. They can learn from their own experience and as well as from their fellow teachers' experiences.

True professionals strive to improve their performance and therefore seek out opportunities for growth and learning by reading new books and journal articles about children, viewing films, and attending workshops, conferences, in-service training, and college courses. They join professional organizations such as the National Association for the Education of Young Children (NAEYC), its local chapter, or other early childhood organizations and participate in their activities.

REFERENCES

Association of Teacher Educators. (1985). *Developing career ladders in teaching.* Reston, VA: Author.

Beatty, J. J. (1992). *Skills for preschool teachers.* Columbus, OH: Merrill.

Clark, C. M., & Peterson, P. L. (1986). Teachers' thought processes. In M. C. Wittrock (Ed.), *Handbook of research on teaching* (3rd ed.) (pp. 255–296). New York: Macmillan.

Jorde-Bloom, P. (1987, September). Keeping a finger on the pulse beat: The director's role in assessing organizational climate. *Child Care Information Exchange*, 31–36.

Jorde-Bloom, P. (1988). *A great place to work: Improving conditions for staff in young children's programs.* Washington, DC: National Association for the Education of Young Children.

Katz, L. G. (1984). The education of preprimary teachers. In L. G. Katz, P. J. Wagemaker, & K. Steiner (Eds.), *Current topics in early childhood education*, Vol. 5 (pp. 1–26). Norwood, NJ: Ablex.

Katz, L. G. (1988). Where is early childhood education as a profession? In B. Spodek, O. N. Saracho, & D. L. Peters (Eds.), *Professionalism and the early childhood practitioner* (pp. 75–83). New York: Teachers College Press.

Katz, L. G., & Raths, J. D. (1985, November-December). A framework for research on teacher education programs. *Journal of Teacher Education, 36*(6), 9–15.

Katz, L. G., & Ward, E. H. (1978). *Initial code of ethics for early childhood education.* Washington, DC: National Association for the Education of Young Children.

Peterson, N. L. (1987). *Early intervention for handicapped and at-risk children: An introduction to early childhood special education.* Denver: Love Publishing Company.

Saracho, O. N. (1984). Perception of the teaching process in early childhood education through role analysis. *Journal of the Association for the Study of Perception, 19*(1), 26–39.

Saracho, O. N., & Spodek, B. (1983). Preparing teachers for multicultural classrooms. In O. N. Saracho & B. Spodek (Eds.), *Understanding the multicultural experience in early childhood education* (pp. 125–146). Washington, DC: National Association for the Education of Young Children.

Spodek, B. (1987). Thought processes underlying preschool teachers' classroom decisions. *Early Child Development and Care, 28*, 197–208.

Spodek, B. (1988). Implicit theories of early childhood teachers: Foundations for professional behavior. In B. Spodek, O. N. Saracho, & D. L. Peters (Eds.), *Professionalism and the early childhood practitioner* (pp. 161–172). New York: Teachers College Press.

Spodek, B., & Saracho, O. N. (1988). Professionalism in early childhood education. In B. Spodek, O. N. Saracho, & D. L. Peters (Eds.), *Professionalism and the early childhood practitioner* (pp. 59–74). New York: Teachers College Press.

Spodek, B., Saracho, O. N., & Davis, M. D. (in press). Professionalism and the preparation of early childhood practitioners. In S. Kilmer (Ed.), *Advances in early education and day care*. Greenwich, CT: JAI Press.

Spodek, B., Saracho, O. N., & Davis, M. D. (1991). *Foundations of early childhood education: Teaching three-, four-, and five-year-old children* (2nd ed). Needham Heights, MA: Allyn and Bacon.

Spodek, B., Saracho, O. N., & Peters, D. L. (1988). Professionalism, semiprofessionalism, and craftsmanship. In B. Spodek, O. N. Saracho, & D. L. Peters (Eds.), *Professionalism and the early childhood practitioner* (pp. 3–9). New York: Teachers College Press.

Appendix A

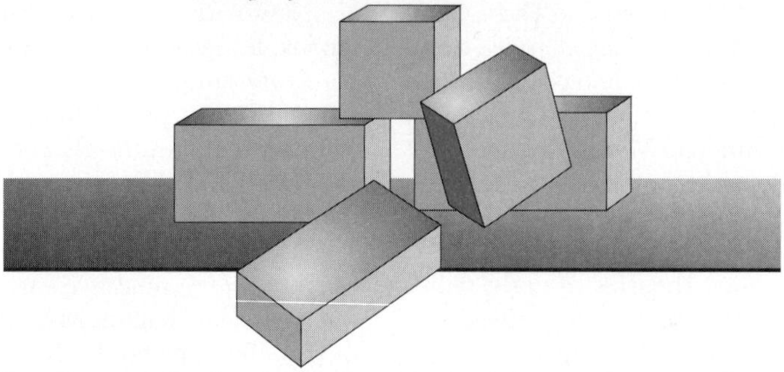

The National Association for the Education of Young Children Code of Ethical Conduct

PREAMBLE

NAEYC recognizes that many daily decisions required of those who work with young children are of a moral and ethical nature. The NAEYC Code of Ethical Conduct offers guidelines for responsible behavior and sets forth a common basis for resolving the principal ethical dilemmas encountered in early childhood education. The primary focus is on daily practice with children and their families in programs for children from birth to 8 years of age: preschools, child care centers, family day care homes, kindergartens, and primary classrooms. Many of the provisions also apply to specialists who do not work directly with children, including program administrators, parent educators, college professors, and child care licensing specialists.

Standards of ethical behavior in early childhood education are based on commitment to core values that are deeply rooted in the history of our field. We have committed ourselves to:

- Appreciating childhood as a unique and valuable stage of the human life cycle
- Basing our work with children on knowledge of child development
- Appreciating and supporting the close ties between the child and family
- Recognizing that children are best understood in the context of family, culture, and society
- Respecting the dignity, worth, and uniqueness of each individual (child, family member, and colleague)
- Helping children and adults achieve their full potential in the context of relationships that are based on trust, respect, and positive regard

The Code sets forth a conception of our professional responsibilities in four sections, each addressing an arena of professional relationships: (1) children, (2) families, (3) colleagues, and (4) community and society. Each section includes an introduction to the primary responsibilities of the early childhood practitioner in that arena, a set of ideals pointing in the direction of exemplary professional practice, and a set of principles defining practices that are required, prohibited, and permitted.

The ideals reflect the aspirations of practitioners. The principles are intended to guide conduct and assist practitioners in resolving ethical dilemmas encountered in the field. There is not necessarily a corresponding principle for each ideal. Both ideals and principles are intended to direct practitioners to those questions which, when responsibly answered, will provide the basis for conscientious decision making. While the Code provides specific direction for addressing some ethical dilemmas, many others will require the practitioner to combine the guidance of the Code with sound professional judgment.

The ideals and principles in this Code present a shared conception of professional responsibility that affirms our commitment to the core values of our field. The Code publicly acknowledges the responsibilities that we in the field have assumed and in so doing supports ethical behavior in our work. Practitioners who face ethical dilemmas are urged to seek guidance in the applicable parts of this Code and in the spirit that informs the whole.

SECTION I: ETHICAL RESPONSIBILITIES TO CHILDREN

Childhood is a unique and valuable stage in the life cycle. Our paramount responsibility is to provide safe, healthy, nurturing, and responsive settings for children. We are committed to supporting children's development by cherishing individual differences, by helping them learn to live and work cooperatively, and by promoting their self-esteem.

Ideals:

I–1.1—To be familiar with the knowledge base of early childhood education and to keep current through continuing education and in-service training.

I–1.2—To base program practices upon current knowledge in the field of child development and related disciplines and upon particular knowledge of each child.

I–1.3—To recognize and respect the uniqueness and the potential of each child.

I–1.4—To appreciate the special vulnerability of children.

I–1.5—To create and maintain safe and healthy settings that foster children's social, emotional, intellectual, and physical development and that respect their dignity and their contributions.

I–1.6—To support the right of children with special needs to participate, consistent with their ability, in regular early childhood programs.

Principles:

P–1.1—Above all, we shall not harm children. We shall not participate in practices that are disrespectful, degrading, dangerous, exploitative, intimidating, psychologically damaging, or physically harmful to children. This principle has precedence over all others in this Code.

P–1.2—We shall not participate in practices that discriminate against children by denying benefits, giving special advantages, or excluding them from programs or activities on the basis of their race, religion, sex, national origin, or the status, behavior, or beliefs of their parents. (This principle does not apply to programs that have a lawful mandate to provide services to a particular population of children.)

P–1.3—We shall involve all of those with relevant knowledge (including staff and parents) in decisions concerning a child.

P–1.4—When, after appropriate efforts have been made with a child and the family, the child still does not appear to be benefitting from a program, we shall communicate our concern to the family in a positive way and offer them assistance in finding a more suitable setting.

P–1.5—We shall be familiar with the symptoms of child abuse and neglect and know community procedures for addressing them.

P–1.6—When we have evidence of child abuse or neglect, we shall report the evidence to the appropriate community agency and follow up to ensure that appropriate action has been taken. When possible, parents will be informed that the referral has been made.

P–1.7—When another person tells us of their suspicion that a child is being abused or neglected but we lack evidence, we shall assist that person in taking appropriate action to protect the child.

P–1.8—When a child protective agency fails to provide adequate protection for abused or neglected children, we acknowledge a collective ethical responsibility to work toward improvement of these services.

SECTION II:
ETHICAL RESPONSIBILITIES TO FAMILIES

Families are of primary importance in children's development. (The term family may include others, besides parents, who are responsibly involved with the child.) Because the family and the early childhood educator have a common interest in the child's welfare, we acknowledge a primary responsibility to bring about collaboration between the home and school in ways that enhance the child's development.

Ideals:

I–2.1—To develop relationships of mutual trust with the families we serve.

I–2.2—To acknowledge and build upon strengths and competencies as we support families in their task of nurturing children.

I–2.3—To respect the dignity of each family and its culture, customs, and beliefs.

I–2.4—To respect families' childrearing values and their right to make decisions for their children.

I–2.5—To interpret each child's progress to parents within the framework of a developmental perspective and to help families understand and appreciate the value of developmentally appropriate early childhood programs.

I–2.6—To help family members improve their understanding of their children and to enhance their skills as parents.

I–2.7—To participate in building support networks for families by providing them with opportunities to interact with program staff and families.

Principles:

P–2.1—We shall not deny family members access to their child's classroom or program setting.

P–2.2—We shall inform families of program philosophy, policies, and personnel qualifications, and explain why we teach as we do.

P–2.3—We shall inform families of and, when appropriate, involve them in policy decisions.

P–2.4—We shall inform families of and, when appropriate, involve them in significant decisions affecting their child.

P–2.5—We shall inform the family of accidents involving their child, of risks such as exposures to contagious disease that may result in infection, and of events that might result in psychological damage.

P–2.6—We shall not permit or participate in research that could in any way hinder the education or development of the children in our programs. Families shall be fully informed of any proposed research projects involving their children and shall have the opportunity to give or withhold consent.

P–2.7—We shall not engage in or support exploitation of families. We shall not use our relationship with a family for private advantage or personal gain, or enter into relationships with family members that might impair our effectiveness in working with children.

P–2.8—We shall develop written policies for the protection of confidentiality and the disclosure of children's records. The policy documents shall be made available to all program personnel and families. Disclosure of children's records beyond family members, program personnel, and consultants having an obligation of confidentiality shall require familial consent (except in cases of abuse or neglect).

P–2.9—We shall maintain confidentiality and shall respect the family's right to privacy, refraining from disclosure of confidential information and intrusion into family life. However, when we are concerned about a child's welfare, it is permissible to reveal confidential information to agencies and individuals who may be able to act in the child's interest.

P–2.10—In cases where family members are in conflict we shall work openly, sharing our observations of the child, to help all parties involved make informed decisions. We shall refrain from becoming an advocate for one party.

P–2.11—We shall be familiar with and appropriately use community resources and professional services that support families. After a referral has been made, we shall follow up to ensure that services have been adequately provided.

SECTION III: ETHICAL RESPONSIBILITIES TO COLLEAGUES

In a caring, cooperative work place human dignity is respected, professional satisfaction is promoted, and positive relationships are modeled. Our primary responsibility in this arena is to establish and maintain settings and relationships that support productive work and meet professional needs.

A—RESPONSIBILITIES TO CO-WORKERS

Ideals:

I–3A.1—To establish and maintain relationships of trust and cooperation with co-workers.

I–3A.2—To share resources and information with co-workers.

I–3A.3—To support co-workers in meeting their professional needs and in their professional development.

I–3A.4—To accord co-workers due recognition of professional achievement.

Principles:

P–3A.1—When we have concern about the professional behavior of a co-worker, we shall first let that person know of our concern and attempt to resolve the matter collegially.

P–3A.2—We shall exercise care in expressing views regarding the personal attributes or professional conduct of co-workers. Statements should be based on firsthand knowledge and relevant to the interests of children and programs.

B—RESPONSIBILITIES TO EMPLOYERS

Ideals:

I–3B.1—To assist the program in providing the highest quality of service.

I–3B.2—To maintain loyalty to the program and uphold its reputation.

Principles:

P–3B.1—When we do not agree with program policies, we shall first attempt to effect change through constructive action within the organization.

P–3B.2—We shall speak or act on behalf of an organization only when authorized. We shall take care to note when we are speaking for the organization and when we are expressing a personal judgment.

C—RESPONSIBILITIES TO EMPLOYEES

Ideals:

I–3C.1—To promote policies and working conditions that foster competence, well-being, and self-esteem in staff members.

I–3C.2—To create a climate of trust and candor that will enable staff to speak and act in the best interests of children, families, and the field of early childhood education.

I–3C.3—To strive to secure an adequate livelihood for those who work with or on behalf of young children.

Principles:

P-3C.1—In decisions concerning children and programs, we shall appropriately utilize the training, experience, and expertise of staff members.

P-3C.2—We shall provide staff members with working conditions that permit them to carry out their responsibilities, timely and nonthreatening evaluation procedures, written grievance procedures, constructive feedback, and opportunities for continuing professional development and advancement.

P-3C.3—We shall develop and maintain comprehensive written personnel policies that define program standards and, when applicable, that specify the extent to which employees are accountable for their conduct outside the work place. These policies shall be given to new staff members and shall be available for review by all staff members.

P-3C.4—Employees who do not meet program standards shall be informed of areas of concern and, when possible, assisted in improving their performance.

P-3C.5—Employees who are dismissed shall be informed of the reasons for their termination. When a dismissal is for cause, justification must be based on evidence of inadequate or inappropriate behavior that is accurately documented, current, and available for the employee to review.

P-3C.6—In making evaluations and recommendations, judgments shall be based on fact and relevant to the interests of children and programs.

P-3C.7—Hiring and promotion shall be based solely on a person's record of accomplishment and ability to carry out the responsibilities of the position.

P-3C.8—In hiring, promotion, and provision of training, we shall not participate in any form of discrimination based on race, religion, sex, national origin, handicap, age, or sexual preference. We shall be familiar with laws and regulations that pertain to employment discrimination.

SECTION IV:
ETHICAL RESPONSIBILITIES TO COMMUNITY AND SOCIETY

Early childhood programs operate within a context of an immediate community made up of families and other institutions concerned with children's welfare. Our responsibilities to the community are to provide programs that meet its needs and to cooperate with agencies and professions that share responsibility for children. Because the larger society has a measure of responsibility for the welfare and protection of children, and because of our specialized expertise in child development, we acknowledge an obligation to serve as a voice for children everywhere.

Ideals:

I-4.1—To provide the community with high-quality, culturally sensitive programs and services.

I-4.2—To promote cooperation among agencies and professions concerned with the welfare of young children, their families, and their teachers.

I-4.3—To work, through education, research, and advocacy, toward an environmentally safe world in which all children are adequately fed, sheltered, and nurtured.

I-4.4—To work, through education, research, and advocacy, toward a society in which all young children have access to quality programs.

I-4.5—To promote knowledge and understanding of young children and their needs. To work toward greater social acknowledgment of children's rights and greater social acceptance of responsibility for their well-being.

I-4.6—To support policies and laws that promote the well-being of children and families. To oppose those that impair their well-being. To cooperate with other individuals and groups in these efforts.

I-4.7—To further the professional development of the field of early childhood education and to strengthen its commitment to realizing its core values as reflected in this Code.

Principles:

P–4.1—We shall communicate openly and truthfully about the nature and extent of services that we provide.

P–4.2—We shall not accept or continue to work in positions for which we are personally unsuited or professionally unqualified. We shall not offer services that we do not have the competence, qualifications, or resources to provide.

P–4.3—We shall be objective and accurate in reporting the knowledge upon which we base our program practices.

P–4.4—We shall cooperate with other professionals who work with children and their families.

P–4.5—We shall not hire or recommend for employment any person who is unsuited for a position with respect to competence, qualifications, or character.

P–4.6—We shall report the unethical or incompetent behavior of a colleague to a supervisor when informal resolution is not effective.

P–4.7—We shall be familiar with laws and regulations that serve to protect the children in our programs.

P–4.8—We shall not participate in practices which are in violation of laws and regulations that protect the children in our programs.

P–4.9—When we have evidence that an early childhood program is violating laws or regulations protecting children, we shall report it to persons responsible for the program. If compliance is not accomplished within a reasonable time, we will report the violation to appropriate authorities who can be expected to remedy the situation.

P–4.10—When we have evidence that an agency or a professional charged with providing services to children, families, or teachers is failing to meet its obligations, we acknowledge a collective ethical responsibility to report the problem to appropriate authorities or to the public.

P–4.11—When a program violates or requires its employees to violate this Code, it is permissible, after fair assessment of the evidence, to disclose the identity of that program.

Appendix B

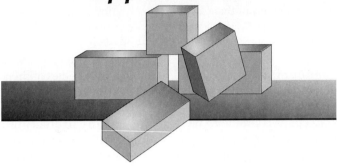

NAEYC Position Statement on Developmentally Appropriate Practice in Early Childhood Programs Serving Children from Birth through Age 8

INTRODUCTION

The quality of our nation's educational system has come under intense public scrutiny in the 1980s. While much of the attention has been directed at secondary and postsecondary education, the field of early childhood education must also examine its practices in light of current knowledge of child development and learning.

The purpose of this paper is to describe developmentally appropriate practice in early childhood programs for administrators, teachers, parents, policy makers, and others who make decisions about the care and education of young children. An early childhood program is any part-day or full-day group program in a center, school, or other facility that serves children from birth through age 8. Early childhood programs include child care centers, private and public preschools, kindergartens, and primary grade schools.

RATIONALE

In recent years, a trend toward increased emphasis on formal instruction in academic skills has emerged in early childhood programs. This trend toward formal academic instruction for younger children is based on misconceptions about early learning (Elkind, 1986). Despite the trend among some educators to formalize instruction, there has been no comparable evidence of change in what young children need for optimal development or how they learn. In fact, a growing body of research has emerged recently affirming that children learn most effectively through a concrete, play-oriented approach to early childhood education.

In addition to an increased emphasis on academics, early childhood programs have experienced other changes. The number of programs has increased in response to the growing demand for out-of-home care and education during the early years. Some characteristics of early childhood programs have also changed in the last few years. For example, children are now enrolled in programs at younger ages, many from infancy. The length of the program day for all ages of children has been extended in response to the need for extended hours of care for employed families. Similarly, program sponsorship has become more diverse. The public schools are playing a larger role in providing prekindergarten programs or before- and after-school child care. Corporate America is also becoming a more visible sponsor of child care programs.

Programs have changed in response to social, economic, and political forces; however, these changes have not always taken into account the basic developmental needs of young children, which have remained constant. The trend toward early academics, for example, is antithetical to what we know about how young children learn. Programs should be tailored to meet the needs of children, rather than expecting children to adjust to the demands of a specific program.

POSITION STATEMENT

The National Association for the Education of Young Children (NAEYC) believes that a high quality early childhood program provides a safe and nurturing environment that promotes the physical, social, emotional, and cognitive development of young children while responding to the needs of families. Although the quality of an early childhood program may be affected by many factors, a major determinant of program quality is the extent to which knowledge of child development is applied in program practices—-the degree to which the program is *developmentally appropriate.* NAEYC believes that high quality, developmentally appropriate programs should be available to all children and their families.

In this position paper, the concept of *developmental appropriateness* will first be defined. Then guidelines will be presented describing how developmental appropriateness can be applied to four components of early childhood programs: curriculum; adult-child interactions; relations between the home and program; and developmental evaluation of children. The statement concludes with a discussion of major policy implications and recommendations. These guidelines are designed to be used in conjunction with NAEYC's Criteria for High Quality Early Childhood Programs, the standards for accreditation by the National Academy of Early Childhood Programs (NAEYC, 1984).

Definition of Developmental Appropriateness

The concept of developmental appropriateness has two dimensions: age appropriateness and individual appropriateness.

1. **Age appropriateness.** Human development research indicates that there are universal, predictable sequences of growth and change that occur in children during the first 9 years of life. These predictable changes occur in all domains of development—physical, emotional, social, and cognitive. Knowledge of typical development of children within the age span served by the program provides a framework from which teachers prepare the learning environment and plan appropriate experiences.
2. **Individual appropriateness.** Each child is a unique person with an individual pattern and timing of growth, as well as individual personality, learning style, and family background. Both the curriculum and adults' interactions with children should be responsive to individual differences. Learning in young children is the result of interaction between the child's thoughts and experiences with materials, ideas, and people. These experiences should match the child's developing abilities, while also challenging the child's interest and understanding.

Teachers can use child development knowledge to identify the range of appropriate behaviors, activities, and materials for a specific age group. This knowledge is used in conjunction with understanding about individual children's growth patterns, strengths, interests, and experiences to design the most appropriate learning environment. Although the content of the curriculum is determined by many factors such as tradition, the subject matter of the disciplines, social or cultural values, and parental desires, for the content and teaching strategies to be developmentally appropriate they must be age appropriate and individually appropriate.

Children's play is a primary vehicle for and indicator of their mental growth. Play enables children to progress along the developmental sequence from the sensorimotor intelligence of infancy to preoperational thought in the preschool years to the concrete operational thinking exhibited by primary children (Fein, 1979; Fromberg, 1986; Piaget, 1952; Sponseller, 1982). In addition to its role in cognitive development, play also serves important functions in children's physical, emotional, and social development (Herron & Sutton-Smith, 1974). Therefore, child-initiated, child-directed, teacher-supported play is an essential component of developmentally appropriate practice (Fein & Rivkin, 1986).

GUIDELINES FOR DEVELOPMENTALLY APPROPRIATE PRACTICE

I. Curriculum

A developmentally appropriate curriculum for young children is planned to be appropriate for the age span of the children within the group and is implemented with attention to the different needs, interests, and developmental levels of those individual children.

A. **Developmentally appropriate curriculum provides for all areas of a child's development: physical, emotional, social, and cognitive through an integrated approach** (Almy, 1975; Biber, 1984; Elkind, 1986; Forman & Kuschner, 1983; Kline, 1985; Skeen, Garner, & Cartwright, 1984; Spodek, 1985).

Realistic curriculum goals for children should address all of these areas in age-appropriate ways. Children's learning does not occur in narrowly defined subject areas; their development and learning are integrated. Any activity that stimulates one dimension of development and learning affects other dimensions as well.

B. **Appropriate curriculum planning is based on teachers' observations and recordings of each child's special interests and developmental progress** (Almy, 1975; Biber, 1984; Cohen, Stern, & Balaban, 1983; Goodwin & Goodwin, 1982).

Realistic curriculum goals and plans are based on regular assessment of individual needs, strengths, and interests. Curriculum is based on both age-appropriate and individually appropriate information. For example, individual children's family/cultural backgrounds—such as expressive styles, ways of interacting, play, and games—are used to broaden the curriculum for all children.

C. **Curriculum planning emphasizes learning as an interactive process. Teachers prepare the environment for children to learn through active exploration and interaction with adults, other children, and materials** (Biber, 1984; Fein, 1979; Forman & Kuschner, 1983; Fromberg, 1986; Goffin & Tull, 1985; Griffin, 1982; Kamii, 1985; Lay-Dopyera & Dopyera, 1986; Powell, 1986; Sponseller, 1982).

The process of interacting with materials and people results in learning. Finished products or "correct" solutions that conform to adult standards are not very accurate criteria for judging whether learning has occurred. Much of young children's learning takes place when they direct their own play activities. During play, children feel successful when they engage in a task they have defined for themselves, such as finding their way through an obstacle course with a friend or pouring water into and out of various containers. Such learning should not be inhibited by adult-established concepts of completion, achievement, and failure. Activities should be designed to concentrate on furthering emerging skills through creative activity and intense involvement.

D. **Learning activities and materials should be concrete, real, and relevant to the lives of young children** (Almy, 1975; Biber, 1984; Evans, 1984; Forman & Kuschner, 1983; Hawkins, 1970; Hirsch, 1984; Holt, 1979; Kamii, 1985; Kline, 1985; Piaget, 1972; Schickedanz, 1986; Seefeldt, 1986; Smith, 1985; Weber, 1984).

Children need years of play with real objects and events before they are able to understand the meaning of symbols such as letters and numbers. Learning takes place as young children touch, manipulate, and experiment with things and interact with people. Throughout early childhood, children's concepts and language gradually develop to enable them to understand more abstract or symbolic information. Pictures and stories should be used frequently to build upon children's real experiences.

Workbooks, worksheets, coloring books, and adult-made models of art products for children to copy are *not* appropriate for young children, especially those younger than 6. Children older than 5 show increasing abilities to learn through written exercises, oral presentations, and other adult-directed teaching strategies. However, the child's active participation in self-directed play with concrete, real-life experiences continues to be a key to motivated, meaningful learning in kindergarten and the primary grades.

Basic learning materials and activities for an appropriate curriculum include sand, water, clay, and accessories to use with them; hollow, table, and unit blocks; puzzles with varying numbers of pieces; many types of games; a variety of small manipulative toys; dramatic play props such as those for housekeeping and transportation; a variety of science investigation equipment and items to explore; a changing selection of appropriate and aesthetically pleasing books and recordings; supplies of paper, water-based paint and markers, and other materials for creative expression; large muscle equipment; field trips; classroom responsibilities, such as helping with routines; and positive interactions and problem-solving opportunities with other children and adults.

E. **Programs provide for a wider range of developmental interests and abilities than the chronological age range of the group would suggest. Adults are prepared to meet the needs of children who exhibit unusual interests and skills outside the normal developmental range** (Kitano, 1982; Languis, Sanders, & Tipps, 1980; Schickedanz, Schickedanz, & Forsyth, 1982; Souweine, Crimmins, & Mazel, 1981; Uphoff & Gilmore, 1985).

Activities and equipment should be provided for a chronological age range which in many cases is at least 12 months. However, the normal developmental age range in any group may be as much as 2 years. Some mainstreamed situations will demand a wider range of expectations. When the developmental age range of a group is more than 18 months, the need increases for a large variety of furnishings, equipment, and teaching strategies. The complexity of materials should also reflect the age span of the group. For example, a group that includes 3-, 4-, and 5-year-olds would need books of varying length and complexity; puzzles with varying numbers and sizes of pieces; games that require a range of skills and abilities to follow rules; and other diverse materials, teaching methods, and room arrangements.

F. **Teachers provide a variety of activities and materials; teachers increase the difficulty, complexity, and challenge of an activity as children are involved with it and as children develop understanding and skills** (Davidson, 1985; Ferreiro & Teberosky, 1982; Forman & Kaden, 1986;

Gerber, 1982; Gilbert, 1981; Gonzalez-Mena & Eyer, 1980; Greenberg, 1976; Hill, 1979; Hirsch, 1984; Holt, 1979; Honig, 1980, 1981; Kamii, 1982, 1985; Kamii & DeVries, 1980; Lasky & Mukerji, 1980; McDonald, 1979; National Institute of Education, 1984; Schickedanz, 1986; Smith, 1982; Smith, 1983; Sparling, 1984; Stewart, 1982; Veach, 1977; Willert & Kamii, 1985; Willis & Ricciuti, 1975).

As children work with materials or activities, teachers listen, observe, and interpret children's behavior. Teachers can then facilitate children's involvement and learning by asking questions, making suggestions, or adding more complex materials or ideas to a situation. During a program year, as well as from one year to another, activities and environments for children should change in arrangement and inventory, and special events should also be planned. Examples of developmentally appropriate learning activities for various age groups follow.

1. Infants and Toddlers

Infants and toddlers learn by experiencing the environment through their senses (seeing, hearing, tasting, smelling, and feeling), by physically moving around, and through social interaction. Nonmobile infants absorb and organize a great deal of information about the world around them, so adults talk and sing with them about what is happening and bring them objects to observe and manipulate. At times adults carry nonmobile infants around the environment to show them interesting events and people. Mobile infants and toddlers increasingly use toys, language, and other learning materials in their play.

Adults play a vital socialization role with infants and toddlers. Warm, positive relationships with adults help infants develop a sense of trust in the world and feelings of competence. These interactions are critical for the development of the children's healthy self-esteem. The trusted adult becomes the secure base from which the mobile infant or toddler explores the environment.

Important independence skills are being acquired during these years, including personal care such as toileting, feeding, and dressing. The most appropriate teaching technique for this age group is to give ample opportunities for the children to use self-initiated repetition to practice newly acquired skills and to experience feelings of autonomy and success. Infants will bat at, grasp, bang, or drop their toys. Patience is essential as a toddler struggles to put on a sweater. Imitation, hiding, and naming games are also important for learning at this age. Realistic toys will enable children to engage in increasingly complex types of play.

Two-year-olds are learning to produce language rapidly. They need simple books, pictures, puzzles, and music, and time and space for active play such as jumping, running, and dancing. Toddlers are acquiring social skills, but in groups there should be several of the same toy because egocentric toddlers are not yet able to understand the concept of sharing.

2. Three-, 4-, and 5-Year-Olds

Curriculum for 3-year-olds should emphasize language, activity, and movement, with major emphasis on large muscle activity. Appropriate activities include dramatic play, wheel toys and climbers, puzzles and blocks, and opportunities to talk and listen to simple stories.

Four-year-olds enjoy a greater variety of experiences and more small motor activities like scissors, art, manipulatives, and cooking. They are more able to concentrate and remember as well as recognize objects by shape, color, or size. Four-year-olds are developing basic math concepts and problem-solving skills.

Some 4-year-olds and most 5-year-olds combine ideas into more complex relations (for example, number concepts such as one-to-one correspondence) and have growing memory capacity and fine motor physical skills. Some 4-year-olds and most 5s display a growing interest in the functional aspects of written language, such as recognizing meaningful words and trying to write their own names. Activities designed solely to teach the alphabet, phonics, and penmanship are much less appropriate for this age group than providing a print-rich environment that stimulates the development of language and literacy skills in a meaningful context.

Curriculum for 4s and 5s can expand beyond the child's immediate experience of self, home, and family to include special events and trips. Five-year-olds are developing interest in community and the world outside their own. They also use motor skills well, even daringly, and show increasing ability to pay attention for longer times and in larger groups if the topic is meaningful.

3. Six-, 7-, and 8-Year-Olds

Six-year-olds are active and demonstrate considerable verbal ability; they are becoming interested in games and rules and develop concepts and problem-solving skills from these experiences. Most 6-year-olds and many 7- and 8-year-olds may be more mature mentally than physically. Therefore, hands-on activity and experimentation is more appropriate for this age group than fatiguing mechanical seatwork.

Seven-year-olds seem to need time to catch up and practice with many newly acquired physical and cognitive skills. They become increasingly able to reason, to listen to others, and to show social give-and-take.

Eight-year-olds combine great curiosity with increased social interest. Now they are able to learn about other, more distant peoples. During first, second, and third grade, children can learn from the symbolic experiences of reading books and listening to stories; however, their understanding of what they read is based on their ability to relate the written word to their own experience. Primary grade children also learn to communicate through written language, dictating or writing stories about their own experiences or fantasies. The same is true of the development of number concepts. Children's mathematical concepts develop from their own thinking during games and real-life experiences that involve quantification, such as cooking or carpentry.

G. **Adults provide opportunities for children to choose from among a variety of activities, materials, and equipment; and time to explore through active involvement. Adults facilitate children's engagement with materials and activities and extend the child's learning by asking questions or making suggestions that stimulate children's thinking** (Elkind, 1986; Forman & Kuschner, 1983; Goffin & Tull, 1985; Kamii & Lee-Katz, 1979; Lay-Dopyera & Dopyera, 1986; Sackoff & Hart, 1984; Skeen, Garner, & Cartwright, 1984; Sparling, 1984).

Children of all ages need uninterrupted periods of time to become involved, investigate, select, and persist at activities. The teacher's role in child-chosen activity is to prepare the environment with stimulating, challenging activity choices and then to facilitate children's engagement. In developmentally appropriate programs, adults:

1. provide a rich variety of activities and materials from which to choose. Such variety increases the likelihood of a child's prolonged or satisfied attention and increases independence and opportunity for making decisions.
2. offer children the choice to participate in a small group or in a solitary activity.
3. assist and guide children who are not yet able to use easily and enjoy child-choice activity periods.
4. provide opportunities for child-initiated, child-directed practice of skills as a self-chosen activity.

Children need opportunities to repeat acquired skills to fully assimilate their learning. Repetition that is initiated and directed by the child, not adult-directed drill and practice, is most valuable for assimilation.

H. **Multicultural and nonsexist experiences, materials, and equipment should be provided for children of all ages** (Ramsey, 1979, 1982; Saracho & Spodek, 1983; Sprung, 1978).

Providing a wide variety of multicultural, nonstereotyping materials and activities helps ensure the individual appropriateness of the curriculum and also

1. enhances each child's self-concept and self-esteem,
2. supports the integrity of the child's family,
3. enhances the child's learning processes in both the home and the early childhood program by strengthening ties,
4. extends experiences of children and their families to include knowledge of the ways of others, especially those who share the community, and
5. enriches the lives of all participants with respectful acceptance and appreciation of differences and similarities among them.

Multicultural experiences should not be limited to a celebration of holidays and should include foods, music, families, shelter, and other aspects common to all cultures.

I. **Adults provide a balance of rest and active movement for children throughout the program day** (Cratty, 1982; Curtis, 1986; Hendrick, 1986; Stewart, 1982; Willis & Ricciuti, 1975).

For infants and toddlers, naps and quiet activities such as listening to rhymes and music provide periodic rest from the intense physical exploration that is characteristic of this age group. Two-year-olds, and many 3s, will need morning and/or afternoon naps, and should also have periods of carefully planned transition to quieting-down or rousing, especially before and after eating and sleeping. Children at about $2\frac{1}{2}$- to 3-years-old become able to maintain brief interest in occasional small-group, teacher-conducted activities, and may enjoy quiet stories, music, and fingerplays together between periods of intense activity. Most 4s and many 5s still need naps, especially if their waking days are very long as they are in some child care situations. Children at this age need planned alternations of active and quiet activities and are usually willing to participate in brief, interesting, small-group activities. Older children continue to need alternating periods of active and quiet activity throughout the day, beyond traditionally provided recess.

The pace of the program day will vary depending on the length of time children are present, but children should never be rushed and schedules should be flexible enough to take advantage of impromptu experiences. The balance between active and quiet activity should be maintained throughout the day by alternating activities.

J. **Outdoor experiences should be provided for children of all ages** (Cratty, 1982; Curtis, 1986; Frost & Klein, 1979).

Because their physical development is occurring so rapidly, young children through age 8 need daily outdoor experiences to practice large muscle skills, learn about outdoor environments, and experience freedom not always possible indoors. Outdoor time is an integral part of the curriculum and requires planning; it is not simply a time for children to release pent-up energy.

II. Adult-Child Interaction

The developmental appropriateness of an early childhood program is most apparent in the interactions between adults and children. Developmentally appropriate interactions are based on adults' knowledge and expectations of age-appropriate behavior in children balanced by adults' awareness of individual differences among children.

A. **Adults respond quickly and directly to children's needs, desires, and messages**

and adapt their responses to children's differing styles and abilities (Bell & Ainsworth, 1972; Erikson, 1950; Genishi, 1986; Greenspan & Greenspan, 1985; Honig, 1980, 1981; Lozoff, Brillenham, Trause, Kennell, & Klaus, 1977; Shure & Spivak, 1978; Smith & Davis, 1976).

Appropriate responses vary with the age of the child. Adults should respond immediately to infants' cries of distress. The response should be warm and soothing as the adult identifies the child's needs. Adults should also respond appropriately to infants' vocalizations, manipulation of objects, and movement, as these are the ways infants communicate. Adults hold and touch infants frequently; talk and sing to infants in a soothing, friendly voice; smile and maintain eye contact with infants. For toddlers and 2-year-olds, adults remain close by, giving attention and physical comfort as needed. Adults repeat children's words, paraphrase, or use synonyms or actions to help assure toddlers that they are understood. As children get older, adult responses are characterized by less physical communication and more verbal responsiveness, although immediacy is still important. Positive responses such as smiles and interest, and concentrated attention on children's activity, are important. Adults move quietly and circulate among individuals in groups to communicate with children in a friendly and relaxed manner.

From infancy through the primary grades, adult communication with children is facilitated by sitting low or kneeling, and making eye contact. With all age groups, adults should also be aware of the powerful influence of modeling and other nonverbal communication; adults' actions should be compatible with their verbal messages and confirm that children understand their messages.

B. **Adults provide many varied opportunities for children to communicate** (Cazden, 1981; Genishi, 1986; Gordon, 1970, 1975; Greenspan & Greenspan, 1985; Lay-Dopyera & Dopyera, 1986; McAfee, 1985; Schachter & Strage, 1982; Schickedanz, 1986.

Children acquire communication skills through hearing and using language, and as adults listen and respond to what children say. Communication skills grow out of the desire to use language to express needs, insights, and excitement, and to solve problems. Children do not learn language, or any other concepts, by being quiet and listening to a lecture from an adult. Listening experiences—when there is something meaningful to listen to such as a story or poetry—can enrich language learning. Most language interaction with infants and toddlers is on an individual basis, although occasionally a group of two or three children may gather to hear an absorbing story. Throughout the preschool years, individual abilities to sit and pay attention will vary considerably, but time periods are short and groups should be small. During kindergarten and the primary grades, children can listen to directions or stories for longer periods of time (gradually expanding as children get older). Individual and small group interactions are still the most effective because children have the opportunity for two-way communication with adults and other children. Total group instructional techniques are *not* as effective in facilitating the development of communication skills and other learning in young children.

Equally important are opportunities for children to engage in two-way communication with others. Infants use crying and body movements to communicate. Adult responses to this communication, including the use of soothing language and descriptions of what is happening, build the foundation for children's ability to use language and their ability to feel good about themselves. Children rapidly expand their ability to understand language in their early years, and from about the age of 2, children can engage in increasingly interesting and lengthy conversations with adults and other children. These one-on-one exchanges are critical throughout the early years. Children's questions, and their responses to questions, particularly open-ended questions, provide valuable information about the individual's level of thinking.

C. **Adults facilitate a child's successful completion of tasks by providing support, focused attention, physical proximity, and verbal encouragement. Adults recognize that children learn from trial and error and that children's misconceptions reflect their developing thoughts** (Cohen, Stern, & Balaban, 1983; Elkind, 1986; Gottfried, 1983: Kamii, 1985; Piaget, 1950; Veach, 1977; Wallinga & Sweaney, 1985; Wellman, 1982; Zavitkovsky, Baker, Berlfein, & Almy, 1986).

Real successes are important incentives for people of all ages to continue learning and maintain motivation. Children learn from their own mistakes. Adults can examine the problem with the child and, if appropriate, encourage the child to try again or to find alternatives. Teachers plan many open-ended activities that have more than one right answer, and value the unique responses of individual children.

D. **Teachers are alert to signs of undue stress in children's behavior, and aware of appropriate stress-reducing activities and techniques** (Dreikurs, Grunwald, & Pepper, 1982; Elkind, 1986; Gazda, 1973; Honig, 1986; McCracken, 1986; Warren, 1977).

Formal, inappropriate instructional techniques are a source of stress for young children. When children exhibit stress-related behavior, teachers should examine the program to ensure that expectations are appropriate and not placing excessive demands on children.

When children experience stress from other sources, adults can find ways to reduce or eliminate the problem, or help children cope with it. Appropriate adult behaviors may include cuddling and soothing a crying infant; offering a toddler a favorite toy; providing books, water play, body movement, music, and quiet times for older children; and physically comforting and listening to the concerns of a child of any age who is in distress. Children's responses to stress are as individual as their learning styles. An understanding adult who is sensitive to individual children's reactions is the key to providing appropriate comfort.

E. **Adults facilitate the development of self-esteem by respecting, accepting, and comforting children, regardless of the child's behavior** (Coopersmith, 1975; Gordon, 1970, 1975; Greenspan & Greenspan, 1985; Kobak, 1979; Kuczynski, 1983; Lickona, 1983; Moore, 1982; Mussen & Eisenberg-Bert, 1977; Riley, 1984; Rubin & Everett, 1982; Smith & Davis, 1976; Stone, 1978).

Understanding behavior that is not unusual for young children, such as messiness, interest in body parts and genital differences, crying and resistance, aggression, and later infraction of rules and truth, is the basis for appropriate guidance of young children. Developmentally appropriate guidance demonstrates respect for children. It helps them understand and grow, and is directed toward helping children develop self-control and the ability to make better decisions in the future.

Adult behaviors that are *never* acceptable toward children include: screaming in anger; neglect; inflicting physical or emotional pain; criticism of a child's person or family by ridiculing, blaming, teasing, insulting, name-calling, threatening, or using frightening or humiliating punishment. Adults should not laugh at children's behavior, nor discuss it among themselves in the presence of children.

F. **Adults facilitate the development of self-control in children** (Asher, Renshaw, & Hymel, 1982; Hoffman, 1975; Honig, 1985; Kopp, 1982; Lytton, 1979; Miller, 1984; Moore, 1982; Read, Gardner, & Mahler, 1986; Rogers & Ross, 1986; Schaffer, 1984; Stone, 1978; Wolfgang & Glickman, 1980; Yarrow, Scott, & Waxler, 1973; Yarrow & Waxler, 1976).

Children learn self-control when adults treat them with dignity and use discipline techniques such as

1. guiding children by setting clear, consistent, fair limits for classroom behavior; or in the case of older children, helping them to set their own limits;
2. valuing mistakes as learning opportunities;
3. redirecting children to more acceptable behavior or activity;
4. listening when children talk about their feelings and frustrations;
5. guiding children to resolve conflicts and modeling skills that help children to solve their own problems; and
6. patiently reminding children of rules and their rationale as needed.

G. **Adults are responsible for all children under their supervision at all times and plan for increasing independence as children acquire skills** (Stewart, 1982; Veach, 1977).

Adults must constantly and closely supervise and attend every child younger than the age of 3. They must be close enough to touch infants when awake, catch a climbing toddler before she hits the ground, be aware of every move of a 2-year-old, and be close enough to offer another toy when 2-year-olds have difficulty sharing. Adults must be responsible for 3- to 5-year-old children at all times, in an environment sufficiently open to permit it. Children older than 5 may be deemed, on individual bases, mature enough to leave the classroom or run independent errands within a building. This should happen only with the adult's permission and specific knowledge.

Children in all early childhood settings must be protected from unauthorized (by the guardian/family) adults and older children. Parents should be welcome visitors in the program, but provisions should be made for limited access to buildings, careful and close supervision of outdoor play areas, and policies which demand that visiting adults check with the administrative office before entering the children's areas. Constant adult vigilance is required with children birth through age 8 years. Young children should not be given the burden of protecting themselves from adults.

III. Relations Between the Home and Program

To achieve individually appropriate programs for young children, early childhood teachers must work in partnership with families and communicate regularly with children's parents.

A. **Parents have both the right and the responsibility to share in decisions about their children's care and education. Parents should be encouraged to observe and participate. Teachers are responsible for establishing and maintaining frequent contacts with families** (Brazelton, 1984; Croft, 1979; Dittmann, 1984; Honig, 1982; Katz, 1980; Lightfoot, 1978; Moore, 1982; Weissbourd, 1981).

During early childhood, children are largely dependent on their families for identity, security, care, and a general sense of well-being. Communication between families and teachers helps build mutual understanding and guidance, and provides greater consistency for children. Joint planning between families and teachers facilitates major socialization processes, such as toilet learning, developing relationships, and entering school.

B. **Teachers share child development knowledge, insights, and resources as part of regular communication and conferences with family members** (Brazelton, 1984; Croft, 1979; Dittmann, 1984; Lightfoot, 1978).

Mutual sharing of information and insights about the individual child's needs and developmental strides help both the family and the program. Regular communication and understanding about child development form a basis for mutual problem solving about concerns regarding behavior and growth. Teachers seek information from parents about individual children. Teachers promote mutual respect by recognizing and acknowledging different points of view to help minimize confusion for children.

C. **Teachers, parents, agencies, programs, and consultants who may have educational responsibility for the child at different times should, with family participation, share developmental information about children as they pass from one level or program to another** (Lightfoot, 1978; Meisels, 1985; Read, Gardner, & Mahler, 1986; Ziegler, 1985).

Continuity of educational experience is critical to supporting development. Such continuity results from communication both horizontally, as children change programs within a given year, and vertically, as children move on to other settings.

IV. Developmental Evaluation of Children

Assessment of individual children's development and learning is essential for planning and implementing developmentally appropriate programs, but should be used with caution to prevent discrimination against individuals and to ensure accuracy. Accurate testing can only be achieved with reliable, valid instruments and such instruments developed for use with young children are extremely rare. In the absence of valid instruments, testing is not valuable. Therefore, assessment of young children should rely heavily on the results of observations of their development and descriptive data.

A. **Decisions that have a major impact on children, such as enrollment, retention, or placement, are not made on the basis of a single developmental assessment or screening device but consider other relevant information, particularly observations by teachers and parents. Developmental assessment of children's progress and achievements is used to adapt curriculum to match the developmental needs of children, to communicate with the child's family, and to evaluate the program's effectiveness** (Cohen, Stern, & Balaban, 1983; Goodwin & Goodwin, 1982; Meisels, 1985; Standards for Educational and Psychological Testing, 1985; Uphoff & Gilmore, 1985).

Scores on psychometric tests that measure narrowly defined academic skills should never be the sole criterion for recommending enrollment or retention in a program, or placement in special or remedial classes. Likewise, assessment of children should be used to evaluate the effectiveness of the curriculum, but the performance of children on standardized tests should not determine curriculum decisions.

B. **Developmental assessments and observations are used to identify children who have special needs and/or who are at risk and to plan appropriate curriculum for them** (Meisels, 1985).

This information is used to provide appropriate programming for these children and may be used in making professional referrals to families.

C. **Developmental expectations based on standardized measurements and norms should compare any child or group of children only to normative information that is not only age-matched, but also gender-, culture-, and socioeconomically appropriate** (Meisels, 1985; Standards for Educational and Psychological Testing, 1985; Uphoff & Gilmore, 1985).

The validity of comparative data analysis is questionable in the absence of such considerations.

D. **In public schools, there should be a developmentally appropriate placement for every child of legal entry age.**

No public school program should deny access to children of legal entry age on the basis of lack of maturational "readiness." For example, a kindergarten program that denies access to many 5-year-olds is not meeting the needs of its clients. Curriculum should be planned for the developmental levels of children and emphasize individual planning to address a wide range of developmental levels in a single classroom. It is the responsibility of the educational system to adjust to the developmental needs and levels of the children it serves; children should not be expected to adapt to an inappropriate system.

REFERENCES

These references include both laboratory and clinical classroom research to document the broad-based literature that forms the foundation for sound practice in early childhood education.

Almy, M. (1975). *The early childhood educator at work.* New York: McGraw-Hill.

Almy, M. (1982). Day care and early childhood education. In E. Zigler & E. Gordon (Eds.), *Daycare: Scientific and social policy issues* (pp. 476–495). Boston: Auburn House.

Asher, S. R., Renshaw, P. D., & Hymel, S. (1982). Peer relations and the development of social skills. In S. G. Moore & C. R. Cooper (Eds.), *The young child: Reviews of research* (Vol. 3, pp. 137–158). Washington, DC: NAEYC.

Bell, S., & Ainsworth, M. D. S. (1972). Infant crying and maternal responsiveness. *Child Development, 43,* 1171–1190.

Biber, B. (1984). *Early education and psychological development.* New Haven: Yale University Press.

Brazelton, T. B. (1984). Cementing family relationships through child care. In L. Dittman (Ed.), *The infants we care for* (rev. ed.) (pp. 9–20). Washington, DC: NAEYC.

Cazden, C. (Ed.). (1981). *Language in early childhood education* (rev. ed.) Washington, DC: NAEYC.

Cohen, D. H., Stern, V., & Balaban, N. (1983). *Observing a recording the behavior of young children* (3rd ed.). New York: Teachers College Press, Columbia University.

Coopersmith, S. (1975). Building self-esteem in the classroom. In S. Coopersmith (Ed.). *Developing motivation in young children.* San Francisco: Albion.

Cratty, B. (1982). Motor development in early childhood: Critical issues for researchers in the 1980s. In B. Spodek (Ed.) *Handbook of research in early childhood education.* New York: Free Press.

Croft, D. J. (1979). *Parents and teachers: A resource book for home, school, and community relations.* Belmont, CA: Wadsworth.

Curtis, S. (1986). New views on movement development and implications for curriculum in early childhood education. In C. Seefeldt (Ed.). *Early childhood curriculum: A review of current research.* New York: Teachers College Press. Columbia University.

Davidson, L. (1985). Preschool children's tonal knowledge: Antecedents of scale. In J. Boswell (Ed.), *The young child and music: Contemporary principles in child development and music education. Proceedings of the Music in Early Childhood Conference* (pp. 25–40). Reston, VA: Music Educators National Conference.

Dittmann, L. (1984). *The infants we care for.* Washington, DC: NAEYC.

Dreikurs, R., Grunwald, B., & Pepper, S. (1982). *Maintaining sanity in the classroom.* New York: Harper & Row.

Elkind, D. (1986, May). Formal education and early childhood education: An essential difference. *Phi Delta Kappan,* 631–636.

Erikson, E. (1950) *Childhood and society.* New York: Norton.

Evans, E. D. (1984). Children's aesthetics. In L. G. Katz (Ed.) *Current topics in early childhood education* (Vol. 5, pp. 73–104). Norwood, NJ: Ablex.

Feeney, S., & Chun, R. (1985). Research in review. Effective teachers of young children. *Young Children, 41*(1), 47–52.

Fein, G. (1979). Play and the acquisition of symbols. In L. Katz (Ed.), *Current topics in early childhood education* (Vol. 2). Norwood, NJ: Ablex.

Fein, G. & Rivkin, M. (Eds.). (1986). *The young child at play: Reviews of research* (Vol. 4). Washington, DC: NAEYC.

Ferreiro, E., & Teberosky, A. (1982). *Literacy before schooling.* Exeter, NH: Heinemann.

Forman, G., & Kaden, M. (1986). Research on science education in young children. In C. Seefeldt (Ed.), *Early childhood curriculum: A review of current research.* New York: Teachers College Press, Columbia University.

Forman, G., & Kuschner, D. (1983). *The child's construction of knowledge: Piaget for teaching children.* Washington, DC: NAEYC.

Fromberg, D. (1986). Play. In C. Seefeldt (Ed.), *Early childhood curriculum: A review of current research.* New York: Teachers College Press, Columbia University.

Frost, J. L., & Klein, B. L. (1979). *Children's play and playgrounds.* Austin, TX: Playgrounds International.

Gazda, G. M. (1973). *Human relations development: A manual for educators.* Boston: Allyn and Bacon.

Genishi, C. (1986). Acquiring language and communicative competence. In C. Seefeldt (Ed.), *Early childhood curriculum: A review of current research.* New York: Teachers College Press, Columbia University.

Gerber, M. (1982). What is appropriate curriculum for infants and toddlers? In B. Weissbourd & J. Musick (Eds.), *Infants: Their social environments.* Washington, DC: NAEYC.

Gilbert, J. P. (1981). Motoric music skill development in young children: A longitudinal investigation. *Psychology of Music, 9*(1), 21–24.

Goffin, S. & Tull, C. (1985). Problem solving: Encouraging active learning. *Young Children, 40*(3), 28–32.

Gonzalez-Mena, J., & Eyer, D. W. (1980). *Infancy and caregiving.* Palo Alto, CA: Mayfield.

Goodwin, W., & Goodwin, L. (1982). Measuring young children. In B. Spodek (Ed.), *Handbook of research in early childhood education.* New York: Free Press.

Gordon, T. (1970). *Parent effectiveness training.* New York: Wyden.

Gordon, T. (1975). *Teacher effectiveness training.* New York: McKay.

Gottfried, A. (1983). Research in review. Intrinsic motivation in young children. *Young Children, 39*(1), 64–73.

Greenberg, M. (1976). Research in music in early childhood education: A survey with recommendations. *Council for Research in Music Education, 45,* 1–20.

Greenspan, S., & Greenspan, N. T. (1985). *First feelings: Milestones in the emotional development of your baby and child.* New York: Viking.

Griffin, E. F. (1982). *The island of childhood: Education in the special world of nursery school.* New York: Teachers College Press, Columbia University.

Hawkins, D. (1970). Messing about in science. *ESS Reader.* Newton, MA: Education Development Center.

Hendrick, J. (1986). *Total learning: Curriculum for the young child* (2nd ed.). Columbus, OH: Merrill.

Herron, R., & Sutton-Smith, B. (1974). *Child's play.* New York: Wiley.

Hill, D. (1979). *Mud, sand, and water.* Washington, DC: NAEYC.

Hirsch, E. (Ed.). (1984). *The block book.* Washington, DC: NAEYC.

Hoffman, M. L. (1975). Moral internalization, parental power, and the nature of parent-child interaction. *Developmental Psychology, 11,* 228–239.

Holt, B. (1979). *Science with young children.* Washington, DC: NAEYC.

Honig, A. S. (1980). The young child and you—Learning together. *Young Children, 35*(4), 2–10.

Honig, A. S. (1981). What are the needs of infants? *Young Children, 37*(1), 3–10.

Honig, A. S. (1982). Parent involvement in early childhood education. In B. Spodek (Ed.), *Handbook of research in early childhood education.* New York: Free Press.

Honig, A. S. (1985). Research in review. Compliance, control, and discipline (Parts 1 & 2). *Young Children, 40*(2), 50–58; *40*(3), 47–52.

Honig, A. S. (1986). Research in review. Stress and coping in children (Parts 1 & 2). *Young Children, 41*(4), 50–63; *41*(5), 47–59.

Kamii, C. (1982). *Number in preschool and kindergarten.* Washington, DC: NAEYC.

Kamii, C. (1985) Leading primary education toward excellence: Beyond worksheets and drill. *Young Children, 40*(6), 3–9.

Kamii, C., & DeVries, R. (1980). *Group games in early education.* Washington, DC: NAEYC.

Kamii, C., & Lee-Katz, L. (1979). Physics in early childhood education: A Piagetian approach. *Young Children, 34*(4), 4–9.

Katz, L. (1980). Mothering and teaching: Some significant distinctions. In L. Katz (Ed.), *Current topics in early childhood education* (Vol. 3, pp. 47–64). Norwood, NJ: Ablex.

Kitano, M. (1982). Young gifted children: Strategies for preschool teachers. *Young Children, 37*(4), 14–24.

Kline, L. W. (1985). *Learning to read, teaching to read.* Newark, DE: LWK Enterprises.

Kobak, D. (1979). Teaching children to care. *Children Today, 8,* 6–7, 34–35.

Kohlberg, L., & Mayer, R. (1972). Development as the aim of education. *Harvard Educational Review, 42,* 449–496.

Kopp, C. B. (1982). Antecedents of self-regulation: A developmental perspective. *Developmental Psychology, 18,* 199–214.

Kuczynski, L. (1983). Reasoning, prohibitions, and motivations for compliance. *Developmental Psychology, 19,* 126–134.

Languis, M., Sanders, T., & Tipps, S. (1980). *Brain and learning: Directions in early childhood education.* Washington, DC: NAEYC.

Lasky, L., & Mukerji, R. (1980). *Art: Basic for young children.* Washington, DC: NAEYC.

Lay-Dopyera, M., & Dopyera, J. (1986). Strategies for teaching. In C. Seefeldt (Ed.). *Early childhood curriculum: A review of current research.* New York: Teachers College Press, Columbia University.

Lightfoot, S. (1978). *Worlds apart: Relationships between families and schools.* New York: Basic.

Lickona, T. (1983). *Raising good children.* New York: Bantam.

Lozoff, B., Brillenham, G., Trause, M. A., Kennell, J. H., & Klaus, M. H. (1977, July). The mother-newborn relationship: Limits of adaptability. *Journal of Pediatrics, 91.*

Lytton, H. (1979). Disciplinary encounters between young boys and their mothers and fathers: Is there a contingency system? *Developmental Psychology, 15,* 256–268.

McAfee, O. (1985). Research report. Circle time: Getting past "Two Little Pumpkins." *Young Children, 40*(6), 24–29.

McCracken, J. B. (Ed.). (1986). *Reducing stress in young children's lives.* Washington, DC: NAEYC.

McDonald, D. T. (1979). *Music in our lives: The early years.* Washington, DC: NAEYC.

Meisels, S. (1985). *Developmental screening in early childhood.* Washington, DC: NAEYC.

Miller, C. S. (1984). Building self-control: Discipline for young children. *Young Children, 40*(1), 15–19.

Montessori, M. (1964). *The Montessori method.* Cambridge, MA: Robert Bentley.

Moore, S. (1982). Prosocial behavior in the early years: Parent and peer influences. In B. Spodek (Ed.), *Handbook of research in early childhood education.* New York: Free Press.

Mussen, P., & Eisenberg-Bert, N. (1977). *Roots of caring, sharing, and helping: The development of prosocial behavior in children.* San Francisco: Freeman.

NAEYC. (1982). *Early childhood teacher education guidelines for four- and five-year programs.* Washington, DC: NAEYC.

NAEYC. (1984). *Accreditation criteria and procedures of the National Academy of Early Childhood Programs.* Washington, DC: NAEYC.

NAEYC. (1985). *Guidelines for early childhood education programs in associate degree granting institutions.* Washington, DC: NAEYC.

National Institute of Education. (1984). *Becoming a nation of readers: The report of the Commission on Reading.* Washington, DC: U.S. Department of Education.

Piaget, J. (1950). *The psychology of intelligence.* London: Routledge & Kegan Paul.

Piaget, J. (1952). *The origins of intelligence in children.* (M. Cook, Trans.). New York: Norton. (Original work published 1936)

Piaget, J. (1972). *Science of education and the psychology of the child* (rev. ed.). New York: Viking. (Original work published 1965)

Powell, D. (1986). Effects of program approaches and teaching practices. *Young Children, 41*(6), 60–67.

Ramsey, P. G. (1979). Beyond "Ten Little Indians" and turkeys: Alternative approaches to Thanksgiving. *Young Children, 34*(6), 28–32, 49–52.

Ramsey, P. G. (1982). Multicultural education in early childhood. *Young Children, 37*(2), 13–24.

Read, K. H., Gardner, P., & Mahler, B. (1986). *Early childhood programs: A laboratory for human relationships* (8th ed.). New York: Holt, Rinehart & Winston.

Riley, S. S. (1984). *How to generate values in young children: Integrity, honesty, individuality, self-confidence.* Washington, DC: NAEYC.

Rogers, D. L., & Ross, D. D. (1986). Encouraging positive social interaction among young children. *Young Children, 41*(3), 12–17.

Rubin, K., & Everett, B. 1982). Social perspective-taking in young children. In S. G. Moore & C. R. Cooper (Eds.). *The young child: Reviews of research* (Vol. 3, pp. 97–114). Washington, DC: NAEYC.

Ruopp, R., Travers, J., Glantz, F., & Coelen, C. (1979). *Children at the center. Final report of the National Day Care Study* (Vol. 1). Cambridge, MA: Abt Associates.

Sackoff, E., & Hart, R. (1984, Summer). Toys: Research and applications. *Children's Environments Quarterly,* 1–2.

Saracho, O., & Spodek, B. (Eds.). (1983). *Understanding the multicultural experience in early childhood education.* Washington, DC: NAEYC.

Schachter, F. F., & Strage, A. A. (1982). Adults' talk and children's language development. In S. G. Moore & C. R. Cooper (Eds.), *The young child: Reviews of research* (Vol. 3, pp. 79–96). Washington, DC: NAEYC.

Schaffer, H. R. (1984). *The child's entry into a social world.* Orlando, FL: Academic.

Schickedanz, J. (1986). *More than the ABCs: The early stages of reading and writing.* Washington, DC: NAEYC.

Schickedanz, J., Schickedanz, D. I., & Forsyth, P. D. (1982). *Toward understanding children.* Boston: Little, Brown.

Seefeldt, C. (1986). The visual arts. In C. Seefeldt (Ed.), *The early childhood curriculum: A review of current research.* New York: Teachers College Press, Columbia University.

Shure, M. B., & Spivack, G. (1978). *Problem-solving techniques in childrearing.* San Francisco: Josey-Bass.

Skeen, P., Garner, A. P., & Cartwright, S. (1984). *Woodworking for young children.* Washington, DC: NAEYC.

Smith, C. A., & Davis, D. E. (1976). Teaching children non-sense. *Young Children, 34*(3), 4–11.

Smith, F. (1982). *Understanding reading.* New York: Holt, Rinehart & Winston.

Smith, F. (1985). *Reading without nonsense* (2nd ed.). New York: Teachers College Press, Columbia University.

Smith, N. (1983). *Experience and art: Teaching children to paint.* New York: Teachers College Press, Columbia University.

Souweine, J., Crimmins, S., & Mazel, C. (1981). *Mainstreaming: Ideas for teaching young children.* Washington, DC: NAEYC.

Sparling, J. (1984). *Learning games for the first three years.* New York: Walker.

Spodek, B. (1985). *Teaching in the early years* (3rd ed.). Englewood Cliffs, NJ: Prentice-Hall.

Spodek, B. (Ed.). (1986). *Today's kindergarten: Exploring its knowledge base, extending its curriculum.* New York: Teachers College Press, Columbia University.

Sponseller, D. (1982). Play and early education. In B. Spodek (Ed.), *Handbook of research in early childhood education.* New York: Free Press.

Sprung, B. (1978). *Perspectives on non-sexist early childhood education.* New York: Teachers College Press, Columbia University.

Sroufe, L. A. (1979). The coherence of individual development. *American Psychologist, 34,* 834–841.

Standards for educational and psychological testing. (1985). Washington, DC: American Psychological Association, American Educational Research Association, and National Council on Measurement in Education.

Steward, I. S. (1982). The real world of teaching two-year-old children. *Young Children, 37*(5), 3–13.

Stone, J. G. (1978). *A guide to discipline* (rev. ed.). Washington, DC: NAEYC.

Uphoff, J. K., & Gilmore, J. (1985, September). Pupil age at school entrance—How many are ready for success? *Educational Leadership, 43,* 86–90.

Veach, D. M. (1977). Choice with responsibility. *Young Children, 32*(4), 22–25.

Wallinga, C. R., & Sweaney, A. L. (1985). A sense of *real* accomplishment: Young children as productive family members. *Young Children, 41*(1), 3–9.

Warren, R. M. (1977). *Caring: Supporting children's growth.* Washington, DC: NAEYC.

Weber, E. (1984). *Ideas influencing early childhood education: A theoretical analysis.* New York: Teachers College Press, Columbia University.

Weissbourd, B. (1981). *Supporting parents as people.* In B. Weissbourd & J. Musick (Eds.), *Infants: Their social environments.* Washington, DC: NAEYC.

Wellman, H. M. (1982). The foundations of knowledge: Concept development in the young child. In S. G. Moore & C. R. Cooper (Eds), *The young child: Reviews of research* (Vol. 3, pp. 115–134). Washington, DC: NAEYC.

Willert, M., & Kamii, C. (1985). Reading in kindergarten: Direct versus indirect teaching. *Young Children, 40*(4), 3–9.

Willis, A., & Ricciuti, H. (1975). *A good beginning for babies: Guidelines for group care.* Washington, DC: NAEYC.

Wolfgang, C. H., & Glickman, C. D. (1980). *Solving discipline problems.* Boston: Allyn and Bacon.

Yarrow, M. R., Scott, P. M., & Waxler, C. Z. (1973). Learning concern for others. *Developmental Psychology, 8,* 240–260.

Yarrow, M. R., & Waxler, C. Z. (1976). Dimensions and correlates of prosocial behavior in young children. *Child Development, 47,* 118–125.

Zavitkovsky, D., Baker, K. R., Berlfein, J. R., & Almy, M. (1986). *Listen to the children.* Washington, DC: NAEYC.

Ziegler, P. (1985). Saying good-bye to preschool. *Young Children, 40*(3), 11–15.

Appendix C

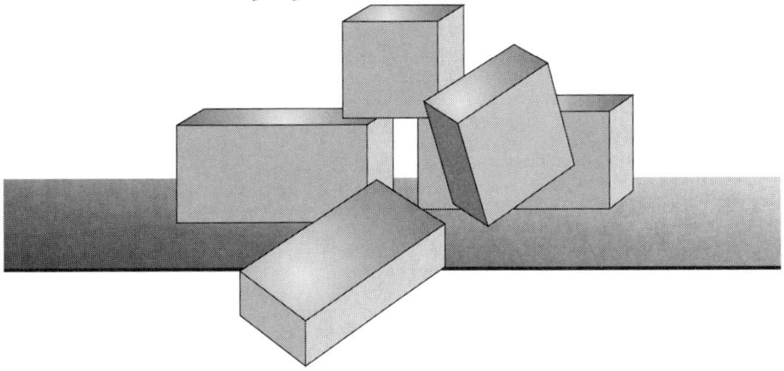

Activity Centers

The following describes the purposes and necessary materials of several activity centers. This list is not in any sense exhaustive. It does indicate the types of activities from which young children can profit, in order to stimulate teachers' own creative ideas.

DRAMATIC PLAY

1. Provide a colorful tablecloth and a vase of flowers to serve as a stimulus for housekeeping play. On some days, simply placing dishes on the table invites creative dramatic play. While traditional female roles may be acted out, you can also encourage the expression of nontraditional roles. For instance, put on a table empty cans of baby powder, cotton balls, towels and wash cloths, clean doll clothes, and a dishpan with about two inches of water in the bottom. Both boys and girls can use these props to care for dolls.
2. Grapefruit-size balls of homemade play-dough, rolling pins, and cookie cutters set up on the table in the housekeeping center are great simulators of dramatic play.
3. Lay out a big bowl, fruits to peel and cut up, and a knife for making fruit salad.
4. Dishes and other equipment from the housekeeping center that need washing frequently provide useful work that five-year-old boys and girls can do well. Put warm sudsy water in plastic dishpans or small buckets. Lay out sponges, scouring pads, and dishtowels. Remember that the job really needs doing and is not just busywork.
5. Put out child-size brooms and mops. Playing with them will be more interesting if they are brought out only now and then.
6. Set up rags and a spray bottle filled with water near a mirror that needs cleaning.
7. Invite the boys to imitate daddy as he shaves or trims his beard. Put a table against a wall below a long mirror hung horizontally. On the table arrange empty razors, old-fashioned shaving brushes and cups with a mild bar of soap for the lather, combs, and safe scissors.
8. To encourage boys' play in the housekeeping center, engage their help in rearranging the equipment every now and then.

9. Invite some of the children to play store in an area set up for this purpose. Provide cans and cartons with the labels and pictures of products, brown paper bags, homemade play money, and a cash register. Leave this area set up for several days, as long as the children are creative and constructive in their play. A trip to a supermarket to observe how real supermarkets are organized and how they function might lead to more elaborate play.
10. Help children understand the roles of doctors, nurses, and dentists, and their relation to these health professionals, by encouraging them to play out their feelings. Set up an area as doctor's office or as a hospital with beds. Stimulate play by providing a stethoscope, plastic syringes, empty plastic bottles, face masks, bandages, and cotton balls. Reading books about medical practitioners or visiting a doctor's office, drug store, or hospital will help enrich this play.
11. Set up a post office center using a large cardboard box with dividers labeled with each child's name. Lay out envelopes and magazines. Old stamps and play money will increase the possibilities of this play.

Have enough props for children's dramatic play. Be creative in selecting and arranging these props to attract boys and girls.

Materials

blouses	gloves	purses
boys' sports coats	jewelry	ribbons
caps	ladies' hats	scarves
construction workers' hats	long skirts	shoes
	neckties	suitcase
	men's boots	

Figure C–1 Types of Unit Blocks

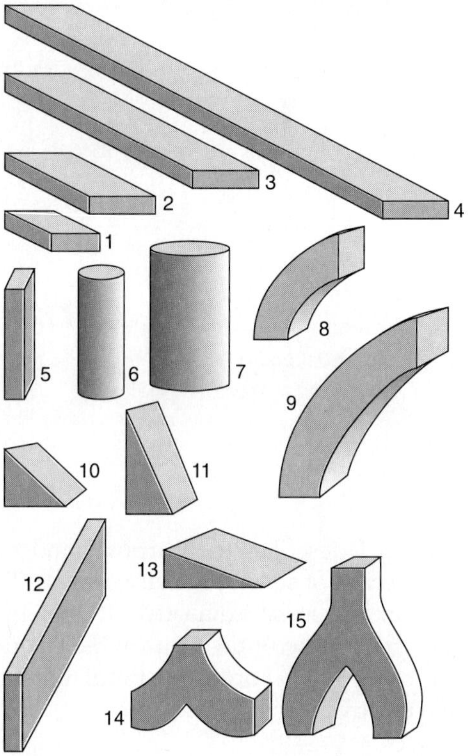

1. Half unit
2. Unit
3. Double unit
4. Quadruple unit
5. Pillar
6. Small cylinder
7. Large cylinder
8. Circular curve
9. Elliptical curve
10. Small triangle
11. Large triangle
12. Floor board
13. Ramp
14. Right-angle switch
15. Y switch

Blocks may come in other sizes and shapes as well.

Source: From Elisabeth S. Hirsch (Ed.), *The Block Book* (Washington, DC: National Association for the Education of Young Children, 1984), pp. 202–203.

BLOCKBUILDING

1. Have enough blocks for children to build appropriate structures. Older children will need more blocks, more varied blocks, and more block accessories than will younger children.
2. Store blocks near toys that can serve as accessories, such as transportation toys, small toy animals and people, and so on.
3. Introduce block building at the beginning of the year. Become involved in building with the children.

MANIPULATIVE PLAY

Encourage children to choose materials, become involved in using the materials, and complete their chosen activity. They should be free to replace items on the table with another type of material.

1. Provide a variety of manipulative materials. Have each set in a container that is clearly labeled so children can see what is available and easily put the materials back when they are through.
2. Match the material available to the children's ability levels. Materials that no longer challenge the children can be stored and replaced with other, more challenging materials.
3. Use task cards to focus children on appropriate ways to use the material.

Materials

beads (assorted shapes and colors)
clock
counting objects
counting stairway
creative snap blocks
design blocks
dominos
flannelboard and/or magnetic board
geometric forms (two- or three-dimensional
hammer and nail set
lacing shoes
landscape peg board
legos (large size for the young)
lock board
matching games
parquetry blocks
pegs and peg boards
picture lotto
pile-up clowns
pull blocks
puzzles of varied difficulty
rising towers
stacking toys
tinkertoy
wood nuts and bolts

SCIENCE

1. Provide children with a science table containing materials they can observe in different ways.
2. Encourage children to ask questions, search for answers, test ideas, and become aware of the world around them.
3. If possible, have pets and growing plants for the children to care for and observe.

Materials

animal cage
aquarium
balance scale
batteries, bulbs, and wire
bird's nest
hot plate
leaves
magnets
magnifying glass
measuring cups
plants, pots, soil, and watering can
prisms (glass)
rocks
rulers
seashells
thermometers

MATHEMATICS

The mathematics center can include various materials to help children explore mathematical concepts. These are discussed in Chapter 14.

1. Set up large dominoes on a table. At first the children will probably build with them, but as they begin to count the dots they will probably match like numbers.
2. Make play money from tag board. Use in situations where paying for things becomes a part of a dramatic play. "You have to pay for the food," says a five-year-old supermarket checker. "That'll be 50 cents." Place the money in a cash register drawer made from a cardboard box near the blocks, in the store, in the housekeeping center, in the post office, or wherever it seems appropriate.
3. Place a tape measure, ruler, and yardstick on a table. Let the children explore their use. Develop task cards that require them to measure different things. Use balance scales, measuring cups, and other devices that allow children to measure different things in different ways.
4. Pair children to compare measurements. A child can compare the weight of a cup of sand with that of a cup of rice. The children can check each other's work.
5. Provide containers that contain the same volume but are of different shapes, such as tall and short quart jars. Have children compare them.

6. Put a small flannelboard on a table. Allow the children to put the shapes together to create great designs.
7. Provide small sticks for children to bundle into groups to 10. Have one stick alone, two tied together with a twist-type closure, three tied together, and the balance loose to invite the completion to 10.
8. Provide 10 small cans on a tray with sticks for grouping by quantity, with one stick in a can, two in another can, and so forth.
9. Encourage experimentation with volume by setting out containers of varying sizes, such as pill bottles, square boxes, round boxes, and so forth. Then provide beads, beans, or any small objects of uniform size to be used to fill the containers. Ask, "Is there enough space in this box for another bead? How many can fit into this box?"

LIBRARY

1. Provide a variety of children's books of different genres.
2. Allow children to browse through books.
3. Arrange to have a parent, volunteer, or older child read to one or more children or listen to them talk about books.

Materials

book jackets
children's books
comfortable places to sit (carpet squares, pillows, if possible a child's rocking chair
display rack
picture collections
recordings of stories, songs, poems

MUSIC

1. Place maracas or other rhythm makers beside the record player for use with rhythmic records. Make maracas from small gourds.
2. Tie full skirts on the girls and long, wide sashes on the boys for their enjoyment as they dance to Spanish rhythms.
3. Place drums created from oatmeal boxes near the record player. A good activity for the preceding day is to make the drums from the oatmeal boxes.
4. Give the children sets of tone bells to enjoy. Later, when they have achieved some familiarity with the bells, arrange one set in ascending scale, and leave another scrambled for the children to line up.
5. Place records of songs with decided rhythms or moods on the record player and encourage the children to move as the music inspires them.

Materials

autoharp
bells
castanets
cymbals
drums
maracas
records, discs, tapes
sand blocks
sticks
tambourines
trianges
xylophone

ART

Every day, during self-directed activity time, the children should have an opportunity to become involved in creative art activities. Teachers should have the media prepared and set out for children to use.

1. Paint on different types and sizes of paper, for example, large pieces of brown wrapping paper, printed newsprint, or wallpaper samples, instead of the usual blank newsprint.
2. Allow children to mix their paint. It is wise to pre-measure the water at first.
3. Use clay or homemade playdough frequently. Place grapefruit-size balls on cardboard clay boards for a small group of children to use.
4. Place trays or cookie sheets at three or four places around a table. Each tray will have finger paint on it. After the children have engaged in this great, messy activity, they can clean each tray in a large tub of water.

Materials

brushes	different sizes of sponges	place for drying pictures
clay	double easels	playdough
construction paper	felt-tip markers	scissors
covered cans for paint	glue	scraps of cloth
crayons	paints	smocks
	paper	

SAND AND WATER PLAY

1. Prepare for water play by covering a table with large towels or placing old rugs under the water play table. Have sponges handy for children to wipe up any spills. Outdoors is also an ideal place for water play.
2. Provide cups, sieves, plastic bottles, and funnels for pouring in a dishpan or tub of water.
3. Lay a rotary beater next to a dishpan of soapy water. Provide a cup and extra pan for scooping off soapsuds as they form.
4. For an experiment with floating, provide corks, balls, boats, cotton balls, rocks, and nails.
5. Painting with plain water and large paint brushes is great outdoors.

Materials

cars and boats	sifters
food coloring	soapsuds
funnels	funnels
hoses	hoses
measuring cups	raincoats or plastic smocks
objects to float and sink	spoons, shovels
plastic containers	trucks
plastic pool, metal tub, or commercial sand-and-water table	

CARPENTRY OR WOODWORKING

1. Provide scraps of soft wood for children to saw pieces from or hammer nails into. At first, do not be concerned with having the children complete a project.
2. Help children plan simple craft projects. Two pieces of wood fastened crosswise can be an airplane. A smaller piece of wood nailed on top of a larger one can become a boat. Later, children can be shown how to saw two corners off one end to represent a bow. Be creative in suggesting other projects.
3. After children have completed a project, they may want to paint what they have made. Tempera paints or water-based household paints allow for reasonably easy clean-up.

Materials

auger	hammers	saws
bit and brace	nails	screwdrivers
bottlecaps	pliers	soft wood
clamps	sandpaper	vice

Appendix D

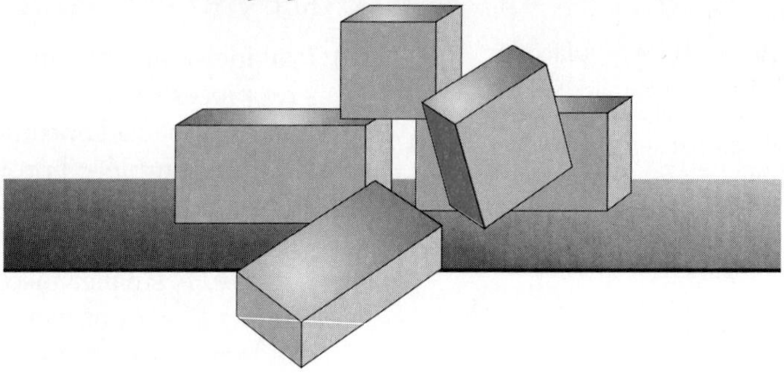

Magazines for Young Children

PRESCHOOL LEVEL

Chickadee: The Canadian Magazine for Children (3–9 years)
Young Naturalist Foundation
56 The Esplanade, Suite 304
Toronto, Ontario, Canada M5E 1A7

This magazine has beautiful illustrations, colorful photographs, and a mix of easy-to-read stories, puzzles, games, things to make, and jokes. It shows animals in their natural habitat. Each issue is devoted to one particular animal or subject.

Children's Playmate Magazine (4–8 years)
Children's Better Health Institute
1100 Waterway Blvd.
P. O. Box 567
Indianapolis, IN 46206

This health-oriented magazine focuses on health practices, exercise, and good nutrition. Numerous stories, poems, jokes, mazes, hidden pictures, word riddles, and recipes are included. Children can write to the doctor to ask questions; answers are published in future editions

Happy Times (3–5 years)
Concordia Publishing House
35585 Jefferson Ave.
St. Louis, MO 63118

This magazine entertains and instructs. It includes stories, recipes, feature articles, crafts, and posters. Special sections focus on the creation of values, sciences, the world, logic, mathematics, and reading preparation.

Highlights for Children (3–12 years)
2300 W. Fifth Avenue
P. O. Box 269
Columbus, OH 43272-0002

The purpose of this magazine is to promote thinking, reasoning, moral sensitivity, basic skills, and creativity. It suggests reading levels and subject matter interests. Cartoons, stories, crafts, puzzles, and activities for a variety of levels are included. Children can send their reactions and original art work, which are published in future editions.

Sesame Street (3–8 years)
Children's Television Workshop
P. O. Box 2896
Boulder, CO 80322

Usually each issue of the magazine concentrates on one theme that reinforces concepts and ideas shown on the television program. Its core areas are language arts, auditory and visual perception, self-expression, and mathematical and reading skills. Most of the content is interactive and consumable. A special section suggests activities relating to the magazine to parents and gives parents practical advice on dealing with children. This magazine can be obtained in either Spanish or English.

Turtle: Magazine for Preschool Kids (2–5 years)
Children's Better Institute
1100 Waterway Blvd.
P. O. Box 567
Indianapolis, IN 46206

The magazine has simple puzzles, pictures to color in, illustrated riddles, and bedtime stories to keep children busy. Children can submit their drawings to be published in future editions.

Your Big Back Yard (3–5 years)
National Wildlife Federation
1412 16th St., NW
Washington, DC 20036

The purpose of this magazine is teach children about nature and about conserving resources. It displays close-up pictures of animals and captions in large print. In each issue, a letter instructs parents how to use the magazine's pictures, games, and puzzles in a creative way.

Lollipops, Ladybugs and Lucky Stars (3–5 years)
Good Apple
Box 299
Carthage, IL 62321-0299

This activities magazine helps develop learning skills. Games are used to teach basic grammatical concepts; the magazine also includes poetry, songs, simple recipes, puzzles and riddles, games for teaching number skills, and bulletin board ideas. Each issue provides a bibliography on a seasonal theme.

Scholastic Let's Find Out (5 years)
Scholastic Magazines
1290 Wall St. W.
Lyndhurst, NJ 07071

This magazine is composed of four parts: sensory experiences, prereading/language arts, social studies, and math/science. Each issue provides a calendar, poster and supplementary materials that support information in that issue. The teacher's edition includes educational applications and suggestions.

SIX- TO EIGHT-YEAR-OLDS

Children six to eight years of age will also enjoy the magazines listed for younger children.

Cricket (6–12 years)
Open Court Publishing Co.
P. O. Box 51144
Boulder, CO 80321-1144

The Electric Company (7–10 years)
Children's Television Workshop
One Lincoln Plaza
New York, NY 10023

Jack and Jill (6–8 years)
Children's Better Health Institute
1100 Waterway Blvd.
P. O. Box 567
Indianapolis, IN 46206

Ranger Rick's Nature Magazine (5–11 years)
The National Wildlife Federation
1412 16th St., NW
Washington, DC 20036

Stone Soup: The Magazine by Children (6–12 years)
Children's Art Foundation
P. O. Box 83
Santa Cruz, CA 95063–9990

TEACHERS AND PARENTS

Kidstuff
Guidelines Press
1307 S. Killian Dr.
Lake Park, FL 33403

Copycat Magazines
P. O. Box 5104
Racine, WI 53405

The Mailbox: Primary Edition
The Education Center, Inc.
P. O. Box 9753
Greensboro, NC 27429

The Good Apple Newsletter
Box 299
Carthage, IL 62321—0299

Index

D

E

N

O

P

Q

R

T